INTRODUCTORY ECONOMICS

INTRODUCTORY ECONOMICS

Barry Harrison
Charles Smith
Brinley Davies

MACMILLAN

First published 1992 by
MACMILLAN PRESS LTD
Houndmills, Basingstoke, Hampshire RG21 2XS
and London
Companies and representatives
throughout the world

ISBN 0–333–54288–6 hardcover
ISBN 0–333–54294–0 paperback

A catalogue record for this book is available from the British Library.

11 10 9 8 7 6 5 4 3
03 02 01 00 99 98 97 96 95

Printed in Hong Kong

CONTENTS

LIST OF FIGURES

LIST OF TABLES

ACKNOWLEDGEMENTS

The authors and publishers wish to thank the following for permission to reproduce copyright material:

The Economic Review, for Figure 2.8 (January 1990) and Figure 8.4, from J. Aylen, 'Cost Curves in the Steel Industry' (September 1989), and for Table 3.2, in E. Symons and I. Walker, 'Fiscal Harmonisation' (May 1990) and Table 38.3, from the Data Supplement (1990).
Hillsdown Group plc for Figure 15.2.
Fiscal Studies for Figure 35.3.
Barclays Bank Review for Figure 37.2.
Finance and Development for Figure 38.2 and for Table 38.5.
Philips for Figure 38.3, from *Philips Certificate Atlas* (1987).
Daily Mirror for the extract on p. 108.
Department of Employment Gazette for Tables 7.2, 17.3 and 27.3 and for Box 27.2.
National Westminster Bank Review for Table 28.2.
Federal Reserve Bank of St Louis Review for Tables 31.1, 31.2 and for material in Box 31.3.
Barclays Country Report for Question 1 on p. 288 and Question 5 on p. 309.
Barclays Economic Review for Tables 32.2 and 32.5.
Lloyds Bank Economic Bulletin for Table 34.3.
Lloyds Bank Economic Profile for Figure 2.1.
Economics (Journal of the Economics Association) for Tables 37.3 and 37.4 and for Figure 37.1.
The Economist for Tables 30.5 and 38.2, for Figure 38.1 and for material in Box 38.5.
BIS Financial Review for Table 34.4, from N. Healey 'The Great EMS Debate 1990 Vintage (May 1990).
The Bank of England for Figures 24.2, 25.1 and 29.4 and Table 24.1.
Bank of England Quarterly Bulletin for Table 30.10.
The Financial Times for Table 33.1.
The IMF for Tables 30.9, 33.2, 38.4, for Figure 30.2 and for material in Boxes 31.1, 31.2, 31.4, 38.2.
The Controller of Her Majesty's Stationery Office for Figures 2.2, 2.5, 2.6, 2.7 14.1, 14.2, 14.3, 14.4, 14.5, 17.7, 17.8, 17.9, 17.10, 28.7, 32.1 and for Tables 2.1, 2.4, 2.6, 2.7, 3.1, 3.2, 14.1, 17.2, 18.1, 19.7, 19.8, 21.3, 29.1, 32.1, 32.3, 32.4, 35.1, 37.2 and for material included in Boxes 13.1 and 35.1.
Nottingham City Council for Figure 24.2.
The EC for Tables 34.1 and 34.2.
The IDA for Figure 38.5.
The Independent for material in Boxes 37.1 and 37.2.
The IBRD for Figures 38.1 and 38.2 and for material in Boxes 37.3, 38.1, 38.3 and 38.4.
The IEA for Table 37.1.
The OECD for Tables 18.2, 18.3, 18.4 and for Figures 18.2 and 18.3.
The Guardian for Figures 14.6, 15.3, 32.2, 33.2 and for material in Boxes 14.1 and 37.5.
The Sunday Times for Figure 16.1.
The Observer for material in Box 16.1.
GATT for Table 30.1.
Macmillan Publishers for material in Box 30.4 and for Table 30.11 from M. Porter, *The Competitive Advantage of Nations.*
UNIDO for Figure 30.2, for Table 30.12 and for material in Box 38.2.
The UN for Table 38.4 and for material in Boxes 31.1, 31.2 and 31.4.
The Evening Standard for Box 4.2.
The Western Mail for Question 1 on p. 117.

Every effort has been made to trace all the copyright-holders, but if any have been inadvertently overlooked the publishers will be pleased to make the necessary arrangement at the first opportunity.

PREFACE

This book is designed to provide a modern and thorough treatment of introductory economics. Although written primarily with the needs of the 'A' level student in mind, it will also be useful to those taking non-specialist courses in economics in universities and polytechnics, as well as those studying for professional qualifications.

The emphasis throughout the book is on clarity, accuracy and relevance. It is hoped that this will stimulate interest and encourage understanding. We have sought to explain the most complex aspects of the subject in a way that is sympathetic to the needs of students at this level, many of whom have no prior knowledge of economics. We have also sought to show the relevance of what can often appear to be abstract theory by providing real-world examples wherever possible to illustrate the importance of theory in understanding the economic environment.

Economic terminology is used throughout the book to enhance understanding of the subject and to enable readers to follow the coverage of economic events in the media. However, we hope readers will find the book free of jargon and we make no apologies for its absence.

There are several features of this book, apart from clarity and accuracy, which we feel will appeal to readers. Each chapter begins with a section entitled **Connections**, which relates the material to be covered in that chapter to other topics covered in the book. This is particularly important in a subject like economics where material covered in one chapter is often related to material covered in other chapters. This is followed by a list of **Key Concepts** that are introduced and discussed in the chapter. There are also **Review Questions** at the end of each chapter which are designed to provide a check on progress and understanding. Most chapters also contain case study or insight material which is set in boxes so as not to interrupt the flow of the text. The boxes often given an application of economic theory or provide an illuminating insight into material covered in the chapter.

We are aware that not all students taking courses in economics have a strong mathematical background and we have therefore devoted a complete chapter to explaining and interpreting typical graphs and charts that are widely used in teaching introductory economics. There is also an explanation of time-series data and we hope this chapter will give confidence to readers who lack a strong mathematical background. More generally we hope it will be useful in preparing all candidates for the data response paper that all major examination boards now set.

The book is also modern in its approach. Recent developments in theory are treated thoroughly and there are separate chapters on the aggregate demand/aggregate supply framework now used in analysing economic policy and on rational expectations. There are also separate chapters on monetary policy, the Economic Community and economic development which provide a careful and detailed analysis of these areas where change has been rapid in recent years.

We are grateful to many people for their help, support and encouragement during the writing of this book. We would like to thank the entire team at Macmillan for their help and encouragement and must place on record our particular thanks to Stephen Rutt. We would also like to thank Stan Goodman of Rickmansworth School, Hertfordshire, John Wigley of Haberdashers' Aske's School, Elstree, and Phyllis Palmer of Dinnington Comprehensive School, Sheffield, for valuable comments on earlier drafts of this book. They are responsible for many improvements to the text, but as we have not always accepted their advice we are unable to implicate them in any errors or omissions that remain. We are also grateful to Keith Povey and his editorial team (Barbara Docherty, Ann Edmondson and Tony Edmondson) for their efforts in ensuring the book's smooth passage to the printer. Finally, we would like to thank our wives and families for all the support and encouragement they have given us during the writing of this book.

BARRY HARRISON
CHARLES SMITH
BRINLEY DAVIES

CHAPTER 1

WHAT IS ECONOMICS?

CONNECTIONS

The subject matter of Chapter 1, and in particular the notion of **scarcity**, is related to all aspects of economics. Perhaps you are studying economics in order to understand the causes of unemployment, inflation or poverty in the Third World. Perhaps you are interested in understanding the economic issues which sometimes appear to dominate the news. What does it mean when we read that the pound is weak against the dollar, and what are the likely effects of this? Why do governments worry about inflation or the price of oil? We hope that by the end of your course you will have some considerable understanding of these, and of many other, economic issues. We hope you will also understand that all economic issues are related to a single problem: what we call the economic problem.

Key Concepts

Centrally planned economy
Choice
Consumer sovereignty
Market economy
Opportunity cost
Price mechanism
Production possibility curve
Resources
Scarcity
The economic problem

What is Economics?

There are many definitions of economics, each trying to encapsulate the fundamentals of the subject. No completely satisfactory definition has yet been derived, but most definitions that have been suggested emphasise the point that economics is about **allocation of scarce resources which have alternative uses**. While most economists would accept this statement, if you are starting economics for the first time you are unlikely to find it helpful as a definition. Let us begin by examining the statement in a little more detail.

The Economic Problem

To the non-economist it might seem confusing to refer to 'the economic problem' as though there were only one such problem. In fact, there are many economic problems. Increases in the rate of inflation or unemployment frequently make headline news, as does the state of the balance of payments. Poverty and income distribution might also be thought of as important economic problems, and in recent years increasing attention has focused on the importance of the environment. These are all economic problems, so why do economists refer to 'the economic problem'?

In fact, all of these economic problems arise because of the existence of **scarcity**, and they are the result of different **choices** made by society. The terms 'scarcity' and 'choice' therefore epitomise the economic problem, and it is to a discussion of these that we now turn.

Scarcity

All societies (with the possible exception of primitive cultures) face the same fundamental problem: unlimited desires but limited ability to satisfy them.

Human beings seem to desire ever higher levels of consumption: as soon as one particular level of consumption is achieved, a new and higher level is desired. There are many possible reasons for this, but the fact is that while there is no limit on the desire for increased consumption, there are clear limits on the means of satisfying these desires at any moment in time. Over time an economy can produce greater and greater levels of output, but this does not alleviate the problem of scarcity since **desires will also have increased**.

All societies possess limited means of production. Economists refer to the means of production as **resources** and these consist of *land*, *labour*, *capital* and *enterprise* or *the entrepreneur*. The nature of these resources is discussed more fully in Chapters 14–16. Here the important point to stress is that all output is created from these resources. Let us look briefly at each in turn.

Land is defined to include all the **free gifts of nature**. It therefore consists of the ores and minerals in the ground, trees and forests and so on.

Labour is defined as **human effort** – both physical and mental.

Capital is defined as any **man-made aid to production**. It therefore includes factory buildings, machinery, processed raw materials and so on.

Enterprise consists of **risk taking and decision making**. The individual (or individuals) who take decisions about what output to produce, and risk funds by undertaking production, are considered to perform a unique economic role and are therefore considered a separate factor of production. We shall see later in Chapter 15 that this factor of production is usually referred to as the entrepreneur.

At any moment in time there are clear limits on the availability of resources. For example, the supply of labour is fixed by the size of the population who are within the working age groups, the length of the working day, the working week and so on. It is a fact that, at any moment in time, these resources are limited, and this limits the quantity of output that can be produced, and compels society to make choices.

Before we move on to consider the nature of the choices which all societies must make, there is an important point which we must emphasise. Because society's resources are limited, the **incomes** received by the owners of these resources will also be limited. It therefore follows that the economic problem cannot be solved by governments simply creating more money. In fact if a government increased the amount of money in circulation this would not affect the total stock of resources: instead, as we shall see on pp. 257–8 it would simply lead to higher prices.

Choice

Because society cannot have all the output which it desires choices have to be made. In fact, there are

Box 1.1 Money isn't scarce

It is sometimes suggested that one way in which the problem of scarcity could be solved is by the government giving everyone more money. In fact it would be very easy for governments to print more money and give some to every individual. However, this would be a fruitless exercise because it isn't money which is scarce: it is the *goods and services that money can buy* which are scarce.

During the German hyperinflation of 1923 (see p. 256) the printing presses broke records daily in the value of notes they produced. By the end of the hyperinflation the amount of currency produced was 400 quadrillion marks each day! Records were similarly broken daily in Hungary during 1945–6 when the average growth of the money supply was 12,000 per cent per month!

Did such increases in the money supply solve the problem of scarcity? The answer, of course, is 'no'. Many people in both Germany and Hungary became poorer during the hyperinflation and many factories and shops closed as a result of it. Far from solving the problem of scarcity, printing more money was a major cause of poverty for many people in Germany and Hungary.

Why does this happen? Money is simply a **claim to output**. When we have money we can use it to buy, or claim, output. If everyone has more money there are **more claims** to the **same level** of output. Inevitably the price of that output rises. Printing more and more money simply leads to ever-increasing rates of inflation.

If it was possible to solve the economic problem by printing money, there would be no need for economists, because no 'economic problem' would exist!

three fundamental choices sometimes referred to as **what**, **how** and **for whom**.

What to produce: This is sometimes referred to as the problem of *product mix*. Since society cannot have all the output it desires it must choose **what output is going to be produced** from its scarce resources. At first glance the answer might seem obvious: we need food, clothing, shelter, and so on. However, the answer is in fact not obvious at all because **more** of one thing means **less** of something else. We have only a limited amount of resources and if more and more of these are devoted to the production of food, less and less are available for the production of other things. Of course we need a certain amount of different foods to survive but, as we shall see on pp. 327–8, in the EC (as well as in other parts of the world) there are food surpluses which in some cases are destroyed. More generally, we must choose whether resources should be used to produce more motor cars or more buses, more hospitals or more schools, and so on. This is an important issue and relates to what economists refer to as the **allocation of resources**.

How to produce: This is sometimes referred to as the problem of *factor combination*. Whatever goods and services society chooses can usually be produced in a variety of ways. A basic distinction is between **capital-intensive** production and **labour-intensive** production. The former uses large amounts of capital **relative** to labour, while the latter uses large amounts of labour **relative** to capital. Motor cars, for example, can be produced by people or by robots. Should power be generated by using oil, coal or nuclear powered generators or should we rely on wind and wave power? Should more of our goods be transported to market using road links or rail links? These decisions clearly affect the efficiency with which we use our resources and the greater the efficiency, the greater the output that can be produced from **any given quantity** of inputs.

For whom to produce: This is sometimes referred to as the *problem of distribution*. How is output to be distributed to ultimate consumers? In other words, who shall consume the goods and services we produce? Since society cannot have all the output it desires, there must be some mechanism for distributing the limited amount of goods and services that is produced among consumers who, in general, desire more. How much petrol should each motorist receive, and how many holidays should each person be permitted?

Again, there are different mechanisms available. It is possible to organise a system of physical rationing where all consumers receive the same amount of goods and services for every member of the family. This is not just a feature of East European economies where rationing is still common but was the basic method of allocating output in wartime Britain. A different method of distribution is to allocate output **through the market** – that is, allow consumers to buy whatever they can afford. This raises another aspect of the problem of distribution, that of **income distribution**. When consumers are free to buy whatever they can afford, those with higher incomes will obtain a greater share of total output than those with lower incomes. Complete physical rationing or distribution through the market are the extremes; in between there are different combinations, and society may choose one particular combination in preference to another.

These basic choices – what, how and for whom – are clearly **interdependent**. Any decision about what to produce also implies a decision about the way that output is to be produced. Similarly, any decision about what to produce also (in general) implies a decision about how that output is to be produced. The way society makes these choices and the implications of its decisions are what the study of economics is really about.

Opportunity Cost

We have already emphasised the point that since resources are limited more of one thing means less of something else. This notion is extremely important in economics and is referred to as **opportunity cost**. Strictly defined, opportunity cost is *the next most desired alternative foregone*: if we use our resources in one way they are not available for use in another. It is important to realise that an opportunity cost does not necessarily imply a money cost: it simply involves an opportunity given up. It is therefore relevant in decisions taken by all economic agents – that is, individuals, firms, other organisations and governments.

All individuals have a limited income and must decide what proportion to spend and what proportion to save. Having decided how much they wish to spend, they must decide how to allocate this between different goods and services which they might wish to buy. How often have you been faced with decisions such as whether to buy one compact disc in preference to another, or one video in preference to another? More generally, how often have you made decisions such as whether to buy a pair of jeans or a

Box 1.2 The peace dividend

The phrase 'peace dividend' has been coined in the USA to express the hope that the new era of disarmament and detente will result in major savings in defence expenditure. These savings might be substantial since the world currently spends about $800bn on defence and about 4 per cent of total world output is accounted for by output related to defence.

Of course, defence can be seen as an insurance against possible attack. But the important point to grasp is that the defence industries are using resources which have an **opportunity cost**. In particular, if industries did not produce defence equipment they could otherwise produce goods for consumption or additional machinery which would make a higher level of production possible.

pair of shoes? In such cases, what you give up is the opportunity cost of what you buy.

The concept of opportunity cost is equally important to firms: when the economic life of an existing machine is over, the firm must consider whether to replace it and if so whether to replace it with a similar machine or whether to change the method of production by adopting a completely different technology. Governments must also consider the opportunity cost of any decision they take. For example, in 1990 the government announced plans to create a new national forest in the Midlands. What is the opportunity cost of this? Obviously resources will be devoted to growing and planting saplings. Forestry workers will be employed in tending and caring for them. Land which was previously put to agricultural use will no longer be available for this purpose, and agricultural output will fall. Similarly, the minerals and ores contained within the land will no longer be available and so on. All of these factors are the opportunity cost or *real cost* of creating the new forest.

Production Possibility Curves

A production possibility curve shows the various combinations of two goods that an economy can produce when its resources are fully employed: it is a diagrammatic representation of the problem of choice. Of course no economy in the world produces only two goods, but this does not diminish the usefulness of the production possibility curve since this is only a simplifying assumption. We can divide an economy's output into output for domestic consumption and output for export, output of goods and output of services, output by the public sector and output by the private sector, output of consumption goods and output of capital goods, and so on. For our purposes we shall simply classify these two goods as good X and good Y. Figure 1.1 shows a typical production possibility curve.

The curve PP_1 shows all combinations of good X and good Y that can be produced by this economy when its resources are fully employed. Points P, A, B and P_1 are points of full employment whereas at point C there are unemployed resources. The production possibility curve is drawn concave to the origin because, although resources have alternative uses, they are not **equally efficient in all uses**. In fact, as more and more of one good is produced, resources which are less and less suited to the production of that good will be used. Because of this, any given input of resources will produce a smaller and smaller increase in total output. This is reflected in the changing production possibilities all the way along the curve.

For example, if the economy is initially at point P producing only good Y, then subsequently undertakes production of OM units of good X, the

Figure 1.1 *A typical production possibility curve*

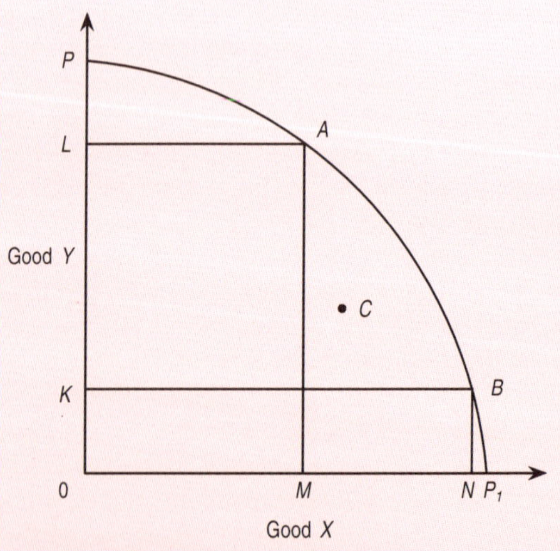

Note its shape and the opportunity cost of producing OM of good X compared with the opportunity cost of producing an additional NP_1 of good X

opportunity cost of this is *PL* of good *Y*. This is the quantity of *Y* given up when the output of *X* increases from zero to *OM*. However, when the output of *X* increases from *ON* to OP_1, an increase in the production of *X* exactly equal to *OM*, the opportunity cost of this is now much greater at *LO* of *Y*. When the output of *X* increases from zero to *OM*, those resources most suited to the production of *X* will be used first. However, as the output of *X* increases we use more and more resources which are better suited to the production of *Y* and are comparatively inefficient in the production of good *X*.

Over time, an economy's production possibility curve will shift outwards, indicating that a higher and higher level of output can be produced. This occurs because productive capacity increases through increased investment, because of population growth or the discovery and exploitation of natural resources, as happened in the UK when the output of oil from the North Sea increased. However, the major source of increased productive capacity is technological advances which make possible the use of ever more sophisticated pieces of equipment (capital) or lead to changes in the techniques of production.

Economic Systems

We have seen that all societies are faced with the same basic economic problem. However, they sometimes adopt different systems to deal with it. In primitive societies choices are made on the basis of custom and habit; things are done in the same time-honoured way they have always been done. Because of this, economists are not much interested in such societies. They are much more interested in the approach adopted in other economic systems. There are two extremes: the market economy and the centrally planned economy.

The Market Economy

This economic system, sometimes referred to as *laissez-faire*, *free enterprise* or *capitalist*, is characterised by freedom of choice and enterprise. In addition, the term 'capitalist' reflects the fact that in this type of economic system, the **means of production** – in particular land and capital – are **privately owned**. The role of the government is therefore very limited in market economies and producers are free to decide what to produce and how to produce it. Because the means of production are privately owned, it is assumed that competition will exist among producers, and that this will ensure that prices are at their minimum levels. We shall see in Chapter 11 that this is not always a realistic assumption. For the moment, we concentrate on the process of resource allocation.

The basic feature of market economies is that resources are allocated through the *price mechanism*. When resources are allocated through the price mechanism consumers are free to purchase any goods offered for sale, **provided they can pay for them**. Subject to certain restrictions designed to protect the public from harm, producers are free to decide what to produce; they simply hire the factors of production. They are guided in their decisions about what to produce, how to produce it, and for whom to produce it by the *profit motive*. This simply means that production is undertaken for profit, and that the aim of producers is to maximise profit – that is, make as much profit as possible from their operations.

To see how resources are allocated through the price mechanism, let us examine what might happen if consumers suddenly demanded more of one particular good, let us call it good *X*, in preference to other goods. The initial effect will be a rise in the price of good *X*. As price rises, producers will be encouraged to increase the production of *X* and will be prepared to offer higher rewards to the factors of production to compete them away from alternatives. Existing producers of good *X* will therefore expand production and new producers will undertake production of good *X*. The end result is that the output of good *X* will increase and the output of alternatives will fall. The implication is that what is produced is decided by the decisions of consumers and the term **consumer sovereignty** is sometimes used to describe this. Producers simply respond to consumer demands because it is in their best interests to do so.

This tells us *what* is produced when resources are allocated through the price mechanism, but it does not tell us *how* that output is produced, or *for whom* it is produced. In fact, the problem of 'how' is easily solved. Since production is undertaken for profit, output is produced using the **least cost method of production**. If any given level of output can be produced using a cheaper method than that which is currently used, it will be adopted, since to do so will increase profit. This means that as technological progress leads to advances in productive techniques, such techniques will be adopted as and when they become available. The implication is that when resources are allocated through the price mechanism, production will *always* be undertaken in the least cost way.

The problem of *for whom* production is undertaken is equally easily solved when resources are allocated through the price mechanism. Output is made available for those who are willing and able to pay for it. Since the desires of society constantly outstrip the ability to satisfy them, we can assume that rational people will be willing to pay for the goods and services they desire. The focus of attention is not therefore willingness, but **ability**, to pay.

However, there is nothing egalitarian about the way the price mechanism operates. Those with the highest incomes will obtain the greatest share of total output. Those with lowest incomes have relatively little power to influence what is produced since they have relatively little buying power. Production is undertaken for profit, and therefore output will be sold to those who are prepared to pay the highest price. Those unable to pay for output will receive nothing!

Nevertheless the price mechanism is widely regarded as an effective way of allocating resources. It functions automatically and provides an elaborate and accurate system of communication between buyers and sellers. Thus when consumers demand changes, producers have an incentive to respond quickly: if they do not, they may lose sales, and therefore profits, to those firms which do respond quickly. However, in practice resources may not always be allocated efficiently through the price mechanism (see Chapter 4).

The Centrally Planned Economy

In centrally planned economies resources are allocated through the *command mechanism* and producers are assigned target levels of output by the government's planning agency. In other words, producers are instructed about **what** to produce and, in many cases, the **quantity** to be produced: it is for this reason that the term 'command' is used to describe the process through which resources are allocated. However, even when the command mechanism is used to decide what is produced, the government's planning agency does not always decide how it is to be produced. It might do so, for example, in order to ensure that all workers were employed. On the other hand, factory managers might be left to make decisions about how to undertake production so as to meet their target level of output. Similarly the government might adopt a system of *physical rationing* as a means of distributing output or it might allow consumers to purchase whatever goods and services they are willing and able to pay for. However, in the latter case the decisions of consumers have no direct influence on the type or the range of goods and services produced. A case study of how the planning is conducted in the Soviet Economy is given on p. 7–8.

The Mixed Economy

Our discussion of economic systems has been confined to the extremes of the market economy and the centrally planned economy. However, in the real world no economy corresponds exactly to either of these two extremes. Some economies more closely resemble market economies than others. Traditionally it has been argued that the economy of Hong Kong has many of the characteristics of a market economy: there is a low level of government involvement in the economy and comparatively few restrictions on the activities of producers. In other cases, such as the UK, there is more direct government involvement in the economy but most output (approximately 80 per cent) is produced by organisations which are owned and controlled by private individuals. Even the economies of Eastern Europe which have traditionally been heavily planned, are now pushing back the frontiers of state involvement in the economy and encouraging the growth of private enterprise.

The economies of the real world are usually referred to as *mixed economies*. In other words, they contain a mixture of private enterprise and state involvement in production and distribution. It is important to note that government intervention in mixed economies does not simply imply that governments decide to finance the production of certain goods and services. They also intervene through the use of taxes and subsidies to influence the price of certain goods and services. The aim is often to discourage or encourage consumption of particular goods and services. In these circumstances, governments work through the price mechanism to influence the allocation of resources. There is this difference in the extent and degree of intervention in different economies. In other words, it is not a question of whether the state intervenes in the economy or not; it is a question of the extent to which the state intervenes in the economy, and this differs from country to country.

Box 1.3 Turning planned economies into market economies

The 1990s has seen rapid change in the former centrally planned economies of Eastern Europe culminating in the collapse of the Soviet Union and the creation of independent states. The main reason for the collapse of the Soviet Union is undoubtedly the failure of planning to achieve anything like the standard of living enjoyed by those who live in the major western economies. The extent of inefficiency in the Soviet Union was made vividly clear in 1990 when Soviet agriculture achieved a record harvest but there were food shortages all over the Soviet Union. In fact, the situation was so bad that food was sent to the Soviet Union from many parts of the world, including the EC, to prevent starvation for many people. The manufacturing sector was equally inefficient and in many cases the techniques of production were unchanged in decades. The result was that many goods taken for granted in the West were simply not available in the East or were badly designed and frequently broke down.

The problems of Eastern Europe did not stem from lack of resources, as is the case with many African countries. Instead, they reflected the failure of planning. Planning involved assigning target levels of output to factory managers. However, if targets were exceeded factory managers were not rewarded financially and instead their targets were increased when the plan was redrawn. They therefore had an incentive to *underproduce* so as to make their own lives easier. Similarly there was little incentive to invest in new technology and/or to improve the quality of the product.

Another problem was that price controls were rigidly applied in an attempt to reduce inequality. This was an important part of communist ideology but it led to a situation where the price consumers paid for many goods and services was well below their free market price and consequently there was overconsumption of some goods and shortages of others. The absence of price signals meant that the planners had to guess how resources could most appropriately be allocated. The existence of long queues and empty shelves was testimony to the failure of planning!

Precise estimates of economic activity in the former USSR are difficult to come by but it is likely that towards the end of the 1980s and into the 1990s the level of production fell considerably, perhaps by as much as 12–15 per cent in 1991. The result has been falling living standards for most people in Eastern Europe. This caused the collapse of the economic plan because it led many of the republics which formerly made up the USSR to believe they could do better if they were free of central control. To put pressure on the Soviet authorities to recognise their independence many republics ceased the export of goods. Because the output of particular goods is concentrated in particular factories this caused shortage of inputs throughout the USSR so that the economic plan disintegrated.

By the 1990s it was clear that economic progress in Eastern Europe required an end to planning and the creation of market economies. This is a tremendously difficult task which involves the reintroduction of private property and the creation of an enterprise culture, this in countries which have no experience of profit and loss accounting, marketing, design, product development and so on, and where the majority of the population have no concept of private property. The first steps in creating a market economy are to reintroduce the right of private ownership supported by the force of law. It is also necessary to create a financial (banking) sector which will channel the funds of savers to industries which need to borrow.

A major change that is necessary to create a market economy is to remove price controls and allow prices to be freely determined. If resources are privately owned, firms will respond to price changes and resources will be allocated through the price mechanism. However, this is fraught with problems. In previous years the shortage of goods in the shops has meant that citizens in Russia and the other republics such as Estonia, Latvia, Lithuania and the Ukraine have tended to save relatively large sums. As price controls have been relaxed and subsidies removed, *most* prices have risen sharply and the value of savings has fallen. In response people have attempted to spend their savings at a time when production cannot respond quickly due to lack of modernisation. The result is that prices have risen even higher. The response of the authorities has been to cut back government spending on goods and services and as they have done so unemployment among those workers who formerly produced these goods and services has risen sharply.

There is a further problem. When most prices in the economy are rising the price mechanism cannot function effectively because producers cannot identify when the rise in price represents a change in society's demand for particular goods in preference to other goods, or a general rise in prices. This implies that shortages of some goods will continue for some time and there seems little the authorities can do to contain rising prices. Even after the cuts in government spending (many of which have been borne by the military) inflation is expected to remain high, perhaps exceeding several hundred per cent in 1993! In these circumstances it is inevitable that for most people their income will buy less and less for some time to come and that living standards will continue to fall.

The transformation from planned economy to market economy also requires large-scale *privatisation* whereby state-owned assets are returned to private individuals and organisations. This, as we shall see on pp. 367–9, is exactly what has happened to many former state-owned industries in the United Kingdom such as electricity and gas which have been privatised. Once an industry is privatised its managers will be guided by the profit motive and will be compelled to respond more quickly and efficiently to changes in consumer demands or risk a rival firm taking their customers away. However, it will take time to modernise industry in Eastern Europe so that it can adjust production in response to changes in consumer demands. It will also take time to alter attitudes so that the entire workforce is more aware of the importance of quality, design, delivery and after-sales service. To achieve this a great deal of emphasis will need to be placed on training. Probably the quickest way to modernise is to allow Western companies to establish subsidiaries in Eastern Europe. Many countries are already doing this!

A particular problem with respect to the balance of payments will exist during the transformation stage from planning to market economy. At present the former planned economies are dependent on Western countries to supply technology. They are also importing a greater volume of consumer goods such as cars and leisure wear. In contrast they have little the West requires and so their exports are relatively low. The result of an excess of imports over exports is a balance of payments deficit. To cope with this the economies of Eastern Europe will need assistance from the international community. This is widely recognised, and Russia, along with other former planned economies such as Hungary and Poland, have become members of the International Monetary Fund (IMF), which, as we shall see on pp. 321–2, provides financial assistance to countries with balance of payments deficits. However, financial assistance from the IMF is conditional on the continued implementation of reforms to achieve market economies. The IMF also insists on the introduction of policies to control inflation and the continuing need of Russia for IMF assistance implies that the control of inflation will remain a priority. The USA and the EC have also been doners of aid to Russia.

The planned economies were also characterised by several environmental problems on a scale unimaginable in the West. Toxic chemicals were routinely dumped into rivers and lakes even where these were close to major cities and towns. Nuclear waste was often buried close to large concentrations of people and there were no controls to restrict the emissions of CO_2 and other environmentally harmful gases into the atmosphere. Since gases released into the atmosphere do not simply cause damage to the environment of the country releasing them, aid from the West is unlikely to continue indefinitely without the establishment of pollution controls in Eastern Europe. A greener Eastern Europe will benefit everybody!

REVIEW QUESTIONS

1 Why is the 'economic problem' a problem?

2 Is the problem of scarcity in the UK greater now than it was in 1970?

3 Apply the concept of opportunity cost to:

(a) A student who stays in full-time education after the age of sixteen.
(b) A firm which borrows funds from a bank to buy a new machine.
(c) A government which finances increased spending on road construction by an increase in taxation.
(d) A home owner who carries out home improvements on a DIY basis in his or her spare time.

4 In what sense is the consumer sovereign in market economies?

5 In a market economy, how will the allocation of resources be affected by technological advances which significantly reduce the cost of producing a particular good?

6 What is 'mixed' in a mixed economy?

CHAPTER 2

THE TOOLS OF ECONOMIC ANALYSIS

CONNECTIONS

In Chapter 2 we shall be examining the role of theories in a social science such as economics. We shall also be studying the uses, presentation and limitations of statistical data in economics. You will find that these two themes are an important feature of this book.

Key Concepts

Bar charts
Graphs
Pie charts
Rounding
Scientific method
Time series
Value judgements

Economics as a Social Science

Economics is often described as a **social science**. It is 'social' because it deals with the behaviour of human beings, in the context of how society makes choices about what output is to be produced, how this output is to be produced and for whom it is to be produced. It is a 'science' because it sets out to analyse economic behaviour by means of the scientific method, which is based on developing theories (hypotheses) to help us understand the events we observe.

A theory comprises four elements:

- A set of consistent and **quantifiable** (measurable) definitions.
- A set of **simplifying assumptions**, sometimes known as a model.
- A set of **logical deductions** from the model.
- A **resulting prediction**, which then represents a theory which can be **tested** against behaviour in the real world.

In the natural sciences theories can be tested through 'controlled' laboratory experiments which can be replicated time and again so that the same results can be demonstrated. However, this is not possible in economics because we are observing human behaviour and a particular set of circumstances can never be perfectly replicated. Economists therefore use **models** to derive theories. A theory is simply a hypothesis which has not yet been contradicted by empirical evidence. As such, it allows us to make predictions about behaviour in the real world. It is possible – indeed, likely – that sooner or later empirical evidence will appear which refutes a theory. When this happens it will need to be discarded or modified, and a search will begin for a new theory.

Where do the ideas for theories or hypotheses 'come from'? A common view is that scientists simply study facts with a neutral, or open, mind until out of a process of prolonged observation a theory ultimately emerges. In fact this approach, which is called the *inductive method*, has played a relatively small part in the develoment of theories. More often than not theories, including those of economics, start with a tentative idea which owes little to induction. We have it on the authority of a distinguished British scientist, Sir Peter Medawar, that 'Hypotheses arise by guess work. That is to put it in its crudest form . . . Hypotheses appear along uncharted by-ways of thought, they are imaginative and inspirational in character . . . The kind of creative process that generates on the one hand poetry as ordinarily understood is also that which operates in the context of science, generating laws and explanations and all else that we recognise as the furniture of scientific thought'.

However, these are deep waters and it is time to make for the shore. From your point of view, as a new student of economics, it is important always to bear in mind two things. First, economists not only need to be able to make **logical deductions** from models, they also require **imagination** and even **intuition**. Secondly, all theories, including those you will be studying in this book, are provisional. Some of today's economic theories may stand the test of time relatively well, others may not. But there is no doubt that in a hundred years the study of economics will probably be very different from what it is now!

However, the question needs to be asked whether the scientific method can be applied to human behaviour. Certainly there are difficulties. One is that controlled experiments (such as those in physics) in which a single factor affecting the result can be isolated and studied, are impossible. This makes it more difficult to link *cause* and *effect*. Another difficulty is that individual human beings often react differently to external events. Fortunately the behaviour of groups of people is more predictable, since a range of individual reactions will often tend to 'average out'. For example, it is difficult to know how an individual will react to a rise in the price of petrol, but we have a good idea of how the motoring public as a whole will react. A third difficulty is that social attitudes and institutions – and hence by implication human behaviour – tend to change over time. Thus a theory which worked well in terms of explaining UK wage bargaining in, say, the 1950s might be much less successful in terms of the 1990s. The final difficulty is that human beings, unlike genes or atoms, are influenced in their behaviour by what they *expect* to happen in the future, and this may influence the way they react to a given change in some economic variable. Nevertheless, economics has had considerable success in explaining some aspects of economic behaviour. However, it is unlikely that economics will ever be an exact science in the way that, say, physics is.

Normative Statements and Positive Statements

An important point arising out of the application of the scientific method to economics is that care must be taken in economic analysis to avoid *normative statements*. These are statements about what ought or ought not to occur in economic matters; they are based on value judgements and are matters of opinion which cannot be tested by reference to facts. For example, it is a matter of opinion whether it is more important for the government to try to reduce inflation or unemployment. *Positive statements*, by contrast, are about what does or does not occur and can therefore in principle be checked by reference to facts. The statement that: 'The rate of inflation in the UK over the last twelve months has been 4 per cent', is a positive statement: it can be checked against the facts and proved to be correct or incorrect.

Positive statements are often of the form, 'If this were to change, that would happen'. It is evident that the successful application of scientific method depends upon the use of positive statements, so that value judgements are avoided and no bias can enter the analysis; normative issues are essentially political and are best resolved through the ballot box. This is not meant to suggest that economics can throw no light on normative issues – for example, society might decide that overcoming inflation was more important than dealing with unemployment. Positive economics can then be brought to bear to study the implications of this choice.

Mathematics and Economics

In economics it is sometimes useful to use mathematical techniques because

- The **behavioural assumptions** which are the basis of an economic theory can often be formulated more precisely by employing mathematics.
- Mathematics is a powerful tool for **deriving logical implications** from the assumptions of economic models.
- The **testing of economic theories** against empirical evidence is assisted by mathematical techniques.

In underlining the role of mathematics in economics we must remember that a theory is as good only as the **assumptions and data** it contains. If these are unsuitable, the theory will be unsuccessful no matter how sophisticated the mathematical and deductive techniques employed.

The Presentation of Economic Data

Tables

We have seen that data plays an important role in the formulation and testing of theories. It is important therefore that all data should be presented in a form which is clear and appropriate. One method of presenting data is in *tabular form* – that is, as a 'table' where figures are arranged in columns and rows. A table has a number of advantages when compared with a straight 'narrative' presentation of data. A table is more concise; it makes it easier to compare figures and to undertake elementary statistical processing such as the calculation of percentages and averages; and it allows the checking of raw data to see if any is missing or inconsistent. These features are illustrated in Table 2.1.

Table 2.1 *UK visible imports by commodity, 1980 and 1989, £m*

Category	1980	1989
Materials	3505	5936
Manufactures	16917	61284
Semi-manufactures	12532	31050
Food and drink	5515	10769
Other	7323	7948
Total	45792	116987

Source: Balance of Payments Pink Book

Figure 2.1 *(a) UK visible imports by commodity; (b) UK volume of imports, 1980 and 1989, pie chart*

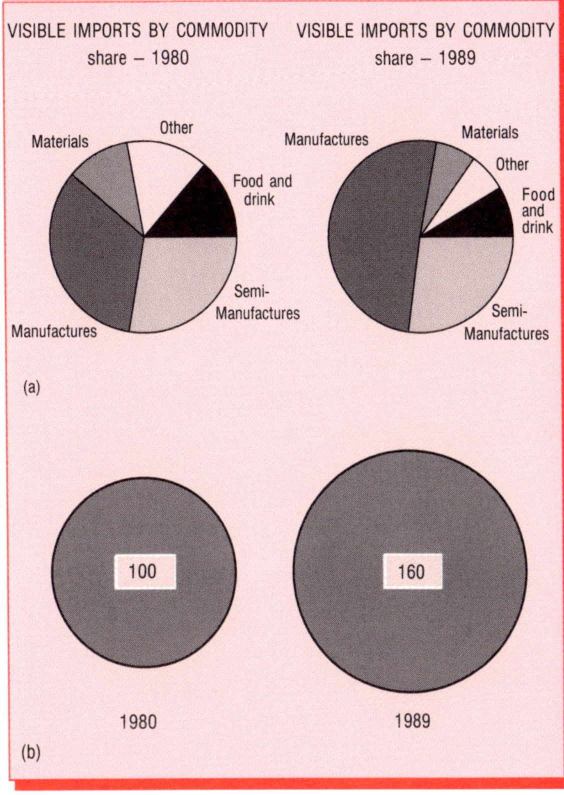

Source: *Lloyds Bank Economic Profile*

Diagrams

Although tables are an important way of presenting economic data, it is sometimes useful to present this in a more vivid diagrammatic form. One method is a *pie chart*, as in Figure 2.1, which shows the changing composition of UK imports between 1980 and 1989. Pie charts are particularly effective at showing the **relative size** of the different components of economic data.

However, pie charts can be quite misleading when used to represent the *magnitude* of data. Consider the volume of UK imports, which in fact increased by 60 per cent from a base of 100 in 1980 to 160 in 1989. In Figure 2.2 this data has been represented by giving the 1989 circle an area which is 60 per cent bigger than the 1980 circle. The problem is that it does not *look* 60 per cent bigger because most people find it difficult to compare different areas. We could if we wished construct the 1989 circle with a 60 per cent bigger diameter but if we did this its area would then be two and a half times greater than that of the 1980 circle! A better way of making this comparison is by constructing a *bar chart*, which we illustrate in

Figure 2.2 *UK volume of imports, 1980 and 1989, bar chart*

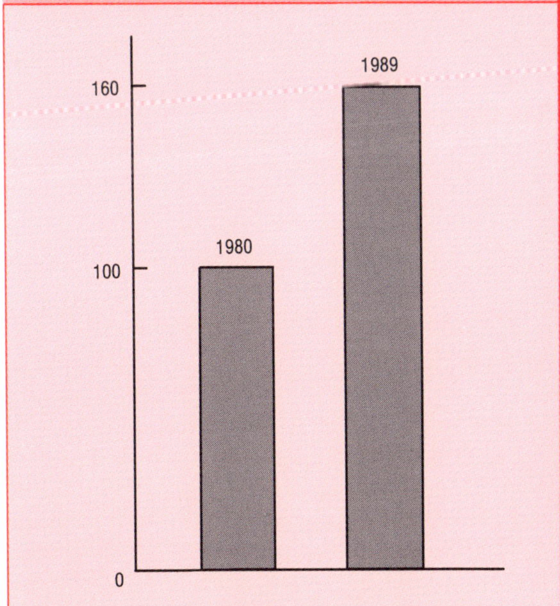

Source: *Economic Trends*

Figure 2.2. We think you will agree that the difference in the level of imports is now readily apparent.

Graphs

Tables and diagrams are very useful, but the most common method employed for presenting economic data is through *graphs*. A graph is a method of representing the relation between two or more 'variables'. For example, suppose it is observed in a market that when the price of a good rises the quantity offered for supply also increases. Price and supply are then examples of *variables*. If we assume the supply of the good to depend upon its price we can further state that supply is the *dependent* variable and price the *independent* variable. Supply is then said to be a *function* of price.

To illustrate, let us take an example. Suppose the supply of rice rises when the market price increases in such a way that when the price, measured in pence, is 20, the supply in kilos is zero; when the price is 30 the supply is 10; when the price is 40 the supply is 20; and so on. In mathematical terms the relationship between the two variables can be expressed by means of the equation:

$$S = P - 20$$

where S is the supply and P the market price.

In order to plot the graph of this equation we have to ask what the quantity supplied would be if the price were 10, 20, 30 and so on. We can present the result as in Table 2.2.

The data in Table 2.2 can now be plotted as shown in Figure 2.3. You will notice that we measure the independent variable, price, along the vertical X axis, and the dependent variable, supply, along the horizontal Y axis. The result is called a **supply curve** even if, as in this example, it traces out a straight line. We can see that the curve we have drawn has a *positive gradient* that is, it slopes upwards from left to right. This reflects the fact that when the **price** of rice rises, the **amount supplied** also rises. In mathematical terms, supply is said to vary *directly* with price.

We can use the same procedure to construct a **demand curve**. Suppose it is observed that buyers' demand for rice, in relation to the market price, is given by the equation

$$D = 100 - P$$

where D is the demand in kilos, and P the price in pence. You can now use the procedure followed

Table 2.2 *Price and quantity supplied*

Price (pence)	Quantity supplied (kilos)
10	–
20	–
30	10
40	20
50	30
60	40
70	50
80	60
90	70
100	80

Figure 2.3 *A supply curve*

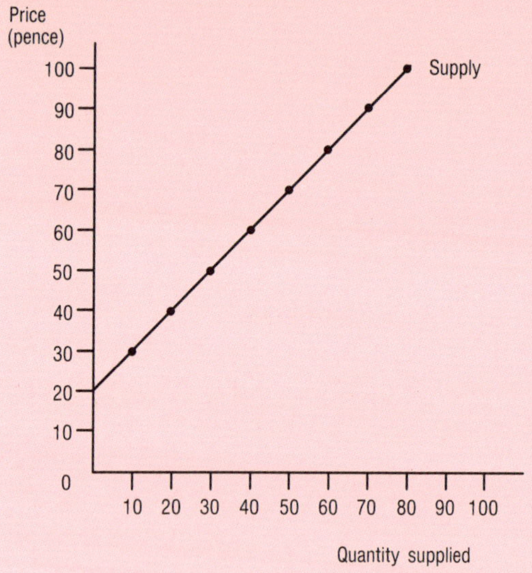

Table 2.3 *Price and quantity demanded*

Price (pence)	Quantity demanded (kilos)
10	90
20	80
30	70
40	60
50	50
60	40
70	30
80	20
90	10
100	0

Figure 2.4 *A demand curve*

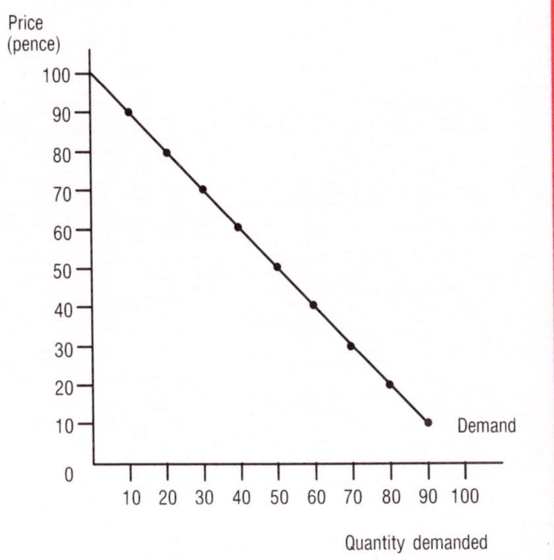

earlier to construct a demand curve. You will observe that the demand curve has a *negative gradient*, reflecting the fact that demand and price 'go in opposite directions': the **lower the price**, the **greater the quantity demanded** by buyers. In mathematical terms, demand and price are said to vary *inversely* with one another (see Table 2.3 and Figure 2.4).

Interpreting graphs

A note of caution must now be sounded about the interpretation of graphs. Consider Figure 2.5. This shows that UK savings fell significantly for the period covered. Now look at Figure 2.6. Here the same fall in savings looks quite dramatic – until we notice that the vertical axis has been changed. First its scale has been altered and secondly a gap has been introduced removing its zero point, the 'origin' of the graph. The effect of changing the axis is to give the quite misleading impression that saving has collapsed. Clearly it is important to be aware that graphs can be deceptive and should be scrutinised carefully before conclusions are drawn from them.

Percentages and Changes in Variables

When measuring the size of one variable relative to another, or when measuring changes in a given variable over time, economists frequently make use of percentages. The term 'per cent' simply means 'per

Figure 2.5 *'Steady decline in savings'*

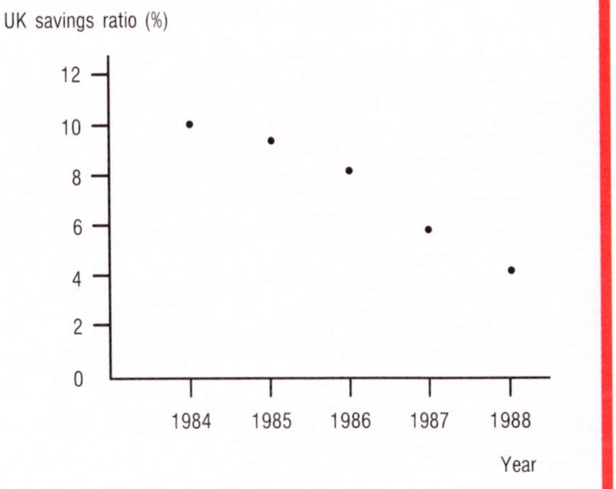

Source: *Economic Trends*

hundred'. For example, 20% is 20 parts of 100, that is:

$$\frac{20}{100} = \frac{1}{5}$$

To convert a fraction to a percentage, we multiply the numerator by 100 and divide by the denominator. So three-quarters as a percentage is:

$$\frac{3 \times 100}{4} = 75\%$$

Figure 2.6 *'Savings collapse'*

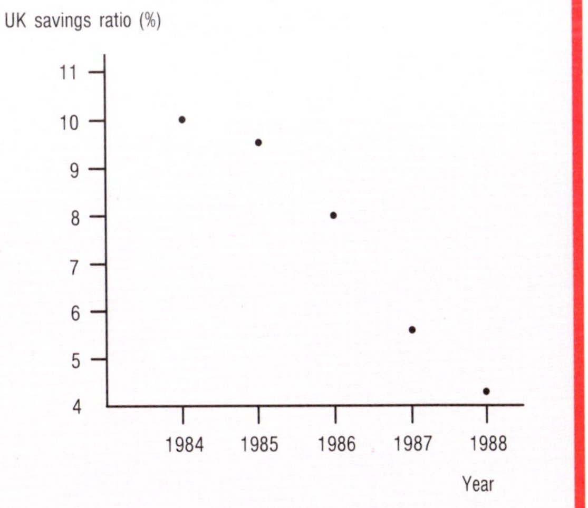

Source: *Economic Trends*

One way of measuring changes over time is in *absolute terms* – for example, if a particular firm increased its output of paper by 1200 tons from 4800 to 6000 tons per week. However, we can often obtain a better insight by calculating *percentage changes*. By 'percentage change' we mean the absolute change in a variable divided by its initial value and multiplied by 100. Thus if paper output increased from 4800 to 6000 tons, the percentage change would be:

$$\frac{1200 \times 100}{4800} = 25\%$$

Most people would find this percentage change more meaningful than the absolute change figure of 1200 tons. It should be noted that whereas absolute changes are measured in **specific units**, percentage changes (like percentages) are **unit-free**.

When studying changes over time we might want to know the percentage changes over a **succession of periods**. We then need to calculate the percentage change from the first period to the second, from the second period to the third, and so on. Percentage changes when expressed in this 'ongoing' form give an indication of the **rate of growth** of the variable being measured. For example, Table 2.4 shows how UK personal income changed between 1987 and 1990.

A word of warning about percentages. Following the March 1991 Budget the rate of Value Added Tax rose from 15 per cent to 17.5 per cent. Some commentators referred to this as an increase of 2.5 per cent. But was it really? Certainly the tax rate had increased by 2.5 *percentage points*. However, the true percentage increase in the amount of tax was actually 2.5 over 15 × 100, that is 16.7 per cent! It is therefore important always to be aware of the distinction between *percentages* and *percentage points*.

Table 2.4 *Increase in personal income on previous year*

Year	Personal income (£bn)	Increase on previous year (%)
1987	285	–
1988	316	10.9
1989	351	11.1
1990	385	9.7

Source: *Economic Trends*

Rounding of Figures

Since all economic data is subject to error and uncertainty (see p. 16) it is generally safe and convenient to employ 'rounded figures' when using data. In Table 2.5 (p. 15) for instance, all the data has been rounded. Clearly this data is not strictly accurate – nevertheless it is good enough for the purpose in hand, which is to establish the underlying trend of the data. When a figure which we are rounding is exactly mid-way between the rounding points, the rule is to round upwards when the first digit is odd, and downwards when it is even. So when rounding to the nearest 100, 750 is rounded up to 800 but 650 is rounded down to 600. A word of caution: remember that you should, where possible, undertake any arithmetical processing *before* you round your figures, otherwise the accuracy of your result is likely to suffer.

Time Series Data and Moving Averages

Data which records the way a given economic variable changes over time (for example, expenditure as in Table 2.5) is known as *time series* data. One important feature of such data is that it is subject to variation, particularly on a **seasonal basis**. There are a number of ways of treating time series data so as to 'smooth out' the variations and isolate the underlying trend. One method is that of *moving averages*. An example will make the method clear. In Table 2.5 the average expenditure on motor vehicles in the four quarters up to the last quarter of 1988 was £3162m. To calculate the corresponding average up to the first quarter of 1989 we delete the first figure in the 1988 series and replace it with the first figure in the 1989 series. The average value of this new set of four observations is seen to have 'moved' to £3233m. In this way a sequence of moving averages can be built up for the period of the data. Figure 2.7 shows clearly how the use of a moving average has the effect of smoothing out variations in time series data and indicating more clearly the underlying trend.

Seasonal Adjustment

When examining time series data one problem is to know whether an observation is influenced wholly

Figure 2.7 *Using a moving average to smooth data*

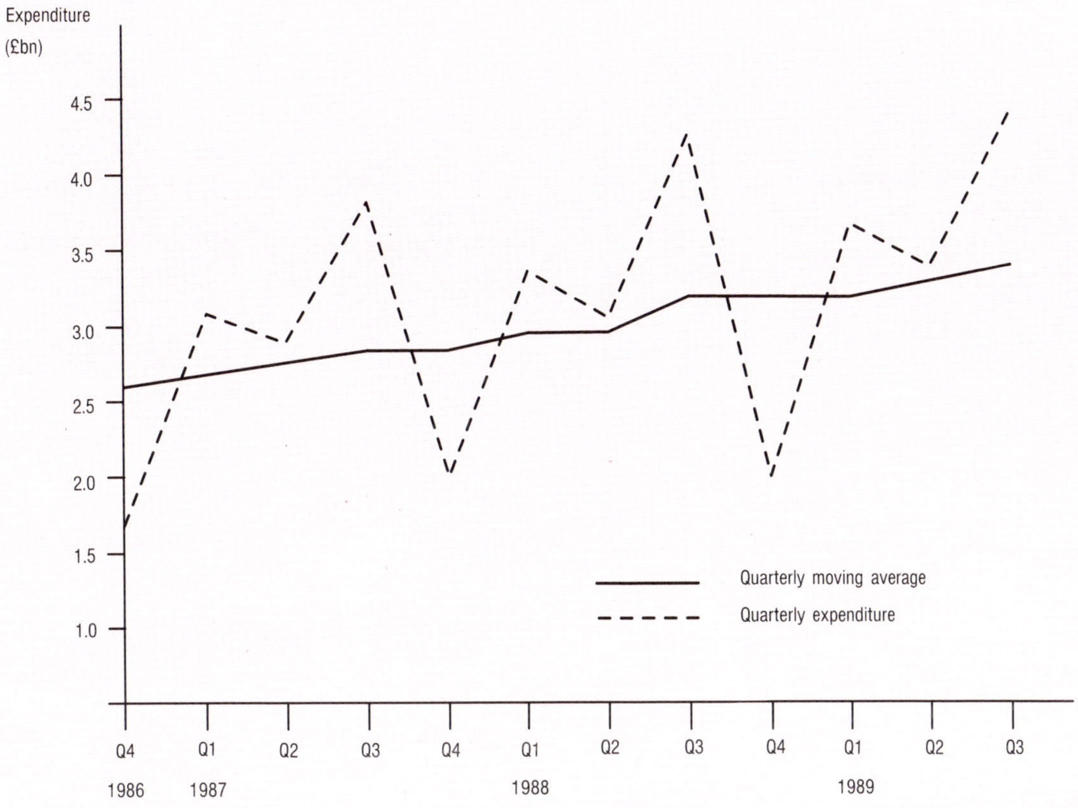

Source: HMSO

by seasonal factors or whether other factors are involved. An advantage of establishing a trend in data is that it makes possible the use of statistical techniques to measure the extent of seasonal factors. These techniques are beyond the scope of this book but as a simplified example let us consider the data in Table 2.5. We can see that the figure for 1987 Q2, at £2885m, shows a fall of £204m on the previous quarter. However, the 'normal' seasonal fall between these two quarters over the three years of the data is in fact £275m. Hence when the seasonal factor is excluded there was in effect a 'rise' in expenditure in the second quarter of 1987.

Data in which, by means of the appropriate statistical techniques, the seasonal element has been removed is called *de-seasonalised* or *seasonally adjusted* data. Seasonal adjustment is commonly used in many areas of economic statistics, for example unemployment statistics. Table 2.6 presents the data from Table 2.5 on a seasonally adjusted basis.

Table 2.5 *Expenditure on motor vehicles: moving average*

		Expenditure (£m)	Expenditure moving average (£m)	Rounded moving average (£bn)
1986	Q4	1729	2611	2.6
1987	Ql	3089	2695	2.7
	Q2	2885	2784	2.8
	Q3	3770	2868	2.9
	Q4	1960	2926	2.9
1988	Ql	3391	3002	3.0
	Q2	3055	3044	3.0
	Q3	4252	3164	3.2
	Q4	1951	3162	3.2
1989	Ql	3672	3233	3.2
	Q2	3386	3315	3.3
	Q3	4438	3362	3.4

Source: HMSO

Table 2.6 *Expenditure on motor vehicles: seasonally adjusted data*

		Expenditure (£m)	Expenditure (£m) (Seasonally adjusted)
1986	Q4	1729	2658
1987	Q1	3089	2793
	Q2	2885	2872
	Q3	3770	2991
	Q4	1960	3048
1988	Q1	3391	3117
	Q2	3055	3078
	Q3	4252	3384
	Q4	1951	3070
1989	Q1	3672	3363
	Q2	3386	3389
	Q3	4438	3494

Source: HMSO

Cross-section Data

Time series data records the way a given variable changes over a period of time. However, economists also frequently use *cross-section data*. This shows the behaviour of a single economic variable across a range of individuals or group of economic agents *at a given point in time*. Because such data breaks up information by some characteristic such as age, gender, or region, it is sometimes called 'dis-aggregated data'. Table 2.7 is a case in point. We can see that for the period in question, while men in manual employment earned more than the average wage, women earned much less; we shall be examining some of the reasons for the low earnings of women in Chapter 17.

The Sources of Economic Data

Economic data is important for two reasons. First it is the starting point for ideas which might eventually develop into economic theories, and can also be used to test these hypotheses. Secondly, data is the basis for the formulation and implementation of *economic policy*. It is therefore doubly desirable that all economic data should as far as possible be accurate and reliable. The extent to which this is achieved will depend partly on the nature of the **sources** of that data. In the UK much economic data comes from government sources, notably the Central Statistical Office and individual government departments. At the international level, data is available from international agencies such as the United Nations, the International Monetary Fund and the International Bank for Reconstruction and Development (World Bank).

Table 2.7 *Average weekly earnings of manual workers in UK manufacturing industry, 1988*

	£
All full-time workers	192.55
Male	213.59
Female	128.82
Part time: female	68.76

Source: HMSO

It is sometimes possible to find already published data which is suitable for use. This is known as *secondary data*: it was first collected by someone else and is now being employed in a secondary use. When treated with care, secondary data can be very useful and is often the only possible source when historical data is required. However, one difficulty with secondary data is that it might have been prepared by a less than reputable organisation. In other words, it should be checked carefully before use. A second difficulty is that the definitions originally employed might be unsuitable, unclear or no longer accessible to the new user. Despite often being cheap and readily available, secondary data will therefore not always be suitable for a particular use. It then becomes necessary to use *primary data*.

Primary data is data which is collected for a particular purpose. The most practical way of obtaining primary data is usually through **sampling**, where data is derived from a small random and representative section of a statistical 'population'. The erratic performance of public opinion polls has given sampling something of a bad name, but sample-based economic data can be quite useful, provided that statistically sound methods of collection and processing are employed. Data which has been checked for safety of sampling and consistency of definitions is sometimes known as *valid data*.

Economic Data and Economic Policy

Governments commonly pursue *economic policies* designed to achieve certain objectives, such as a high level of employment, a sound balance of payments, and so on. The successful pursuit of such policies depends on reliable data. Unfortunately, some economic data in use is actually rather unreliable. There are a number of reasons for this:

- Data **takes time to collect and process**. When it becomes available for use the situation might well have changed and the data will to some extent have become 'out of date'.
- The collection of data is inevitably subject to some **error**.
- Data first collected for one purpose might not be suitable as secondary data for **other purposes**.
- **Differential data** is particularly uncertain. By this term, we mean statistics which arise from the difference between other figures, each of which may contain errors: relatively small statistical adjustments to figures for imports and exports might for example, give the impression that the difference between these aggregates is larger than it actually is.

Box 2.1 How reliable are UK unemployment figures?

One economic statistic which is much in use in the UK as an indicator of the level of economic activity is the total of unemployed people: the lower the figure, the higher the assumed level of activity. But how reliable is this statistic?

In principle, a person is unemployed if he or she is of working age, able and willing to work, but does not have a job. There are two ways in which the number of unemployed people can be measured:

- One method is to ask a sample of the population at regular intervals if they are able and willing to work and if so, whether they are currently employed or unemployed. Information so obtained is **primary data**. (One drawback of this approach is that the criterion of willingness to work is left to the respondent.) This method is used in the USA, but it is not in use in the UK.
- The main method used in the UK is to count the number of people *claiming unemployment benefit* as the basis for determining the level of unemployment. Information so obtained is thus **secondary data**. The major advantage of this method of counting the unemployed is that it is relatively cheap and easy to administer. However, there are several problems with data obtained in this way. First, some of those claiming benefit might not really be seeking work (see p. 363), while others willing to work might have given up claiming benefit. Moreover, when conditions for claiming benefit change (as they often have in the UK) so too does the level of recorded 'unemployment'. This makes it difficult to compare unemployment in one period with unemployment in another period.

It is clear that the unemployment figures should be treated with great caution when used as an economic indicator. In particular, Figure 2.8 shows how the official unemployment data in the UK has been subject to frequent revisions.

Figure 2.8 *Revisions of UK unemployment data*

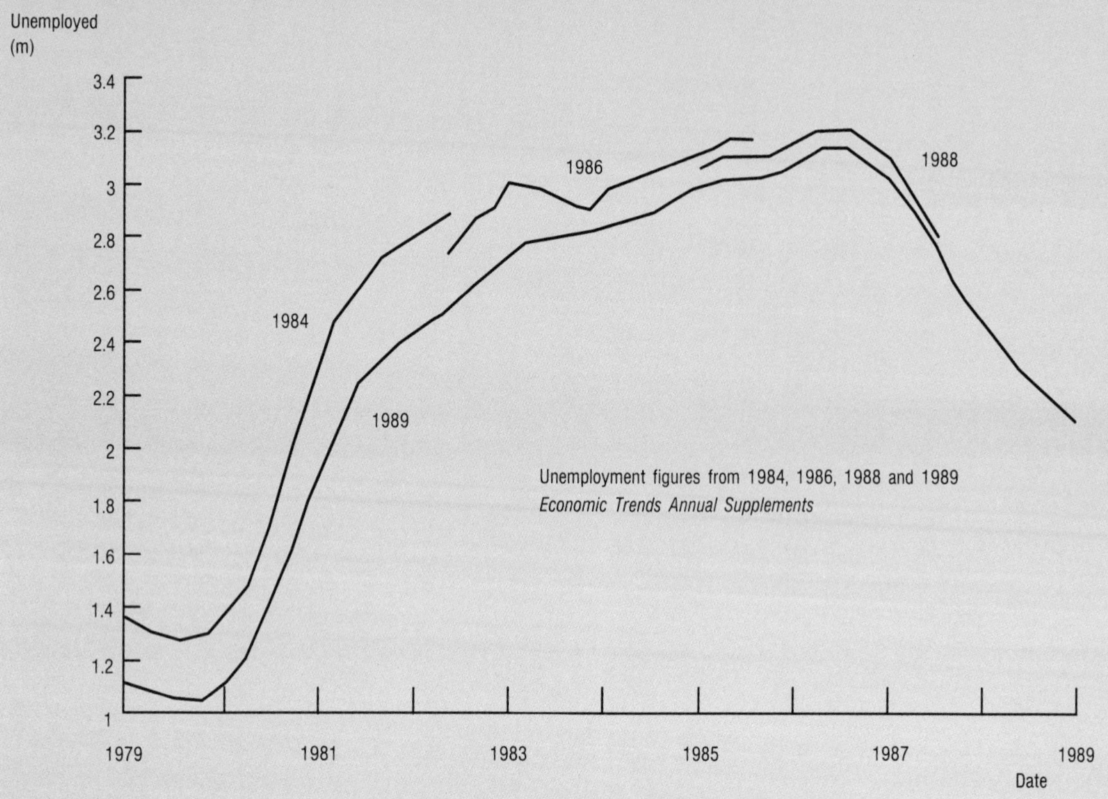

Source: Alan Ingham in the *Economic Review* (January 1990)

REVIEW QUESTIONS

1 Rather than using models would it be better if economists studied the real world as it actually operates when formulating theories?

2 Devise (1) positive and (2) normative statements about the following:

(a) The comparative earnings of nurses and pop stars.
(b) The level of unemployment.
(c) The rate of inflation.
(d) The housing shortage (see p. 47).

3 'Figures from the Institute of Economic Affairs (1991) show that in 1985 the numbers of newly qualified craftsmen, technicians and graduate engineers and technologists in the UK were 35,000, 28,000 and 15,000 respectively. In France the corresponding figures were 92,000, 30,000 and 16,000, while in Germany the figures were 120,000, 43,000 and 22,000'.

Summarise the statistical content of this quotation in tabular form, as a pie chart and as a bar chart. Which form is visually most effective?

CHAPTER 3

DEMAND, SUPPLY AND MARKET PRICE

CONNECTIONS

What determines the price of an HB pencil, an audio tape, or a supersonic airliner? In Chapter 3 we begin to examine how economists study the phenomenon known as *price*. We also introduce the important economic concept of *elasticity* and thus provide the basic economic model which can be used to analyse how prices are determined by **changes in supply and demand**. The model will be used extensively throughout this book.

Key Concepts

Cross elasticity
Demand
Engel curve
Income elasticity
Price elasticity
Quantity demanded
Quantity supplied
Supply

Economists are concerned with the operation of markets and it is therefore useful to begin by examining exactly what the term 'market' implies. In fact we are familiar with markets such as Smithfield, Covent Garden, or local produce markets, but a 'market' in economics is not necessarily tied to a particular location. There are places we can go in order to buy and sell houses, but when we talk about the 'housing market' we are using the word 'market' to describe the *idea* rather than a *place*. For example, an important component of the property market is the local newspaper where property is advertised for sale. A market is simply a set of arrangements which **brings buyers of a good or service into contact with sellers of that good or service**. In this sense, buyers and sellers as referred to as market *participants*.

Demand

Demand is the willingness and ability of consumers to purchase a commodity at a given price, over a particular period of time. This willingness together with the ability is sometimes described as **effective demand**. It does not matter how much we desire something, if we do not have the ability and willingness to pay there can be no effective demand. The inclusion of some **specified time period** is also important. It is meaningless to say that at a price of £10,000, 4000 cars are demanded, unless we know whether this refers to the amount demanded per day, per week, per month and so on.

The Influence of Price on the Quantity Demanded

Price is the most obvious factor that influences demand for any good or service. So important is price that economists have evolved a *law of demand*. This law states that over a given time period and *other things being equal*, the **quantity demanded** of a commodity is **inversely related to its price**. In other words, as the price of a commodity rises, the quantity demanded falls. Economists often illustrate this law by drawing a *demand curve*, as in Figure 3.1. (There is a *possibility* that the demand for certain commodities contradicts the law of demand, giving an upward sloping or 'perverse' demand curve, but for the time being we assume demand curves to be of the orthodox, downward sloping variety. We consider perverse demand curves in Chapter 6.)

Figure 3.1 *Movements along a demand curve*

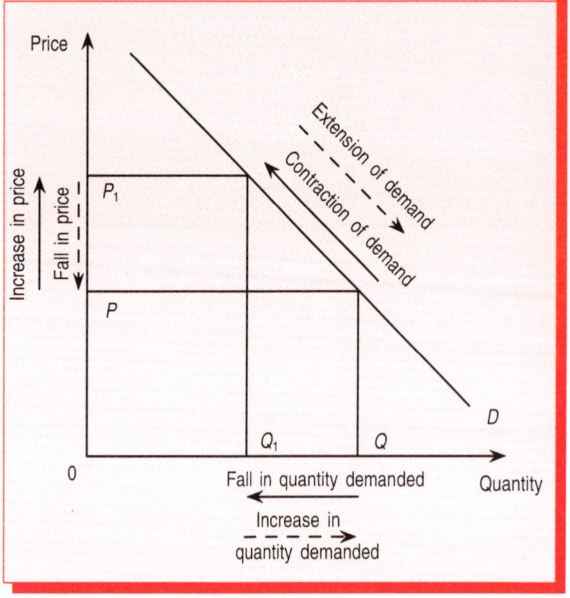

Figure 3.1 shows that any change in price will cause a *movement along* an existing demand curve. The result of this movement, will be an *extension or contraction* of demand, in other words an *increase* or *decrease* in the *quantity demanded*. For example, if price rises from P to P_1, there will be a contraction of demand (a reduction in the quantity demanded) from Q to Q_1. A reduction in price from P to P_2 causes an extension of demand (increase in the quantity demanded) from Q_1 to Q_2.

The Underlying Conditions of Demand

Any factors other than price which might influence demand for a good or service are grouped together as the *underlying conditions of demand*.

When a demand curve is drawn, a relationship is plotted between price and the quantity demanded, *other things being equal*. These 'other things' are the underlying conditions of demand, and if there is a change in any of these conditions of demand then the 'other things being equal' condition is violated and the whole demand curve shifts to a new position. When the demand curve shifts from D to D_1 in Figure 3.2 we say there has been an increase in demand because *more* is now demanded at *any given price* than previously. Conversely, when the demand curve shifts from D to D_2 there has been a reduction in demand because *less* is demanded than previously at *any given price*.

Figure 3.2 *Shifts of a demand curve*

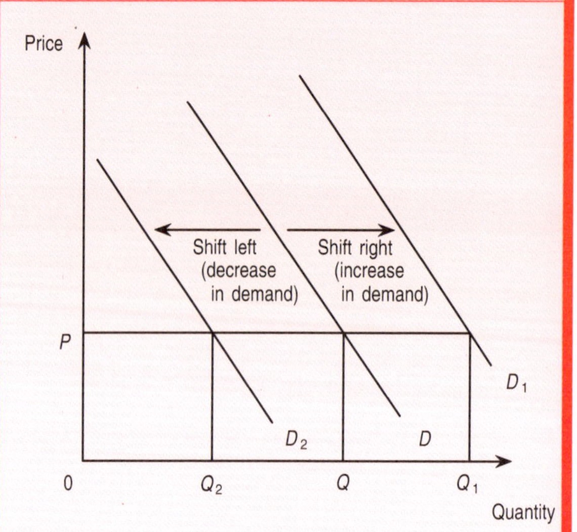

The diagram shows that shifts change the quantity demanded at each and every price. For instance, at price P, a shift from D to D_1 increases quantity demanded to Q_1; a shift to D_2 reduces quantity demanded to Q_2

Let us now examine conditions of demand in more detail.

Income is an important factor in many decisions to buy. Other things being equal, an increase in income will increase the number of goods we can afford. Therefore an increase in income will, in general, shift a demand curve to the right, while a decrease in income will cause a shift to the left. This happens for most goods, and we use the term *normal good* to describe those goods which conform to this relationship. There is a small range of goods, known as *inferior goods*, which people tend to switch away from as incomes rise. The distinction between normal and inferior goods is further discussed on p. 56.

The price of related goods can often affect demand for a particular good. For example, the demand for one brand of coffee is partly related to the price of other brands because they are, to some extent, *substitutes*. In general, a fall in the price of one product can be expected to reduce the demand for its substitute (shift its demand curve to the left) and vice versa.

Other goods might be *complements* – that is, they are *jointly consumed*. Fish and chips are a good example; in this case a fall in the price of one good will lead to an increase in the quantity of that good demanded and will cause an increase in demand (shift the demand curve to the right) for the complement. The opposite is also true, and a rise in the price of one good will cause a reduction in demand for its complement.

Taste is a broad concept which can be used to encompass many influences on demand. Taste is a very personal matter, but sometimes it is possible to identify a fashion or a trend which indicates changes in taste among large numbers of people. For instance, clothes in particular are subject to frequent changes in design. However, changes in taste sometimes occur over longer periods. For example, views on health matters and environmental considerations became much more important during the 1980s and have had a profound effect on the range of 'environmentally friendly' products now produced. When tastes change in favour of a particular product demand for that product will rise, and when they change against a particular product, demand for that product will fall.

Advertising can sometimes have a marked impact on sales, and indeed can influence tastes in favour of certain products. We normally argue that a successful advertising campaign will shift the demand curve for the product which is advertised to the right.

Population change – that is, the size and composition of the population – can exert a long-term influence on demand. For instance, a general increase in the size of a country's population can be expected to increase the demand for most goods and services. Similarly a change in the structure of a nation's population will significantly affect demand for different goods and services. For example, an increase in the number of female births relative to male births would, over time, have a profound effect on demand for certain goods and services.

Movements Along and Shifts of the Demand Curve

We have already stated that a change in price affects demand differently from a change in one of the underlying conditions of demand, and it is worth reinforcing the point at this stage.

Economists make very precise use of language when discussing demand curves. *A change in the quantity demanded* is very different to a *change in demand*. A decrease or increase in the *quantity demanded* refers to a *contraction* or *extension* of demand (a *movement along* the demand curve to the left or right), and can be caused only by a change in *price*, as in Figure 3.1.

A decrease or increase in *demand* refers to a leftward or rightward *shift* of the *whole demand curve*, caused by a change in one of the *underlying conditions of demand*. These shifts in demand are illustrated in Figure 3.2.

These distinctions are very important, and it is essential to become familiar with them. In particular, we use them to explain the **effects** of changes in price.

Supply

Supply is the willingness and ability of producers to make a specific quantity of output available to consumers at a particular price over a given period of time. This willingness together with the ability is sometimes described as **effective supply**.

As with demand, price is probably the main determinant of the amount supplied and economists have formulated a *law of supply* which states that over a given time period and other things being equal, the **quantity** supplied of a commodity is **directly related to its price**. In other words, as the price of a commodity rises, the quantity supplied increases. Economists often illustrate this law by drawing a supply curve, as illustrated in Figure 3.3. Usually, supply curves slope upwards from left to right, showing that producers are more willing and able to produce at higher prices compared with lower prices.

Figure 3.3 *Movements along a supply curve*

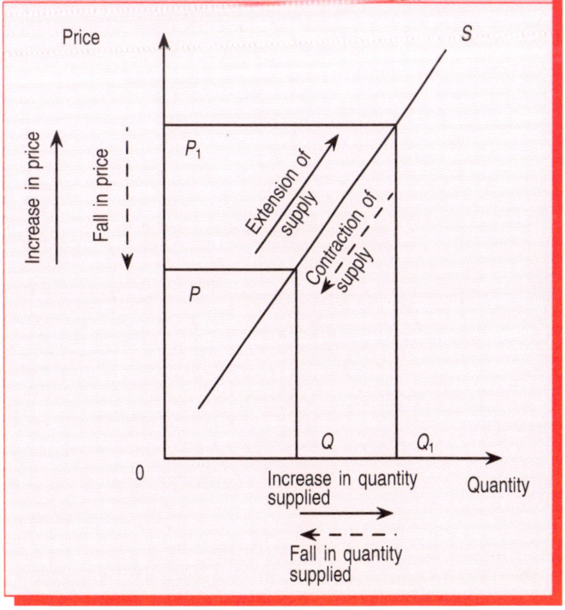

Figure 3.3 shows that any change in price will cause a *movement along* an existing supply curve. The result will be an *extension* or *contraction* of supply, in other words an *increase* or *decrease* in the *quantity supplied*. For example, when price *increases* from P to P_1, quantity supplied increases from Q to Q_1. Conversely, when price decreases from P_1 to P, quantity supplied decreases from Q_1 to Q.

The Underlying Conditions of Supply

The law of supply operates on the assumption that *other things remain equal*. These 'other things' refer to the factors other than price which can affect supply and are known as the *underlying conditions of supply*. Changes in any of these underlying conditions will mean that at each and every price producers will be able to produce either more or less than before, and a new supply curve will need to be drawn. Figure 3.4 illustrates an increase in supply and a decrease in supply. Specifically when the supply curve shifts from S to S_1 we say there has been an increase in supply and when the supply curve shifts from S to S_2 we say there has been a decrease in supply.

The main underlying conditions of supply are as follows.

Money costs of production – that is, the cost of factor inputs (land, labour, capital and enterprise) – has a major influence on supply. In order to purchase these factors of production, money will have to be spent. If at any *given level of output*, there is an increase in costs of production, this will reduce the ability of producers to purchase factors of production at any given price for their product. In consequence the supply curve will shift to the left – that is, there will be a reduction in supply. A fall in costs of production at any given level of output shift the supply curve to the right.

Figure 3.4 *Shifts of a supply curve*

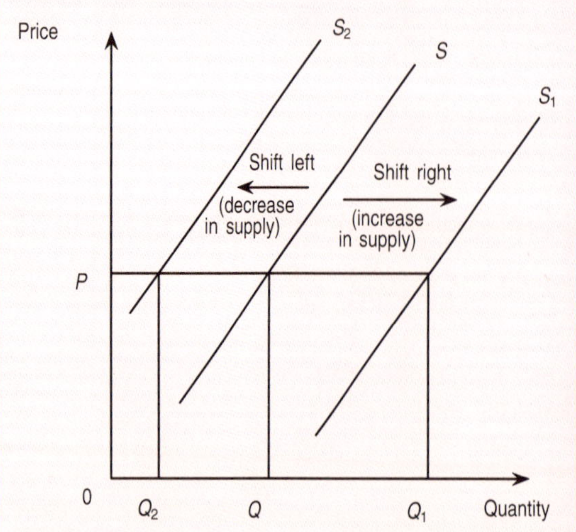

The diagram shows that Shifts change the quantity supplied at each and every price. For instance, at price P, a shift from S to S_1 increases quantity supplied from Q to Q_1; a shift to S_2 reduces quantity supplied to Q_2

Inter-related supply can be an important factor in some cases. Some goods are in *joint supply*, so that variations in the amount of one good produced almost automatically affect the supply of by-products. Thus an increase in the output of beef can be expected to shift the supply curve for leather to the right. Other goods are in *competitive supply*, especially when they have an important raw material in common. Thus liquid milk can be turned into either cheese or butter, and an increase in the amount of cheese produced from a given quantity of milk may reduce the supply of butter.

Events beyond human control in particular may affect the supply of certain agricultural products. In some years there may be good harvests, in others poor harvests because of favourable or unfavourable weather conditions. In consequence, we can visualise the supply curve of various crops shifting to the right (an increase in supply) or to the left (a reduction in supply) depending on the weather conditions. The effects of natural disasters (such as earthquakes, or floods) can also be put into this category, as can occurrences such as the effect on the supply of oil of wars in the Middle East (insofar as these are beyond human control).

Taxes and subsidies can have an important effect on supply. A tax on the production or sale of a good or service can be regarded as an increase in costs and will thus shift the supply curve to the left. A *subsidy* on the production or sale of a good or service can be regarded as a reduction in costs and will thus shift the supply curve to the right. There is a fuller analysis of the effects of taxes and subsidies on p. 344.

Movements Along and Shifts of a Supply Curve

Again it is necessary to stress the importance of using terms precisely. A *change in the quantity supplied* is very different to a *change in supply*. A decrease or increase in the *quantity supplied* refers to a *contraction* or *extension* of supply (a *movement along* the supply curve to the left or right), and can be caused only by a change in *price*. The effect of changes in price on quantity supplied is illustrated in Figure 3.3 on p. 21.

A decrease or increase in *supply* refers to a leftward or rightward *shift* of the supply curve, caused by a change in one of the *underlying conditions of supply*. The effect of changes in the underlying conditions of supply is illustrated in Figure 3.4 on p. 22.

The Determinants of Price

Having examined the determinants of demand and supply, we can bring the demand and supply curves together to show how **price is determined in a free market**. Figure 3.5 combines the demand curve for a particular good with the supply curve of that good.

Figure 3.5 *The determination of equilibrium price*

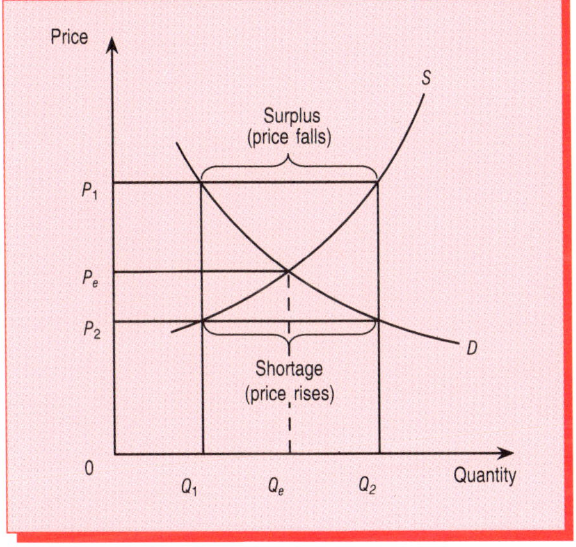

Figure 3.5 is one which is familiar to all economists, and it illustrates the *law of price* which states that markets will tend to settle at an *equilibrium price* where **quantity demanded is equal to the quantity supplied**. In this case, the equilibrium price is OP_e. No other price could be sustained in a market free of government restriction.

If market price is OP_1, the quantity demanded by consumers is OQ_1, while the quantity which producers wish to supply is OQ_2. There is thus a surplus at this price represented by Q_1Q_2. It is well known that a surplus leads to a downward pressure on price, so we can expect market price to fall. At the lower price of OP_2, the quantity supplied is OQ_1, while the quantity demanded is OQ_2. There is therefore a shortage at this price represented by Q_1Q_2. This shortage tends to put upward pressure on price, and we would therefore expect market price to rise.

There is only one price in Figure 3.5 at which the quantity supplied is equal to the quantity demanded, and where there is no surplus or shortage and therefore no upward or downward pressure on price. This is the price OP_e, where the supply and demand curves intersect, and we would expect this market to move towards OP_e with a quantity of OQ_e supplied and demanded. Because consumers and producers are in balance at this price and quantity we refer to this as an *equilibrium* position. The equilibrium price is sometimes referred to by economists as a *market clearing price* due to the absence at this price of surpluses and shortages.

The Effect of Changes in the Underlying Conditions of Demand and Supply

Once price settles at an equilibrium level we can expect it to remain there until something happens to **disturb the equilibrium**. This can only be a change in one or more of the underlying conditions of demand and/or supply which cause demand and/or supply to shift. For example, if we consider the market for lettuces. How would this market be affected by a sudden spell of late frost which destroyed many young plants? Clearly such an occurrence would shift the supply curve to the left, and this would result in a higher price with a lower equilibrium quantity. Suppose, instead, that there were a long spell of warm weather, so that people demanded more lettuces to put in their summer salads. In this case the demand curve would shift to the right, resulting in a rise both in equilibrium price and in quantity.

Altering the Underlying Conditions of Supply or Demand

All sorts of things can happen to alter the underlying conditions of supply or demand, but they can all be reduced to four possibilities: either demand will shift or supply will shift; and the shift will either be an increase or a reduction. These four possibilities are shown in Figure 3.6. Case I illustrates the decrease in supply of lettuces discussed above, while Case IV corresponds with the increase in demand for lettuces.

Figure 3.6 *Altering the underlying conditions of supply and demand: graphical presentation*

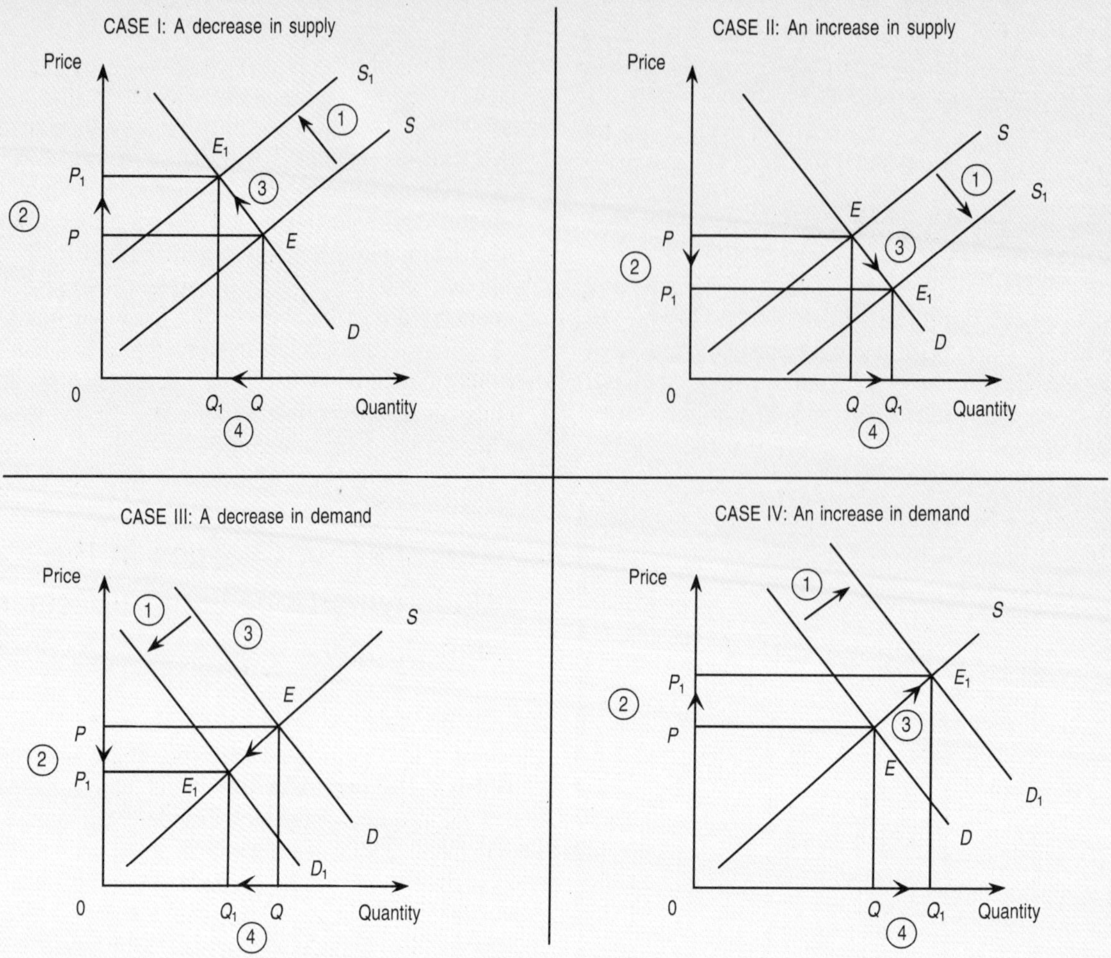

KEY

1 Shift (caused by changed conditions)
2 Change in price (caused by shift)
3 Contraction or extension (caused by price change)
4 Change in quantity

The possibilities are summarised in chart form in Figure 3.7, on the following page.

It is important to note that when a demand curve shifts, there is a *movement along* the supply curve, with the result that the amount supplied and demanded in equilibrium change – although for different reasons. Similarly, a shift in supply is accompanied by a *movement along* the demand curve.

Using Supply and Demand Theory

We are now in a position to use supply and demand theory to analyse simple problems and make predictions. Suppose, for instance, we are asked how the following changes would affect the market for textbooks:

(a) A large fall in incomes.

Figure 3.7 *Altering the underlying conditions of supply and demand: tabular presentation*

Case	Shift	Price	Quantity
I	Supply, left	Increase	Decrease
II	Supply, Right	Decrease	Increase
III	Demand, left	Decrease	Decrease
IV	Demand, Right	Increase	Increase

(b) The introduction of relatively cheap computerised printing methods.

In (a) a fall in income will have at least two effects on this market. First, students will have less money to spend on all goods and services, including textbooks. Secondly, the government will receive less money in tax revenue, and might therefore have to reduce expenditure on school books. The demand curve shifts to the left; price falls and the quantity supplied contracts. In Figure 3.6, Case III provides a suitable diagram which could be used to illustrate this reasoning.

An answer to (b) would incorporate a diagram similar to Case II from Figure 3.6, as in this case the reduction in costs of production can be expected to shift the supply curve to the right.

Elasticity of Demand and Supply

We can now begin to extend and deepen our analysis of markets, and we devote the rest of this chapter to another important tool of economic analysis: that of *elasticity*.

Elasticity is broadly defined as the **responsiveness** of one variable to changes in another. In this section we examine four different types of elasticity: price elasticity of demand, income elasticity of demand, cross elasticity of demand, and elasticity of supply.

Price Elasticity of Demand

Price elasticity of demand measures the **responsiveness of consumers to changes in price**. The general formula for measuring price elasticity is:

$$E_D = \frac{\text{Percentage change in quantity demand}}{\text{Percentage change in price}}$$

where E_D stands for price elasticity of demand. This is sometimes called the *own-price* elasticity to distinguish it from *cross elasticity*, which we will discuss later. Elasticity is expressed as a coefficient and the greater the size of this coefficient, the greater the effect of a change in price on quantity demanded.

Alternatively we can calculate elasticity by applying the following formula:

$$E_D = \frac{P \times dQ}{Q \times dP}$$

(where P is the original price, Q is the original quantity, dP is the change in price, and dQ is the change in quantity). Question 5 on p. 34 provides an opportunity to practice using this formula to calculate elasticities.

Since the vast majority of demand curves slope downwards, the coefficient of price elasticity will generally be *negative*. This is because any *increase* in price will result in a *decrease* in quantity, so that in the elasticity formula if dP is positive dQ will be negative (and vice versa) and a negative divided by a positive gives a negative result. Because we always expect E_D to be negative, we often omit the negative sign.

If we calculate the coefficient of elasticity and find it to be greater than 1, we describe this as *elastic* demand. This means that a change in price has a relatively large impact on quantity demanded. Coefficients between 0 and 1 are said to be *inelastic*, with price changes having relatively little effect on quantity demanded.

Price elasticities along a straight line demand curve

Consider the demand curve shown in Figure 3.8.

The formula $\frac{P \times dQ}{Q \times dP}$

tells us that elasticity will have a different value at every point on a straight line demand curve like that shown in Figure 3.8. Why is this? Consider what happens when P is increasing. Any *given change* in P represents a smaller percentage change in the original price. However, the percentage change in Q becomes larger and larger. For example, in terms of Figure 3.8 when price rises from £2 to £4, elasticity of demand is:

Figure 3.8 *Elasticity of demand when price rises from £2 to £4*

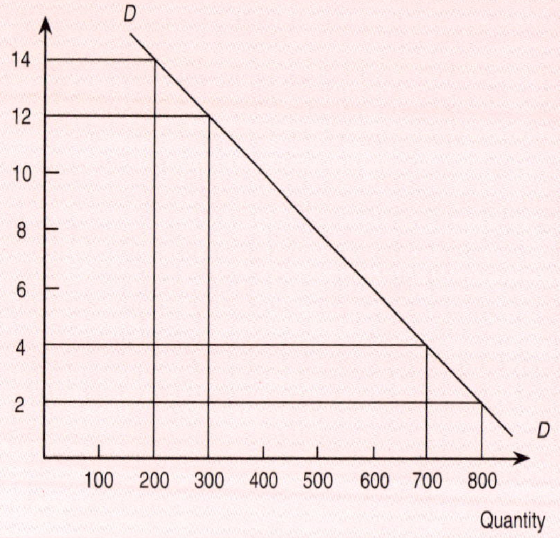

$$\frac{P \times dQ}{Q \times dP} = \frac{2 \times 100}{800 \times 2} = 0.125$$

but when price rises from £12 to £14, elasticity of demand rises to

$$\frac{P \times dQ}{Q \times dP} = \frac{12 \times 100}{300 \times 2} = 4$$

In this case *the same given change in price has a proportionately greater effect on quantity.*

Despite this, some straight line demand curves have a constant elasticity. Panels (a) and (b) of Figure 3.9 illustrate these exceptions. Panel (c) illustrates another demand curve with constant elasticity: one that has elasticity equal to unity along its entire length.

Factors influencing price elasticity of demand

What is it that determines whether one commodity has a higher elasticity of demand than another? There are several possible influences, including the following.

The proportion of income spent on a good is an important factor in determining elasticity of demand. A family holiday takes up a more substantial part of a family budget than a box of matches. Therefore there is likely to be more response to a 10 per cent change in the price of holidays than a 10 per cent change in the price of a box of matches.

The availability of substitutes will influence elasticity of demand. If a good has many substitutes consumers are able to switch to an alternative as its price rises or an alternative can be readily abandoned as its price falls. The situation is different where a good has few substitutes, or where those substitutes which do exist are not close substitutes. It should be noted that as we broaden our *definition* of a good, so we reduce the number of substitutes and therefore reduce the price elasticity of demand. Thus the demand for pork is more price elastic than that for meat, and the demand for meat is more elastic than that for food. Similarly the demand for a certain brand of washing powder can be expected to be more price elastic than the overall demand for all washing powders.

Figure 3.9 *Demand curves with constant elasticity*

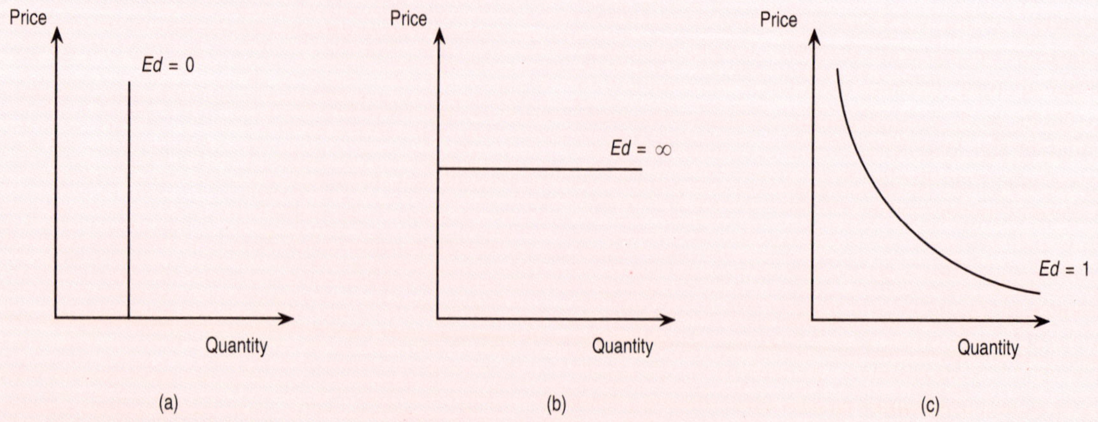

The durability of a good might affect elasticity of demand in some cases. A 'durable' good is one which can be consumed time and again. Television sets and refrigerators are durable goods, whereas cigarettes and food are not. For some goods, such as motor cars, durability enables car owners to postpone the purchase of a replacement. This durability also gives cars a secondhand value, which might encourage an owner to sell his or her existing car to purchase a new one. Thus, if a car owner finds that the price of new cars has risen, then he or she might react by deciding not to buy a new one and might try to run the existing car for a little longer. If, on the other hand, car dealers make some sort of 'special offer' amounting to a reduction in their prices, potential customers might be encouraged to purchase a new car immediately. In other words, the owners of older cars might be **responsive** to changes in the price of new cars.

The number of uses for a good is an important determinant of elasticity in some cases. Where a good has many uses, it is possible that small reactions by consumers purchasing for particular uses can 'add up' to a large overall reaction. Electricity, for instance, has a number of uses and is sold on several markets. It is used in the home for heating and lighting, in industry to power machines, in transport to drive trains, and so on. Each of these markets might be fairly price inelastic, but it is quite possible that the overall demand for electricity will be less inelastic than its demand for any particular use.

Addictive goods such as alcohol, cigarettes (and, some nutritionists would add, sugar and chocolate) are habit-forming. This helps to reduce the responsiveness of consumers to changes in price.

The time period under consideration is important and, in general, demand is more elastic the longer the time period under consideration. During the oil price shocks of the 1970s, the demand for Middle East oil products was fairly inelastic, and the industrialised countries suffered due to their inability to react quickly to price changes. However, since that time alternative sources of energy have been developed, so that in the long term demand has proved to be more elastic than in the short term.

These influences are offered as *possibilities*, and for many commodities it would be very difficult to define precisely what affects price elasticity of demand. Some of these influences will tend to counteract each other; a very durable good might have very few substitutes, for instance.

It is sometimes suggested that whether a good is a necessity or luxury is a possible influence on price elasticity. We would recommend avoiding this argument for several reasons. First, some economists use the words 'necessity' and 'luxury' to refer to items which are income inelastic and income elastic respectively, so to use these terms in connection with price elasticity can cause confusion. Secondly, many economists are unhappy about linking the words 'necessity' and 'luxury' to *any* measure of elasticity, as it causes problems of definition. For example, should cigarettes be defined as a necessity and meat as a luxury? Thirdly, it can be argued that the terms 'necessity' and 'luxury' are superfluous, and we can live quite normal lives as economists without them. If we accept that goods which we think of as necessities are in fact goods with few substitutes, and luxuries are goods with many substitutes, then this so-called influence on price elasticity is already covered in our discussion above.

A word of warning is appropriate here. The factors influencing elasticity should not be confused with the underlying conditions of demand. The former are concerned with *movements along* the demand curve; while the latter are related to the *position* of the demand curve with changes causing *shifts* of the demand curve.

Total expenditure and price elasticity

If we multiply the price of a good by the number of units consumed, then the result measures the *total expenditure* or *outlay* of consumers. The total expenditure of consumers will, of course, have the same value as the *total revenue* received by the sellers of the good.

There is an important relationship between total expenditure on a good and price elasticity of demand. This relationship summarised thus:

- $Ed > 1$ a *rise* in price leads to a *fall* in total expenditure.
- $Ed > 1$ a *fall* in price leads to a *rise* in total expenditure.
- $Ed < 1$ a *rise* in price leads to a *rise* in total expenditure.
- $Ed < 1$ a *fall* in price leads to a *fall* in total expenditure.
- $Ed = 1$ a rise or fall in price leaves total expenditure *unchanged.*

This tells us that if we look at the *total expenditure before and after a price change*, we can estimate whether demand is elastic, inelastic or unity. Conversely, if we know whether demand is elastic, inelastic or unity at the current price, we can predict whether a price change will increase or reduce total revenue. To see why this is so, consider Figure 3.10.

In general there are six possibilities. Price can either rise or fall, and demand can either be elastic, inelastic or unity. These six posibilities and their effect on total expenditure are illustrated in Figure 3.10, which shows that in each case the actual result is the same as the expected result. The reader is invited to select other price changes than those we have considered, to compute the relevant elasticity values and compare the actual effect on total revenue with the expected effect.

Income Elasticity of Demand

We can examine the effect of changes in income on the demand for a good (price and other conditions of demand remaining constant) by drawing a graph with income on the vertical and demand on the horizontal axis. This kind of demand curve is known as an *Engel Curve*, after the nineteenth-century Prussian statistician Ernst Engel who first studied relationships between income and expenditure. Usually an increase in income will increase demand, and so the Engel curve for *normal* goods slopes upwards from left to right. Goods with a downward sloping Engel curve, which people tend to switch away from as incomes increase, are known as *inferior goods* – not because they are necessarily shoddy or of poor quality, but because people regard them as **less desirable as their incomes rise**.

Income elasticity of demand E_Y is the **degree of responsiveness of consumers to a change in income**. It can be measured using the formulae:

Box 3.1 The significance of price elasticity of demand

It is not difficult to see why a knowledge of price elasticities of demand would be very useful to various decision makers. Within firms, local authorities and central government, decisions which affect prices are constantly being taken and, as we have seen, changes in price will affect both quantity demanded and total expenditure. A city council, for instance, might wish to know whether it could reduce traffic congestion in its city centre by subsidising fares on the municipal bus service. Price elasticity of demand will play at least some part in determining the success, or otherwise, of this policy. If demand for bus services is inelastic, then a substantial price reduction will be necessary in order to make any noticeable difference to the number of passengers travelling by bus. On the other hand, if demand is elastic, then the subsidy could be self-financing, because the revenue lost to the council from the lower price will be more than compensated for by extra expenditure from new passengers.

Consider the following policy options, and decide to what extent price elasticity of demand will determine whether the decision makers in question will achieve their objectives:

1 A farmer wants to know if the planting of a larger acreage of crop would be worthwhile.

2 The Chancellor of the Exchequer is considering increasing government revenue by imposing VAT on a product which at the moment is untaxed.

3 British Rail is considering increasing its prices for commuter services while reducing off-peak fares, and hopes to increase both the number of passengers carried and total revenue.

4 The Post Office is considering the viability of offering a special cheap stamp for delivery of Christmas cards.

In case 1, the farmer would need to consider the effect on crop prices of the increased output. If demand is elastic total revenue will rise, but to increase profits it must rise by more than the additional costs involved in increasing the acreage, planting and harvesting the crop. An indirect tax, such as that mentioned in case 2 will have the effect of increasing price to consumers and will increase government revenue if demand is elastic. In case 3 it is assumed that commuters are unresponsive to price increases, while the demand for off-peak travel is more elastic so that a price decrease will lead to a substantial increase in the quantity demanded. In case 4 the Post Office might consider that the demand for stamps for Christmas cards is more elastic than the demand for stamps for other mail. Whereas a price *increase* might increase the total revenue from other mail, a price *decrease* might have the same effect in the case of Christmas mail.

$$E_Y = \frac{\text{Percentage change in quantity demanded}}{\text{Percentage change in income}}$$

or

$$\frac{Y \times dQ}{Q \times dY}$$

where Y = original income, Q = original quantity, dY = change in income, dQ = change in amount demanded.

For normal goods income elasticity of demand is *positive*: as income rises demand for most goods and services rises. However, it is important to take care with the sign of the coefficient of income elasticity of demand, because inferior goods have a *negative* income elasticity of demand. Inferior goods are considered in further detail (along with goods known as *Giffen goods* and *Veblen goods*) in Chapter 6. The most frequently quoted examples of inferior goods are bread and potatoes, and coarse grades of rice in countries where this item replaces the potato as a staple part of the diet. It might be that certain services and consumer durables have negative income elasticities: bus travel and black and white television sets are possibilities.

Income elasticity of demand has great significance for the different industries in the economy. We shall see in Chapter 36 that in the UK a major aim of all governments is to raise incomes. For industries with an income elastic demand for their products, this implies **rising demand**. However, those with a negative income elasticity of demand will be forced to **contract**. However, it is not just incomes in the UK which have implications for UK industry: rising incomes in other parts of the world will affect the demand for UK goods which are sold abroad (exports). Here again, if demand for UK goods is income inelastic in other countries, then as incomes abroad rise demand for certain UK industries' output will fall and they may therefore decline. This has implications for the balance of payments, for employment, and for the standard of living in the UK.

Cross Elasticity of Demand

The cross elasticity of demand between two goods X and Y attempts to measure the **responsiveness of consumers of** X to a change in the price of Y, using the formulae

$$E_C = \frac{\text{Percentage change in the quantity demanded of good } X}{\text{Percentage change in the price of good } Y}$$

Figure 3.10 *Price changes and total revenue*

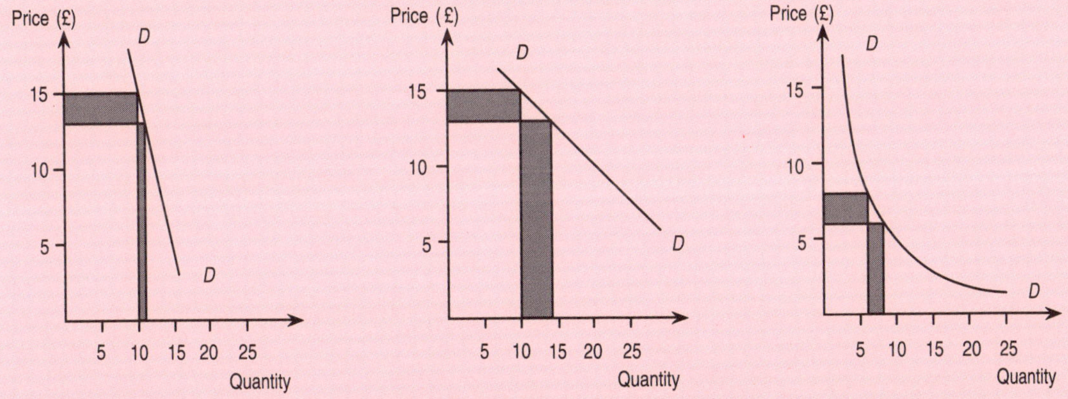

Price falls from £15–£13
Ed = 0.75 (Ed < 1)
Total expenditure falls

Price rises from £13–£15
Ed = 0.59 (Ed < 1)
Total expenditure rises

Price falls from £15–£13
Ed = 3 (Ed > 1)
Total expenditure rises

Price rises from £13–£15
Ed = 2.33 (Ed > 1)
Total expenditure falls

Price falls from £15–£13
Ed = 1
Total expenditure unchanged

Price rises from £6–£8
Ed = 1
Total expenditure unchanged

where E_C = the cross elasticity of demand of good X with respect to good Y, or

$$E_C = \frac{P \times dQ}{Q \times dP}$$

where P = original price of good Y, Q = original quantity demanded of good X, dQ = change in quantity demanded of good X, dP = change in price of good Y.

The main point to remember is that substitutes, like tea and coffee, have **positive cross elasticity** (because a rise in the price of one good causes an increase in demand for the substitute) while complements, like fish and chips have **negative cross elasticity** (because a rise in the price of one good causes a fall in demand for the complement).

Examples of elasticities

Table 3.1 shows estimated elasticities of demand for certain foodstuffs.

Concrete figures for items other than foods are more difficult to obtain, but a table of demand elasticities based on the UK government's Family Expenditure Surveys between 1973 and 1984 is given in Table 3.2.

The columns in Table 3.2 show own-price elasticities, cross elasticities, and income elasticities. The numbers on the diagonal give the own-price elasticities; the off-diagonal elements are the cross price elasticities, and the last but one line shows the income elasticities. The last line gives the proportion of household expenditure that is devoted to each item; 33.5 per cent on food, 1 per cent on spirits, etc.

Table 3.1(a) *Income and own-price elasticities of demand*

Item	Income elasticity of demand (1987)	Price elasticity of demand (1982–7)
Liquid milk	–0.13	0.13
Cheese	0.26	–1.53
Carcase meat	0.21	–1.17
Bread	–0.18	–0.25
Fruit	0.66	–0.53
Potatoes	–0.43	–0.14

Table 3.1(b) *Cross elasticities of demand*

	Cattle meat	Sheep meat	Pig meat
Cattle meat	–	–0.06	0.10
Sheep meat	0.15	–	0.03
Pig meat	0.25	0.03	–

Source: HMSO, *Household Food Consumption and Expenditure* (1987); HMSO, *Annual Report of The Food Survey Committee.*

Elasticity of Supply

Unlike the demand side, where there are three types of elasticity to consider, economists usually only distinguish one type of supply elasticity, measuring the **responsiveness of market supply to changes in the price of the product**. The elasticity of supply, E_S, is measured using the formulae:

$$E_S = \frac{\text{Percentage change in quantity supplied}}{\text{Percentage change in price}}$$

or

$$E_S = \frac{P \times dQ}{Q \times dP}$$

where P = original price, Q = original quantity supplied, dP = change in price, dQ = change in quantity supplied.

Because supply curves normally slope upwards from left to right, elasticity of supply is usually positive. The main types of elasticity of supply are shown in Figure 3.11.

Factors influencing elasticity of supply

What determines whether a good has a relatively elastic or inelastic supply? The main influence is the *time factor*, with other influences generally involving the extent to which *the time factor can be overcome.*

The time factor is an important determinant, of elasticity of supply and economists identify three supply periods: the *momentary period*, the *short period* and the *long period*. Let us take the supply of tomatoes as an example. Certain *factors of production* are required for the production of tomatoes. Some of

Table 3.2 *Estimated own-price, cross and income elasticities*

Price elasticities	Beer price	Wine price	Spirits price	Food price	Fuel price	Clothing price	Transport price	Service price	Other price
Beer	−1.42	−0.08	0.24	0.10	0.52	−0.03	0.10	−0.16	−0.17
Wine	−0.40	−0.51	−0.61	−0.43	0.78	−0.05	−0.91	−0.10	0.15
Spirits	0.96	−0.57	−2.59	0.09	0.16	0.40	0.61	00.5	−1.27
Food	0.03	0.00	0.02	−0.54	−0.02	0.02	0.00	0.02	−0.03
Fuel	0.21	0.08	0.03	−0.10	−0.02	0.02	−0.23	−0.06	0.11
Clothing	−0.03	0.00	0.06	−0.18	−0.14	−0.67	−0.16	−0.39	0.16
Transport	0.00	−0.05	0.05	−0.34	−0.27	−0.10	−0.64	−0.01	−0.16
Services	−0.08	−0.00	0.01	−0.35	−0.17	−0.23	−0.04	−0.78	−0.04
Other	−0.07	0.02	−0.11	−0.26	0.07	0.15	−0.14	0.4	−0.69
Income elasticities	0.88	2.07	2.18	0.49	0.59	1.29	1.52	1.68	0.99
Shares	0.043	0.010	0.010	0.335	0.115	0.083	0.160	0.136	0.108

Source: Symons and Walker, 'Fiscal Harmonisation', *Economic Review* (May 1990).

hese factors – such as land, greenhouses, irrigation equipment, and the tomato plants themselves – are *fixed* over shorter time periods, because it takes some time to bring more of these factors into productive use. Other factors – such as fertilisers, water, and (to some extent) labour – are relatively *variable* which means that the amount of these factors devoted to tomato growing can be varied relatively quickly. We examine these concepts in more detail in Chapter 7 in our treatment of the *law of diminishing returns*. Here it will suffice to say that in the *momentary time period* all factors of production are fixed; in the *short run* some factors are fixed while others are variable; and in the *long run* all factors are variable.

It follows that in the *momentary* time period, the supply of tomatoes is fixed: that is to say, the *elasticity of supply is zero*. For example, on any particular day growers send a certain quantity of tomatoes to market and no matter what happens to price supply cannot be varied on that day.

In the *short run*, tomato growers can increase their use of variable factors in order to exploit their fixed factors more intensively. They can increase the temperature of their greenhouses, and apply more water and fertiliser in an attempt to boost production. The supply curve for tomatoes is thus more *elastic in the short run* than in the momentary period.

In the *long run* all factors of production are variable: the tomato grower can purchase more land, more greenhouses and more tomato plants. As we shall see when we study economies of scale in Chapter 7, beyond a certain level of output this is likely to prove more productive than attempting to squeeze more output out of fixed factors, and so in the long run supply is *more elastic* than in the short run.

Factor specificity and mobility can also have a major effect on elasticity of supply. Some of the factors used in tomato growing can be described as *specific* because they have a narrow range of uses, while others, such as land or greenhouses, are *non-specific* in the sense that they have a wider range of uses. *Mobility* is closely related to specificity, and refers to the ease with which factors can be adapted to new uses, and to the possibility of moving some factors from one place to another: we examine these concepts in more detail in Chapter 14. The reader will notice that we have not specified an *actual time period* in our discussion of the short and long run above. Whether the time difference between the short run and long run will be six weeks, six months, six years or any other length of time will be largely determined by the *mobility of factors* in any particular industry. For instance, it might be easier for the producers of tomatoes, who live in the countryside,

Figure 3.11 *(Price) elasticity of supply (E_s)*

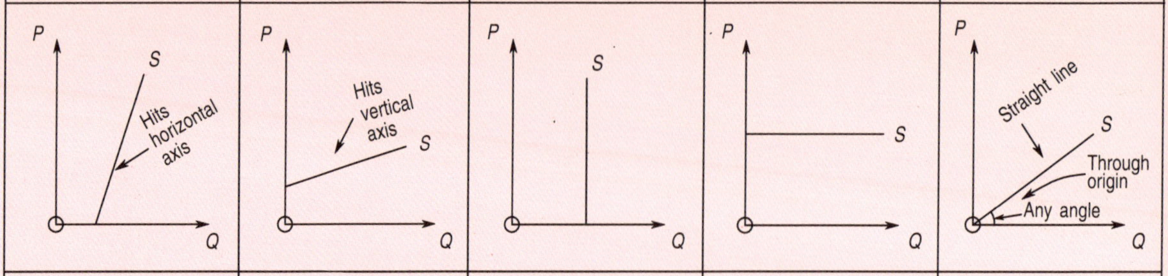

Relatively inelastic supply	Relatively elastic supply	Perfectly inelastic	Perfectly elastic supply	Unit supply elasticity
$0 < Es < 1$	$1 < Es < \infty$	$Es = 0$	$Es = \infty$	$Es = 1$
Quantity supplied changes less than proportionally to (by a smaller percentage than) price	Quantity supplied changes more than proportionally to (by a larger percentage than) price	Quantity supplied remains the same whatever the price	Suppliers will produce an unlimited quantity at the existing price	Quantity supplied changes in proportion to (by the same percentage as) price

to purchase extra land for tomato growing than it might be for the owners of a commercial car park in a crowded city centre to acquire land to make more parking spaces available.

The behaviour of costs as output changes has an important influence on elasticity of supply. If a tomato grower wishes to increase the output of tomatoes, then more factors of production have to be purchased. The ability to purchase factors of production is largely governed by the *cost* of those factors. As we shall see in Chapters 7 and 8, the costs involved in increasing output vary according to certain economic principles. Here we need mention only that if tomato growers find that if costs rise steeply as output rises so that there are heavy costs involved in purchasing extra factors of production, then this is likely to reduce the elasticity of supply of tomatoes.

The ability to store the product also affects elasticity of supply. Fresh tomatoes cannot be stored over long periods of time, whereas the producers of frozen meat, for example, can carry stocks for several months. This means that meat producers are more able to react to price rises by releasing stocks, or to price falls by building up stocks.

Spare capacity is important, and some firms maintain unused assets to enable them to react more quickly to market changes. Since tomato growing is strongly influenced by the demands of the growing season, and the number of plants to be planted has to be decided several months in advance of the crop being harvested, it is difficult for market gardeners to keep capacity in reserve. By way of contrast, during a time of depressed demand for cars, manufacturers tend to practice 'labour hoarding'. Rather than dismiss workers and find themselves short of labour when the market picks up, they are more likely to cancel overtime, or put their workers on a three-day week, so that output can be adjusted more quickly in response to rising demand.

Barriers to entry might affect the elasticity of supply of certain goods. In particular some industries restrict the entry of new firms into the market, and this influences the responsiveness of supply to changes in price (see p. 94).

Box 3.2 Elasticity of supply in the momentary period, the short run and the long run

Consider Figure 3.12. The initial equilibrium is at point E, D is the initial demand curve, S_{M1} is the initial momentary supply curve, S_{MR} is the short run supply curve and S_{LR} is the long run supply curve.

Figure 3.12 *Elasticity of supply in the momentary period, the short run and the long run*

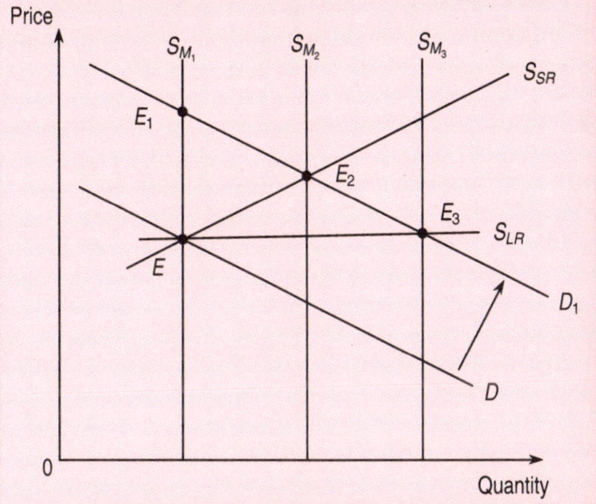

An increase in demand from D to D_1 raises price and provides an incentive for producers to supply more output. However, supply cannot respond in the momentary period and the new equilibrium is at point E_1. In the short run adjustment in output is possible because producers can increase the input of certain factors of production. Short run equilibrium is therefore established at point E_2 with S_{M2} as the new momentary supply curve. If producers believe the increase in demand is permanent they will increase the input of all factors of production and the final equilibrium will be at point E_3 on the long run supply curve with S_{M3} as the appropriate momentary period supply curve.

REVIEW QUESTIONS

1 Consider the following supply and demand schedules:

The supply of and demand for lettuces in Borchester during August

Price (p)	*Quantity demanded*	*Quantity supplied*
48	1000	16000
40	3600	12600
32	6000	10000
24	8000	6000
16	10000	4000
8	14000	2500

On graph paper, plot the supply and demand curves associated with these schedules, then answer the following:

(a) If market price were at a level of 40p, what would you expect to happen to price, and why?
(b) If market price were at a level of 16p, what would you expect to happen to price, and why?
(c) At what price would you expect the market to eventually settle, and why?

2 Use supply and demand analysis to predict the likely changes in the price and quantity of:

(a) tinned peaches after an increase in the price of tinned apricots;
(b) cream when there is a large fall in the price of strawberries;
(c) butter following publicity that consuming butter adversely affects health;
(d) beef following an epidemic which kills cattle;
(e) butter following a large increase in the price of cheese;
(f) flowers on the day before Mother's Day;
(g) ice cream during a hot summer;
(h) lamb when the price of wool rises considerably;
(i) cheese following an increase in the wages of dairy workers.

3 Why is a second-hand book generally cheaper than a brand new copy? Under what circumstances might a second-hand book attract a substantially higher price than a new one?

4 'An increase in price reduces quantity demanded, while a fall in demand reduces price.'

A non-economist might find this statement contradictory. By distinguishing between shifts of a demand curve and movements along a demand curve, explain the apparent contradiction.

5 Consider the following demand schedule:

Price (pence)	*Quantity (units)*
3	100
5	50
6	30

Calculate the price elasticity of demand for a change in price from:

(a) 3p to 5p;
(b) 5p to 3p;
(c) 5p to 6p;
(d) 6p to 5p;
(e) 3p to 6p;
(f) 6p to 3p.

Comment on your results.

6 A demand curve makes a parallel shift to the right. Has price elasticity of demand increased or decreased at each price? Explain your answer.

7 The Chancellor of the Exchequer is advised that the price elasticity of demand for milk is 1.2 for low income groups and 0.23 for high income groups. Why might this information help to lead to the conclusion that milk is a suitable item to be subsidised by the government?

CHAPTER 4

THE PRICE MECHANISM AND MARKET FAILURE

CONNECTIONS

The price mechanism is central to the study of microeconomics, and in particular is closely related to the discussion of economic systems in Chapter 1, and also to Chapter 5, where we examine some modifications (such as price controls and rationing) to the market mechanism. In Chapter 4 we also examine the concept of **market failure**. This is related to the reasons for government intervention in the economy which we examine in Chapter 36; we examine the particular case of monopoly as a source of market failure in Chapter 11.

Key Concepts

Externality
Merit good
Optimum allocation of resources
Public good
Rationing by price
Signalling
Social cost

The *price mechanism* is said to operate where the problems of *what how* and *for whom* to produce are determined by market forces. In market economies, as we have seen in Chapter 1, the price mechanism is the main means of allocating resources.

The Functions of Price

During 1989–90 huge changes in the political structure of Eastern Europe and the Soviet Union signalled moves towards market economies in those countries. These moves were supported by millions of people who felt that market forces would improve their quality of life. In order to understand the attraction of free markets to the citizens of these countries, and also to appreciate that markets are not without their problems, it is necessary to discuss the advantages and disadvantages of allowing resources to be allocated through the price mechanism.

The Rationing Function

Price can be used to **ration** goods and services, and **reward** factors of production.

Price Rations Goods and Services

At any given moment in time, the supply of goods and services is relatively fixed. In the longer run the supply of some commodities is more elastic than others, but economic goods are always *scarce* in relation to people's demand for them. The supply of goods and services therefore has to be apportioned among many potential consumers. How does rationing take place? In Box 4.1 on p. 36 we have mentioned the use of the *queue* as a rationing mechanism in certain circumstances. Other possibilities include a *rota* system, where people take it in turns to use goods and services, or a *lottery* where goods and services are allocated to the lucky winner. These mechanisms are used in our society to a limited extent, but it is *price* which is used in the vast majority of cases. So, for example, when a box of breakfast cereal appears on the shelf of a supermarket, the question of who will consume it is

Box 4.1 Analysing the queue

Although it is sometimes said to be a peculiarly British phenomenon, and while British tourists often feel that its principles are imperfectly understood in certain countries, the social phenomenon known as the *queue* is found all over the world.

The premise underlying the queue is that of *first come first served*. In a way, this is a very democratic principle. Like many commonplace happenings to which we rarely give a second thought, the idea that regardless of income, social status, or any other consideration one must wait one's turn is a fascinating idea worthy of investigation. Our habit of expressing the value of commodities in terms of a price is yet another.

We have used the phrase 'social phenomenon' above as a reminder that such things as money, prices, and queues have not been handed down to us by divine intervention: they are human inventions which serve a purpose and have their advantages, disadvantages, and alternatives.

Driving through the London Borough of Wimbledon during late June or early July can be an interesting experience. An orderly and good-natured queue winds its way for several miles along the pavements of this leafy suburb. To an economist's eye this is an exercise in resource allocation. A scarce resource (places in the crowd watching a tennis tournament) are being rationed, partly by price, as an entry charge is made, and also by time, as a queue has been formed by people willing to pay the price.

largely determined by price. In a country like Britain there is little likelihood of such an item being allocated in any other way. In planned economies it is not unusual to see queues forming for basic groceries: this is due to the inability of the bureaucrats making basic decisions of *what, how* and *for whom* accurately to match the demands of consumers with the output of producers, so that **excess demand occurs at the ruling price**. In Chapter 5 we discuss the possibility of *black markets*, which have been a special feature of centrally planned economies, occurring when there is a mismatch between supply and demand.

However, even in economies like the UK there are problems in resource allocation when the price mechanism is prevented from discharging its role. A case in point is the problem of traffic congestion in towns which appears to be worsening with every year that passes. It is a typical example of a case where something in **limited supply** (roadspace) faces increasing pressure of **demand**. One solution to the problem would be to instal a meter in each vehicle which, together with an electronic device buried under the road surface, would register every time a car entered the central area of a city. The motorist could then be sent a regular bill in order to pay a fee for entering the city centre. Clearly, this solution to traffic congestion depends on the availability of suitable technology, but once installed the system could be very flexible, with different charges incurred at different times of day, for example.

Figure 4.1 shows that if the market works perfectly, the streets of the city centre would never be empty of cars; but neither would they be congested. At the equilibrium price (*Pe*) the quantity of roadspace demanded (*Qe*) would be equal to the supply of roadspace in the city centre (*Qe*). Of course this depends on the pricing authority accurately gauging the mood of the market, and charging a suitable price. It would soon find out if it had made a mistake. If price were too high there would be an excess supply of roadspace, too few cars to pay the costs of running the system. If price were too low, there would be an excess demand at that price, and the problem of congestion would continue. The advantage of road pricing would be that, once

Figure 4.1 *The market working perfectly*

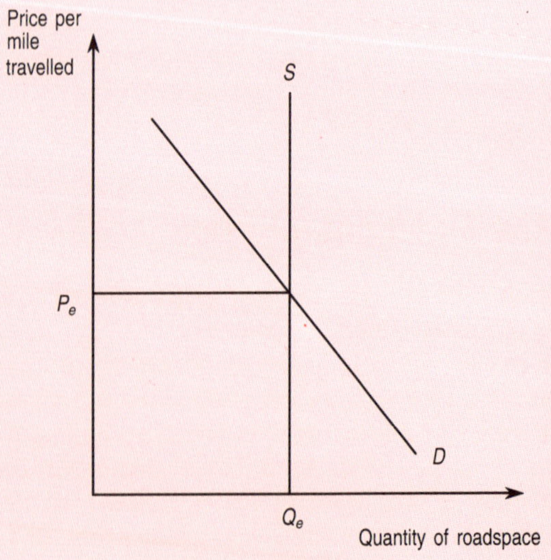

established, the system would be a very efficient mechanism for rationing the scarce resource: a minimum of bureaucracy would be needed.

There would also be disadvantages: the price mechanism is very sensitive to effective demand but does not recognise the concept of *need*. Therefore, if it were taken to extremes, people with the ability to pay to take vehicles into the city centre would be given priority over local residents, disabled people, and emergency services. Probably some compromise would have to be reached where special categories of road user could carry a sticker or device which would exempt them from all or part of the road charges.

Another disadvantage of allowing resources to be allocated through the price mechanism is that there are certain goods and services which, if they are provided at all, must be provided *communally*, as it is difficult, or even impossible, to price them individually. These goods are known as 'public goods' and street lighting, defence and the police force are examples. Much more is said about these on p. 40 but the point to be stressed here is that if the price mechanism operated freely these goods would not be produced because no-one would pay individually for them.

Price Rewards Factors of Production

The question of who can afford to buy a box of breakfast cereal is not entirely determined by the price of the item itself. It is also affected by the *distribution of incomes* between consumers. It is possible to think of the four 'rewards' to the factors of production, or factor incomes – namely rent, wages, interest and profit – as being a 'price': the price paid for the factor services of land, labour, capital and enterprise respectively.

When the price of a good rises, rewards to the factors of production rise, and this attracts them away from other uses. Such rewards give spending power to the recipients: it gives them the ability to command a greater volume of goods and services.

When demand for an industry's output is rising, workers in that industry are likely to find that they are able to earn higher wages than those in declining industries. Before the Second World War, the main means of long distance transport in Britain was the railway. The drivers of main line expresses such as the *Flying Scotsman* were relatively highly paid; indeed they were regarded as the elite of the British workforce, and given a certain amount of attention by newspapers and documentary film makers. If today's mass media had been in existence they might have been given very glamorous treatment. Since the Second World War there has been a shift in demand away from public transport in favour of private transport, particularly the motor car. Today, even the most experienced train drivers on important Inter-City routes find that their wages are nowhere near the top of the league while many jobs have been lost in the associated locomotive works in places such as Swindon, Derby and Darlington. At the same time, because of the level of demand for motor cars, even quite unskilled work in the motor car industry has become relatively highly paid.

In the 1960s many school leavers, after training, earned relatively high wages as comptometer operators. The comptometer was a mechanical calculator which could add, subtract, multiply and divide at great speed when used by a skilled operator. However, in the 1970s the development of micro-computers and hand-held calculators depressed the wages of comptometer operators and reduced the profits that could be made from the manufacture of the machines. Meanwhile, the earnings of people whose skills were increasingly demanded in the electronics industries were quickly rising.

As we discuss in Chapter 16, market forces are not the *only* influence on incomes, but they are a *major* influence.

The Signalling Function

Price can be used to allocate resources between different sectors of the economy. It is sometimes said that changes in price both *indicate* and *motivate*. Price *indicates* changes in demand, and provides a means by which consumers can signal their changing preferences to producers; it also indicates changes in supply, and allows producers to send signals to consumers, showing what is available on the market, and on what terms. Price also *motivates* producers to respond to changes in consumer demand.

Price Indicates Change in Demand

When consumer demands alter, price is a means by which consumers can send 'messages' to producers. Prices allow the community to indicate a change in its preferences for some commodities in relation to others, and the extent to which particular commodities are demanded. It can be argued that the rise in house prices in Britain in recent years partly reflects the demands of families for owner occupation. Meanwhile, the rented sector has contracted, partly due to the inability of landlords to charge a sufficiently high rent to make the business adequately profitable because of falling demand for rented accommodation.

Price Indicates Changes in Supply

Price is a means by which producers can send 'messages' to consumers when there are changes in the underlying conditions of supply. If the cost of producing a good or service rises, this can be signalled to consumers who can decide whether they are willing to pay the higher price, or whether they wish to switch to alternatives. For example, a wage increase in an industry which is not matched by an increase in productivity will increase costs of production in that industry. We have seen on p. 22 that changes in costs of production will shift the supply curve for a good or service. In Figure 4.2, *SS* and *DD* are the original supply and demand curves for a particular good and the initial equilibrium price is *P*. If the costs of producing the good now increase at all levels of output, supply will shift to S_1S_1 and price will increase from *P* to P_1.

If, following a price increase, consumers are willing to pay the higher price then their response will be minimal; whereas if they feel that the conditions upon which goods are now being supplied are unacceptable, they will switch to alternatives or cease consumption. Clearly price and cross elasticities of demand have a role to play here, because they affect the extent to which consumers react to price signals. In this case the effect of the price increase is a reduction in sales from *Q* to Q_1. A reduction in costs of production would have exactly the opposite effect.

Figure 4.2 *The 'polluter pays' principle*

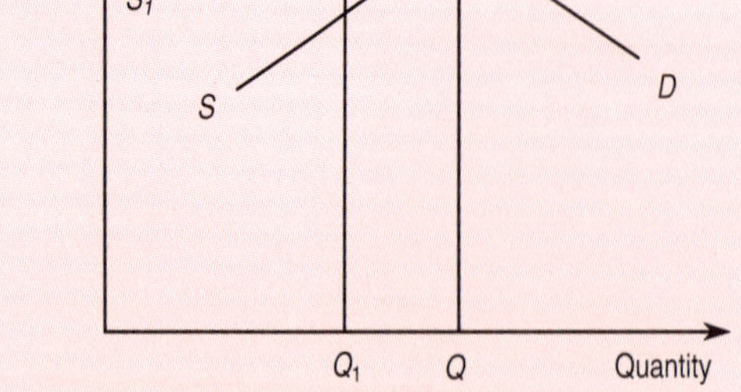

If the consumer pays the full social cost of production when there are negative externalities, price will rise and quantity demanded will fall

Price Motivates Producers to Alter Supply in Response to Changes in Demand

The idea of profit as an *incentive* to producers is an important part of price theory. When demand increases, price increases and supply extends. It is the *profit motive* which causes this extension in supply. For example, it has been estimated that in certain parts of the UK, there is a large unsatisfied demand for recreational facilities such as golf courses. This demand is reflected in the fees which existing course owners can charge, and is encouraging land owners to apply for planning permission to build golf courses. Firms would not enter into such ventures unless they had examined the prospects carefully and were reasonably certain that they would be profitable. The implication is that the price mechanism is an efficient and accurate indicator of consumer preferences.

However, reliance on the price mechanism causes some concern when it leads to results which are not easily reversed – for example, the loss of good agricultural land when farm prices in certain commodities are depressed. It might be that the price mechanism is offering a short-term plan of action which might be detrimental in the long term. Some scientists are predicting that 'global warming' might make it difficult for certain countries, including Britain, to grow their traditional crops. We might find that while it was quite easy to switch land out of food production in response to short-term price changes in order to construct golf courses or housing estates, it could well be much more difficult to regain the use of land for farming in the event of any future food shortage.

An Optimum Allocation of Resources

We have seen how the price mechanism discharges its role in allocating resources. However, it is some

Box 4.2 MP defends ticket tout 'stockbrokers'

Tory MP Teresa Gorman today hailed Wimbledon ticket touts as 'stockbrokers in cloth caps' who should not be stopped from trading.

'Those who attack them are condemning the normal system of buying and selling in this country and they are picking on people because they are easy scapegoats and are not organised to answer back'. said Mrs Gorman, who represents Billericay.

Mrs Gorman denounced as 'absurd' a Bill to be presented to the Commons tomorrow by Liberal Democrat sports spokesman Menzies Campbell which would make it an offence to sell tickets without a licence.

However, time restrictions mean that the Bill has little chance of reaching the statute books. 'It is the fault of the Wimbledon authorities if they do not price their tickets according to the market and what the market will stand', said Mrs Gorman.

'They should keep some tickets back and grade them according to the quality of the match on a particular day.

'That is what the touts do. They buy cheap and sell at a profit. They may have cockney accents, but they are doing precisely what people do in the City – take a gamble on what they buy in the hope they can sell it at a profit.

'On the Stock Exchange it is called speculating on futures. This is a free country with free people conducting free transactions on free streets. I don't see why anyone should try to make it illegal'.

However, touts are about as popular with most tennis fans as a monsoon.

Outside Wimbledon today touts were asking £450 for 'two together' to see Boris Becker on Centre Court compared with a face value of £20.

A £39 ticket for the men's singles final would cost £1000.

However, the emergence of stars such as Monica Seles and Jennifer Capriati to challenge the pre-eminence of Steffi Graf has added up to £100 to the previously depressed price of a black market ticket in advance for the women's final.

Long-suffering Wimbledon fans arriving up to six hours before the scheduled start of play can be expected to be harassed from the moment they step off the Tube at Southfields all along the one-mile approach to the grounds on Church Road.

Touts have even been known to loiter in public toilets offering to buy or sell any spare tickets.

Press photographers refused to take pictures on the opening day of the championships in a row over seat allocation.

At previous championships each newspaper or agency was allowed two reserve seats which enable photographers to come and go for the best pictures without fear of losing their place.

Now all photographers' seats are open and the number of passes available for pictures has been halved.

Source: *Evening Standard* (25 June 1990).

times argued that the price mechanism operates so as to achieve an *optimum* allocation of resources. An optimum allocation of resources exists when it is impossible to make one member of society better off without making at least one other member of society worse off by changing the allocation of resources – that is, by producing a different range of goods and services.

At its simplest level this implies that the price mechanism ensures that, from the alternatives available, the goods and services **society most desires** are produced. How does this happen? Because any change in socity's preferences for different goods and services will lead to price changes. These price changes will encourage producers to vary the amount of the different goods and services they produce until, given the prices of the different goods and services produced, society's preferences are met.

Market Failure

Despite the appealing logic of the argument, the free operation of the price mechanism will never achieve an optimum allocation of resources. This is referred to as *market failure* because the price mechanism fails to allocate resources to their optimum use. In other words, there is a *suboptimal* allocation of resources. Let us examine the reasons for market failure.

Externalities

When resources are allocated through the price mechanism, consumers decide which goods and services to purchase on the basis of their money price. Similarly producers make decisions about what to produce on the basis of money prices, in particular, the price consumers are prepared to pay for the product and the costs of hiring the factors of production to produce the product. However, these prices do not always reflect the *true value* of the product to society or the *true cost* of producing the product. Consuming and producing certain products often has side effects which do not simply affect the consumer or the producer: these side effects are referred to as *externalities* and their existence is an important source of market failure.

Externalities are **costs** (negative externalities) or **benefits** (positive externalities) which are **not reflected in free market prices**. They can arise from acts of consumption or acts of production. An example of a positive consumption externality would occur if one person had himself or herself vaccinated against a contagious disease, thus reducing the risk of passing on the disease to someone else. Similarly a person who has their car converted to use unleaded petrol improves the environment for everyone. An example of a negative consumption externality occurs when people smoke in a public place, because they impose passive smoking on others.

Similarly there are examples of externalities from production. For example, a firm which offers training to workers benefits society because the greater skill of the workforce improves its productivity which is a major factor in raising the standard of living for all (see p. 362). A negative production externality occurs when a firm pollutes a river with its toxic wastes, thus depriving anglers of the use of the river; more seriously, the drinking water of local residents might also be affected.

Let us consider the case of a firm polluting a river to see the implications of externalities for the allocation of resources. A firm which discharges its waste materials into a river is treating the environment as a free resource. It is imposing a cost on society as a whole, rather than simply on consumers of the product. Consumers are not therefore paying the true cost of the product. If the firm was forced to treat its waste materials so that they were harmless before discharging them into the river, its costs of production would rise. It would therefore charge a higher price for its product and in consequence consumers would desire less of it. Resources would then be released for the production of other goods and services .

To illustrate the point economists distinguish between the *private cost* and the *social cost* of production. The private cost is simply the money cost of production, and it refers to the cost of raw materials, the cost of labour and all other money costs that firms must pay in order to undertake production. Social cost, on the other hand, is the private cost of production *plus* the value of externalities. Let us consider Figure 4.3.

In Figure 4.3 *D*, is the demand curve for a particular good. S_p is the supply curve when only private costs are considered. S_s is the supply curve when the full social costs of production are considered. It is clear that when the full social costs of production are considered price is higher and output lower than when supply is based simply on the private costs of production. In this case, if society were forced to pay the full social cost of producing this product, they would consume $Q–Q_1$ less of it than if they simply paid the private cost of production. When prices do not reflect negative externalities society 'overconsumes' in relation to the optimum, and therefore the market fails to allocate resources optimally in such cases. More generally, you might like to consider the effect on the allocation of resources when there are positive and negative externalities in consumption as well as positive externalities in production.

Public Goods

These have strong externalities, and pure public goods have the properties of *non-excludability* and

Figure 4.3 *Social cost*

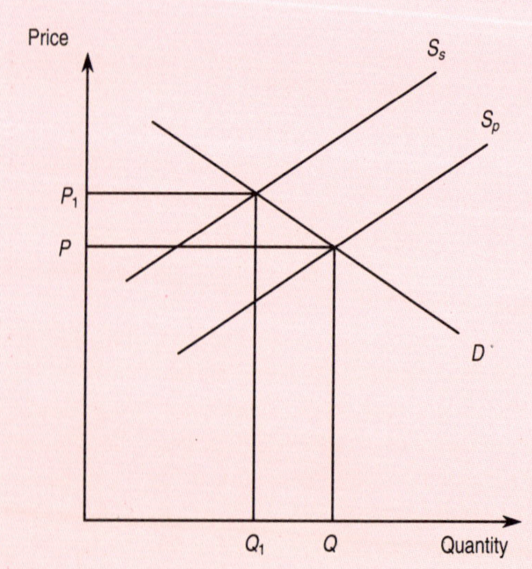

non-rivalrousness. (Note that although economists have adopted the habit of referring to these items as goods, very often they are in fact services.) Public goods are 'non-excludable' because, as is sometimes said: *provision at all means provision for all*. Examples include defence, street lighting, lighthouses, and drains. In each case, once the facility is provided, it is **impossible to exclude individuals from using it**. In other words, such goods are non-excludable and therefore their prices cannot be attributed to particular consumers. Public goods are 'non-rivalrous' because **one person's use of the public good does not deprive any other person of such use**. If Mr *A* benefits from the 'Queen's peace' which is maintained by the armed forces, he in no sense 'uses up' this peace and there is still exactly the same amount left for everyone else to consume.

It is is the non-excludability of public goods which makes them non-marketable. Without the ability to exclude non-payers, the private sector would be unwilling to supply them. However, while it is very likely that the main way of financing public goods will be through general taxation, public goods are not necessarily provided by the government; lighthouses on the British coast for example, are provided by Trinity House, a registered charity; while drains are provided by the water companies which are public limited companies. However, many people feel that in order to avoid a preponderance of *free riders* – that is, consumers who use a public good without contributing towards its cost – public goods should, in general, be provided by the government and financed out of general taxation. Payment is therefore *averaged* among the whole community, rather than being billed to the *marginal* consumer.

Merit Goods

These confer benefits on **society in excess of the benefits conferred on individual consumers**. For example, health care and education benefit the individuals who receive them, but there are also benefits to society from having a healthy, well-educated workforce. If merit goods were provided through the market, insufficient would be consumed in relation to the optimum. The government therefore encourages consumption of merit goods by subsidising them to lower their market price, or by providing them free of charge to consumers.

It is important to note that unlike public goods, merit goods could be produced by the private sector. This happens in the case of such things as education and health care at the national level, and recreation facilities, such as public parks, at the local level. In each of these cases examples of private provision are easy to find, but it is believed that if these goods were supplied entirely through the market, they would be *underconsumed* and this again implies a suboptimal allocation of resources. The government therefore uses tax revenues to ensure an optimal provision of merit goods.

Demerit Goods

These are goods which impose **negative externalities on society** rather than just on the individual consumer. Cigarette smoking is often cited as an example. The dangers of smoking cigarettes are well-known, but the price consumers pay for a packet of cigarettes is not related to the costs of providing the health care their actions will, on average, necessitate. These costs are, in part, borne by the tax payer. Again, provision through the market leads to a sub-optimal allocation of resources, because the market price is less than the true price of consumption and therefore encourages overconsumption in relation to the optimal level.

It is often said that government intervention to encourage the consumption of merit goods and to discourage consumption of demerit goods is *paternalistic*.It implies that the government knows best and therefore acts to reduce *consumer sovereignty*. The competitive pricing system can be criticised as it takes account only of *effective demand* – that is, demand backed by the money to pay. It does not respond to people's *needs*, and where society judges that certain facilities, such as hospital treatment, should be allocated according to need rather than on the basis of effective demand, then some modification of the price mechanism is deemed necessary.

Monopoly

We shall see in Chapter 11 that a monopoly exists when there is a single supplier of a good or service. As the only supplier of this good or service, the monopolist has the power to influence the price by increasing or reducing market supply. This gives a monopolist considerable power, and it is usually argued that he will use this power to achieve maximum profit from his operations. It is argued that by restricting market supply monopoly causes market failure, because society is deprived of some output which it values more highly than the output which it currently consumes. In other words, the allocation of resources could be improved if the monopolist expanded production (see p. 97).

Disadvantages of the Price Mechanism

Apart from criticisms of market failure there are other possible problems of allowing resources to be allocated through the price mechanism.

Instability in the Economy

The argument is that, left to its own devices, the market system is subject to periods of *boom* and *slump*, historically referred to as the *trade cycle*: the boom is associated with periods of inflation whereas the slump is characterised by heavy unemployment. As we shall see in Chapter 28 inflation imposes costs on society, and it is clear that when workers are unemployed the economy is producing at below its maximum productive potential. Because of this, all governments intervene to some extent in order to regulate the economy and to try to iron out the peaks and troughs in economic activity. Although there is some disagreement among economists about the nature and extent of intervention, very few people would seriously dispute the principle of at least a minimal level of government intervention.

Inequality in the Distribution of Income and Wealth

The free operation of markets leads to vast inequalities in the distribution of *income* and *wealth*. Those with physical assets such as capital and land earn relatively large incomes while the vast majority, with only their labour to sell, earn relatively low incomes. Some idea of what this implies is given the experience of Britain during the Victorian period. Here, a few fortunate individuals were able to consume to excess, but the vast majority lived in poverty.

To avoid what is considered an undesirable distribution of income and wealth the government uses the tax and benefit system (see p. 152) to redistribute income and wealth. We shall see in Chapter 36 that supplementary benefit is available to those on relatively low incomes along with a host of other concessions – for example, free prescriptions to those on pensions, and so on. The progressive taxation of income and levying no VAT on food for household consumption (a major item of expenditure for those on lower incomes) are examples of how the tax system is used to redistribute income.

REVIEW QUESTIONS

1 Give some examples of circumstances where 'rotas' and 'lotteries' are used to ration scarce resources.

2 Why do universities and other higher education institutions insist on certain 'A' level grades as an entry requirement? Could the student loan scheme be described as a movement towards using the price mechanism?

3 Examine the arguments for and against the use of the price mechanism as a means of overcoming traffic congestion at places such as the Severn Bridge.

4 During the Christmas shopping period of 1989 British Rail received some criticism when it increased its fares into certain cities on Saturday mornings in order to reduce overcrowding on trains. In what ways could this policy be criticised, and are these criticisms justified?

5 Suppose the country is faced with a petrol shortage. What are the arguments for and against using the price mechanism to remove the shortage?

Figure 4.4 *Supply and demand conditions for car parking in a busy town centre*

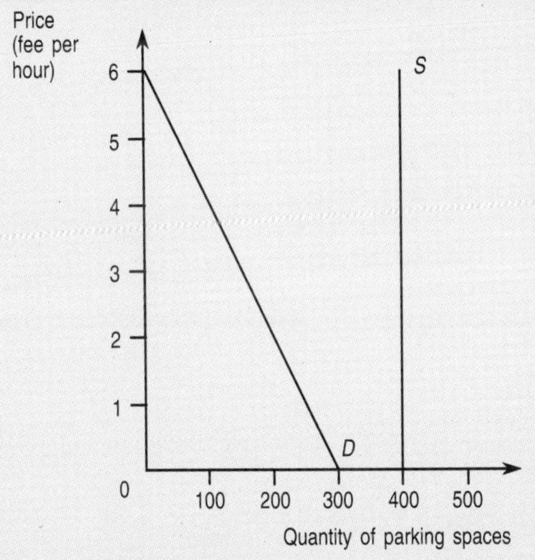

6 Figure 4.4 shows the supply and demand conditions for car parking in the centre of a busy town.

(a) Why is it difficult in the circumstances shown for the city council to use market forces as a guide to what the price of car parking should be? What price would the council wish to charge in order to:
   (i) encourage maximum use of the car park;
   (ii) obtain maximum revenue?

(b) Suppose the demand for car parking spaces increases by 200 at each and every price. What price is the council now likely to charge? Explain your answer.

7 Public goods are non-rivalrous and non-excludable. Discuss the extent to which each of the following should be regarded as public goods.

(a) Radio and TV broadcasts.
(b) Secondary school places.
(c) University places.
(d) Hospital beds.
(e) Roads.

8 Why would the non-excludability of pure public goods make their provision an unattractive proposition for a profit-making entrepreneur?

9 Why might the social costs of a car journey exceed the private costs?

10 Why might the social costs of building a factory in an area of high unemployment be less than the private costs?

11 How would you decide whether to make a charge for a government service or to provide it free to the user?

CHAPTER 5

SOME APPLICATIONS OF PRICE THEORY

CONNECTIONS

In Chapter 5 we show how concepts from Chapters 3 and 4 can be used to gain insights into various ways in which market forces influence economic decisions.

Key Concepts

Agricultural support schemes
Black market
Price controls
Rent controls

Price Controls

Let us begin by investigating what is likely to happen when prices are set at a level which is **not the free market equilibrium price**. In such cases, there must be some sort of *pricing authority*. This authority could be the government – although to be accurate it is more likely to be a government department such as the Ministry of Agriculture; or it could be an agency of the government, such as the Milk Marketing Board; or it could be a private body such as a sports federation; or even a profit making organisation such as the promoters of a pop concert. We shall see that whatever form the pricing authority takes, it is not likely to be able to fix a price which differs very much from the market equilibrium level unless it can completely control *either* supply *or* demand. Consider Figure 5.1

If the market is allowed to operate freely, the equilibrium price and quantity will be *OPe* and *OQe*, because the supply curve *S* and demand curve *D* intersect at *E*. At this price there is neither a surplus nor a shortage.

Figure 5.1 *Maximum and minimum price controls*

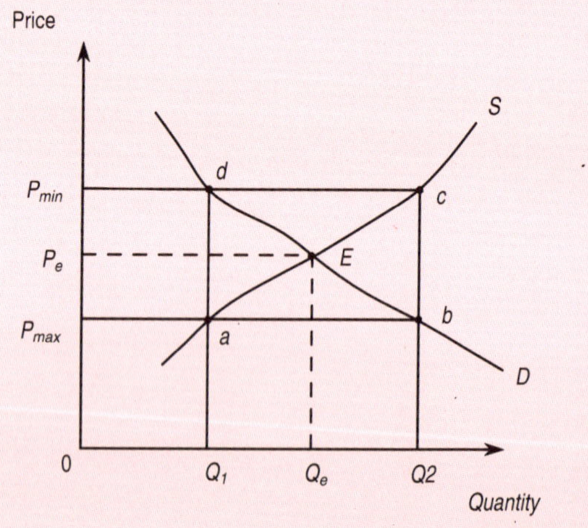

Maximum Price Controls

If a pricing authority decides that the equilibrium price is too high, it might set a 'ceiling' price: that is, a maximum price, as shown by the horizontal line P_{max}. How can the pricing authority take steps to ensure that this price is not exceeded? Figure 5.1 shows that at a price of OP_{max}, quantity supplied is OQ_1 and quantity demanded is OQ_2. There is therefore a shortage at that price of Q_1Q_2. In order to maintain this price, the pricing authority must either reduce demand so that it equals supply at point *a*, or reduce supply so that it equals demand at point *b*.

Reducing the amount demanded could be achieved in various ways: one possibility would be by physical rationing, as has happened in the UK during wartime, when food and clothing were among a number of items rationed, and also during the Suez crisis of 1956 when petrol was rationed. Achieving an equilibrium at point *a* results in a lower price to consumers, together with a lower quantity demanded: it is therefore a suitable position to attempt to reach when the intention is to conserve limited stocks while giving as many people as possible the ability to pay. During the Second World War, for instance, there were shortages of food, clothing and other essential items. Unrestrained demand could easily have led to inflation, and the government felt it very important to ensure that people should feel that the whole nation was involved in making sacrifices for the war effort. Great care was taken to make the public feel that limited stocks of commodities were distributed fairly: even the King and Queen had ration books! The ability to pay was therefore not the only criterion for purchasing goods; the limited stocks were rationed by making it necessary to accompany payment with a certain number of 'points' or ration coupons. A disadvantage of this type of physical rationing is that it involves administrative costs; and if it is not fully supported by the public it might lead to the development of a black market, which we examine later in this chapter.

Equilibrium point *b* is more suitable when the pricing authority wishes a lower price to be coupled with as *high* a level of consumption as possible. Thus suppliers will be subsidised in order to shift the supply curve *S* to the right so that it passes through *b*. Examples of items which might be suitable targets for this kind of intervention include orange juice and milk for babies; dental treatment; eye tests; and other items known as *merit goods*, which (it is considered) would be under-consumed if supplied at their full market price (see p. 41).

Minimum Price Controls

If a pricing authority decides that the equilibrium price is too low, it can set a 'floor' price, or a minimum price as shown by the horizontal line P_{min} in Figure 5.1. At this price there is a surplus of Q_1Q_2, and so the pricing authority must either increase demand to point *c*, or reduce supply to point *d*.

Point *c* combines a higher price than the free market equilibrium with a higher quantity supplied. It is therefore suitable in cases where there is a surplus of a product which is regarded as useful or desirable, and where consumption is therefore encouraged. The pricing authority cannot *force* people to buy the product, but at a time of milk surpluses, for instance, the Milk Marketing Board might encourage people to purchase more milk with an advertising campaign, or pensioners might be encouraged to use up some of the EC's butter mountain by being given vouchers which they can exchange for this commodity in the shops. At times the pricing authority might add to demand by purchasing surpluses itself. We examine the advantages and disadvantages of such activities in Chapter 34 when we discuss the CAP (see p. 327).

Point *d* combines a higher price than the free market equilibrium with a lower quantity. In order to reduce supply to this point the pricing authority could impose prohibitions, quotas or penalties on producers. A prohibition means that a product is simply banned, and so supply could disappear entirely. *A* quota means that no more than a certain amount of the product can be made, so that in effect the supply curve becomes vertical at point *d*. A penalty means that firms can be fined for producing more than their quota; or the penalty might take the form of a tax on the product. An example would be the milk quotas which have been used to limit the supply of milk in the EC: some farmers have suffered bankruptcy as a result, but those farmers remaining in business have benefited from higher prices. Another good whose equilibrium might occur at point *d* is tobacco, or any other *demerit* good, which a pricing authority (in this case the government) decides is harmful and ought to be consumed less. This reduction in consumption is achieved by taxation. The effect of a tax on the supply of a good is examined more fully on p. 344.

Figure 5.1 is very important; there are many instances in micro-economics where the workings of the market can be illustrated by some variant of this diagram. It is useful to remember that a pricing authority has only two basic options: it can set a price either below equilibrium, or above equilibrium. Then there are a further two options: either demand or supply has to be controlled, or at least influenced in some way. This gives four possible outcomes:

- lower price, lower quantity than would occur in a free market;
- lower price, higher quantity than would occur in a free market;
- higher price, higher quantity than would occur in a free market;

- higher price, lower quantity than would occur in a free market.

Which of these outcomes is preferred will depend on circumstances: the type of good or service involved, and the ultimate aims and objectives of the pricing authority. Some of these circumstances will be apparent in the market conditions discussed in the rest of this chapter.

Black Markets: Tickets for a Big Event

The term 'black market' began to be widely used in Britain during the Second World War when, under cover of the 'blackout', the 'spiv' would deal in rationed goods, often charging outrageously high prices. Another infamous market of this type appeared in the USA during the prohibition of the 1920s when there was a dangerous and profitable trade in 'bootleg' liquor.

In recent years many people have come up against black market conditions when attempting to purchase tickets for important events such as rugby internationals, tennis championships, soccer cup-ties, pop concerts, and other major events. Supply and demand analysis gives interesting insights into the workings of the 'spivs' or 'touts' who handle tickets at prices many times above their face value. In Chapter 4, some evidence of the activities of touts at Wimbledon was provided in Box 4.1.

As we shall see in the following example, a black market can exist when three sets of circumstances come together. First, the price of a commodity is kept below market equilibrium by a pricing authority. Secondly, the pricing authority introduces a rationing system other than price, and this system does not work perfectly. Thirdly, if unofficial dealings in the commodity are illegal, then some holders of the commodity and some potential customers are prepared to break the law. It might be that while these activities are not strictly illegal they can carry some degree of risk (it has been known for ticket touts to be physically attacked by irate fans). Black market prices can be expected to be relatively high, partly due the risks involved.

Suppose a promoter wishes to stage a snooker championship and hires a venue for the final capable of holding 4000 spectators. The supply curve for tickets at the final will be vertical or totally inelastic, as shown by the line *S* in Figure 5.2.

It would be possible for the organiser to plot a demand curve. If entry to the final were free, it might

Figure 5.2 *Inelastic supply and demand determined price*

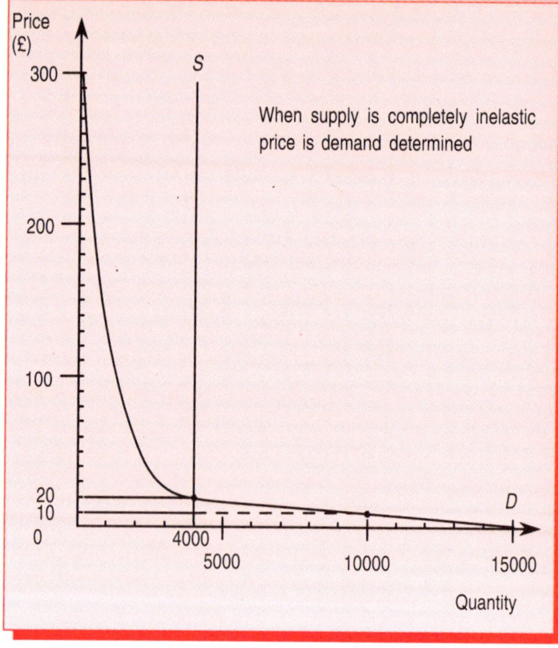

be estimated that 15,000 people would wish to come and watch. At the other extreme, it might take a price as high as £300 per seat to ensure that nobody would turn up. Between these two points the demand curve might trace a path as shown by the line *D* in Figure 5.2.

The point of intersection of the supply and demand curves indicates that a price of £20 would enable every seat to be filled, and there would therefore be no surplus or shortage at that price. However, the promoter might decide that the main source of profit for this event is going to be the sale of television coverage rights and that income from sales of seats is likely to be a relatively insignificant part of total revenue. A policy decision might then be made to allow regular supporters of snooker to purchase tickets at a lower price. The promoter might decide that a price of £10 is reasonable: and if this decision is made then the promoter effectively adopts the role of a pricing authority. Figure 5.2 shows that at the price of £10, the quantity demanded is 10,000, and so there is an excess demand of 6000. In order to allocate the 4000 available tickets among potential customers numbering 10,000, the pricing authority must take steps to ration supply. This could be done by using the queue, or by a 'draw' whereby postal applications are picked from a hat. Another possibility is that bona fide snooker clubs around the country might be allocated tickets, with individual club committees deciding how to allocate them between members.

The idea behind these arrangements is to ensure that tickets are available to 'genuine' snooker fans at prices they can afford. But suppose that for various reasons the system is not very efficient in achieving this aim. For example, some people given the right to purchase tickets held by snooker clubs might not wish to travel to the final. Let us suppose that 500 tickets end up in the hands of people who are prepared to sell them to ticket touts at as high a price as possible. Inspection of Figure 5.2 shows that there are a number of potential customers who are willing to pay relatively high prices, and who might have been disappointed when applying for tickets. If these customers can be brought into contact with the ticket touts then we have a potential black market.

The Price of New Houses

Suppose a labour shortage resulted in building labourers and bricklayers being able to command substantially increased wages. Housebuilders would therefore face increased costs. How would this affect the price of new houses? The answer predicted by economic theory is perhaps surprising: it is that prices might not change significantly in some areas.

Why is this? An important feature of housebuilding is that there is a highly organised second-hand market, and that the second-hand commodity is far more numerous than the new commodity. To use economic terminology, new houses and second-hand houses are *close substitutes*; indeed many home buyers would actually prefer to buy a house in an established area rather than on a new estate, and the *stock* of existing houses is large compared with the *flow* of newly built houses. These factors taken together mean that the costs of building new houses are an *insignificant* determinant of prices on the housing market as a whole. The vast majority of houses were built in the past, and their building costs have already been paid. The price of a second-hand house is therefore decided by the interaction of supply and demand, with demand being influenced by such things as incomes, mortgage interest rates, tastes (people's preferences for owning their own homes) and so on. So, in the rising cost situation described above, the price of existing houses acts in effect as a *maximum price control* which prevents housebuilders from increasing the price of new houses substantially above prices on the market as a whole. The supply of new housing falls because of the increase in costs, but any increase in prices is prevented because consumers turn to substitutes and demand for new housing falls. This process is illustrated in Figure 5.3.

Figure 5.3 *The supply of and demand for new houses*

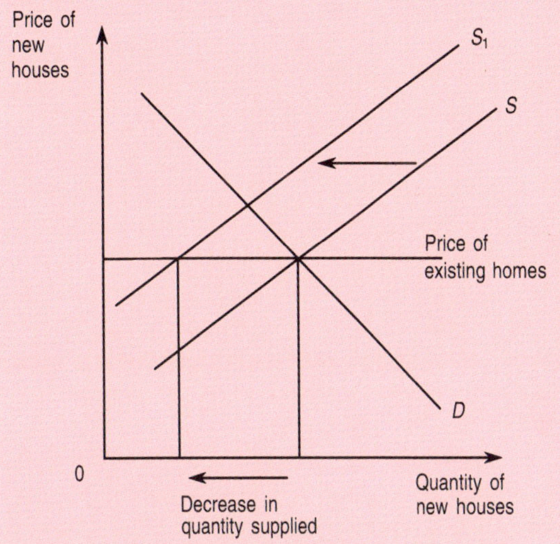

Initially the price of new houses is similar to the price of second-hand houses. The increase in costs shifts the supply curve to the left, but builders are unable to increase the price of new houses above that of existing houses. Quantity supplied is decreased instead.

Rent Controls

Sometimes maximum price controls are held in place over a period of years. Until quite recently, rent controls in the UK put a ceiling on the price landlords could charge for rented accommodation. When such regulations are first introduced, supply may be relatively inelastic, as shown by supply curve S in Figure 5.4, and the resulting shortage may be relatively small.

Landlords cannot quickly sell their houses in order to invest their money in other activities. However, if their rate of return falls below what they could receive from alternative investments (such as government bonds) then they can be expected to attempt to leave the housing market. After some time the supply curve will shift left and become more elastic at each and every price, like S_2 in Figure 5.4. At this price there is an increasing shortage of rented accommodation, which can be predicted to worsen unless the government can shift supply to the right – for example, by building more council houses. Until

Figure 5.4 *Shortage of rented property and rent controls*

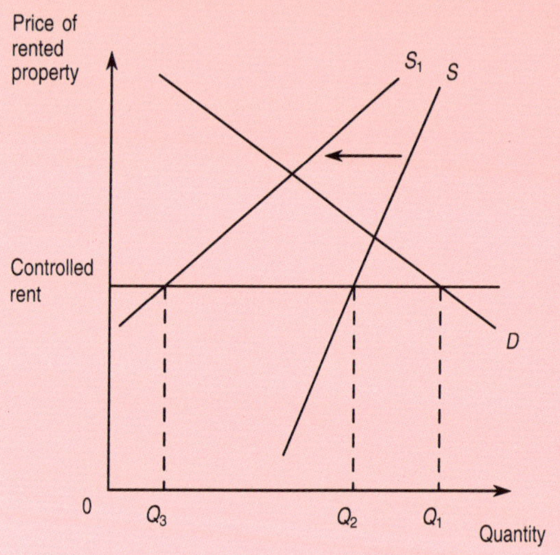

Over time, the shortage of rented property at the controlled rent increases from Q_2Q_1 to Q_3Q_1

this happens, the shortage is rationed by council house waiting lists, which might work on the basis of time (first come first served) or on some system of priorities, such as a 'points system' where families with young children, say, might accumulate more points than childless couples and thus accelerate towards the front of the queue.

In short, rent controls, which are meant to assist the poor who cannot afford their own homes, may in fact harm those very same people by causing increasing shortages of rented accommodation – unless the government is committed to making good the shortfall in privately rented housing with an investment in public housing subsidised by the taxpayer.

Agricultural Support Policies

There are various types of agricultural products, including livestock, fruit, vegetables and arable crops. Many of these products form a staple part of people's diets, and some of them (including corn, wheat and potatoes) have relatively low price elasticities of demand. Some also are purchased as inferior goods, which results in their demand curve tending to drift to the left as incomes and living standards increase. Where price elasticity is low, shifts in supply can cause large fluctuations in price, and most agricultural products suffer from a tendency for the supply curve to be unstable. Such things as droughts, frosts, and epidemics can cause sudden shifts of the supply curve to the left and large price increases; while in some years weather conditions can be so perfect that supply shifts dramatically to the right and sometimes the costs of gathering in the harvest are not covered by the equilibrium market price.

There is often a conflict or tension between the consumer and producer of agricultural products. The consumer wishes to pay prices which are as low as possible for as large a quantity as possible, whereas the producer might find that market conditions are such that incomes are higher in years when there are bad harvests than in years when there are good harvests. Thus we have the curious phenomenon that a plentiful supply may actually harm farmers by reducing their income.

Since the Second World War all western governments have protected their farmers. They have done this for admirable reasons: no-one would wish to go back to the years of shortages and rationing which were experienced by many people during the war. Governments have therefore felt a need to achieve some degree of self-sufficiency in food production to avoid shortages, and to protect farm incomes in order to achieve long-term stability in managing food supplies. However, it also has to be said that governments have had some less praiseworthy motives, in attempting to pacify the politically vocal farming lobby, and responding to pressure from the powerful agriculture-related chemical and pharmaceutical industrial interests.

Figure 5.5 shows a situation where in a free market equilibrium price would settle at OP_e. If it is considered that this price is too low to maintain farmers' incomes at an acceptable level, then the government has three broad options: it can do nothing and leave the market to the forces of supply and demand; it can attempt to maintain a minimum price by reducing supply; or it can attempt to maintain a minimum price by increasing demand.

Option 1: Do Nothing

At an equilibrium point E, supply is equal to demand and there is no shortage or surplus at the market clearing price of P_e. If free market forces are left to operate, only those farmers who are able to make a profit at this price will stay in business; others will switch to other lines of production. In the short term we might be presented with the spectacle of farmers ploughing perfectly good crops into the ground because their costs are not covered by the revenue from sales. Those crops which do reach the market

Figure 5.5 *The operation of an agricultural support scheme*

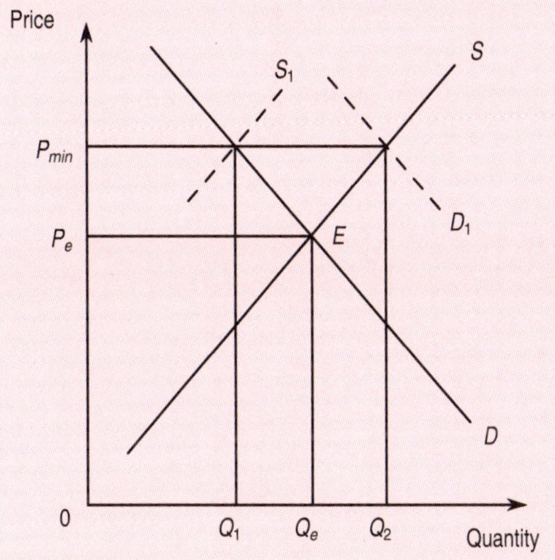

benefit the consumer with a relatively low price: however, when the next season comes, prices may well rise due to the smaller numbers of producers operating.

Option 2: Maintain a Minimum Price by Reducing Supply

The minimum price, or floor price, is shown in Figure 5.5 by the horizontal line $P_{\min}$. At this price, quantity demanded is Ql, while quantity supplied is Q_2. At the price of Pmin, therefore, there is a surplus of Q_1Q_2. The government, or one of its agencies, could try to shift the supply curve to the left to S_1. In this way the Potato Marketing Board has introduced licensed acreage schemes, where farmers are prevented from producing potatoes without permission, and the EC has, through the Milk Marketing Board, introduced milk quotas. Such arrangements mean that the 'invisible hand' of the market no longer makes decisions about *what*, *how* and for whom. The government agency has to allocate licences and quotas, and this may be done in a way which farmers see as arbitrary or unfair. Often, quotas and licences will be allocated to those farmers who already operate the largest concerns. Many farmers, both large and small, have invested heavily in capital equipment in order to make themselves more efficient and productive; they depend on a high volume of output in order to repay the interest on loans taken out for this purpose. At the same time, developments in fertilisers and drugs have greatly increased productive capacity, thus making it very difficult for farmers to keep within quotas, even if they try. The overall result is that smaller farms have either closed or been absorbed into huge agribusinesses concentrated in the hands of fewer owners. Such trends not only have economic consequences, but also have environmental and ecological effects with social costs: many people are concerned about such things as the loss of hedgerows, soil erosion, and the pollution of waterways.

Option 3: Maintain Price by Increasing Demand

If one of the aims of government is to avoid food shortages then it is reasonable to shift the demand curve to the right, as shown by D_1 in Figure 5.5. In this way, farmers can dispose of a higher quantity while maintaining the price $P_{\min}$. There are two main methods of increasing demand: a system of deficiency payments, or a system of intervention purchasing.

Deficiency Payments

This was the essence of the 'cheap food' policy which operated in the UK before entry into the EC. Prices in the shops were allowed to fluctuate to some extent, but whenever the equilibrium price fell below the agreed floor price, the government paid the farmers a sum of money which increased their revenue to that which they would have received from the agreed floor price $P_{\min}$. In effect, the demand curve as seen from the producers' viewpoint (the 'seller-perceived' demand curve) shifted to the right to D_1.

The deficiency payment was financed by general taxation, and so the taxpayer was subsidising both the producer and the consumer. The producer benefited from a guaranteed income; the consumer benefited because a quantity OQ_2 was available at a price in the shops of OP_e; but there were two main disadvantages: the possibility that inefficient farmers were kept in business by the subsidy and, of course, the cost to the taxpayer.

Intervention Purchases

One of the principles guiding the Common Agricultural Policy of the EC was that the burden of agricultural support borne by the taxpayer should be reduced and transferred to the consumer of agricultural products. The idea was that the government would act as a 'swing consumer and supplier': adding to demand by purchasing surpluses during years of good harvests, while stabilising prices by releasing stocks during times of shortage. Prices in the shops would more accurately reflect market conditions, and so consumers could expect at times to pay more for their food, but supplies would in the long term be safeguarded.

However, in practice the intervention purchasing system has not eliminated surpluses: it has merely transferred their ownership from the farmer to the government. It has always been regarded as sensible for governments to keep *buffer stocks* in reserve, but huge butter mountains, wine lakes, and warehouses full of dried milk and frozen beef are expensive to maintain, and difficult to dispose of.

REVIEW QUESTIONS

1 What conditions are necessary for a black market to exist?

2 Figure 5.6 represents the market for a commodity where the demand curve is *D* and which is supplied both by domestic producers whose supply curve is shown by S_d and by a large number of producers in other countries whose supply curve (S_w) can be regarded as being horizontal at the world price, P_w. *OM* represents the output of domestic producers, and *MN* represents imports.

Figure 5.6 *Horizontal world supply curve*

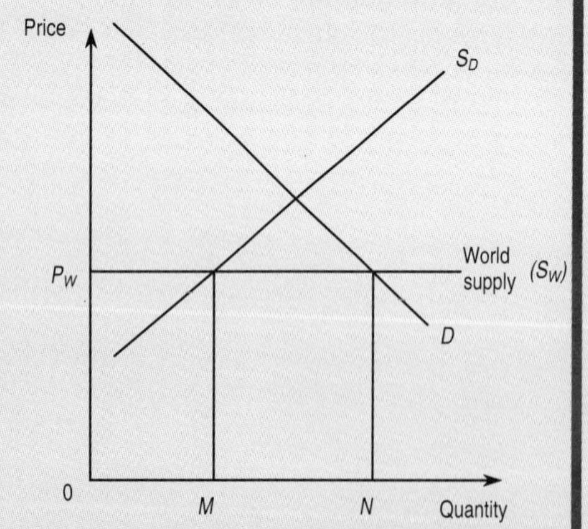

(a) Explain why the world supply curve is horizontal, and why it in effect imposes a ceiling price on domestic producers if there is free trade.
(b) Use Figure 5.6 to predict the effect of an import tariff on:
(i) domestic output;
(ii) imports;
(iii) the price paid by consumers.
(c) Who benefits and who loses from a tariff?

3 Why does the EC sometimes supply butter and cheese at a reduced price to certain targeted groups such as senior citizens?

4 Use supply and demand curves to show how it can be predicted that as the Soviet Union moves towards a market economy queues for certain commodities might get shorter, but prices will rise.

CHAPTER 6

THE BASIS OF DEMAND

CONNECTIONS

Market demand, the total demand of all consumers of a particular product, was examined in Chapter 3. In Chapter 6 we are more concerned with *individual demand*, the demand for a **particular product by a single consumer**. We assume that individuals demand goods and services in order to obtain maximum satisfaction from their limited incomes.

Until now, we have treated the law of demand *inductively*, in that we have based it upon observation of how consumers generally respond to price changes. In this chapter we examine ways in which the law of demand can be based on a *theoretical* footing. We show how economists can put forward basic *assumptions* about human behaviour and then use *deductive* methods to arrive at the conclusion that demand curves will usually slope downwards from left to right.

Key Concepts

Budget line
Giffen good
Income effect
Inferior good
Indifference curves
Marginal utility
Substitution effect
Veblen good

The Law of Diminishing Marginal Utility

For over 200 years economists have assumed that there is a pleasurable state or feeling called *utility* which is affected by every act of consumption. Jeremy Bentham (1748–1832) was the founder of a branch of philosophy known as *utilitarianism*, and several eminent nineteenth-century economists, including David Ricardo (see p. 282) and Alfred Marshall (see p. 58) were heavily influenced by his thinking, in particular by his idea that the satisfaction gained from consuming a commodity could be measured in units known as *utils*.

The amount of utility added to total utility by purchasing the last unit of a good or service is known as *marginal utility*, and economists believe that marginal utility usually **diminishes as consumption increases**. This is known as the *law of diminishing marginal utility*. Two holidays per year are better than one in terms of total satisfaction received, but not twice as good; three are better than two but not 50 per cent better, and so on. Similarly, after working all morning, the first glass of orange juice at breaktime yields very high utility; a second one might also be very thirst-quenching, but it will not provide as much utility as the first since we will not be as thirsty as we were before our first drink, and so on.

The law of diminishing marginal utility can be used to explain why it is that an individual's demand curve slopes downwards from left to right. Suppose a consumer received 50 utils from consuming one unit of a commodity, an additional 30 utils from consuming a second unit, an extra 25 utils from consuming a third unit and another 20 utils from consuming a fourth unit. It is reasonable to suppose that the satisfaction gained is closely linked to the sacrifices which the consumer is willing to make in order to obtain extra units. If, for example, the consumer is prepared to pay one penny for each util received, then this individual will be prepared to buy one unit of this commodity when the market price is 50p, but will be prepared to pay only 30p for a second unit, 25p for a third unit and so on. This information could easily be presented in the familiar form of a downward sloping demand curve.

A disadvantage of using the law of diminishing marginal utility to analyse consumer behaviour is that it is necessary to assume that this very subjective and personal concept, utility, can be accurately **measured**. Another disadvantage is that it is not easy to demonstrate the precise effects of an income constraint – that is, the existence of a limited income – on consumer spending. *Indifference analysis* is a technique which overcomes these objections.

Indifference Analysis

An *indifference curve* is a type of graph which shows various combinations (or 'bundles') of two goods which give equal utility. In other words, the consumer is *indifferent* as to which bundle he or she consumes, and therefore to which position he or she occupies on the indifference curve.

Suppose a consumer is given a combination of two goods, *X* and *Y*. For the sake of argument *X* could be apples and *Y* could be pears. To begin with the consumer has 10 pears but no apples. The consumer can then be asked to give up pears, which are taken away one by one, with enough apples being given in compensation each time to maintain the *same level of satisfaction*, or utility, as before. Table 6.1 gives different combinations of apples and pears, each combination giving equal utility. This level of utility does not have to be measured precisely; it is sufficient for the consumer to know that a combination of 8 pears and 2 apples, for example, gives exactly the same utility to 7 pears and 4 apples.

Table 6.1 *Combinations of apples and pears giving an equal level of utility*

Pears		Apples
9	+	1
8	+	2
7	+	4
6	+	7
5	+	10
4	+	15
3	+	22
2	+	32
1	+	58

When the first pear is taken away, the consumer is willing to accept just one apple in compensation. The *marginal rate of substitution*, or the rate at which one good is substituted for another, is 1 apple to 1 pear. This is because the consumer has a fairly large number of pears and does not miss one very much (its marginal utility is relatively low). However, when the consumer has fewer pears, the marginal utility of a pear increases, and a larger number of apples is required in compensation. For example, when the consumer is down to 2 pears, the marginal rate of subtitution is 26 apples for an additional pear. This change in the marginal rate of substitution is a reflection of the law of diminishing marginal utility.

The combinations shown in Table 6.1 can be used to plot an indifference curve, as in Figure 6.1.

Note the shape of the indifference curve: it slopes downwards from left to right and is convex when viewed from the origin. Appendix 1 at the end of this chapter demonstrates that the gradient of the indifference curve at any point measures the marginal rate of substitution, and depends upon the ratios of marginal utilities of the two goods. The gradient of the indifference curve is less at point *B* in Figure 6.1 than it is at point *A*. This indicates that the marginal rate of substitution of good *X* for good *Y* has increased.

Indifference Maps

It is possible to draw a whole 'family' of indifference curves for an individual consumer as in Figure 6.2, which illustrates what is known as an *indifference map*.

Although we have shown only three indifference curves here, it would be theoretically possible to draw an infinite number of indifference curves on the indifference map of any consumer of two or more goods.

The main features of an indifference map can be summarised as follows:

- Each indifference curve on the map shows different combinations of goods, each combination giving an **equal level of total utility**.
- Each indifference curve is **convex to the origin**. This is due to the law of diminishing marginal utility (or the marginal rate of substitution).
- An indifference curve to the right of another on the indifference map indicates a **higher level of total utility**. A diagram reinforcing this point (Figure 6.11) is given in Appendix 2 to this chapter.

Figure 6.1 *An indifference curve*

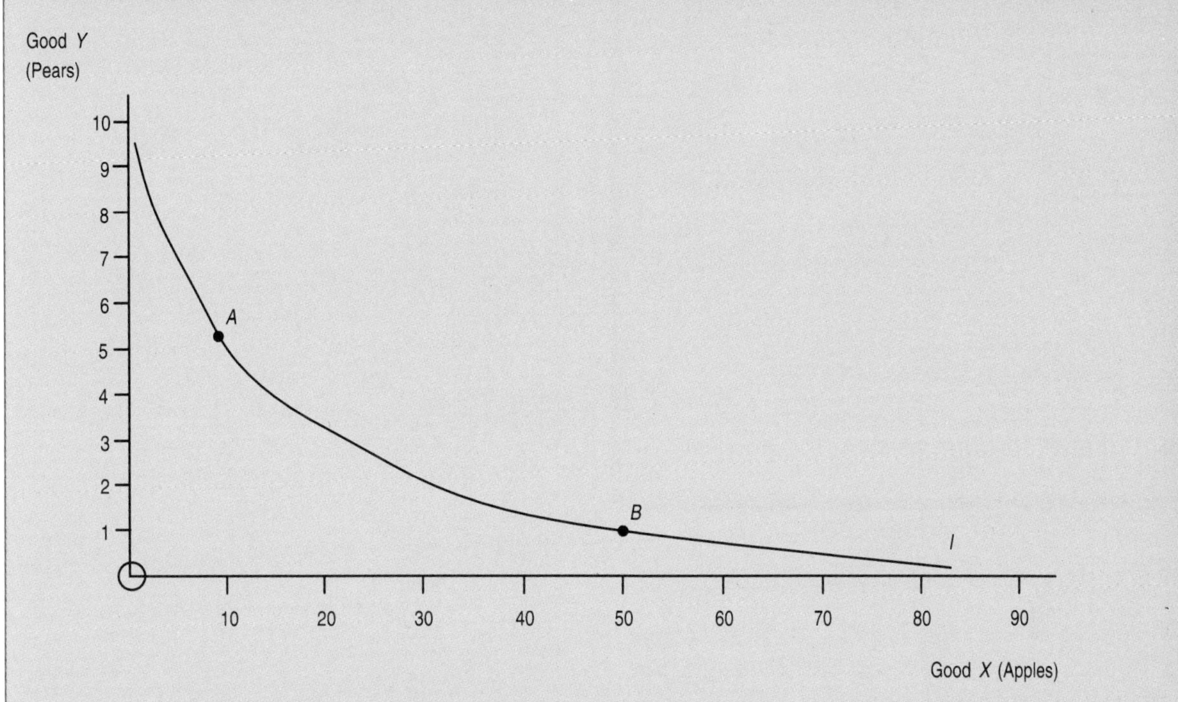

- Indifference curves **cannot intersect with each other**. This rule can be deduced from the other three features: it follows as a logical conclusion, and is proved in Appendix 3 to this chapter.

Budget Lines

We now come to a particular strength of indifference analysis, which is that it can be used to show very clearly the *income constraint*: the effect on consumers of the fact that their incomes are limited.

Again, let us assume that a consumer has a choice between just two goods, *X* and *Y*. The amount of any good which can be bought depends on two things: consumer income and the price of the good. Suppose the consumer decided to spend the whole of his or her income on good *Y*, then he or she might be able to afford *OM* units of *Y*, as shown in Figure 6.3.

If, on the other hand, the consumer decided to spend the whole of his or her income on good *X*, then *ON* units could be purchased. *M* and *N* are extreme points, where the consumer has bought no units of one good and spent the entire income on the other good. If we join these extremities, then the straight line *MN* is a *consumption possibility frontier*, or a *budget line*, which shows different combinations of two goods which the consumer can afford. Appendix 1 to this chapter shows that the gradient of the budget line is determined by the ratio of prices of the two goods, and Figure 6.4 shows the effect on the budget line of various changes in price and income.

Figure 6.2 *An indifference map*

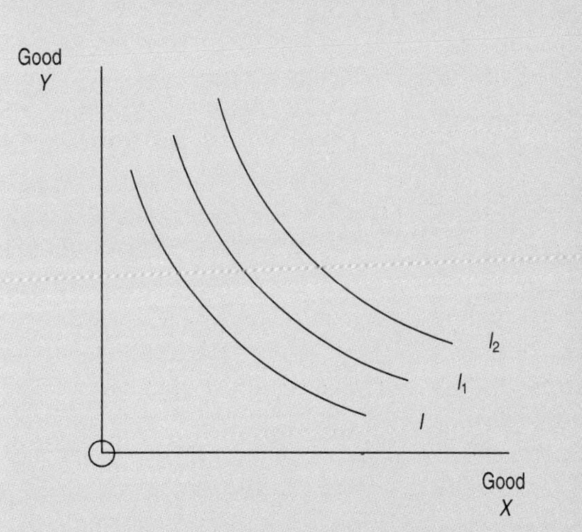

Figure 6.3 *A budget line*

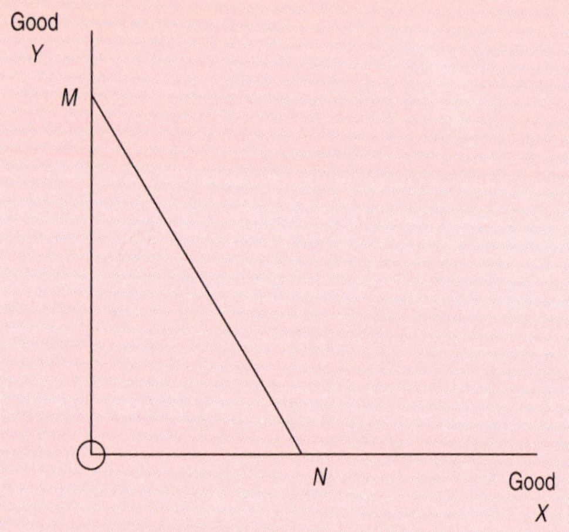

Choosing a Combination of Goods

We now have two quite powerful tools of economic analysis: an indifference map and a budget line. Figure 6.5 demonstrates how these tools provide a framework which economists can use to show how a consumer would divide a given income between two products in order to obtain the maximum possible level of utility.

The consumer will aim to consume a bundle of goods on an indifference curve which is as far to the right on the indifference map as possible, because this will maximise utility. When a budget line is superimposed onto an indifference map, there will be a large number of indifference curves positioned so that they cut the budget line: these curves can be represented by I_1 in Figure 6.5. Similarly, I_2 represents indifference curves which are to the right of the budget line. Indifference curve I is a *unique* indifference curve: it is the only curve which touches the budget line *MN* at a *tangent*. (A curve touches a straight line at a tangent when they meet at an infinitely small point, without crossing. This idea is further discussed in Appendix 1 to this chapter.) There can be no other indifference curve touching *MN* at a tangent, because if there were it would have to cross the curve I at some point, and as discussed earlier, one of the features of indifference maps is that indifference curves cannot intersect. Indifference curve I is therefore the curve furthest to the right which the consumer can reach given the prices currently charged for *A* and *B* and the consumer's current income. Since the consumer can reach only one point on this curve, we can conclude that this point defines the quantity of goods *X* and *Y* which

Figure 6.4 *Changes in the budget line*

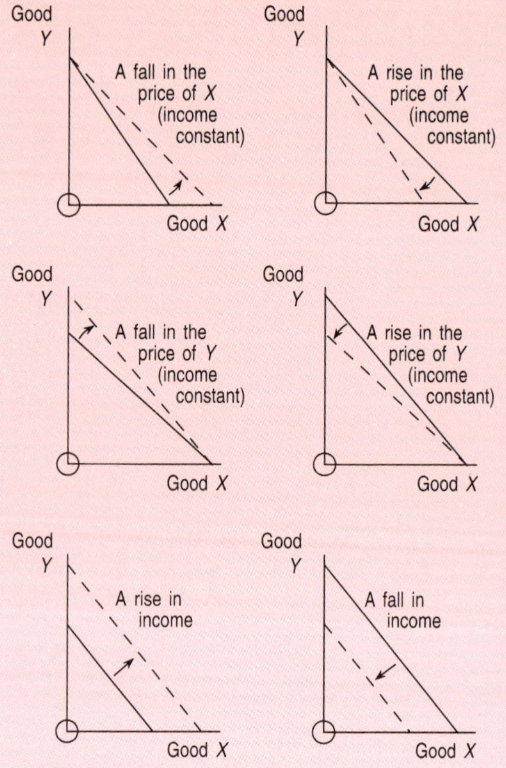

the consumer will purchase. In Figure 6.5, therefore, the consumer achieves maximum satisfaction by purchasing *OY* units of good *Y* and *OX* units of good *X*.

Figure 6.5 *Consumer's maximum possible level of utility*

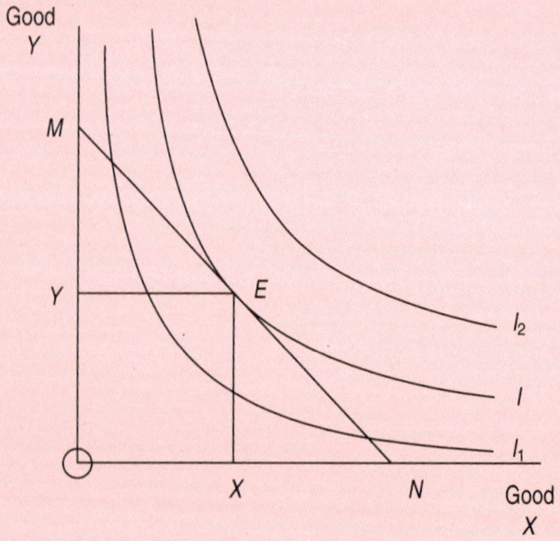

The Effect of a Change in Income

Remember from p. 20 that a normal good is defined as a commodity which people tend to purchase more of as their incomes increase. Figure 6.6 shows the indifference map for a normal good, and shows that as income increases, the consumer can increase consumption of both good X and good Y.

Figure 6.6 *Indifference map for a normal good*

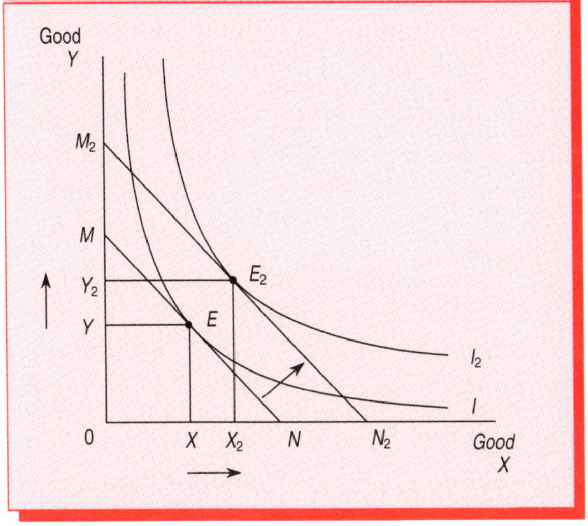

On p. 20 we argued that there is a small class of goods known as inferior goods. In Figure 6.7, good Y is a normal good, while good X is inferior (bread or potatoes are often quoted as examples). Note how the indifference curves are bunched together in the top left hand corner of the indifference map, and tend to diverge in the bottom right hand corner. This shows two things. First, somewhere off the top left hand corner of the map, the indifference curves converge towards a basic minimum amount of good X, below which consumption will not fall. Thus even the wealthiest families will purchase at least some bread and potatoes. Secondly, consumers have strong preferences for good Y over good X. As quantities of good Y are taken away, relatively large amounts of good X are required by consumers to restore their levels of total utility, thus the indifference curves rapidly flatten out towards the bottom right hand corner of the indifference map and diverge from each other as they point towards infinity. In other words, since good X is *inferior*, but good Y is *normal*, consumers regard good X as a very poor substitute if they are offered it in compensation for giving up successive units of good Y. In consequence, as income increases, more of good Y is purchased, but *less* good X is purchased.

Figure 6.7 *Normal and inferior goods*

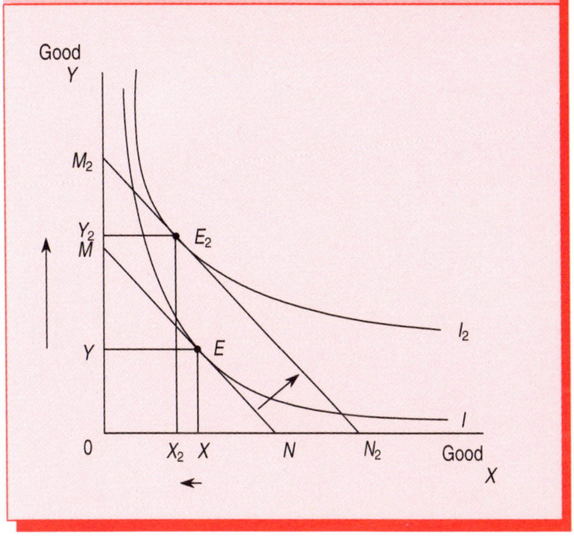

Deriving a Demand Curve

Figure 6.8 shows how the indifference curve is related to the downward sloping demand curve. At the original point of tangency, E, the consumer is in equilibrium purchasing goods X and Y so that their ratios of marginal utility to price are equal. As the price of X falls, this equilibrium is disturbed, and the consumer has to increase the consumption of X in order to reduce its marginal utility and thus restore equilibrium. This sounds complicated, but indifference analysis has the virtue of providing a simple visual demonstration of the effect of a price change. As the price of X falls point N of the budget line MN moves to the right along the X axis, and the quantity demanded of good X increases as the budget line makes a tangent with an indifference curve further to the right on the indifference map. Figure 6.8 shows how these tangency points can be used to plot the downward sloping demand curve with which we are familiar.

The Substitution and Income Effects of a Price Change

Indifference analysis enables us to go beyond Figure 6.8 and to examine the response of consumers to changes in price in greater depth, by analysing it in terms of the *substitution* and *income* effects of the price change.

The substitution effect occurs because a change in price of a commodity alters the **attractiveness of that commodity compared with its substitutes**.

Figure 6.8 *The indifference curve and the downward sloping demand curve*

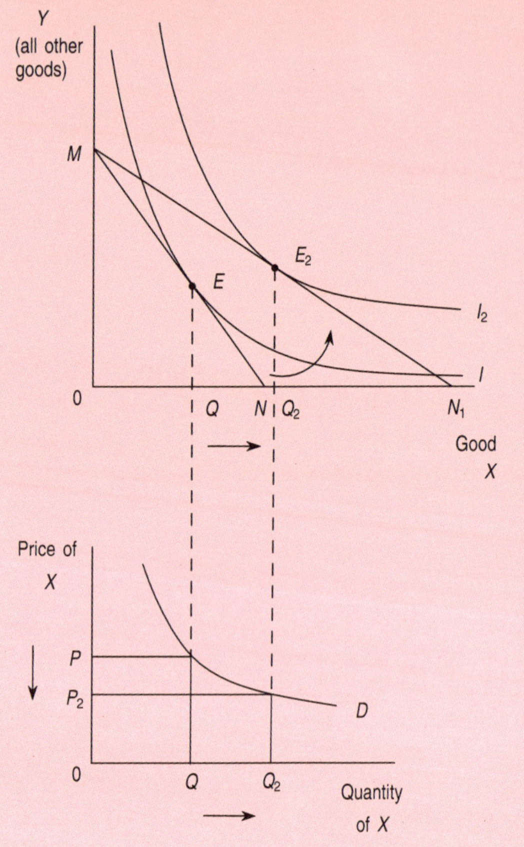

If, for instance, the price of apples falls, then apples become rather more attractive compared with pears, and people will substitute apples for pears. The extent to which they do this will depend on the *closeness* of the two substitutes as perceived by consumers.

The income effect occurs because a change in price alters the *real income* of consumers. If, for example, the price of apples falls, then the consumer can buy the same amount of apples as before, and still have spending power to spare. This increased real income can be spent on all goods, including apples. An interesting and important point to note from Figure 6.8 is that when the price of X falls the consumer purchases more of X, but purchases **more of** Y as well. Thus the fall in the price of X enables the consumer to move to an indifference curve further to the right of the indifference map than before (this would be impossible without an increase in real income), and to purchase more of all goods, including good X.

The diagram in the top right hand corner of Figure 6.9 on p. 57 shows how much of a change in quantity is due to the substitution effect, and how much is due to the income effect. In Figure 6.9, we adopt the convention of regarding the vertical axis as referring to *all other goods*. We are therefore no longer restricting our analysis to two goods, but we are examining the choices available to the consumer between good X and everything else on the market.

Following the fall in the price of X, the budget line MN swings to MN_2, and quantity demanded changes from OQ to OQ_2. How much of this change in quantity QQ_2 is due to the substitution effect, and how much is due to the income effect? To discover this, we take the new budget line MN_2 and give it a parallel shift backwards so that it touches the original indifference curve at a tangent. Thus the dotted budget line M_1N_1 touches indifference curve I at tangency point E_1. What we have done is to extract the income effect. When the consumer moves from equilibrium point E to E_1 he or she is substituting X for other goods, because X has become more attractive compared with its substitutes. The consumer therefore *moves along* the *existing* indifference curve, consuming more of X and less of other goods. When the consumer *shifts* from E_1 to E_2 he or she is consuming more of X and more of other goods, and attaining a higher total utility by consuming on an indifference curve further to the right. Along the horizontal axis, the distance QQ_1 therefore represents the change in quantity due to the substitution effect of the price change, and Q_1Q_2 represents the change in quantity due to the income effect.

Normal, Inferior, Giffen and Veblen Goods

Figure 6.9 summarises the main properties of four types of good. These goods can have a demand curve which slopes upwards or downwards, together with an Engel curve which slopes upwards or downwards, giving four possibilities in total.

Column I in Figure 6.9 contains four demand curves (price/quantity graphs). Goods of types (1) and (2) have *orthodox* demand curves, which have negative price elasticity and slope downwards from left to right. Goods of types (3) and (4) have *perverse* demand curves, which have positive price elasticity and slope upwards from left to right, violating the law of demand.

Figure 6.9 *Types of good*

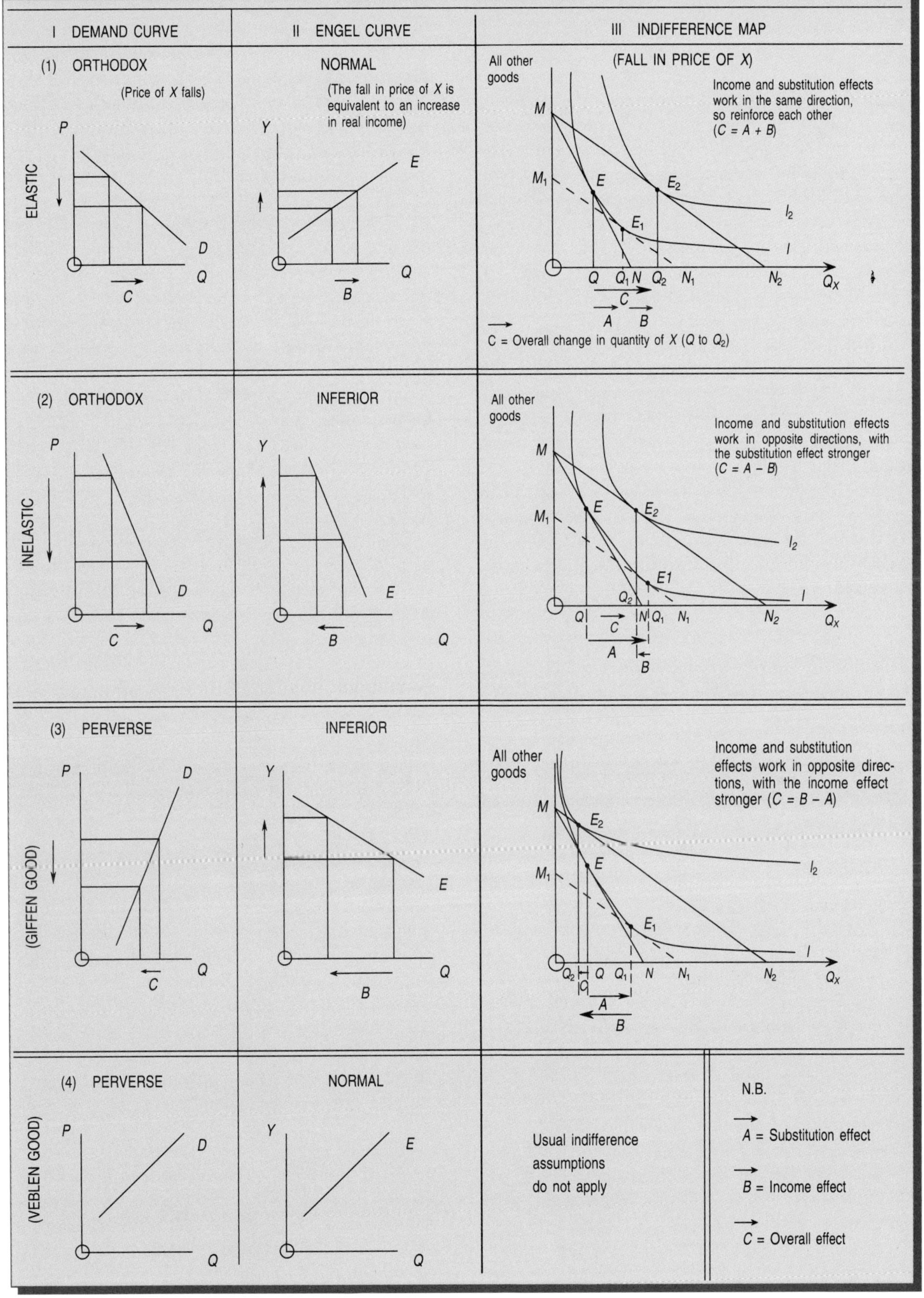

In Column II we have plotted Engel curves (income/quantity graphs). A *normal* good is one whose consumption increases as income increases, hence a normal good has positive income elasticity and its Engel curve slopes upwards from left to right, as in (1) and (4) in Figure 6.9. *Inferior* goods, on the other hand, have negative income elasticities of demand and downward sloping Engel curves, as in cases (2) and (3) in Figure 6.9. This is how we define a *normal* good: whether a good is normal or inferior describes how the consumption of a good varies with *income*. We must be wary of using these terms in other circumstances; in particular, we should use the words 'orthodox' or 'perverse' to describe only how consumers respond to changes in *price*.

In case (1) we have *orthodox-normal* goods, with negative price elasticity and positive income elasticity. The indifference map shows that the substitution and income effects of a price change **reinforce each other**. Most goods and services are of this type.

Case (2) shows *orthodox-inferior* goods, with negative price elasticity and negative income elasticity. Here the indifference map shows how the substitution and income effects **work in opposite directions**, but because the substitution effect is the stronger, the overall effect ensures that the good still obeys the law of demand. Bread, black and white TV sets, and cheap cuts of meat are plausible examples.

Perverse-inferior goods, as shown in case (3), are commonly termed *Giffen Goods*, with positive price elasticity and negative income elasticity. The shape of the indifference map, with indifference curves very tightly bunched towards the top left corner, and diverging dramatically towards infinity in the bottom right corner, shows that the consumer has **very strong preferences for other goods over good** X – or, to put it another way, the consumer regards good X as very inferior indeed. The substitution and income effects of a price change **work against each other** and, because the income effect is assumed to be stronger, the overall effect is such that the demand curve violates the law of demand. Thus in Giffen's alleged example, poor families in Ireland in the nineteenth century were supposed to find that when the price of potatoes rose, they had insufficient remaining real income to purchase more expensive items such as bacon, so they spent any remaining income on more of their basic foodstuff, potatoes, instead. When the price of potatoes fell again, as happens to good X in Figure 6.9, families deserted potatoes in large numbers and spent their increased real income on anything else other than potatoes: hence the perverse demand curve.

Finally, in case (4) we have *perverse-normal* goods with positive price elasticity and positive income elasticity of demand. These goods require us to suspend our belief in the economist's basic assumptions about consumer behaviour and consider the possibility that the **utility from consumption of a good might increase with its price**: people want them *because* they are expensive. These goods are

Alfred Marshall (1842–1924)

Alfred Marshall has been described as the father of modern microeconomics, that is, the study of how individual choices are made and individual goods are produced and priced.

Marshall was the son of a Bank of England cashier who wanted his son to enter the Ministry. However, Marshall turned down a theological scholarship at Oxford in order to study Mathematics at Cambridge. He completed his master's degree at Cambridge in 1865 and taught mathematics there for nine years.

Marshall was soon drawn to the study of economics and translated much of classical microeconomics theory into mathematical equations, though he limited his use of mathematics in his published works. In 1885 he was appointed to the Chair of Political Economy, a position he held until his retirement in 1908. During this time he dominated microeconomic thinking in England and in 1890 published his *Principles of Economics*.

In this book, Marshall established many of the principles and concepts which form the core of courses in modern microeconomic theory. So pervasive was his influence that his simple geometric slip in which he reversed the price and quantity axes in his diagrams, thus placing the dependent variable on the x axis, is almost universally followed by economists today when teaching the theory of supply and demand (see p. 20).

Marshall was a man of tremendous energy though it is difficult to assess his contribution to the development of economic thought. He delayed publication of some of his work and chose to destroy work for which he no longer had any use.

purchased for ostentatious reasons and give utility to the consumer by impressing other people. Thus goods purchased for ostentatious reasons have a perverse demand curve for a very different reason from Giffen's potatoes, which are a staple diet for the poor. It might also be the case that consumer ignorance might play a part in producing a perverse demand curve, if consumers believe that the price is a reflection of quality. Thus a perfume priced at £5 might sell less well than an identical product priced at £50.

Goods of the type just described are sometimes called *Veblen Goods*, after the economist who studied aspects of consumer psychology such as this, and it is important to note that purchasers of such goods need relatively high levels of income, hence the *normal* Engel curve coexisting with the *perverse* demand curve. In the Veblen case the utility obtained from consuming a good depends partly on one's own satisfaction, but also stems from the satisfaction derived from displaying wealth. We therefore find that the market demand curve is no longer the simple summation of individual demand curves, and we are likely to be prevented from using our usual analysis in terms of substitution and income effects, and from employing an indifference map.

Box 6.1 Do you love someone enough to give them your last Rolo?

The copywriters at the advertising agency which dreamed up this slogan on behalf of the Rowntree Mackintosh chocolate manufacturing company might not have realised that they were expressing a corollary of the law of diminishing marginal utility.

The law of diminishing marginal utility is a *behavioural relationship*: it depends upon our making basic assumptions about human behaviour. We are assuming that as we obtain more of a commodity, **each additional unit provides less extra utility than the previous one**. It therefore follows that as we sacrifice units of a commodity, each extra unit given up represents more of a sacrifice than the previous unit given up.

The law of diminishing marginal utility is therefore encapsulated in the suggestion that you would have to love someone very much to give them your last piece of chocolate. As we acquire more pieces of chocolate our marginal utility diminishes; it follows that as we give up pieces of chocolate the marginal utility sacrificed each time will increase.

It should not be assumed that economic behaviour is always based upon greed or selfishness. People can obtain utility by giving as well as by receiving. Thus a person who gives a sum of money to charity might receive utility from this use of his or her income in much the same way as if he or she had purchased commodities. Similarly, we can receive utility by making someone a present of a piece of chocolate, and where the utility lost from the chocolate is less than the utility gained from the act of giving, then this is a relatively easy thing to do. Thus the giving up of your first Rolo involves comparatively little sacrifice, since the total utility from the remaining Rolos in the packet would be relatively high. But you would have to love someone very much to give up your last Rolo!

REVIEW QUESTIONS

1 The *paradox of value* was a problem which preoccupied many economists during the early stages of the development of economics as a social science. The question was posed along the following lines: why is it that water, which is essential to human life, is cheap, whereas diamonds, which are inessential, have a high price?

Distinguish carefully between total and marginal utility, and use this distinction to explain the paradox of value.

2 Adam Smith stated that taxes should involve taxpayers in *equality of sacrifice*. Progressive taxes are related to the ability to pay, so that people on higher incomes pay a higher percentage rate of tax on each additional pound earned than do those on lower incomes. In what way does the law of diminishing marginal utility provide a justification for the use of progressive taxes?

3 Refer to Table 6.1 on p. 52. Describe carefully how the marginal rate of substitution would alter as the consumer was asked to give up apples with pears being offered as a substitute. Explain *why* the marginal rate of substitution varies at different points along an indifference curve.

4 Carefully explain the following statements:

(a) All Giffen goods, if they exist at all, are inferior, but not all inferior goods are Giffen goods.

(b) A Rolls Royce car might have a perverse demand curve, but it is not a Giffen good.

5 Examine Figure 6.9 on page 57 and consider whether the demand curves and Engel curves shown there have positive or negative price and income elasticities of demand. Then complete Figure 6.10 by placing each of the following types of good in the appropriate cell of the matrix: orthodox–normal good; orthodox–inferior good; perverse–inferior ('Giffen') good; perverse–normal ('Veblen') good (we have filled in the first cell for you).

Figure 6.10 *Matrix box*

		PRICE ELASTICITY OF DEMAND	
		NEGATIVE	POSITIVE
INCOME ELASTICITY OF DEMAND	POSITIVE	ORTHODOX–NORMAL GOOD	
	NEGATIVE		

Appendix 1

The Principle of Equi-marginal Returns

Refer to Figure 6.11 which shows the equilibrium position for maximum utility for a consumer using combinations of goods X and Y. With a budget line MN tangential to the indifference curve I at point E, he or she consumes OY units of good Y and OX units of good X.

Figure 6.11 also shows the budget line. If the consumer receives an income, which we can call A, then if he or she chooses to spend the whole of A on

Figure 6.11 *Equi-marginal returns*

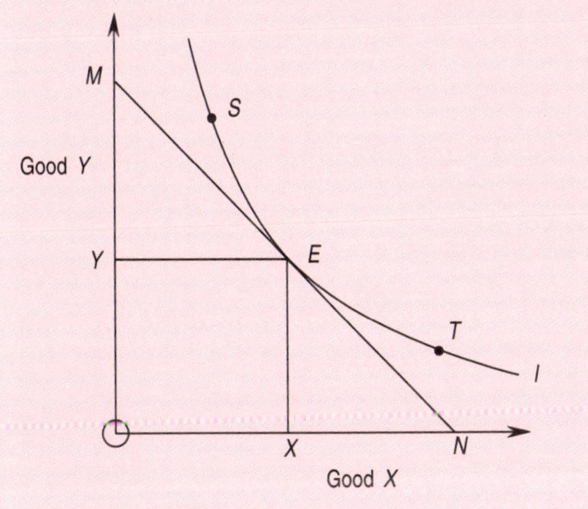

good Y, he or she could afford OM units. The actual number of units which OM represents depends upon the price of Y. If we denote the price of Y as P_Y, then

$$OM = A/P_Y \qquad (1)$$

Similarly, if he/she spends the whole of his/her income on good X, with a price of P_X, then

$$ON = A/P_X \qquad (2)$$

The budget line MN shows various combinations of X and Y which the consumer can afford. Its gradient or slope is determined by the relative prices of X and Y, since the gradient is given by the tangent of angle MNO, or

$$\text{Gradient of } MN = OM/ON = (1)/(2)$$

$$= A/P_Y \times P_X/A$$

$$= P_X/P_Y \qquad (3)$$

The gradient of the curve at any point gives the marginal rate of substitution of X for Y, that is, the terms upon which the consumer will sacrifice marginal units of Y in return for substitute units of X. At point S the gradient is steeper than at point T, where the consumer is giving up a marginal unit of a lower total amount. The way in which the marginal rate of substitution alters along the indifference curve is therefore a result of the law of diminishing marginal utility.

In the same way that a small section of the earth's surface – for example the apparently flat floor of a room – can disguise the curvature of the earth's surface, so a magnified indifference curve would appear to be a straight line at the point of tangency E. If, at this point, we were to take a small amount of good Y (that is, δY) away from the consumer then the consumer loses a certain amount of utility (say U imaginary units). The consumer is therefore 'pulled below' the indifference curve I to a position of lower total utility. We restore him/her to indifference curve I by giving him/her δX units of good X. Hence:

The marginal utility of δY units of good Y = U

Therefore the marginal utility of 1 unit of good Y $= U/\delta Y$, and

$$\delta Y = U/\text{marginal utility of good } Y \qquad (4)$$

Similarly,

$$\delta X = U/\text{marginal utility of good } X \qquad (5)$$

Now the gradient of I at point E is given by

$$\text{gradient} = \delta Y/\delta X = (4)/(5)$$

$$= MU \text{ of good } X/MU \text{ of good } Y \qquad (6)$$

For the consumer to achieve the highest possible level of total utility given his limited income, he consumes at point E where the gradient of I is equal to the gradient of the budget line, so that

equation (6) = equation (3),

i.e., $P_X/P_Y = MU$ of good X/MU of good Y.

Cross-multiplication gives:

MU of good *X*/Price of *X* = *MU* of good *Y*/Price of *Y*.

This could be extended to other goods, so that the *MU* of good *W* over the price of *W* is equal to the *MU* of good *V* over the price of *V* and so on. This is what economists call the **principle of equi-marginal returns**, which suggests that in order to obtain maximum utility from a limited income, a consumer will purchase goods so that the ratio of marginal utility to price is equal in each case. If price changes, quantity demanded will be adjusted in order to re-establish the ratio. For example, if price increases, consumers will increase marginal utility by reducing the quantity demanded: hence the demand curve slopes downward from left to right.

Note

Some economists would argue with our assumption that the shape of the indifference curve (convex to the origin) can be inferred from the law of diminishing marginal utility. This is because this law, like many other economic laws, has an 'other things equal' condition. It states that as more of a good is consumed, the extra utility obtained from each unit gets smaller, *other things being equal*. We might well decide that 'other things' should include the quantity of all other goods being consumed: but when we draw an indifference curve we are *reducing* the quantity of at least one other good while we increase the consumption of the good under scrutiny. It might be that the utility we get from pears, say, depends in some way upon the utility we get from apples, and that their marginal utilities therefore cannot be considered entirely separately.

However, as we show in Chapter 6 and its appendices, it is *possible* to derive the principle of equi-marginal returns quite effectively by assuming that a convex indifference curve 'reflects' the law of diminishing marginal utility. In the United States they sometimes say: 'If it works, then don't fix it.' If you study economics at a much higher level, you might one day come across mathematical models which can 'prove' that the shape of indifference curves can be regarded as completely distinct from the notion of diminishing marginal utility. At the level at which you are presently studying, however, we know from experience with our own students that our simpler model can be a great aid to understanding. There is a lot to be said for this approach: people studying physics to a high level might well agree that they would have got very confused if they had been taught Einstein's theory of relativity before they understood Newton's laws of motion.

Appendix 2

Indifference Curves and Total Utility

To prove that an indifference curve to the right of another indifference curve yields a higher level of total utility. . .

On indifference curve I_1 in Figure 6.12, the consumer can combine OY_1 units of Y with OX units of X. On indifference curve I_2, the consumer can consume OY_2 units of Y with OX units of X. The combination $OY_2 + OX$ clearly gives a higher total utility than $OY_1 + OX$; therefore an indifference curve to the right of another yields a higher level of utility.

Figure 6.12 *Indifference curves and total utility*

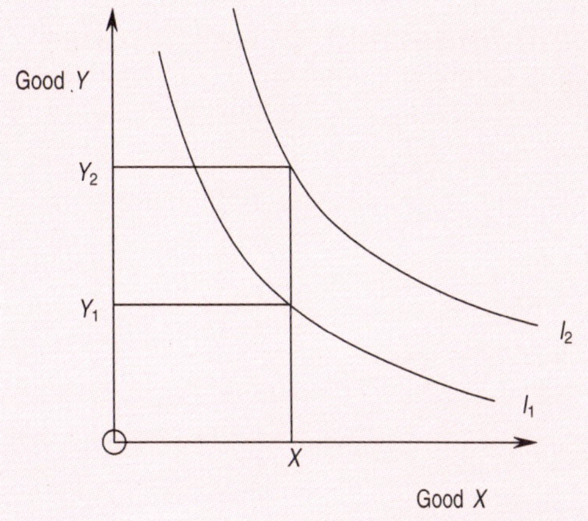

Jeremy Bentham, 1748–1832

Jeremy Bentham was a British philosopher and social reformer. He studied law and qualified as a lawyer, but never practiced; instead he taught at London University and in some ways was regarded as an eccentric. He was ahead of his time: he supported votes for women, he was a rationalist, and he disapproved of the monarchy. He designed a model prison called a 'panopticon' and also a new type of teapot which ensured that all cups of tea from the first poured to the last were of equal strength. His lasting influence was greater than many other thinkers of the day. At a time when British society suffered from gross inequalities and life for many was hard and violent government reaction was often to repress civil liberties. Bentham's followers were responsible for much of Britain's early reform legislation.

In his book *Introduction to the Principles of Morals and Legislation* (1789) he defined his philosophy of *utilitarianism*, which was based on the premise that the object of government should be 'the greatest happiness of the greatest number'. Modern economists can trace the roots of much of their thinking on economic welfare to this theory: and of course the idea of the 'util' with the implication that 'utility' can be measured has its origins here also. Bentham's philosophy was not selfish, because he stressed that utility could be obtained not just from 'hedonistic' pleasures but also from the satisfaction of helping others.

Appendix 3

Non-intersection of Indifference Curves

To prove that indifference curves cannot intersect. . .

Figure 6.13 shows an impossible situation where two indifference curves cross. This is impossible because at point *A* indifference curve I_2 is to the right of I and therefore has a higher level of utility, whereas at point *B* it is to the left of I_1 and has a lower level of utility. This contradicts the principle that an indifference curve maintains the same level of utility along its length, and therefore indifference curves cannot intersect.

Figure 6.13 *Non-intersection of indifference curves*

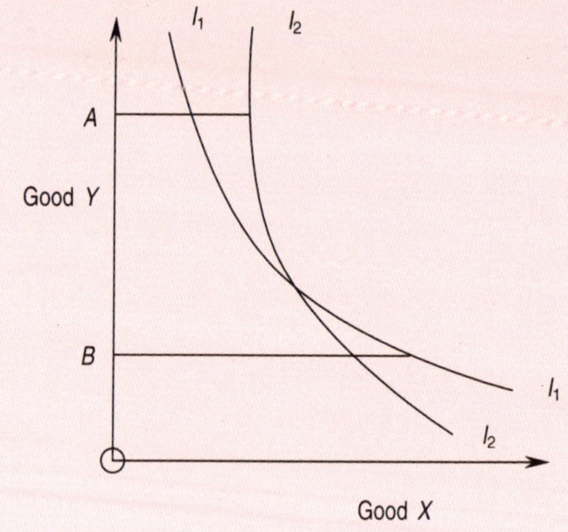

Appendix 4

The income and substitution effects of a price change

Beneath the indifference diagram in Figure 6.14 we have derived a downward sloping demand curve and shown how this is related to (a) the cross demand curve between the substitutes for X and X itself; (b) the Engel curve for good X, showing how consumers of X respond to income changes. Compare this diagram with Figure 6.8 on p. 56.

In (a) we can see that the fall in the price of X is equivalent in the minds of consumers to an increase in the price of the substitutes for X. The extent of the increase in quantity demand is therefore determined by the cross elasticity of demand for good X with respect to its substitutes.

In (b) we notice that the fall in the price of X is equivalent to an increase in real income; the extent of the increase in quantity demanded is therefore determined by the income elasticity of demand for good X.

The overall change in quantity (c) is thus equal to the substitution effect plus the income effect.

Figure 6.14 *The demand curve, the cross demand curve, and the Engel curve*

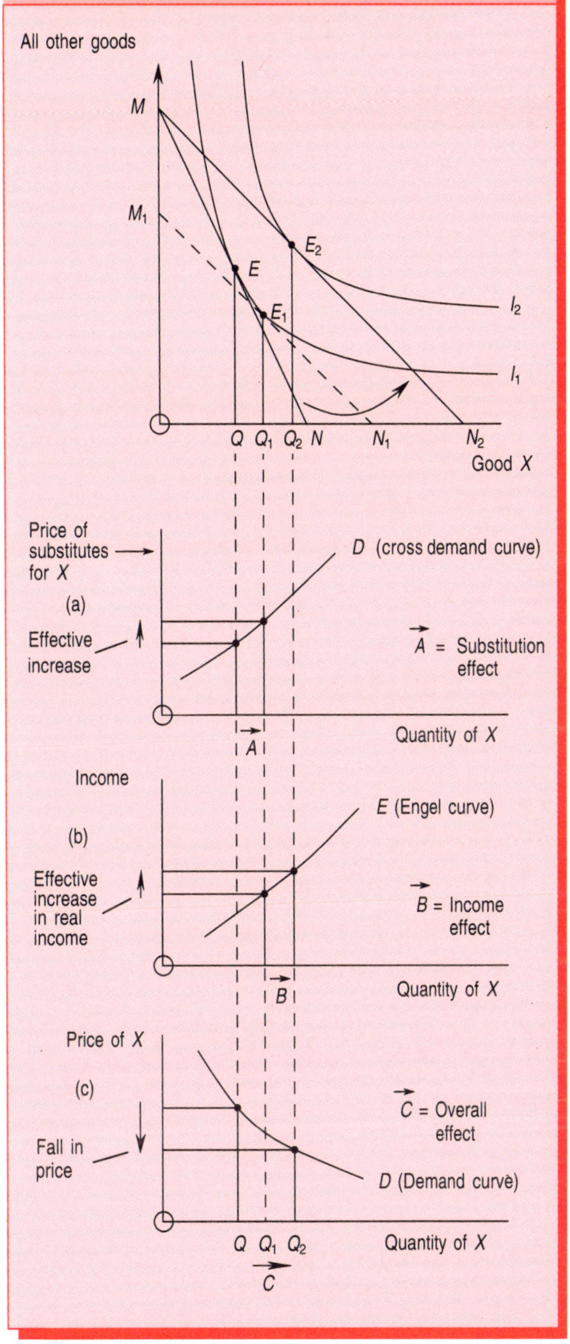

CHAPTER 7

THE LAWS OF RETURNS

CONNECTIONS

The sections on *increasing* and *diminishing returns* along with the sections on *economies* and diseconomies of scale in Chapter 7 provide a foundation for our analysis of costs in Chapter 8. It is also a foundation for our discussion of the theory of the firm which begins in Chapter 10.

Key Concepts

Diminishing returns
Diseconomies of scale
Economies of scale
Fixed and variable factors of production
Increasing returns
Integration
Marginal product and average product
The short run and the long run

It is important to distinguish *fixed factors* of production from *variable factors* of production. Fixed factors of production are those whose input **cannot readily be changed**. For example, skilled labour might be a fixed factor of production because it takes time to train workers in the skills required. The input of variable factors, on the other hand, can be altered **with comparative ease**. This classification of the factors of production is the basis of the very important distinction economists make between the *short run* and the *long run*. The short run is defined as a period of time during which it is possible to alter only the input of **variable factors**. In other words, if we can identify any factor of production whose input cannot readily be altered we are dealing with a short run situation. The long run is defined as a period of time during which the input of **all factors of production** can be changed. In the long run, therefore, **all factors are variable** and there are no fixed factors.

The Laws of Returns

The distinction between the short run and the long run is important because as firms change the input of factors of production they will change the level of output produced by those factors. However, the change in output might not be *proportional* to the change in factor inputs. In fact, the behaviour of output as factor inputs change depends on whether we consider a short run situation when only the input of variable factors can be changed, or a long run situation when the input of all factors of production can be changed.

The short run behaviour of output as more variable factors are combined with a fixed amount of at least one other factor of production is generalised in two important laws: *the law of increasing returns* and *the law of diminishing returns*.

- *The law of increasing returns* tells us that as more units of a variable factor of production are used with a fixed amount of at least one other factor of production, output will initially rise *more than proportionately*.
- *The law of diminishing returns* tells us that beyond a certain point further employment of variable factors will result in a *less than proportional* rise in output. In fact, it is possible that, beyond some point the level of output will actually **fall** if more variable factors are employed!

Before we can analyse the way in which output changes in the short run as the input of variable factors changes we need to introduce two important concepts: *marginal product* and *average product*. Marginal product is the change in total product, or output, that occurs when **one more unit of a variable factor** is employed. For example, if a firm increases its workforce from 10 workers to 11 workers and total product rises from 200 units per day to 242 units per day, then the marginal product of the eleventh worker is 42 units per day. Average product, on the other hand, is **total product divided by number of employees**. In our example above, average product when 10 workers are employed is 20 units per day and this rises to 22 units per day when 11 workers are employed.

A Numerical Example

To illustrate the laws of increasing and diminishing returns let us consider a numerical example. For simplicity we assume that an increasing number of workers is combined with a fixed amount of capital. Table 7.1 shows how output changes as more workers are employed and this information is used to construct Figure 7.1.

Table 7.1 *Output change as more workers are employed*

No. of workers	Total product	Average product	Marginal product
1	2	2	2
2	6	3	4
3	12	4	6
4	24	6	12
5	45	9	21
6	60	10	15
7	63	9	3

It can be seen that up to the employment of the sixth worker the firm experiences increasing average returns – that is, average product is rising. However, with the employment of the seventh worker diminishing average returns set in. These changes in average product are important and are usually referred to as changes in *productivity*: in our example above, productivity is rising until the seventh worker is employed.

Figure 7.1 *Marginal and average product of labour*

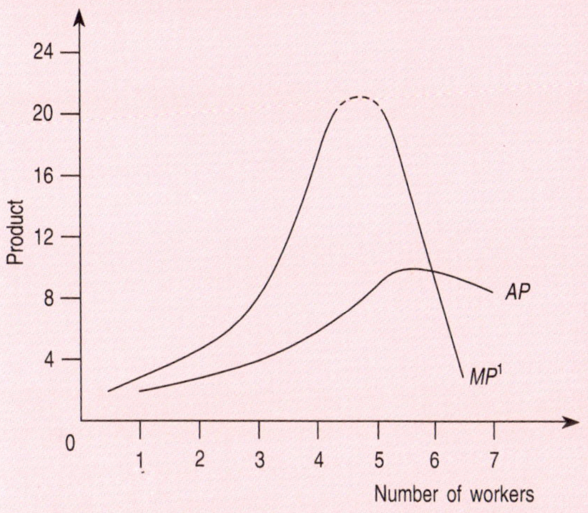

[1] Marginal product is plotted at the mid-point of each worker

The behaviour of marginal product is also extremely important because changes in marginal product tell us the *rate* at which total product is changing. For example, the firm experiences increasing marginal returns until after the employment of the fifth worker, and up to this point total product is rising *at a faster rate*. In other words, the employment of each worker up to and including the fifth worker results in an increase in total product greater than the increase which resulted from employing the preceding worker. For example, when the second worker is employed total product rises from 2 units to 6 units, but when the third worker is employed total product rises from 6 units to 12 units. However, when the sixth worker is employed the firm experiences *diminishing marginal returns* and marginal product falls from 21 units to 15 units. This tell us that total product is now rising *at a slower rate*.

Why Do Returns Change?

We would expect changes in the input of variable factors to result in changes in the level of output. But why does output not change proportionately? In fact we shall see on pp. 118–19 that specialisation has a profound effect on productivity. This implies that as firms employ more workers or more specialised items of capital, for example, the increased scope for specialisation will result in a *more than proportionate* rise in output. However, there are limits to the gains from specialisation and beyond some point, as more units of a variable factor are combined with a fixed amount of another factor, there is less scope for further specialisation because of the existence of fixed factors. In consequence firms experience diminishing marginal returns and as marginal product falls it ultimately pulls down average product.

Economies of Scale

The laws of increasing and diminishing returns govern the short run behaviour of output as the input of variable factors changes. However, in the long run there are no fixed factors and firms can change the input of all factors of production. When firms change the input of all factors of production, we say that there has been a change in the *scale of production.* It is argued that as firms initially change the scale of production output will rise more than proportionately. However, in this case there has been a change in the input of *all* factors of production and therefore the short run laws of returns as described above do not operate. In the long run, if output rises more than proportionately as factor inputs are changed, we say that firms experience *economies of scale.* There are many sources of economies of scale. Here we group them into particular categories.

Technical Economies

Scope for increased specialisation

We have already seen the effect of increased specialisation on the behaviour of output as the input of variable factors is changed. In the long run, because there are no fixed factors of production there is greater scope for specialisation. This does not imply that there are no limits on the gains from specialisation: it simply means that the point at which factor proportions become less favourable and firms experience diminishing returns can be delayed until a higher level of output is reached. In modern industrial complexes there are many examples of the gains from increased specialisation. In the car industry, for example, the production line operates so that workers perform only a small number of highly repetitive tasks. It is often suggested that individual workers find this boring, but there is no doubt that increasing the scale of production has made greater specialisation possible and has had a favourable impact on average product.

Indivisibilities

Some items of capital equipment are indivisible into smaller units and can be used efficiently only at relatively large levels of output. For example, in large supermarkets EPOS stock control systems are used to constantly monitor changes in stock so that firms can order new stock in the most efficient quantities and at the optimum time. Such a system of stock control is not feasible in a small corner shop. Similarly in the car industry the production line cannot be broken down into smaller units and used by smaller producers. Only large firms can use these indivisible units of capital which makes possible a higher average product compared with smaller producers.

Increased Dimensions

If the external dimensions of a container are increased, the cubic capacity increases more than proportionately. Because of this the transport costs per unit fall as larger vehicles or ships are used – provided, of course, that vehicles or vessels are filled to capacity. If we double the external dimensions of a tanker it will carry eight times as much oil but it will not require an eightfold increase in fuel to power the ship or eight times the number of crew to man her. Consequently average product tends to increase as the size of vehicles and vessels increases. Similarly larger supermarkets with their larger stockrooms can hold proportionately more stock than smaller firms so that their stockrooms have a higher average product per cubic foot than smaller stockrooms.

Principle of Multiples

Modern production often requires the use of more than one machine but different machines often work at different speeds. Larger firms can combine machines in different proportions so that all machines operate at their optimum level. For example, a particular production process requires the use of three machines *A*, *B* and *C* such that machine *A* can process 2 units per hour, Machine *B* can process 3 units per hour and machine *C* can process 4 units per hour. For small firms with only a single unit of each machine the total hourly output is 2 units per hour because this is the speed of the slowest machine. However, larger firms can combine these in an optimum combination so that all machines are fully operational each hour of each day. In this example the firm would require 6 units of machine

A, 4 units of machine *B* and 3 units of machine *C* which makes an hourly output of 12 units possible. Clearly in this case average product per hour is greater than in the former case.

Marketing Economies

In large organisations the marketing department has responsibility for a wide range of functions including purchasing, sales and advertising, each of which can often confer economies of scale on larger firms.

Bulk-buying

An important source of economies to large firms arises from the fact that large firms place large orders for many items which they purchase, such as raw materials. Because they place large orders they are often able to negotiate substantial discounts compared with smaller firms.

Distribution

We have already seen that large firms can gain economies from increased dimensions in the distribution of their output. However, they may also gain other economies. For example, large firms are likely to receive large orders for their own products, but it costs exactly the same to raise an invoice for a relatively large as for a relatively small order.

Advertising

Large firms which produce several products gain an important advantage over smaller producers in terms of advertising because each product of the firm advertises all other products. The unit cost of advertising a single product is therefore likely to be smaller for a larger firm than for a smaller firm.

Financial Economies

Large firms are often able to negotiate loans at lower rates of interest than smaller firms. On average, larger firms are less likely to be forced to close than smaller firms; they are therefore less of a risk and this is one reason larger firms can often obtain funds at a lower rate of interest than smaller firms. However, they are also less of a risk in another way because their size often enables larger firms to pledge more assets by way of security against loans and here again they can often negotiate lower rates of interest than smaller firms.

Risk-bearing Economies

Large organisations often diversify into several different product lines and as a result are often able to withstand adverse trading conditions in one particular market better than smaller firms. If demand for a particular product falls, larger diversified firms will be able to concentrate their efforts in other markets. However, smaller firms which are reliant on a contracting market may very well be forced to close.

Another risk-bearing economy stems from the risk of running out of stock. All firms hold stocks of raw materials and finished products in order to meet sudden changes in demand for their products. However, larger firms are able to hold proportionately smaller levels of stock than smaller firms because, for example, a given change in demand for the product represents a smaller proportion of total sales for larger than for smaller firms.

Diseconomies of Scale

Just as firms experience diminishing returns in the short run when the input of variable factors increases beyond a certain point, so in the long run they experience *diseconomies of scale* when the scale of production is increased beyond a certain point. Again this is an indication that there are limits to the advantages of size. However, diseconomies of scale are unlikely to occur for technical reasons: after all, if an organisation wishes to expand it can always duplicate its existing plant. So what are the sources of diseconomies of scale?

Poor Communications

As organisations grow it is possible that managerial functions will be performed less efficiently. In large organisations there will no doubt be several departments so that it becomes necessary to devote more time and energy to communication and consultation. It is likely that errors will occur either because work is duplicated or not done at all because different departments believe work will be performed by someone else. In any case it is likely that large organisations will be unable to respond quickly to changes in consumer tastes.

Poor morale

It is sometimes argued that in large organisations workers lose a sense of identity and take less pride in their work. The suggestion is that there is a greater incidence of spoiled work in large organisations and that greater expenditure is incurred on quality control. There is some evidence that larger organisations have a worse industrial relations record than smaller organisations and that this reduces their overall level of efficiency.

X-Inefficiency

The term 'X-inefficiency' is vague but is usually taken to imply that resources rarely operate at their most efficient level unless there are powerful incentives for them to do so. This is thought to be primarily related to the level of competition in an industry, but to some extent probably also depends on the size of an organisation: the larger the organisation, the greater the effect of X-inefficiency.

The Growth of Firms

The existence of internal economies of scale provides a major force encouraging firms to grow. However, there are different ways in which firms can grow. Broadly these can be classified as *internal* growth, when firms finance an expansion of capacity by ploughing back their own profits, or *external* growth, when firms *amalgamate* or *integrate* with other firms. Such amalgamations may be by mutual agreement, in which case firms *merge*, or they may be the result of an acquisition or *takeover*, when one firm acquires control of another firm by obtaining at least 51% of its equity (see p. 84). Whether it is the result of a merger or a takeover, integration can be either *vertical* or *horizontal*, and vertical integration can either be *backwards* or *forwards*.

Backward integration occurs when one firm amalgamates with another firm supplying an input: in other words, backward integration occurs when a firm amalgamates with another firm which is closer to its raw material supplies. *Forward integration* occurs when the opposite happens: here, a firm amalgamates with another firm which is closer to the retail end of the chain of production. *Horizontal integration*, on the other hand, occurs when one firm amalgamates with another firm which is at the same stage of production in the same industry as the original firm. Figure 7.2 illustrates the implications of integration.

Figure 7.2 *The implications of integration*

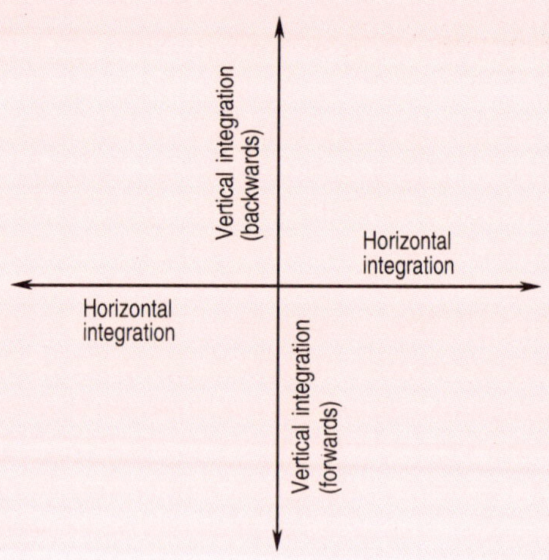

Motives for Vertical Integration

Vertical integration may occur for several reasons:

Security

This is a major factor motivating vertical integration either backwards or forwards. In the case of backward integration the motive may be to safeguard the supply of some vital component input. However, firms are unlikely to be solely concerned with protecting the supply of components; they are also likely to be concerned at ensuring that components are of a particular *quality*. Backward integration guarantees supply and ensures control over quality. Similarly forward integration may be motivated by the desire to safeguard the retail outlets for the product, so that once produced the firm can distribute its product to consumers.

Efficiency

Vertical integration may be motivated by nothing more complicated than a belief by management that they can perform a particular stage of the productive process more efficiently than it is already being performed. There may be various reasons for this: incompetent management, or the possibility that economies of scale might be reaped after amalgamation. Whatever the reason increased efficiency is a major factor encouraging amalgamations of all types. If a particular stage of production can be performed more efficiently, the combined value of the firm's assets after amalgamation will exceed the value of the two individual firms.

Improved Image

It is sometimes suggested that a major reason motivating forward integration is the desire to improve the image of the product by improving the nature of the retail outlets and thus encouraging sales. This was a major factor encouraging the breweries to take over many of the public houses through which their products are distributed.

Monopoly

Another possible motive for integration is that it may give a firm a monopoly over the supply of certain component inputs required by other firms in the industry, or it might give control over the retail outlets through which all firms distribute their products. In the UK such motives are unlikely to exist because governments, while mindful of the need to allow firms to reap economies of scale through growth are also concerned to protect the public from possible exploitation by a monopolist.

Motives for Horizontal Integration

Monopoly

Since firms which integrate horizontally are at the same stage of production, a possible motive for such integration may be to achieve a monopoly. For example, if one firm gains complete control of the raw material supplies vital for a particular productive activity it will have created a monopoly position. However, as explained above, this is unlikely to be a motive for horizontal integration in the UK at present.

Efficiency

Again, as explained above, a major factor encouraging horizontal integration is the possibility that efficiency will increase after amalgamation. This is more likely with horizontal than with vertical integration because there is more scope for economies of scale, particularly technical economies (see p. 68–9), in the latter than in the former case.

Diversification

Despite the emphasis on horizontal and vertical integration, a large number of amalgamations do not fall neatly into either category. It seems that as firms grow they often prefer to diversify and in a few cases establish vast *conglomerate* enterprises. Such growth may result in economies of scale being reaped but it seems that the major reason for such diversified growth is **security**. A firm which produces only a single product for a single market is pursuing a high risk strategy: if demand for the product falls, the firm could easily be forced to close. In 1991 Ford UK announced its first pre-tax loss for 23 years because the recession had resulted in a substantial reduction in demand for new cars. Although Ford UK has not ceased production of cars this does show how vulnerable firms can be when demand for their product falls.

Survival of Small Firms

In this chapter we have concentrated on the importance of growth and economies of scale. However, in many activities we find that small firms are common and they apparently survive and prosper. In fact there are many reasons for this:

Self-employment

Many individuals wish to be self-employed and start up their own business. Many large firms which are household names today started in this way. Sainsbury's, Marks and Spencer, Boots and the John Lewis Partnership all started life as small businesses and still bear the name of their founder(s) today. In most cases individuals are initially restricted in the size of their business organisations by lack of finance. There seems to be no limit on the number of people willing to start their own business and lack of finance will almost certainly ensure that such businesses remain small scale.

Small Markets

Small firms supply small markets. If we wish to explain why small firms survive we must look to those factors that restrict the size of the market. One obvious factor is the nature of the product. For example, in the case of personal services such as hairdressing small firms prosper. Similarly small family run restaurants and hotels are often popular with consumers.

Convenience

In retailing, the local corner shop often survives because it provides consumers with convenient shopping hours for the purchase of individual items. Such shops also sometimes offer regular customers credit and will undertake delivery of groceries.

Nature of Activity

In some cases the nature of the activity restricts the growth of firms. Repair work, for example, is individual and there are few advantages in size. The same is true of window cleaning and in these cases production tends to be small scale.

Small Firms in the Economy

In the UK in 1986 there were some 2.47 million small businesses and Table 7.2 gives information on the different categories of firm in terms of employment and turnover. The figures for 1979 are in brackets.

Table 7.2 *UK firms, employment and turnover, 1986 and 1979*

Employment size	No. of businesses (%)	Total employment (%)	Total turnover (%)
1–5	83.0 (79.1)	18.7 (12.4)	9.0 (5.8)
6–10	7.7 (10.0)	7.2 (6.7)	4.4 (3.3)
11–19	5.7 (6.1)	10.0 (7.6)	7.4 (3.6)
20–49	1.8 (2.6)	6.7 (6.9)	7.3 (5.3)
50–99	0.8 (0.9)	6.9 (5.3)	10.5 (7.8)
100–199	0.6 (0.8)	9.9 (10.2)	18.2 (16.4)
200–499	0.3 (0.3)	11.9 (8.1)	13.8 (8.2)
500+	0.1 (0.2)	28.7 (42.8)	29.4 (49.6)

Source: Department of Employment Gazette (May 1990) (adapted)

Since 1979 attention has focused on the growth of the small firm sector as workers who have been made redundant have been encouraged by the government to start their own business. It is significant that in 1986 over 96 per cent of the total number of firms employed less than twenty people and accounted for some 20 per cent of turnover. In 1979 95.2 per cent of all firms employed fewer than 20 people.

REVIEW QUESTIONS

1 Why do firms experience increasing returns as they employ additional units of a variable factor?

2 What is the difference between increasing returns to scale and increasing returns?

Question 3 is based on the following matrix which shows the output available when different combinations of capital and labour are employed

Units of labour					
	4	40	80	120	160
	3	36	72	108	144
	2	30	60	90	120
	1	20	40	60	80
	Units of capital	1	2	3	4

3 Does the firm illustrated above experience:

(a) Increasing, diminishing or constant marginal returns to labour?
(b) Increasing, diminishing or constant marginal returns to capital?
(c) Economies or diseconomies of scale?

4 What economies of scale might exist in retailing?

5 What type of integration is involved in each of the following cases?

(a) A publisher takes over a papermill.
(b) A tobacco company amalgamates with a manufacturer of potato crisps.
(c) A tyre manufacturer amalgamates with a car producer.

Question 6 is based on the Table 7.3 which shows how output varies when an increasing amount of labour is used with a fixed amount of other factors.

Table 7.3 *Output variation with increasing amounts of labour and fixed amounts of other factors*

No. of workers	Total product	Average product	Marginal product
1	1	–	–
2	3	–	–
3	8	–	–
4	20	–	–
5	30	–	–
6	36	–	–
7	40	–	–

6 Complete Table 7.3 and then identify the point at which:

(a) diminishing average returns are experienced;
(b) diminishing marginal returns are experienced.

CHAPTER 8

COSTS AND REVENUE

CONNECTIONS

In Chapter 7 we studied the laws of production in the short run and the long run. In Chapter 8 we shall be building on these laws to study the way in which a firm's costs are likely to behave in the short run and in the long run as **output changes**.

We shall also be looking at the pattern of a firm's **revenue** and examining how this, in conjunction with its cost structure, influences the amount of profit earned.

Key Concepts

Average cost
Average revenue
Fixed cost
Marginal cost
Marginal revenue
Variable cost

Costs in the Short Run: Fixed Costs and Variable Costs

Costs are **payments made by firms to the factors of production**. For example, in order to obtain labour a firm needs to pay wages, in order to obtain land a firm has to pay rent and so on. In the short run the availability of some factors may be fixed. The costs of these factors are therefore *fixed costs*. Since the input of fixed factors does not change as output changes, **fixed costs do not vary as output changes**. Indeed fixed costs are incurred even if a firm produces no output at all! Because fixed costs are not directly related to output, they are sometimes referred to as *indirect, overhead or supplementary* costs. Examples of fixed costs are mortgage payments, insurance, interest on loan capital, rent on premises, depreciation on assets and certain types of labour, particularly managerial staff.

There are other factors of production, (for example, some types of labour), whose inputs *can* be varied in the short run. The costs of hiring factors which are variable are therefore referred to as *variable* costs. These are zero when output is zero and then rise directly with the level of output because in order to increase output more variable factors are employed. Variable costs are sometimes described as *direct* or *prime* costs. Examples of variable costs are raw materials, power and wages of direct labour.

The *total* cost of any given output is made up of the cost of employing both fixed and variable factors of production. Hence total cost equals the **sum of fixed costs and variable costs**. When a firm's output is zero, total cost is equal to fixed costs since variable costs will be zero. As output expands total cost will rise as variable costs increase, but as we shall see on p. 75, costs will not change proportionately with output.

Average (Unit) and Marginal Costs

For any given level of output average costs of production are obtained by dividing total cost by the number of units produced. The three measures of *average* or unit cost are as follows:

$$\text{Average fixed costs } (AFC) = \frac{\text{Total fixed cost}}{\text{Number of units of output produced}}$$

$$\text{Average variable costs } (AVC) = \frac{\text{Total variable costs}}{\text{Number of units of output produced}}$$

$$\text{Average total costs } (ATC \text{ or } AC) = \frac{\text{Total cost}}{\text{Number of units of output produced}}$$

It follows that average total costs = average fixed costs + average variable costs: that is, $ATC = AFC + AVC$

Marginal cost is defined as the change in total cost when output is expanded by one unit; marginal cost is therefore entirely a variable cost. For example, if total cost rises from £5000 to £5050 when output is increased by one unit, marginal cost is £50.

The Behaviour of Short-Run Variable Costs

This is very much governed by **increasing and decreasing factor returns**, based on the law of variable proportions which we studied in Chapter 7. The data we shall be using in Table 8.1 relates to the use of one factor of production only, namely labour, but since the law applies to all factors, our analysis of variable cost can be generalised to include returns to all factors of production and all variable costs. For simplicity we assume that the cost of labour is £200 per worker. We see that up to the employment of the fourth worker average product is rising, which indicates increasing returns to labour. The effect of this is seen to be that average labour cost – that is, variable cost per unit of output – falls. This must be so, for since each worker is producing more but still being paid the same wage of £200, the variable cost of *each unit* of output produced must be falling. Table 8.1 shows that when the fifth worker is employed decreasing returns set in and average product falls. Since each worker is now producing less, but being paid the same amount, the variable cost per unit of output now increases. It follows that when average product is at a maximum, average variable cost will be at its minimum, and vice versa.

Table 8.1 also provides an explanation of the behaviour of marginal cost. Consider the employment of the second and third workers respectively. This is associated with a change in marginal product from 90 to 110 units – that is, whereas the employment of the second worker adds 90 units to total of output, the employment of the third worker adds 110 units to output. Hence, for the reason indicated above, the extra cost of the 110 additional units of output will be less than that of the additional 90 units, and marginal cost will be falling. However, when the input of labour reaches four workers marginal product is seen to fall, and marginal labour cost per unit of output will therefore increase. Thus when **marginal product is at a maximum, marginal cost will be at a minimum**.

The short run relationship between costs and returns is illustrated in Figure 8.1. It will be observed that marginal and average cost constitute a kind of

Table 8.1 *The behaviour of variable and marginal cost*

No. of workers	Total product (output)	Average product	Marginal product	Total variable cost (£)	Average variable cost (£)	Marginal cost (£)*
0	0	0		0	–	
			50			4
1	50	50		200	4	
			90			2.2
2	140	70		400	2.9	
			110			1.8
3	250	83.3		600	2.4	
			100			2.0
4	350	85		800	2.3	
			70			2.9
5	420	84		1000	2.4	
			30			6.7
6	450	75		1200	2.7	

* The value of marginal cost per unit of output described in Table 8.1 is that obtained over a range of output. The derivation of marginal cost in its more precise context of a one-unit change in output is indicated in Table 8.2

mirror image of marginal and average product. It will also be seen that the marginal cost curve cuts the average variable cost curve *at its lowest point*. If, at a given level of output, marginal cost is below average variable cost, then an increase in output must add a smaller amount to total variable cost than the previous average; the new average variable cost will thus be less than the previous average variable cost. In other words, **average variable cost will be falling**. Conversely if marginal cost is above average variable cost, the cost of extra units of output will exceed the previous average, and so the new average variable cost will be greater than the old; **average variable cost will therefore be rising**. If then, at a given output level, marginal cost is equal to average variable cost, the average variable cost will be neither rising nor falling – that is, it will be at a **minimum**. For the same reason when marginal cost is equal to average total cost, the latter will be at a **minimum** (see Figure 8.2, p. 77).

Figure 8.1 *Short run relationship between costs and returns*

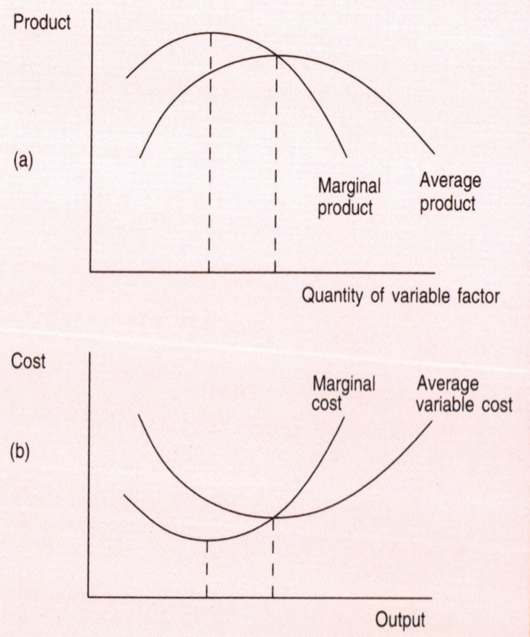

The Behaviour of Average Fixed Cost and Average Total Cost

Table 8.2 shows that average fixed cost declines continuously as output expands. This must be so because as output expands, total fixed cost will be spread over a larger and larger level of output. Note that since average fixed cost is associated with the use of fixed factors of production, its behaviour is *not* governed by increasing and decreasing returns based on the law of variable proportions.

Table 8.2, in which new variable cost data has been employed for convenience, shows us that the behaviour of average total cost is more complex since, as you will recall, total costs include both fixed and variable costs. We can see that average fixed cost falls continuously as output expands and that initially average variable cost also falls. At this level of output then average total cost is **falling**. However, beyond a certain point further expansion of output results in increasing average variable cost. Once the rise in average variable cost more than offsets the fall of average fixed cost, **average total cost will rise**; this is seen to occur at an output of 6 units in both Table 8.2 and Figure 8.2.

Table 8.2 *Behaviour of average total cost*

Units of output	*TFC* (£)	*AFC* (£)	*TVC* (£)	*AVC* (£)	*TC* (£)	*ATC* (£)	*MC* (£)
0	50	–	0	–	50	–	
1	50	50	30	30	80	80	30
2	50	25	55	27.5	105	52.5	25
3	50	16.7	77	25.7	127	42.4	22
4	50	12.5	102	25.5	152	38	25
5	50	10	132	26.4	182	36.4	30
6	50	8.3	169	28.2	219	36.5	37
7	50	7.1	216	30.9	266	38	47
8	50	6.3	278	34.8	328	41	62
9	50	5.6	363	40.3	413	45.9	85

The Behaviour of Average Costs in the Long Run

In the short run the existence of fixed factors of production means that a firm can increase output only by increasing the input of variable factors.

Figure 8.2 *Graphical representation of unit and marginal costs*

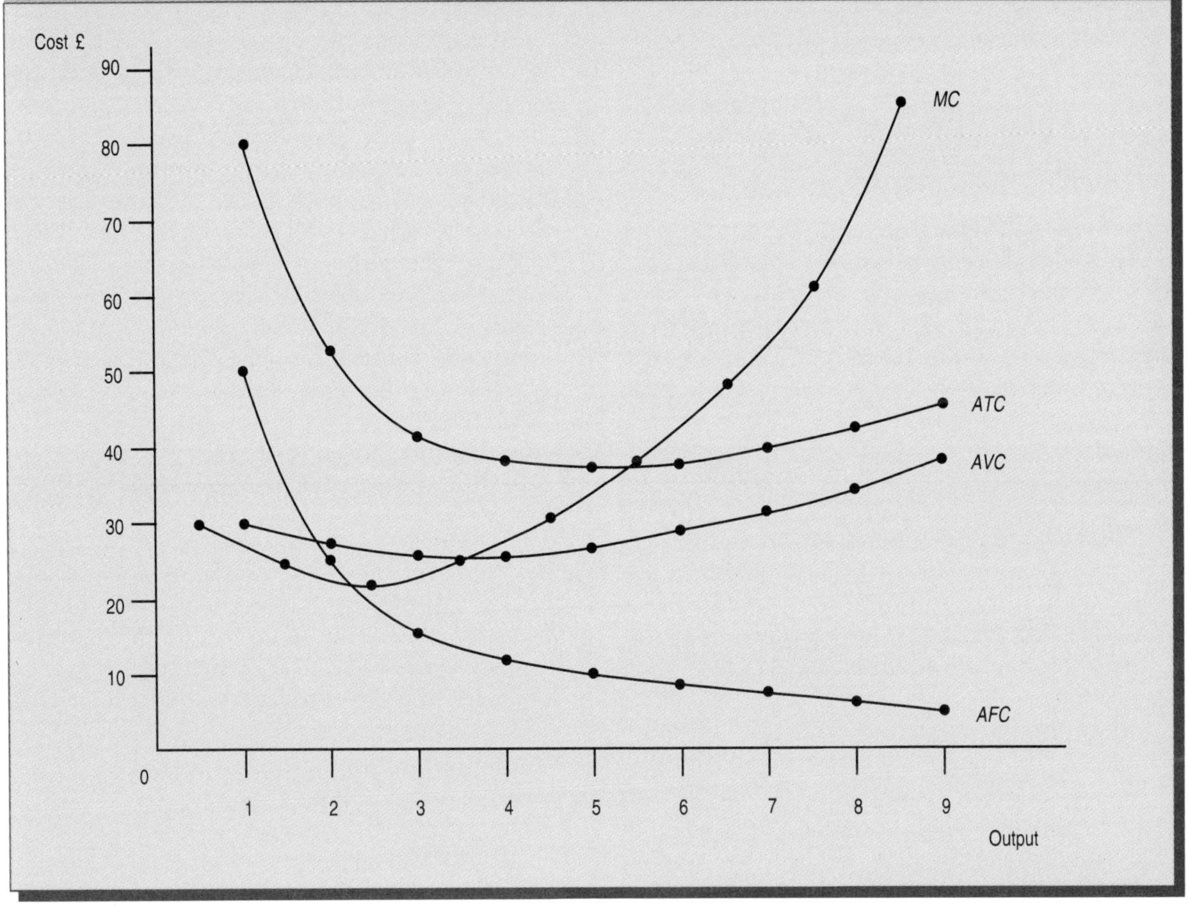

However, in the long run, by definition, all factors of production become **variable**. Hence the *capacity* or *scale of operations* of a firm can be increased (for example, through the installation of new equipment) to produce any required level of output in the most efficient way. Alternatively, a firm can reduce the scale of its operations by not replacing factors of production as they wear out or become obsolete.

In Figure 8.3, each *SAC* curve is a short run average cost curve showing how, at a given scale of operation, average costs vary with output. Assume that at its initial scale of operation the firm's short-run average cost curve is represented by SAC_1, and that output OQ_1 is being produced at an average cost of OC_1. Now suppose that, due to an increase in demand, the required level of output increases to OQ_2. In the short run the firm is limited to its current level of capacity and the only way it can meet the new level of output is therefore by increasing its input of variable factors. The effect of this is to increase short run average cost to OC_2. However in the long run the firm can increase the input of *all* factors and increase its scale of operations. Thus a

Figure 8.3 *Short run average cost curves*

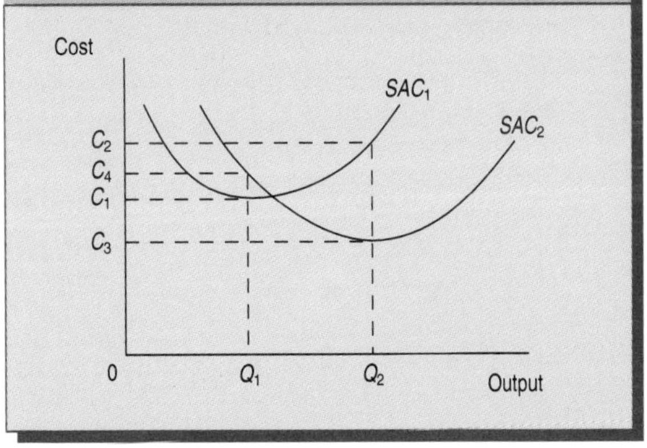

clothes manufacturer might install extra sewing machines in its existing premises or construct and equip a new workshop. By expanding its capacity a firm moves onto a new short run cost curve, say SAC_2. We can see that for the output OQ_2 there is an improvement in cost efficiency since the average cost of production is reduced from OC_2 to OC_3. Note, however, that if the required output were to return to

OQ_1 the average cost result from expanding the scale of operation would be OC_4, which is a higher average cost than at the initial scale of operation.

The Long Run Average Cost Curve

In the example just discussed we confined our analysis for simplicity to just two scales of output. However, there are likely to be many available scales of output open to a firm, each with its associated short run cost structure. Hence by adjusting capacity a firm can minimise the cost of producing any given level of output. The *long run cost curve* then consists of a series of such points on the different short run cost curves. This is shown in Figure 8.5 by the curve *LAC*, which is a tangent to the *SAC* curves. The *LAC* curve is sometimes referred to as an *envelope curve*, because it supports an infinite number of *SAC* curves, each reflecting a different level of capacity. In the long run a firm's capacity can be in principle adjusted to achieve any point on its *LAC* curve which, for this reason, is also known as a *planning curve*. It will be observed that the *LAC* curve as shown is broadly U-shaped. This is due to the influence of **returns to scale**. Up to the scale of operation *OQ*, the firm illustrated is experiencing

Box 8.1 The cost of making steel

The analysis of costs which we have undertaken can be applied in practice to many industries, one of which is steel-making. There are two major steel-making methods, which operate at different capacities and differ substantially in their costs structures.[1]

The 'arc' method uses an electric arc furnace to convert scrap metal into molten metal, which is then rolled into shape. Arc furnaces are cheap to build but have high variable costs and are designed to operate at a relatively low scale of production. About one-quarter of UK steel-making is accounted for by arc furnaces.

Figure 8.4 *Short run cost structures: European BOS v arc (late 1988 input price)*

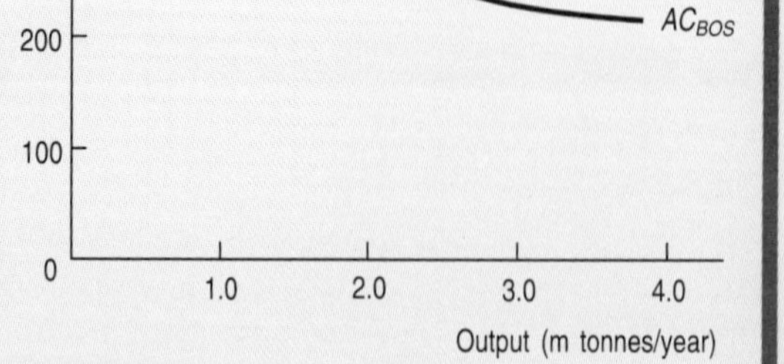

Source: Jonathan Aylen in the *Economic Review* (September 1989)

The alternative production method is known as the 'basic oxygen steel' (BOS) method. BOS furnaces are fuelled by coke and the iron from the blast furnace is turned into steel with the help of oxygen blasts in the converter. BOS plants, which account for three-quarters of UK steel production, are expensive to build but have low variable costs and are designed to operate at a relatively large scale of production.

The relationship of the short run cost structures for the two rival processes is illustrated in Figure 8.4. We can see that the short run average cost for BOS plants is below that for arc plants when both are operating close to their capacity: the minimum cost for arc produced steel is $245 compared with $220 for BOS steel. However, when the two types of plant are operating below their respective capacities, the cost differential between them is reduced, or even reversed. Moreover, arc producers with their relatively low set-up costs are able more easily than their rivals to enter the market quickly in boom times. These two factors have enabled the arc producers to survive as a 'competitive fringe' to the UK steel industry.

The data in Figure 8.4 also provides us with a starting point for the construction of a long run average cost curve. Given the cost data on plants operating at scales of production intermediate to those examined above, it would in principle be possible to derive a cost envelope defining long run average cost conditions in the UK steel industry.

[1] This section draws heavily on Jonathan Aylen, *The Economic Review* (September 1990).

improving efficiency due to economies of scale. Long run average cost is therefore falling. Beyond *OQ* diseconomies of scale set in, efficiency declines, and long run average cost rises. The level of output *OQ* corresponds to minimum long run average cost and is known as the *optimum scale of operation*.

The Firm's Revenue

We have studied costs in some detail since their behaviour is an important factor in determining the level of output produced by a firm. The other factor which the firm needs to take into account is the behaviour of its **revenue** – that is, the receipts obtained from the sale of output. Just as we drew a distinction earlier in this chapter between average and marginal costs, so we now distinguish between average and marginal revenue.

Average revenue is total revenue divided by the number of units sold, that is,

$$\text{Average revenue } (AR) = \frac{\text{Total revenue}}{\text{Total output}}$$

Assuming a firm sells its output to all customers at the same given price, average revenue will be constant.

Marginal revenue is defined as the change in total revenue resulting from an increase or decrease of one unit in sales of output. For example, if total revenue rises from £4000 to £4080 when sales increase by one unit, marginal revenue is £80.

Table 8.3 illustrates the behaviour of average revenue and marginal revenue as sales change. For simplicity we assume the firm sells its output at a constant price.

Table 8.3 *Behaviour of average revenue and marginal revenue as sales change*

Units of output	*TR*	*AR*	*MR*
0	0	–	–
1	50	50	50
2	100	50	50
3	150	50	50
4	200	50	50
5	250	50	50
6	300	50	50
7	350	50	50
8	400	50	50
9	450	50	50

The Firm's Profit

Profit is defined as a firm's total revenue minus its total costs. The relationship between revenues, costs and profit at various levels of output is illustrated in Table 8.4. It will be observed that the level of output which *maximises profit* – that is, yields greatest total profit – is 7 units per week.

Any firm which is to remain in an industry in the long run will need to earn a certain mimimum level

Figure 8.5 *Long run average cost curve*

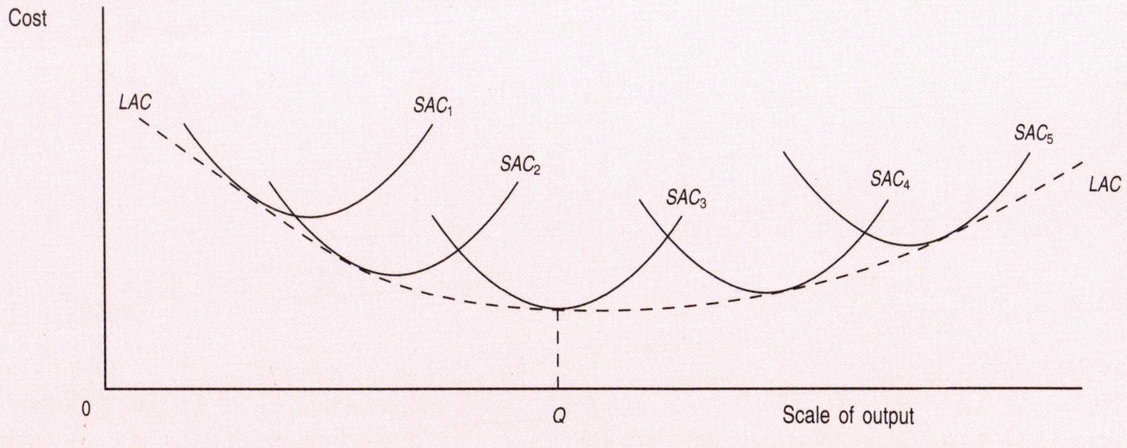

of profit which is known as *normal profit*. This is regarded as the cost of the entrepreneur and if profit falls below normal in the long run, we shall see on p. 90 that entrepreneurs will choose to leave the industry rather than remain in production. Any profit in excess of normal profit is known as *super-normal profit*. A firm earning less than normal profit – that is, *subnormal profit* – will in the long run leave the industry. Normal profit thus represents the **opportunity cost of the entrepreneur** and is therefore treated by economists (but not accountants) as a cost of production: it is the cost of keeping the entrepreneur in his or her current line of work. We shall be examining the significance of normal profit in more detail in later chapters.

Table 8.4 *Relationship between revenues, costs and profit at various levels of output*

Units of output	TR (£)	TC (£)	Profit (£)
0	0	50	–50
1	50	80	–30
2	100	105	–5
3	150	127	23
4	200	152	48
5	250	182	68
6	300	219	81
7	350	266	84
8	400	328	72
9	450	413	37

The Break-even Level of Output

We have seen that the relationship between costs and revenue is important because ultimately it determines the amount of profit earned by a firm. An important concept in this context is that of the *break-even point*. The break-even point is defined as the level of output where total cost exactly equals total revenue. The break-even point may also be expressed in terms of the relationship between average revenue and average cost. For example, suppose a firm's average revenue is £40, its total fixed cost is £1000 and average variable costs are constant at £30. The firm is thus able to earn a revenue 'surplus' over variable costs of £10 per unit, which can be set against its fixed costs. Hence an output of 100 units would enable the total fixed costs of £1000 to be met, and this output would therefore constitute the break-even point. It is clear that, other things being equal, the higher the total fixed cost, the greater will be the break-even point. For example, assuming no change in average revenue and average variable costs, a doubling of total fixed costs would double the break-even level of output.

Box 8.2 Break-even circulation in the newspaper industry

The costs of producing a quality 'broadsheet' newspaper like the *Independent* are substantially more than for a 'tabloid' such as the *Sun*. We would therefore expect the break-even level of circulation for the *Independent* to be much greater than for the *Sun*. In fact, the reverse is the case! The *Independent* can make a profit on a daily circulation (about half a million copies) which would leave the *Sun* with a large financial loss. One of the reasons for this is the superior revenue performance of the *Independent*, which is related to its relatively affluent readership compared with that of the *Sun*. First, readers of the *Independent* are willing to pay a higher price for their paper. Secondly, advertisers are willing to pay more to target the readership of the *Independent*. Whereas advertising receipts constitute only 30 per cent of a typical tabloid's total revenue, they amount to 70 per cent of a typical quality paper's revenues. Thus a quality newspaper like the *Independent* has a much *lower* break-even circulation than a tabloid like the *Sun* (see Figure 8.6).

In recent years break-even circulation levels in the newspaper industry have been falling because of the disappearance of restrictive labour practices and the introduction of new technology, both of which have reduced cost levels, including those of setting up a newspaper. This has allowed the emergence of several new national titles, for example *Today* and *The European*. With the advent of computer desk top publishing, further reductions in costs may make it possible for newspapers to be launched with even lower break-even levels of circulation – provided they can attract sufficient advertising revenue.

Figure 8.6 *Break-even circulation*

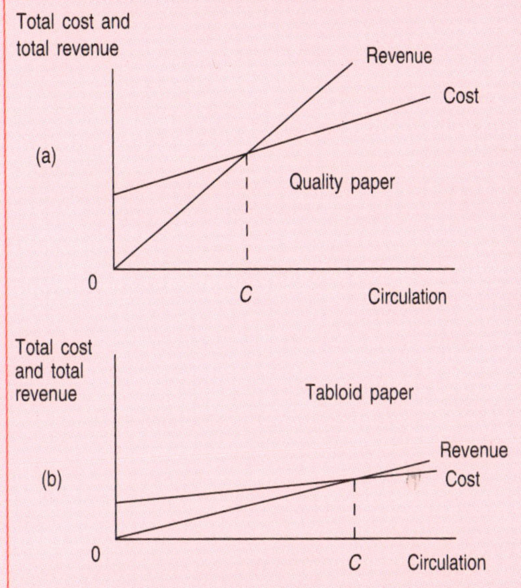

REVIEW QUESTIONS

1 Draw a graph to illustrate the relationship between long run and short run average costs for a firm experiencing constant returns to scale at all outputs.

2 Calculate *MC*, *AVC* and total fixed costs for the data below:

Output	*Total cost*
0	20
1	25
2	30
3	35
4	40
5	45
6	50
7	55
8	60

3 If, for a particular firm, *AVC* and *AR* are constant at £80 and £90 respectively, calculate the break-even level of output if total fixed costs are:

(a) £4000
(b) £2000
(c) zero

4 A market research survey suggests that a reduction from £500 to £480 in the price of a particular make of mountain bike would lead to an increase in the quantity sold from 30 to 33 per week. It is estimated that total profit would then be maintained at £3000 per week. On the basis of this data calculate:

(a) The price elasticity of demand for the bike.
(b) the average total cost per bike at a weekly output of:
(i) 30 units;
(ii) 33 units.
(c) If the price elasticity of demand was in fact -0.5, and assuming the same cost data as above, what effect would the price reduction have on total profit?

5 You are planning the introduction of a new airline service between London and Manchester and are faced with the following costs per flight:

Fuel charges	£2000
Interest and depreciation	£500
Insurance	£1000
Landing charges	£500
Labour	£900

(a) From the above data distinguish between fixed and variable costs, giving reasons for your choice.
(b) Given a maximum seating capacity of 55 persons per aircraft, what is the minimum price per seat which you must charge to avoid making a loss?

6 A firm finds that over the range of output from 0 to 100 tonnes total physical product is given by the following formula:

$$TPP = 5 \times E$$

where *TPP* is total physical product (in tonnes per time period) and *E* is the number of workers employed on a production line. Draw a graph showing the marginal and average physical product of the first 20 persons employed on the production line. What sort of path would be followed by the graphs showing the marginal and average costs of production?

CHAPTER 9

THE FINANCE OF INDUSTRY

CONNECTIONS

In Chapter 9 we refer to joint-stock companies and we build on our basic discussion in Chapter 15. We also refer to certain institutions connected with the raising of finance by firms. These institutions and their functions are discussed more fully in Chapter 23.

Key Concepts

- Debentures
- Equity
- Gearing ratio
- Hire-purchase
- Joint-stock company
- Leasing
- Plough-back profit
- Preference shares
- Stock Exchange

Firms need to raise finance because there is a time lag between the costs incurred in producing output and the revenue received from sales. The length of this time lag will depend on several factors, such as the type of product produced and whether trade credit is granted to the customers. However, the major factor is probably the *type of costs* incurred in production. In general, for most firms expenditure on wages and raw materials can be recovered relatively quickly, whereas the purchase of additional factory premises may take many years to recover. This is why a distinction is made in the balance sheets of firms between *fixed assets*, such as buildings and plant and *current assets* such as stock and work-in-progress.

This is an important distinction because efficient financing implies that **fixed** assets require **long-term finance**, whereas **current** assets require **short-term finance**. The asset side of the balance sheet shows the way in which a business has **used** its funds and the liabilities side will show the way in which the business has **obtained** its funds. Because of the way in which transactions are recorded, assets will always exactly equal liabilities, but for all firms it is important that *current assets* are available to meet *current liabilities*, otherwise the firm's creditors will force its closure. In other words, although any balance sheet will show that assets exactly equal liabilities in total, fixed assets are not available to meet current liabilities.

Sources of Finance

Short-term Finance

Bills of exchange are a major source of trade credit. When firms have produced their output they require funds to finance further production. However, retailers do not always have funds to purchase this output and require credit so as to allow time to sell the output and so generate the funds to pay the producer. This problem can be solved by using a *bill of exchange*. The *drawee* of the bill (that is, the debtor) agrees to pay the *drawer* (that is, the creditor) an agreed sum on a specified date. This gives retailers a period of time, usually up to six months, to sell goods and thus generate the funds to pay for them. However, this still leaves the producer without the funds needed to finance further production. In fact, as we shall see below, such bills of exchange can often be sold to banks for less than the full amount due – that is, they can be discounted.

Bank borrowing is an important source of short-term finance for all firms. In particular, firms rely on bank *overdrafts*. This is simply an agreement whereby the bank will provide loans up to some specified limit but firms pay interest only on the balance borrowed. Firms can therefore draw from and pay into their account and pay interest only on the day-to-day amount they are overdrawn. At any given time, therefore, the amount borrowed might be relatively small, but overdrafts are nevertheless extremely important since they are the major source of *marginal* finance for firms when other sources of funds are more difficult to obtain. In other words, they provide an important mechanism which, assuming overdraft funds are available, enables firms to ensure that **current assets match current liabilities**.

Discounting bills of exchange is another way in which banks provide short-term finance. We shall see on p. 216 that bills of exchange are IOUs given between traders and that banks (as well as other financial institutions) will buy these for less than their face value – that is, *discount* them. In fact, the role of the banks in discounting bills of exchange goes beyond the actual process of discounting. For a fee, they will also *accept* bills of exchange. This simply means that they will accept responsibility for non-payment in the event of default by the drawee. In effect, this represents a guarantee to the drawer because all risk is accepted by the bank and when this happens a bill will be readily discounted.

Factoring occurs when credit is advanced against the security of an unpaid bill from the sale of output. Usually 80 per cent of the unpaid bill is advanced and a charge of between 1–2.5 per cent of the full amount is made for the service.

Medium-term Finance

Firms usually require medium-term finance to purchase particular assets such as additional machinery. In such cases firms will probably prefer to match the length of time over which funds are borrowed to the expected life of the asset.

Bank finance in the form of a *loan* is one form of medium-term finance. Here firms negotiate a loan for a specific amount to be repaid within a specified period of time. Usually sums are repaid on a regular basis in addition to interest charges which will almost certainly need to be paid regularly.

Hire-purchase is often used by small and medium sized businesses to purchase items of capital equipment. This is not strictly a source of funds because the procedure is for the hire-purchase company to buy the capital item on behalf of a business but to allow the business concerned to use the machine and to pay for it by making regular instalments. The advantage for the firm is that it obtains the use of the business asset without having to raise all of the funds to pay for it immediately. The assets can then be put to use generating funds with which repayment can be made. The disadvantage is that despite the fact that sums may have been repaid, the asset remains the property of the finance house until the final instalment is received. In addition interest charges are likely to be higher than those made on other sources of funds and any discount that might have been available for a cash purchase is foregone.

Leasing is similar to hire purchase but in this case the user of the equipment never becomes the owner. The supplier of the equipment, premises or vehicles retains ownership and is responsible for the maintenance and repair of whatever is leased. This technique is increasingly common in the business world especially in the case of cars and electronic equipment.

Long-term Finance

Long-term finance is required for the purchase of fixed assets. In the case of smaller businesses such as sole proprietors where there is only a single owner of the business or partnerships where there are only a few owners (in most cases the legal maximum is 20), long-term finance is usually provided by savings of the individuals concerned. There is little we can say about such funds and in this chapter we concentrate on long-term finance for joint-stock companies.

Equity, or ordinary share capital, is the basic form of long-term company finance. The equity holders, along with the *preference shareholders*, are the owners of a company. The term 'shareholder' indicates that they own a share of the company; their stake in the ownership is determined by the proportionate number of shares they hold.

The equity holders in any company are important because it is they who have voting rights at the AGM in proportion to the amount of equity they hold. At the AGM the board of directors is elected and policy decisions for the coming year are outlined. In addition, the equity holders have voting rights in the event of any extraordinary general meeting.

Because it is the equity holders who have voting rights, it is necessary to control at least 51 per cent of the equity to control a company.

Although equity holders ultimately control the company, they have little influence on its day-to-day activities, which are in the hands of salaried managers. The senior managers will of course have a seat on the board of directors and will therefore be subject to re-election by the shareholders at the AGM. However, the AGM is rarely well-attended and few shareholders vote against the recommendations of the board.

Although the equity holders have voting rights they receive their share of company profits, announced as a dividend per share, only after the debenture holders and preference shareholders have received their entitlement in full. In years when profits are relatively low the company may not pay equity holders a dividend at all! Similarly, in the event of forced closure, or *liquidation*, the assets of the company will be sold and the debenture holders and preference shareholders will receive the face value of their investments before the equity holders receive anything.

Preference shareholders are also owners of a company but they have no voting rights at the AGM. They receive a fixed maximum return, expressed as a fixed return of the face value of their shares. In this way preference shareholders have preference in the distribution of profits over equity holders. However, there is no guaranteed minimum return on preference shares and in years when profits are relatively low preference shareholders may also receive nothing. Additionally, in the event of liquidation preference shareholders will receive the full face value of their stake in the company before the ordinary shareholders receive anything. In these circumstances there is no obligation on the company to make up for any unpaid dividend in years when profits are relatively high.

Debentures are long-term loans to a company; the debenture holders are therefore creditors of the company. These loans are highly secure because they are usually tied to specific assets such as property, and in the event of company liquidation the proceeds from the sale of these assets must be used to redeem debenture holders for the full amount of their investment before they can be used for any other purpose. Debenture stock holders therefore receive the full face value of their stock holding before any class of shareholder receives anything. Additionally, as company creditors, debenture holders receive the full return on their holdings of debenture stock before all classes of shareholders receive any kind of return. This is important because interest on debt is an obligatory payment: failure to meet this obligation will result in creditors taking action, perhaps calling in a firm of liquidators to recover lost interest as well reimbursement of debt.

Internal finance is by far the most important source of additional business funds. One reason for this is that using retained profits is the cheapest source of funds, although it is not costless since firms forgo any interest that could be earned on such funds. However, it is also alleged that reliance on internal funds indicates an inability to obtain funds from the investing public or the financial institutions. This implies that the investing public and the financial institutions in the UK are *risk averse* – that is, unwilling to invest in new business projects. This is a controversial issue which cannot be resolved here. All we can do is indicate the importance of the different sources of company finance as in Table 9.1.

Table 9.1 *Sources of funds for UK industrial and commercial companies in 1990*

	£million
Internal	24958
Bank borrowing	18903
Market capital issues	11967
Other	10287

Source: Financial Statistics

The Gearing Ratio

The *gearing ratio* measures the proportion of debt to equity plus debt in the capital structure of the company, and the higher this proportion the more **highly geared** the company is. This ratio has two important implications. First, when the capital stock of a company consists mainly of loan capital (debt) the dividend paid to equity holders will tend to be quite volatile. In some years it might be relatively high while in others it might be relatively low. This might make the company vulnerable to a takeover if, in years when profits are depressed equity holders are tempted to sell their stake in the company. Secondly, the higher the gearing ratio the greater the risk to the company that it will be forced into liquidation because it has a heavy debt burden to meet. As we saw in our discussion of debentures, unless interest charges are met creditors can force the company to sell its assets to meet these charges and redeem outstanding debt. A company with a high gearing ratio might therefore be forced to close if there was a drop in sales – even if this was only a temporary drop!

The Stock Exchange

The main function of the Stock Exchange is to provide a **market where shares in public companies can be traded**. This is important because once a company has issued shares they are irredeemable by the company except in the case of liquidation. An investor buying shares cannot therefore subsequently resell them to the company. If there were no means of reselling shares, few people would ever buy them in the first place and this implies that it would be extremely difficult for firms to obtain long-term finance and therefore to grow and reap the benefits of economies of scale. By providing a ready market in shares (and other long-term securities such as government bonds; see p. 218) investors know that if they wish to sell their shares they can readily do so. This undoubtedly encourages greater investment in public companies than would otherwise be the case. However, it is important to note that only those public companies which are given a Stock Exchange *listing* or *quotation* can be traded on the Stock Exchange.

How the Stock Exchange Works

Only registered brokers are allowed to buy or sell securities on behalf of the public. In other words, any individual wishing to buy or sell securities quoted on the Stock Exchange must do so through a **registered broker**. Whether securities are bought or sold it is the responsibility of the broker to obtain the best possible deal for the client. To do this, brokers operate a dealing room with up to the minute information on the latest prices recorded for purchases or sales of securities. In fact, the use of electronic equipment has now made it possible to buy or sell securities on stock exchanges throughout the world – it is now possible for brokers to conduct their business 24 hours a day if they so wish! For an individual wishing to buy or sell securities the implication is that the broker will now be able to obtain the best deal for the client whether this be in Tokyo, New York or London.

But how are the prices of the different securities determined? In fact, the prices of securities in the different stock markets are determined by the **interaction of supply and demand**. If, at the existing price, more investors are selling a particular type of security than are buying it, the price of that security will tend to fall. The opposite will happen if demand for a particular type of security is rising. Since a given type of security is a homogeneous good it will tend to have the same price in the long term, whoever is buying or selling it and wherever it is bought or sold.

REVIEW QUESTIONS

1 What is the difference between an ordinary share and a preference share?

2 Does a debenture holder own part of a joint 'stock company'?

3 Why is the gearing ratio important to firms?

4 What is 'exchanged' on the Stock Exchange?

5 Is ploughing back profit a costless source of finance for firms?

CHAPTER 10
PERFECT COMPETITION

CONNECTIONS

In Chapters 3 and 4 we examined the idea of a *market* and introduced the concept of *market failure*. Then, in our discussion of internal and external economies of scale in Chapter 7, we examined the distinction between a *firm* and an *industry* and in Chapter 8 we examined the behaviour of costs and revenue as output and sales change. We now begin to study the *theory of the firm* which will occupy us until Chapter 14, and we shall draw on our knowledge of all the concepts introduced earlier.

Key Concepts

Allocative efficiency
Equilibrium of the firm
Normal profit
Productive efficiency
Profit maximisation
Shut down point
Subnormal profit
Supernormal profit
The firm
The firm's supply curve
The market

Perfect competition is a market structure where the decisions and actions of an individual firm, or an individual consumer, will have no effect on market price. However, before we discuss the nature of perfect competition it is important to stress that the term perfect competition simply implies that there are no restrictions on competition. It does not mean that perfect markets are in any sense ideal or desirable. You will recall from Chapter 2 that any statement about the desirability of a particular market is a value judgement and is therefore not something which can be subjected to economic analysis. With this in mind we set out the assumptions on which our model of perfect competition is based.

Assumptions

Perfect competition can exist in a market only **if the following conditions are satisfied**:

- There is a **very large number of buyers and sellers**, each so small in comparison to the market as a whole that no individual can alter market price by his or her own actions.
- Units of the good sold by different sellers are **identical**; in other words, the product is *homogeneous*. This means that buyers have no preference for the products of one firm over those of another; they regard these products as perfect substitutes. Therefore there is no need for persuasive advertising or product differentiation.
- **Buyers** have **perfect knowledge**: they know what goods are available, and at what prices. **Suppliers** also have **perfect knowledge**: they know the products produced by their rivals, and the prices charged for them.
- Consumers are assumed to be **price conscious buyers** and are **indifferent from which producer** they purchase the product.
- There are **no barriers to entry into or exit from the market**. New sellers will not be prevented from starting a business or closing down and leaving a particular market. It can be deduced from this that institutions such as trade

unions – and, indeed, the government – have a very small role to play in a perfect market.

- Producers aim to **maximise profit** – that is, their aim is to make as much profit as possible.

Market Conditions

The assumptions of perfect competition imply that a particular relationship exists between the firm and its market. This relationship is illustrated in Figure 10.1.

Figure 10.1(a) shows the market demand curve for the product. In other words, it shows the **total amount of this product demanded by consumers at different prices**. It is a normal downward sloping demand curve showing that for *the industry as a whole* **quantity demanded increases as price falls**. The seller-perceived demand curve, on the other hand (Figure 10.1(b)) is horizontal – i.e., it is perfectly elastic demand with respect to price. It hits the vertical axis at the current market price (P in Figure 10.1(a)). What is stopping the producer from charging a price such as P_1 which is higher than P? The answer is *perfect knowledge* and the *homogeneous product*, because if a higher price were charged customers would know immediately that a lower price was available elsewhere, and that the product for sale at the lower price was a perfect substitute for the more expensive product. What then is stopping an individual producer from undercutting its rivals and charging a price such as P_2 which is lower than P? The answer is that there is nothing stopping a firm doing this, but there is absolutely no point. The firm's output is small compared to the industry as a whole, and so its entire output can be sold at the current market price of P. At a price lower than P the firm would not therefore maximise profit. Thus over any feasible range of output, the demand curve for the product of the individual firm is perceived to be horizontal.

Equilibrium of the Firm and Industry

We have seen already seen in Chapter 3 that free markets have a tendency to establish an **equilibrium price**. 'Equilibrium' simply means a state of rest that will continue indefinitely until it is disturbed – in the case of a free market by a change in demand and/or a change in supply.

However, in this chapter we are not simply concerned with equilibrium in the market; we are also concerned with equilibrium of the firm. Since we have assumed that firms aim to maximise profit, they can be in equilibrium only when they achieve this aim. So when do firms maximise profit? For all firms, profit maximisation is achieved when marginal revenue (MR) equals marginal cost (MC). This must be so because if $MR > MC$ the firm adds more to revenue than it does to costs by increasing output and sales. When this happens profits will rise. On the other hand, if $MR < MC$ the firm adds more to costs

Figure 10.1 *Relationship between the market and the firm in perfect competition*

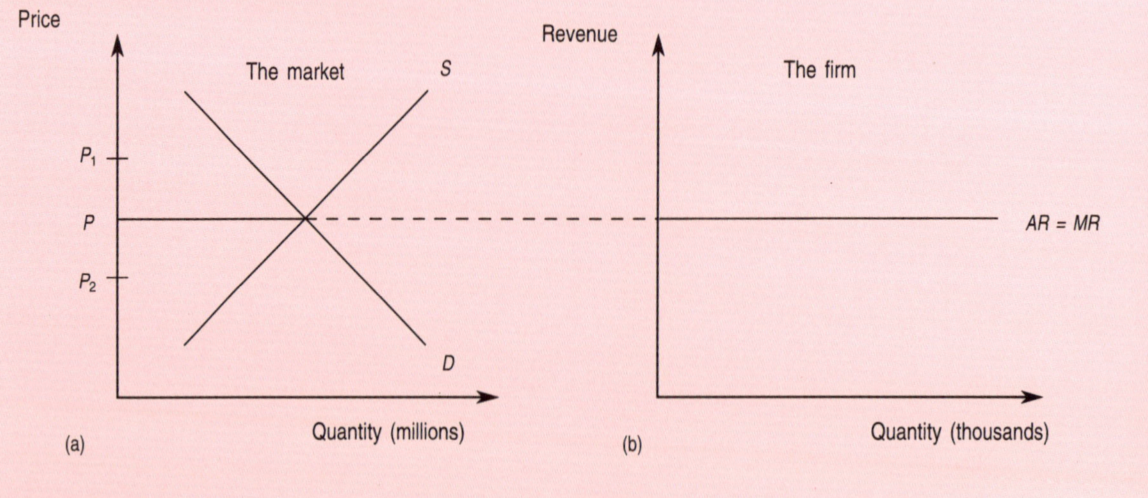

than it does to revenue by expanding output and sales. When this happens profits will fall. It follows that when $MC = MR$ the firm maximises profit. In other words, the firm **is in equilibrium when $MC = MR$.**

In Figures 10.2 and 10.3 panel (b) in the centre shows both how price is determined in the short run and how the market adjusts between the short and long run; the panel (a) on the left shows the equilibrium of a firm in the short run.

Let us examine Figure 10.2 in detail.

Figure 10.2(b) shows how market price is determined by the interaction of the market supply and market demand curves. Once established, the market price is taken by the individual firm as given and beyond its control. The firm therefore perceives its demand curve as being perfectly elastic at the current market price, *OP*.

To understand how equilibrium is achieved in perfect competition remember that the individual

Figure 10.2 *Equilibrium of the firm: firms entering the industry*

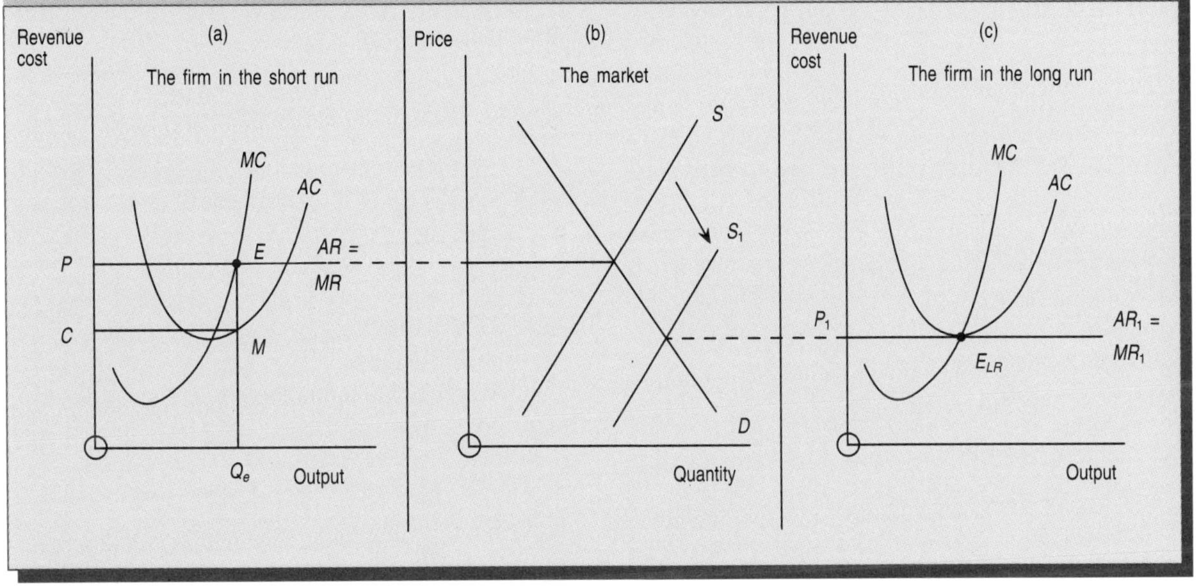

Figure 10.3 *Equilibrium of the firm: firms leaving the industry*

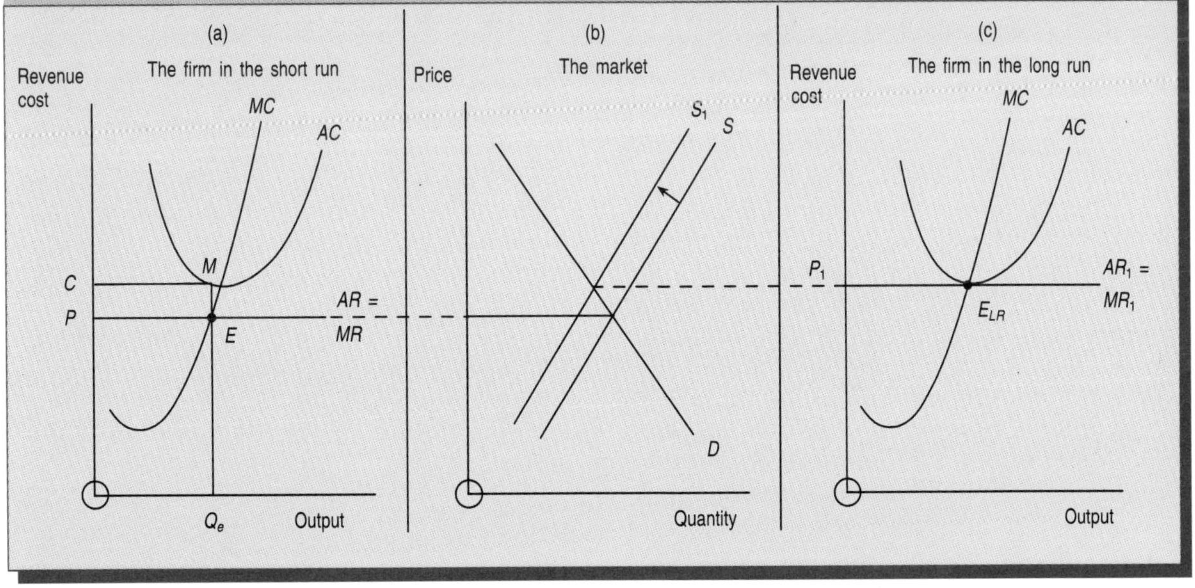

firm has no control over what happens to market demand, market supply or market price. Because the firm sells its entire output at the ruling market price, average revenue (*AR*), (that is price per unit) and marginal revenue (*MR*) (that is, the addition to total revenue from the sale of one more unit) are constant as sales increase. Indeed, since the price of the last good sold is equal to the price of all previous goods sold, *MR* is always equal to *AR* in perfect competition. Since the firm has no power to influence market price it simply adjusts output so as to maximise profit *given the current market price.*

But how much profit will the firm earn? This depends on the price of the product and the costs of production. When the cost curves are superimposed onto the revenue curves, the firm will either have relatively low costs and be profitable, or it will have relatively high costs and be unprofitable. In Figure 10.2(a) the firm (which we take to be typical of most firms in this industry) has costs which are generally low compared with market price. In order to determine the quantity to produce, the firm looks for point *E* where $MC = MR$ as this gives the profit maximising level of output OQ_e. The price received for selling one unit of output is *OP*; thus the revenue received for selling OQ_e units is measured by the area $OPEQ_e$. The level of average cost is discovered by finding where the vertical line through Q_e and *E* cuts the *AC* curve. This is at point *M*, and the average cost of producing one unit is therefore measured by distance *OC* in Figure 10.2(a). The total cost of producing OQ_e units is represented by area $OCMQ_e$. Since

$$\text{Total profit} = \text{Total revenue} - \text{Total cost}$$

the total profit of producing output OQ_e and selling it at a price *OP* is equal to area *CPEM*. This is *supernormal* profit (remember from Chapter 8 that *normal* profit is included in Total Cost.)

Thus the firm in Figure 10.2(a) is in *equilibrium*, meaning that it has no incentive to alter its level of output because at its current level of output it is maximising profits. However, if this firm is typical of other firms in the industry, then we can see that the industry as a whole is not in equilibrium. For the industry to be in equilibrium there would have to be no incentive for the number of firms in the industry to change – i.e., for existing firms to leave, or new firms to enter the market for this particular product. In this case the existence of supernormal profits acts as an incentive for new firms to enter the market.

It is possible to identify several markets in the UK today which, while they might not be characterised by perfect competition, do provide examples of industries where supernormal profits are being made and where new firms are therefore eager to enter the market. The development of hypermarkets on out-of-town retail parks is a case in point (similarly there are industries where the typical firm is making losses and there is an exodus of producers – coal and steel for example).

We now need to consider Figure 10.2(b). As new firms enter the industry, the supply of the product increases. The supply curve *S* shifts to the right, reducing the market price to OP_1 (as always we assume that all other things, including the conditions

Box 10.1 The firm and the market

People often associate competition with *price cutting*. In order to understand the theory of perfect competition, it is necessary to understand the idea of *price taking*.

When studying perfect competition theory for the first time it is often helpful to understanding to take part in what historians call an 'empathy exercise'. For example, imagine you are the owner of a small market garden producing lettuces in competition with a large number of similar firms, any one of which could increase or decrease its output without having any effect on the prices generally charged for lettuces by other market gardeners. How would you go about deciding on your price? If you find that the best guide to what you should charge is in fact what everyone else is charging, and you find that by charging this price you can sell all your lettuces, then the chances are that you are selling on a market which has most of the features which economists use to define a 'perfect market': you are a *price taker*. If, on the other hand, you find that you have to undercut the prices of your rivals in order to sell all your lettuces, then there are probably some imperfections in your market.

People who deal on the Stock Market, which is often quoted as a near example of a perfect market, are similarly not concerned with undercutting each other's prices. The successful dealer will be the one who has the skill of determining whether a given share price is *over-valued* or *undervalued*: in other words, whether its actual price corresponds to the **true current market price**.

of demand, remain equal). In the long run, supply will increase and price will fall until there is no longer any incentive for firms to enter the market: that is, until $AC = AR$, and firms are earning only normal profit.

Figure 10.3(a) shows a similar process at work, but this time starting with the possibility that the market price illustrated in Figure 10.3(b) is such that the typical firm is making losses in the short run. (Note that in this case, by producing where $MC = MR$ the firm is *minimising losses*, which involves the same principle as maximising profits.) Figure 10.3(a) shows the short run equilibrium of the firm, making losses equivalent to the area *PCME*. These losses act as an incentive for firms to leave the industry – remember that there is freedom of both entry and exit. In the long run the least efficient firms are forced to leave the industry thus causing a reduction in market supply. Figure 10.3(b) illustrates this with supply shifting to the left and price increasing to P_1; Figure 9.3(c) shows the long run equilibrium, with firms which remain in the industry making only normal profits.

Inspection of Figures 10.2(c) and 10.3(c) will reveal that whether firms begin by making supernormal profits or losses in the short run, the long run outcome is similar in certain respects. Profitable industries will expand, and loss making industries will contract, but in either case, at the long run equilibrium position E_{LR}

$$P = AR = AC = MR = MC$$

It is only under perfect competition and in the long run that these five criteria are equal simultaneously. Under other forms of competition it might be possible for two or three of these, but not for *all* of them, to be equal at once.

In order to appreciate the importance of this long run equilibrium condition under perfect competition, we must introduce the idea *of economic efficiency*.

Efficiency

In Chapter 1 we discussed the basic economic problems of *what*, *how* and *for whom* to produce. The idea of *economic efficiency* is mainly concerned with the first two of these problems. What to produce is seen by economists as being related to what is known as *allocative efficiency*, while how to produce is linked to *productive efficiency*. Let us examine these two types of efficiency in turn.

Allocative Efficiency

Allocative efficiency occurs when the pattern of goods and services being produced is such that it is impossible to make one person better off without making someone else worse off. This criterion of economic efficiency was first suggested by the Italian economist Vilfredo Pareto and is sometimes known as *Pareto Optimality*.

We have seen that under perfect competition when the firm is in equilibrium price is equal to marginal cost, or

$$P = MC$$

and we already know from our study of individual demand in Chapter 6 that when the *consumer* is in equilibrium price is equal to marginal utility, or

$$P = MU$$

It therefore follows that in a perfect market, marginal cost is equal to marginal utility, or

$$MC = MU$$

This means that the producer and consumer are in a finely balanced equilibrium with each other. The cost in terms of time, effort and factors of production put into attracting resources away from alternative uses and producing a given good or service is exactly compensated by the price paid by the consumer, and this price exactly reflects the satisfaction received in consuming the good. There is no *welfare loss*; the utility of one group in society exactly matches the costs of all other groups. In other words, the consumer is paying an amount for the last unit consumed which exactly equals society's valuation of the resources used to provide the last unit. How do we know this? Because marginal cost measures the cost of competing additional resources away from alternatives and in perfect competition $P = MC$. It follows that perfect competition, were it to exist, would result in allocative efficiency.

Productive Efficiency

This is also known as *technical efficiency*, and means that output is produced at the lowest possible cost. Since the marginal cost curve passes through the lowest point of the average cost curve, productive efficiency is achieved at that level of output where marginal cost equals average cost, or

$$MC = AC$$

If average cost is above marginal cost, then resources are being used inefficiently; they are either being underutilised, with spare capacity going to waste, or overutilised, with output suffering from diminishing returns (as discussed in Chapter 7). Since in perfect competition, when the firm is in long run equilibrium $MC = AC$, we can conclude that firms are producing at their technically most efficient level.

We can now begin to see why the model of perfect competition is so important to economists. It is the only market model which simultaneously achieves allocative and productive efficiency and it does this *automatically*. There is no overall coordinating body that has to *decide* to try to achieve this result; instead, the result is achieved by thousands of consumers and producers pursuing their own self-interest by maximising their utility. Economists refer to the *invisible hand* of market forces, and describe this process as one of 'enlightened self-interest', where it is argued that individual actions which might be seen as selfish can ultimately benefit society.

The Supply Curve Under Perfect Competition

We have considered the distinction between the demand curve for the individual firm and the market demand curve. We now need to examine the relationship between the output of a firm and the market supply curve. Figure 10.4 shows the cost curves of an individual firm in perfect competition. Remember that Average Total Cost is equal to Average Variable Cost plus Average Fixed Cost. Three prices are considered, P_1, P_2 and P_3.

Supply in the Short Run

At a price P_1, the profit maximising level of output is OQ_1. In producing this output the firm covers all its costs and makes supernormal profit. Suppose price falls to P_2, so that the profit maximising level of output falls to OQ_2. The firm does not cover all of its costs at this price and output combination. Nevertheless, in the short run the firm will still undertake production because by doing so it covers its variable costs and makes a contribution towards its fixed costs. Remember, if the firm ceased production altogether it would still incur fixed costs and therefore at a price of P_2 it makes a smaller loss by continuing production than if it withdrew from the

Figure 10.4 *Marginal cost and the supply curve*

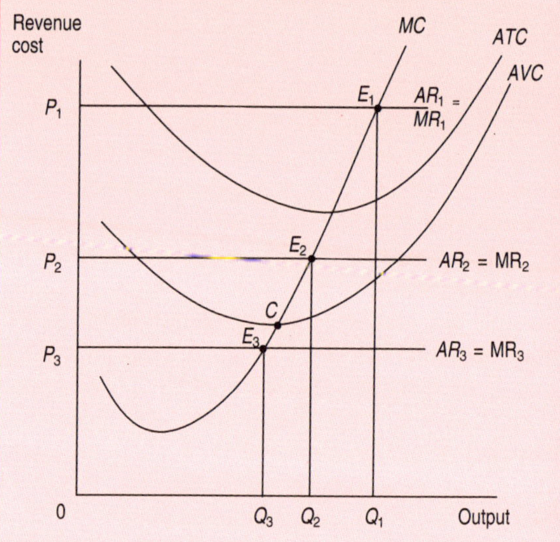

industry. However, such losses cannot continue indefinitely and in the long run the firm will be forced to leave the industry unless it can earn at least normal profit. The situation is different if price falls to P_3. In this case the firm is unable even to cover its variable costs. Thus the more goods the firm produces the greater the loss. Clearly, the rational course of action here would be to cease production immediately. In practice, it might be possible to find instances of firms which remain in production even when variable costs are not being covered.

Point C in Figure 10.4 is usually referred to as the *short run close down point* of the firm. The minimum point on the AVC curve is therefore the lowest price at which the firm will be able to continue in production in the short run.

We therefore reach the following conclusions.

- Under perfect competition, the short run supply curve of a firm is that part of its marginal cost curve **above the point where marginal cost is equal to average variable cost**. (It is also true that firms under other forms of competition need to cover variable costs in the short run but, as we shall see later, it is not possible to derive a supply for these firms.)
- A firm can continue in production in the short run if **price is less than average total cost**, provided that **average variable cost is covered**. In the long run, however, all costs must be covered.
- A market supply curve can be derived by adding together the output of individual firms **at each**

and every price above the level of average variable cost for each firm.

Supply in the Long Run

We have seen that in the short run a firm will remain in the industry as long as variable costs are covered. However, in the long run *all* costs have to be covered. The theory of perfect competition tells us that in long run equilibrium price is equal to average cost, and firms are just making normal profits. What if something happens to disturb this equilibrium? Take, for instance, the possibility of an increase in demand.

Figure 10.5(b) shows this increase as a shift in demand from D to D_1 which would raise market price from OP to OP_1. The firm in Figure 10.5(a) would earn supernormal profit, attracting new firms into the industry and shifting supply in Figure 10.5(b) from S to S_1. Price would fall back to OP, but the equilibrium quantity supplied would increase from OQ to OQ_1. Thus the long run supply curve is the horizontal line through the market price OP.

Figure 10.5 would seem to suggest that in the long run prices are static. In the real world, in many industries, the long run supply curve does *not* appear to be horizontal. The price of colour television sets, for example, has fallen (in real terms) over the last 20 years, and yet the quantity supplied has risen, thus indicating a *downward* sloping long run supply curve. An important influence here is the existence of *economies of scale*. As we saw in Chapter 8, long run cost curves can be horizontal, but they can also be upward or downward sloping. If costs alter in the long run then the long run supply curve is not necessarily horizontal.

Figure 10.5 *Supply in the long run*

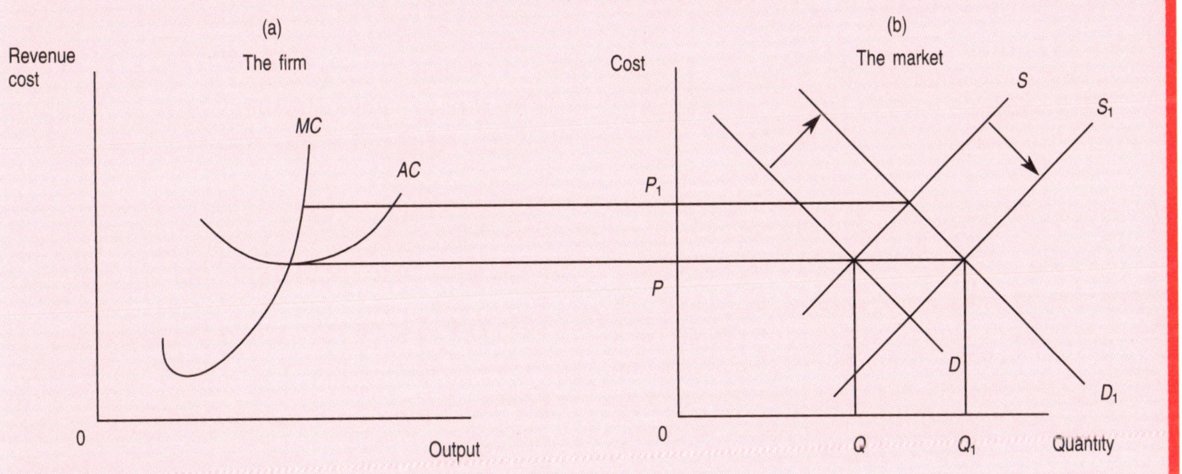

REVIEW QUESTIONS

1 Define and distinguish between the following terms: firm, industry and market.

2 Explain how economists distinguish between the *short run* **and** *long run*. Why are these concepts important to the theory of perfect competition?

3 Explain why a firm which is making losses in the short run might *increase* its output in the long run while the output of the industry *falls*.

4 Why are there no significant economies of scale in perfect competition?

CHAPTER 11

MONOPOLY

CONNECTIONS

The treatment of monopoly in Chapter 11 follows on from the discussion of *economic efficiency* in Chapter 10 by comparing the efficiency of monopolies with that of firms under perfect competition. Since a pure monopoly is unlikely to exist in practice, legislation to control monopoly is more likely to be aimed at *oligopolies*, where a market is dominated by small group of large firms. This market form is discussed in Chapter 13

Key Concepts

Barriers to entry
Monopolies and Mergers Commission
Natural monopoly
Restrictive trade practices
Welfare loss

A monopoly, in the strictest sense, occurs when a single firm or small group of firms who coordinate their activities **controls the entire market supply** of a good or service for which there are **no close substitutes**. This is sometimes referred to as 'pure monopoly'; while this provides an *economic* definition of monopoly, it is often in practice necessary to use a *legal* definition of monopoly. In the UK, for example, a firm is regarded as a monopoly if it controls **25 per cent** of the total market supply of a particular good or service. An important feature of pure monopoly is that because there is a single firm which controls market supply this firm can make decisions about price. Whereas under perfect competition the firm is a price taker, under monopoly there is some degree of *price making*.

Economists are interested in monopoly primarily because of its effect on the allocation of resources. (We deal with this in detail on p. 97.) However, a frequent criticism of monopoly is that it is characterised by the existence of supernormal profit even in the long run. This implies the existence of barriers which prevent the entry of new firms into the industry. Indeed the essence of monopoly power is the ability to **restrict entry**, and we begin our analysis of monopoly by considering the different barriers to entry.

Sources of Monopoly

Legal Restrictions

Some public sector services are *statutory monopolies*, which means that their position is protected by law. In the UK it is illegal, for example, to compete with the Post Office in the delivery of letters (although not parcels). The Milk Marketing Board acts both as a monopoly in selling milk to the dairies and as a *monopsony* (a single buyer) in purchasing milk from farmers.

A monopoly position might also be protected by a patent which prevents other firms from producing an identical good during the life of the patent. However, similar products can often be produced and it is easy to exaggerate the protection afforded by patents.

Capital Costs

Certain businesses, such as international airlines and chemical companies, have relatively high set-up costs. In such cases the minimum efficient scale of production might be very high indeed and this creates a formidable barrier to entry since the relatively high fixed costs incurred represent the cost of entry. In addition where substantial economies of scale are available it is sometimes the case that the market is most efficiently served by a single producer. This situation is sometimes referred to as *natural monopoly* and it is important not to confuse this with the monopoly that stems from natural factor endowments, as discussed below.

Natural Factor Endowments

Sometimes firms within a particular country between them control a major proportion of the world output of a commodity: nitrates from Chile, coffee from Brazil and gold from South Africa are cases in point. In these circumstances a particular country has a monopoly in the supply of a particular commodity due to natural factor endowments and it is impossible to obtain supply of the commodity from any other source.

Agreements Between Producers

While we might find that a single firm has a monopoly in the supply of a particular commodity, it is also possible to find a number of firms acting together to *create* a monopoly. The most highly formalised agreements are *cartels*, when firms jointly agree the level of output each member of the cartel will produce and the price to be charged for the product. Such agreements are illegal in the UK but a well-known international cartel is the Organisation of Petroleum Exporting Countries (or OPEC). This organisation has had varying degrees of success over the years in fixing output quotas for member countries and establishing a uniform price per barrel for oil. The main problem, as with any cartel, is to persuade all members to follow a single, uniform course of action. Invariably this will represent a compromise and will not necessarily be equally favourable to all members. When an individual member can do better on its own it has an incentive to break with the cartel and for this reason cartels tend to be unstable.

Tariffs and Quotas

It can happen that a firm has a dominant position in its home country, but faces competition internationally. A tariff raises the price of goods imported into the domestic economy and a quota restricts the volume that can be imported. They therefore protect domestic industry from international competition. (Tariffs and quotas are discussed more fully on p. 290.)

The Theory of Monopoly

Market Conditions

In our analysis of perfect competition, there was a difference between the market demand curve and the demand curve for the output of an individual firm. When the firm acts as a *price taker* it views its demand curve as being horizontal, with average revenue equal to marginal revenue. However, under monopoly there is only one firm in the industry and so there is **no difference between the demand curve for the industry and the demand curve for the firm**. Since we assume a normal demand curve it is necessary for the monopolist to reduce price in order to increase the quantity sold. In other words, in order to increase sales the monopolist must reduce the price of *all* goods sold and therefore marginal revenue will always be less than average revenue under monopoly. Reference to Table 11.1 will confirm this

Table 11.1 *Market conditions and monopoly*

Output sales	Price (*AR*)	Total revenue	Marginal revenue
			20
1	20	20	
			16
2	18	36	
			12
3	16	48	
			8
4	14	56	

Monopoly Equilibrium

In order to maximise profit the monopolist will produce where $MC = MR$. In Figure 11.1, this gives an output of OQ and a price of OP where a vertical line from the quantity axis meets the AR curve. At this price and output combination, the monopolist earns supernormal profit of $PRSC$.

Figure 11.1 *The equilibrium of a monopolist*

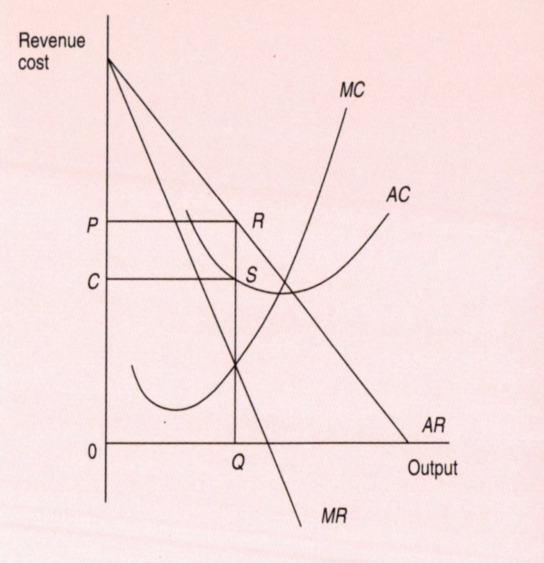

Under perfect competition, this supernormal profit would be temporary. In the long run new firms would be attracted into the industry and the short run supernormal profits would be competed away. However, under monopoly there are barriers which prevent new firms from entering the industry and a single firm remains the only supplier. Supernormal profits are therefore a feature of both short run and long run equilibrium under monopoly.

The existence of long run supernormal profit implies considerable power in the market place. However, the monopolist does not have complete market power. A firm with a pure monopoly has complete control over supply, but it cannot control demand. It can try to influence demand, for example increasing its expenditure on advertising. In fact it is sometimes suggested that huge corporations can manipulate the tastes of consumers, a state of affairs described as *producer sovereignty*. It is undoubtedly true that the millions of pounds spent each year on advertising can influence preferences, and can stimulate people's wants. However, as long as elasticity of demand for the product of a monopolist is greater than zero there is still some vestige of consumer sovereignty.

Some Important Points Regarding the Theory of Monopoly

- A monopolist will always produce at a point where **demand is elastic**.

A profit maximising monopoly will never produce at a point where demand is inelastic. Instead it will reduce output to push price into the upper price ranges where demand is elastic. Reference to Figure 11.1 will show that marginal revenue falls continuously as price falls and can be positive or negative. Marginal cost, on the other hand, may fall or rise but it is always positive because there is always a factor cost involved in producing any economic good. It follows that the profit maximising equilibrium position of the firm where, $MC = MR$, must occur where MR is **positive**. Demand is elastic where MR is positive.

- **It is impossible to derive a supply curve** for a monopolist.

We have seen in Chapter 9 that under perfect competition the firm's supply curve can be drawn by plotting the points of intersection of price (average revenue) and marginal cost at different levels of output. Since average revenue is always equal to marginal revenue under perfect competition these points coincide with the profit maximising level of output at different prices. However, we cannot do the same under conditions of monopoly because here marginal revenue is not equal to average revenue, and so different demand conditions can give rise to different prices for any given output. Figure 11.2 is used to illustrate this point.

Figure 11.2 *Monopoly price and quantity*

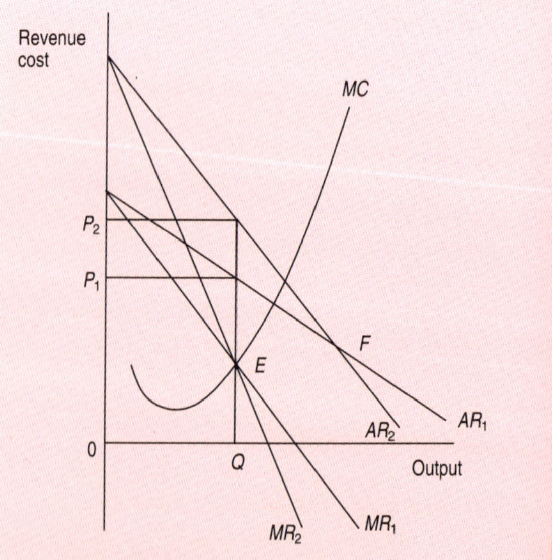

If the marginal revenue line is rotated about point E in a clockwise direction, then at prices above point F the demand curve AR_2 is less elastic at each price than AR_1.
Price rises from OP_1 to OP_2.

Figure 11.2 shows that the price charged for output OQ depends on the position of the demand curve. The demand curve AR_1 is more elastic at each and every price than AR_2 and the monopolist would charge either OP_1 or OP_2 for the output OQ, depending on which demand curve applies. Thus the price charged by the monopolist for the profit maximising level of output depends not only on marginal cost, but also on the **conditions of demand**. If there is no direct relationship between price and quantity supplied there is no unique supply curve.

- A lump-sum tax on the profits of a monopolist will leave **price and output unchanged**.

Suppose a government decided to levy a lump-sum tax of 50 per cent on monopoly profits. How would a monopolist react? It might seem that the simplest thing to do would be to raise price. However, inspection of Figure 11.1 (p. 96) will remind us that the monopolist makes maximum profit if output is OQ when $MC = MR$. If the firm increases price it moves from its equilibrium position and profit will fall. The monopolist will therefore leave price and output unchanged: it is better to have 50 per cent of maximum profits than 50 per cent of less than maximum profits!

Perfect Competition Versus Monopoly

Figure 11.3 can be used to predict the effect of a monopoly taking over an industry which was previously perfectly competitive.

$AR_m(D_p)$ is the monopolist's demand curve and the market demand curve under perfect competition. MR is the monopolist's marginal revenue curve. MC is the combined marginal cost curves of all firms in the perfectly competitive industry. In other words, we have simply added together the marginal cost curves of all firms in the industry. We know that in perfect competition the marginal cost curve of a firm is also its supply curve, and therefore the combined marginal cost curves of all firms in the industry must be the industry's supply. Equilibrium occurs when supply equals demand and therefore in perfect competition OP_c would be the equilibrium price and OQ_c the equilibrium output of the industry. If the industry is monopolised and costs are unchanged the monopolist would produce where $MC = MR$, giving an equilibrium price of OP_m and an equilibrium quantity of OQ_m. We shall relax our assumption that costs are unchanged when an industry is monopolised shortly,

Figure 11.3 *Perfect competition versus monopoly*

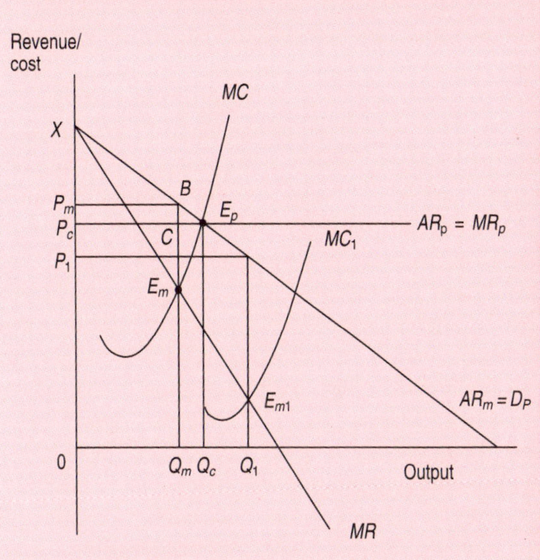

but first let us consider the implications of our analysis thus far.

- Under monopoly, **price is higher and output lower** than under perfect competition, assuming that costs are unchanged during the process of monopolisation.
- Under monopoly **price is greater than marginal cost** and so **allocative efficiency is lower** than under perfect competition.

In Figure 11.3 consumer surplus falls from area P_cXE_p to P_mXB. Area P_cP_mBC represents a direct transfer of welfare from consumers to the producer, while area BCE_p is lost to both groups and is known as a deadweight loss. Its existence implies that society's resources are not used in a way that would achieve maximum allocative efficiency.

- Under monopoly **productive efficiency is lower** than under perfect competition. Productive efficiency occurs at the lowest point on the AC curve, which is where firms produce in the long run under perfect competition. It is only by pure chance that a monopoly will produce here. In Figure 11.3, for the sake of clarity, we have omitted the average cost curves. However, we know that in long run equilibrium under perfect competition, the MC curve passes through the minimum point of the AC curve and this occurs when $MC = AR = MR$ i.e., at point E_p. It therefore follows that output OQ_m (under monopoly) is produced at a higher unit cost than output OQ_c (under perfect competition), and there is unused capacity of Q_mQ_c.

These considerations represent a powerful case against monopoly. However, we have assumed that the combined cost curve under perfect competition is identical to that under monopoly. In fact, it is more likely that a monopoly will gain from economies of scale and under these circumstances it is possible to predict a social gain from monopolisation. This might happen if the monopolist is able to benefit from economies of scale. If economies of scale exist under monopoly the monopolist's marginal cost curve will shift from MC to MC_1. In equilibrium this implies quantity (OQ_1) and lower price than was obtained under perfect competition. However, the monopoly firm still has not achieved full allocative efficiency, because price is still higher than marginal cost. Neither has it achieved full productive efficiency, because average cost will be above the minimum level on the new average cost curve. Despite this, society still gains from monopoly under these circumstances. The point is that further gains are available but are not reaped under monopoly.

Contestable Markets

It can be argued that all markets will operate efficiently if they are *contestable markets*: it is argued that firms can benefit from the advantages of large scale production, while consumers are protected from the disadvantages of monopoly by the *threat* of new entrants into the industry. For a market to be fully contestable new entrants would have to face costs similar to those of existing firms, and firms leaving the market would be able to recoup most of their capital costs. The knowledge that a market is contestable compels producers to keep prices and costs as low as possible. In the UK, two examples of markets which might possibly be seen as being contestable in this way are provided by the independent broadcasting franchises which are periodically allocated to competing companies by the authorities; and the relationship between the National Health Service and the pharmaceutical companies which supply the NHS with drugs.

Government Monopoly Policy

Policy Options

Monopolies can either be **removed**, or they can be **reformed**. The removal of monopolies (for instance, by simply passing laws banning them) would clearly remove the disadvantages, but it would also remove any advantages. Where possible, it might be better to remove the conditions which give rise to monopoly, such as the barriers to entry which discourage competition.

A policy of reform on the other hand, allows a monopoly to continue, if it can be proved to be 'in the public interest'. This option is aimed at keeping the advantages, while limiting in some way the harmful effects of the disadvantages. The reform of monopolies can be attempted in three ways: by replacement, regulation or restriction.

Replacement could be attempted by substituting a public monopoly for a private monopoly: that is, through nationalisation. If it is accepted that some degree of monopoly is unavoidable – for instance, in the supply of water by a natural monopoly – then it

William J. Baumol (1922–)

William J. Baumol was born the son of immigrant parents in New York in 1922. He studied as an undergraduate at the College of the City of New York (CCNY). After the war he applied for a postgraduate place at the LSE but was rejected. Apparently no-one had heard of the CCNY but Baumol persisted and was finally offered a place on the master's programme. Within weeks he was transferred to the PhD programme and was offered a part-time teaching appointment which became full-time the following year.

After being awarded his Phd he moved to Princeton, New Jersey, as assistant professor but was subsequently given a full professorship in economics. He has spent most of his career at Princeton and is regarded as one of the foremost theoreticians in microeconomics.

Baumol has a diverse range of interests and has had a lifelong interest in the performing arts. As well as economics he has taught wood sculpture to undergraduates at Princeton – a course that was particularly popular with students! His writings in economics have had a marked impact in several branches of the subject and throughout his career he has been a critic of models assuming profit maximisation. In the 1960s he developed the sales maximisation model and more recently he has proposed the theory of contestable markets.

could be argued that any profits should be returned to the community at large by means of state ownership and government control of the enterprise on behalf of the taxpayer.

Regulation would involve the government laying down conditions which had to be met by the monopolist. These might take the form of *performance indicators*. The government might lay down minimum standards for such things as productivity or the quality of consumer service, and might set up a 'watchdog' agency to ensure that these standards were met.

Taxation might be chosen as a means of regulating a monopoly, in recognition of the fact that in the absence of competition monopolies might have considerable influence on prices. Any monopoly profits which are judged to be 'excessive' could be taxed at a penal rate. Alternatively, *price controls* might be implemented to stop the profits from becoming excessive in the first place.

Restriction of monopolies refers to a policy of controlling the growth of existing monopolies, and discouraging the formation of new ones (for instance, by limiting mergers and takeovers). Restriction can either be carried out by *administrative* means (using a statutory body or *commission*): or by *legal* means (using a court of law).

The work of a *commission* is carried out in private, although its findings are made public. Such a commission may have a great deal of flexibility and discretion over what it investigates. However, its decisions are unlikely to be legally binding; instead, they may only be regarded as 'recommendations' which can be ignored by the government and the other parties concerned.

The work of a *court* is carried out by judges, in public. Its main advantage is that its decisions must be obeyed, as they are legally binding. However, its terms of reference may be very narrow because it will be obliged to follow strict rules.

Table 11.2 *Main instruments of UK monopoly policy*

Institution	Founded	Monopoly policy functions
DEPARTMENT of TRADE and INDUSTRY (DTI)	1973 (Formerly the Board of Trade)	Secretary of State can refer existing firms and proposed mergers to MMC
MONOPOLIES and MERGERS COMMISSION (MMC)	1948 (Monopolies) 1956 (Mergers)	Investigates and reports on monopolies and mergers (if referred)
RESTRICTIVE PRACTICES COURT (RPC)	1956	Decides whether referred agreements are against the public interest
OFFICE of FAIR TRADING (OFT)	1973	Director-General can initiate an investigation into 'anti-competitive' practices, and can refer agreements to RPC
EUROPEAN COMMUNITY (EC)	1957 (Britain joined in 1973)	European Commissioner for competition has powers to prevent various restrictive practices, monopolies and mergers
REGULATORY AUTHORITIES	1980s/1990s (on privatisation)	Act as 'Watchdogs' on privatised industries – e.g., OFTEL (telecommunications)

Monopoly Policy in the UK

Table 11.2 shows the main institutions which are concerned with the implementation of monopoly policy in the UK.

It is possible to regard monopoly policy in the UK in the twentieth century as having passed through four phases, during which attitudes towards monopoly have reacted to changed economic and political conditions. Note that a distinction can be made between **public** monopolies (nationalised industries), and **private** monopolies (limited companies). The four phases can be outlined as follows:

- Before the Second World War, **both private and public monopolies were encouraged**. It was hoped that this would help to protect British industry against international competition and lessen the effects of the economic depression of that time. Many large enterprises which are in operation today, such as British Rail, British Airways and the BBC, can trace the history of their present organisation back to the 1930s, when the government of the day actively encouraged them to take up a monopolistic position.

- Immediately after 1945 the Labour government, being committed to a policy of export-led growth and full employment, **discouraged private monopolies** (which according to economic theory reduce output and increase prices). However, certain **public monopolies**, such as railways and coal, were **encouraged** in line with the government policy of nationalisation. The Monopolies Commission and Restrictive Practices Court were established during this period, thus giving a two-pronged approach to private monopolies, but public monopolies were excluded from their terms of reference.
- In the 1960s and 1970s, the **stop go macroeconomic policies** (see p. 358) of both Conservative and Labour governments were reflected in the microeconomy by policies towards both public and private monopolies which were confused and contradictory. By now it was realised that the control of *potential* monopolies which could be created by mergers and takeovers was just as important as the control of *actual* monopolies. In consequence the Monopolies Commission had its powers extended to become the Monopolies and Mergers Commission (MMC). But in the 1960s government policy towards mergers was particularly ambiguous. There was a case-by-case approach: some were referred to the MMC, some were not. For instance, the Westminster Bank was allowed to merge with the National Provincial to form the National Westminster Bank. However, a proposed merger between Lloyds and Barclays was disallowed after an unfavourable report by the Commission. Meanwhile, an organisation known as the Industrial Reorganisation Corporation (IRC) was created by the government – in order to encourage mergers! The IRC was particularly active in the motor industry, assisting car manufacturers to amalgamate to form the two groups which are today known as Rover and Peugeot.

  By 1970 many commentators were predicting that the MMC would be disbanded. However, it was given a new lease of life by Britain's entry into the EC, and the need for Britain to adopt European standards of monopoly control.
- Through the 1980s, when privatisation and deregulation were central to Conservative government policy, **public monopolies were clearly discouraged**, but policy towards private monopolies was still somewhat contradictory. In 1980 the powers of the MMC were extended to cover nationalised industries. The MMC also benefited from the growth of 'consumerism' with increased public awareness of monopolistic practices and general demand for government action to protect the interests of consumers. However, the MMC was still restricted by the traditional case by case approach of UK governments towards monopolies. At the same time, mergers between large companies reduced competition and the power of multinational conglomerates grew. There was also a trend towards joint ventures, for instance between British and Japanese car manufacturers, which might reduce competition, and there was a growing awareness that action by single countries to limit monopoly power was no longer sufficient: there had to be action on an international scale: for example, within the EC.

The Current Position

The Monopolies and Mergers Commission

The Commission's independence has been increased by the existence of the Office of Fair Trading, which was established in 1973. Today, the Commission investigates cases of **dominant firm monopolies**, where a firm controls 25 per cent of the output of an industry, which are referred not only by the Secretary of State for Trade and Industry (who is a politician) but also by the Director-General of Fair Trading (who is a permanent public official).

The MMC might recommend, for instance, that prices should be reduced, or that costs should be lowered. It is then up to the Secretary of State to either accept or reject the Commission's recommendations. It should not be assumed that the MMC will automatically criticise a monopoly; it is empowered to support a monopoly if it thinks that it is in the public interest. For example, it might support a monopoly if it thinks that consumers benefit from economies of scale which would be lost if the monopoly were broken up.

With respect to mergers, the MMC can investigate only those mergers which are referred to it by the Secretary of State, and only a small percentage of mergers are referred. The government is sometimes accused of failing to have a consistent policy on mergers, and some takeover bids, such as the 1989 takeover of the Harrods Store, cause a great deal of controversy.

The Restrictive Practices Court

This court was set up in 1956 to consider restrictive trade practices, or agreements between firms – for example, an agreement between two petrol companies to increase their prices at the same time might be viewed as a restrictive trade practice.

Any agreement between firms has to be registered with the Director-General of Fair Trading. The agreement is automatically assumed to be against the public interest unless it can satisfy one of eight conditions known as *gateways*. For example, it might be claimed that to abandon an agreement will increase unemployment, or that the agreement is necessary to protect the public from harm. In fact, the Court has found against most agreements which have come before it and many agreements are voluntarily abandoned before they come to court.

Evaluation

A common criticism of UK monopoly policy is that it is too prone to political interference, and that it is too slow and ineffective to have any significant effect on mergers. While the MMC has had a powerful impact in certain cases, only a small proportion of Britain's monopolistic practices have been investigated.

As the 1992 measures take effect in Europe, it is possible that the major impetus for the regulation and restriction of monopolies in the UK will increasingly come from the EC, and our discussion of the Single Market is relevant to the future of policies aimed at encouraging competition (see p. 324).

REVIEW QUESTIONS

1. British Gas is a monopoly. Why, then, does it spend so much money on television advertising?
2. Is it possible for a monopoly to make losses?
3. Make a list of the advantages and disadvantages of monopolies. Are monopolies necessarily undesirable?
4. Compare the effects on a monopolist of a specific tax on its output and a lump-sum tax on its profits.
5. Why are patents granted to manufacturers who develop new products or techniques? Do patents restrict or encourage competition?

CHAPTER 12

PRICE DISCRIMINATION

CONNECTIONS

Price discrimination is not just a piece of abstract theory: it attempts to explain aspects of the behaviour of certain producers in the real world of imperfect competition.

Our discussion of price discrimination in Chapter 12 is related to several topics which were dealt with earlier in this book: you will find the theory of price discrimination much easier to understand if you review monopoly (particularly the equilibrium output of a profit maximising monopolist), restrictive trade practices, and price elasticity of demand. There are also links with the following topics: product differentiation, oligopoly and consumer surplus.

Key Concepts

Consumer surplus
First degree price discrimination
Market seepage
Second degree price discrimination
Third degree price discrimination

Price discrimination occurs when the *same consumer is charged different prices* for the same product or when *different consumers are charged different prices* for the *same product*, subject to the condition that these prices cannot be justified by differences in the cost of supplying the product.

The aim of price discrimination is to *increase the profits* of the discriminating firm. We should note, however, that the practice of price discrimination sometimes increases costs. For example, British Rail, incurs administrative costs in running its various Railcard schemes. If these extra costs were to cancel out the extra revenue obtained, then price discrimination would not take place because the aim of higher profits would be defeated.

Conditions Under Which Price Discrimination Can Take Place

Price discrimination is profitable only when *all three* of the following conditions exist:

- The product is supplied by a monopolist.

There must be at least *some degree* of monopoly power in the market. The supplier must have some ability to *make* rather than *take* prices. The greater the degree of competition to supply a good or service, the less likely is the existence of price discrimination.

- It must be possible to split consumers into separate markets.

The discriminating supplier needs to **identify different markets** among his customers. Separation of markets can be achieved in one of three important ways.

Separation by distance, ensuring that customers are **geographically separate**. The international dumping of cheap goods is a case in point. A company in Taiwan might be able to produce ladies' shoes relatively cheaply, as long as it can produce them in their tens of thousands, and so benefit from economies of scale. The home market in Taiwan is too small to absorb such large numbers, so the excess is dumped in Europe at prices which are related to local market conditions (prices which undercut competition in each country) rather than at prices which reflect the costs of production and transport.

Separation by time keeping customers apart by **serving them at different times**. Consider the case of a hotel which charges high rates to business clients during the week, but offers 'bargain breaks' to tourists at the weekend. It is likely that running costs are *higher* at weekends (staff will require overtime payments for working on Sundays) although prices are lower. Assuming the business clients and tourists receive the same standard of service, price discrimination is possible because consumers are separated by time.

Separation by type of customer using some easily identified **feature of the customers themselves**. Customers might be classified according to age, sex, income, occupation, or some other criterion. We have already seen that British Rail uses Railcards to keep recognisable categories of customer (such as families, senior citizens or young persons) separate. Senior citizens and students often qualify for discounts on purchases they make at certain retail outlets, and so on.

No matter which method is used to separate the markets, it is absolutely essential to the success of price discrimination that there should be no 'seepage' or resale between the markets. Suppose, for instance, that potatoes are supplied to customers in North Shields at a price which is 30p. per bag dearer than in South Shields. Any seepage between the two markets (people from South Shields travelling north in large numbers to buy the cheaper potatoes, or people from North Shields travelling south to sell their potatoes at a profit) would cause this price discrimination quickly to collapse.

The tendency for buyers who buy at lower prices to resell to buyers who pay higher prices is known as arbitrage. If arbitrageurs are active in the market, the prices charged to each group of buyers will soon **converge**.

The two conditions discussed so far make price discrimination *possible*; they do not necessarily make it *profitable*. For price discrimination to be profitable a third condition must be satisfied. We now turn our attention to this.

- Each separate market has a **different price elasticity of demand**.

If the elasticity of demand in each market was identical at each and every price, then a monopolist would simply charge a common price in both markets. Why is this? Remember from p. 79 that profits are maximised when $MC = MR$. Now if elasticity of demand is equal at each and every price in both markets, it can be shown that MR is equal at each and every price in both markets. In this case there would be a common profit maximising price in both markets and price discrimination would not maximise profit.

Figure 12.1 *Perfect price discrimination*

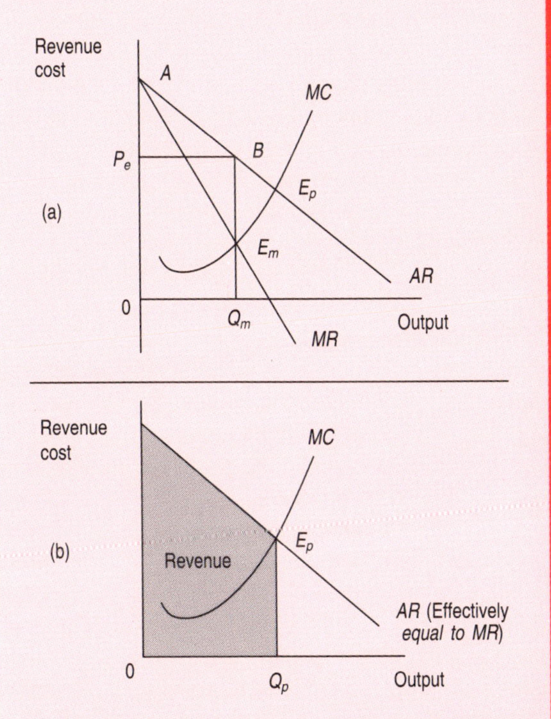

(a) The monopolist charges all customers the same price P_e, and produces at point E_m where $MC = MR$. If each unit of output can be sold at a different price, then extra units of output can be sold *without* reducing the price of existing units. This means that the demand curve AR also becomes the marginal revenue curve, and the prefectly discriminating monopolist will increase both output and profits by producing at point E_p.

The monopolist can not only gain an extra revenue of ABP_e from selling output Q_e at differentiated prices, but he can also make extra profit of BE_mEP by expanding output and sales from Q_m to Q_p.

(b) Total receipts under perfect price discrimination.

First Degree Price Discrimination

This is sometimes referred to as 'perfect price discrimination', because the monopolist discriminates to the extent that each unit is sold for the maximum obtainable price. It is possible for first degree price discrimination to take place when different consumers are charged different prices for the same product, or when the same consumer is charged different prices for the same product. First degree price discrimination is illustrated in Figure 12.1.

In this case a different price is charged for each unit sold. This will clearly succeed in raising monopoly profit compared with selling the good or service at one price, because for any given level of output the monopolist earns greater revenue from discrimination than is available when a single price is charged.

In order to discriminate as perfectly as this, a producer would need extremely accurate information on the willingness and ability of **all consumers to pay different prices**. The monopolist could then set price so as to eliminate any consumer surplus. In other words, each consumer would pay the maximum they were willing to pay for the good or service produced. In practice, it is unlikely that a producer will have this degree of information about consumers and therefore cases of first degree price discrimination will be rare indeed!

Second Degree Price Discrimination

This occurs when the same consumer pays a certain price for some units of a commodity and a different price for further units of the commodity. Most households in the UK experience this kind of discrimination in their consumption of electricity. Electricity prices are subject to a two part tariff which simply means that a higher price is paid for the first units consumed and thereafter a lower price is paid for however many other units are consumed. This type of price discrimination is illustrated in Figure 12.2.

Figure 12.2 shows the demand for a particular good by a given household over, say, a month. The first 100 units are sold at a price of P and the next 300 units are sold at a price of P_1. Here again, monopoly profits rise because, by discriminating, the monopolist is able to increase the revenue obtained from selling a *given quantity* of output. Effectively, the monopolist has reduced the amount of consumer surplus gained. The importance of this point is examined more fully on p. 105.

Figure 12.2 *Second degree price discrimination*

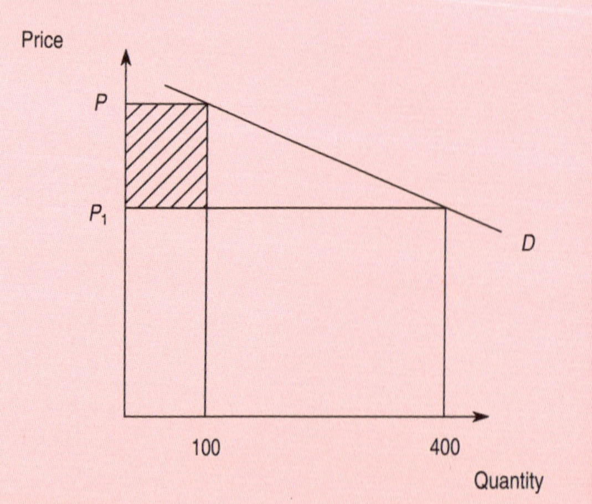

The hatched area shows the revenue gain compared with selling 400 units at the single price of P_1.

Second degree price discrimination has the same aim as first degree price discrimination, that of raising profit by reducing consumer surplus. However, in this case much less information is required by the monopolist since no attempt is made to eliminate consumer surplus completely. Instead the aim is simply to transfer a part of consumer surplus to the monopolist. Accurate information on the extent of consumer surplus is not necessary, merely some knowledge that it exists!

Third Degree Price Discrimination

Third degree price discrimination occurs when the same product is sold to different consumers at different prices. This is probably the most common form of price discrimination.

Figure 12.3 illustrates the relevance of price elasticities and shows two distinct markets (market (a) and market (b)) and the overall demand curve when the individual demand curves are added together (market (c)). Note that in markets (a) and (b), the quantity demanded is different at any given price, and therefore at any given price the elasticity of demand will be different in each case.

In market (c) the monopolist's equilibrium output is *Qc* and the single profit maximising price is *Pc*. In other words, the monopolist produces where $MC = MR$ and earns a total profit equal to the shaded area *z*. If a single price were charged this would be the maximum profit the monopolist could earn. If he tried to sell his output at a higher price, quantity demanded would contract along *AR* (the demand curve); the monopolist would move away from the equilibrium point *Ec* and the profit rectangle (area *z*) would be reduced in size.

However, it is possible to increase profit through *price discrimination*. In this case, the monopolist could take the output Q_c and sell it in two separate markets at different prices. In market (a), the monopolist has identified a group of consumers with relatively low price elasticity of demand for his product. They are less responsive to price changes and therefore willing to pay higher prices than consumers in market (b), where demand is relatively more elastic.

The problem for the monopolist is to decide how much output to sell in market (a) and how much to sell in market (b). In fact, the monopolist simply equates marginal revenue in each market with the marginal cost of producing *Qc* units of output. Thus the marginal cost of production *OM* is projected back

Figure 12.3 *Third degree price discrimination*

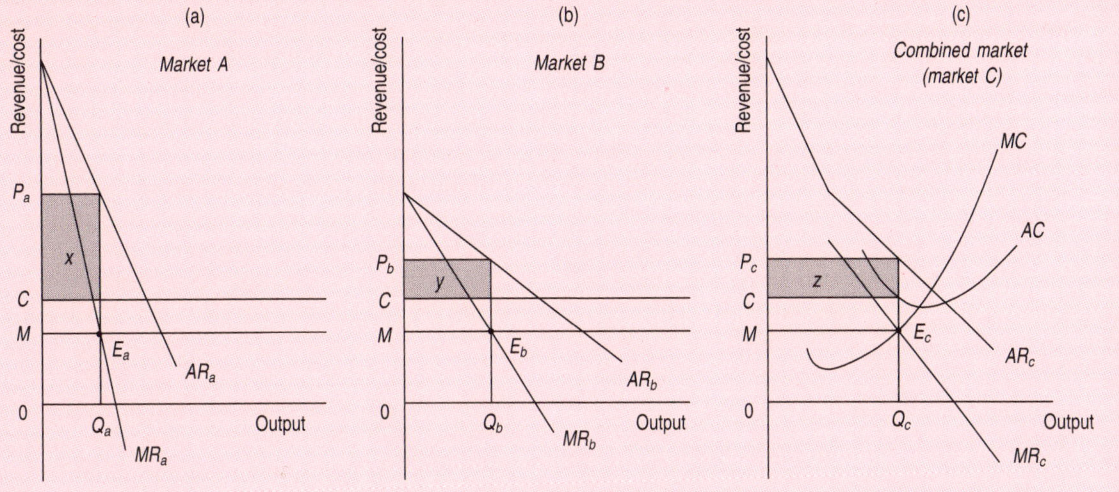

The profit gain from price discrimination is $(x + y) - z$

from the combined market as a horizontal line to enable the monopolist to find the equilibrium points E_a and E_b where $MC = MR$ in each of the individual markets (a) and (b). Similarly, the average cost of production, *OC*, is projected back from the combined market as a horizontal line to enable the monopolist to calculate profit (area x in market (a), and area y in market (b)) from discrimination.

Price discrimination will be a success, from the monopolist's point of view, if total profits increase as a result. In the example in Figure 12.3, the monopolist has succeeded because

$$\text{Area } x + \text{Area } y > \text{Area } z.$$

To sum up: the diagram in Figure 12.3 of the combined market shows us the total quantity the monopolist can produce; the diagrams for market (a) and market (b) show us how much of this output can be sold in each of the separate markets, and at which prices. The market with the lower price elasticity is where consumers are less responsive to price changes, and where the monopolist can therefore charge a higher price.

Disadvantages of Price Discrimination

We have seen that the main advantage of price discrimination from the producer's point of view is that it increases profits. We shall now evaluate price discrimination from the consumer's point of view.

Price discrimination represents a *transfer of welfare* from the consumer to the producer: it can be argued that the producer gains at the consumer's expense. One way of measuring the consumer's loss of welfare is to attempt to measure the loss of *consumer surplus*. Consumer surplus can be regarded as *utility* which a consumer receives free of charge, although he or she is willing to pay for it.

It might be possible, at least in theory, for a monopolist to establish a separate market for each and every unit of his product. This would be a system of *perfect price discrimination* where the marginal revenue for each good would be the price at which it was sold. The monopolist's output would then be the same as the perfectly competitive output, but there would be one important contrast with perfect competition: no consumer would receive any consumer surplus.

If we all had to pay the maximum we were willing to pay for everything we bought, so that we never received consumer surplus, then our incomes would purchase fewer goods and services and there would be a massive drop in our living standards. The total sum of human welfare might remain the same – but producers would gain at the expense of consumers.

Advantages of Price Discrimination

Contrary to what might be expected, price discrimination is not always against the consumer's interests.

There are circumstances in which discrimination can benefit consumer and producer alike.

A major advantage of price discrimination is that it can sometimes turn a loss making monopoly into a profitable one. This situation can be illustrated in terms of Figure 12.4.

Given the *AR* and *AC* curves in Figure 12.4 there is no level of output at which the monopolist can avoid a loss if a single price is charged for his output. In the absence of discrimination this good would not therefore be supplied in the long run. This might not seem a bad thing. After all, if society is unwilling to pay a sufficiently high price to attract resources into the production of this commodity it would seem that allocative efficiency could be improved if resources were used to produce an alternative which society valued more highly than the monopolist's product.

However, we have seen in Chapter 4 that some goods confer positive externalities on society which are unpriced by market forces. The existence of such positive externalities implies that the good conferring them would be underconsumed in relation to the optimum level in a free market. If the good illustrated in Figure 12.4 confers positive externalities then society may gain from discrimination.

In Figure 12.4, the producer's equilibrium point is at *E* and output is OQ_e; but the price of OP_e does not cover the cost of *OC*. Losses are measured by the rectangular area *x*. Under normal circumstances, economic theory would predict that this enterprise would close down in the long run. However, along the demand curve *AR* to the left of point *B* there are consumers who are willing to pay a price that is higher than OP_e.

If instead of charging a single price OP_e, the monopolist charges some consumers a higher price of OP_{e1}, a loss can be transformed into a profit. The shaded area *y* shows the additional revenue that would be available to the producer if he were able to charge a two-part tariff. Since area *y* is greater than area *x*, then the loss-making monopolist now makes a profit at his present level of output.

In the days before the NHS it was not uncommon for doctors to charge their patients different prices. The wealthier patients were charged higher prices and no doubt some patients were charged less than the full cost of the doctor's service. If the doctor served an isolated community then the ability to discriminate might mean the difference between the the non-provision of medical care in the community and provision. For example, if Figure 12.4 shows the situation facing the doctor in an isolated community it is clear that in the absence of discrimination this community will be without medical care in the long run.

Figure 12.4 *Profits and losses (a) without and (b) with discrimination*

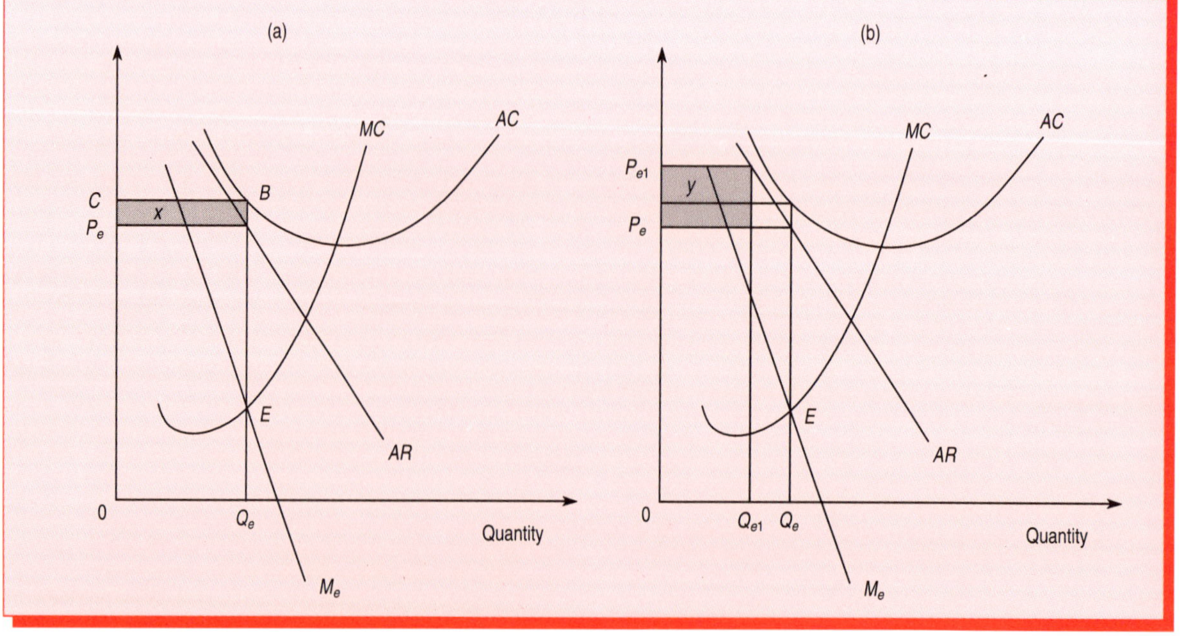

Box 12.1 It isn't always price discrimination when firms charge different prices for different products

Consider the following examples, which are often given as instances of price discrimination.

- The differences in price for first class and standard class rail travel.
- Different rates for the consumers of off-peak and peak-time electricity.

In the first example, passengers are receiving the same product in the sense that they are travelling to the same destination. But are they all receiving *exactly* the same service? First class seats are larger, more comfortable, and have more leg room than standard class seats. The costs of running a first class carriage are therefore shared among fewer passengers than those of a standard class carriage. In addition, passengers who travel first class often receive additional comforts, such as waiter service.

British Rail could argue that these services cost more and that these costs should be reflected in a higher price. On the other hand there might be an *element* of price discrimination if the price differences are not *entirely* justified by cost differences, but it cannot be argued that the difference between first class and standard class ticket prices is *completely* due to price discrimination.

With respect to the second case the demand for electricity fluctuates throughout the day and it cannot be stored. Demand is heaviest in the evenings when people come home from work, turn on the lights and television, cook their tea, and heat the water to wash up. The electricity generating companies must keep plant and equipment in reserve able to cope with the heaviest demand on the coldest and darkest day of the year. For much of the time this is spare capacity which is idle and unused. It can therefore be argued that on-peak consumers impose higher costs on the industry than off-peak consumers, and that on-peak charges should reflect these higher costs.

Thus Powergen and other electricity suppliers do not practise price discrimination by charging different prices for peak and off-peak consumption of electricity. They are merely trying to use their generating capacity more efficiently by matching supply more closely to demand.

- Lower cost travel on British Rail

Imagine you are travelling from Bristol to London on the train. You have bought a ticket using your Young Person's Railcard. The man opposite you is a soldier returning from leave; his ticket has been obtained using a Forces Travel Warrant. The gentleman next to him has bought a 'Supersaver' ticket. The lady next to you has used a coupon cut from a detergent packet, and her young daughter has a cheap travel voucher because she belongs to the 'Rail Riders Club'. On the other side of the aisle the girl's grandmother is travelling with a Senior Citizen's Railcard. These passengers are sharing a substantially similar service; all are imposing similar costs on the provider, and yet six different customers have paid six different prices.

- West Wales Coal Merchants

In 1980, a local consumer group in Dyfed found that coal in their area was 30p per bag more expensive than in London. This was surprising, because customers in West Wales lived on the doorstep of some highly productive anthracite mines, whereas coal of any description had to be transported many miles to reach London. It was discovered that certain coal merchants were operating a *cartel* which discriminated against local customers by charging them higher prices. Clearly, once this came to light it was difficult for this *restrictive trade practice* to continue.

REVIEW QUESTIONS

1 Consider whether or not each of the following is a case of price discrimination. Give your reasons in each case, and for each instance of price discrimination, state how the conditions (such as avoiding separation between markets) have been achieved:

(a) The Ford Motor Company offers a fleet of Ford Fiestas to the British School of Motoring at a substantial discount.
(b) Industrial users of electricity are charged a different price to domestic users.
(c) Business travellers flying from London to Madrid by scheduled air services pay higher prices than holidaymakers on a package deal.
(d) A concert is advertised with seats at no fewer than *nine* different prices.
(e) Surplus butter from the EC is sold cheaply to Russia, and is given away to British senior citizens.
(f) Parents pay different contributions towards their children's university education, depending on income.

Question 2 is based on the following article:

A Large Beef About Oxo

Are you paying too much for Oxo cubes? It has come out in a court case that Brooke Bond's export price for Oxo cubes is 42 per cent cheaper than shops in Britain pay. On the face it that should mean that a packet of Oxo selling at around 38p in your local shop should cost only 22p.

Brooke Bond could not explain its double pricing because all its experts are busy giving evidence at the trial.

The defendants are accused of trying to buy Oxo at the cheaper export price in order to sell it in Britain at a profit.

Surely the real crime is that firms operate such two-faced pricing systems in the first place.

I look forward to hearing Brooke Bond's explanation when its experts can spare me the time.

Source: *Daily Mirror* (28 October 1987)

(a) How does your knowledge of price discrimination enable you to analyse the behaviour of Brooke Bond with respect to the pricing of Oxo cubes?
(b) One of the conditions for price discrimination to exist is a 'separation of markets' with no 'seepage' between markets.
  (i) Explain how this condition seems to have broken down in the Oxo case.
  (ii) Would you agree that the continuation of price discrimination partly depends on consumer ignorance?
  (iii) Suggest why the company appears to be willing to go to the expense of a court case in order to maintain separate markets.
(c) Apart from the condition referred to in (b), how are the other conditions for price discrimination likely to apply to Oxo?
(d) What possible reasons might Brooke Bond put forward to try to justify their pricing policy, and how might these differ from an economist's analysis of the matter?

CHAPTER 13

IMPERFECT COMPETITION

CONNECTIONS

We can think of perfect competition (with its large number of sellers) and monopoly (with its single seller) as being two extreme market forms. Other types of market, known as imperfect competition, fall within these two extremes.

Key Concepts

Advertising
Kinked demand curve
Monopolistic competition
Non-price competition
Oligopoly
Price leadership
Product differentiation

Imperfect competition covers two broad market forms:

Monopolistic competition is a market with a **large number of suppliers and a differentiated product**. Each firm has a limited degree of monopoly power, because it has a monopoly over its own brand of the product.

Oligopoly is a market with a **small number of large scale suppliers**. In general, it is assumed that each firm produces a differentiated product.

Monopolistic Competition

The Nature of Monopolistic Competition

Monopolistic competition, as the name suggests, combines some aspects of both perfect competition and monopoly. The theory of monopolistic competition was developed during the 1930s by Joan Robinson in Britain and Edward Chamberlin in the USA. These economists worked independently and simultaneously developed a more realistic analysis of the behaviour of firms than was provided by the theories which describe perfect competition and monopoly.

The main market conditions of monopolistic competition are:

- There are many firms but each is large enough to have **some influence on the price it charges for its product**.
- There are **few** (if any) **barriers to exit from, or entry to**, the market.
- Each firm produces a product which is **slightly differentiated** from that of rival producers.

The first two of these assumptions correspond closely to conditions for perfect competition, while the third results in some degree of monopoly. In other words, each firm has a monopoly over its own brand of the product. Monopolistic competition is common in the service sector where there are relatively few barriers to entry, and where firms can be profitable without necessarily benefiting from economies of scale. Some product markets, such as the manufacture of much clothing, are also monopolistically competitive.

The Importance of Product Differentiation

Product differentiation is an important feature of monopolistic competition and persuasive advertising is one of the main ways of achieving and reinforcing such differentiation. By creating a *brand image* persuasive advertising inspires loyalty among consumers for the products of one firm rather than those of another. However, it is important to note that a *differentiated* product is not necessarily a *different* product. The difference can be real or imagined. For example, there may be no substantial difference between the chemical formula of an inexpensive unbranded aspirin and a more expensive, widely advertised headache tablet sold under a brand name. What is important is that people *think* that there is a difference, and this psychological difference is the key to product differentiation (although there may well be many instances where there is a real difference as well).

In monopolistic competition it is product differentiation that enables a firm to act in some respects as a monopolist. For example, it might be impossible for the chocolate manufacturer Mars PLC to monopolise the world supply of confectionery; but it *is* the only supplier of Mars Bars. As we saw in Chapter 11, the fewer the substitutes for a product, the greater the monopolist's power to make profits. Thus persuasive advertising, which attempts to convince people that there is really no substitute for Mars Bars, is successful if it creates brand loyalty.

Product differentiation might be based on factors other than brand loyalty. For instance, in the case of corner shops it is based on location since consumers clearly take the convenience of a local store into account when deciding where to shop. The local grocer therefore provides a different service in the minds of consumers compared with other shops. Similarly, a hairdresser, a restaurant, a solicitor's practice or an optician might all have special features which differentiate their services from those of competitors, and which give them some control over the prices which they can charge.

The Firm in the Market

Under monopolistic competition, customers have preferences for the product of a particular firm, but they are aware of the existence of substitutes. The firm therefore finds that if it raises its price it will lose some, but not all, of its customers; and if it reduces its price it will attract some, but not all, of the customers of other firms. However, being only one of a large number of firms, individual market share is small and the actions of one firm have no effect on the prices charged by other firms. There is an element of price taking, but the firm can also decide its own prices, at least to some extent. Thus, the demand curve faced by the firm slopes downward from left to right. Figure 13.1 shows the firm in equilibrium in monopolistic competition.

Figure 13.1 *Short run equilibrium under monopolistic competition*

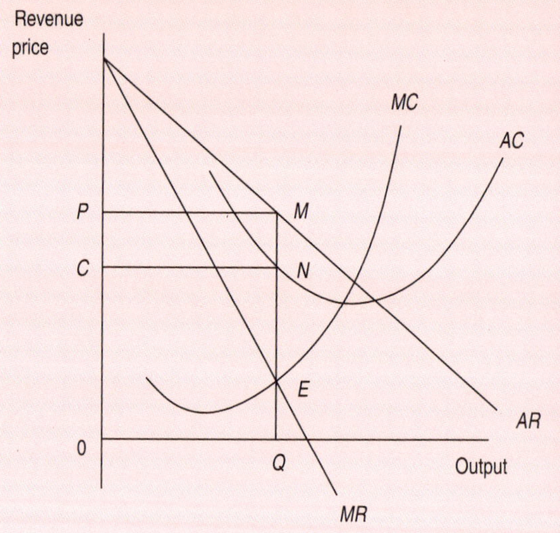

The firm is in equilibrium producing where $MC = MR$ and is making supernormal profits of *PMNC*. However, the industry is not in equilibrium because there are no barriers to entry and the supernormal profits are an incentive for new firms to enter the industry.

As new firms enter the industry, the demand of consumers is shared among a larger number of suppliers, and so the individual firm's demand curve gradually shifts to the left. It might also become more elastic due to the increased number of substitutes. Firms will go on entering the industry until supernormal profits are competed away and all firms earn only normal profit. The firm's long run equilibrium output is illustrated in Figure 13.2.

The firm is in equilibrium because it is producing where $MC = MR$. The price the firm charges for its output is *OP* and it produces an output of *OQ* units. However, the industry is also in equilibrium because the firm is earning only normal profit since it is producing where $AC = AR$. Effectively what has happened is that the influx of competitors has shifted the individual firm's demand curve leftwards and simultaneously increased its elasticity at all points. The demand curve goes on shifting in this way until it becomes tangential to the *AC* curve at the firm's equilibrium output.

Figure 13.2 shows that, as under monopoly, the firm under monopolistic competition has excess capacity because it is not producing at the point of minimum average cost. It is therefore *productively*

Figure 13.2 *Long run equilibrium under monopolistic competition*

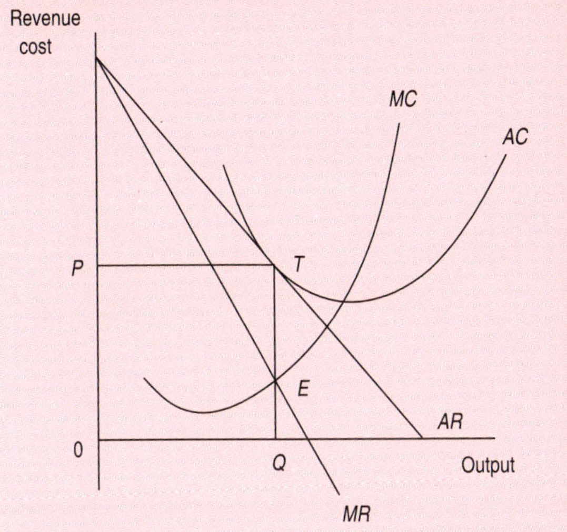

inefficient. The firm is also *allocatively inefficient* because price is greater than marginal cost. However, price is equal to average cost and so it could be argued that in the long run prices are more closely related to costs under monopolistic competition than they are under pure monopoly.

Oligopoly

Market Conditions

Under oligopoly, there are a few sellers each operating on a large scale. Firms might be producing identical products, in which case we refer to **perfect oligopoly**, but more commonly products are differentiated and we refer to **imperfect oligopoly**.

Oligopoly is often referred to as *competition among the few*. But how few is 'few'? The answer, as we shall see on p. 112, is few enough to ensure that the actions of one firm will affect other producers in the industry. However, before we analyse the implications of this for oligopolistic behaviour, it is useful to look at the causes and extent of oligopoly.

The Extent of Oligoply

The emergence of oligopoly as the most prevalent market form in the industrialised world is easily explained. The increasing availability of economies of scale, particularly in manufacturing, has encouraged the growth of large scale production. Inevitably, as firms grow, the number of firms supplying a market falls. This is precisely why oligopoly has emerged as the most common market form.

Economists use various ratios to measure the degree of industrial concentration. One which is often quoted is the *Five Firm Concentration Ratio* (known as C5 for short). This shows the percentage of the total output of an industry which comes from the five largest producers.

Table 13.1 *Concentration ratios in selected industries*

Industry	% share of 5 largest firms
Toys and sports goods	16
Footwear	37
Soft drinks	45
Bread, biscuits, cakes	55
Motor vehicles	92
Tobacco	99

Source: Census of production, (1986)

Table 13.1 shows C5 figures from the 1986 UK Census of Production. These figures are *unadjusted*, which means that they do not allow for the fact that imports might be an extra source of supply for domestic consumers. Concentration ratios are useful in indicating whether an industry is oligopolistic, but it should be borne in mind that they show the *combined* output of the five largest firms: they tell us nothing about the relative size of the output of those firms. In fact, no single statistic can be relied upon by itself to indicate the degree of competition within a given industry. C5 figures are a first approximation.

The Kinked Demand Curve

Observers often state that oligopolistic markets exhibit price rigidity. Anyone who follows the price of petrol over a period of time, for example, will notice that prices often remain more or less stable for weeks or even months. Subsequently one or two companies will announce a price increase, and within days the industry as a whole will have adjusted its price upwards; or, occasionally, other firms will refuse to change prices and the companies who originally tried to increase their prices will be forced reduce them again. A similar pattern can be observed in the raising and lowering of mortgage rates by banks and building societies in the UK. How can we explain this?

Remember that because there are only a few producers, oligopolistic markets are characterised by a high degree of *interdependence*. Because of this, firms can no longer make decisions without considering the effect of these decisions on other firms in the industry. This has important implications for the way in which the firm perceives the nature of its demand curve. In particular, it is sometimes suggested that because there is uncertainty over the way rivals will react to any price change initiated by a firm, oligopolists perceive their demand curve to be *kinked* at the ruling market price, as in Figure 13.3.

Figure 13.3 *The oligopolist's 'kinked' demand curve*

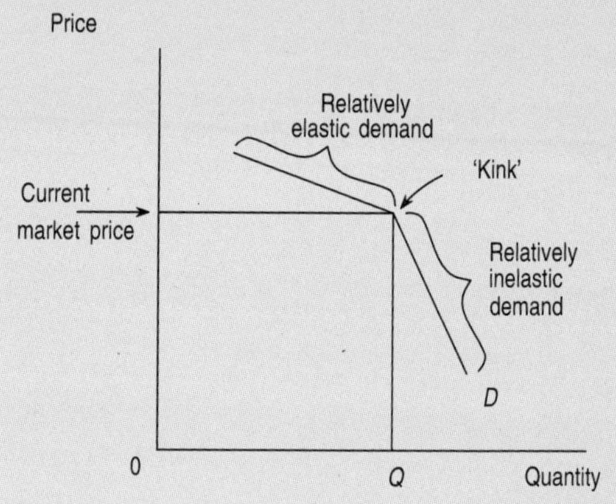

Box 13.1 Price stability in the ceramic sanitaryware industry: a case of the kinked demand curve?

One of the distinctive features of the ceramic sanitaryware industry is that there is a marked degree of similarity between the major manufacturers' list prices for a substantial part of the ceramic sanitaryware manufactured and supplied in the UK and this similarity has persisted for many years as a result of price changes of the same or nearly the same amounts taking place simultaneously (or nearly so).

All four companies told us that the particular products whose prices we are considering, being made to British Standard specifications, are so similar in dimensions, appearance and quality that the products of the different companies are virtually indistinguishable. We accept their argument that because of this, and because of their customers, mainly builders' merchants, are well-informed, price-conscious buyers who normally deal with more than one of the manufacturers, it is essential for each of the manufacturers to ensure that his list prices are never materially higher than those of his competitors for comparable products. It is important for the manufacturers to retain the custom of builders' merchants, many of which are large businesses with substantial bargaining power; and it is the competition for this business which ensures that list prices for comparable products can never be materially different as between different manufacturers, or at least that any material differences cannot persist. In our view none of the manufacturers is in a position to set its own list prices for similar patterns of BSS ware without having full regard to those of its competitors and it is primarily competitive considerations and input costs similar for all manufacturers which influence each of them in determining such prices and which result in their being largely uniform.

Further evidence that, at least in the present circumstances of excess capacity, list prices for similar patterns of standard products are determined as a result of competitive pressures is in fact that on two occasions, in 1975 and 1976, individual companies increased their list prices in the expectation that their competitors would do so to the same extent, but were quickly forced to rescind or reduce their increases when they found that their competitors did not do so. Moreover, Armitage Shanks, the only company required to notify price increases to the Price Commission, has on more than one occasion been prevented by competition from increasing prices to the extent allowable as a result of increased costs.

Source: HMSO, *A Report on the Supply in the United Kingdom and Export from the United Kingdom of Ceramic Sanitary Ware*, Cmd 7327 (August 1978).

Suppose the oligopolist decides to increase price. There is a danger that rivals will *not* follow suit, thus leaving the firm isolated, and encouraging customers to switch to the output of other producers. In this way the firm making a price increase could lose sales to rival firms. If, on the other hand, an oligopolist decides to reduce price, other firms will almost certainly be compelled to match the price cut to avoid losing sales as customers switch to the cheaper substitute. This implies that the individual firm considers its demand curve to be *relatively elastic for a price rise* but *relatively inelastic for a price fall*. The kinked demand curve therefore provides a possible explanation of price rigidity in oligopolistic markets, since it implies that firms are frightened to increase price because rivals might not follow suit, but see no benefit of reducing price because rivals will be compelled to follow suit!

The Effect of an Increase in Costs

However, the kinked demand curve has other implications. An ordinary downward sloping demand curve, as we have seen on p. 26 gradually becomes less elastic as price falls. The demand curve for the oligopolist, on the other hand, becomes less elastic *suddenly* at the kink. This would result in the *MR* line suddenly changing to a completely different position, as shown in Figure 13.4. The broken line between the discontinuous *MR* curve is referred to as the *region of indeterminacy* because when price is at the kink in the demand curve, marginal revenue is indeterminate. Marginal revenue is indeterminate because when price is *P*, the oligopolist is simultaneously at a common point on two demand curves. The relevant demand curve *for a price rise* is *DAD* and the relevant demand curve *for a price fall* is therefore D_1AD_1.

The region of indeterminacy provides a possible explanation of price rigidity in oligopolistic markets even when costs of production change. When costs increase, conventional supply and demand analysis would predict a fall in output with an increase in price. However, Figure 13.4 suggests that, within limits, the oligopolist can absorb the higher costs. As long as marginal costs fluctuate within the region of interminacy the existing price and output combination (*P* and *Q* respectively) remain the profit maximising combination. This behaviour can be seen in practice when the price of crude oil rises, and petrol companies wish to increase price, but no company wants to be the first to do so. However, if costs move so that the equilibrium point moves out of the region of indeterminacy, the profit maximising firm is likely to find the pressure to adjust price unbearable.

Figure 13.4 *The oligopolist's absorption of a rise in costs*

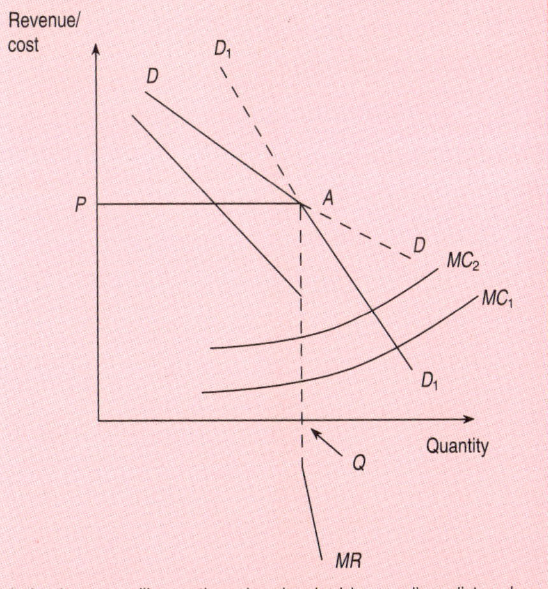

A rise in costs will sometimes be absorbed by an oligopolist and so will have no effect on price or output

The Effect of an Increase in Demand

How might an oligopolist react to an unexpected increase in demand? In a perfect market, using supply and demand analysis, we would expect an increase in market price accompanied by an increase in output. However, Figure 13.5 shows that the oligopolist might react to the change in demand by adjusting output while keeping price constant. He might prefer this because of the risks associated with price changes. For example, if demand shifts in Figure 13.5 from AR_1 to AR_2, the 'kink' in the demand curve moves horizontally to the right. The equilibrium points E_1 and E_2, where $MC = MR$, occur in the 'vertical' portion of the marginal revenue lines MR_1 and MR_2, thus enabling the oligopolist to maintain the price at OP while increasing output from OQ_1 to OQ_2. This can be done to some extent, but if the shift in demand is so great that the equilibrium point moves off the new region of indeterminacy, then the oligopolist is forced to consider a price change, with the attendant risks from the reactions of rivals.

Figure 13.5 *The oligopolist's reaction to changes in demand*

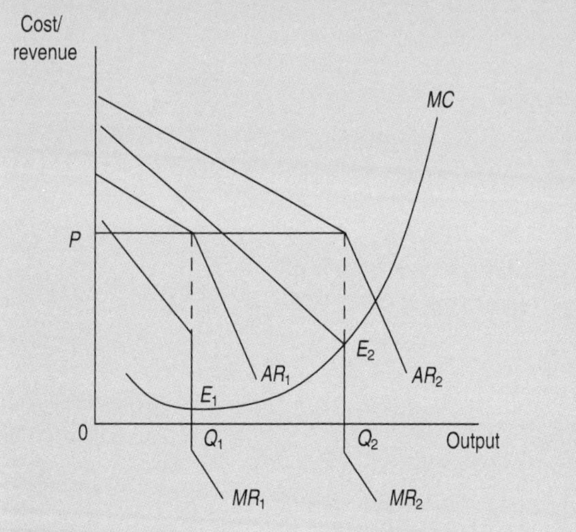

The oligopolist can react to changes in demand by adjusting output, without altering price

Criticisms of the Kinked Demand Curve

- In practice, it might be that price rigidity in oligopolistic markets is more apparent than real. Anyone wishing to buy a new car, for example, will find that the practice of offering *discounts* is widespread. While the published catalogue price of a certain model might remain unaltered for comparatively long periods, individual dealers have the flexibility to offer price reductions, or items such as 'free' insurance, cheap credit, or AA membership, all of which amount to a price reduction.
- Another criticism of the kinked demand curve is that while it assumes that oligopolists perceive a kink at the current market price, it does not explain how the current market price is arrived at in the first place. How, then, can we explain the determination of the ruling price? One possibility is some form of *price leadership*.

Price Leadership

Price leadership occurs when one producer sets a price which is then accepted as the market price by other producers. There need be no formal agreement to do this, it is sufficient for other firms to believe that this is the best way of protecting or increasing their profits.

Dominant Firm Price Leadership

Price leadership might result from the existence of a *dominant supplier*, which by virtue of its size has more power to influence market supply than other

Box 13.2 The car industry is an oligopolistic market

On the face of it, the car industry is an oligopolistic market. There is product differentiation, strong branding, customer loyalty, and price making. In Western Europe there are seven major European-owned firms, and in the USA there are three. Companies in Japan and other countries bring the total up to less than 20 significant producers. With this number of firms, collusion is possible: Rover, for example, has strong links with Honda. On the whole, however, the car industry is not tightly collusive. On the contrary, it is extremely competitive. For instance, British manufacturers have had drastically to alter their working practices and invest massively in new technology in order to compete with the highly efficient Japanese producers; and there are new entrants from countries like Korea and from Eastern Europe with lower labour costs and hence relatively low prices.

Price leadership in the car industry tends to be barometric rather than of the dominant-firm kind. In practice, there might be no consistent price leader: on one occasion Ford might be the first producer to change its prices; another time it might be Rover. Often price changes are carried out by a method sometimes referred to as *iteration*: a step-by-step process of trial and error, where a tentative price change might be quickly reversed if an oligopolist misjudges the state of the market. Such behaviour is consistent with the theory of the kinked demand curve. It is sometimes said that while a perfect competitor is a *price taker*, and a monopolist is a *price maker*, an oligopolist is a *price searcher*: although the firm has some influence over price, the fact that it must judge how its rivals will react means that it lacks the pure monopolist's power to set prices in a straightforward manner and must act in a more roundabout and circumspect way.

firms in the industry. In other words this dominant firm might act as a *swing producer*, varying output in order to maintain a particular price. For example, in the case of OPEC, Saudi Arabia is the dominant oil producer and frequently adjusts output so as to maintain the price of oil at a particular level.

Barometric Price Leadership

There is also the possibility of a *barometric* price leader, where some firms have the reputation of employing the best accountants and market analysts. Because of this, these firms are more aware of changes in market conditions than other firms, and when they change prices others tend to follow. The term 'barometric' is therefore used to imply that these firms can accurately measure changes in the pressure of demand.

Price Leadership and the Kinked Demand Curve

If there were a strongly established and infallible leader, then price leadership would have the effect of removing the 'kink' from the kinked demand curve, certainly when the market is viewed from the angle of the price leader, although not necessarily from the point of view of other firms. The price leader would know that it could quote a new price and other firms would be sure to follow. It could therefore select the price and output combination which would maximise its own profits and clear its production lines. Other firms would satisfy any residual, or left over, demand. They would continue to do this as long as they felt that the price resulting from price leadership was in their best long-term interests. The outcome would be the same sort of near-monopoly price and output that would result from formal collusion, as we shall now discuss.

Collusion

When a small number of rivals sell a similar product, they may come to the conclusion that it is in their interest to *collude* rather than compete. In Chapter 10 we discussed the nature of *cartels*, where groups of firms enter into agreements to set agreed prices for their products. Cartels are very formal arrangements and members of the cartel agree on output quotas to maintain the agreed price. Quotas may be decided by geography, productive capacity, pre-cartel market share, or on some other basis. The motive for cartel formation is to reduce the uncertainty in oligopolistic markets by reducing the unpredictability of rivals' reactions to changes in price; it thus increases the profits of the group as a whole.

However, once a cartel is formed, individual members have an incentive to 'cheat' on other members by secretly undercutting the cartel price. For the individual firm, membership of a cartel will almost certainly mean an undertaking to reduce output because it will be necessary to reduce output in order to raise the market price. The individual

Box 13.3 The market for petrol is oligopolistic but there is no collusion

Petrol is often cited as an example of a product which is sold in an oligopolistic market. Features include: a small number of suppliers, product differentiation, persuasive advertising, price stickiness, and sporadic price wars. Motorists will also be familiar with non-price competition in the form of trading stamps, air miles tokens, wine glasses, and other 'free gifts'.

Nevertheless there is often considerable similarity in pump prices for different brands of petrol and during the 1980s this led to allegations of price fixing which culminated in an investigation by the Office of Fair Trading. Sir Gordon Borrie, the Director General of Fair Trading concluded in his report that 'excess profits do not appear to be generated at the retail, wholesale, or refining stages of the industry'.

The report found that 'UK pump prices are primarily governed by international prices'. The report also stated that 'neither the absolute levels of UK petrol price nor the way they react to international price changes have been unreasonable over the period we studied'. It went on 'we have found no evidence of collusion among the principal wholesalers to fix pump prices, nor was a collusion theory required to explain the way in which prices moved. We have found no monopoly profits either in wholesaling petrol or in the downstream business as a whole'.

firm will therefore have spare capacity and could earn higher profits by expanding output. The firm will earn a profit on the additional sales, but will increase the profits of its *existing* sales because of the reduction in fixed costs as output expands. For this reason cartels tend to be fragile agreements and often do not last long.

OPEC (the Organisation of Oil Exporting Countries) is probably the most economically significant and certainly the most famous example of collusion in modern times. It has thirteen member states who between them account for 60 per cent of total world oil production, and 90 per cent of total world oil exports. Saudi Arabia, which possesses approximately 25 per cent of the world's known oil reserves, has been the dominant supplier and has often acted as the swing producer. It has adjusted output to maintain a predetermined market price and other countries have followed its lead. It is very difficult to counteract the influence of a supplier with such a dominant position. However, in 1976 a split developed in the organisation and, because of a decision by Saudi Arabia and the United Arab Emirates that oil price rises should be kept to a minimum, a system of dual pricing was attempted.

Because the end result of successful collusion is to create a situation similar to a monopoly, with its resulting loss of economic efficiency, cartels and similar agreements are illegal in many countries including the UK and the USA. It should be borne in mind, however, that *cooperation* is not necessarily the same thing as *collusion*. Producers who *cooperate* can often point to outcomes which are to their mutual benefit and ultimately benefit the general public. For example, this might apply to firms which shared common research facilities or who agreed between themselves on improved safety standards or reductions in the use of processes which damaged the environment. Firms might also cooperate in the development of new products such as the arrangements between Rover and Honda. In contrast to this, firms which *collude* are trying to improve their own position at the expense of the consumer.

REVIEW QUESTIONS

Question 1 is based on the following extract:

Oil price tumbles 14 dollars a barrel

By GEORGE SIVELL, City Editor

NORTH SEA oil prices fell below 14 dollars a barrel yesterday for the first time since the 1986 oil crisis. At one stage yesterday a barrel of North Sea crude could have been had for as little as 13.85 dollars, a fall of a dollar on the day.

Concern in the City over the oil price has mounted in the past few days as it has become clear that the relatively mild European winter and continued strong production by the Opec cartel have left oil stocks at the highest level for five years.

Opec production is now estimated at just below 17 million barrels a day for January and just above for February.

These levels are still within the agreement which was rolled over at the December Opec meeting but the pressure still remains on prices because certain states are coming under pressure to offer discounts to their main customers.

Such has been the level of discounting that prices on the oil markets are now four dollars adrift of the official Opec price of 18 dollars a barrel.

Prices have held to an average 18 dollars over the past year but dipped to just below 16 dollars in mid-December on dismay that Opec had failed to agree firmer production quotas or pricing controls.

Opec is not due to meet again until June and in the meantime Saudi Arabia, which took up any production slack, has complicated matters by abandoning its role as a swing producer.

Before the oil price crisis of 1986 the Saudis would always cut output when production accelerated and prices weakened.

But Saudi Arabia actually increased production from an estimated four million barrels in January to 4.3 million barrels in February.

"March is going to be a very severe test for the oil market," said one analyst last night.

Source: *The Western Mail*, 3 March 1988

(a) On what grounds would the extract lead to the conclusion that oil is not bought and sold in a perfect market?

(b) Saudi Arabia is described in the extract as a 'swing producer'. Explain this term, and describe how the abandoning of this role destabilises oil prices.

(c) Describe the effects on the price and output of oil of the events of August 1990 when Iraq invaded Kuwait.

2 Since *excess capacity* is a prediction of the theory of monopolistic competition, does it necessarily follow that society would benefit from a reduction in the number of firms in such a market?

3 Under monopolistic competition price taking does not occur. Explain why it is nevertheless likely that firms will have only very limited control over the market clearing price.

4 It can be argued that the banking industry, which was once very oligopolistic and collusive in the UK, is now much more competitive. What factors have influenced this trend?

5 Is collusion between firms necessarily undesirable?

6 Describe and account for differences in expenditure on advertising between industries.

CHAPTER 14
LABOUR

CONNECTIONS

We have already seen that the production of any good or service uses up scarce resources. In this chapter we are concerned with the human input which economists refer to as labour. However, labour does not work in isolation and in this sense there is a connection between labour and the other factors of production: land, capital and enterprise. In addition, since inputs are related to output, this chapter is related to Chapter 7 on Production.

Key Concepts

Ageing population
Dependency ratio
Division of labour
Mobility
Monopsony
Optimum population
Participation rate

The Division of Labour

In 1776 the modern social science of economics was inaugurated by Adam Smith in his book *An Inquiry Into The Wealth of Nations*. One of the important themes covered by this work was the idea of *specialisation*, or the *division of labour*. The division of labour involves breaking down the process of production into **specialised tasks**. Adam Smith described specialisation within a pin factory thus: 'One man draws out the wire, another straights it, a third cuts it, a fourth points it, a fifth grinds it at the top for receiving the head; to make the head requires three distinct operations; to put it on is a peculiar business, to whiten the pins is another; it is even a trade by itself to put them into the paper; and the important business of making a pin is, in this manner, divided into about eighteen distinct operations . . . each person making four thousand eight hundred pins in a day. But if they had all wrought separately and independently . . . they could certainly not each of them have made twenty, perhaps not one pin in a day; that is . . . perhaps not the four thousand eight hundredth part of what they are at present capable of performing, in consequence of a proper division and combination of their different operations'.

In the modern world even a cursory glance inside factory premises reveals the extent of specialisation. However, specialisation is not confined to manufacturing and is also common in the service sector. In solicitors' offices there is often specialisation in the different branches of legal affairs. The same is common in the offices of accountants and so on. So why is specialisation so common?

Advantages of Specialisation

The main advantage is that division of labour leads to *increased output per head* – that is, higher productivity. Using division of labour, a *given set of factors* can produce a far greater amount of goods and services. This leads to an increase in real income because the same factor inputs now achieve a higher volume of output.

Division of labour makes possible the *mass production* techniques of large factories, production lines, and high volume output. As we saw in Chapter 8, this results in lower costs per unit of output. When they were hand-built by craftsmen, motor cars were available only to a small minority of wealthy people. It was Henry Ford's use of division of labour

Adam Smith (1723–90)

Adam Smith is widely regarded as the founder of economics as an academic discipline. He was born the son of a customs official in Kirkaldy, Fife, in Scotland. He was educated at Glasgow College and showed such promise that he was awarded a scholarship to Oxford.

After completing his studies Smith was appointed professor of moral philosophy at Glasgow University. He was a popular lecturer and his notes show he lectured on jurisprudence, military organisation, taxation and 'police'. The latter refers to the administration of domestic affairs and is now refered to as economic policy.

In 1759, he published *The Theory of Moral Sentiments*, a book that was to change the course of his life. It brought him to the attention of Lord Townsend, later to become Chancellor of the Exchequer, who appointed him tutor to his stepson. As a result Smith travelled extensively in Switzerland and France where he met Voltaire, Rousseau and Quesnay, some of the greatest philosophers of the age.

It was in France that Smith started work on his influential book, *The Wealth of Nations* and it took ten years to complete. This was a pathbreaking work in which Smith argued in favour of economic liberalism, that is free enterprise within countries and free trade between countries. He argued that government intervention in economic life was at best unnecessary and at worst harmful to the functioning of the economy. He insisted that by pursuing their own self-interest each individual also pursued the best interests of society as a whole. Firms would produce those products society demanded and individuals would specialise in those tasks to which they were particularly suited.

During his life Smith suffered from chronic absent-mindedness. On one occasion he went for a stroll in his backgarden wearing a dressing gown and walked fifteen miles down a country road before realising where he was! Despite this he was an intellectual giant and his book influenced governments on both sides of the Atlantic and provided the intellectual background for the economic freedom which characterised the nineteenth centry. He started work on two more books but we shall never know what was in them. He had his writings burnt shortly before his death!

techniques on the 'Model T' production lines in Detroit which first began to bring cars within the budget of ordinary families in America. The same techniques were brought to Britain with William Morris's plant at Cowley, Oxford. Without division of labour and its associated capital-intensive mass production techniques, not only would we produce fewer goods and services, but the *range* of goods and services available to the average person would be substantially reduced. The list of goods and services which are mass produced is almost endless and includes clothes, electrical goods, furniture and food. Even houses and package holidays can be regarded as being mass produced to some extent.

But *why* does division of labour increase productivity? One reason is that *practice makes perfect*: people who perform the same tasks every day become very adept at performing a very narrow range of tasks and are able to increase the speed at which they perform them. Specialisation also makes possible a more efficient use of time, because the worker stays more or less in the same position and does not have to spend time moving to different parts of the factory, setting up different pieces of equipment and so on. However, probably the main reason for increased productivity is that capital is used more efficiently. Specialised machinery can be developed, and machinery can be kept in use constantly instead of intermittently as would happen if each worker performed different tasks on different machines. Thus it is possible to stand at the end of the line in a car factory, for instance, and observe a car being completed every few minutes as a result of the efforts of a workforce of specialists. If the same workforce did not specialise, it would take each worker weeks to complete a single car. Remember from Chapter 8, that there is an important relationship between productivity and costs.

Disadvantages of Specialisation

Monotony is often a problem when workers perform repetitive tasks. It is argued that production workers take little pride in their work and that the resulting decline in standards is wasteful because a greater proportion of the workforce needs to be engaged in quality control.

Strikes are sometimes associated with monotony and where workers specialise it is possible for a small group of workers, performing a key function, to bring the entire production line to a standstill. The high degree of *interdependence* associated with mass production techniques therefore enables a small group of workers to cause considerable disruption to production. It is perhaps no coincidence that industries which are famous for their production line techniques are sometimes prone to poor labour relations.

A decline in craftsmanship has been suggested as another disadvantage of division of labour because specialisation and mass production results in the creation of a standardised product. This is true but, as we saw above, specialisation has vastly increased the *range of goods and services* available to most people. Whether consumers prefer this is easy to see. For example, the engine compartment of a Ferrari is craftsman built and has a plaque bearing the name of the person who built it, but a glance at the company's prices will quickly cause the casual observer to reflect on some of the advantages of division of labour and mass production! Similarly every packet of frozen trout produced on a fish farm looks identical, but it is worth remembering that 20 years ago the average family living in a British urban area would never have seen a trout of any description!

Unemployment is alleged to result from specialisation because it becomes easier to replace labour with capital. In fact, substituting capital for labour has had a liberating effect by eliminating many of the monotonous and repetitive tasks formerly performed by labour. It can be argued that by increasing real income, division of labour will lead to an increase in demand and output generally, so that if jobs are lost in one factory, different jobs are created in other factories.

The Limits to Specialisation

Adam Smith recognised that specialisation was limited by *the extent of the market*: there is little point in producing vast quantities of goods if they cannot be sold. One factor of considerable importance is the availability of effective transport and distribution systems: if goods cannot be transported and distributed efficiently only small local markets can be served. For some goods the availability of efficient transport and distribution networks makes an international market possible.

At a more basic level we shall see on p. 208 that the size of the market can also be limited by lack of an efficient *monetary system*. In the absence of money, trade would almost certainly require a system of barter which would severely limit the size of the market.

Mobility of Labour

If an economy is to change and develop, the factors of production need to be adaptable or *mobile*. There are two types of mobility: *geographical* or lateral mobility (which refers to the movement of a factor from one location to another), and *occupational* or vertical mobility (which refers to the change of use to which a factor is put). Despite this, we must remember that the movement of labour from one occupation to another does not always take place directly: we shall see that it is not always easy for a redundant coalminer to retrain for work on the production line of a TV factory, for example. More often, the transfer of labour between one occupation and another is achieved at the entry stage. A declining industry will cease to take on young people leaving education, while the expanding industries will recruit new entrants; thus while the occupational profile of an area might change over time, this does not necessarily imply that relatively large numbers of workers are retraining in new skills.

Table 14.1 shows the extent of geographical mobility of labour in the UK during 1988.

Clearly Table 14.1 shows evidence of considerable geographical mobility but in practice there are many factors which limit the extent of such mobility. Before we consider these, let us look at why a high degree of mobility is thought important.

Advantages of a Mobile Labour Force

The need for geographical mobility is linked to the *regional problem*, or the fact that some parts of the country are relatively prosperous and tend to have lower levels of unemployment compared to other areas. If workers are geographically mobile they are able to move away from the depressed areas where there is surplus labour to areas which have employment opportunities. Similarly if workers are occupationally mobile they will be able to move to those occupations where labour shortages exist. If workers are unable to move, the imbalance between demand for labour and supply of labour in certain areas will

Table 14.1 *Internal migration: moves within areas (based upon NHS registrations)*

Area	1988			
	Within area	With rest of UK		
		In	Out	Net
	Movements (thousands)			
England and Wales	1880	78	57	+21
North	32	51	55	−4
Yorkshire & Humberside	59	95	88	+7
East Midlands	30	108	90	+17
East Anglia	13	70	54	+15
South East	583	265	320	−55
Greater London	210	172	248	−75
Remainder	156	309	289	+20
South West	51	145	110	+35
West Midlands	75	88	95	−8
North West	103	103	105	−2
Wales	24	65	49	+16
Scotland	81	50	64	−14
Northern Ireland	:	9	17	−7
	Movement rates (per 1000 population)			
England and Wales	37	2	1	+0
North	10	17	18	−1
Yorkshire & Humberside	12	19	18	+1
East Midlands	8	27	23	+4
East Anglia	6	34	27	+7
South East	34	15	18	−3
Greater London	31	26	37	−11
Remainder	15	29	27	+2
South West	11	31	24	+8
West Midlands	14	17	18	−1
North West	16	16	17	−0
Wales	9	23	17	+6
Scotland	16	10	13	−3
Northern Ireland	:	6	11	−5

Source: HMSO, *Population Trends* (Winter 1989)

tend to result in firms competing for labour, thus driving up wages which some economists argue is an important cause of inflation (see p. 255).

There are other advantages of a mobile labour force. The factors which determine demand for any product are constantly changing and if producers are to be able to respond by increasing their output of those goods and services where demand is rising it is important that they are able to recruit additional workers. This is much easier to achieve if the labour force is mobile. Again this will help restrain pressure on prices, but in a country like the UK which is dependent on exports to pay for its imports, it is important to be able to respond to any increase in demand for UK exports. Failure to do this will result in foreign customers purchasing the output of other countries.

Another important factor is that technology is constantly changing the skills required by employers. If the labour force is mobile it will be able to adapt quickly to technological advances; here again, this has implications for the level of output UK firms produce as well as for the price and competitiveness of UK output.

Disadvantages of a Mobile Labour Force

Clearly mobility is important, but we must not neglect to mention that too high a degree of mobility might also be undesirable. For example, there are problems with the movement of workers between regions. One problem is that movement of workers into a relatively small number of regions will increase pressure on the social infrastructure (hospitals, schools, roads, etc.) of those regions. It could be argued that this is a waste of resources, because the areas from which workers move will have underutilised resources. However, there is another factor to consider. In our discussion we have not yet considered the question of *which* workers move. In fact it is likely to be those which are most employable – that is, young workers who are adaptable or skilled workers. These are precisely the workers firms will require if they are to be encouraged to move to the depressed areas which is the aim of government regional policy.

There might also be problems with too high a degree of occupational mobility. Firms invest in training workers, and if workers move away to different areas or retrain in different skills the degree of labour turnover might discourage firms from undertaking training. This is potentially very serious and a major problem facing the UK at the present time is its failure to undertake training to the same extent as those countries with whom the UK competes in international markets.

Barriers to the Geographical Mobility of Labour

The availability and cost of suitable housing is an obvious barrier. When a substantial amount of housing was provided by the public sector, and families had to join a long waiting list for a council house, it was often suggested that increased home ownership would increase labour mobility. However, during the 1980s many council houses were sold to sitting tenants and some observers have suggested that whatever their other economic and social benefits, council house sales have not significantly increased geographical mobility. This, it is argued, is because the cost of living can vary significantly between regions, and people attempting to move to a more prosperous area to find work are likely to find themselves attempting to sell a house in an area where house prices are low, and purchase one where costs are high. It is now sometimes argued that an increase in the size of the privately rented sector might be a way of increasing mobility in the future.

Social barriers also restrict geographical mobility of labour. Many people are reluctant to leave areas where they have family ties and social contacts; often parents may not wish to disrupt the schooling of their children, especially in the crucial times preceding public examinations. Another barrier might be that many people are simply unaware of opportunities which exist in other areas: improved information services through Job Centres is a way in which this can be overcome to some extent.

Barriers to Occupational Mobility of Labour

Specialisation might be a barrier to occupational mobility. When workers specialise they acquire a limited range of skills and it is not always easy to transfer these to other occupations. This can be a serious problem if an industry goes into decline and skills specific to that industry cannot be transferred to other situations. This helps explain the growing emphasis on the role of education and training in society. It is often said that whereas it was once possible for a worker to regard himself or herself as being trained for life, the modern worker may need to be trained and re-trained several times during a working life in future, which will further reduce mobility. On the other hand, because workers often specialise in a narrow range of tasks, re-training is often a relatively simple and inexpensive matter.

The length of training required can also pose a formidable barrier to mobility. Where a long period of training is necessary (for instance, in the training of doctors or solicitors) it is not easy to increase movement of labour into these occupations. In addition, there may be substantial costs involved in training which will further reduce mobility.

Special abilities are required for some jobs and it is not always easy to acquire these. For instance few of us have the ability to become an international tennis player and no matter how hard we work at it we are unlikely ever to acquire the level of skill required.

Population

Economists are interested in population studies for all sorts of reasons. In Chapter 38, for example, we examine population problems in less-developed countries. In the following section we are interested in population as it affects the labour supply in the UK.

The Size and Structure of the UK Population

Figure 14.1 shows some of the main features of, and trends in, the UK population.

The size of the population of the UK has steadily increased since 1801, the year of the first official census. However, the size of the population has grown less rapidly during the twentieth century. The factors determining the size of the population are the *birth rate* (the number of live births per 1000 of the population per year), the *death rate* (the number of deaths per 1000 of the population per year) and *net migration* (emigration minus immigration).

In recent years, medical progress, higher incomes and living standards, improved working conditions and healthier diets have tended to increase people's life expectancy and the death rate has declined. At the same time, due to various changes in society, including better family planning methods, better job prospects for women, and a tendency to have smaller families, the birth rate has declined. For any country the birth rate minus the death rate is the *natural rate of increase* of the population. Where the birth rate exceeds the death rate the population rises, and vice versa. Perhaps of more relevance to the UK is that a lower death rate coupled with a lower birth rate leads to an *ageing population*. This implies that the

Figure 14.1 *Population change and its components, England and Wales, 1971–2 to 1987–8*

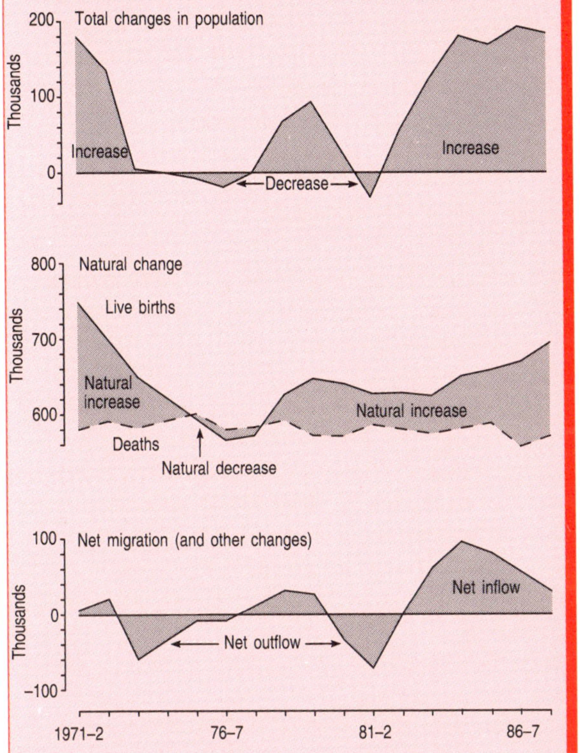

Source: HMSO, *Population Trends* (Winter 1990)

Figure 14.2 *UK density of population per square mile*

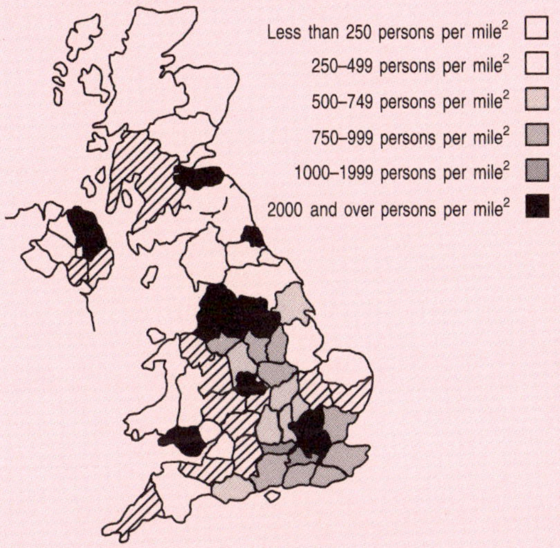

UK Population		(m)
1841	:	20.3
1921	:	44.2
1921	:	55.7
1991	:	57.5 (est)
2001	:	59.0 (est)

Source: 1981 Census of Population *Annual Abstract of Statistics* (1987)

average age of the population has increased and we discuss the consequences of this on p. 126.

The geographical distribution of the UK population has two main features: first, it is urban, with over 80 per cent of the population living in towns and cities. Second, it is dense, with more people per square kilometre than most other developed countries. The North West and South East regions are the most densely populated (see Figure 14.2).

The sex distribution of the population is such that females slightly outnumber males. This occurs despite the fact that male births exceed female births, as a result of the tendency for women to live longer than men (see Figure 14.3, on p. 124).

The occupational distribution of the UK has followed the same pattern in the twentieth century as that of many developed countries. There has been a relative decline in employment in the *primary sector* (extractive and agricultural industries), with an increase in the *secondary sector* (manufacturing and construction) as countries have become industrialised. In recent years, due to increased mechanisation and higher living standards resulting in people spending more of their income on activities such as leisure, banking and insurance, the *tertiary sector* in the UK (service industries) has become larger than the secondary sector. Employment in the different sectors is illustrated in Figure 14.4.

The Dependency Ratio

The *dependency ratio* is an important statistic and measures the proportion between the numbers in the working age groups and the numbers in the non-working age groups. Thus the

$$\text{Dependency ratio} = \frac{\text{No. below school leaving age} + \text{No. over retirement age}}{\text{No. between school leaving age and retirement ages}}$$

In the UK, as the number of retired people has increased, so the dependency ratio has increased in recent years. A rising dependency ratio is important because it implies that the working population must produce *more output to support the non-working population*.

Figure 14.3 *UK proportion of males and females, by age group*

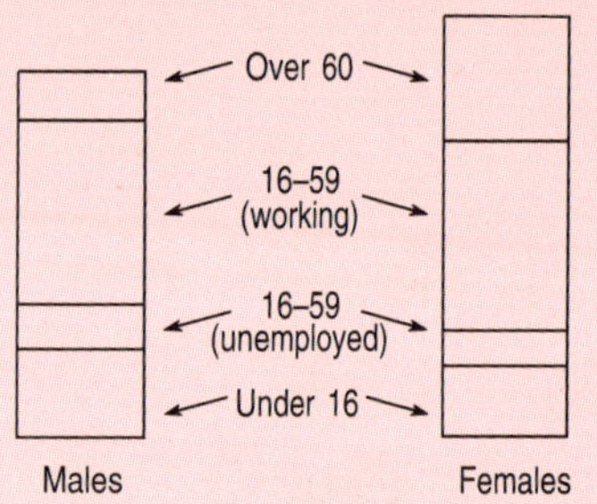

Source: *Annual Abstract of Statistics* (1987)

The Participation Rate (or Activity Rate)

The participation rate measures the percentage of the labour force who are *economically active* – that is, those people who are of working age and who are either employed, self-employed, serving in the armed forces or seeking employment. It is possible for changes in the participation rate to increase the size of the labour force even when other population variables are static or falling. For example, in recent years the increased tendency for women to stay on in further and higher education and enter a career, thus postponing starting a family, has enabled the size of the labour force to increase at a faster rate than the population as a whole. Similarly many companies believe that by encouraging older women who have had children to return to the labour market, the participation rate can be increased sufficiently to overcome staff shortages. Similarly, policies aimed at providing equal opportunities for disabled persons can encourage participation from people who were previously wrongly regarded as having little to contribute to the level of economic activity.

Figure 14.4 *Percentage of workforce in primary, secondary and tertiary industry, 1987*

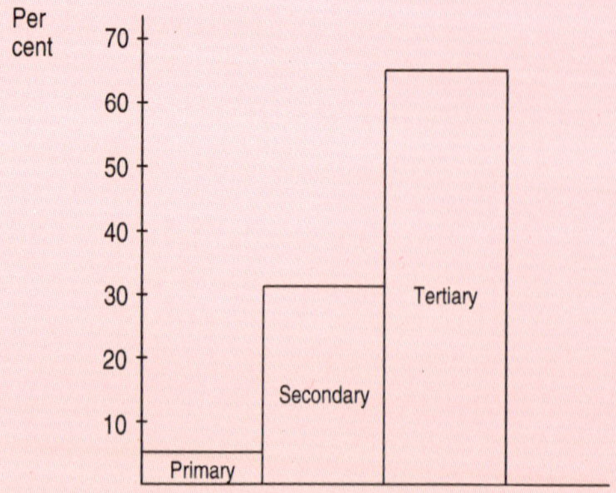

Source: *Monthly Digest of Statistics*

Optimum Population

The term 'optimum population' describes that number of people which, when combined with other resources, gives the maximum output of goods and services per head of the population (see Figure 14.5).

In Figure 14.5 the optimum point is reached at *OA* when output per head is *OY*. The actual level of optimum population depends on the balance between existing resources. A sparsely populated country may be 'overpopulated' if it lacks resources other than labour. A densely populated country may be 'underpopulated' if it has unused land and capital. Underpopulated countries have in the past sought to reach their optimum by encouraging mass immigration. For example, in the 1950s, it was possible to emigrate from the UK to Australia paying just £10 for the sea voyage. Overpopulated countries can reach their optimum either by a reduction in population, or by an increase in productivity, for instance through the use of improved technology. The idea of an optimum population is linked to the law of diminishing returns (see p. 66).

In practice it may be very difficult to decide whether any given country is below or above its

Figure 14.5 *Optimum population*

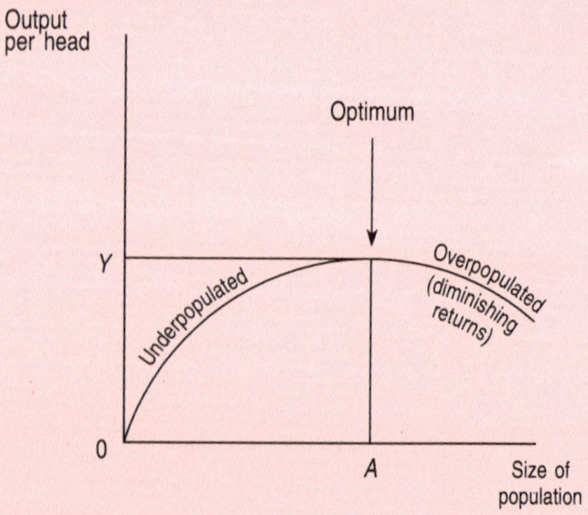

Figure 14.6 *(a) Age structure of UK, 1891 and 1988; (b) age structure of EC, 1990 and projected 2020*

(a)

(b)

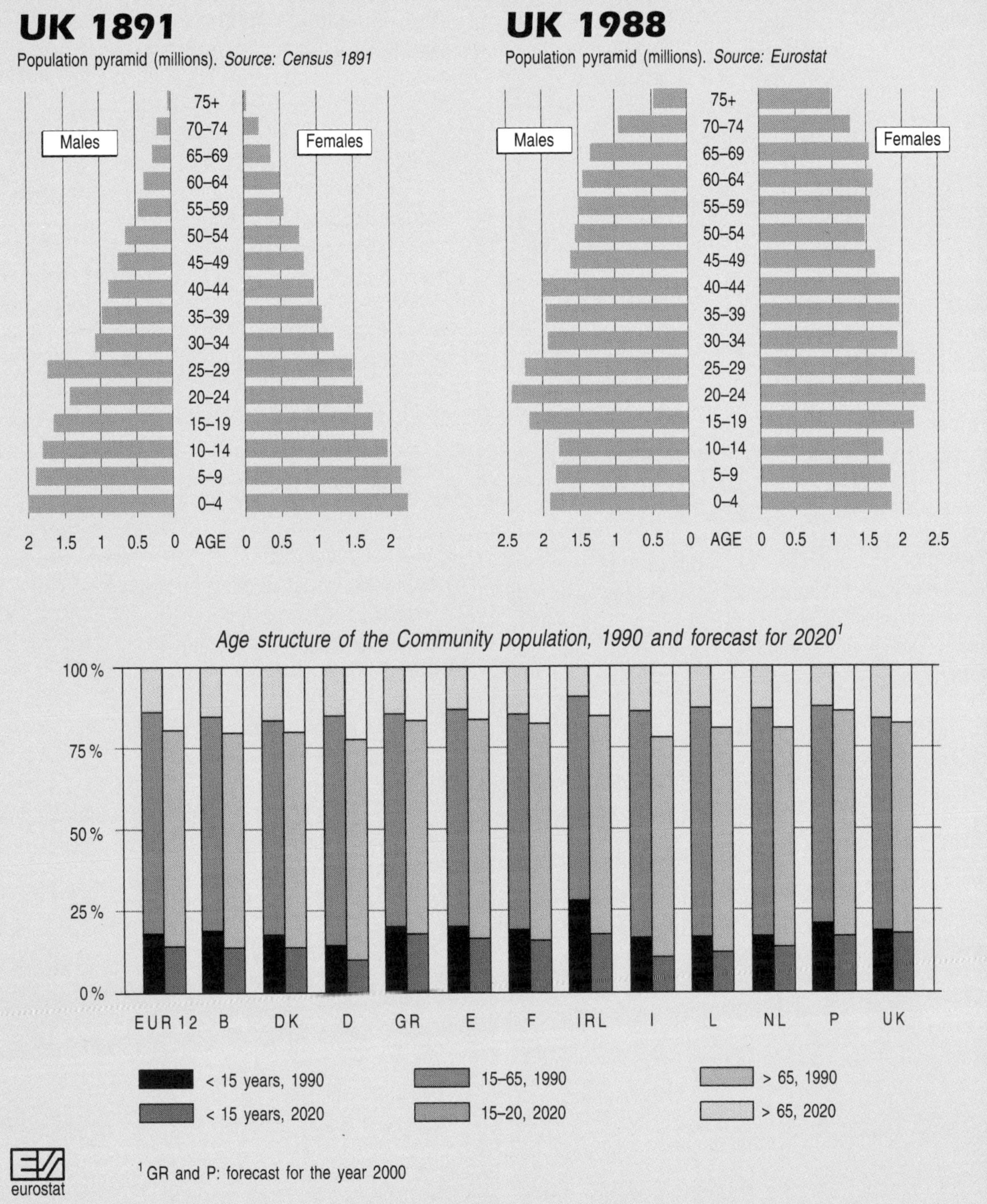

Between 1990 and 2020, the proportion of the population of the Community accounted for by people under 15 years of age will fall by 3%, while the proportion of persons aged over 65 will increase from 14% to 20%.

This shift in age structure will be across the board, but not the same in all the countries. The proportion of persons aged under 15 will be the highest in Portugal and the lowest in Germany and Italy.

It is more disturbing to note that the proportion of the population of working age will fall in 10 Member States.

Sources: (a) *Guardian* 'EG' Supplement (23 April 1991); (b) *Eurostat* (1990) optimum. Many relevant factors such as developments in technology and education are constantly changing, and as these change, they change the productivity of labour and therefore the size of the optimum population.

Consequences of an Ageing Population

An ageing population can be caused by a fall in the *death rate* so that, on average, people live longer. On the other hand, it could be caused by a decline in the *birth rate*, so that there was a fall in the number of live births. Figure 14.6 illustrates the changing age structure of the UK between 1891 and 1988 and shows the projected change in the age structure of Europe from 1990 to 2020. The UK, as well as Europe generally, has an ageing population.

It is often argued that an ageing labour force, caused by a decline in the death rate, will be less adaptable than a younger labour force. However, this is not necessarily true. Older workers have many qualities that increase their adaptability. They are often more willing to undertake re-training because their responsibilities necessitate that they have regular employment. They also have more experience of the world of work. Many employers value their older workers for their interpersonal skills. The B & Q organisation, for example, which has staffed an entire store with older workers believes that they have more patience and a better relationship with the public than many younger staff.

The changing age structure of the population implies that firms need to change their outputs – that is, there will be a reallocation of resources, in order to satisfy a different pattern of demand. For example, if the death rate has fallen, housebuilders will need to plan well ahead to supply smaller houses suitable for retired people rather than growing families. If the birth rate has fallen, on the other hand, fewer baby clothes will be required.

Governments will need to plan ahead. A reduction in the death rate implies heavier demands on the health and social security services. State and private pension schemes will also need to be redesigned. In this sense the changed dependency ratio will increase the burden on workers and taxpayers. At the other extreme a reduction in the birth rate implies possible labour shortages in the future as a smaller number of school leavers enter the labour market.

Box 14.1 Case Histories

Case History 1: Recruitment

When companies realised there was going to be a sharp fall in the number of school leavers entering the labour market in the late 1980s and early 1990s, they had to think of new ways to attract recruits.

A year ago, Marks and Spencer gave its shop staff a 26 per cent pay increase to persuade them not to move to other jobs. Other retailers – which in the past have relied heavily on teenage recruits – also gave pay increases above the rate of inflation. B & Q, the Do-it-Yourself chain, offered jobs to people who could work only during term-time. They also opened a store a Macclesfield, Cheshire, staffed only by 'mature' workers – people over the age of 50, many of whom had retired from previous careers.

Over the last few months, however, the mood of employers has changed. The recession has meant that profits are falling and they want to save money. With unemployment rising sharply, they feel less inclined to spend money to retain staff: why bother, when they can recruit cheaply from the dole queue?

Midland Bank is a good example. It had planned to set up 300 creches by 1993, making it easier for women with small children to return to work. But last month it emerged that Midland will stop opening creches at the end of this year. By then, there will be only 130.

Case History 2: Products

Ten years ago, Top Shop sold clothes mainly for teenagers. At that time there were plenty of them: nearly one million 16 year olds in the population. But Top Shop realised that the number of people in their teens was going to fall. By the early 1990s, there would be fewer than 750,000 people aged 16 at any given time. That meant Top Shop would have fewer potential customers. So it gradually changed the range of its clothes to appeal to older customers – women in their twenties rather than teenagers.

Other companies use demography, too, to predict what the demand will be for their goods. Toy manufacturers look at birth rates to see whether they should make board games aimed at schoolchildren or building blocks for toddlers.

The over-50s already control more than 70 per cent of the country's savings. Ken Dychwald, an American who advises on the implications of having more elderly people in the community, predicts that by the year 2000 cars will have larger wing-mirrors and clearer dashboard markings, television serials will have fewer changes of scene and household appliances will be simpler – all to appeal to an older market

Source: Guardian, Education Supplement (23 April 1991)

REVIEW QUESTIONS

1 How does the degree of specialisation affect productivity?

2 In what ways, if any, might the mobility of labour be affected by (i) the introduction of a National Curriculum in UK schools, (ii) an increased tendency for people to buy their own homes, with a corresponding reduction in the size of the privately rented housing sector?

3 The more specialised a factor of production the higher its productivity, but the lower its mobility. Why is this?

4 How would you assess whether Britain was overpopulated or underpopulated?

5 Why might (a) companies producing goods and services, and (b) local and central government, be interested in whether future trends will show an expanding, declining, or ageing population?

6 For what reasons might some of the less prosperous regions of the UK find that they have even fewer 15–19 year olds than other areas during the 1990s? What problems might they face as a result?

7 Analyse the arguments for and against someone who reaches the age of 18 in the year 2000 leaving school for a mechanical apprenticeship rather than going to university to read for a degree.

CHAPTER 15
ENTERPRISE

CONNECTIONS

The factor of production *enterprise* is provided by the *entrepreneur*. Chapter 15 is therefore connected very much with the earlier chapters on the theory of the firm (Chapters 9–13) and examines the role of the entrepreneur in the firm.

Key Concepts

Cost-plus pricing
Enterprise
Ownership and control
Risk taking
Sales maximisation
Satisficing

What is an Entrepreneur?

Economists have had great difficulty defining precisely what is meant by the *entrepreneur*. There is total agreement that the entrepreneur is a factor of production but it is certainly more difficult to describe the nature of the entrepreneur's services than of any other factor of production. Even when economists agree on certain distinguishing features of the entrepreneur they often disagree on which of these features should be given most prominence as being more important than the others.

Economists have identified several features of entrepreneurship. These include the *initiative* required to identify needs and opportunities; the ability to make a *creative response* to those needs and opportunities; the *capacity to work* long and hard; and the willing acceptance of the *risk* which exists due to the uncertainties of the business world.

The entrepreneur is unique among factors of production in having **no guaranteed reward**. He or she brings together the other factors and organises them so that the production of goods and services can take place, and *assumes responsibility for the risks involved*: if the enterprise is successful, the reward is **profit**. If the enterprise fails, the firm makes a **loss** and may not be able to continue as a business.

As well as the function of risk taking, the following functions, among others, have been identified by various economists: exercising overall *control*; making day-to-day *decisions*; *organising* economic resources; *innovating* and bringing about change; *identifying markets*; being the *owner* of an enterprise; *seeking profits*. This last function is particularly important to economists, as such a large part of microeconomic theory rests upon the basic assumption that the overall objective of a firm will be to *maximise profits*. Profits, after all, are the *incentive which brings entrepreneurship into existence*, and provides an incentive for people to adopt enterprising attitudes and perform entrepreneurial functions. We shall argue later in this chapter that it is possible that as firms grow in size and complexity some of these functions become separated from each other. For example, it is often said that there is a divorce between ownership and control in large companies: this may mean that the people who in effect run the firm are not always committed to the goal of profit maximisation. Figure 15.1 summarises the man features of the principal forms of business under private enterprise.

The main point to note in considering Figure 15.1 is that a firm is not necessarily a **company**. A company is a firm which has taken out *limited liability*. With sole traders and partnerships, there is little difference from a legal point of view between the firm and its owners. The firm is not taxed separately from its owners, for instance, and if the firm cannot repay debts its owners may ultimately

Figure 15.1 *Types of business organisation (private sector), UK*

Unit	*Ownership*	*Decision making/ Control*	*Main sources of funds*	*Liability*	*Disposal of profits*	*Duration*
Sole Trader	One proprietor	Owner	Owner, savings, loans Ploughed-back profits	Unlimited (no distinction between firm's assets and owners)	To owner	Firm ceases to exist on death of owner
Partnership	2–20 owners	Partners	Partners' funds as agreed. Loans. Plough-back	Unlimited	To partners as agreed	Dissolved as agreed in terms of partnership
Limited Company: Private (Ltd) or Public (PLC)	Minimum 2 shareholders	Directors, managers, shareholders	Shareholders, (PLCs have access to Stock Exchange). Loans. Plough-back	Limited (firm's assets are distinct from assets of owners)	Directors allocate between shareholders; and plough-back	On liquidation/ winding up

be forced to sell personal assets in order to raise the necessary money. With limited companies, on the other hand, a firm has an existence separate to that of its owners. If a firm has limited liability, then there is a restriction on an owner's loss in a business to the amount of capital invested in it. If a limited company is liquidated (closed down and its assets sold) because it is unable to repay debts, shareholders will not have to sell personal assets, such as their own homes, in order to pay company debts.

Entrepreneurship in Large Firms

In small firms it is relatively easy to locate the functions of the entrepreneur. Often they are carried out by a small group of people, or even by an individual, as in our three case studies in Box 15.1 on pp. 133–5. As firms expand, the functions of the entrepreneur become more difficult to locate, and when firms become very large, the functions of the entrepreneur can become diffused and spread between many people and groups of people. Many large public limited companies have budgets similar to those of many governments, and it is worth taking this comparison a few steps further. Theoretically, there are several parallels between the way in which a country is governed and the way in which a business is controlled.

Like many countries, a company has a 'written constitution', its Articles of Association and Memorandum of Association. These are documents signed on the creation of a company when it is first registered. Among other things, they set out the rights and duties of the shareholders and other groups within the company, and the rules which govern their behaviour – for example the voting of directors or the calling of meetings. There is some degree of 'democracy' within a company. There is an 'electorate', the shareholders, but instead of one person, one vote the general rule is one share, one vote. There is a type of 'parliament' in the form of the Annual General Meeting (AGM), which elects from within its own ranks a 'cabinet', the Board of Directors, whose responsibility is to control the general direction of the company's activities. In order to make *executive* company decisions or *manage* the company's affairs, 'civil servants', known as executives or managers are employed. They implement company policy on a day-to-day basis and thus have the responsibility of *decision making* as opposed to overall *control*, which is the responsibility of directors.

The Position in Theory

To summarise so far: the functions of the entrepreneur are carried out in large companies as follows: ownership and risk taking are ultimately the responsibility of shareholders, who between annual meetings delegate their powers of control to directors, who are themselves likely to be shareholders and therefore part owners of the firm. Decision making is carried out by managers who are employees rather than owners of the firm.

The Position in Practice

It is often claimed that in large companies there is a **divorce between ownership and control**, and that effective control has passed from shareholders to directors and from directors to managers. Let us examine the validity of this assertion, and its implications for the theory of the firm.

The absentee rate at shareholders' meetings is well above 90 per cent, and institutional investors (insurance companies, pension funds and so on) are the most powerful influences among shareholders today. Individual investors, who might have relatively small sums invested in several companies, are unlikely to think it worthwhile attending meetings. So although the AGM has the power to make significant changes within a company, such as removing directors and replacing them, in practice these powers are rarely used, and a dramatic display of shareholder power is rare enough to attract widespread publicity when it does happen. This line of argument can be used to support the view that shareholders have relinquished power to directors.

It can be further argued that directors, in their turn, are in a weak position compared with managers. A typical board of directors meets once a month in order to receive reports and determine general policy. A directorship is traditionally a part-time appointment, and many directors sit on the boards of several companies. Managers, on the other hand, are full-time professionals, and are salaried employees of the company. They are in constant touch with the day-to-day workings of the company, and it is hardly surprising, given the complexity of the modern business world, that the opinions and outlook of managers have an increasing influence on the decisions of boards of directors.

There has, in fact, been a blurring of the distinction between directors and managers: most firms now have a Managing Director and other hybrid 'Executive Directors'. Sometimes a board has a Chairman who is a director, and the post of Managing Director or Chief Executive is held separately. When they are combined, then the holder of this position, being a major shareholder as well as a salaried manager, is likely to be placed in an extremely powerful position within a large company.

Implications for the Theory of the Firm

Salaries are not always linked to profits, and so managers may pursue goals other than those designed to maximise profits. It is possible, for example, that managerial salaries are linked to the *rapid growth* of a company. Successful mergers and takeovers may well be taken as a sign of success, and managers rewarded accordingly, even if the increase in scale does not substantially increase company profits. Rapid growth may lead to *diversification*. Managers may see it as a sign of success to preside over a conglomerate producing as wide a range of products as possible. Figure 15.2 shows some of the brand names controlled by one such enterprise.

Some products in the range will inevitably be more profitable than others, and the fact that the products, although diverse, belong to a family of types of output makes it possible for managers to be flexible in their view of the levels of profitability required. A certain amount of *cross-subsidisation* can take place, meaning that the profits of more successful lines can be used to keep less profitable goods and services in production. Cross-subsidisation can also be used to create a **loss-leader**: a good which attracts customers to make an initial purchase which is then followed by expenditure on more profitable lines. Loss-leaders can, in addition, be used to try to drive out and undercut competition. Yet another use of cross-subsidisation occurs when a firm may believe that a currently unprofitable product has a good long-term future if supported in the short run. Or it may be that a firm is willing to support an established brand name through a fairly long period of decline. Sometimes a firm values the prestige of an item which has a long standing base of customer loyalty: for instance, the publishers of a 'quality' newspaper have been known to use some of the profits from a popular tabloid in order to enable the serious title to continue in existence.

Figure 15.2 *Brand names and trade marks owned by Hillsdown Group plc*

Source: Hillsdown Group plc

Another item other than profit which managers may try to maximise is *sales revenue*. If costs rise more or less in step with sales, then profits may not increase; but it may well be that buoyant sales figures can, for instance, cause a surge in the quoted share price of a company and create an aura of success that to some extent disguises an underlying lack of profitability. This possibility is further discussed in Box 15.1.

The management of some companies may be sensitive to the *external costs and benefits* of the good or service that it supplies. Recent advertising by banks, building societies and large insurance companies, for example, appears to attempt to draw attention away from their role as profit making companies, and create an image of these enterprises as public benefactors, serving the community, supporting small businesses, enhancing the quality of life of individuals and families. Similarly, publicity from the oil, gas and petrochemical industries attempts to suggest that they are as concerned with the protection and even improvement of the environment as with any other objective. A realistic view of such activities might be that, however they dress it up, the real underlying aim is still closely related to profits.

Managers may be interested in maximising a whole set of non-monetary rewards known as *managerial utility*. They may be seeking status, power, or 'perks' such as a large office or a company car. Some commentators allege that this is a peculiarly British phenomenon, where managers tend to set great store by being given a key to the executive washroom, or being allowed to use a separate restaurant. But even in the supposedly egalitarian Japanese system, a sign of managerial success is to be allowed to operate an expense account, which can effectively double the income of a manager.

Finally, there is the possibility that managers do not attempt to maximise anything, but instead aim at a reasonable return on a range of criteria. This is known as *satisficing*. A powerful monopoly, for example, might find that by pressing its advantages in the marketplace and maximising profits it attracts unwelcome attention to itself and creates the threat of government action. Some managers, faced with various demands from different quarters – including shareholders, politicians, pressure groups, trade unions, and public opinion at large – may to some degree opt out of the competitive world and seek a relatively quiet life. Others may find that the complexity and pace of commercial life makes it too hectic to keep a complete check on what is going on. Far from the 'perfect knowledge' and accurate plotting of costs and revenues depicted in economic theory, managers' pricing and output decisions may amount to something more like inspired guesswork and trial and error methods (sometimes known as *iteration*).

Cost-plus pricing is a method of setting price where average cost is calculated and a percentage rate of profit or *mark-up* is added to determine the final selling price. Economists suggest that this method of deciding prices is more likely to happen in markets where firms have few competitors. Different firms supplying different markets will have different ideas of what constitutes a reasonable rate of return, or mark-up. Managers using cost-plus pricing may not be ignoring profits altogether, but neither are they maximising profits in the textbook sense by aiming to produce where marginal cost equals marginal revenue.

Box 15.1 Market Share

Maximising market share

In April 1991 a UK holiday tour operator, International Leisure, went out of business. In a discussion on the *Today* programme on BBC Radio 4 it was suggested that one of the factors contributing to the failure was that in Britain, where there are more than 700 tour operators (compared with six or seven in countries like France and Germany) tour operators have been competing for *market share* rather than for profits. It was stated that the profit on each holiday sold is often less than one pound! This means that when unforeseen circumstances happen, such as airport delays or foreign currency fluctuations, holidays are often sold at a loss. It was suggested that holiday prices would have to rise in order for firms to aim for a profit on each holiday sold.

A large number of producers selling a differentiated product, with little or no 'supernormal' profit, corresponds to the economic model of *monopolistic competition.* Those firms unable to make a 'normal' profit due to their costs being generally higher than those of other firms are likely to have to leave the industry. If the UK holiday tour industry became more *oligopolistic*, as is apparently the case on the continent, would consumers and producers necessarily be better off?

Maximising sales

An example of problems which can arise when profit maximising is not a prime objective is given by the experience of the Equity Funding Corporation in the USA between 1964 and 1973.

This corporation is listed in the Guinness Book of Records as being involved in one of the earliest, and largest computer frauds in history, involving some $2 billion. Company executives noticed that short-term share prices in the company were strongly influenced by announcements of increased sales of insurance policies. In other words, investors were impressed by gross sales figures, and did not look too closely at underlying costs and other details which would have indicated whether the company was running along lines which would give a real profit, as opposed to a performance on paper.

Over a ten-year period, names and addresses were collected (allegedly from sources such as obituaries and gravestones) and over 64,000 fake insurance policies were created on the company's computers. The fraud apparently came to light when investigators realised that if the company's projected growth rates in sales were believed it would eventually issue more life policies than there were lives to insure.

Investors were therefore measuring success in terms of figures which bore little relation to the real performance of the company.

Case Studies

Case Study 1 The Creative Technology Team

Up and down the UK there are estimated to be about 1 million regular users of a machine known as the Amstrad PCW (Personal Computer Word Processor). The brain child of someone often mentioned in connection with entrepreneurship, Alan Michael Sugar, these machines were launched in 1985, and most have been purchased as inexpensive word processors. A substantial part of this textbook was written on a PCW. What many users do not realise is that their PCW is not just a glorified electronic typewriter, it is quite a powerful computer also. Compared with the industry standard PC, the PCW is slow and idiosyncratic; its programs are generally incompatible with other computers, and even its discs are a non-standard 3″ size (rumour has it that Sugar happened to find that he was able to purchase a job lot of 3″ disc drives when the PCW was being designed). The word processing software was contracted to a programming firm known as Locomotive Software of Dorking, and the whole package, including 'Locoscript' software and a printer, was made available for around £400.

It was not long before other groups of entrepreneurs identified opportunities provided by the existence of such a large base of potential customers. They included Creative Technology of Uttoxeter, a group of people who exemplify the initiative, drive and risk-taking of the entrepreneur.

Creative Technology consists of Richard Bland, Don Taylor, Simon Hargreaves, Nik Holmes and Gill Brownhill. The firm began as a partnership in the mid-1980s, basically a small group of friends who no longer wished to work for other people although initially, to bring money into their own firm, they remained employed part-time. Each partner developed specific projects, for example Nik Holmes experimented with a loop amplifier hearing aid, but the crunch came after about a year when it was decided to concentrate resources on producing software. There was a gap in the market for a high quality desktop publishing programme for the PCW, which would incorporate graphics and page design as well as make use of text generated by Locoscript or other word processors. Simon Hargreaves had already written such a program for another model of computer, for which he had won an Amstrad prize for programming in 1982. A major influence on the decision to develop a DTP program was the fact that the production of a unit of software requires comparatively little capital investment: progamming is a labour-intensive activity, and so it was possible to launch the project with a bank loan of £5000. At first the package, known as Microdesign 2, sold steadily, but in small quantities. It received excellent notices in the specialist computer press, whose reviewers marvelled at Microdesign 2's ability to achieve printed results on a £400 computer which were of comparable quality to those achieved on an Apple Macintosh, which is widely recognised as the market leader among DTP computer systems. A problem was that PCW users tend not to be computer-minded, and only a minority of them read computer magazines. Here is where the firm benefited from a commodity which eludes many entrepreneurs, that of good luck. After Microdesign 2 had been available for six months, it received a favourable review in the *Guardian*, and then sales soared to over 500 per month, so that by the second anniversary of its launch, in 1991, it had sold over 10,000 copies. By this time a PC version was available for industry-compatible computers, and so Creative Technology found itself heading for further rapid expansion. It began to develop new products and at the time of writing it was celebrating the launch of a successful piece of hardware, a hand-held scanner whose first production batch had sold out within months, and the firm was advertising for additional staff.

With a turnover in six figures and rising, the firm had to alter its structure to some extent. A limited company, with unsalaried directors, was created to exist alongside the partnership. The limited company deals with other firms and with the public in order to obtain components, manufacture products and market them. The partnership carries out research and development and sells office resources, expertise and consultancy services to the limited company, paying its members and employees out of partnership profits. Thus the partners have managed to acquire a degree of limited liability (see p. 128) without losing their much valued informal management structure which they describe as 'broadly cooperative' where the possibility of one person making a decision and going ahead without the agreement of the others would be unthinkable.

Richard Bland, who handles the firm's finances, states that the element of limited liability has reduced risk to some extent, but believes that entrepreneurship always involves some degree of risk existing in the background. 'If you don't want that risk, you don't start your own business', he says, 'You just carry on working for someone else'. The other essential quality he believes entrepreneurs need is 'Not minding working very hard, and having faith in what you're doing. When we developed Microdesign 2 we worked 80 hours a week, in order to get it right'. Richard tends to be critical of so-called 'enterprise agencies' which have been set up to encourage entrepreneurship. He believes that they are over-bureacratic. 'One of these agencies promised us a loan of £2000, and at that time it would have made a crucial difference; we really needed the money. But by the time they sent us a cheque we were turning over £20,000 a month and we no longer needed the loan!'

Talking to any member of the Creative Technology team gives a distinct impression that this is a firm bursting with ideas and with a clear sense of purpose. They are determined to keep their independence and not to allow themselves to become bogged down in what they see as the bureaucratic attitudes of large organisations. 'People who work in corporate computing do so because it's their day's work', says Richard Bland, 'While we work here because we want to do it. We feel that we are fulfilling the needs of our customers with technology, and whatever happens we never want to stop being creative'.

Case Study 2 The Ice Cream Sellers

Ben and Jerry began an ice cream company in 1978 in an old garage in Burlington, Vermont. Within a few years they were being described in the American press as 'tycoons' and were invited to the White House to receive a Business of the Year award. What was the secret of their success?

First of all, they worked hard. Ben and Jerry were brought up in the suburbs of New York. They tried various jobs in an inner-city environment and then moved to a rural part of New England. They sent off for a correspondence course on ice-cream making and taught themselves the craft. Then they took the risk of putting their entire $8000 savings into equipment. Ben and Jerry realised that there was a gap in the market for 'real' ice cream. Commercially produced ice creams use powerful mixing machines which mean that 50 per cent of what you buy is actually air. Ben and Jerry's ice cream contains only 10 per cent air – and it also contains real cream, real eggs, and real fruit. It aimed at a quality market, and it also aimed at a young market. This was achieved by using coupons on the wrappers to support ecological causes, such as alternative energy and conservation of the rainforests, and is being further supported by a range of 'light' ice-creams, low in cholesterol and sugar.

Ben and Jerry achieved national prominence when the giant Pillsbury food company tried to operative a restrictive trade practice, an 'exclusive dealership' by threatening not to supply retailers who sold Ben and Jerry's products. The resulting court case was reported in the media as a victory for free enterprise, and incidentally gave Ben and Jerry's brand name an incalculable amount of publicity.

Ben and Jerry are friendly with a well known British entrepreneur. Anita Roddick, founder of the Body Shop. They have formed an organisation called Act Now, which aims to link 'ecologically minded' firms around the world. Currently they are campaigning to reduce pollution from car exhausts, and as a step in this direction Anita Roddick has decreed that no Body Shop executive shall have a company car which is any larger than a Volkswagen Golf.

Case Study 3 The Morris Minor Manufacturer

The Morris Minor motor car was designed by Sir Alec Issigonis (who also created the Austin Mini) during the Second World War, and was in production throughout the 1950s and 1960s until it was replaced by the Morris Marina in 1971. Today, there are 250,000 Morris Minors still in use around the world, including some 80,000 in the UK, where they have become collector's items and are now appreciating in value.

In the early 1970s there was a property boom followed by a collapse in the market, and many property speculators suffered a sudden failure of their business. One such was Mr Charles Ware, who with the small amount of money he managed to salvage, opened the Morris Minor Centre in Bath, Avon, and began working as a restorer of the car. He had realised that the Morris Minor had a tremendously loyal following. One customer even purchased an entire set of spare parts and constructed a complete car – the only non-Morris Minor parts he used were the door handles. The Bath Centre became a place of pilgrimage for afficionados from all over the country.

In April 1991 Mr Ware announced that he had teamed up with Mr Dhanapala Samarasekara to build a Morris minor factory in Sri Lanka. The factory would cost £100,000 to set up: a small amount in car manufacturing terms, resulting from the fact that the Durable Car Company will be deliberately geared towards labour-intensive production: within four years it was hoped that 1000 people would be employed. Mr Samarasekara stated in a radio interview that the Morris Minor was ideal for Sri Lanka because of its proven reliability, together with its low-level technology. There were no modern gadgets such as electronic ignition; if the car broke down in any part of Sri Lanka traditional skills could be used to repair it – for example, a broken fan belt could be temporarily replaced by a piece of rope. The project had the support of the Sri Lankan government, who were enthusiastic about its use of local resources. Mr Ware told the TV news that 95 per cent of operations would be carried out manually and that the plant would consume a minimal amount of electricity. 'We are investing in people', he said, 'Not in machinery'. So here is an example of the entrepreneur 'bringing together the factors of production' in a way which displays a remarkable ability to seek out opportunities, and a great degree of adaptability to local conditions.

REVIEW QUESTIONS

1 Explain how a public limited company forms part of the private sector of the industry.

2 To what extent could a registered charity such as the RSPCA be regarded as an enterprise? Who carries out the functions of the entrepreneur within such an organisation?

3 If a company devotes resources to sponsoring a symphony concert, is this a sign that the firm is not maximising profits? In what way could it be argued that such sponsorship has a direct link with profitability?

4 Consider the article in Figure 15.3, which appeared in the *Guardian*:

(a) To what extent does this article reinforce the view that there is a divorce between ownership and control?

(b) Many school pupils now take part in 'enterprise' activities. Is it possible to learn how to be enterprising?

5 Is entrepreneurship possible within large organisations? Suppose you were employed by a multinational car manufacturer. What opportunities might there be for you to display the characteristics of entrepreneurship?

Figure 15.3 What motivates tycoons

The British Psychological Society hears what motivates tycoons, and the risks in moving staff

Entrepreneurs' spur to success

Chris Mihill
Medical Correspondent

Tycoons who founded multi-million pound empires are more likely to be poorly educated, come from deprived backgrounds and have had mothers with strong personalities, a study of successful people has found.

The personality of entrepreneurs is significantly different from that of senior managers and company chairmen who worked their way up the corporate ladder.

A unique study of what motivates elite businessmen and the forces that shaped their drive has been carried out by a mature PhD student, Reg Jennings, which involved detailed interviews with some of the richest and most powerful business people in this country and the United States.

The four-year study consisted of an analysis of self-reported characteristics of 19 entrepreneurs and 22 managers, two of whom were women.

The entrepreneurs included Lord Young, the former Trade and Industry secretary, George Davies of Next, businessman Owen Oyston, publisher Eddie Shah, Gerald Ronson of the Heron group, financier Peter de Savary, and Jeffrey Archer.

The managers included Anthony Pilkington of Pilkington glass, Lord McAlpine, Julian Smith of W H Smith, Sir Adrian Cadbury of Cadbury Schweppes, Sam Whitbread of the brewing firm, and Denis Thatcher.

Mr Jennings, of Lancaster University, told the annual meeting of the British Psychological Society in Bournemouth at the weekend that the hardest part was getting access to the people. Once he had done so, they were happy to talk, although reluctant to fill in personality questionnaires.

An analysis of their characteristics found the entrepreneurs had higher reserves of energy, were more creative thinkers, more risk-seeking, but becoming bored with routine. They were more likely to attribute their success to luck.

They also strongly believed their early years of poverty had shaped their ambition, and, in particular, that their mothers had been a strong influence.

Mr Jennings said the entrepreneurs "gave not a damn for education," usually having left school at 15. The managers had usually been to the best schools.

The entrepreneurs sought excitement and saw adversity as a challenge.

Lord Young said: "I spent a very miserable year in 1973 when I thought I was rich and didn't know what to do. Very luckily for me the 1974 bank crash wiped me out and I woke up one morning full of the joys of spring because I knew what I had to do."

One tycoon said being Jewish in a poor area and being beaten up nearly every day of his school life had acted as the spur to prove himself.

Owen Oyston, Peter de Savary and Jeffrey Archer all said their mothers had influenced them strongly.

Mr Oyston commented: "I was ill for years at school. My mother was the driving force. She created in me an uneasiness about not working and the pressure for me to really prove to the world what I had in me."

By contrast, Denis Thatcher said: "As a businessman I am still, and always have been, the professional director. The decision-maker, yes, but not with the flair of the real entrepreneur."

Source: *Guardian*, 15.4.91

CHAPTER 16
LAND AND CAPITAL

CONNECTIONS

Land is often discussed in connection with the law of diminishing returns, which we covered in Chapter 7, and with economic rent, which we deal with in Chapter 18. Capital accumulation is important in influencing the standard of living and we discuss the importance of this in Chapters 18, 36 and 38.

Key Concepts

Fixed capital
Investment
Non-renewable resource
Working capital

Land

Features of Land as a Factor of Production

To the economist, *land* includes all natural resources which can be used in production, and which might be regarded as 'gifts of nature'. It therefore refers to the earth's surface, and natural features such as soil, forests and the minerals beneath the earth; it also refers to the oceans, natural resources in the sea (such as fish) and minerals under the sea bed (such as oil), and the resources of other waterways.

Mobility of Land

Land is **geographically immobile**, even in the long run. It has been known for large amounts of capital to be moved geographically – an entire steel works was once dismantled in the UK and relocated in Southern Africa. However, it would be impossible to move an entire farm from one place to another, or to relocate a coal mine to somewhere without coal reserves underground.

On the other hand, a great deal of land is very **occupationally mobile**. Since the uses to which land is put can be changed, land has a certain amount of vertical or occupational mobility. Farmland, for instance, can be used for housing, or a Ministry of Defence rifle range may be turned over to agriculture. Box 16.1 illustrates a dramatic change of land use.

Land as a Non-renewable Resource

In recent years there has been increasing interest in 'renewable' resources: in the power industries, for instance, this is interpreted as referring to the harnessing of energy from sources such as solar cells, hydroelectric or tidal schemes and wind generators. It also underlines schemes for recycling valuable earth resources such as aluminium, glass and paper. To what extent can land itself (as opposed to its natural resources) be regarded as 'renewable', and in what sense is it 'recyclable'?

Land is important as a factor of production, not just because of the minerals and other resources yielded by the earth and its waterways, but also because of its ability to be **built upon**. In a densely populated country like the UK there is a tremendous amount of pressure upon land, and the opportunity costs of using land can be very high. Some of the older industrial areas have large amount of what has been termed 'derelict' land, which was once thought to be so scarred by heavy industry as to be of no further economic use. In other words, land in these areas was regarded to some extent as a 'non-renewable resource': a factor which could be used once and once only. Industrialists, housebuilders, and others seeking land preferred to look for 'greenfield' sites. However, in recent years land prices have risen dramatically at certain times, as shown in Figure 16.1

Figure 16.1 *Rises in land prices, UK, 1987–8*

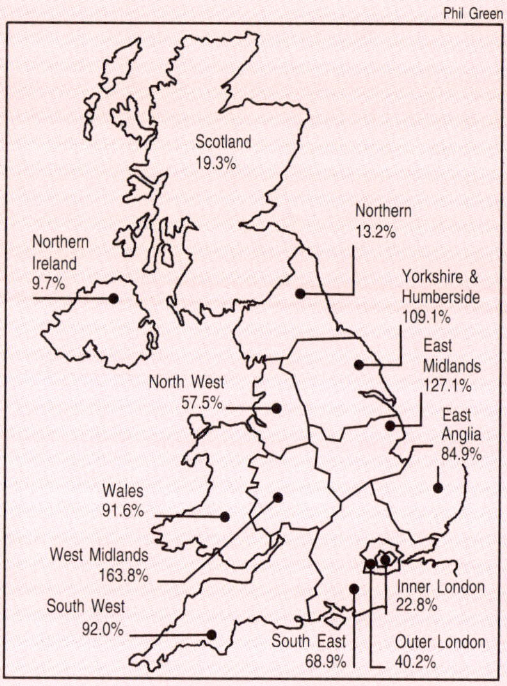

Source: The Sunday Times

Such price increases have helped to create a great deal of interest in bringing derelict land back into use, whether for housing, industry, commerce or recreation. Examples are the revitalisation of the dockland areas in some of the older ports, including those in the East End of London, and land clearance schemes in old mining areas.

However, recycling of land can be a very long-term process, and it can be very difficult to wean housebuilders and industrialists away from their favoured greenfield locations. Successive Secretaries of State for the Environment have become embroiled in controversy over plans to build new villages in areas previously designated as belonging to green belts, while it has been suggested by environmental groups that inner city areas and disused industrial sites contain more than enough open space for foreseeable housing and industrial needs. One thing is certain: argument will continue for many years to come!

Capital

'Capital' is defined as those assets created by the factors of production with the sole purpose of **making further production possible**; in other words, they are *producer goods*. In some cases it is possible to question the extent to which capital is actually distinct from land. In order for land to provide a productive service, it is usually also necessary for there to be an expenditure on capital goods: thus a farmer's field might well be unproductive unless criss-crossed with a drainage system, which eventually becomes indistinguishable and inseparable from the land itself. Furthermore, to be productive land may require repeated applications of fertiliser.

A further possible source of confusion stems from the use of the word 'capital'. Capital is sometimes used in everyday speech to mean *money*. However, economists do not regard money as a factor of production, and in the case of firms money is required to purchase real assets, such as machinery, which are capital.

What is Capital?

Businesses often recognise *two types of capital.*

Working capital (sometimes known as *circulating capital*) is required for the everyday running of the business and is constantly changing its form: every transaction that takes place changes the form of working capital – selling goods, for example, involves a reduction of stock and an increase in liquidity.

Fixed capital consists of real assets, such as plant, machinery, tools, factories, shops, offices, and so on.

How is Capital Accumulated?

Two important features arise out of the description of capital which we have given above.

First, the accumulation of capital involves a *sacrifice*, since resources are used to make capital goods instead of consumer goods for immediate use. In other words, capital accumulation has an opportunity cost in terms of forgone current consumption. The phrase 'capital accumulation involves abstention from current consumption' is widely used by economists to indicate the opportunity cost involved. In a modern economy like the UK, this implies that capital

Box 16.1 Villagers demand return of 'stolen' common land

Common land campaigners are launching a nationwide bid to have thousands of acres requisitioned by the Government during and just after the Second World War returned as public open space, writes Sarah Lonsdale.

The land, taken over primarily for military and agricultural use, was requisitioned 'for the best of reasons in the Forties and Fifties', say countryside bodies. But much of it is no longer of strategic use to the Government and should be returned to the public, they say.

Pill Heath, in the parish of Hurstbourne Tarrant, near Andover, Hampshire, was bought by the Ministry of Agriculture in 1952 after it had been farmed by the Ministry during the war. Before the war it had formed part of more than 200 acres of common in the parish.

It was declared surplus to requirements in 1988 and is for sale. Hampshire County Council and the local branch of the Ramblers Association are keen to have the land returned as common, but the money to purchase it has not been found.

Roland Clark, who lives on the borders of the heath – 43 hilltop acres of open scrub and grassland, with commanding views of the Test Valley – has been campaigning for the common's return and says the Ministry has a moral duty to consider the wishes of the local people.

Brian Wright, chairman of the Common Land Cause, which is to start pressurising for more requisitioned commons to be returned to their original status, has discovered that the Ministry acted unlawfully when purchasing Pill Heath. By some quirk of history, the parishioners were lords of the manor under the soil of the common – a unique circumstance recorded in documents from the now defunct Court Baron.

However, the Ministry only paid parishioners for the loss of common rights. Although the order for the common's purchase was given in Special Parliamentary Procedure in 1952, no money was handed over until 1961. 'The three-year period during which the Government had to hand over the money had lapsed well before then,' said Mr Wright.

'Like Greenham and other commons, Pill Heath was acquired by the government in a roundabout and questionable way', said Mr Wright. 'We now aim to highlight this loss of thousands of acres of public land which the Government has a moral duty to return as it becomes surplus to requirements, rather than sell it to private enterprise'.

Leslie Pope, of the pressure group Commons Again, which is fighting the Ministry of Defence over its attempts to buy common rights over Greenham Common, said: 'Every bank holiday people rush off to the Lake District or Exmoor to enjoy the countryside, when all over the country there is land on people's doorsteps which should now be made available as public open space again'.

A spokesman from the Ministry of Agriculture was unable to comment on Pill Heath. However, the Ministry's view is that the maximum amount of money should be obtained from the sale of land of this type.

Source: *Observer* (31 March 91)

accumulation requires **saving by the community**. This is analysed more fully in Chapter 19.

Secondly, capital enhances the *productivity* of the other factors of production, and it is this enhanced productivity which represents the benefit gained from the sacrifice involved in creating capital: we consume less today in order to create capital so that we can consume more tomorrow. The process of capital creation is usually referred to as *investment*, and we analyse this in Chapter 21.

Occupational Mobility of Capital

Capital assets tend to be more *specific* than land, labour or enterprise. This means, essentially, that they have less occupational mobility: it is more difficult to change their use. Many tools are designed to do particular jobs. A mould for making plastic egg cups, or a jig for cutting out the wooden frames for three-piece suites, are examples of fairly specific capital. A computer is far less specific, as it can be used in a variety of situations for a range of tasks; the software which it runs is likely to be more specific, controlling a production line or turning the computer into a word processor, for example. The extent to which the capital employed by a firm is specific might vitally affect entrepreneurial decisions. For instance, a firm making clothing faced with reduced demand for men's suits could fairly easily switch production to make, say, overalls or ladies' dresses, because sewing machines are to some extent non-specific. This kind of switch might be more difficult for a car manufacturer faced with changed demand conditions, as production lines tooled up to make family cars, for example, might not easily be converted to making vans. Because of the specificity of the capital the firm faced with reduced demand might have to build up stocks, go onto reduced time working, or even shut down.

Geographical Mobility of Capital

Is capital geographically mobile? This depends what we mean by 'capital'. If we think of capital in monetary terms, then capital has become far more mobile in recent years than it ever was before. With improved communications and computer networks linking the financial markets of Japan, North America and Europe, dealing in securities takes place almost continuously around the clock over the different time zones of the world. Many governments, especially the Thatcher government of the 1980s, reduced and removed restrictions on international monetary movements. However, we have argued above that as economists we should attempt to think of capital in real terms, rather than in monetary terms. Whether real physical assets can be moved geographically obviously depends upon their nature.

Box 16.2 The opportunity cost of capital accumulation

Figure 16.2 shows a technique sometimes used by economists to illustrate the choices between producing consumer goods and capital goods.

Figure 16.2 *Production possibility curve for consumer and capital goods*

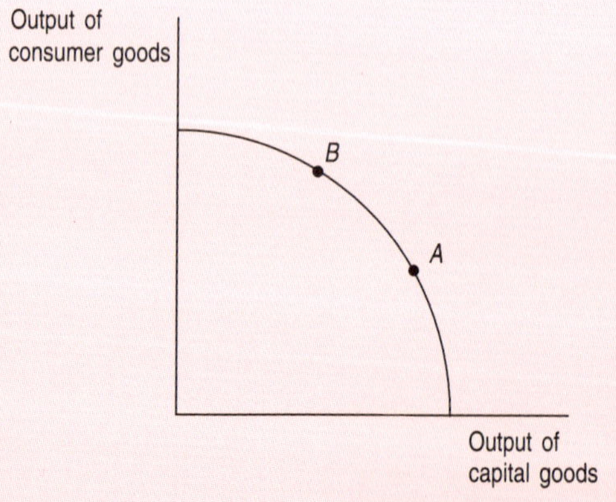

The production possibility curve was introduced in Chapter 1. This particular version shows several economic principles. Its shape, convex to the origin, shows the **immobility or specificity of capital**; the fact that if resources designed to produce consumer goods are diverted towards the output of capital goods, then there will be diminishing returns, as the factors are not perfectly mobile. Figure 16.2 also shows the opportunity cost or sacrifice involved in investment. An example of this sacrifice is shown by recent events in Eastern Europe.

In the twentieth century the Soviet Union moved rapidly from being an undeveloped agrarian economy towards being an industrial economy and a defensive superpower. Investment in steelworks, hydroelectric plant, and other industrial and social infrastructure was achieved at the expense of consumer goods. It has become a cliche in the Western press to say that Russians now have an insatiable appetite for consumer goods: for private cars, fast food, denim jeans, and so on. Perhaps people are less willing to sacrifice present consumption in favour of investment. How the long-term development of the Soviet economy will be changed by this remains to be seen. In Figure 16.2, an increased preference for current consumption over increased investment is indicated by a short-term movement from point *A* to point *B*. In the longer term, this could reduce the rate of increase of productive capacity, and so slow down the ability of the production possibility curve to shift to the right.

The most important capital asset in the lives of many families is the family house; this is an example of an asset which is geographically immobile. But having said that, there are instances of buildings which have been moved brick by brick, and on the plains of the American mid-west it is not uncommon to see an entire house creeping to a new location on the back of a huge transporter. The building of oil rigs in the North Sea is an example of how the movement of real capital assets can follow a movement of monetary assets. The moving of funds to the UK by an American or Dutch oil company intent on investing in the North Sea will precede the purchase of the necessary capital goods, and will be followed eventually by the movement of real capital assets to the desired location: it is when the real capital goods are purchased that investment in the economic sense, takes place.

REVIEW QUESTIONS

1 Is land a renewable or non-renewable resource? Explain your answer.

2 The Bible tells us to turn 'swords into ploughshares', and there is much talk nowadays of the 'peace dividend' (see p. 4). What are the practical problems involved in such changes, and how can they be illustrated by the use of a production possibility curve?

3 Is a screwdriver an example of fixed or working capital?

CHAPTER 17

THE DISTRIBUTION OF FACTOR INCOMES

CONNECTIONS

Having examined the nature of the factors of production in preceding chapters, we now turn to the study of **factor incomes** – that is, the rewards for providing factor services. We examine wages, interest, rent and profit. To do this we use the supply and demand techniques explained in Chapter 3 and the marginal analysis explained in Chapters 7 and 8. We use the sum of all factor incomes received during the course of a year to estimate the value of output produced during the year in Chapter 18.

Key Concepts

Collective bargaining
Economic rent
Interest
Isoquant
Marginal productivity theory
Monopsony
Profit
Quasi-rent
Supply of labour
Transfer earnings
Wages

Wages

Why do airline pilots receive more pay than bus conductors? Why do doctors earn more than nurses? Why do teachers earn more than road sweepers? To economists, as well as to the individuals concerned, these are important questions and they immediately bring into focus the nature of *wage differentials*. How can we explain the existence of these differentials? In fact, as we shall see, economists rely on supply and demand techniques. We begin with a discussion of the marginal productivity theory of labour, because this is important in explaining the demand for labour.

The Marginal Productivity Theory of Labour

It is important to note at the outset that the demand for any type of labour is a *derived demand*. It is derived from the demand for the product that labour produces: if there is no demand for a particular product, there will be no demand for labour to produce it.

The *marginal productivity theory* is based on certain assumptions:

- The firm sell its product in a **perfectly competitive market**. It is therefore a price taker and changes in its output have no affect on market price.
- There is **perfect competition in the factor market**, so that the firm can recruit as many workers as it wishes at the ruling wage rate.
- **All workers are homogeneous** so that any individual worker's contribution to output does not depend on the individual employed.

Marginal revenue product (MRP) is the amount added to total revenue when the firm sells the output of an additional worker. Since we have assumed perfect competition in the product market, all output will sell at a constant market price and therefore MRP will equal *marginal physical product* (MPP)

Table 17.1 *Physical product and revenue product*

Number of Workers	Total Physical Product	Marginal Physical Product	Average Physical Product	Price of Product	Total Revenue Product	Marginal Revenue Product	Average Revenue Product
		3				15	
1	3		3	5	15		15
		4				20	
2	7		3.5	5	35		17.5
		8				40	
3	15		5	5	75		25
		13				65	
4	28		7	5	140		35
		17				85	
5	45		9	5	225		45
		15				75	
6	60		10	5	300		50
		3				15	
7	63		9	5	315		45

multiplied by the price of the product. Table 17.1 is used as a basis for illustration.

As the firm employs more workers it initially experiences increasing returns but beyond the employment of the fifth worker these give way to diminishing returns. Since the price of the product is constant at £5, the *shape* of the *MPP* and *MRP* curves are identical as are the shapes of the *APP* and *ARP* curves. The importance of *MRP* can be illustrated by reference to Figure 17.1.

The rule the entrepreneur will follow is the **profit maximising rule** established in Chapter 8 – that is, *MC* is equated with *MR*. Since the wage rate is constant as the firm employs more workers, the marginal cost of employing additional workers is constant. In Figure 17.1 when the wage rate is *OW* the firm is in equilibrium when *OQ* workers are employed. If fewer workers were employed, the firm would add more to revenue than to cost by increasing employment since *MRP* > *MC*. The opposite is

Figure 17.1 *The profit maximising number of workers employed*

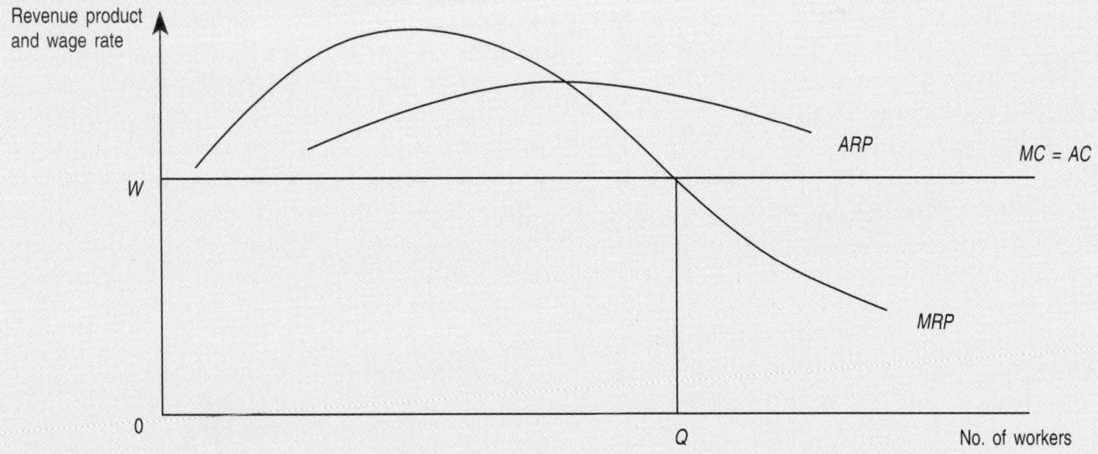

true if the firm employs more than OQ workers. Similar reasoning tells us that when the wage rate is OW_1 the firm will be in equilibrium when OQ_1 workers are employed and when the wage rate is OW_2 the firm will be in equilibrium when OQ_2 workers are employed.

The Demand for Labour

It is clear that when the wage rate falls the firm will employ more workers. However, the marginal productivity theory takes the wage rate as given; it does not tell us how the wage rate is determined. The marginal productivity theory is not therefore a theory of wage determination; nevertheless, it does provide an explanation of why the demand for labour by an individual firm is inversely related to the wage rate. In other words it enables us to derive the individual firm's demand for labour curve and since this is the normal shape we can assume that the industry's demand for labour curve is the normal shape. Clearly this is *part* of a theory of wage determination, but a complete theory must also provide an explanation of the **supply of labour**.

The Supply of Labour

The supply of labour in an economy depends crucially on the size of the population. Other things being equal, the larger a nation's population, the larger the labour force. In particular, social and cultural influences such as the number of years of compulsory education, the retirement age, the provision and size of state retirement benefits, the attitude of society to working women and so on are relevant.

While the absolute size of a nation's population is an important issue, we are more concerned here with the supply of labour to a particular occupation or industry. We cannot begin by analysing the behaviour of an individual because, as we shall see on p. 351, the effect of a rise in wages on the number of hours an individual is prepared to work is unpredictable. In some circumstances an individual will be prepared to work longer hours in response to a pay rise but in other circumstances the same individual will work fewer hours in response to a a pay rise. Nevertheless, we can be sure of one thing: a rise in wages in one industry relative to other industries will increase the supply of labour to that industry. Some individuals will undoubtedly be prepared to work longer hours but workers will also be attracted away from other occupations. The supply of labour to an industry will therefore vary directly with the **wage rate offered** by that industry.

The Determination of the Wage Rate

In a particular industry or a particular labour market, wages are determined by the **interaction of the forces of supply and demand**. We have seen in our preceding analysis that demand and supply curves for labour will be the normal shape and therefore in any labour market the wage rate will tend towards the equilibrium rate which equates supply of labour with demand for labour. This is illustrated in Figure 17.2

Figure 17.2 *The equilibrium wage rate in an occupation*

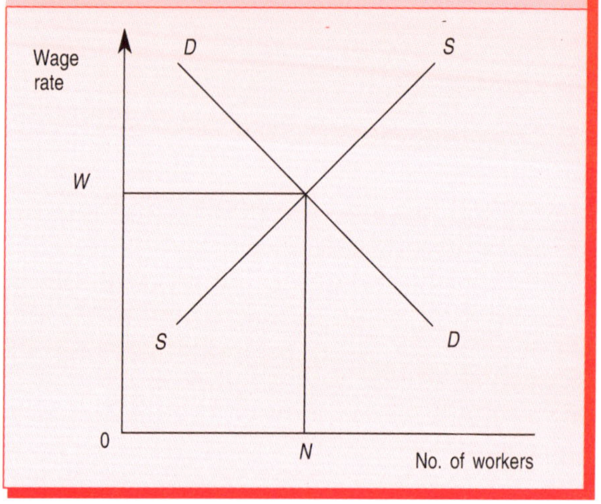

In Figure 17.2 the curve SS shows the supply of labour to a particular industry and DD shows the demand for labour by the same industry. The equilibrium wage rate is OW. Any wage rate different to this is unsustainable. For example, at a wage rate above OW the supply of labour exceeds the demand for labour and therefore in a free market the wage rate will fall. At a wage rate below OW there will be excess demand for labour and therefore the wage rate will rise. Once equilibrium is established at OW it will change only if there is a change in the conditions of demand and/or the conditions of supply in this labour market.

Changes in the Wage Rate

In Figure 17.3 supply and demand are initially given by SS and DD respectively and the equilibrium wage

Figure 17.3 *Changes in the wage rate*

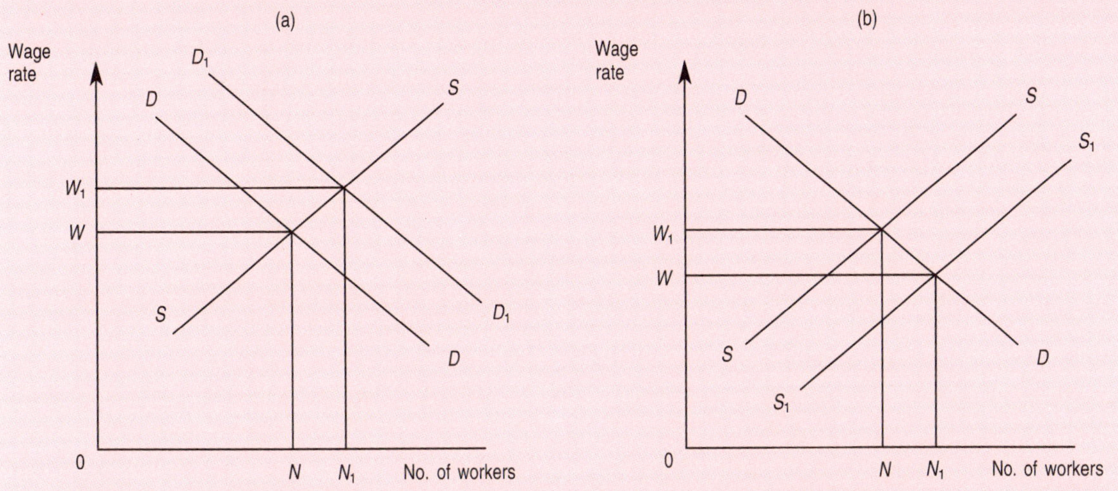

(a) The effect on the wage rate and number of workers employed of an increase in demand for labour

(b) The effect on the wage rate and number of workers employed of an increase in the supply of labour

rate is OW. In Figure 17.3(a), a shift in demand from DD to D_1D_1 is an increase in demand for labour in this labour market, and a shift in demand from D_1D_1 to DD is a reduction in demand for labour. In Figure 17.3(b) a shift supply from SS to S_1S_1 is an increase in supply of labour in this labour market, and a shift in demand from S_1S_1 to SS is a reduction in supply of labour.

It is clear from Figure 17.3(a) that an increase in demand results in an increase in the wage rate in this labour market and a reduction in demand has the opposite effect. It is also clear from Figure 17.3(b) that a reduction in supply results in an increase in the wage rate while an increase in supply results in a reduction in the wage rate. But what might cause these changes in demand for and supply of labour?

Causes of a Change in Demand for Labour

- *A change in the productivity of labour* is a major cause of changes in the demand for labour. If all other things remain equal, an increase in the productivity of labour implies that the firm has a greater output to sell *at any given price*. In these circumstances *MRP* will increase and therefore at any given wage rate the firm will demand more workers and will increase its number of employees until *MC* equals the increased *MRP*. In terms of Figure 17.3(a) this implies a shift in demand for labour from DD to D_1D_1 and an increase in the wage rate from OW to OW_1. A reduction in productivity will have the opposite effect.
- *A change in the price of the product* is also a major cause of changes in the demand for labour. Again if all other things remain equal, an increase in the price at which the firm sells its product implies an increase in *MRP* and therefore an increase in the demand for labour at each and every wage rate. Again the final effect will be an increase in the wage rate from OW to OW_1. A reduction in the price of the product will have the opposite effect.

Causes of a Change in the Supply of Labour

What might change the supply of labour to a particular industry, or to industry as a whole?

- *Changes in legislation*: Increasing the school leaving age, or reducing the retirement age will reduce the potential number of recruits to industry by reducing the participation rate (see p. 124).
- *Changes in people's preferences for work over leisure*: If people become either more willing or less willing to work longer hours, this can affect the supply of labour in general. It can affect the supply of labour to particular industries depend-

ing upon the type of work being done and the working conditions. It might be more difficult to persuade people working underground in a coal mine, for example, to work overtime compared with people working in an office environment. Recent studies have shown that working hours are generally longer, and holidays shorter and less frequent in the UK than in many European countries. It is difficult to say whether this indicates that British people value leisure less than their continental counterparts, or whether they are simply unaware of the benefits to which workers in other countries are entitled, or too poorly organised to negotiate similar conditions for themselves.

- *Social changes*: These include the increased desire of women to pursue careers, and changed attitudes in society generally making it more acceptable for women to go out to work on equal terms to men. Such changes have been assisted by improved techniques for family planning and better medical facilities enabling women safely to postpone the starting of a family until later in their lives. In certain countries governments have been very active in encouraging schemes such as maternity leave, paternity leave and workplace nurseries. Some have also promoted measures to enable disabled persons who were previously regarded as unemployable to work alongside the able-bodied.
- *Measures to remove barriers to the mobility of labour*: These barriers, and the measures which can help to remove them, are discussed on p. 122. The provision of education and training facilities is receiving particular attention at the moment, especially the perceived need to encourage more young people to stay on in full time education after the age of 16. The proportion of young people doing this is significantly lower in the UK compared with the USA, Japan, and most of western Europe. If more people remained in education to improve their qualifications this would reduce the size of the overall working population and thus reduce the supply of labour in general. However, the supply of labour to particular industries (those that require a highly trained and educated workforce) would be increased.
- *Changes in the power of trade unions*: Particularly relevant here is the power of trade unions and professional bodies to operate a **closed shop**. As discussed on p. 153 these powers have been eroded in recent years, thus lessening the ability of unions and professional bodies to control the supply of labour to particular industries.
- *Population changes*: Changes in the size of the population, the age structure of the population and the geographical distribution of the population can all have dramatic effects on the supply of labour. There is a great deal of comment at the moment on the effects of the 'demographic time bomb' and this is discussed on p. 126.

Elasticity of Demand for Labour

We have seen that in a free market wage rates are determined by the interaction of demand for labour and supply of labour. But in analysing why one group of workers is paid more than another group of workers it is important to identify the factors that influence **elasticity of demand** for labour. Remember, if demand for labour is inelastic the quantity of labour demanded will change less than proportionately as the wage rate changes. The main factors that influence elasticity of demand for a particular type of labour are:

- *Elasticity of demand for the product*: Labour is a **derived demand.** It is derived from demand for the product which labour produces. Clearly if demand for the product which labour produces is inelastic, the demand for labour is also likely to be inelastic. If we consider the case of air travel and bus travel we might expect the demand for air travel to be less elastic than the demand for bus travel. After all, there are fewer substitutes for air travel than for bus travel. If this is true the demand for airline pilots will be relatively inelastic with respect to the wage rate because airlines are able, to a certain extent, to pass on wage increases in the form of higher prices to air travellers. The same is unlikely to be true of bus travel where substitutes are more readily available. Here the ability of firms to pass on wage increases is likely to be more limited and therefore the demand for bus drivers is likely to be more elastic than the demand for airline pilots.
- *The proportion of labour costs to total costs*: This is an important determinant of elasticity of demand for labour. In the case of labour-intensive industries where labour costs account for a significant proportion of total costs, demand for labour is likely to be relatively elastic. For example, if labour costs account for 70 per cent of total costs than a 10 per cent rise in labour costs will lead to a 7 per cent increase in total

costs. However, if labour costs account for only 5 per cent of total costs then a 10 per cent rise in labour costs implies an increase in total costs of only 0.5 per cent.

Here again the airlines tend to be more capital-intensive than bus companies. The aviation industry has invested billions of pounds in aircraft, maintenance facilities, air traffic control equipment and so on. Bus companies also need to invest in capital equipment, but the support facilities required to keep a bus on the road are not so great as those required to keep a plane in the air. If refusal to grant a wage rise therefore results in a strike, the effect on the average fixed cost of an airline company would be proportionately greater than the effect on the fixed costs of a bus company.

- *Elasticity of substitution*: The ease with which other factors can be substituted for labour is an important determinant of the elasticity of demand for labour. For example, where it is easy to substitute capital for labour then as wages rise firms will increasingly substitute capital for labour. To some extent capital can be substituted for labour in the case of airline pilots because of the development of automatic pilot systems. However, since no aircraft leaves the ground without at least one pilot on board the scope for such substitution is limited. However, capital can be substituted for labour because of the development of larger aircraft capable of carrying more passengers without requiring an increase in the number of pilots. The same is true of buses.

However, in both cases the scope for substitution is limited. The same is not true of bus conductors and in many towns and cities bus conductors have been replaced by machines from which passengers purchase tickets before making their journey. In other places a change in working practices has led to 'one person operation' where the bus driver also sells tickets.

Elasticity of Supply of Labour

Elasticity of demand for labour exerts a powerful influence on the wages of different groups of workers. However, elasticity of supply is also important because it determines the effect of any change in demand for labour on the wage rate and the numbers employed. For example, if supply of a particular type of labour is inelastic an increase in demand for that type of labour will result in a relatively large increase in wages but a relatively small change in the number of workers employed. This can be seen if we consider Figure 17.4(a) and Figure 17.4(b). In both cases *SS* and *DD* are the original supply and demand conditions in different labour markets. When demand for labour increases to D_1D_1, the same increase in each market, it is clear that the effect of this is different in each market. In market (a) there is

Figure 17.4 *Elasticity of supply of labour and wages*

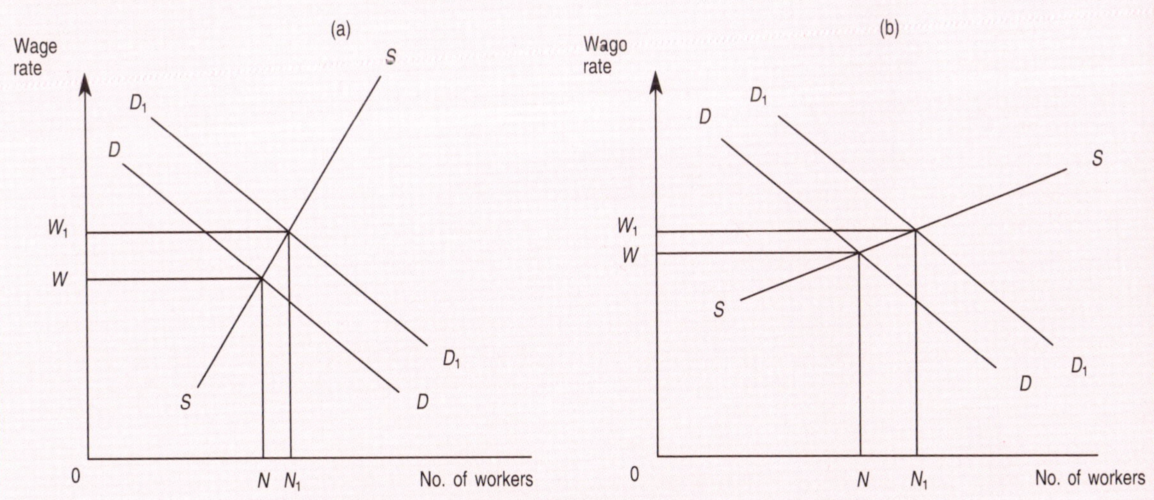

The effect on the wage rate and number of workers employed of a given change in demand for labour with different conditions of supply

a more than proportional increase in the wage rate, but relatively little impact on the numbers employed, whereas in market (b) there is relatively little change in the wage rate but a more than proportional increase in the numbers employed.

The main determinants of elasticity of supply are easily summarised:

- *Length of training*: Where it takes a relatively long period of time to train workers supply will be relatively inelastic in response to an increase in the wage rate. For example, it takes several years to train as a doctor or a chartered accountant and in such cases it is difficult to increase the numbers available for employment in the short run. However, the same is not true of doctors' receptionists or air hostesses who can be trained in a relatively short period of time.
- *Special aptitudes*: Some occupations require particular ability levels while others require special particular skills. For example, not everyone has the ability to become a doctor and few people possess the skill required to become an international golfer. In such cases supply is less elastic than the supply of labour to occupations such as shop assistants where fewer special aptitudes are required.
- *Mobility of labour*: We have seen on p. 122 that there are many barriers to mobility of labour and if the population is occupationally immobile in particular this implies that the supply of labour to an occupation will be relatively inelastic. However, where an industry is highly localised and the population is geographically immobile, supply of labour to that industry may be relatively inelastic.

The Case of Monopsony

There are some industries where there is a single buyer, or *monopsonist*. For example, the coal industry in the UK is a case of monopsony in the labour market because the National Coal Board (NCB) is virtually the only purchaser of coal miners. Monopsony is an interesting case because it might seem that when there is only a single buyer of labour the workforce would be at a severe disadvantage in negotiating pay and conditions. In fact, even in these circumstances it may sometimes be possible for a trade union to negotiate an increase in the wages of its members and simultaneously increase the numbers employed. To see why let us consider Figure 17.5 in which we assume there is a monopsonistic buyer of labour and imperfect competition in the labour market.

Figure 17.5 *The effect of a monopsonist on the wage rate*

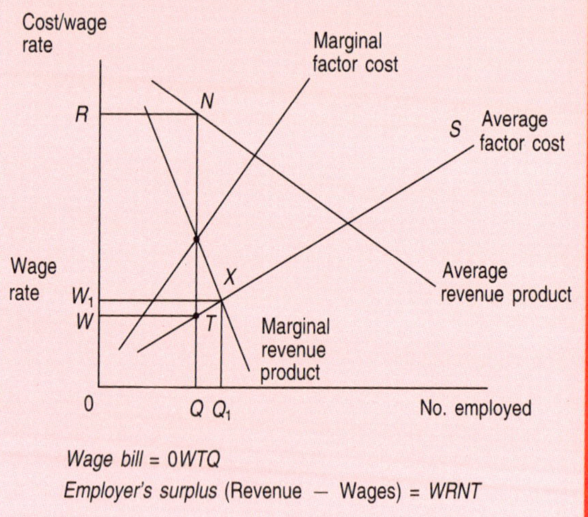

Because there is imperfect competition in the labour market the monopsonist is obliged to pay a higher wage rate to attract additional employees. The marginal cost of labour is therefore greater than the average cost of labour. For example, if the firm employs ten workers at a wage rate of £400 per week but is forced to increase the wage rate to £410 per week in order to attract an additional worker, the marginal cost of the eleventh worker is £810 but the average cost of employing eleven workers is only £410. In Figure 17.5 the marginal cost of labour intersects the *MRP* curve of labour when *Q* workers are employed and the wage rate, that is, the average cost of labour is *W*.

However, at a wage rate of *W* workers receive less than their *MRP* and therefore contribute a surplus of revenue product over the wage they receive. When *Q* workers are employed this surplus is equal to *TN* per worker. If a trade union is now formed it might be able to persuade the employer to pass on part or all of this surplus to the workforce. If the labour market were perfectly competitive the equilibrium wage would be W_1 because this is where the MRP curve for labour intersects the (constant) average cost = marginal cost of labour. The firm would therefore employ and Q_1 workers. A trade union might therefore refuse to supply workers at a wage rate of less than W_1 and therefore the supply of labour to the firm becomes W_1XS. Since the monopsonist aims to maximise profits the firm must increase its employment of workers to Q_1 because this is where the new *MC* curve intersects the *MRP* curve. The trade union has therefore succeeded in raising the wage rate and the numbers employed!

Collective Bargaining

In our discussion of monopsony we discussed a particular situation. However, it is possible to look at the role of a trade union more generally. Trade unions are able to influence the supply of labour when there is a high degree of union density in an industry. The procedural arrangements through which unions negotiate on behalf of their members is referred to as *collective bargaining* because the union bargains collectively on behalf of its membership with the employer, particularly over pay and conditions. This strengthens the bargaining hand of labour, because the alternative would be for each worker to negotiate individually with the employer.

Economic Rent

In the nineteenth century Ricardo developed a theory of rent which depended on the idea that land was fixed on supply and had no cost of production since it was a gift of nature. Ricardo therefore alleged that rent on land is determined entirely by **demand**. This led to him to reason that when the demand for corn is high relative to available supplies, and corn prices rise, there will be an increased demand for land and rents will increase. Thus high corn prices should not be blamed on landlords, their high rents are an *effect* rather than a *cause* of high corn prices. Ricardo's famous conclusion was that the price of corn is high not because the rent of land is high, but rather the rent of land is high because the price of corn is high: in other words, rent is not **price determining**, it is **price determined**.

Modern economists find the notion of *economic rent* has useful applications, not only to land but to all factors of production. The term 'rent' in popular usage describes the payment made for the use of a good belonging to someone else: a TV set, a car or a horse, for example. *Economic rent* is not quite the same thing. It is defined as a *surplus*, being any payment received by a factor of production over and above the minimum payment necessary to keep it in its present occupation. This minimum payment or supply price is known as *transfer earnings* and it represents an opportunity cost; if the reward to a factor of production falls below its transfer earnings the factor will transfer to its next well paid occupation. For example, a teacher might be willing to work as a teacher for a minimum of £900 a month. If his wage fell below that level he would seriously consider a transfer to what he regards as his 'second-best' occupation, as a driving instructor. His transfer earning is therefore £900 per month, and if his actual earnings are £1200, then his economic rent per month is £300. The most important feature of economic rent is that it is a **surplus**, so that in principle its payment is not necessary to ensure a supply of a particular factor.

Figure 17.6 *Transfer earnings and economic rent*

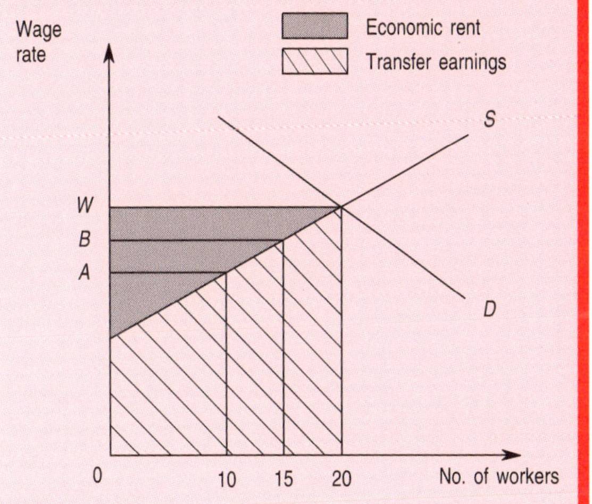

Figure 17.6 shows the demand for and supply of a particular factor, in this case labour. The tenth worker is willing to work for a wage of *OA*, so his or her transfer earnings are *OA*. If the actual wage rate is *OW*, then his or her economic rent is given by *AW*. However, the fifteenth worker does not enter this labour market until wages rise to *OB*, this being his or her transfer earning, and *BW* is this worker's economic rent. The twentieth worker can be described as the marginal worker; he or she is the last person to enter the labour market at the current wage level, and receives no economic rent, only transfer earnings. Total transfer earnings on this market are equal to the hatched and total economic rent is given by the shaded area.

Figure 17.6 is consistent with Ricardo's notions of economic rent, because it shows that the earnings received by factors are strongly influenced by **demand**. Employers will demand factors which are capable of being used profitably, their demand

Box 17.1 Economic rent and the elasticity of supply

If the supply curve in Figure 17.6 were to become steeper (if its supply elasticity *at every price* were to decrease) then the area of the graph representing rent would increase, while transfer earnings would increase. Thus a factor with zero supply elasticity would earn all economic rent, while a factor with infinite supply elasticity would receive all of its income in the form of transfer earnings. These possibilities are illustrated in Figure 17.7.

Figure 17.7 *Transfer earnings and economic rent*

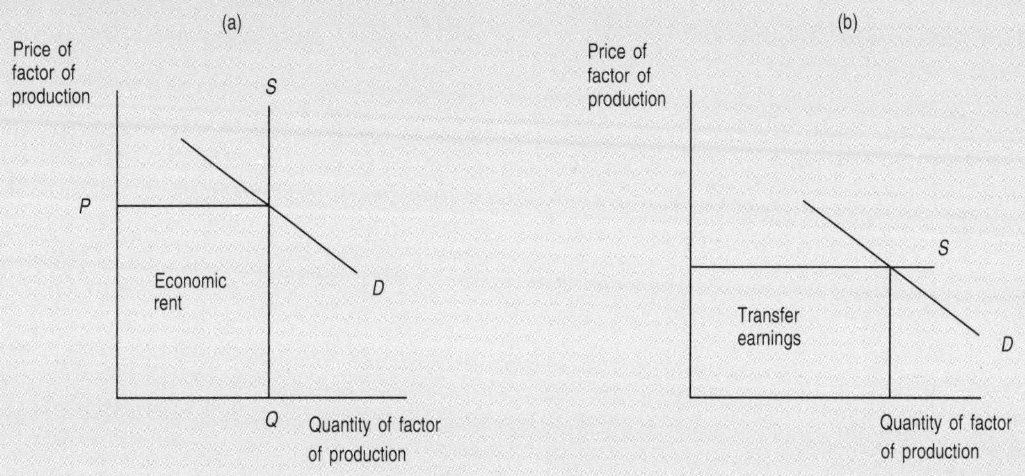

called Terry Griffiths won the world professional snooker championship for the first time, and received a fairly modest money prize measured in four figures. Ten years later he won the championship for the second time, and received a *five*-figure prize, accompanied by the promise of a number of sponsorship and advertising contracts each worth tens of thousands of pounds. Economic rent provides a worthwhile explanation of this remarkable transformation in the fortunes of successful professional snooker players.

Figure 17.7(b) helps to explain why certain factors which have a virtually unlimited supply (e.g., unskilled workers) receive a relatively low income, which may not increase noticeably as demand increases. In a recession employers shed unskilled labour, whereas in a boom they hire unskilled labour, while the workers themselves find that they receive more or less the minimum amount for which they are willing to work. Figure 17.7(a), on the other hand, provides an insight into the very high payments received by certain factors which can be regarded as unique: pop stars, famous film actors, top ranking sports persons, and so on.

The world of professional snooker provides a suitable case study. Today in the UK, there are many thousands of occasional snooker players, but very few people who can play with such skill and consistency that other people are prepared to pay to watch. In the mid-1970s, an ex-bus driver called Terry Griffiths won the world professional snooker championship...

At any one time there is only one world snooker champion; at the time of his greatest successes we can therefore argue that no-one could quite do what Terry Griffiths could do. We could therefore draw his supply curve as vertical through the point where quantity equals 1. He had a transfer earning; and if his wages from snooker fell too low then he might possibly have considered going back to being a bus driver. However, at the time of his second world championship success the difference between transfer earnings and actual earnings was so large that Figure 17.7(a) would be appropriate, with all earnings regarded as economic rent. The great difference between his 1970s earnings and his 1980s earnings is therefore entirely explained by a shift in demand to the right as the televised popularity of snooker increased dramatically.

Similarly, the demand for the services of pop stars such as Madonna has become not just nation-wide, but world-wide, and this demand has been satisfied by a massive investment in capital equipment. This capital is television equipment linked to cable and satellite systems. During Madonna's 1990 European tour, for example, several thousand people paid at the turnstiles to see her Barcelona concert. Many millions of people, however, paid to see the concert televised on television. They paid indirectly, through mechanisms such as the TV licence fee in the UK, or through purchasing the goods which are advertised on commercial television. The revenues from these sources are used to acquire the TV rights of such events, and so the demand for the services of these performers comes not directly from individuals, but from huge communications corporations. When these corporations with their huge buying power shift the demand curve to the right, the earnings of these fortunate individuals rise dramatically.

for factors being derived from the public's demand for goods and services which will affect both price and profitability. Hence Figure 17.6 shows that rent is price determined, not price determining.

Quasi-rent

Sometimes factors of production earn economic rent in the short term which *disappears* in the long term. This is known as *quasi-rent*, and arises mainly in cases where supply takes some time to catch up with demand. Take, for example, the provision of centres for ten-pin bowling. This pastime has enjoyed two waves of success in the UK: first in the late 1950s and early 1960s, when about 100 bowling alleys were built, many of which were closed so that by 1974 there were less than 40 left. The owners of these facilities presumably felt that despite the slump in demand they were still making a reasonable return, in other words receiving their transfer earnings, and so they did not follow the trend of converting their premises into supermarkets or warehouses.

Then, during the 1980s, certain sections of the entertainment industry such as the First Leisure Corporation realised that ten-pin bowling could cash in on the boom in demand for American-style leisure activities such as fast food outlets and multi-screen cinemas. They did this through a change of image, together with innovations such as computerised scoring which revitalised the market, and the demand for ten-pin bowling increased dramatically. The game has been described as 'easy to play, but difficult to master', which entrepreneurs would recognise as a perfect recipe for keeping the customers coming back, even when prices are relatively high. In the short run, therefore, the owners of existing bowling alleys found that with some investment to go up-market as 'bowling centres' they could quite easily capitalise on the boom, and begin earning surpluses over and above transfer earnings: that is, they began receiving economic rent. However, in the long run these economic rents can disappear through increased competition or by other means. By 1991 there were already 250 bowling centres in the UK, with more being built. Once supply begins to catch up with demand, we can expect prices to fall and surpluses to be reduced.

Another way in which the economic rent can disappear in the long run is by being converted into a **cost**. Suppose the proprietor of a bowling centre rents premises on a seven-year lease and during that seven years profits increase due to a boom in this sector of the leisure industry. Upon renewal of the lease, the landlord could well try to negotiate an increased payment on the grounds that the value of the site has been increased by its higher earning power. If the landlord is successful, a short run surplus has been turned into a transfer earning or opportunity cost in the long run.

The Taxation of Economic Rent

It is often suggested that economic rent is a suitable target for taxation because being a surplus it could, in theory, be taxed away completely without losing the factor service which would still be receiving its transfer earning. Thus, when oil companies have received unexpected surpluses from time to time, and when banks have received increased profits during times of high interest rates, there have been suggestions that a once and for all windfall profits tax would be appropriate: on one occasion in the 1980s the government levied such a tax In practice, economic rent is not easy to tax because it is difficult to measure.

Profit

Economists regard profit as a *reward for enterprise* and a *reward for risk-bearing*. Remember that in Chapter 8 we distinguished between *normal profit*, which is the minimum rate of return required to keep the entrepreneur in his or her present line of business; and there is *supernormal profit*, which is a surplus over and above normal profit. Careful consideration of these definitions should make it clear that normal profit is, in fact, the **transfer earnings of the entrepreneur**, while supernormal profit is the entrepreneur's **economic rent**. We can therefore argue that normal profit is a *reward for enterprise* which brings the entrepreneur into production. Although it is no means certain that an entrepreneur will earn normal profit, it is even less certain that there will be any supernormal profit. So the idea of profit as a 'reward for risk-bearing' corresponds, at least to some extent, to the idea of supernormal profit because it provides the incentive to undertake the risks of production.

However, to an accountant, profit is a *residual* concept, or a *remainder* which is calculated by subtracting the cost price of goods and services from their selling price. These costs and revenues are expressed in purely monetary terms and give a figure known as *gross profits*. Once various expenses are deducted a figure called net profit is arrived at. If this figure is a positive number, a business is regarded as profitable.

An economist might take a rather different view of profitability, because there is an opportunity cost, as well as money costs, to consider. Suppose for example a landlord invests £100,000 in property and receives £10,000 in rent. After deducting expenses an accountant might consider the enterprise to be profitable. An economist, on the other hand, is more likely to consider the alternatives to which the £100,000 could have been put – or, in other words, the opportunity costs. For instance, it might be estimated that if £100,000 had been invested in gilt-edged stock the return could have been greater than £10,000, and so in this sense the enterprise can be viewed as being unprofitable.

Interest

Traditionally, interest is regarded as a **reward to the factor capital**. However, in practice it is not so easy to assign rewards such as interest, rent and profit to particular factors. We have already seen that elements of economic rent are found in various types of income. When a lender charges a rate of interest as a 'price' for the use of borrowed money, that price has a number of components. There is a payment for risk, because some borrowers are a better risk than others. There is payment for the trouble involved in creating a loan (for example, the loss of liquidity which a bank will experience, and the expense of servicing a loan). There is also an element of compensation, since the lender is for a time deprived of his or her money. Finally, there may be an element of speculation, with the lender choosing to be a creditor in preference to, say, investing in the equity of companies.

In practice, interest and profit are very difficult to distinguish from each other. In Chapter 18 where we study the measurement of the national income, we find that under the *income method* there are entries in the national accounts for wages, rent and profit, but no separate entry for 'interest'. This is because interest is regarded as being, in effect, a subset of profit: in other words, dividends and interest payments are paid out of company profits. In companies, retained profits are ploughed back or kept within the firm for further expansion, while distributed profits are paid out to shareholders. The determination of interest rates is considered in Chapter 28.

The Personal Distribution of Income and Wealth

Figure 17.8 shows how income in the UK is divided between individuals.

Table 17.2 *The effect of state intervention on the distribution of personal income*

% of original income	*Bottom fifth*	*Middle fifth*	*Top fifth*
1976	0.8	18.8	44.4
1985	0.3	17.2	49.2
% of disposable income	*Bottom fifth*	*Middle fifth*	*Top fifth*
1976	7.0	18.2	38.1
1985	6.5	17.3	40.6

Source: Social Trends (1988)

Figure 17.8 *Distribution of personal income, UK, 1989*

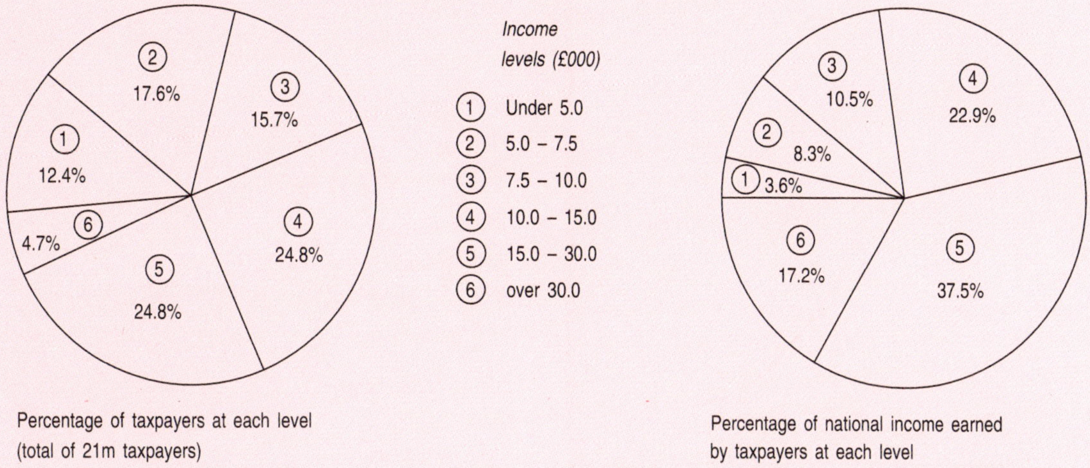

Source: *Social Trends* (1990)

Note that the pie-charts do not concern themselves with people whose income is so low that they pay no tax at all. Even so, we find that the figures reveal significant inequalities. For example, in the highest income bracket shown we find that 4.7 per cent of taxpayers earn 17.2 per cent of national income, while in the lowest income bracket 12.4 per cent of taxpayers earn only 8.3 per cent of total income. These figures are, however, gross figures. They do not make allowances for income tax or state benefits.

Figure 17.9 *Distribution of marketable wealth, UK, 1987*

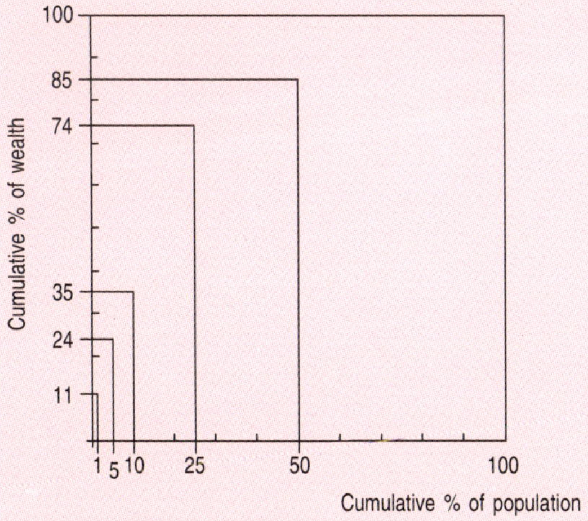

Source: *Social Trends* (1990)

Table 17.2 shows that the very unequal distribution of income thrown up by market forces is reduced to some extent by government action.

In 1976, for instance, the quintile group (the fifth of the population) with the lowest incomes received only 0.8 per cent of total income, that is to say, for every £100 earned, only 80p went to this group while the top fifth of the population received £44.40. After income tax and state benefits were taken into consideration, however, £7 went to the lowest fifth and £38.10 to the top fifth. Table 17.2 confirms the widely held view that both original and disposable incomes became more unequally distributed during the 1980s; in other words, the gap between rich and poor has become wider, both before and after taxes and benefits have been taken into account. However, there has been sufficient economic growth to ensure that the *level* of income received by the lowest quintile group has risen.

On p. 144 we discuss some of the reasons why people earn different wages. However, it is sometimes said that the quickest way to become wealthy in Britain is to have wealthy parents. One reason why income is so unequal is that the ownership of wealth, which generates income from profits and rents, is even more unequal; and inherited wealth is taxed comparatively lightly compared with the earnings which can be used to build up a stock of wealth during a person's lifetime.

Figure 17.9 shows that the most wealthy 1 per cent of the population owns 11 per cent of the

Figure 17.10 *Functional distribution of income, UK, 1960 and 1987*

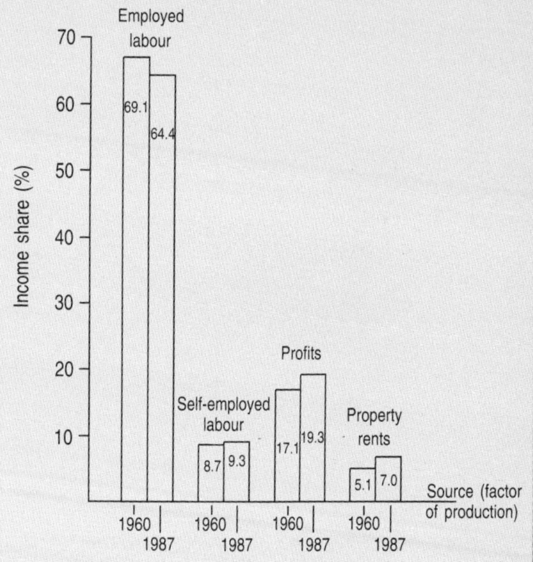

Source: *UK National Accounts* (1989)

nation's marketable wealth, and 50 per cent owns 85 per cent. The profit and rent which this wealth provides for its owners plays a large part in determining the distribution of **pre-tax income**.

Figure 17.11 *Membership of TUC-affiliated trade unions, 1970–90*

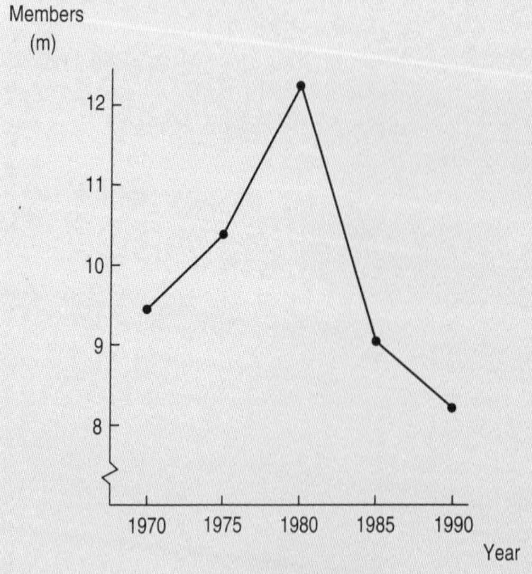

Source: TUC (1990)

The Functional Distribution of Income

Figure 17.10 shows the factor (or functional) distribution of income in the UK and compares this distribution in 1960 and 1987.

Note that the headings shown do not correspond exactly with the definitions of factor services and factor incomes as generally used by economists. Profits in Figure 17.10 include interest on capital, and rent here refers to the return on land and buildings. It is *not* economic rent – though, of course, an element of economic rent might be included.

We can see that the share of income going to employed labour has fallen in the time period shown, possibly reflecting a decline in the power of trade unions or the impact of higher levels of unemployment on wage bargaining. During the 1980s the power of trade unions was weakened by legislation (see p. 359) but membership also declined substantially as Figure 17.11 shows.

Income Distribution

Figure 17.12 shows a method which can be used to measure inequalities in the distribution of income.

The curved line is known as a *Lorenz Curve*. It plots the cumulative percentage of income recipients (ranked from poorest to richest) against the cumulative percentage of total income. The straight line

Figure 17.12 *A Lorenz Curve*

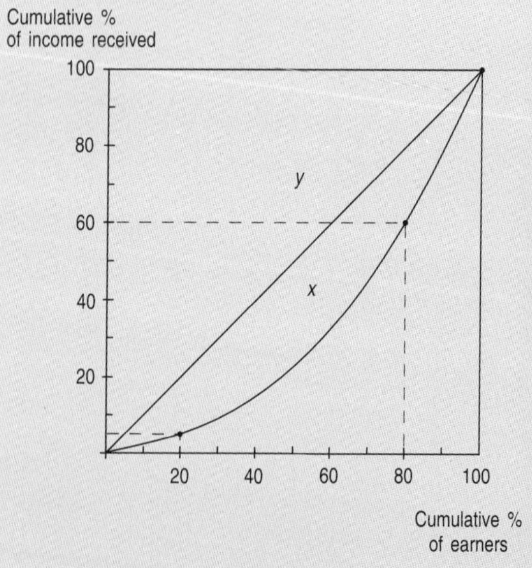

diagonal represents an equal distribution of income: along this path the poorest 20 per cent (or quintile) of the population would receive 20 per cent of total income; the poorest 40 per cent would get 40 per cent of total income, and so on. If the actual relationship follows a path similar to the curved line then this indicates that incomes are unequally distributed. In this particular case, the poorest 20 per cent earn 5 per cent of total income, while the top 20 per cent receive 40 per cent of total income.

The ratio between areas x and y on the graph is known as the *Gini coefficient*, or G (x is the area between the Lorenz curve and the diagonal; y is the area above the diagonal, $G = x/y$). If $G = 0$, then the Lorenz curve is a diagonal, and there is a completely equal distribution of income. As G increases and gets closer to 1, so the distribution of income becomes less equal. This could occur, for instance, if more people received nothing, because then the lower end of the Lorenz curve would move along the horizontal axis to the right. The top right hand end of the Lorenz curve always touches the top right hand end of the diagonal (100 per cent of the population must receive 100 per cent of total income) but if the top quintile groups receive a higher proportion of income, the Lorenz curve moves further to the right in its upper regions before it reaches the top right hand corner. If one person received all of the income and everyone else received nothing, then the area below the Lorenz curve would be almost the same as the area below the diagonal and G would be very near to 1. It should be clear that G cannot be greater than 1.

REVIEW QUESTIONS

1 Why is the productivity of the average American worker likely to be higher than that of a worker in Russia?

2 A trade union negotiates a wage rate which is greater than marginal revenue product. Use a diagram to illustrate that not all members of the union can expect to benefit from this in the long run. How might an increase in productivity alter this diagram?

3 For a time in the late 1970s and early 1980s some airlines stopped training new pilots. Use supply and demand analysis to predict how the wages of pilots subsequently altered during times of increased economic activity.

4 Are the promoters of a recital by Pavarotti able to pay the artist high wages because of the high ticket prices they can charge for admission, or are they forced to charge high ticket prices because of the artist's ability to command high fees?

5 Explain why land prices are much higher in New York City than on the plains of the American mid-west.

6 Examine the two Lorenz curves A and B in Figure 17.13.

Which of these Lorenz curves shows a more unequal distribution of income? Carefully justify your answer.

7 A person inherits £50,000 and uses it to buy a shop. At the end of the first financial year an accountant finds that sales receipts were £40,000 and costs were £36,000 and reports that profits were therefore £4,000. Explain why an economist might not agree that this represents a true picture of the shop's profitability.

8 Suppose that a local firm were negotiating a wage deal with a trade union, and asked you as an economist for advice. Write a report showing how economic theory might be relevant to the negotiations.

Figure 17.13 *Lorenz curves of income earned and earners*

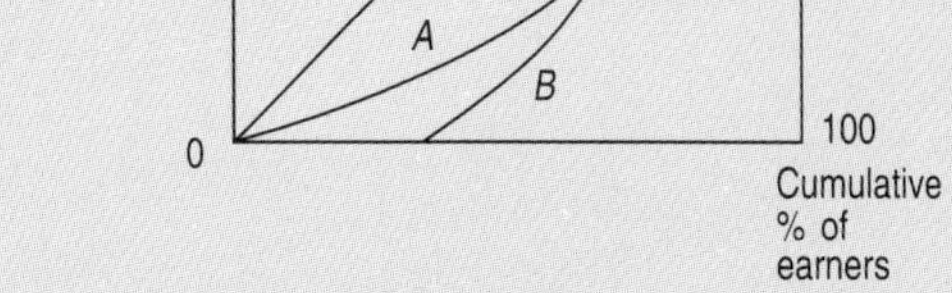

9 Examine the figures in Table 17.3.

(a) What are the difficulties involving comparing male and female wages?

(b) Why do women tend to have inferior pay to men? Are these reasons purely economic?

(c) Can legislation improve the wages of women? Does the data support the view that the Equal Pay Act of 1970 has been effective?

Table 17.3 *Male and female earnings and employment*

	1973			1988		
Occupational group	**Female–male differential***	**Proportion of female employment†**	**Male earnings, as % of average** male earnings‡	**Female–male differential***	**Proportion of female** employment†	**Male earnings as % of average** male earnings‡
Clerical and related	70.7	49.0	103.6	80.2	59.2	109.0
Selling	46.0	7.8	111.5	55.9	8.4	127.3
Catering, cleaning, etc.	72.4	14.5	76.3	82.5	12.5	77.4
Materials processing: excluding metals	63.1	3.9	95.9	68.4	2.2	94.8
Making and reparing: excluding metal, electrical	58.5	8.4	104.8	66.2	6.4	98.6
Processing, making and repairing: metal, electrical	61.5	4.1	105.9	69.6	2.0	104.1
Repetitive assembling and related	61.2	10.6	100.7	72.8	8.2	93.5
Transport operating, storage and related	70.5	1.6	89.7	79.9	1.1	87.9
All identified occupations	65.7	100.0	100.0	79.1	100.0	100.0

Notes: *Average hourly earnings (excluding overtime pay and overtime hours) of adult women in full-time employment as percentage of average hourly earnings of adult men in full-time employment.
† Females in occupational group as % of all females in identified occupations.
‡ Male hourly earnings in occupational group as % of average male earnings in all identified occupations.

Source: Department of Employment

CHAPTER 18

NATIONAL INCOME AND ITS MEASUREMENT

CONNECTIONS

How national income is **measured** is important in understanding the determination of national income. Measures of national income are also used in measuring living standards, and in assessing whether a country is considered developed or less developed. The rate at which national income grows from year to year is one way in which **economic growth** is measured.

Key Concepts

Gross national product (GNP)
Gross domestic product (GDP)
National income
Standard of living
Real income
Nominal income
Personal disposable income

National income is the basic measure of **economic activity**. It represents the **total output of an economy over a given accounting period**, usually a year. It is clear that because production is a continuous process, national income is a *flow* rather than a *stock*. Any attempt to measure the flow of output is an extremely difficult task. Some idea of the enormity of this task is provided by the fact that in the UK on any single day of the year there will be several million transactions that add to national income! Before we consider how national income can be measured, let us look more closely at some of the problems involved in its measurement.

The Problems of Measurement

Units of Measurement

As we have just noted, national income is a measure of the flow of output an economy produces over a given period of time. But in advanced economies like the UK there are millions of different types of goods and services produced each year. How can we add together such diverse goods and services as pork pies, haircuts and ships? To add these together we need a common denominator, and the only feasible approach is to use the **price paid** for each good or service purchased as a **measure of its value**.

The task of measuring national income therefore involves adding together the money value of all output produced by an economy over a twelve-month period. However, this is not as straightforward as it might appear and there are several points to emphasise.

The Problem of Double Counting

National income does not consist of the full value of every single item that is produced in an economy, since the **output** of some firms is the **input** of others. National income consists of *final output* only. It therefore excludes the value of all *intermediate* inputs, and great care must be taken when compiling the statistics to avoid *double counting* – that is, counting the same output twice. Flour bought for use in the home is a final good, but flour bought by the baker is an intermediate good, it is *part* of final output. Similarly electricity used in the home is a final good, but it is an intermediate good for almost every other good and service produced within the economy. This poses a problem when calculating national income. If all goods and services are included in the calculation there will be *double counting* because intermediate goods will be counted twice. If we count the final value of the output of the steel industry and the final output of the motor vehicle industry, then the value of steel used in the production of motor vehicles will be counted twice. Just as surely there would be double counting if the total output of millers (flour) and bakers (beard) were included or the final value of the electricity generating authorities and the final value of all other goods and services.

To avoid double counting we must include only the value of **final output** in the calculation of national income. Alternatively we must sum the *value added* at each stage of production. Either method of calculation will yield exactly the same result, as Figure 18.1 shows.

Figure 18.1 *Value added at each stage of production*

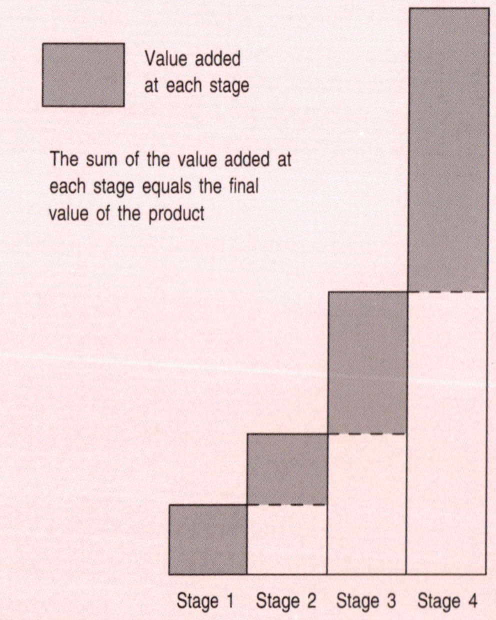

Stage 1: Landowner sells trees to sawmill owner
Stage 2: Sawmill owner cuts trees into timber sheets and sells to furniture manufacturer
Stage 3: Furniture manufacturer turns timber sheets into furniture and sells to retailer
Stage 4: Retailer sells furniture to consumer

Figure 18.1 shows the value added at each stage of a particular productive process and the final value of the output produced. It is clear that the sum of all values added at each stage is exactly the same as the value of the final output produced.

Non-market Goods and Services

A whole range of productive activities are undertaken by central and local government, which clearly add to national income but which are not sold through the market mechanism. The maintenance of law and order provided by the police force, education and health care, are all activities which contribute to national income, but which are not priced by market forces. How are such activities to be valued for purposes of computing national income statistics? In fact, they are valued at *resource cost* – that is, the **cost of the resources used to produce these activities** is taken as a measure of their value.

Transfer Payments

Care must be taken when assessing the contribution to national income made by central and local government, since not all of their expenditure contributes directly to national income. Part consists of *transfer payments*: these are simply transfers of wealth from one individual or organisation to another which are not payments made in respect of any productive activity. Unemployment benefit, retirement pensions and student grants are all examples of transfer payments, and since they are not made in return for any productive activity they must be excluded from any calculation of national income. Similarly gifts to charity or payments of pocket money from parent to child are not part of national income.

Second-hand Goods

National income is the flow of **current output**; at the time of production the value of a good is included in national income. However, if that good is then sold to someone else, to include the latter transaction in national income will result in the good being counted twice. For example, if a car is produced in one year and sold to a customer, the value of this transaction is included in national income. However, if the car is then sold to someone else, to include the full value of this transaction would mean that the value of the car had been counted twice. Of course, if the car is sold by a dealer, the dealer provides a service which *is* part of national income. The dealer's profit is therefore included in national income, but not the full value of any sales he or she makes.

Defining National Income

The value of output produced within a nation's frontiers is referred to as *gross domestic product* (GDP). This is an important concept and is often used in estimating changes in the productivity of domestic resources. However, *gross national product* (GNP) is the value of output produced using resources owned by a particular nation, wherever these are located. For example, many UK companies have subsidiaries located in different countries and part of their incomes are remitted to the parent company in the UK. This is referred to as *property income from abroad*. Similarly many foreign companies are located in the UK and remit part of their incomes abroad. This is referred to as *property income paid abroad*. The difference between these flows is recorded in the national accounts as *net property income from abroad* and adding this to GDP (or deducting it if it is negative) gives us a value for GNP.

However, neither GDP nor GNP provides an entirely accurate measure of national income because neither takes account of the fact that during the process of production existing capital assets will have *depreciated*. Economists refer to the creation of capital assets as *investment* and *depreciation* refers to the **loss in value of capital assets over time**. Depreciation may be caused by wear and tear on assets, but it is more likely to be caused by technological progress which makes the continuing use of some assets uneconomic. In other words, some capital equipment will have been superseded by more efficient capital equipment, and in order to remain competitive firms will have to adopt these newer technologies. Part of current production is therefore devoted to maintaining the capital stock and simply replaces capital equipment that has been scrapped. *Gross investment* refers to the total output of capital goods within a given period of time, whereas *net investment* refers to the net addition to the capital stock – that is, gross investment minus depreciation. The term 'gross' in gross domestic product and gross national product implies that no account has been taken of depreciation. When depreciation is deducted from gross national product we arrive at *net national product* (NNP), and conceptually this is a more accurate measure of national income.

Despite the fact that NNP is conceptually the superior measure of national income, which is the most appropriate measure depends on the purposes for which statistics are required. For example, if we are interested in the productivity of resources within the UK, GDP is the more relevant statistic. On the other hand, if we are interested in the value of output becoming available for consumption by UK residents, GNP is more relevant. In fact, for most purposes GNP is the more widely used aggregate.

Measuring National Income

A useful framework of analysis used by economists is the *circular flow of income*. This is an extremely important identity which tells us that the output produced by the factors of production is equal to the incomes paid to those factors of production. This, of course, is true by definition since we have assumed that output is valued at resource cost. However, it is also true that the value of output produced must, by definition, be equal to the amount spent on that output net of any taxes and subsidies. Thus we have the basic accounting identity:

$$\text{Income} \equiv \text{Output} \equiv \text{Expenditure}$$

This provides the conceptual basis for measuring national income.

The Expenditure Method

This approach to national income measurement sums the **total expenditures on goods and services produced by the economy**. For convenience, these are grouped into four categories according to the type of expenditure undertaken. Each of these in now considered.

Consumers' expenditure includes spending by private individuals on goods and services such as food, clothing, travel, medicine and so on. As Table 18.1 shows, this is the largest component of total expenditure and in 1989 consumers' expenditure accounted for £328,453m which was approximately 74 per cent of GNP.

Investment is the creation of real capital assets such as machinery, hand tools, office equipment and so on. In Table 18.1 we can see *gross domestic fixed capital formation* was £100,472m in 1989. However, under our heading of *investment* we must also include *additions to stock and work in progress* (£3102m in 1989). Remember that national income is the **flow of output produced** – even though not all of that output will have been sold. Firms' investment in stock is therefore included as part of gross investment (see Box 18.1).

Table 18.1 *National income 1989, UK, (£m)*

Output[1]		Income		Expenditure	
Agriculture, forestry, fishing	6561	income from employment	284399	Consumers' expenditure	328453
Energy & water supply	22619	Income from self-employment	53126	General government final	
Manufacturing	97380	Gross trading profits of		consumption	
Construction	30274	companies	65639	of which: Central government	60850
Distribution, hotels & catering,		Gross trading surpluses of		Local authorities	38576
repairs	62133	public corporations	6576	Gross domestic fixed capital	
Banking, finance, insurance,		Gross trading surpluses of		formation	100472
business services & leasing	86628	general government enterprises	192	Value of physical increase in	
Transport and		Rent	31568	stocks & work in progress	3102
Communications	30074	Imputed charge for con-			
Public administration, defence		sumption of non-trading capital	3840	Total Domestic Expenditure at	
& compulsory social security	29571	*Less* stock appreciation	7598	market prices	531453
Ownership of dwellings	25482	Statistical discrepancy		Exports	123396
Education & health services	42547	and income adjustment	1032	*Less* imports	142527
Other services	29715	Gross Domestic Product		Gross Domestic Product	512322
Statistical discrepancy		at factor cost	438744	Statistical discrepancy	920
and income adjustment[2]	1032	Net property income from		Net property incomes from	
Gross Domestic Product at		abroad	4582	abroad	4582
factor cost	438744			*Less* taxes on expenditure	80136
Net property income from		Gross National Product	443396	Subsidies	5668
abroad	4582	*Less* capital consumption	56186		
				Gross National Product	443356
Gross National Product	443356	National income	387170	*Less* capital consumption	56186
Less capital consumption	56186				
				National income	387170
National income	387170				

[1] The contribution of each industry to GDP after providing for stock appreciation.
[2] The statistical discrepancy includes all errors and ommissions. It has a different rate in the expenditure estimates than in the estimates for output and input because estimations of GDP are build up from independent data on incomes expenditure. The statistical discrepancy is the difference between these estimates, but there is no implication that expenditure estimates are superior in accuracy.

Source: HMSO, *National Income and Expenditure* (1989)

Box 18.1 Changes in stock and national income

In business accounting, any increase in the value of stocks between the beginning and the end of the accounting period will enter into profit. However, if this convention were adopted in national income calculations it would mean that any increase in the money value of stocks in the year would be seen as adding to national income, even if the *physical volume* of stocks had remained constant or declined. To be consistent with other flows measured, only additions to national income arising from the economic activity of the period are included – that is, physical volume rather than money value. If this was not done there would be a discrepancy between income, output and expenditure. Remember that national income is a measure of the value of output produced in a given accounting period. If prices rise, this does not change the value of output **that has already been produced**.

So, in calculating the main aggregates, the estimated value of the physical increase in stocks is included. Any difference between this and the book value of stocks is ignored. It arises from stock appreciation (which is not part of national income) as distinct from the physical increase in the value of stocks (which is part of national income). Note that as long as prices are rising, stock appreciation will always be positive.

Government expenditure includes all spending by central and local government on the different goods and services they are responsible for providing. It does not include transfer payments. A detailed analysis of government spending is given on pp. 346–50, but we can note here that *general government final consumption expenditure* includes expenditure on education, defence, roads, the health service and the police force. In 1989 general government final consumption expenditure was £99,426m.

Net exports refers to total export revenue from the sale of goods and services abroad, minus expenditure on goods and services produced abroad (that is, expenditure on imports). Exports are produced with factors of production owned by a particular country. The fact that this output is sold abroad does not affect the rewards paid to the factors of production. It is for this reason that the value of exports is part of national income. Exactly the opposite reasoning tells us why expenditure on imports, although undertaken by domestic residents, is not included in calculations of domestic national income. Such expenditure provides rewards for factors of production abroad.

Market Prices and Factor Cost

Adding together the values of all of these expenditures will of course give GDP at *market prices*. For some purposes this might not be adequate and it is often more useful to measure GDP (and GNP) at *factor cost*. The problem is that market prices do not always reflect factor rewards. We have seen in Chapter 6 that a tax on a product will raise its price. However, the tax is a payment to the government and is not a reward to the factors of production. The factors of production will therefore receive the market price of the product they produce *minus* the value of the tax. Conversely, a subsidy will reduce the market price of a product. The factors of production will therefore receive the value of the subsidy *plus* the market price of the product they produce.

To obtain GDP at *factor cost* we therefore deduct the value of indirect taxes and add on the value of subsidies. To obtain GNP at factor cost we add *net property income from abroad* to GDP at factor cost and to obtain NNP we deduct *depreciation* from GNP at factor cost.

The Income Method

To calculate national income by the *income method* we must add together **all of the incomes received from producing the current year's output**. We have already seen that it is necessary to exclude transfer payments from any calculation of national income since these are not factor incomes. However, care must also be taken to ensure that *gross* incomes, rather than *net* incomes, are used in the calculation. In other words, we must use incomes *before* the payment of any tax on those incomes. Why is this? Remember we are measuring the value of output produced in the current year and this is equal to the gross amount earned by the factors of production. The factors of production do not receive the full value of their output because the government levies taxes on the incomes they receive. However, this does not diminish the value of the output the factors of production produce, or the amount consumers pay to purchase this output.

Let us look at the factor incomes we must consider when using the income method to calculate national income.

Income from employment is the reward to the factor of production labour and consists mainly of wages and salaries. However, it also includes other payments made by employers, in particular national insurance contributions and any payments made by the employer into a pension fund for the employees' benefit on retirement. These are costs of employing labour, just as wages and salaries are costs of employing labour. As Table 18.1 shows p. 160, income from employment is by far the largest category of income.

Income from self-employment must, in part, also be considered a return to labour. However, not all of this represents a wage or salary. Part is undoubtedly profit, and as such is more properly considered a return to the entrepreneur. In practice, it is impossible to distinguish what proportion of income from employment is a wage and what proportion a profit. The actual proportions probably depend more on how each is treated for purposes of tax liability rather than on any consideration of economic principles!

Profits are an important factor income and are strictly the return to the entrepreneur. We have already noted that part of the income from self-employment is profit, but in the official statistics profit appears as the *gross trading profits of companies*, *gross trading surpluses of public corporations* and *gross trading surpluses of other public corporations*. As we have seen on pp. 79–80, for accounting purposes profit is usually treated as the amount left over after all other costs are deducted from revenue. This tells us that whether profit is distributed to shareholders or retained by firms as an undistributed surplus has no affect on its contribution to national income.

Rent, for purposes of national accounting, consists of payment for the use of assets such as private dwellings and land. However, a notional amount is also included in the case of owner-occupiers. In other words, it is assumed that owner-occupiers rent their property from themselves. Failure to include this notional sum would result in measured national income falling as a result of an increase in owner-occupation.

Summing the value of incomes in this way yields GDP. To obtain GNP we simply add *net property income from abroad*, and if NNP is required we simply deduct *depreciation* from GNP.

The Output Method

Here we sum the value of **final output**. We have already seen on p. 158 the need to avoid *double counting*. However, there are also other factors to bear in mind. Exports are part of national output even though they are consumed by overseas residents; in calculating the value of output, exports must therefore be included. However, the value of imports are excluded and particular care must be taken to deduct the value of *imported raw materials* which are used in the production of final output. By taking account of net property income from abroad and depreciation we can obtain GNP and NNP respectively by the output method.

Exclusions From National Income

National income statistics provide a measure of the value of output produced by an economy over a period of one year. However, these statistics are not complete and in this section we consider some of the reasons for this.

Self-provided Output

A great deal of productive activity is undertaken by people for their own benefit and is not sold to consumers. Many people grow their own fruit and vegetables, paint their own houses, clean their own windows, and so on. Many people are DIY enthusiasts and produce a great many things for their own home. In all of these cases resources are used and an output is produced, but it is impossible to assess the value of this output because it is unrecorded. The greatest omission here is the value of the home-maker's output. Cleaning, shopping, cooking, nursing sick children, and so on, are activities often carried out by a spouse, but which are again unrecorded in the national income statistics.

Such under-recording of the true level of output clearly reduces the reliability of national income statistics. However, the real value of these activities is unlikely to change significantly from one year to the next and since they are permanently omitted the statistics provide an accurate picture of the way national income is changing. For most purposes, this is all that is required. Despite this, there is no doubt that over time the real value of these activities does change significantly, and this affects the reliability of national income comparisons in the longer term.

The Underground Economy

In any economy certain transactions go unrecorded or their value is deliberately under-recorded. There may be several reasons for this, but the most obvious are that the transaction is illegal or the motive is tax evasion. These transactions are referred to as the 'underground economy' or 'black economy', and for whatever reason they are not reported, these transactions represent a contribution to national income and their omission reduces the reliability of the statistics.

The very nature of the underground economy makes it difficult to assess its magnitude. However, one obvious way in which the size of the underground economy may be measured is to compare the estimates of GNP derived from expenditure estimates with those derived from income estimates. If the underground economy is significant we would expect to find that the estimates of expenditure were significantly greater than the estimates of income. After all, whether income is declared or undeclared, it will almost certainly be spent. Estimates of the size of the black economy in the UK suggest it is equal to between 4 and 8 per cent of GNP.

This is comparatively low, and in less developed countries the underground economy will count for a much greater percentage of GNP than it does in the UK. In such economies the banking sector is not well-developed and therefore a great many transactions are paid for in cash. However, even in some developed economies the underground economy accounts for a greater proportion of GNP than it does in the UK. For example, it is estimated at between 10 and 15 per cent of GNP in the USA and in excess of 25 per cent of GNP in Italy. However, such estimates are not perfect and must be treated with caution because money earned in the underground economy might also be spent in the underground economy. The extent to which this happens is likely to vary between countries and make comparisons of this nature less reliable.

Voluntary Work

In some countries, such as the UK, a great deal of charity work is done, particularly in the form of community work. This is done on a voluntary basis and so has no effect on the value of recorded national income. Here again the effect is that the official statistics under-record the true value of output produced.

Nominal Income and Real Income

'Nominal income' refers to national income expressed in money terms. Thus Table 18.1 (p. 160) shows that in 1989 nominal GNP in the UK was £443,356m. However, 'real income' refers to the volume of output produced, and economists are often interested in analysing changes in real income or total output between one year and another year. The term 'real' therefore refers to the fact that the data have been adjusted for changes in the level of prices. This is true whether we refer to real income, real wages, real rate of interest or any other *real* variable. Clearly, if we wish to know how real income has changed between one year and another, we cannot simply compare nominal income in both years because between the two years prices will have increased. It is possible for nominal GNP in one year to be twice that of nominal GNP in another year, but if prices are also twice as high, the level of output will be unchanged.

The problem is solved by using *index numbers*. These are considered in detail on pp. 248–50, but for present purposes it is sufficient to know that they are a technique used by economists to measure changes in the **average price level**. The average price level in one year is given the notional value of 100 and the price level in subsequent years is measured as a *percentage increase* on this. Let us take an example to see how index numbers can be used to obtain an estimate of the change in real income between one year and another year.

Suppose nominal income in year 1 is £500m and that it increases to £750m by the end of year 5. Suppose also that over the same period prices have risen by 25 per cent. Thus we have:

Year	*Nominal income (£m)*	*Index of prices*
1	500	100
5	750	125

To obtain an estimate of real income we must remove the contribution of higher prices to nominal income. In other words, we must measure nominal income in year 5 at *constant prices*. This is a relatively easy calculation. Since prices have increased between year 1 and year 5 in the ratio 1:1.25, nominal income in year 5 must be reduced in the same ratio. Thus:

$$\frac{£750\text{m} \times 100}{125} = £600\text{m}$$

National income in year 5 measured at constant year 1 prices is therefore £600m. In other words, if there had been no change in prices between year 1 and year 5, nominal income in year 5 would have been £600m. This implies that the volume of output in year 5 is 20 per cent greater than it was in year 1. So although nominal income has increased by 50 per cent between year 1 and year 5, real income has increased by only 20 per cent.

Personal Income and Personal Disposable Income

We have already seen that national income is a measure of the value of output produced or factor incomes received. However, for some purposes it is useful to have a measure of the value of total income received regardless of its source. For example, we have already seen that there are transfer payments which increase the incomes of their recipients. In addition, some groups have a claim on factor income which they do not receive. For example, shareholders are the owners of a company but they do not always receive the total profits earned by the company because a great deal of profit is retained by firms to finance additional investment. *Personal income* reflects gross receipts of income rather than gross earnings of factor income. Personal disposable income is simply gross personal income less payments of personal income tax.

We can calculate personal income in the following way. (The figures for the UK in 1989 are given below the appropriate category.)

Personal income	=	income from employment	+	income from self-employment	+	interest rent profit	+	transfer payments
£441,334m	=	£284,399m	+	£53,126m	+	£45,264m	+	£58,545m

If we deduct taxes and social security contributions, etc. (which in 1989 amounted to £89,237m) from personal income we obtain personal disposable income which in 1989 was equal to £352,097m.

Personal disposable income is an extremely important concept and is the main determinant of consumption expenditure by households. In other words, changes in personal disposable income will cause changes in consumer spending and, as we shall see later, this will have a powerful impact on such economic variables as the rate of inflation and the level of employment in an economy.

Measuring Economic Welfare

GNP statistics are used as a basis for estimating the standard of living in different countries, and because of this it is sometimes suggested that they provide a measure of **economic welfare**. The basic measure of living standards is GNP per head or *per capita income*; this is simply GNP divided by total population. However, whether such a statistic accurately reflects the standard of living is debatable for three broad reasons. First, the standard of living is influenced by many factors which are not included in our estimates of GNP; second, estimates of GNP include the market value of all goods and services produced, regardless of their contribution to the standard of living; and third, as we have seen on p. 160, estimates of the true value of GNP are imprecise.

What Factors Influence the Standard of Living?

Clearly many factors are relevant here. Some are tangible, but several are intangible. Of the **tangible influences** the availability of goods and services for consumption is clearly an important factor affecting welfare. Indeed, it is the most important factor affecting *material welfare*. However, it is not just *current output* which is relevant here. The level of material welfare in the present also depends on *past output* of goods and services. A television produced last year is not part of current output, but it still gives satisfaction and therefore adds to current welfare! In this sense the ever-increasing number of cars on our roads, or homes with consumer durables such as television sets, home computers, automatic washing machines, dishwashers, refrigerators and freezers that were unavailable to the majority of people even a few decades ago are all evidence of an increasing standard of living. However, a more comprehensive view of economic welfare includes the effect of **intangible factors**, which we now consider.

Leisure Time

An intangible factor which influences economic welfare is the availability of leisure time. If everybody worked a 60-hour week, output would certainly increase above its current level, but welfare would not increase to the same extent. The gain is increased output, but the cost is a reduction in leisure time.

Externalities

The effect of externalities on welfare is becoming an increasingly important consideration. It is possible to increase production by using more and more resources, but if this adds to pollution the effect on economic welfare from increased production will not be entirely favourable. In recent years the 'greenhouse effect' (sometimes referred to as 'global warming') has become the most widely publicised aspect of pollution. The main cause of the greenhouse effect is burning fossil fuels for power. As production increases, more power will be required and this will compound the greenhouse effect. It is widely felt that the consequence will be rising food prices because of changing weather and land use patterns. It is also predicted that the total land space will fall because the polar ice caps will melt. It could be argued that these are considerations for the future rather than the present, but there also effects relevant to the present. For example, there is no doubt that burning fossil fuels and car exhaust emissions are major causes of *acid rain* which is directly responsible for the emergence of dead forests and dead lakes.

The problem is that these externalities are an important consideration in assessing welfare, but they are not reflected in the estimates of *per capita* income. It is of course difficult to quantify the value and extent of externalities, but it remains true that if production generates externalities then the benefits of increased production do not lead to an equivalent increase in welfare.

Is it Reasonable to Include the Value of All Output?

We have already seen on p. 158 that non-market public sector output is valued at resource cost. This is true of health care and education, for example. Now both of these clearly contribute to welfare, but what is the value of their contribution? In fact, it is easy to argue that using resource cost as the measuring rod underestimates the true contribution of these merit goods to welfare. There are also problems in assessing the contribution of investment in additional capacity to society's welfare. If more resources are devoted to the production of machinery and so on, this will increase the amount of output that can be produced *in the future*. However, increased capital output means lower consumption output and this implies a current reduction in material living standards. A change in the pattern of production may leave measured GNP unchanged, but it may alter society's current welfare.

Qualitative Changes in Output

Measures of welfare take no account of the *qualitative changes* in output that take place over time. Even if measured GNP is the same from one year to the next, welfare will increase if there are changes in the quality of output. For many consumer durable goods there have been impressive improvements in quality during the last two decades or so. This is true of the performance of dishwashers, television sets, pocket calculators and so on. Failure to take account of such qualitative changes reduces the reliability of GNP *per capita* as a measure of living standards.

International Comparisons of the Standard of Living

Per capita income statistics are sometimes used to compare the standard of living between different countries. Such comparisons are misleading for a variety of reasons, which we summarise here.

Differences in Compilation

There may be substantial differences in the accuracy with which the statistics are compiled between different countries. We have already mentioned on p. 162 that the size of the underground economy may vary substantially between countries. Two countries with a similar level of GNP per head may have vastly different standards of living if there is a substantial difference in the size of the underground economy. The same is true if there are differences between countries in the contribution of spouses to running the home and child-rearing.

Differences in the Distribution of Income

The distribution of income between two countries may differ widely even if these countries have similar levels of *per capita* income. In this case, there will be differences in the *actual* standard of living for the population of both countries – even though the *average* standard of living as measured by *per capita* income was equal.

Range of Goods Produced

Countries with similar *per capita* incomes may produce a substantially different range of goods and services. Some countries devote relatively large amounts of resources to military expenditure, while for others a larger proportion of GNP consists of goods and services for household consumption. Such differences have an important bearing on material living standards, which is masked by simple comparisons of *per capita* income.

There may be other differences which are masked by simple comparisons of *per capita* income. For example, two countries may have similar *per capita* incomes but because of climatic differences may devote different amounts of resources to the provision of heating and lighting. The fact that some countries need not devote resources to the provision of heating and lighting without loss of comfort implies that more resources can be devoted to the production of other goods and services. Here again simple comparisons of GNP *per capita* may mask differences in the standard of living between countries. Similarly, there may be differences in the proportion of GNP which consists of investment output rather than consumption output, as discussed on p. 165.

Levels of Medical Provision

Comparisons of *per capita* income ignore the availability of medical facilities to the population. This has a major impact on the quality of life and if medical facilities are not widely available many people may suffer as a result. This is particularly relevant if we compare living standards in the developed world with the less developed world. In the latter case many people suffer problems which could easily be cured by a minor operation; blindness caused by cataracts is a case in point. Comparisons of living standards might therefore be more accurate if they included some measure of the number of doctors per head, the number of hospital beds per head, and so on.

Conversion into a Common Currency

For purposes of comparison it is essential that GNP *per capita* of different countries be converted into a common currency, and the most widely used currency for this purpose is the American dollar. However, actual exchange rates as quoted on the foreign exchange market are influenced by a variety of factors and may not accurately reflect the purchasing power of one currency in another country. For example, if the exchange rate for sterling against the dollar is £1 = $2, then for comparisons of *per capita* it is important that £1 buys in the UK the same amount of goods and services that $2 buys in the USA. In reality this is unlikely to be the case, and instead of using market exchange rates for purposes of comparing *per capita* incomes, economists often use *purchasing power parities*. These measure **how many units of one country's currency are needed to buy exactly the same basket of goods** as can be bought with a *given amount* of **another country's currency**. However, although superior to market rates of exchange, purchasing power parities are only an approximation and any inaccuracy in the units of conversion will distort the dollar value of *per capita* income in every country except the USA (see Box 18.2).

Uses of National Income Statistics

National income statistics are collected for a variety of reasons. They are the most complete records of the performance of the economy which have yet been developed, and they provide a great deal of useful information. We shall see in Chapter 36 that governments have various economic objectives such as the achievement of a particular level of employment and increased economic growth. Variations in real national income have an important bearing on both of these. For example, if real national income increases from one year to the next, and there is no change in the techniques of production, we would expect to see unemployment falling. Similarly, the rate at which real national income is changing is taken as a measure of economic growth. Since governments adopt policies which are designed to achieve their economic objectives the more knowledge they have of the current state of the economy, the more precisely they will be able to formulate their policies.

National income statistics are also important in measuring the standard of living. We have seen that *per capita* income is an imprecise measure of the standard of living, but it does nevertheless reflect the amount of goods and services available for consumption per head, and this is an important component of the standard of living for all countries. Documentaries on the television of conditions in many Third World countries provide vivid reminders of the suffering caused by a low level of output per head, and in particular a low level of food production per head. Similarly, the low standard of living in many East European countries reflects, among other things, a low *per capita* income.

Because they provide a measure, however imprecise, of the standard of living in different countries, *per capita* income statistics are used by international bodies and governments to determine which countries are in greatest need of economic aid or other forms of assistance. *Per capita* income statistics are also one of the statistics used by international bodies such as the IMF to determine each country's membership quota and by the Commission of the EC as a basis for assessing contributions to the EC budget (p. 325).

Box 18.2 Output and living standards compared

Measurement problems

Each country needs to measure its own output of goods and services to calculate its GDP. But each country values goods in its own currency (sterling, dollars, or francs, for example). To make comparisons between countries it is necessary to convert these GDP measures to a common currency. This is often done using market exchange rates. But these fluctuate from year to year, indeed from day to day, and often by large amounts. Even more fundamentally, market exchange rates make no proper allowance for differences in relative prices between countries, as every tourist knows.

International comparisons based on output measures converted to a common currency using market exchange rates can, therefore, produce misleading, and often idiotic results. For example, on this basis GDP per head in the UK would appear to have fallen from 80 per cent of that in the USA in 1980 to only 50 per cent in 1985. Yet over these five years average GDP growth per head in the UK has actually grown by 2 per cent more than in the USA.

Purchasing power parities

One way round this problem is to use (PPPs) which, as their name suggests, measure how many pounds, dollars or francs, for example, people need to buy the same basket of goods and services in the UK, USA or France. If people bought only one good, the PPP would simply be the relative price of that item in the two countries. (For example, if a loaf of bread costs 50p in the UK and $1 in the US, then the PPP of sterling in relation to the US dollar for this one item would be $2 = £1.)

International organisations, like the OECD* and Eurostat**, calculate PPPs by first defining a single wide-ranging international basket of goods and services and then measuring its cost in different countries. Calculating PPPs based on a basket of goods and services covering the whole economy is obviously a major task, so it is undertaken only periodically, normally every five years. The OECD and Eurostat latest fully researched estimates for 1985 are shown in Table 18.2.

Table 18.2 *PPPs and exchange rates, 1985*

	Currency units per £	
Country	PPPs	Market exchange rates
US	1.75	1.28
Canada	2.19	1.76
Japan	395	306
UK	1.00	1.00
Belguim	77	76
Denmark	17.0	13.6
France	12.8	11.5
West Germany	4.4	3.7
Greece	135	177
Ireland	1.21	1.22
Italy	2230	2450
Luxembourg	79	76
Netherlands	4.4	4.2
Portugal	116	218
Spain	167	218
Austria	30	26.5
Finland	10.5	8.0
Norway	14.9	11.0
Sweden	14.4	11.0

Source: OECD Eurostat

Using PPPs

Table 18.3 shows estimates of GDP in nineteen OECD countries, converted from national currencies to sterling using PPPs.

On these figures the US economy is by far the largest in the world. Its output in 1985 was almost three times greater than that of Japan and a fifth higher than the combined output of the twelve countries of the EC. Japan in turn produced almost twice as much as the largest Community country,

* Organisation for Economic Co-operation and Development
** The Statistical Office of the European Communities

West Germany. Figure 18.2 illustrates the relative output of the USA, Japan and the EC.

Table 18.3 *GDP 1985, £bn**

Country	GDP
US	2250
Japan	800
West Germany	425
France	355
UK	350
Italy	305
Canada	215
Spain	170
Netherlands	95
Belgium	60
Sweden	60
Austria	45
Denmark	35
Greece	35
Norway	35
Finland	30
Portugal	30
Ireland	15
Luxembourg	5

*Converted to sterling using PPPs

Source: OECD Eurostat

Figure 18.2 *Shares in GDP, main industrialised countries, 1985*

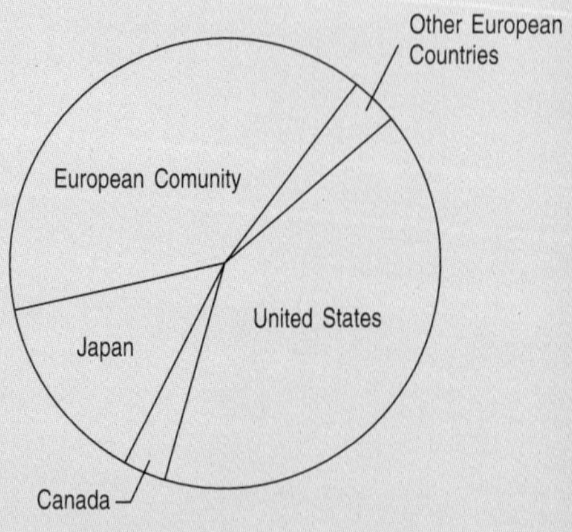

Source: OECD Eurostat

The UK has the fifth largest economy among the group of developed countries. Its GDP in 1985 was close to that of France, which has the fourth largest economy.

Living standards

Living standards are better measured by GDP per head. These are shown in Table 18.4.

Table 18.4 *GDP, 1985, £ per head**

Country	GDP per head
US	9400
Canada	8500
Norway	8000
Luxembourg	7800
Sweden	7200
Denmark	7000
West Germany	6900
Japan	6600
Finland	6500
France	6500
Netherlands	6500
UK	6200
Belgium	6100
Austria	6000
Italy	5400
Spain	4400
Ireland	4000
Greece	3400
Portugal	3000

*Converted to sterling using PPPs.
Source: OECD Eurostat

On this measure, living standards are highest in the USA and Canada. Japanese living standards are about 30 per cent below those in the US, and over 20 per cent below Canadian living standards.

The UKs in a group of 'middle-income' European countries and has a GDP per head roughly the same as that in France, Belgium and the Netherlands. This group of countries are some way behind the Scandinavian countries and West Germany, but ahead of the southern European countries. Figure 18.3 shows the UK's GDP per head in sterling relative to that of a range of other countries, based on PPPs and market exchange rates.

Figure 18.3 *GDP per head, main industrialised countries, 1985*

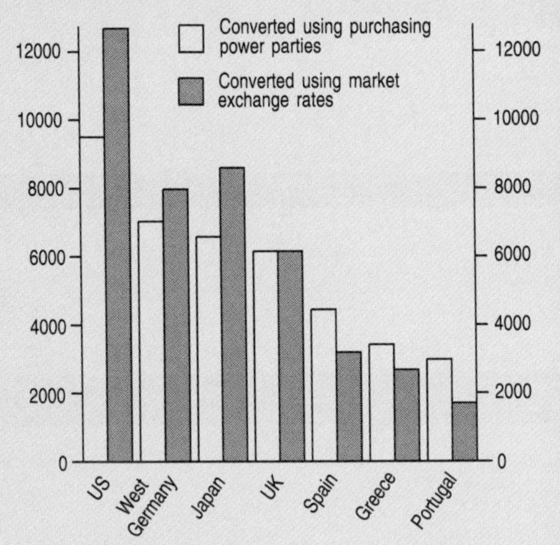

Source: OECD Eurostat

Some of these countries have higher relative prices than the UK, some have lower. Figure 18.3 gives some indication of the misleading impression that using market exchange rates can give.

(Box extract from *Economic Progress Report*, March–April 1987.)

REVIEW QUESTIONS

1 When will GNP > GDP?

2 Can personal disposable income ever be greater than GNP?

3 You are given the following information about a particular economy.

Year	*Nominal income (£m)*	*Index of prices*
1	100,000	100
2	120,000	110

What has happened to real income over the period shown?

4 Which of the following are transfer payments?

(a) A soldier's pay while serving abroad?
(b) A gambler's winnings?
(c) A student's grant?
(d) A son's earnings while employed in his father's business?

5 The following data refer to the UK economy in 1984 (all figures are in £m):

Income from employment	180342
Depreciation	38371
Total domestic expenditure at market prices	391470
Rent	18937
Net property income from abroad	3304
Exports	91736
Imports	91852
Taxes on expenditure	52578
Subsidies	7797

(a) What is meant by the term 'total domestic expenditure at market prices'?
(b) What is the value of (i) GDP at market prices; (ii) GNP at market prices; (iii) NNP at factor cost?

6 Why are leisure time and externalities important in estimating the standard of living?

7 Apart from estimates of *per capita* income, how else might we compare the standard of living of people in different countries?

CHAPTER 19

THE DETERMINATION OF NATIONAL INCOME

CONNECTIONS

In Chapter 19 you will be studying the **macro-economic process of income determination**. We will be referring extensively to national income and the circular flow of income which we discussed in Chapter 18 and to investment which we shall discuss in Chapter 21.

Key Concepts

Consumption function
Planned and realised investment
Planned and realised saving
Propensity to consume
The equilibrium level of income
The multiplier

The Model of Income Determination

The model of income determination explained in this chapter follows the analysis in a very influential model put forward in the 1930s by the English economist John Maynard Keynes. Keynes suggested that the main factor behind short-term fluctuations in national income was changes in the **total amount that people and businesses want to spend on goods and services in the economy as a whole**. Total planned spending is referred to as *aggregate demand*. In this chapter we analyse the predicted effects on economic activity of changes in aggregate demand in terms of a simple 'two-sector' model* consisting of households and businesses.

The two underlying conditions are:

- All prices and wages are **constant at a given level of national income**.
- At these prices and wage levels, there are **unemployed people seeking work** and **businesses with spare capacity which it would be profitable to use.**

These conditions (which in many respects were appropriate to those existing in the 1930s) mean that any change in the money value of national income will imply an equivalent change in real income and employment. Also, since increases in output and employment will be forthcoming, we do not need to consider the 'supply side' of the economy. In other words, in this model changes in national income are caused by changes in aggregate demand. (In Chapter 22 we relax these two conditions and develop our analysis correspondingly.)

The Determination of Aggregate Demand

Having established the basic condition of our model we now turn to the determination of aggregate demand. In a two-sector model aggregate demand consists of two elements which we shall now consider in turn:

* In Chapter 20 the analysis is extended to 'three-sector' and 'four-sector' models.

1 Consumption Expenditure by Households

'Consumption' means spending on consumer goods like food, clothes, household electrical equipment and so on. In the UK consumption spending by households is the main component of aggregate demand, accounting for over 60 per cent of the total. There are a number of factors which are likely to affect consumption and we examine these later on p. 78. However, one key factor is the level of households' *personal disposable income*. By 'disposable income' we mean the income households receive from employment, *plus* transfer payments from government *minus* taxes paid to the government. Since our two-sector model does not contain a government sector, all income is disposable income and this must either be **spent** or **saved**. For simplicity we shall assume that the relationship between planned consumption and income is given by the equation or *consumption function*:

$$C = 50 + 0.75Y$$

where C is planned household consumption and Y is the level of income. (We assume that all variables in this chapter and Chapter 20 are in £m.) This equation tells us that:

- Households have a basic or *autonomous* level of planned consumption expenditure of 50, which does not vary with income and will be undertaken whatever the level of income (if necessary by dissaving – that is, using past accumulations of saving).
- If their income increases, households will plan additional *induced* consumption equal to three-quarters of *any increase* in income: we say that households have a *marginal propensity to consume* (*MPC*) of 0.75.

In symbols we can write:

$$MPC = \frac{\Delta C}{\Delta Y}$$

where ΔC is a change in consumption
and ΔY is a change in the level of income.

Take care not to confuse the marginal propensity to consume with the *average propensity to consume* (*APC*). The *APC* is simply total consumption divided by total income – that is,

$\frac{C}{Y}$ where C is total income and Y is total consumption.

The corollary of the marginal propensity to consume is the *marginal propensity to save* (*MPS*). Since income must either be spent or saved, it follows that if the *MPC* is 0.75, the *MPS* must be 0.25. Similarly the total amount saved divided by the total level of income is the average propensity to save, or *APS*.

In symbols we can write:

$$MPS = \frac{\Delta S}{\Delta Y} \text{ and } APS = \frac{S}{Y}$$

where ΔS is a change in savings
and ΔY is a change in the level of income.

We use the term 'planned consumption' (and planned saving) because we do not know at this stage what the *actual* or *realised* level of consumption expenditure (or saving) will be.

2 Investment Expenditure by Businesses

'Investment' means spending on producer goods such as machinery and additions to stock. In the UK, this constitutes about one-quarter of aggregate demand. The level of business investment depends on a number of factors (see p. 190). One of these is how fast the demand for output is likely to increase in the future. The connection between business investment and the current *level* of income and expenditure is, however, quite weak and for simplicity we assume that investment is entirely *autonomous* – that is, it is determined *independently* of income. In other words, we assume that investment is constant at all levels of income. Our investment equation is taken to be:

$$I = 100$$

that is, businesses are planning to invest £100m.

Since in our two-sector model aggregate demand consists of consumption spending by households plus investment spending by businesses, we can now combine the two equations above to obtain a function for aggregate demand. Thus:

$$\begin{aligned}\text{Aggregate demand } (AD) &= C + I \\ &= 50 + 0.75Y + 100 \\ &= 0.75Y + 150\end{aligned}$$

Our aggregate demand function, together with its consumption and investment components can be presented in tabular form, as in Table 19.1.

Table 19.1 *Aggregate demand in a two-sector economy*

National income (£m)	Consumption (£m)	Investment (£m)	Aggregate demand (£m)
100	125	100	225
200	200	100	300
300	275	100	375
400	350	100	450
500	425	100	525
600	500	100	600
700	575	100	675
800	650	100	750
500	725	100	825
1000	800	100	900
1100	875	100	975

In graphical terms, our three functions become as in Figure 19.1.

Figure 19.1 *Consumption, investment and aggregate demand*

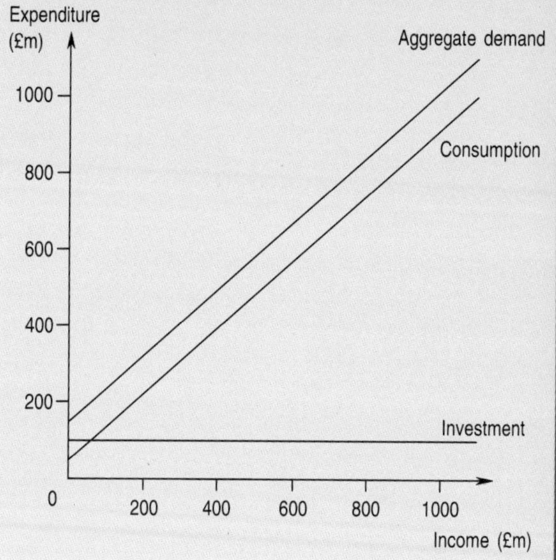

The Equilibrium Level of National Income

Equilibrium is a state of balance where there is **no net tendency to change**. National income will therefore be in equilibrium when there is no tendency for it to rise or fall. Consider Table 19.2.

Column 1 gives different possible levels of national income, while columns 2, 3 and 4 calculate, in terms of our equations, consumption, investment and aggregate demand for different values of national income. Column 6, which shows unplanned changes in business stocks, is important in helping us to understand the concept of national income equilibrium. Suppose planned and realised national income is, say, £400m. This means that businesses are paying out £400m of income to the factors of production. However, when income is £400m, column 4 shows that expenditure is £450m. Hence businesses will be experiencing an *unplanned fall*

Table 19.2 *The equilibrium level of national income*

National income (£m) (1)	Consumption (£m) (2)	Investment (£m) (3)	Aggregate demand (£m) (4)	Aggregate demand minus NI (£m) (5)	Unplanned change in stocks (£m) (6)	Tendency of change in NI (£m) (7)
100	125	100	225	125	−125	increase
200	200	100	300	100	−100	increase
300	275	100	375	75	−75	increase
400	350	100	450	50	−50	increase
500	425	100	525	25	−25	increase
600	500	100	600	0	0	no change
700	575	100	675	−25	25	decrease
800	650	100	750	−50	50	decrease
500	725	100	825	−75	75	decrease
1000	800	100	900	−100	100	decrease
1100	875	100	975	−125	125	decrease

in their stocks of £50m. Their likely response in this situation is to raise output, which in turn will generate more income for factors of production. £400m is thus *not* an equilibrium level of income.

Equally we can test £700m as a possible equilibrium level of income. Table 19.2 shows that while businesses are paying out £700m to the factors of production, they are getting back as expenditure on their output only £675m. Hence they will be experiencing an *unplanned increase* in stocks and will respond by reducing output. £700m is not therefore an equilibrium level of income.

In this example, the equilibrium level of income is £600m. At this level of income, planned expenditure by households and businesses (£500m + £100m) is also £600m. In other words, firms are selling an amount which exactly equals the amount they plan to sell. £600m is therefore the equilibrium level of output.

The equilibrium level of income can easily be calculated using simple algebra. We know that:

$AD = Y$ in equilibrium

But

$AD = C + I$

Therefore, in equilibrium $C + I = Y$

Hence $50 + 0.75Y + 100 = Y$

$0.75Y + 150 = Y$

$Y = 600$

The equilibrium level of national income is £600m.

Figure 19.2 *The equilibrium level of income in a two-sector economy*

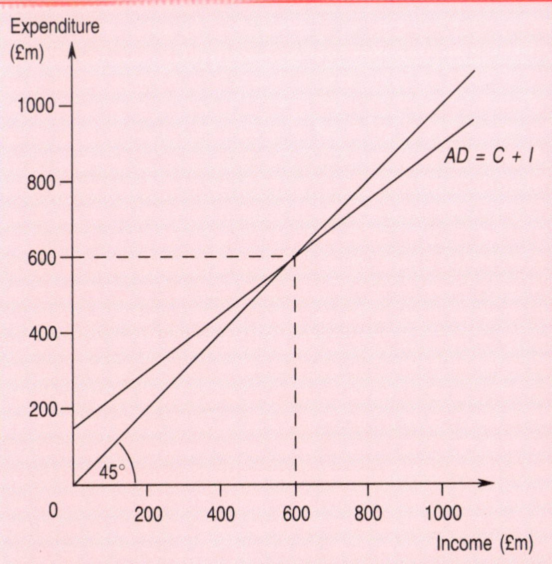

A Graphical Presentation of National Income Equilibrium

In Figure 19.2 planned expenditure by households and businesses ($C + I$) is represented by the line AD. Note that both axes in the diagram have the same scale and therefore the 45° line will show equal values of expenditure and income. Equilibrium occurs where aggregate demand cuts the 45° line because planned expenditure exactly equals planned output at that point.

An Alternative View of National Income Equilibrium

In the example above the equilibrium level of income was £600m. Another way to arrive at this outcome would be by examining the relationship between *planned saving* and *planned investment*. Savings are defined as any part of income received by households which is not spent on consumption. (For simplicity we omit business savings in the form of retained profits.) In other words, savings are not used to purchase other goods and services, they represent a *withdrawal* or a *leakage* of potential spending from the circular flow of income. Investment spending by businesses, on the other hand, does not arise from the spending of households. It is therefore an *injection* of expenditure into the circular flow of income. In our model the economy can be in equilibrium only when *planned investment injections equal planned savings leakages*. This must be so because:

- If planned investment injections into the circular flow of income *exceed* planned savings leakages from it, planned expenditure will exceed planned output. As a result, businesses will experience *unplanned reductions* in stocks and will expand output. National income will therefore **increase**.
- If planned investment injections are less than planned savings leakages, planned expenditure will be less than planned output. Businesses will experience *unplanned increases* in stocks and will reduce output. National income will **fall**.

Hence national income can be in equilibrium only when **planned investment** (injections) **exactly equals planned savings** (leakages). Table 19.3 and Figure 19.3 present the outcome in terms of the data in our model.

Table 19.3 *Planned investment exactly equals planned savings*

National income (£m)	Saving (£m)	Investment (£m)	Saving minus investment (£m)	Unplanned change in stocks (£m)	Tendency of change in NI (£m)
100	−25	100	−125	125	increase
200	0	100	−100	100	increase
300	25	100	−75	75	increase
400	50	100	−50	50	increase
500	75	100	−25	25	increase
600	100	100	0	0	no change
700	125	100	25	−25	decrease
800	150	100	50	−50	decrease
500	175	100	75	−75	decrease
1000	200	100	100	−100	decrease
1100	225	100	125	−125	decrease

Figure 19.3 *Savings, investment and equilibrium*

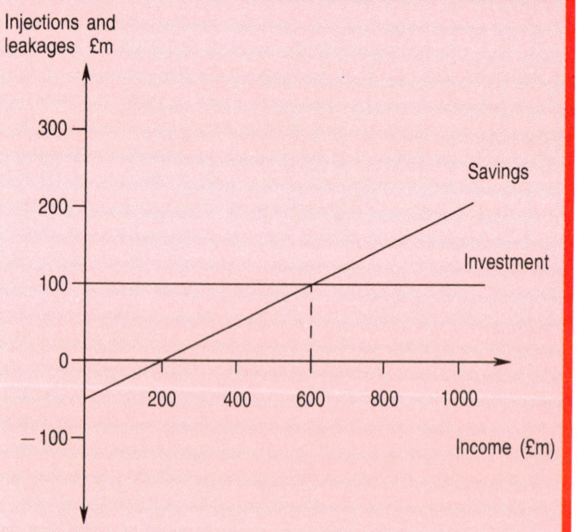

A Change in Aggregate Demand: the Multiplier Effect

Suppose businesses increase their planned investment spending from 100 to, say, 200. Aggregate demand will therefore be £100m higher. How will this affect the level of income? The increase in expenditure will initially cause an unplanned reduction in stocks. Firms will respond to this by increasing output and therefore factor incomes will rise. But how much will incomes rise? Initially an increase in aggregate demand of £100m will generate an extra £100m of income. However, the final change in income will be much greater than this. To see why, let us suppose the extra investment was for plant and equipment. Incomes of factors of production in businesses making these will rise by £100m. But some of this extra income *will be spent* on goods and services, generating a further increase in income, part of which will also be spent on goods and services and so on. In terms of the data in our model, where the *MPC* is 0.75, income will change in the following way:

ΔI = £100m
ΔY =
£100m + £75m + £56.25m + £42.1875m . . . + . . . = £400m

Mathematically, the figures above constitute a 'series' which would in the end sum to a total of £400m. The initial increase of £100m in aggregate demand has therefore generated a total increase in incomes of £400m. The increase in income is therefore four times greater than the initial increase in aggregate demand. The cumulative process which brought this about is known as *the multiplier effect.* The 'multiplication factor' of four is called the *multiplier coefficient* or *k*.

The Multiplier and Saving

In the multiplier sequence above, for each increase in **income** there was a corresponding increase in **consumption**. However, since increases in income were not fully passed on, there must also have been increases in **savings**. This provides us with a different way of examining the multiplier sequence.

ΔI = £100m
ΔY = £100m + 75m + £56.25m + . . . + . . . = £400m
ΔS = £25m + £18.75m + . . . + . . . = £100m

We saw above that national income will be in equilibrium when planned investment equals planned savings. In this example business investment rose by £100m and this caused national income to rise until households were persuaded to increase their savings by £100m. In other words, income goes on rising until planned leakages (savings) are brought into equality with planned injections (investment). At the higher level of aggregate demand, the new equilibrium level of national income is £400m higher, at £1000m.

The Multiplier Coefficient

In the multiplier process examined above, the initial increase in *AD* was £100m and the resulting increase in *Y* was £400m. Hence the multiplier coefficient was 4.0.

The value of the multiplier coefficient (*k*) can be obtained by using a simple formula:

$$k = \frac{1}{1-MPC}$$

In the example above the *MPC* was 0.75, therefore

$$k = \frac{1}{1-MPC} = \frac{1}{1-0.75} = \frac{1}{0.25} = 4.0$$

The higher the *MPC*, the greater the *proportion* of extra income which is spent on consumption, and therefore the greater the multiplier effect. This is illustrated in Table 19.4

Table 19.4 *MPC, proportion of extra income spent on consumption, and the multiplier effect*

Marginal propensity to consume (*MPC*)	Multiplier coefficient ($k = 1/1-MPC$)
0	1.00
0.1	1.11
0.2	1.25
0.3	1.43
0.4	1.67
0.5	2.00
0.6	2.50
0.7	3.33
0.8	5.00
0.9	10.00
1.0	infinity

You should use your calculator to 'test' the values of *k* in Table 19.4 by constructing multiplier-process 'sequences' for different values of *MPC*, in terms of an increase in initial aggregate demand of £100m.

A Change in Aggregate Demand – Tabular and Graphical Representations

We saw above that an increase in aggregate demand will induce a process of income generation via the multiplier effect. The outcome can also be presented in tabular and diagrammatic forms, see Table 19.5 and Figure 19.4.

Figure 19.4 *An increase in aggregate demand*

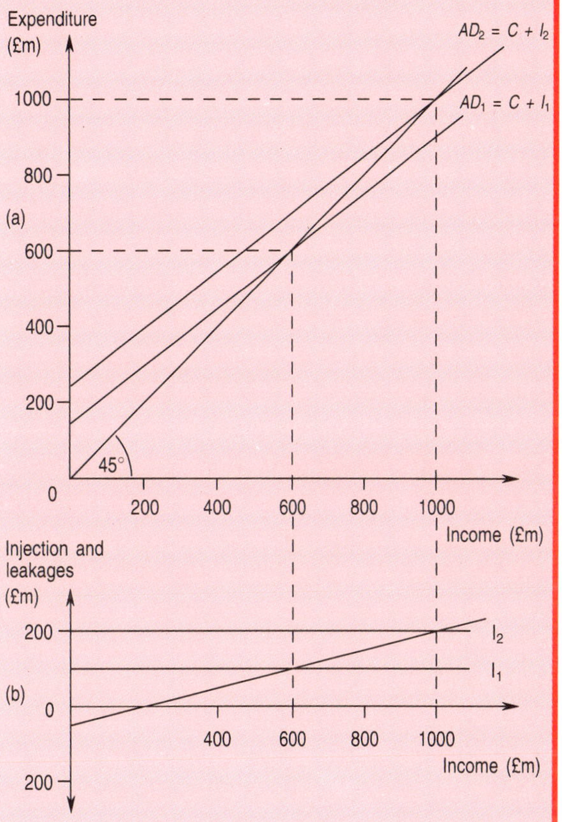

The effect of the £100m increase in aggregate demand is the same in either presentation, national income increases via the multiplier, from £600m to £1000m.

The 'Backward Multiplier'

In our next example we examine the effect on national income of a fall in aggregate demand initiated by a *decrease* in planned investment from £100m to £50m.

Table 19.6 (on p. 177) shows that the reduction of £50m in aggregate demand leads to an *unplanned increase* in business stocks at the original equilibrium income level of £600m (p. 172) and the establishment of a new level of income of £400m. Thus the effect has been a fall in income of £200m. The value of the multiplier coefficient *k* is therefore

Table 19.5(a) *Planned investment, unplanned investment and the equilibrium level of income*

National income (£m)	Consumption (£m)	Planned investment (£m)	Aggregate demand (£m)	Aggregate demand minus NI (£m)	Unplanned change in stocks (£m)	Tendency of change in NI (£m)
100	125	200	325	225	−225	increase
200	200	200	400	200	−200	increase
300	275	200	475	175	−175	increase
400	350	200	550	150	−150	increase
500	425	200	625	125	−125	increase
600	500	200	700	100	−100	increase
700	575	200	775	75	−75	increase
800	650	200	850	50	−50	increase
500	725	200	925	25	−25	increase
1000	800	200	1000	0	0	no change
1100	875	200	1075	−25	25	decrease

Table 19.5(b) *Planned savings, unplanned investment and the equilibrium level of income*

National Income (£m)	Planned Saving (£m)	Investment (£m)	Saving minus investment (£m)	Unplanned change in stocks (£m)	Tendency of change in NI (£m)
100	725	200	−225	225	increase
200	0	200	−200	200	increase
300	25	200	−175	175	increase
400	50	200	−150	150	increase
500	75	200	−125	125	increase
600	100	200	−100	100	increase
700	125	200	−75	75	increase
800	150	200	−50	50	increase
500	175	200	−25	25	increase
1000	200	200	0	0	no change
1100	225	200	25	−25	increase

$$\frac{-200}{-50} = 4.0$$

The fall in income generated by the multiplier also has the effect of inducing households to undertake the reduction of £50m in planned savings required to match the initial fall in planned investment. The fall in equilibrium resulting from reduced aggregate demand income can also be shown graphically (see Figure 19.5).

The Equality of Investment and Saving

National Income (Y) is either consumed (C) or saved (S); and National Expenditure (Y) consists of consumption spending (C) plus investment spending (I). Thus

$$Y = C + S$$
$$Y = C + I$$

therefore $S = I$.

Figure 19.5 *The effect of a reduction in aggregate demand*

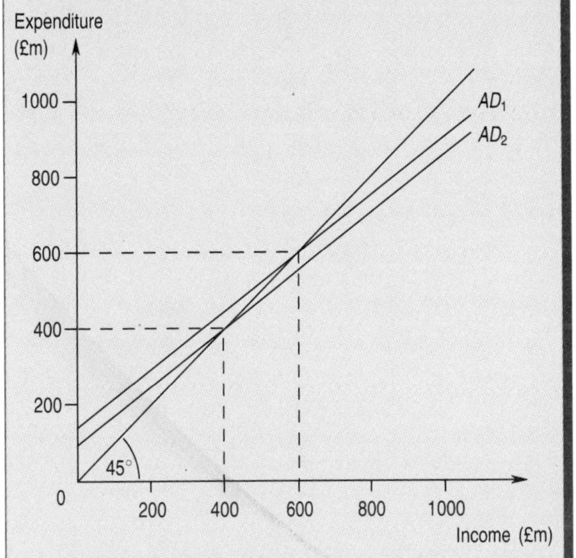

This implies that in our two-sector economy **savings always equals investment**. But why should savings always equal investment? After all savings and investment are undertaken for very different motives and by very different agents (businesses and households). In fact, the identity S = I refers to *realised saving* and *realised investment*. It does not imply that *planned savings* and *planned investment* are always equal.

Consider Figure 19.6. Here planned saving decreases initially by £50m at all levels of income. Since there is no corresponding reduction in planned investment, businesses will experience an *unplanned* fall in their stocks (lower planned household savings mean increased consumption). This reduction in stocks will represent *unplanned disinvestment* of £50m by businesses. In other words *realised* saving and realised investment will be equal even though planned saving and planned investment are not equal. Businesses react to unanticipated expenditures by households by expanding output. However, planned investment will exceed planned savings until equilibrium is restored when national income has risen to £800m.

Figure 19.6 *A reduction in planned savings*

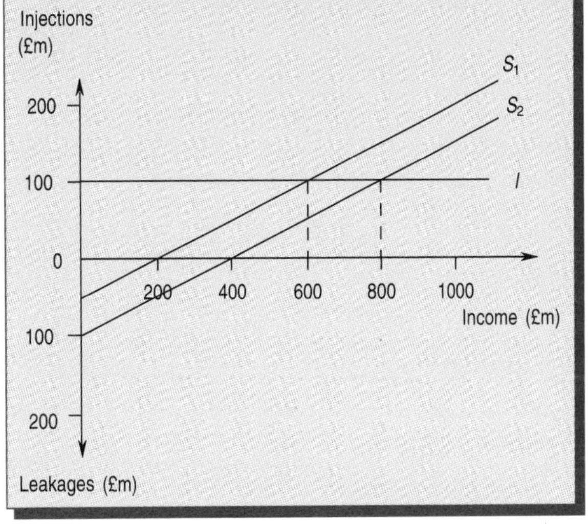

Table 19.6 *A reduction in aggregate demand*

National income (£m)	Consumption (£m)	Investment (£m)	Aggregate demand (£m)	Aggregate demand minus NI (£m)	Unplanned change in stocks (£m)	Tendency of change in NI (£m)
100	125	50	175	75	−75	increase
200	200	50	250	50	−50	increase
300	275	50	325	25	−25	increase
400	350	50	400	0	0	no change
500	425	50	475	−25	25	decrease
600	500	50	550	−50	50	decrease
700	575	50	625	−75	75	decrease
800	650	50	700	−100	100	decrease
500	725	50	775	−125	125	decrease
1000	800	50	850	−150	150	decrease
1100	875	50	925	−175	175	decrease

The Keynesian Consumption Function and Real World Data: A Look at the Evidence

The Keynesian consumption function is based on the assumption that **changes in consumption are determined by changes in income**. However, empirical data does not 'fit' the Keynesian consumption function at all well. Consider the UK data in Table 19.7.

The data suggests that the relationship between consumption and income is not as straightforward as the Keynesian analysis implies. This has led economists to formulate alternative versions of the consumption function.

Modern Theories of the Consumption Function

Although the Keynesian consumption function has an appealing logic economists were questioning its validity before the end of the 1940s. Here we examine three alternative versions of the consumption function.

The Duesenberry Relative-income Hypothesis

National income data published by the American economist Kuznetz in 1939 showed that, contrary to the Keynesian view, the *APC* (*C*/*Y*; see p. 171) over a period of 60 years in the United States *had remained constant* – even though real income per head had risen greatly over that period. Yet the same data did show that high income families consume a lower proportion of income than poor families – which would imply a Keynesian-type *falling APC* as United States income levels rose over time. This apparent inconsistency led the American economist Duesenberry to postulate his *relative-income hypothesis*. In summary, this suggests that if one individual's income rises, his *APC* will indeed tend to fall. But if everybody's income rises, each individual will be under pressure to consume more to 'keep up with the Jones's' – so the *APC* of the community *as a whole* will, over time, tend to remain constant, as in Kuznetz's data.

On the Duesenberry view, a less equal distribution of income, such as occurred in the UK in the 1980s, ought to lead to more 'emulatory consumption' and a higher *APC*. This view seems to fit the UK experience. Keynes took the opposite view: since the rich have a lower propensity to consume than the poor, a transfer of income from poor to rich should reduce the community's *APC*.

The Friedman Permanent-income Hypothesis

This hypothesis assumes that what households desire is a stable consumption pattern over time. However, household incomes often fluctuate. What people tend to do therefore is base their *present*

Table 19.7 *Disposable income, consumption and savings, 1983–90*

Year	Total personal disposable income (£m)	Consumers' expenditure (£m)	Consumption ratio (%)	Personal saving (£m)	Savings ratio (%)
1983	206,130	185,895	90.2	20,235	9.6
1984	221,446	198,895	89.8	22,551	10.2
1985	239,781	217,023	90.5	22,758	9.5
1986	260,133	238,922	91.8	21,206	8.2
1987	279,333	263,421	94.3	15,912	5.7
1988	315,983	298,796	94.6	17,187	5.4
1989	351,438	326,489	92.9	24,949	7.1
1990	384,814	349,421	91.8	35,393	9.2

Source: CSO

consumption on their *expected average long-term income* – what Friedman calls their *permanent income*. Suppose an individual receives an unexpected salary bonus from his employer. As this is temporary or 'transitory' income it will make little difference to his permanent income. So he will tend to save most of it for use at another time when his income turns out to be unusually low. Positive transitory income will tend to lead to saving and negative transitory income to dissaving, so the change in consumption, that is the *MPC*, will be quite low.

If our individual has reason to believe the bonus will be regularly repeated it becomes part of his permanent income and therefore available for consumption. The *MPC* and the associated multiplier will then be greater than they were in the case of transitory income.

We should note that the permanent income hypothesis leaves room for an expectations effect. If households come to believe that their income over a period of future years will be greater than they previously anticipated, increased permanent income should lead to a higher propensity to consume. It may be that the observed rise in UK household consumption ratios during the long boom of the middle and late 1980s owed something to this effect.

The Life-Cycle Hypothesis

Developed by Modigliani and Ando, this theory of the consumption function is similar to the permanent income hypothesis. The main distinction is that households are assumed to estimate their likely permanent income over their whole life time and this is then associated with a 'life-cycle' pattern of consumption.

In essence, permanent income represents a household's average expected lifetime income stream – that is, what it could afford to consume at a steady rate over a household's lifetime. Actual income is likely to rise until near retirement, then fall to pension level. A household will therefore tend to dissave in its early and final years and save in its middle years (when, for example, children grow up and leave home). The life-cycle hypothesis implies that the net savings of the community as a whole will be related to its growth of income. When this is high, 'this' generation's middle-aged households will save more than the 'last' generation's: the *APC* will be correspondingly lower.

The Consumption Function (Continued): Determinants of Autonomous Consumption

In the section above we examined income related factors which might affect the level of planned consumption. In this section we study autonomous factors, that is, all determinants *except* income. Whereas changes in income generally move households *along* the consumption function, changes in autonomous factors *shift* the consumption function itself.

Consumer credit. This mainly affects consumer expenditure on consumer durables like washing machines, furniture and cars. One factor is the *quantity* of credit on offer from financial intermediaries such as banks, finance houses, building societies and so on. The greater this is, the more likely households are to overspend on their disposable income and increase their consumption level. The other factor is the *cost* of credit – the rate of interest: the lower this is, the more households can borrow, given the need to meet future interest payments and loan repayments. A lower rate of interest might also discourage households from saving. Evidence suggests that the rate of interest has quite a weak effect on consumption (see, for example, Paul Turner, *Economic Review*, November 1987).

Price expectations. When households expect a higher rate of inflation this might encourage the purchase of consumer durable goods sooner rather than later when they become more expensive. If this happens, autonomous consumption will increase. However, we cannot be certain that this will happen. In the UK, for example, during the relatively high inflation of the early 1970s the proportion of income spent on consumption fell, while during the relatively low inflation of the early and middle 1980s the proportion of income spent on consumption increased. It is therefore possible that the expectation of higher inflation might lead households to *save more* (that is, consume less) because it causes uncertainty about future real income and difficulties for household management. Conversely a low inflation rate which facilitates household management could reduce 'precautionary' saving and boost consumption.

Household Wealth

In the late 1980s the level of household wealth in the UK rose substantially (Table 19.8).

Table 19.8 *Household wealth, 1984–8 (personal sector balance sheet, year-end, £bn)*

Category	1984	1985	1986	1987	1988
Dwellings	461.4	527.3	620.6	738.7	964.3
Financial assets	554.0	628.1	744.0	830.0	920.7
Financial liabilities	174.1	204.8	240.0	283.4	340.0
Net wealth	841.3	950.6	1124.5	1285.3	1545.0

Source: CSO

We can see that there was an increase in the value of financial assets such as shares in joint stock companies and in the value of dwellings, due to the rise in property values. How will an increase in household wealth affect consumption? In terms of the permanent income and life-cycle models, more wealth means that households can spend more over a period of time, meeting any shortfall in income by using some of their extra wealth. For example, they might sell shares which they possess, or they might remortgage any property they own. In effect, their permanent income will be increased and there will be a corresponding increase in consumption.

Determinants of the Propensity to Save

In the final sections of this chapter we have been examining factors which might affect the rate of planned consumption for a given level of income. It is sometimes appropriate to shift the focus of analysis from consumption towards the *savings* function of households. Since household income is either consumed or saved, it is clear that any factor leading to an increase in induced or autonomous consumption will bring about a corresponding fall in autonomous saving. Conversely, a lower level of consumption will imply a higher level of saving. Hence it is in principle possible to re-examine the determinants of consumption described in the sections above and 'recast' them in terms of their effect on planned household saving.

We recommend that, as an aid to understanding, you do this as an exercise, presenting the outcome in the form of a summary sheet. A refinement which you will wish to include is that aggregate saving includes business savings in the form of retained profits.

REVIEW QUESTIONS

1 A hypothetical two-sector economy is initially in equilibrium, with $MPS = APS = 0.25Y$ and investment is £100m. Subsequently MPS falls to $0.2Y$.

(a) Construct a graph to show the original equilibrium level of income and the new equilibrium level of income after the fall in MPS.

(b) Why is there no change in investment in response to the decline in planned saving?

2 In a hypothetical economy which is initially in equilibrium, the consumption function is:

$$C = 100 + 0.8Y$$

where C denotes consumption and Y income. The level of investment is 100. Why is 600 not an equilibrium level of income? What is the actual equilibrium level of income?

3 The data below relate to a hypothetical economy for which column '*n*' shows the values of the variables when a state of equilibrium has been attained

	Weeks 1	2	3	4	'*n*'
Income (=output)	200	180	164	151.2	100
Exante investment	20	20	20	20	20
Exante savings	40	36	32.8	30.2	20
Consumption goods produced	180	160	144	131.2	80
Consumption goods demanded	160	144	131.2	130	80
Exante savings minus *exante* investment	20	16	12.8	10.2	0

(a) Calculate the MPC and MPS.

(b) Explain the process of ajustment which is taking place.

(c) What conditions are necessary for equilibrium to be attained?

CHAPTER 20

NATIONAL INCOME DETERMINATION: THE FOUR-SECTOR ECONOMY

CONNECTIONS

In Chapter 20 we extend our analysis of income determination developed in Chapter 19 to incorporate a government sector (the three-sector economy) and an international sector (the four-sector economy). It is important that you have a thorough understanding of the material covered in Chapter 18 and especially Chapter 19 before you embark on this chapter.

Key Concepts

Balanced budget multiplier
Four-sector economy
Marginal propensity to import
Marginal rate of taxation
Three-sector economy

In Chapter 19 we examined the process of income determination in a two-sector model containing only households and businesses. We saw that the condition for equilibrium level income could be stated in terms of two alternative propositions:

- The expenditure-income approach

Aggregate demand = national income. When these are equal, planned expenditure by businesses and households is just sufficient to purchase the planned output of businesses and there is therefore no tendency for national income and output to change.

- The injections-leakages approach

Planned investment (injections) **by businesses equals planned savings** (leakages) **by households**. When these are equal there will be no tendency for national income and output to change.

Income Determination in a Three-sector Model: the Government Sector and Aggregate Demand

In this chapter we shall eventually be examining the determination of national income in terms of a four-sector model containing households, businesses, a government sector and a foreign trade sector. We begin however by applying our two equilibrium approaches to a three-sector economy consisting of households, businesses and a government sector. This model is known as a *closed economy*. In a two-sector model aggregate demand consists of two elements: consumption expenditure and investment expenditure. In a three-sector model, aggregate demand (*AD*) consists of three elements: consumption expenditure (*C*), investment expenditure (*I*) and *government expenditure (G)*. That is:

$$AD = C + I + G$$

In the UK the government is a large source of expenditure. However, not all government expenditure contributes *directly* to aggregate demand. About one-third consists of *transfer payments* such as social security payments, family income supplements and so on, which are simply transfers of income *within* the community. The remainder of government expenditure takes the form of direct payments to factors of production for services rendered. It therefore represents expenditure on real output and is therefore a component of aggregate demand. In Chapter 19 we saw that households' consumption is assumed to be mainly dependent on the level of income, whereas business investment is assumed to be independent of income. Which do you think government spending is? Since it mainly reflects perceived requirements for schools, housing, defence, and so on, there is no automatic reason why government expenditure should vary with the level of national income. In other words, government expenditure is normally assumed to be autonomous – that is, unrelated to the level of income.

The Equilibrium Level of National Income in a Three-sector Model

We know that the equilibrium level of national income occurs when *planned expenditure equals planned output*. In terms of simple algebra we can write:

$$AD = C + I + G$$

but

$$AD = Y \text{ in equilibrium}$$

therefore

$$C + I + G = Y \text{ in equilibrium}$$

Using the notation followed in Chapter 19, let us assume the following data:

$$C = 50 + 0.75Yd$$
$$I = 100$$
$$G = 40$$

You will notice that we have introduced a new term, *Yd*, which means households' *disposable* income. As we saw on p. 163, disposable income excludes taxation paid to the government. In the income-determination model in this chapter we shall assume that households pay taxes equal to 20 per cent of their gross income. Disposable income will thus be 80 per cent of national income. Again in simple algebra we can write:

$$\begin{aligned} Yd &= Y - \text{T} \\ &= Y - 0.2Y \\ &= 0.8Y \end{aligned}$$

Our consumption function can now be restated in the following way:

$$\begin{aligned} C &= 50 + 0.75\,Yd \\ &= 50 + 0.75\,(Y - 0.2Y) \\ &= 50 + 0.75\,(0.8Y) \\ &= 50 + 0.6Y \end{aligned}$$

The equilibrium level of income is now easily calculated:

$$C + I + G = Y \text{ in equilibrium}$$

Thus

$$50 + 0.6Y + 100 + 40 = Y$$
$$190 + 0.6Y = Y$$
$$190 = 0.4Y$$
$$Y = 475$$

The equilibrium level of income is 475

A Change in Government Expenditure

Let us assume that government expenditure now increases from £40m to, say, £90m. Aggregate demand is now £50m higher and national income will increase to a new and higher equilibrium.

$$C = 50 + 0.6Y$$
$$I = 100$$
$$G = 90$$

Hence

$$50 + 0.6Y + 100 + 90 = Y \text{ in equilibrium}$$
$$240 + 0.6Y = Y$$
$$240 = 0.4Y$$
$$Y = 600$$

The new equilibrium level of income is 600

Figure 20.1 illustrates in graphical terms the effect on national income of the increase in government expenditure.

Figure 20.1 *An increase in aggregate demand in the three-sector model*

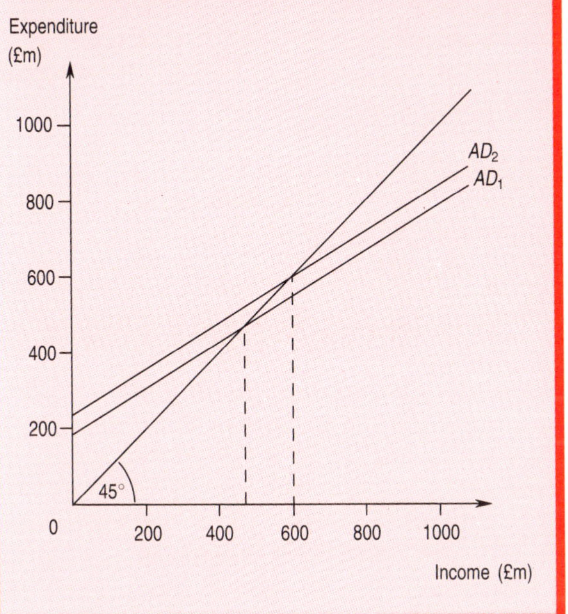

The Three-sector Multiplier

In this example an increase of £50m in government expenditure results in an increase of £125m in national income. Hence there was a government expenditure initiated multiplier effect of:

$$k = \frac{\Delta Y}{\Delta AD} = \frac{125}{50} = 2.5$$

How does this result fit our general formula,

$$k = \frac{1}{1 - MPC} ?$$

In our example we know that $C = 50 + 0.6Y$, hence the marginal propensity to consume out of national income is 0.6. Thus the value of the multiplier becomes:

$$k = \frac{1}{1 - MPC} = \frac{1}{1 - 0.6} = \frac{1}{0.4} = 2.5$$

We can see that this general formula for the multiplier still holds for a three-sector model. Note, however, that the relevant *MPC* is not the propensity to consume out of *disposable* income (0.75 in this example), but the propensity to consume out of *national* income ($0.75 \times 0.8 = 0.6$).

The Three-sector Model: the Injections and Leakages Approach to Income Determination

The second way of looking at national income equilibrium is in terms of the equality of *injections and leakages* with respect to the circular flow of income. In a two-sector model injections take the form of business investment and leakages take the form of household saving. In a three-sector model the position is a little more complicated. We have already identified *government expenditure* as an autonomous element of aggregate demand. As such, it represents an injection into the circular flow of income. Hence for a three-sector model:

Total injections into circular flow of income $= I + G$

A leakage is a **withdrawal of potential spending** from the circular flow of income. In our two-sector model, savings were the only leakage. In a three-sector model there is a second form of leakage, namely *government taxation (T)*. There are two types of taxation, direct and indirect. Both are leakages from the circular flow of income. *Direct taxes*, such as income tax and corporation tax, reduce the potential spending of households and businesses, since part of the value of output is withdrawn from the factors of production. *Indirect taxes*, such as VAT, reduce the receipts of businesses in relation to total planned expenditure and therefore deprive factors of production of part of total spending. The total tax leakage from the circular flow of income is therefore the amount paid in direct taxes *plus* the amount paid in indirect taxes. For simplicity, we shall assume that only direct taxes are levied.

Using the values for *I*, *G*, *S* and *T* given on p. 182, let us calculate the equilibrium level of national income by equating planned leakages and planned injections:

$$I + G = S + T$$
$$100 + 40 = -50 + 0.25Yd + 0.2Y$$
$$140 = -50 + 0.8\,(0.25Yd) + 0.2Y$$
$$140 = -50 + 0.2Y + 0.2Y$$
$$140 = -50 + 0.4Y$$
$$190 = 0.4Y$$

The equilibrium level of national income is 475

We saw earlier that if government expenditure increases from £40m to £90m, the new equilibrium level of national income can easily be determined as £600m. Since income would have risen by £125m (from £475), the multiplier is:

$$\frac{\Delta Y}{\Delta AD} = \frac{125}{50} = 2.5$$

You can check this through the general formula:

$$k = \frac{1}{1-MPC} = \frac{1}{1-0.6} = \frac{1}{0.4} = 2.5$$

Alternatively, we can recast the general formula into a new form:

$$k = \frac{1}{MRL} = \frac{1}{0.2 + 0.2} = \frac{1}{0.4} = 2.5$$

where *MRL* is the marginal rate of leakage from gross income.

It is significant that the three-sector multiplier coefficient, at 2.5, is considerably lower than the two-sector value in Chapter 19, which was 4.0. This is because we now have *two* leakages – savings by households and taxation by the government, each with a marginal rate of $0.2Y$. This gives us a combined rate of leakage of $0.4Y$. In the two-sector model there was only *one* leakage – savings, at a rate of $0.25Y$, so the multiplier was 4.0.

Figure 20.2 illustrates the effect of increased government spending in terms of the injections-leakage approach.

The Balanced Budget Multiplier

The data in our three-sector model assumes that the effect of taxation is to reduce the level of both household saving and household consumption. This leads us to an important concept known as the 'balanced budget multiplier'. This multiplier shows the effect on national income of *equal changes in government expenditure and taxation*. It may be expected that since government expenditure is an

John Maynard Keynes (1883–1946)

Keynes was born in Cambridge the son of an economist. His brilliance was apparent at a very early age and throughout his life he was dazzling at everything he did. He was a brilliant classical scholar and mathematician. He excelled at bridge and was an accomplished mountaineer. He was a member of the influential Bloomsbury Group and made a fortune for himself by buying and selling on the foreign exchange and commodity markets – allegedly from his bed before he even went to work! However, he is best remembered as an economist.

After graduating, Keynes took the civil service exams. His second place score prevented him obtaining the position he wanted in the Treasury and instead he was appointed to the India Office. Interestingly his lowest score in the exam was on the economics paper and he suggested afterwards that this was because 'The examiners presumably knew less than I did'! Few would disagree with this statement now.

During the First World War Keynes was called to the Treasury to assist in planning the financial implications of the war. In 1919 he was a representative of the Treasury at the peace conference of Versailles but resigned over the terms of reparations imposed on Germany. He argued that Germany would never be able to meet the harsh economic conditions imposed and that the consequence of imposing severe reparations on Germany would be a continuing source of instability in Europe and might even precipitate another war!

After his resignation from the Treasury, Keynes returned to Cambridge and accepted a lecturing appointment. It was during this time that he produced his most influential works culminating in his *General Theory of Employment, Interest and Money*. Keynes was deeply concerned at the hardship, poverty and suffering caused by the economic depression of the 1930s and in the General Theory he argued that goverments should increase their own spending so as to lift an economy out of depression. His book had a world-wide impact on economic policy though his influence has now declined.

Keynes returned to the Treasury in the Second World War and represented the UK at the conference which met in 1944 at Bretton Woods, New Hampshire, to establish the post-war international financial system. Unfortunately he died of a heart attack in 1946 and never witnessed the unprecedented growth of world trade and living standards that characterised the fifties and sixties.

Figure 20.2 *The equilibrium level of income: planned injections equals planned leakages*

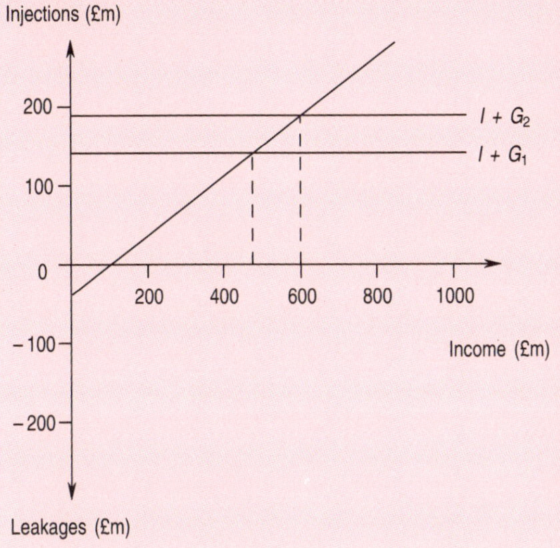

injection and taxation a leakage, the net effect will be zero and that national income will remain unchanged. In fact, this is not the case. Suppose, in terms of our model, there is an increase in government expenditure of £100m, financed entirely by an increase in taxation of £100m. We can analyse the outcome of this double change in two stages.

- The £100m increase in government expenditure will lead to a multiple increase in income. Since the *MPC* is 0.6, this will take the form

  $Y = 100 + 60 + 36 + \ldots + \ldots = 250$

- The £100m increase in taxation will lead to a multiple contraction of income. The effect is not, however, as straightforward as the change in government expenditure. In terms of income determination what is relevant is the *part* of any increase in taxation which is financed by a *decrease in consumption*. Since any increase in taxation will be partly financed by a reduction in household saving the *net* increase in leakages will therefore be less than the increase in taxation.

In our example *MPC* is 0.6. Any reduction in disposable income will therefore result in a fall in consumption (equal to 0.6 of the fall in disposable income) and a reduction in saving (equal to 0.4 of the fall in disposable income). An increase in leakages through taxation is therefore partly financed by a reduction in leakages through savings. In this case, the net increase in leakages is equal to $0.6T$, because one-fifth of the increase in taxation is financed by a cut in savings. The associated contraction in incomes will therefore take the form:

$$Y = -(60 + 36 + 28.8 + \ldots + \ldots) = -150$$

The net result of the equal increases in government spending and taxation is therefore that national income increases by only (250 − 150) = 100. Since this is equal to the initial increase in government expenditure the balanced budget multiplier always has a value of 1.

Income Determination in a Four-sector Model: the Foreign Trade Sector and Aggregate Demand

In an open economy aggregate demand includes expenditure by foreigners on domestically produced goods and services. Aggregate demand thus includes the *total of all expenditure on exports*. Since the level of exports depends mainly on conditions abroad (tastes and incomes there, for example) export expenditure (X) is assumed to be independent of the level of domestic income: like investment and government expenditure it is *autonomous*. In our model, we shall assume that the level of export expenditure is £80m. However, there is a complication because some consumption, investment and government expenditure is on imports, and therefore does not generate domestic income. To arrive at aggregate demand for domestic production we must *subtract the import content* of C, I and G.

Hence aggregate demand = $C + I + G + (X - M)$

The level of a country's expenditure on imports will be related to the level of its disposable income. The higher incomes rise, the greater the level of expenditure on imports. For simplicity we assume that $M = 0.125Yd$. However, we know from p. 182 that $Yd = 0.8Y$ and therefore $M = 0.125(0.8Y) = 0.1Y$. In other words, one-tenth of gross national income is spent on imports.

We can now examine the four-sector model of income determination using the planned values we have already established. To recap, these are:

$$C = 50 + 0.75Yd$$
$$I = 100$$

$G = 40$
$S = -50 + 0.25Yd$
$T = 0.2Y$
$X = 80$
$M = 0.125Yd$

and since $Yd = Y - T$ then

$C = 50 + 0.6Y$
$S = -50 + 0.2Y$
$M = 0.1Y$

Given these planned values what is the equilibrium level of income? Using the expenditure-income approach:

In equilibrium

$$C + I + G + (X - M) = Y$$
$$50 + 0.6Y + 100 + 40 + (80 - 0.1Y) = Y$$
$$270 + 0.5Y = Y$$
$$Y = 540$$

The equilibrium level of income is 540

We can check this result, since we know that in equilibrium planned injections must equal planned leakages:

$$I + G + X = S + T + M$$
$$100 + 40 + 80 = -50 + 0.2Y + 0.2Y + 0.1Y$$
$$270 = 0.5Y$$
$$Y = 540$$

The equilibrium level of income is 540

Figure 20.3 illustrates the equilibrium level of income.

Figure 20.3 *The equilibrium level of income in a four-sector economy*

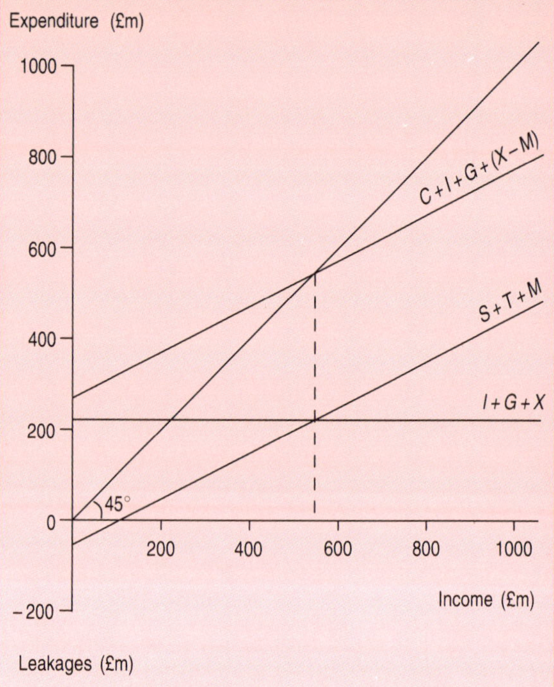

An Increase in Export Expenditure

An increase in planned exports will lead to a corresponding increase in aggregate demand. Suppose, in terms of our model, planned exports rise by £60m, from £80m to £140m, we can easily calculate the effect on national income. In equilibrium:

$$C + I + G + (X - M) = Y$$
$$50 + 0.6Y + 100 + 40 + (140 - 0.1Y) = Y$$
$$330 + 0.5Y = Y$$
$$Y = 660$$

The equilibrium level of income is 660

In graphical terms, an increase of 60 in export expenditure leads to an upward shift of 60 in the aggregate demand schedule, $C + I + G + (X - M)$ and in the injection schedule $C + I + G$. The outcome is presented in Figure 20.4.

It might be thought that since equality between injections and leakages has been restablished at $Y = 660$, the relationship between exports and imports will not be changed. However, this is not so. An increase in export expenditure will, through the multiplier process, increase domestic income. This in turn will raise all leakages (taxation, savings and import expenditure). This implies that the increase in realised imports will be *less than* the increase in exports: the balance of trade with the rest of the world will have improved.

The Four-sector Multiplier

In our example, an increase in export expenditure of £60m led to an increase in income of £120m. Clearly

Figure 20.4 *The effect of an increase in exports*

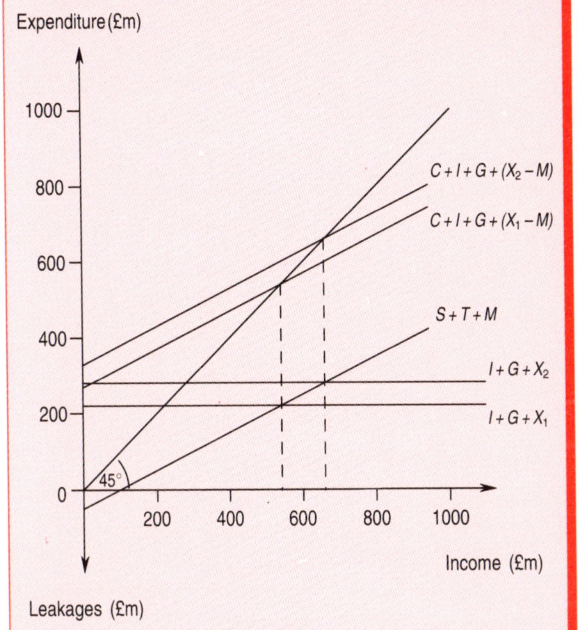

there has been a multiplier effect and in this case the value of the multiplier is:

$$k = \frac{\Delta Y}{\Delta AD} = \frac{120}{60} = 2.0$$

The value of the multiplier in the four-sector economy is calculated in the same basic way, as explained on p. 184.

$$k = \frac{1}{MRL}$$

But in this case *MRL* is the leakage from gross income from saving, taxation and import expenditure.

$$k = \frac{1}{0.2 + 0.2 + 0.1}$$

$$= \frac{1}{0.5}$$

$$= 2$$

Box 20.1 What is the value of the multiplier in the UK?

The multiplier is an important element in the Keynesian theory of income determination since it suggests that changes in national income are likely to be significantly greater than the changes in aggregate demand which initiated them. Keynes seems to have assumed that the multiplier would have a value of about 2. In fact, the evidence suggests that the multiplier's value is considerably less. There are two ways one can seek to calculate the 'true' value of the multiplier.

The 'static' method

We estimate for a given period the ratios of the main leakages to income and employ the appropriate formula to calculate the multiplier. Consider the following 1989 values for the UK leakages which have been derived from the 1990 *Blue Book on National Income and Expenditure*:

Direct taxation as a proportion of GDP at market prices	0.21
Savings as a proportion of personal disposable income	0.05
Indirect taxes as a proportion of consumption at market prices	0.23
Imports as a proportion of consumption at factor cost	0.52

If we assume an increase in GDP of 100 we can use this information to calculate the total value of leakages from GDP.

	£	Leakages (£)
GDP at market prices	100.00	
Direct taxes (including national insurance)		21
Personal disposable income	79.00	
Savings		3.95
Consumption at market prices	75.05	
Indirect taxes		17.26
Consumption at factor cost	57.79	
Imports		30.05
Domestic consumption at factor cost	27.74	
Total leakages		72.26

Since the total of leakages is 72.26, the ratio of total leakages to income is

$$\frac{72.26}{100} = 0.72$$

Hence our estimate for the value of the multiplier in the UK in 1989 is:

$$\frac{1}{\text{Total leakages ratio}} = \frac{1}{0.72} = 1.38$$

The econometric method

The static method, while providing a useful guide to the value of the UK multiplier, cannot be considered a true measure. It employs real data but applies it in terms of a highly simplified model. We would ideally prefer a measure of the *empirical* multiplier as it exists in the actual UK economy. We might in principle attempt to obtain this by observing a significant change in aggregate demand (for example, the increase in UK business investment in 1987) and then appraising the resulting changes in national income over a period of time. The difficulty, of course, is that this procedure would inevitably fail to take account of factors other than the change in business investment which might also be influencing the level of national income.

To avoid this problem, economists employ *econometric methods* to estimate the value of the multiplier (and other important economic variables). These entail the construction of complex computer-based economic models which embody actual UK data and in which one or more variables at a time can be changed, with the resulting 'simulated' outcomes observed under a variety of assumptions. The value of the multiplier thus obtained is generally around unity – that is, much less than that implicit in the Keynesian model of income determination.

REVIEW QUESTIONS

1 Explain the difference between an *endogenous* variable and an *exogenous* variable. Using examples from the national income model outlined in this chapter, distinguish between endogenous variables and exogenous variables.

2 How is the equilibrium level of national income determined in a closed economy?

3 The following data refer to a hypothetical economy:

Consumption = $100 + 0.8Yd$
Investment = 150
Government = 200
Exports = 200
Taxation = $0.2Y$
Imports = $0.05Yd$
where Y is the level of national income.

(a) Find the equilibrium level of national income, using both the aggregate-demand and injection-leakages approaches. Illustrate your answer with the appropriate graphs.
(b) Is there a budget surplus or budget deficit at the equilibrium level of income?
(c) Is the balance of trade in deficit or surplus at the equilibrium level of income?
(d) What is the value of the multiplier in this economy?
(e) If exports increase to 250, what is the new equilibrium level of income?
(f) In the original situation, if the government introduced transfer payments by 200, what is the new equilibrium level of income?

4 Why is the balanced budget multiplier equal to 1?

CHAPTER 21

INVESTMENT

CONNECTIONS

We have seen in Chapters 19 and 20 that investment is an important component of aggregate demand and changes in investment can produce significant changes in national income. In Chapter 21 we focus on the determinants of investment, particularly private sector investment. We shall therefore draw on our knowledge of the entrepreneur from Chapter 15.

Key Concepts

Accelerator
Cost-benefit analysis
Discounting to present value (DPV)
Expectations
Marginal efficiency of capital

In economics, production is defined as any activity which leads to the satisfaction of wants. Goods and services which satisfy wants directly (a Mars Bar or a haircut) are known as *consumer goods*. Goods which are used in the production of other goods such as machinery are known as *producer goods* or *capital*. Expenditure by businesses or by the government on producer goods is called *investment*.

Discounting to Present Value (DPV)

DPV techniques are useful in estimating the *present value* of revenue earned at some *future* time. This may be important in decisions about investment because firms incur most of the costs of investment in the **present** but do not receive revenue until some point in the **future**. In some cases the time difference is significant. For example, in the case of the Channel tunnel costs were incurred several years before the tunnel was expected to be operational. However, to assess the return on an investment it is necessary to compare **like with like**. In other words we need to have a common denominator; **discounting to present value** performs this role.

It is probably easiest to think of DPV as the opposite of interest rate compounding. For example, if the rate of interest is 10 per cent and £100 is invested for three years, the amount repayable in three year's time will be as shown in Table 21.1

Table 21.1 *Discounting to present value*

Amount invested (£)	Rate of interest (%)	Gross amount + interest (£)
Year 1 100	10	100(1.1) = 110.0
Year 2 110	10	110(1.1) = 121.0
Year 3 121	10	121(1.1) = 133.1

Alternatively, we could calculate the amount repayable in three years' time directly in the following way $£100(1.1)^3 = £133.1$. DPV simply reverses this procedure. If we were offered £133.1 in three years' time, how much would we be prepared to lend today? If we can be certain that the rate of interest will be 10 per cent for three years, the answer of course is £100.

In DPV calculations, the rate of interest is referred to as the *rate of discount* because we are *discounting* revenue received in the future, to *present values*. Now we can use this technique to estimate the *net* return (revenue *minus* cost) on an investment. For example, if a firm is considering an increase in fixed investment of £5m and the future returns after deducting variable costs are expected to be:

Year 1	Year 2	Year 3	Year 4	Year 5
£1.6m	£1.6m	£1.4m	£1.2m	£1.2m

For simplicity, let us assume that after the five-year period the investment has no scrap value and that the appropriate rate of discount is 10 per cent. If we simply add the returns on the investment it looks like an attractive proposition because the net return is estimated at £7m. However, we must remember that the return on our investment is not received until the future – we don't receive the final £1.2m until five years' time. If we discount the future returns to present value we find that this investment is not such an attractive proposition after all. In this case, we have:

$$\frac{£1.6m}{(1.1)} \quad \frac{£1.6m}{(1.1)^2} \quad \frac{£1.4m}{(1.1)^3} \quad \frac{£1.2m}{(1.1)^4} \quad \frac{£1.2m}{(1.1)^5} = £5.39m$$

It still seems as though the investment will be profitable because the *present value* of the future returns on the investment exceed the present cost of £5m. However, the future returns are only estimates, which may be subject to a wide margin of error. It is also possible that the firm may have underestimated the variable costs it will incur in the future. There is also a risk that the rate of discount will prove to be inappropriate. If interest rates in the economy rise above 10 per cent this implies that the present value of future returns will be understated if we apply a discount rate of 10 per cent.

Determinants of Investment

Before we consider our theories of investment, it is useful to consider some of the factors that **influence entrepreneurs in their decisions to invest**.

The Rate of Interest

Firms undertake investment for profit. The rate of interest is therefore likely to influence investment, either because firms borrow funds to finance investment projects, or because they forego interest by financing investment with their own funds. In this case, as we have seen above, changes in the rate of interest will change the present value of future returns and so will influence the investment decision. In particular, a rise in the rate of interest will tend to reduce investment by firms, while a reduction in the rate of interest will encourage investment.

Nevertheless, we must be careful not to exaggerate the effect of changes in the rate of interest. For one thing, it is often difficult to estimate precisely a project's likely profitability: an element of guesswork will be involved. Often we cannot do better than derive a wide range of possible rates of return, in which case a relatively small change in interest rates is likely to have little effect. Secondly, tax allowances on interest charges reduce the cost to businesses of changes in interest rates.

Expectations

Expectations are thought to be a powerful determinant of investment. Firms undertake investment in the expectation of profit and therefore they must estimate expected revenue. In practice, expectations are often coloured by the general mood of optimism or pessimism in the business community and on the Stock Exchange and there is a great deal of uncertainty surrounding investment decisions. We have seen in Chapter 15 that this is the nature of **entrepreneurial risk**, and it arises because it is impossible accurately to forecast either demand or costs. For example, demand would be affected if there was a change in the price lists of competing firms or a change in income tax which altered disposable income. Estimates of costs would be affected if there were unanticipated increases in wages or raw material inputs. When firms borrow to finance investment, a change in the rate of interest will affect their costs. Furthermore, we shall see in Chapter 33 that changes in the exchange rate will alter demand for goods which are exported and the costs of firms which use import raw materials.

Despite this, research suggests it is common for managements to accept projects which would have been rejected outright on straight profitability grounds. Take the huge sums invested in London's Dockland in the 1980s. In the general scramble for development, cool appraisal was less significant than the mood of the time – what Keynes called the 'animal spirits' of entrepreneurs.

Innovation and Technical Change

It was the American economist Schumpeter who first suggested that *innovation*, which is related often to *technical change*, might be an important determinant of investment. By 'innovation' we mean the introduction of *new* production processes such as the compact disc and the *big bang* computerisation of the London Stock Exchange. Process innovation often takes the form of *capital deepening*, where the amount of capital per worker is increased rather than *capital widening* where more capital is employed with more workers.

There is a tendency for sales of all goods to follow an identifiable pattern, known as the *product life cycle*, and eventually decline partly because of changes in consumer tastes but often because changes in technology make possible the production of new and improved goods. Because of this it is necessary for existing producers to invest in research and development and introduce new models to defend their market share as sales of existing models decline. For example, in the 1970s, demand for the VW Beetle was tailing off. To defend its market share VW invested heavily in two successors to the ageing Beetle, namely the Golf and the Polo. At the time of writing these are themselves becoming out of date and VW are investing in new models again.

Theories of Investment

The Accelerator

This *accelerator* relates **changes in investment** to **changes in consumer demand**. Consider a firm producing designer T-shirts with £200,000 worth of fixed capital. Demand and sales have been steady for some time but this year they have risen substantially. One way of reacting to this would be to invest in more equipment, assuming the net return is adequate.

As so often in economics, we can analyse the outcome in terms of a model based on three conditions:

- the capital has an average life of **ten years**;
- the capital stock has been built up evenly so that **10 per cent comes up for replacement each year**;
- the firm is operating with a **capital–output ratio of 2:1**. That is, it needs £1000 of equipment to be able to produce £500 worth of shirts per year. Table 21.2 shows us the mechanics of the accelerator.

In years 1 and 2 the capital situation is in equilibrium with sales of 100, a capital stock of 200 and capital replacement of 20. In year 3 sales have increased to 110 and the firm now requires 220 of capital. It therefore undertakes two blocks of investment, the usual 20 of capital replacement plus an extra 20 of net investment to get capital up to its target of 220. As sales continue to increase, it repeats the process in year 4, increasing capital to 240; and similarly in year 5.

Note what has happened. Sales have increased by (about) 10 per cent per year. Yet *total investment has doubled*, while net investment has gone from zero to 20 per year. Investment generated by the accelerator is known as *induced investment*, because it has been brought about by **changes in the rate of change of expenditure**.

Table 21.2 *The mechanics of the accelerator*

Year	Sales	Existing capital	Required capital	Replacement investment	Net investment	Total investment
1	100	200	200	20	0	20
2	100	200	200	20	0	20
3	110	200	220	20	20	40
4	120	220	240	20	20	40
5	130	240	260	20	20	40
6	130	260	260	20	0	20
7	120	260	240	0	0	0

In year 6 sales level off and in year 7 they fall off slightly. The result is a collapse of investment. We call this violent response of investment to changing sales the *accelerator effect* or *acceleration principle*. Look at years 3, 4 and 5. Sales are *growing* at a steady rate but net investment is *constant*. We can see that the level of net investment is related to the *rate of change* of sales, and that is why it is so unstable.

In practice, the accelerator will not affect investment as dramatically as indicated here. If firms are operating with excess capacity they will be able to increase output merely by drawing into use assets which are currently working at less than full capacity. In this case, the higher level of sales will have no effect on investment. In addition, firms will increase investment in response to higher sales only if they are confident that the higher level of sales represents a permanent increase in demand, rather than simply a temporary increase. In the latter case, they will prefer to lengthen waiting lists. Similarly, if firms have stocks of output these can be released to meet any increase in demand. Even if the increase in sales is expected to be permanent, the accelerator may not operate. Instead firms might choose to:

- introduce a **faster output** rate by means of piece rates, bonuses, and so on;
- introduce **shift working** to get more hours per day fròm the equipment;
- keep some equipment going **for more than 10 years**.

There is also the possibility of *supply bottlenecks*: capital suppliers may be unable to deliver as quickly as needed. For example, if resources are fully employed in the economy it may be difficult to increase the output of capital goods.

The Marginal Efficiency of Investment

We have seen how changes in the rate of interest affect the return from investments. But how do we select an **appropriate rate of discount**? In fact, the term 'marginal efficiency of investment' (*MEI*) denotes the rate of discount which would make the present value of the expected net returns from a capital asset just equal to its supply price. In other words, if a firm purchased a capital asset for £1m, the marginal efficiency of investment is that rate of discount which would reduce the future net earnings to a present value of £1m. The implication is that if the *MEI* is greater than the rate of interest purchasing the capital asset will be profitable, and vice versa.

In fact, we can construct a *marginal efficiency of investment schedule* which shows the behaviour of *MEI* as investment increases. As we would expect, as investment increases *MEI* falls because firms experience diminishing returns as their purchases of capital increase. *MEI* will also probably decline because as firms increase their purchases of capital assets, they will need to sell higher levels of output, and this will depress output prices. The combined effect of these factors is to reduce the expected rate of return on additional investment. The implication is that for any individual firm, the equilibrium rate of interest exists when investment has been pushed to the point at which *MEI* = the rate of interest. This is illustrated in Figure 21.1.

Figure 21.1 *The equilibrium level of investment*

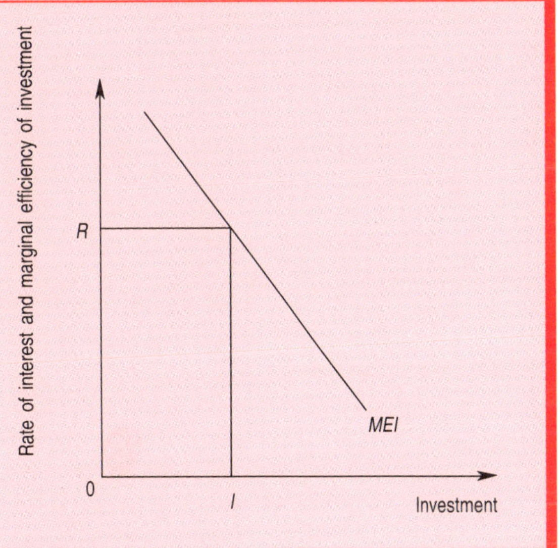

In Figure 21.1 the rate of interest is *R* and the level of investment by the individual firm is *I*. Once this point is reached firms will increase their level of investment only if the rate of interest falls or if the *MEI* increases, perhaps because technological progress or buoyant expectations about the future level of demand increases the expected future returns and therefore shifts the *MEI* outwards.

Cost-benefit Analysis

Cost-benefit analysis (CBA) is a method of **appraising the return on investment expenditure.** It attempts to set out the *social costs* and *social benefits* of an investment. The aim is to identify not only the obvious monetary costs and benefits, but also to place a monetary value on the positive and negative *externalities* (see p. 40). When all of these factors are taken into account the losses and gains in *economic welfare* to society as a whole can be estimated. Because of its approach, cost-benefit analysis is more relevant to decisions about investment in the public sector than the private sector.

Shadow Prices

But how can we measure the value of these externalities, many of which, by their very nature, are *intangible*? One method is to use a technique referred to as *shadow pricing*. This attempts to assess the opportunity cost of a resource, including an estimate of any externalities generated. For example, a major social benefit in considerations about the desirability of building the Victoria Underground Line was time savings. When trying to put a value on time savings we can easily identify an opportunity cost; an hour saved travelling to a business meeting across London is an hour which the traveller can use in the service of the company he or she works for, and can therefore be valued at an hour's wages.

Suppose British Rail is thinking of building a new high-speed railway line to link London with the Channel Tunnel. It does some research and finds that the costs of construction are so high that revenue from the tickets sold to passengers using trains to the continent is unlikely to be sufficient to make the project pay for itself. It the decision were allowed to rest on a purely *financial* appraisal (one that takes account only of those costs and revenues that affect British Rail's financial accounts), then the Tunnel link might never be built. What is needed is a contribution from the public purse. But why should the general public be expected to contribute?

Resource Allocation

An economist might be able to show that if the line were built, it would provide benefits to passengers over and above the fares paid, and therefore would improve the allocation of resources. The demand curve for travel on the line is downward sloping, and so whatever the equilibrium price is, most passengers would be prepared to pay more than they actually pay; in economic terminology, they receive *consumer surplus*; and financial appraisal does not recognise the additional benefits to passengers that this consumer surplus represents. Neither does financial appraisal recognise the *external* costs and benefits of building the railway line – that is to say, it does not recognise that a railway line can have costs and benefits to non-users as well as to users. Cost-benefit analysis attempts to put a value on some of the items which are overlooked by regular financial appraisal.

In appraising the high-speed rail link between London and the Channel Tunnel, for example, the construction costs would not simply be measured against the revenue from ticket sales, but an attempt would be made to place a value on reductions in travelling times, reduced road congestion and air pollution, fewer road accidents, and so on. These would represent benefits, and some of them might be considerable; the Road Research Laboratory has estimated that the cost to the taxpayer of one fatal road accident, in terms of police attendance, hospital treatment, state support for dependents, etc. is over £600,000, and if we were to take into account such things as the loss of potential earnings of the deceased person the social costs would be even higher.

A new railway line would also impose costs, including the increased nuisance of noise to people living close to the line. The railway planners have so far found it very difficult to find a route for this line which is both economically and socially acceptable. It could be that part of the reason for this is the government's insistence that there should be minimal state involvement in the scheme and that it should be appraised on ordinary investment criteria. Perhaps a CBA approach, attempting to look in the broadest way at the benefits and costs to society as a whole, would have more chance of gaining public acceptance.

Measuring Costs and Benefits

A problem which CBA shares with other investment appraisal techniques is that the costs of investment are incurred **before the good or service becomes available for consumption**, whereas the benefits often occur over a very considerable period. For example, try and estimate the economic life of the rail link between London and the Channel Tunnel. The further we look into the future, the more difficult it becomes to estimate the value of the benefits. Even when they are estimated, we cannot simply compare the value of benefits received in the future with costs incurred in the present to determine whether the project is viable. The value of future benefits must be *discounted* to their present value. But how do we decide an appropriate rate of discount when capital is expected to have a relatively long life?

CBA and Decision Making

One point to stress is that even if a CBA calculation shows an excess of benefits over costs, this does not necessarily imply that a project should go ahead. Critics of CBA might argue that it is possible to define costs and benefits so widely and loosely as to construct a case for or against any expenditure proposal. Its supporters would argue that such an argument takes a mistaken view of the nature of CBA. A CBA calculation is simply and aid to decision taking, since it shows whether a project is thought to make a worthwhile use of scarce resources. There will always be other priorities making demands on resources, and it is not an economist's job to choose between priorities. Whether other projects should be given preference remains a political decision.

Consider investment in urban light railways, a number of which now exist or are being planned in

Box 21.1 Investing in London's Dockland Light Railway

The Victoria Underground Line was constructed in the 1960s to reduce travel congestion in central London. By the 1980s another London railway investment was under consideration, this time to service London's Dockland which, following the closure of the docks and the decline of the local clothing trade, had become an area of depopulation and urban decay. In the 1980s the government set in hand policies to redevelop the dockland into a commercial centre to rival the city and the West End. This redevelopment would require substantial investment in property construction and in transport infrastructure. Responsibility for property investment was left to private sector capital, though the government also promoted development through tax concessions and land subsidies. The main transport project undertaken was the construction of the Dockland Light Railway (DLR) which was completed in 1988 with a capacity of 4000 passengers per hour. The investment cost of the DLR was £77m and this was met out of government funds.

Commercial development of Dockland was extremely rapid and the DLR soon proved incapable of handling increased passenger demand. The government therefore announced plans to extend the DLR in stages up to 1995, at a financial cost of £900m. Since estimated passenger revenues would amount to £300m, £600m would be required to cover costs, including the large initial capital investment. The government now decided to rely as far as possible on *private capital* for financing the required investment, and by negotiating substantial funds from property companies, who were reaping substantial external benefits in the shape of increased development opportunities made possible by infrastructure improvements.

However, this 'mixed investment' approach ran into difficulties. In the first place, the property companies' profits had fallen sharply due to the collapse of property prices associated with the recession of the early 1990s. Secondly, the property companies were reluctant to fund transport improvements since it was difficult to quantify the benefits for them, and they were also worried that later developers would benefit from an improved transport system which, unlike earlier developers, they had not funded. A process of bargaining now set in between the government and the property developers and the uncertainty which this caused undermined confidence in the future of the Docklands.

Meanwhile travellers were experiencing increasing difficulty travelling to Docklands by rail, road or even by water (on Thames river boats). Plans were also announced to extend the London Underground Jubilee Line through the docklands, a scheme which would generate favourable externalities over a wide area of London. However, as in the case of the proposed LDR extension, the government was reluctant to commit public investment funds until it had squeezed the maximum amount from the private sector. Then, in 1991, the government's approach appeared to change, for it announced it would now be prepared to commit unconditionally substantial investment funds for both the DLR and the Jubilee Line extensions. In effect, it was admitting that the policy of 'clawing back' externalities had not really worked.

various British and foreign cities. Apart from directly providing a service for users, such railways often provide *indirect* benefits to the community. For example, users of other modes of transport, such as roads and conventional rail services, may experience reduced congestion and so save on travel time. Also, opportunities for commercial development may be created in the area served by the new railway.

REVIEW QUESTIONS

1 At a market rate of interest of zero, would the level of business investment be infinite?

2 (a) Using economic analysis and the information in Table 21.3, how might you explain observed changes in net fixed investment?
(b) What other factors may have influenced the level of net fixed investment in the period shown?

3 The data below refers to a hypothetical investment project with a life of two years and no final resale value.

Cash flow year 1	£1035
Cash flow year 2	£1058
Supply price of project	£1600

If the market rate of interest is 15 per cent, determine the viability of the project by estimating:

(a) the present value of the cashflows.
(b) the net present value of the project;

How would your appraisal be affected by a rise in the rate of interest to 25 per cent?

Table 21.3 *Investment and GNP, 1978–88*

Year	GNP at 1985 prices (£b)	Gross investment at 1985 prices (£b)	Gross investment (% of GNP)	Net fixed investment at 1985 prices (£b)	Net fixed investment (% of GNP)
1978	322.2	54.9	17.0	20.6	6.3
1979	331.8	56.4	17.0	21.3	6.4
1980	322.4	53.4	16.6	17.0	5.3
1981	320.1	48.3	15.1	10.7	3.3
1982	325.8	50.9	15.6	12.2	3.7
1983	338.8	53.5	15.8	13.6	4.0
1984	347.3	58.1	16.7	17.1	5.2
1986	358.1	60.3	16.8	18.5	5.0
1987	390.1	66.9	17.1	23.2	5.9
1988	406.7	75.7	18.6	29.8	7.3

Source: HMSO, UK National Accounts (1989)

CHAPTER 22

AGGREGATE DEMAND AND AGGREGATE SUPPLY

CONNECTIONS

Chapter 22 draws on and extends the analysis of Chapters 20 and 21 on income determination. In this chapter we are concerned with the simultaneous determination of real output and the price level, whereas in Chapters 19 and 20 we were concerned purely with the determination of income since we assumed that the price level was **constant at all levels of income**. The analysis in this chapter also draws on Chapter 18, which explained the meaning of national income and its measurement. We shall also draw on this chapter in our discussion of rational expectations in Chapter 29.

Key Concepts

Actual rate of inflation
Expected rate of inflation
Natural rate of output
Price level
Real balance effect
Supply shock

The Aggregate Demand Curve

In Chapter 20 we assumed that the price level was constant. In this chapter we take a more realistic approach, and allow the price level to vary – as indeed it does in the real world. The aggregate demand curve in this chapter (and in Chapter 29) therefore shows the level of real national output that will be demanded at each and every price level. It is usually argued that the demand for real output will be inversely related to the price level – that is, as the price level falls the demand for real output will increase. There are three reasons for this, and each is analysed in turn.

The Real Balance Effect

Changes in the price level cause changes in the **real value of money balances**. As the price level rises a given quantity of money exchanges for a smaller volume of real output, and vice versa. In other words, the purchasing power of money balances falls as the price level rises and economists refer to this as the 'real balance effect'. It seems reasonable to assume that as the price level rises economic agents will cut back on their expenditures because the real value of their money balances has fallen. In contrast, a fall in the price level increases the wealth of individuals and organisations who are holding money balances, and in consequence they will increase their spending on goods and services. The real balance effect therefore provides one reason for the inverse relationship between the price level and real output.

Changes in Interest Rates

When the average price level rises it is likely that individuals will carry larger money balances to finance their expenditures. Similarly business organisations will require larger money balances to conduct their activities. Since the supply of money is constant, it is impossible for all economic agents to increase their money balances simultaneously: the attempt to do so simply creates a shortage of money at the existing price level. No doubt this will result in a fall in savings as economic agents attempt to restore the purchasing power of their money balances. As savings fall interest rates are likely to rise; as a result, firms are likely to cut back on their investment expenditures and households are likely to cut back on their demand for many consumer durables such as cars and household utilities which are often financed with credit. Here again a higher price level, by driving up interest rates, causes a reduction in real spending on goods and services.

Net Exports

An increase in the price level will make domestic output less competitive against foreign output. In consequence domestic residents will cut their spending on domestic output and will switch to cheaper foreign substitutes. Import expenditure will therefore increase. The opposite is true of foreigners. As the domestic price level rises they will cut their demand for exports and therefore export earnings will fall. For analytical purposes the difference between export earnings and import expenditure is sometimes referred to as *net exports,* and when the domestic price level rises, net exports will fall. Once again, this implies that as the price level rises the demand for real output will fall.

The combined effect of these factors gives an inverse relationship between the price level and the demand for real output. This is illustrated in Figure 22.1.

Figure 22.1 shows a typical aggregate demand curve. As the price level falls the demand for real output increases. For example, if the average price level is P, a total of Y units of real output will be demanded. However, at the lower average price level P_1, a total of Y_1 units of real output will be demanded.

Aggregate Supply

In the Keynesian models which we studied in Chapters 20 and 21 the price level was assumed to be constant and output was demand determined. This implies that aggregate supply is perfectly elastic up to the full employment point. In this chapter, we relax the assumption of a constant price level and take a more realistic approach by allowing aggregate supply to vary with changes in the price level. In addition, the behaviour of aggregate supply is not as straight forward as the behaviour of aggregate demand, because we must distinguish between aggregate supply in the **short run** and aggregate supply in the **long run**. The determinants of aggregate supply are different in each case. Let us begin by looking at aggregate supply in the short run.

Figure 22.1 *A typical aggregate demand curve showing an inverse relationship between real output and the price level*

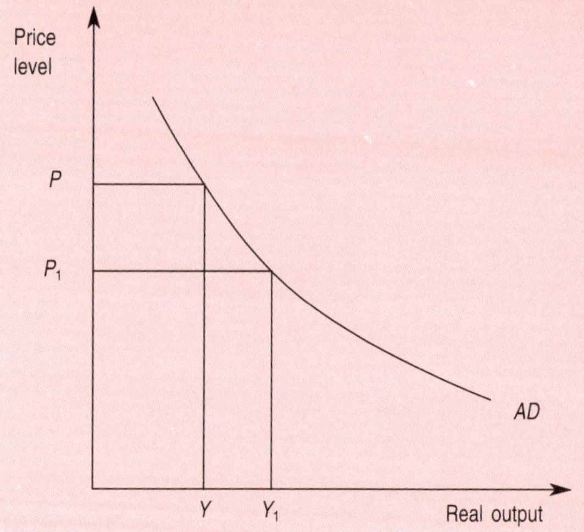

Aggregate Supply in the Short Run

Firms undertake production on the basis of an expected price for their output. However, costs are incurred *in anticipation* of sales. This is the risk of production since firms cannot know beforehand how much their output will sell for. This is important, because if the *actual* price achieved exceeds the *expected* price, firms will experience a higher than anticipated level of profit and this will encourage an increase in output. This implies that in the short run, at least for part of its range, the aggregate supply curve slopes upward from left to right with respect to price.

We have stressed that the short run aggregate supply curve slopes upward from left to right *for part of its range* because at any point in time there is a **physical limit** on the output of goods and services. This limit is imposed by the decreasing availability of idle resources as production increases, and the limit is reached when all resources are fully employed. At the point of full employment the short run aggregate supply curve will become vertical. At the full employment level of output further increases in the price level have no effect on output. It is impossible to increase the output of an economy beyond this point.

Aggregate Supply in the Long Run

Just because the aggregate supply curve slopes up from left to right in the short run, it does not necessarily follow that the long run aggregate supply curve will behave in the same way. In the short run the actual price level differs from the expected price level. It is this which causes output to increase (or decrease) in the short run. However, if all other things remain equal, the higher price level will come to be accurately and confidently expected by firms. In other words, the **expected** price level will coincide with the **actual** price level. This is important because in the long run the costs incurred by firms will rise as economic agents react to the higher prices they now pay for the goods and services they purchase. For example, wage rates will be negotiated upwards and suppliers will draw up new lists incorporating higher prices.

To understand the implications of this let us assume that initially the expected price level and the actual price level coincide. Subsequently there is an unanticipated increase in the price level which generates an increase in output. Over time as costs rise, profits will fall back to their original level. But if profits fall back to their original level, output will also fall back to its original level. Remember, the higher level of output in the short run was possible only because the *unanticipated* increase in the price level led to higher profits for firms. As soon as costs increase in line with final prices, the incentive to produce the higher output disappears and therefore output will return to its original level. In these circumstances the level of output produced will be at its *natural rate* and deviations from this are possible in the short run only if the actual price level deviates from the expected price level. Figure 22.2 shows the short run and long run aggregate supply curves of an economy.

The short run aggregate supply curve of this economy is given by AS_S and AS_L is the long run aggregate supply curve. The output level Y_n is the natural rate of output.

Figure 22.2 *Aggregate supply in the short run and the long run*

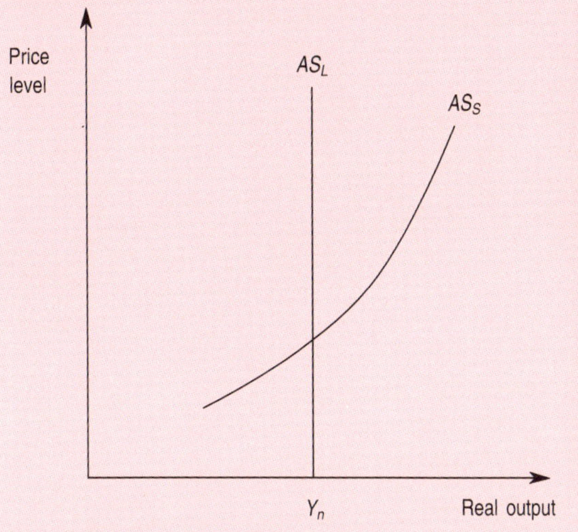

Long Run Equilibrium

In the long run the natural rate of output is the equilibrium rate of output for the economy. This is the level of output to which the economy will tend in the long run. The implication is that in the long run the average price level has **no effect on the level of output**. Any unanticipated price increase in the short run will be offset in the long run by an increase in costs as contracts are renegotiated. In the long run the output of an economy does not depend on the price level, but on such factors as the supply of labour and the skills possessed by the labour force, the capital stock, technological progress which improves the productivity of capital and so on. These factors are not influenced by changes in the average price level, and neither therefore is the aggregate supply of an economy. In the long run therefore the aggregate supply curve of an economy is vertical at the natural rate. Figure 22.3 shows the relationship between aggregate demand, the short run aggregate supply curve and the long run aggregate supply curve.

Aggregate demand is given by AD, AS_S is the short run aggregate supply curve and AS_L is the long run aggregate supply curve. The economy is equilibrium producing the natural rate of output Y_n and the price level is P. Note that the natural rate of output is not the same as the level of output achieved in the short run when all resources are fully

Figure 22.3 *Short and long run equilibrium between aggregate demand and aggregate supply*

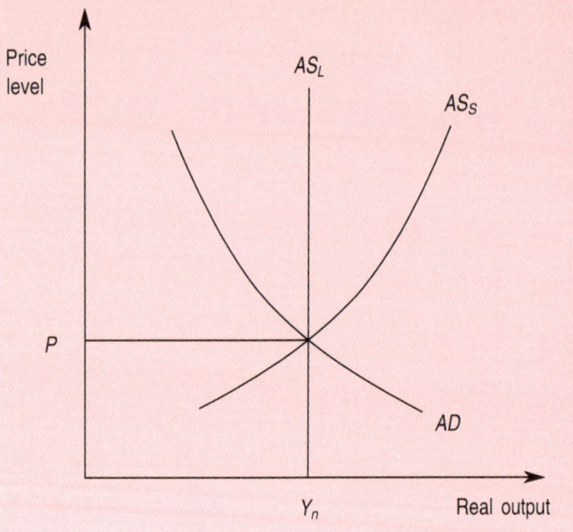

employed. At the natural rate of output there are unemployed resources caused by lack of mobility and other labour market rigidities (see pp. 359–63). For the moment, it is sufficient to understand that the natural rate of output differs from that achieved when all resources are fully employed.

Factors Causing a Change in Aggregate Demand

The aggregate demand curve shows the quantity of goods and services demanded at any given price level. However, this curve is based on the assumption that all other factors which might affect demand for goods and services apart from the price level are held constant. In practice the other factors which might affect aggregate demand – such as the level of income, the real rate of interest, the exchange rate and so on – will not remain constant. Let us explore the factors that may cause changes in aggregate demand in more detail

A Change in Income

This is one of the main factors affecting aggregate demand. If technological progress shifts the natural rate of output to a higher level this implies an increase in long run aggregate supply. It also implies an increase in the **real income of the community**. If real income rises, aggregate demand rises because the higher level of output will provide the community with higher incomes (remember from p. 159 that output = income). If real income rises, the aggregate demand curve will therefore shift outwards from *AD* to AD_1 in Figure 22.4 and if real income falls aggregate demand will shift from *AD* to AD_2 in Figure 22.4.

However, some economists, often referred to as *monetarists*, argue that a rise in *nominal income* caused by an increase in the money supply will also lead to an increase in aggregate demand. If the money supply increases economic agents will be holding increased money balances, and in consequence they will increase the amount they spend on goods and services.

Although it seems clear that a rise in income will lead to a rise in consumption, economists are not completely agreed on the way in which an increase in income leads to an increase in consumption. Nevertheless, at present the most widely accepted view is the *permanent income hypothesis* outlined on p. 178.

The Rate of Interest

We have seen on p. 197–8 that an explanation for the downward sloping aggregate demand curve is that as the price level rises the rate of interest will rise and this will reduce expenditures. However, as we

Figure 22.4 *A change in aggregate demand*

In terms of Figure 22.4, if aggregate demand increases from *AD* to AD_1 nominal income will rise, and if aggregate demand falls from *AD* to AD_2 normal income will fall

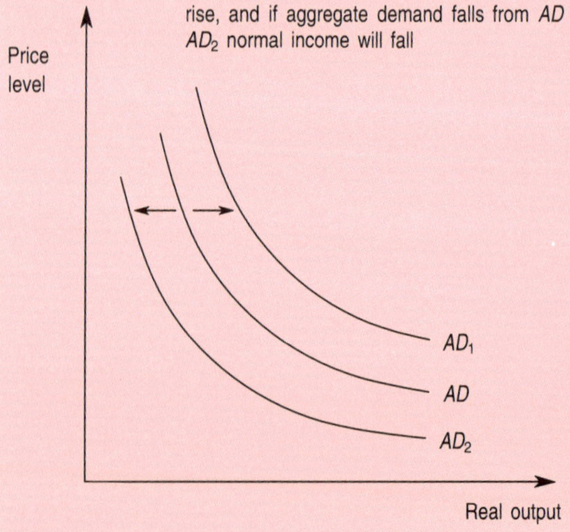

shall see on p. 245, interest rates change for many reasons. A change in the price level is simply one possible cause. When the rate of interest changes and all other things, including the price level, remain constant, this changes the *real cost* of lending or borrowing. Specifically if the rate of interest falls and the price level remains constant, firms will be more willing to borrow to finance increased investment and individuals will be encouraged to borrow in order to purchase consumer durables. The implication is that a fall in the rate of interest when the price level is constant will lead to an increase in aggregate demand (aggregate demand rises from AD to AD_1 in Figure 22.4), and a rise in the rate of interest when the price level is constant will lead to a fall in aggregate demand (aggregate demand shifts from AD to AD_2 in Figure 22.4).

A Change in the Exchange Rate

We shall see on p. 312 that changes in the exchange rate cause changes in the price of exports and imports. Specifically if the exchange rate falls the price foreigners pay for exports will fall and the price domestic residents pay for imports will increase. The natural consequence of this is that exports will increase and imports will fall, despite the fact that there has been no change in the domestic price level. This implies that aggregate demand will increase at each and every price level when the exchange rate falls (aggregate demand rises from AD to AD_1 in Figure 22.4).

The opposite will happen if the exchange rate rises. In this case the price foreigners pay for exports will increase while the price domestic residents pay for imports will fall. In consequence demand for exports will fall while demand for imports will rise although the change in the exchange rate will have no direct effect on the domestic price level. This implies that aggregate demand will fall at each and every price level when the exchange rate rises (aggregate demand falls from AD to AD_2 in Figure 22.4).

A Change in the Expected Rate of Inflation

An increase in the expected rate of inflation, other things being equal, will tend to increase aggregate demand. If economic agents expect the rate of inflation to rise in the future they will also expect the value of their real money balances to fall in the future. As a consequence they will bring forward any of their spending plans which they able to. It is for this reason that an increase in the expected rate of inflation causes a rise in aggregate demand and a reduction in the expected rate of inflation causes a reduction in aggregate demand.

A Change in Business Expectations

Expectations of the future will also affect investment decisions. If business decision takers feel more confident about future sales they will be encouraged to increase the level of their investment. Aggregate demand will therefore rise. Conversely, an air of business pessimism will discourage investment and aggregate demand will fall.

Government Policy

As we saw in Chapter 20, changes in fiscal policy can exert a powerful influence on aggregate demand. Traditionally it has been argued that if all other things remain equal an increase in government spending on goods and services implies an outward shift of the aggregate demand schedule – that is, a shift from AD to AD_1 in Figure 22.4. However, an increase in transfer payments or a reduction in the taxation of incomes, by increasing disposable income, will increase consumption spending, and again this implies an increase in aggregate demand. Cutting other taxes such as VAT will also increase spending power and will generate an increase in aggregate demand.

In more recent years the emphasis has changed and fiscal policy now focuses on the effect of government borrowing caused by an excess of spending over revenue from taxation (that is, a budget deficit) on the money supply. In particular it has been argued that a budget deficit causes an increase in the money supply, and that this is the route through which aggregate demand increases. Whatever the case, there is no disagreement that a budget deficit will shift the aggregate demand curve outwards. The opposite will happen if the government cuts its expenditure and/or raises the rate of taxation.

Factors Causing a Change in Aggregate Supply

Most of the factors which affect the position of the aggregate supply curve in the short run also affect the position of the aggregate supply curve in the long run. Since aggregate supply tends to increase in the long run as the productive capacity of an economy grows, Figure 22.5 shows the effect of this on the short run and long run aggregate supply curves of an economy.

Figure 22.5 shows the initial short run aggregate supply curve AS_S of an economy, and the initial long run aggregate supply curve AS_L. Subsequently, an increase in aggregate supply shifts the short run aggregate supply curve from AS_S to AS_{S1} and the long run aggregate supply curve from AS_L to AS_{L1}.

Although many of the factors which affect short run aggregate supply also affect long run aggregate supply, we can identify two situations when there will be a shift in the short run aggregate supply curve which will have no effect on the long run aggregate supply curve. These are the first two factors discussed below.

A Change in Costs of Production

The short run aggregate supply curve shows us the level of output that will be produced at any given price level. Like any supply curve, it is based on the assumption that the cost of producing any given level of output does not change. If costs change, firms will change the amount they are willing to supply *at any given price level*. An increase in labour costs or raw material costs will, other things equal, reduce the amount firms are willing to supply at any given price level. In Figure 22.5, the short run aggregate supply curve will therefore shift upwards from AS_{S1} to AS_S. However, an increase in the cost of producing any given level of output does not alter the long run aggregate supply curve, which remains at AS_L whatever happens to costs in the short run. A reduction in costs of production will have the opposite effect on the short run aggregate supply curve but again will have no effect on the long run aggregate supply curve.

Figure 22.5 *A change in aggregate supply in the short run and the long run*

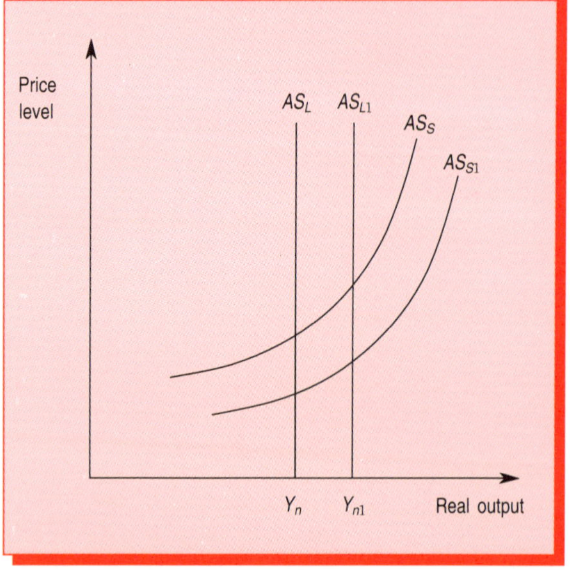

A Supply Shock

Supply shocks are occurrences which temporarily cause an **increase or decrease in current output**. We saw on p. 22 that favourable weather conditions will cause a bumper harvest while unfavourable conditions will cause a shortage. For countries with a large agricultural sector the effect on aggregate supply will be significant. More generally, a natural disaster such as a major flood will also adversely affect aggregate supply. However, these occurrences are only temporary and with the return of more normal conditions aggregate supply will revert to its previous level. In terms of Figure 22.5 an adverse supply shock will initially shift aggregate supply from AS_{S1} to AS_S, but as conditions return to normal aggregate supply will return to its original position of AS_{S1}. A positive supply shock such as a bumper harvest will have the opposite effect. In either case, there is no effect on the long run aggregate supply curve which remains at AS_L.

Investment and technological progress

A major influence on aggregate supply in the short run and the long run is investment and technological progress. Investment in additional capital assets improves productivity in the economy. If other things remain equal, an increase in productivity will shift the aggregate supply curve from AS_S to AS_{S1} in Figure 22.5 for exactly the same reasons that any market supply curve shifts a change in productivity change costs of production (see p. 22). Similarly technological progress which makes it possible to substitute capital for labour and more efficient capital for less efficient capital improves productivity. No doubt you will also realise that increased investment in the latest technologies, because it raises productivity, will also shift the long run aggregate supply curve from AS_L to AS_{L1}.

The Discovery of Raw Materials

An important factor determining the productive potential of an economy is the availability of raw materials. The discovery of additional raw materials which are accessible will **expand the productive base of the economy**. As more raw materials become available the initial effect will be to lower their cost to businesses and this implies a shift in the aggregate supply curve from AS_S to AS_{S1}. Remember that as costs of production fall, with a constant price level the profit from producing any given level of output increases and therefore firms will be encouraged to expand their output. In addition, since more raw materials are now available, the natural rate of output will increase from Y_n to Y_{n1}.

The Supply of Labour

Other things being equal, an increase in the supply of labour will shift the short run aggregate supply curve and the long run aggregate supply curve outwards. In the short run, if all other things remain equal, an increase in the supply of labour will bid down the wage rate and therefore raise the profit to firms from producing any given level of output. The short run aggregate supply curve in Figure 22.5 will thus shift from AS_S to AS_{S1}. However, in the longer run, the increased supply of labour will make possible increase the natural rate of output, since it will expand the productive base of the economy.

Human Capital

'Human capital' refers to the **skills of the labour force**. The more highly skilled the labour force, the greater its productivity. In this context education, training and health care have an important bearing on aggregate supply. For example, in the short run an increase in training initiatives which raises the skill levels of the labour force will shift the aggregate supply curves outwards in both the short run (a movement from AS_S to AS_{S1} in Figure 22.5) and the long run (a movement from AS_L to AS_{L1} in Figure 22.5).

Incentives

In recent years considerable emphasis has been placed on the importance of incentives in improving the supply-side of the economy (see Chapter 37). The basic argument is that if incentives can be increased the factors of production will increase their productivity. If this is the case, incentives will shift the aggregate supply curve in Figure 22.5 from AS_S to AS_{S1} and the long run aggregate supply curve from AS_L to AS_{L1}.

The Effect of a Change in Aggregate Demand

In the long run the level of real income is fixed at the natural rate. It follows that in the long run changes in aggregate demand cause changes in nominal income only by changing the price level. However, depending on whether the change in aggregate demand is anticipated or unanticipated it may encourage a short run increase in aggregate supply.

An Unanticipated Increase in Aggregate Demand

To understand the effect of an unanticipated change in aggregate demand let us consider Figure 22.6. Aggregate demand is initially given by AD and AS_S

Figure 22.6 *The effect of an unanticipated increase in aggregate demand on price and output in the short run and in the long run*

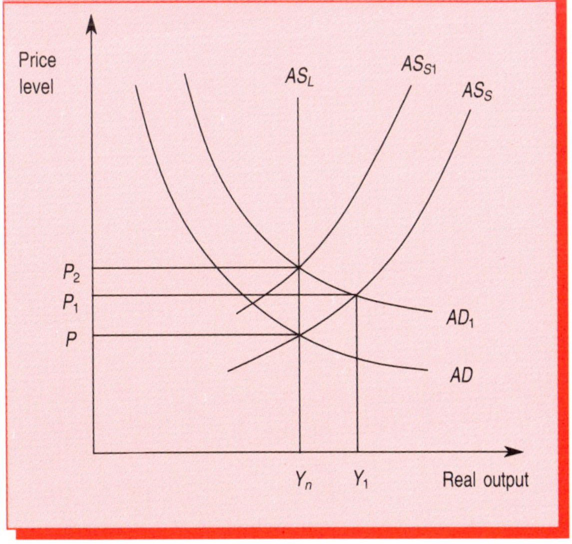

is the initial short run aggregate supply curve. AS_L is the long run aggregate supply curve and the economy is initially in equilibrium with aggregate demand equal to short run and long run aggregate supply. The equilibrium level of output is the natural rate Y_n and the price level is P.

Now suppose the government increases its expenditure on goods and services in an attempt to increase the level of real income above Y_n. This will shift the aggregate demand curve from AD to AD_1. In response to the increased demand, firms will increase the amount they produce and a new equilibrium will be established at Y_1 with a higher price level of P_1.

However, this is not the long run equilibrium position for the economy because the increase in aggregate demand will cause the actual price level to deviate from the expected price level. Remember that it this which persuades producers to increase their output because it increases their profits from doing so. However, over time contracts will be renegotiated with the result that wages and other costs, such as raw material costs, will increase. This will shift the aggregate supply curve to AS_{S1}. Here aggregate demand (AD) equals short run aggregate supply (AS_{S1}) and long run aggregate supply (AS_L). The economy is therefore again in long run equilibrium. Output returns to the natural rate, and the change in aggregate demand has not therefore led to a change in real income. However, the increase in demand has led to a **permanently higher price level** of P_2. This is the only long run effect of an unplanned increase in aggregate demand. (You may note in passing that the above analysis explains why many economists claim that it is impossible for governments to 'spend their way out of' a recession.)

An Unanticipated Reduction in Aggregate Demand

What would be the result of an unanticipated reduction in aggregate demand? Exactly the opposite sequence of events to that explained above. We can see this by reference to Figure 22.7.

Aggregate demand is initially given by AD and AS_S is the initial short run aggregate supply curve. AS_L is the long run aggregate supply curve and the economy is initially in equilibrium with aggregate demand equal to short run and long run aggregate supply. The equilibrium level of output is the natural rate Y_n and the price level is P.

Figure 22.7 *The effect of an unanticipated reduction in aggregate demand*

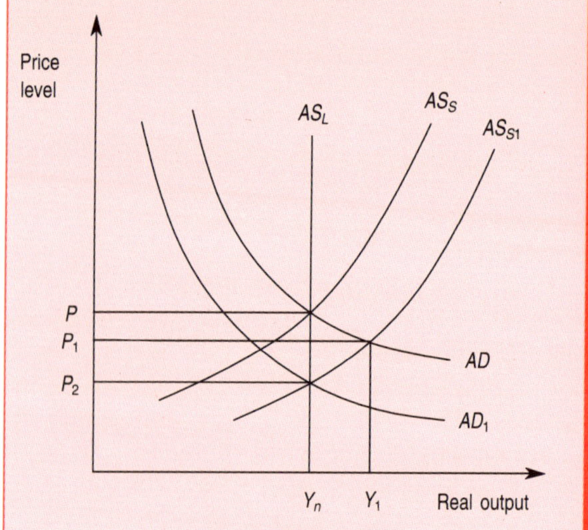

Now suppose consumers become more optimistic about the future rate of inflation, and expect it to fall. They will react by cutting back on their consumption expenditures at the existing price and output level, preferring to wait until prices fall. As a result aggregate demand will fall from AD to AD_1. The fall in demand implies that the actual price will be less than the expected price and in response firms will cut back on the amount they produce. A new equilibrium will be established at Y_1 with a lower price level of P_1. The economy moves into recession.

However, this is not the long run equilibrium position for the economy because the lower output firms produce implies a lower demand for resources. This will cause a fall in input costs when contracts are renegotiated and this in turn implies a shift in the aggregate supply curve from its original position AS_S to AS_{S1}. Long run equilibrium is restored when output has returned to the natural rate Y_n and aggregate demand (AD) equals short run aggregate supply (AS_{S1}) and long run aggregate supply (AS_L). Again, real income is unchanged in the long term but the price level has fallen to a **permanently lower level** of P_2. Again, the fall in the price level is the only long run effect of an unplanned reduction in aggregate demand.

It is important to note that factor prices, wages, raw material costs and so on, may not adjust quickly to a fall in aggregate demand. Many economists argue that factor prices are *inflexible* downwards. This does not imply that factor prices never fall; it simply means there may be a considerable time-lag involved before they do fall. If this is the case the adjustment to a reduction in aggregate demand will be lengthy and will result in factors of production being unemployed for longer periods than would otherwise be the case. The costs of adjustment in terms of unemployment will therefore be heavier and the recession longer than if factor prices adjusted quickly.

The Effect of a Change in Aggregate Supply

The effect of a change in aggregate supply depends on its cause, and we must take care to distinguish between those changes in aggregate supply which have only a short run effect on output and those which have a short run *and* a long run effect. Here we analyse three causes of a change in aggregate supply. In each case we assume that *all other things remain equal.*

Supply Shocks

On p. 202 we defined a supply shock as a random event such as a bumper harvest which caused an unanticipated change in aggregate supply. The effect of this is to shift the short run aggregate supply curve outwards, implying an increase in output and a fall in the equilibrium price level as shown in Figure 22.8.

Figure 22.8 *The effect of a supply shock on output and prices in the short and long run*

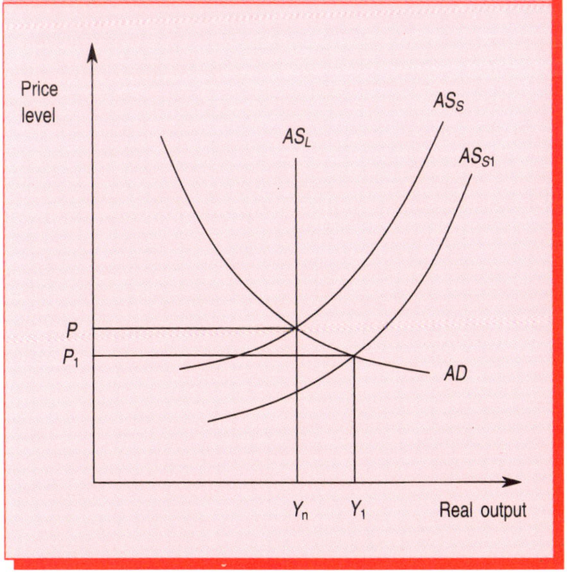

Aggregate demand is initially given by AD, short run aggregate supply is given by AS_S and AS_L represents long run aggregate supply. The economy is initially in long run equilibrium with output at Y_n and the price level at P. Subsequently a bumper harvest shifts the short run aggregate supply curve from AS_S to AS_{S1}. Short run equilibrium is established at output Y_1 and the price level falls to P_1. However, a single bumper harvest does not change the productive potential of the economy and therefore there is no change in the natural rate of output. As soon as agricultural conditions return to normal the short run aggregate supply curve returns to AS_S and long run equilibrium is restored at the original equilibrium position – that is, output at Y_n and a price level of P. The opposite will happen if freak conditions produce a poor harvest.

An Increase in Wages

We have seen on p. 202 that an increase in wages will shift the short run aggregate supply curve upwards. In other words, because firms now have higher costs of production they will produce less *at any given price level.* The effect of this is analysed in Figure 22.9

Aggregate demand is initially given by AD, short run aggregate supply is given by AS_S and AS_L represents long run aggregate supply. The economy is initially in long run equilibrium with output at Y_n and the price level at P. Subsequently a wage

Figure 22.9 *The effect of an increase in wages on prices and output in the short and long run*

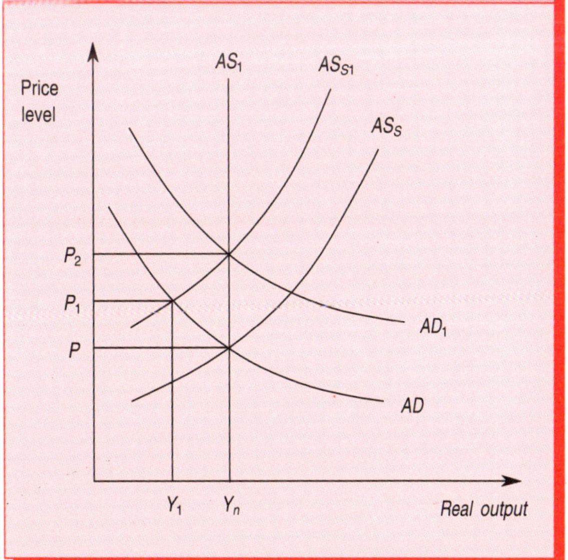

increase shifts the short run aggregate supply curve from AS_S to AS_{S1}. Short run equilibrium is established at output Y_1 and the price level rises to P_1. However, since wages have now increased consumption, expenditures by recipients of higher wages will increase. Therefore aggregate demand will increase at each and every price level. If the entire increase in wages is spent on increased consumption aggregate demand will shift to AD_1 and long run equilibrium will be restored at Y_n but the price level will be higher at P_2.

Even if the entire increase in wages is not spent on additional consumption but is partly saved, aggregate demand will still shift to AD_1 because the increased saving will pull down interest rates and encourage firms to increase investment. In this case, the adjustment to long run equilibrium is more complex since the increase in investment will cause a shift in the short run and long run aggregate supply curves. The adjustment to long run equilibrium following an increase in investment is discussed in the following section.

Figure 22.10 *The effect of an increase in investment on prices and output in the short and long run*

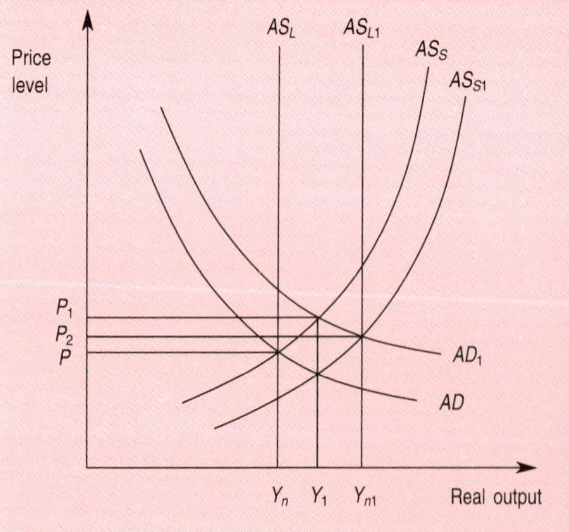

Increased Investment

We have seen on pp. 200–1 that a reduction in the rate of interest at each and every price level will encourage firms to increase their level of investment. The effect of this on the economy is discused in terms of Figure 22.1.

Aggregate demand is initially given by AD, short run aggregate supply is given by AS_S and AS_L represents long run aggregate supply. The economy is initially in long run equilibrium with output at Y_n and the price level at P. Subsequently a fall in the rate of interest generates an increase in investment and shifts the aggregate demand curve to AD_1. Short run equilibrium is established at output Y_1 and the price level rises to P_1. However, the increased investment also raises the productive capacity of the economy and this will shift both the short run aggregate supply curve and the long run aggregate supply curve. In Figure 22.10 short run aggregate supply shifts to AS_{S1} and long run aggregate supply shifts to AS_{L1}. In this case, the final equilibrium is a higher level of output at Y_{n1} and a lower price level at P_2.

In practice, we have no way of knowing whether the price level will be higher or lower when long run equilibrium is restored compared with the initial equilibrium. It might be, but we cannot be certain because we do not know what the *actual* changes in aggregate demand and aggregate supply will be. However, we do know that an increase in investment will increase the productive potential of the economy, and therefore we can be certain that when long run equilibrium is re-established there will be a higher natural rate of output. We have already seen on p. 164 that if output rises faster than population, the standard of living will improve. This explains the attraction of increased investment both as an anti-inflationary strategy and a source of improved living standards.

REVIEW QUESTIONS

1 What will be the effect on aggregate demand of each of the following? Assume all other things remain equal in each case.

(a) A strike in the docks which prevents the loading and unloading of exports and imports.
(b) Technological advances which improve the productivity of capital.
(c) A decrease in the expected rate of inflation.
(d) A budget deficit.

2 How would the slope of the aggregate demand curve in an economy differ if the real balance effect was (i) relatively strong; (ii) relatively weak?

3 Is the natural rate of output the full employment level of output (i) in the short run; (ii) in the long run?

4 When will the output of an economy be at the natural rate?

5 Show diagrammatically what effect an unanticipated increase in exports would have on price and output in an economy in the short run and the long run.

6 What effect will each of the following have on the price level of an economy?

(a) An unanticipated increase in the world price of oil. Assume the country is (i) an exporter of oil; (ii) an importer of oil.
(b) An increase in the expected rate of inflation.
(c) Technological progress which improves the productivity of capital.
(d) A substantial reduction in income tax.

CHAPTER 23

MONEY AND THE CREATION OF BANK DEPOSITS

CONNECTIONS

In Chapter 23 we will be studying the **functions of money** and identifying those assets which **function as money** in a modern economy. This is important background material for Chapter 25 when we look at the official measures of the money supply currently used in the UK. It is also important for our discussion of the monetary implications of the PSBR in Chapter 37 and monetary policy in Chapter 36.

Key Concepts

Bank deposits
Bank deposit multiplier
Bank loans
Fractional banking
Liquidity
Medium of exchange
Money supply
Reserve assets
Unit of account

The Functions of Money

Throughout history money has taken various forms. Metals such as gold and silver have been widely used as money, but stones, shells, beads, salt, slaves and cattle have all been used as money at one time or another. As we shall see later in this chapter, money in the modern world consists of notes, coin and bank deposits. In fact, we have no difficulty in *identifying* money. We can all recognise it and scarcely a day goes by when we do not use it. The problem is *defining* money. In fact, it has not proved easy to define money and economists rely on the functional definition that *money is as money does*. This tells us that money is any asset which **performs the functions of money**. But what are the functions of money?

A Medium of Exchange

One of the primary functions of money is to act as a *medium of exchange*. This simply means that it is *acceptable* in payment for goods and services. Without money trade would be based on *barter*: for example, a farmer might be willing to trade grain for cloth or a potter might be willing to trade jugs for shoes. However, trade would require a *double coincidence of wants*, that is, each person would have to **possess** what the other person **required**. Furthermore, they would have to agree on a **mutually acceptable rate of exchange** between the commodities traded: how many kilos of grain per yard of cloth, and so on.

The use of money enables us to avoid these difficulties. Each person simply exchanges their output for money and then exchanges money for the goods and services they require. The process of exchange is therefore simplified. It is no longer necessary to seek out a double coincidence of wants and then to negotiate a rate of exchange. However, this does not adequately convey the full implications of the role money performs as a medium of exchange.

Without money the gains from *specialisation and exchange* which characterise modern economies would be impossible. Mass production requires the existence of a mass market, and this would be impossible if trade was conducted on the basis of barter. Markets would tend to be small and localised and therefore the benefits of economies of scale would not be realised. This implies an inefficient use of resources and this inefficiency would be compounded because time and effort would be spent seeking out a double coincidence of wants. If money is used it is no longer necessary to seek out a double coincidence of wants and the time and effort saved can therefore be put to alternative uses.

A Unit of Account

Because money is used in exchange it also acts as a means of **expressing the value of different goods and services**. In the UK, the price of all goods and services is expressed in pounds sterling and this enables us to compare relative values. If a pair of shoes costs £50 and a pair of shorts costs £10, then we know that the shoes are two and a half times as valuable as the shorts.

Such comparisons are important to consumers and firms in making decisions about consumption and investment. Money is a common denominator, capable of expressing the current value of all expenditures. In the absence of money, comparisons would be infinitely more difficult, since every good and service would need to be expressed in terms of every other good and service to have complete information. Thus a pair of shoes might be worth 10lb of steak, 5 tins of paint, 4 shirts, 3 pairs of slippers, and so on. We are sure you will agree a single unit of account is a much easier way of comparing relative values!

A Standard for Deferred Payments

This function of money is closely related to its unit of account function. We are simply making the point here that the use of money enables trade to take place at a price agreed today, but that payment is to be made in the future. In the absence of money it would be very difficult to agree what would constitute an acceptable rate of payment in the future. One problem is that we do not know with certainty what goods we will have available in the future. Nor do we know what goods we will require. This problem is solved by agreeing a money price which, on payment, can be converted into those goods and services which are required at that time.

A Store of Value

Money provides a means of storing wealth. It is often easier and more convenient to store wealth in the form of money than in other goods such as antiques. The main problem with storing wealth in a form other than money is that such assets are less *liquid* than money. An asset is more liquid the easier and more quickly it can be transformed into other goods and services without any appreciable loss in its nominal value. Since money is a medium of exchange it follows that it is the most liquid asset of all. Because money provides immediate purchasing power, most people store at least part of their wealth in the form of money.

Components of the Money Supply

As we shall see on pp. 225–7, in the UK (and in all other modern economies) there are several official measures of the money supply. Here we look only at the broad components of the money supply.

Notes and coin are acceptable in exchange for goods and services and are therefore part of the money supply. However, notes in particular are intrinsically worthless; they are simply pieces of paper. Coin has intrinsic value since the metals used in its manufacture have alternative uses but, even here, the value of the metal is considerably less than the value of the coin. This is important because it implies that notes and coin are relatively cheap to produce and their purchasing power exceeds their resource cost. This is because they are *fiat money* – that is, they derive their value because *by law* they are legal tender.

Important though notes and coin are, they are not the largest component of the money supply in modern economies. In this sense *bank deposits* are far more significant. Bank deposits function as money because they are acceptable in payment for goods and services. However, the means of transferring bank deposits from one person to another – that is, cheques – are not money. A cheque is simply an instruction to a bank to transfer money from one account to another account and a cheque that cannot be honoured against a bank deposit is worthless. A cheque is not therefore money; it is the bank deposit which is acceptable in payment.

It is sometimes asked whether *credit cards* are money since many purchases are made using these. In fact, credit cards are a means of obtaining credit and using this to finance expenditure, but they are not money. In other words, they substitute for money at the time purchases are made. However, payment must ultimately be made by movement of bank

Box 23.1 Why are bank deposits money?

Money is anything which is acceptable in settlement of a debt. But, paradoxically, the main asset used to settle debts in modern economies is **other debts** after all, bank deposits are liabilities that the banks owe to their customers. Furthermore, we shall see below and on p. 211 that banks create liabilities against themselves when they make loans to their customers. In so doing, they are exchanging a debt which is not money for one which is money because bank deposits are acceptable in settlement of a debt. In other words, when a bank grants a loan it is effectively buying a debt which is not usable as money (otherwise it would be spent) in exchange for a debt which is usable as money. So why are banks able to create money? The answer is that their liabilities are acceptable in settlement of a debt because everyone has confidence that, on demand, these liabilities can be converted into cash. So long as this confidence is maintained, bank liabilities will always be acceptable in settlement of a debt, and will always therefore be money.

deposits, initially when the credit card company pays traders, and subsequently when users of credit cards pay the credit company.

But what if credit bills are unpaid? As we shall see below, banks can create deposits and if they do so to settle the claims of traders, the use of credit cards can lead to an increase in the money supply. In this sense credit cards function as money only *to the extent that credit bills are unpaid*. However, unpaid credit bills are not recorded in the official measures of the money supply because it is impossible to calculate the amount of credit outstanding at any moment in time.

The Creation of Bank Deposits

In terms of the total value of all transactions made in the UK, bank deposits are far more significant than cash. But how are bank deposits created? In fact, bank deposits are created in two main ways: when a customer deposits funds, and when a bank makes a loan.

When a Customer Deposits Funds

When funds are deposited with a bank a deposit is automatically created. In accounting terms, the bank acquires an *asset* and a *liability*. The asset is clearly the funds deposited with the bank. However, the depositor also has a claim against the bank. After all, any funds deposited can also be withdrawn. In these circumstances bank deposits fall.

When a Bank Makes a Loan

A bank can make a loan in two basic ways. One way is to grant borrowing facilities to a customer for an agreed amount or up to an agreed limit. When this happens, the bank's assets and liabilities rise by equivalent amounts. When a loan is granted the customer has a claim against the bank for the full amount of the loan. This is the bank's liability. However, the bank also has a claim against the borrower. In many cases banks do not grant loans without some sort of security such as property deeds or insurance policies (for small amounts this is not usually required). In these circumstances the bank's asset is simply the borrower's assurance that repayment will be made on or by an agreed future date.

Another way in which a bank may make a loan is to *buy a security*. As we shall see on pp. 214–15, securities are simply IOUs which are bought and sold in organised markets. When a bank buys a security, it is in effect granting a loan until the security matures and is redeemed – or, of course, until the bank sells the security to somebody else. In this case the bank's asset is the security, and its liability is the loan granted when the security is purchased.

The Multiple Expansion of Bank Deposits

Fractional Banking

History has taught bankers that at any one time only a small proportion of the total funds deposited with them will ever be withdrawn, and in general inflows exceed outflows. This gives banks the opportunity to make profits by expanding their loans. In other words, they simply lend *part* of the total amount deposited with them. They hold the remainder for *prudential reasons* – that is, to meet withdrawals of cash by their customers. For example, if banks hold 10 per cent of all funds deposited with them for prudential reasons, this implies that they can lend 90 per cent of total deposits. This is what the term *fractional banking* means: only a fraction of total deposits are required by banks to meet day-to-day withdrawals by their customers. This is important since, for any bank, lending is its most profitable activity: banks pay to attract deposits from one set of customers, and then charge others for the use of these funds.

The Implications of Bank Lending

It is important to note that banks can *lend only what is deposited with them*. Any bank that created deposits in excess of the funds deposited with it would quickly find that it could not meet the demands of its depositors for cash. Because of this, it is sometimes said that banks cannot create deposits; they simply lend funds that are deposited with them. Nevertheless, any deposit of cash received by a single bank will create the potential for a multiple increase in the volume of bank deposits by the banking system *as a whole*.

To explain the multiple expansion of deposits we use a simplified balance sheet referred to as a 'T account', so called because it looks like the letter 'T'. By convention, assets always appear on the *left* side of the balance sheet and assets on the *right* side. We assume that banks wish to maintain a ratio of 10 per cent cash to total deposits – that is, for prudential reasons banks will lend only a maximum 90 per cent of all deposits lodged with them.

Let us begin by considering the balance sheet of Bank *A* which has just received a cash deposit of £100,000. The change in Bank *A*'s balance sheet as a result of this deposit is shown in Figure 23.1.

The bank's assets are the cash deposit it has received, and its liabilities are the funds it owes to its depositors. But if it requires only 10 per cent of all deposits made with it to honour withdrawals by customers, 90 per cent of any additional deposit will

Figure 23.1 *Deposit of £100,000 in Bank A's balance sheet*

Bank *A*

Assets		Liabilities	
Cash	+ £100,000	Deposits	+ £100,000
Total	+ £100,000	Total	+ £100,000

Figure 23.2 *Withdrawal of £90,000 from Bank A's balance sheet*

Bank *A*

Assets		Liabilities	
Cash	+ £10,000	Deposits	+ £100,000
Loans	+ £90,000		
Total	+ £100,000	Total	+ £100,000

be available for lending. In this case Bank *A* will be prepared to lend £90,000 to customers requiring loans.

If there are willing borrowers, granting a loan will change the nature of Bank *A*'s assets, though not its liabilities. In granting a loan to a customer the bank simply creates a deposit in the customer's name (or else credits the customer's account with the agreed amount) but this does not change the amount the bank owes to its *existing* depositors. However, since no customer will negotiate a loan that is not required to finance expenditures, we can assume that any loan Bank *A* grants will result in that quantity of funds being withdrawn. After £90,000 has been withdrawn, Bank *A*'s balance sheet will appear as in Figure 23.2.

In granting a customer a loan, Bank *A* exchanges one asset for another asset – that is, it has exchanged cash for a claim against the borrower. However, this is not the end of the process. The person borrowing the £90,000 will spend it and will draw a cheque against the bank deposit created in his (her) name. The recipient of the cheque will pay it into his (her) bank account. Let us assume this is held at Bank *B* so that the transaction will result in a transfer of funds from Bank *A* to Bank *B*. We can represent the change in Bank *B*'s balance sheet in Figure 23.3.

Bank *B* now has additional cash deposits and just as Bank *A* was prepared to lend 90 per cent of any additional cash deposits, so Bank *B* will be prepared

Figure 23.3 *Transfer of funds from Bank A to Bank B: Bank B's balance sheet*

Bank *B*

Assets		Liabilities	
Cash	+ £90,000	Deposits	+ £90,000
Total	+ £90,000	Total	+ £90,000

to lend £81,000 – that is, 90 per cent of £90,000. If this happens Bank *B*'s cash reserves will fall as cash is withdrawn to finance expenditures. The change in Bank *B*'s balance sheet is shown in Figure 23.4.

As money is spent it will flow back into the banking system and will result in a further round of deposit creation. Even if funds flow back to Bank *A* or Bank *B* they will be indistinguishable from any other inflows and so the process will continue until the entire initial deposit of £100,000 is held to meet day-to-day withdrawals by customers. Figure 23.5 shows how, simply by relending part of any deposits

Figure 23.4 *Fall in Bank B's cash reserves after a loan*

Bank *B*

Assets		Liabilities	
Cash	+ £9,000	Deposits	+ £90,000
Loans	+ £81,000		
Total	+ £90,000	Total	+ £90,000

Figure 23.5 *Multiple increase in total bank deposits*

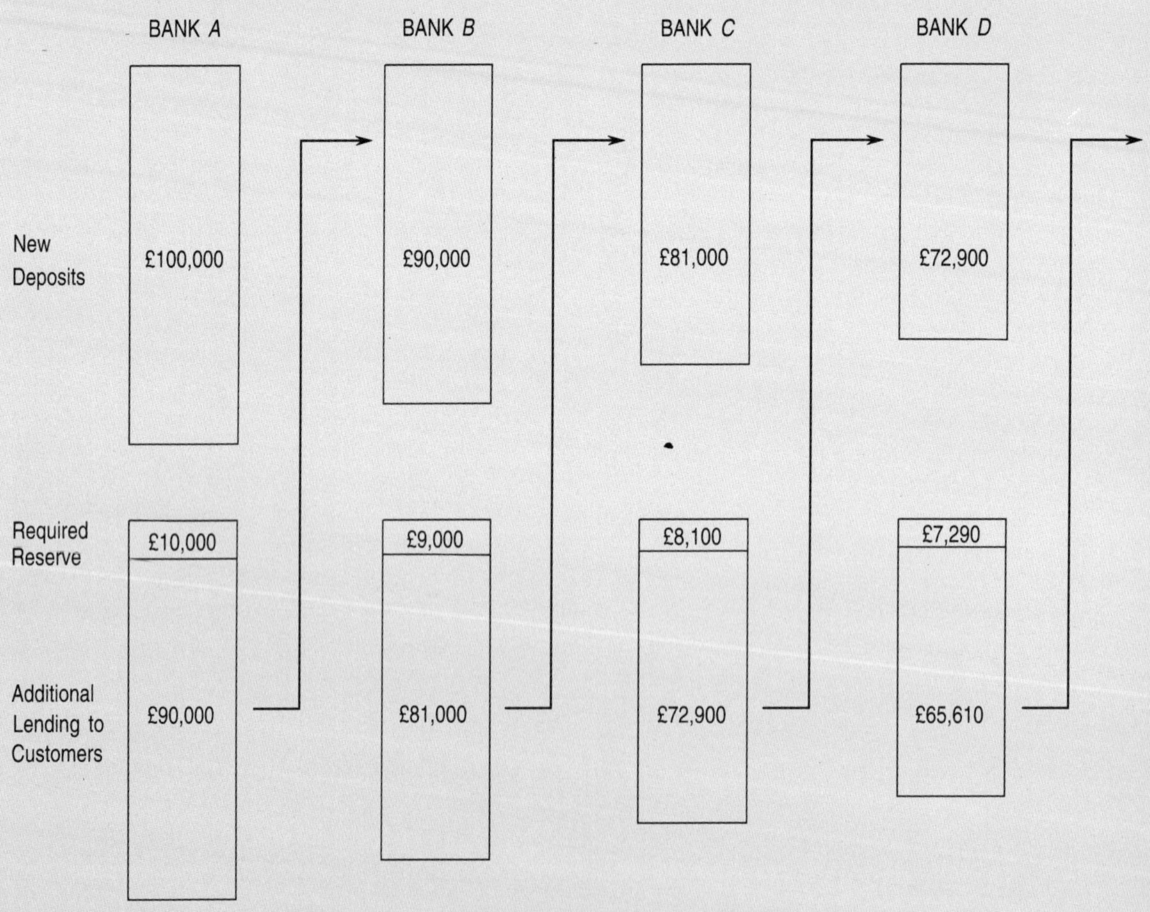

The multiple expansion of bank deposits. Banks hold 10 per cent of any sums deposited with them as reserves and lend the remainder. [Note in this example we assume that additional loans created by one bank flow to a different bank. In so far as they flow back to one of the banks above they will be indistinguishable from any other inflows and 90 per cent will still be lent to customers.]

made with them, the banking system creates a multiple increase in total bank deposits.

But what is the final increase in total deposits following an initial deposit? Since the entire initial deposit of £100,000 is held for prudential reasons, it must constitute 10 per cent of the total deposits created. This implies that an initial deposit of £100,000 leads to an ultimate increase in total bank deposits of £1,000,000.

In fact, if we know what proportion of deposits banks hold as reserves, we can always calculate the final increase in total deposits following an initial deposit. Perhaps you will recognise that the growth of deposits shown in Figure 23.5 is a *geometric series*. We can find the sum of this series by multiplying the first term in the series by:

$$\frac{1}{\text{Reserve ratio}}$$

In this case, the reserve ratio is 10 per cent so we have:

$$\frac{1}{0.1} = 10$$

The final change in total bank deposits following an initial deposit of £100,000 is therefore 10 × £100,000 = £1,000,000. However, the important point to note is that in this case the bank deposit multiplier is 10 and in general it can always be calculated in the way described above – whatever the value of the reserve ratio.

Our analysis of the creation of bank deposits tells us that it is quite correct to say that banks lend only whatever is deposited with them: deposits are not created because banks lend money which they do not have. Nevertheless, the banking system is able to create deposits in excess of the cash deposited therein, because not all of the money deposited with the banks will be withdrawn by customers at any one time.

Despite this, there are limits on the ability of banks to create deposits. The most obvious limitation is that there may be no willing borrowers. If no-one wishes to borrow funds from a bank, there can be no multiple expansion of deposits. Another factor is the degree of *confidence* people have in the banking system. If there are no depositors, banks cannot create deposits because they will have no reserve assets. The availability of reserve assets therefore constrains the ability of banks to create deposits, as does the proportion of reserve assets they hold for prudential purposes. The greater the proportion of assets held as reserves, the lower the ability of banks to create deposits.

There are other factors which limit the ability of banks to create deposits. In particular, just as banks make loans to some customers and this creates the potential for a multiple expansion of bank deposits, other customers repay loans made in the past. Such repayments must be deducted from loans made over any given period to obtain the *net increase* in bank deposits. Net flows of funds to the banks therefore constrain their ability to create deposits, and if repayments exceeded new loans, bank deposits would actually fall!

REVIEW QUESTIONS

1 Why are banks able to lend a portion of any funds deposited with them?

2 Why are banks unable to lend sums in excess of the amount deposited with them?

3 Why are sight bank deposits money?

4 Are cheques money?

5 If all banks in a particular economy maintain a ratio of 12½ per cent

(i) What is the size of the bank deposit multiplier?

(ii) What is the maximum increase in total deposits following an initial deposit of £1000?

CHAPTER 24

THE MONETARY SECTOR

CONNECTIONS

In Chapter 24 we build on material covered in Chapter 23 and explore the different institutions in the *monetary sector*. We shall draw on material covered more fully in later chapters including Interest Rates (Chapter 26), The Balance of Payments (Chapter 32) and Exchange Rates (Chapter 33).

Key Concepts

Bills of exchange
Certificates of deposit
Discount market
Eurocurrency market
Financial intermediary
Inter-bank market
Merchant bank
Money market
Non-bank financial intermediary
Parallel money market
Retail bank
Treasury bills

'The monetary sector' is the term used to describe those institutions which participate in the sterling money market. This is essentially a market in short-term funds – that is, loans and deposits of up to one year maturity. The minimum amount lent or borrowed is £100,000. In Chapter 3 we described a market as any arrangement which brings buyers and sellers of a particular product into contact. The function of the money market is to bring those individuals and organisations with funds to lend into contact with those individuals and organisations who wish to borrow funds. However, this does not imply that there is a particular meeting place where those with funds to lend and those who wish to borrow meet. In fact, a great deal of borrowing and lending is conducted over the telephone between individuals who deal with each other on a day-to-day basis. Neither is there a single type of loan arranged through the money market. Instead there are many different submarkets which together make up the money market. The issue is complicated because, as we shall see, most institutions actively participate in more than one of these submarkets.

The Securities Traded in the Money Market

Before we look at the institutions which participate in the money market and the specific markets in which they participate, let us look at the securities traded on the money market. This is important because funds are 'sourced' or obtained by issuing securities. These are simply IOUs, or promises to pay out a particular sum usually at some specified future date. The securities traded on the London Money Market are often referred to as *negotiable bearer documents*. The term 'negotiable' implies that they can be bought and sold at prices which are negotiable, while the term 'bearer document' implies that the bearer, or owner, receives any interest due and is paid the appropriate amount when the security *matures* – that is, when it is redeemed.

Securities can take a variety of forms, but it is the fact that they are all negotiable bearer documents which makes the money market, where these securities are traded, possible. As we shall see on pp. 219–24 the different securities give rise to the different submarkets which make up the London Money Market. Securities are either sold *at a discount* or are *interest bearing*. When securities are issued at a discount they are sold at less than their maturity value, the difference being the reward for holding them. By reducing the price at which they are sold their attractiveness to investors can therefore be increased. Interest bearing securities, on the other hand, pay their holder interest as the reward for holding them. In this case, their attractiveness to investors can be increased by increasing the rate of interest paid on them.

The distinction is important because securities which are sold at a discount usually mature in a relatively short period of time with three months and six months being the most popular duration. These securities are usually referred to as *bills*. Interest bearing securities, on the other hand, mature after a longer period of time, often five years or more. These securities are known as *bonds*. Bills are by far the most important securities traded on the London Money Market with bonds being traded mainly on the capital market (see p. 86). It is useful to look at the specific securities traded on the London Money Market.

Treasury Bills

These securities are issued weekly by the Bank of England on behalf of the government and are sold by *tender* – that is, they are sold to the highest bidder. Normally Treasury bills mature 91 days after issue and, because there is no default risk, they are highly liquid assets. They are issued to meet the government's short-term borrowing requirement (though, as we shall see in Chapter 25, the amount of Treasury bills issued can be varied in accordance with the dictates of the government's monetary policy). A Treasury bill is illustrated in Figure 24.1.

Figure 24.1 *A Treasury bill*

Commercial Bills of Exchange

These are IOUs given by a buyer of goods (the **drawee** of the bill) to a supplier of goods (the **drawer** of the bill) promising a fixed sum of money at some specified future date in payment for the goods. Effectively they are a means of granting **trade credit**. The usual practice is for the drawer to have the bill accepted by one of the financial institutions which then assumes responsibility for payment in the event of default by the drawee (see p. 222). The bill can then be sold at a discount on the money market.

Local Authority Bills

Local authority bills are usually issued by tender, normally with an original maturity of three months or six months. They are used to finance the short-term borrowing requirements of local authorities that arise because of a difference between local authority spending and local authority revenue. Figure 24.2 illustrates a local authority bond issued by the City of Nottingham.

Certificates of Deposit

Certificates of deposit are issued mainly by banks and building societies in denominations ranging from £50,000 to £500,000, though larger sums can also be raised. They are negotiable bearer documents and are usually issued at a fixed rate of interest. Certificates of deposit have original maturities of three months to five years but only those with one year or less to maturity are traded on the money market. These certificates have become increasingly important in recent years as retail banks have practised *liability management* (see p. 222).

Figure 24.2 *A local authority bond*

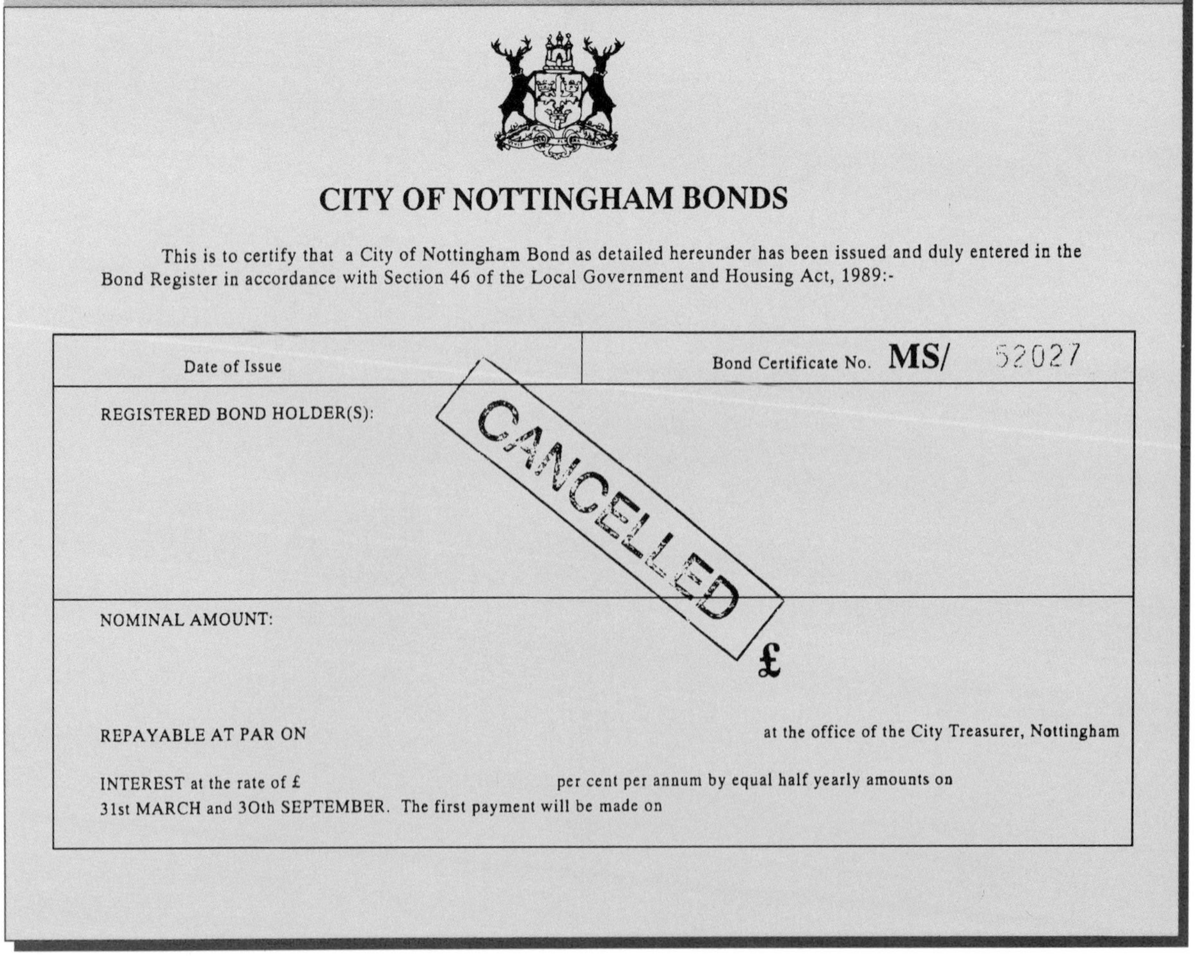

CITY OF NOTTINGHAM BONDS

This is to certify that a City of Nottingham Bond as detailed hereunder has been issued and duly entered in the Bond Register in accordance with Section 46 of the Local Government and Housing Act, 1989:-

Date of Issue

Bond Certificate No. MS/ 52027

REGISTERED BOND HOLDER(S):

CANCELLED

NOMINAL AMOUNT:

£

REPAYABLE AT PAR ON at the office of the City Treasurer, Nottingham

INTEREST at the rate of £ per cent per annum by equal half yearly amounts on 31st MARCH and 30th SEPTEMBER. The first payment will be made on

Financial Intermediaries

All participants in the money market are **financial intermediaries**. This simply means they accept deposits and make loans. You are no doubt very familiar with some financial intermediaries. The high street banks such as Barclays and Lloyds, and the building societies are all financial intermediaries. All financial intermediaries perform two main functions: *maturity transformation* and *risk reduction*. Let us consider each in turn.

Maturity transformation. Savers often require access to their funds at quite short notice. In some cases this means immediate withdrawal but in others it may mean withdrawal after, say, seven days' notice. Borrowers on the other hand, often require funds for quite long periods of time and will rarely borrow funds which they may be called upon to repay immediately or after a short period of notice. Financial intermediaries bridge the gap. They borrow short and lend long. They can do this, because, as we saw in Chapter 23, inflows will at least match outflows and even if they do not any financial intermediary can always attract additional inflows by offering depositors a higher rate of interest than other financial intermediaries.

Risk reduction. Whenever funds are lent there is always a risk that the lender will default. However, an individual can eliminate the risk of default if funds are deposited with a financial intermediary. When a financial intermediary lends funds there is still a risk of default but financial intermediaries are better able than an individual to assess the degree of risk in any particular lending arrangement. We would expect this, since they employ analysts and accountants to advise them. However, they are also better able to insure themselves against the consequences of default. For an individual making a small number of loans, the consequences of a single borrower defaulting might be catastrophic. However, a financial intermediary, by lending to many customers, is able to withstand the effect of a few defaulters. Indeed, by including a small mark-up in the rate of interest they charge all borrowers financial intermediaries are able to pass on the cost of default. An individual, lending only on a small scale, could not do this because there are insufficient borrowers over which to spread the risk of default.

Traditionally, we distinguish between bank financial intermediaries and non-bank financial intermediaries. At one time the basis of the distinction was that the liabilities of bank financial intermediaries, such as bank deposits were money (see pp. 209–10) whereas the liabilities of the non-bank financial intermediaries were not. In fact, this distinction is now very blurred indeed though a distinction continues to be made for drafting and applying legal regulations. Currently in the UK bank financial intermediaries are defined to include the Banking Department of the Bank of England, the clearing banks, the discount houses, the accepting houses and other wholesale banks. The non-bank financial intermediaries include the building societies, the National Savings Bank, most finance houses, pension funds, insurance companies and unit trusts. Let us look more closely at the institutions which act as financial intermediaries. We begin with a discussion of the functions of the Bank of England.

The Bank of England

The Bank of England is at the heart of the monetary sector in the UK. It is referred to as the central bank (or simply the Bank) which confirms its dominant role and, although the functions may vary, all countries have their own central bank. The Bank of England performs two main functions: it is banker to the government and it is banker to the banking system. Before we discuss these functions in more detail, we should note that although the Bank of England is banker to the government, it carries out its day-to-day activities independently of the government. In general, the Treasury, under the Chancellor of the Exchequer, is responsible for setting the overall framework of economic and monetary policy and the Bank of England has responsibility for seeing that these policies are carried out by the City's financial institutions. Let us examine the particular functions the Bank of England performs.

Issue of Notes

The Bank of England is the sole note issuing authority in England and Wales. The Scottish and Irish banks retain the right to issue their own notes. However, they cannot issue notes without limit; for each note issued by these institutions they must hold an equivalent Bank of England note as backing. Nevertheless, the Bank makes no attempt to regulate the issue of notes for purposes of monetary control or economic management. As we shall see on p. 221, notes constitute a relatively small part of the total money supply in the UK and the Bank of England simply responds passively to changes in the public's demand for cash. We may note that the government, if it so desires, is able to restrict the issue of notes because when the Bank increases the note issue it must ensure that it holds an equivalent amount of government securities. It is for this reason that the note issue in the UK is referred to as a *fiduciary issue*.

Implementation of the Government's Monetary Policy

A major function of the Bank is to implement the government's monetary policy which, as we shall see on pp. 329–31, primarily involves controlling the rate of interest at present, though in the past the Bank has attempted to control the growth of the money supply. However, this implies that unless the government wishes to see a change in monetary policy, the Bank does not play an active part in the operation of monetary policy. In fact, as we shall see on pp. 229–30, the Bank operates in the bill (short term securities) market on a daily basis so as to ensure that interest rates are not disturbed in a way that is counter to government policy.

Issue and Redemption of Government Stock

Quite apart from its short-term borrowing, the government also issues longer-term debt known as *gilt-edged stock*. These stocks involve borrowing over periods from five to 40 years and interest is paid twice yearly. The purpose of such borrowing is primarily to meet any shortfall in tax revenues over expenditure by the government. In years when revenue exceeds expenditure, as in 1988–89 and 1989–90, some of this stock can be redeemed early. It is the responsibility of the Bank to arrange the issue and redemption of stock and to pay interest to holders of stock.

Manage the Exchange Equalisation Account

The Exchange Equalisation Account is where the nation's reserves of foreign currency are held. The Bank, in accordance with government policy, intervenes in the foreign exchange market so as to influence the value of sterling against other currencies such as the dollar and the Deutschemark. We shall see on p. 315 that in order to prevent sterling falling against other currencies, the Bank will intervene and use its reserves of foreign currency to prevent, or reduce, the extent of the fall in sterling. Conversely, if sterling is rising against other currencies and the government wishes to avoid or reduce the extent of this, the Bank will buy foreign currency and so add to the reserves.

Manage the Government's Accounts

As well as the other functions it performs for the government, the Bank receives inflows of funds paid into the government's account, for example from the payment of taxes, and makes payments on the government's behalf such as payments to the National Giro which distributes pensions, social security payments and so on.

Banker to the Banking System

As banker to the banking system, the Bank of England performs additional functions.

Supervision of the Clearing System

Each day, the high street banks receive claims on other banks which often exceed several hundred million pounds. Instead of each bank settling its indebtedness to every other bank, they simply 'swop-off' claims against each other and settle the residual balance. This is known as the *clearing process*, and it takes place each working day in London at the Clearing House. It plays a crucial part in the functioning of the banking system and all banks (and building societies) which are not clearing banks maintain deposits with at least one bank which is a clearing bank so that claims against it can be settled. In order to settle any claims outstanding after cheques have ben cleared, banks maintain deposits at the Bank of England which are transferred from the account of one bank to the account of another bank to settle any indebtedness. It is for this reason that the Bank of England is sometimes referred to as *banker to the banking system*.

Lender of Last Resort to the Banking System

The Bank of England stands ready to lend to the banking system in the event that an individual bank has insufficient cash to meet demands by its customers. The aim is to maintain confidence in the banking sector. Usually, lender of last resort assistance is provided through the discount market, but exceptionally the Bank may deal directly with a bank seeking assistance. However, when making such assistance available the Bank reserves the right to charge a punitive rate of interest, thus deterring banks from any excessive lending that might necessitate their use of the lender of last resort facility.

Exercise of Prudential Supervision of the Banking System

The Bank exercises prudential control over the banking system so as to safeguard the interests of depositors. Banks, after all, are custodians of other people's money, and in the absence of prudential supervision they may very well operate in a way that is not entirely consistent with the interests of depositors. The prudential arrangements which safeguard the interests of depositors have been considerably improved in recent years and the Bank is currently concerned with three areas:

Capital adequacy, to ensure that the bank has sufficient reserves to cover the possibility of default by creditors. The increase in the volume of Third World debt and the corresponding increase in the risk of default (see p. 379) has made this a particularly important issue in recent years.

Liquidity, to ensure that banks maintain a sufficient stock of liquid assets – that is, assets which can easily be converted into cash – to meet any unanticipated increase in demand for cash by the public and to ensure orderly trading in the City's financial markets.

Foreign currency exposure, which refers to the extent to which an individual bank holds deposits of, or lends in, foreign currency. Such banks are exposed to the risk of loss due to adverse movements in the exchange rate (see p. 315). Here again, the risk of such losses has implications for the adequacy of banks' capital reserves. The Bank therefore imposes limits on the volume of assets and liabilities in foreign currency that a bank can hold.

The Discount Market

One of the principle intermediaries in the money market is the Discount Market. This consists of nine discount houses which are unique to the UK financial system and perform several important functions. Let us examine these.

Discounting Securities

The traditional function of the discounting houses is, of course, *discounting*, whereby they purchase short-term securities, such as commercial bills of exchange and treasury bills at less than their maturity value. In fact, the discount houses are the principle *market makers* in bills in the London Money Market. This simply means that they are always prepared to buy and sell bills. The difference is profit for the discount houses.

In discounting bills, the discount houses are effectively making short-term loans. For example, if a commercial bill with three months to maturity is purchased or discounted for £975,000, the discount houses is making a three-month loan of £975,000 to the drawer of the bill. If the maturity value of the bill is £1m, the discount house is charging a rate of interest of (£1m − £975,000 × 100 × 4) ÷ £975,000 ≃ 10.3%. (Note that we have multiplied by 4 to convert our rate of interest from a three-month rate into an annual rate.)

The importance of the discount market as a source of short-term finance must not be underestimated. Manufacturers produce their output in anticipation of sales. However, traders often require time to sell this output to customers before they are able to pay the manufacturer. This poses a problem for manufacturers because they will usually require funds to finance further production but by accepting a bill of exchange they are granting traders credit. The dilemma is resolved by *discounting* the bill of exchange. The trader is allowed credit and the manufacturer obtains funds with which to finance further production. The absence of a discount market may seriously disrupt the flow of production in some cases – though, of course, this particular aspect of the work of the discount market could be performed by other financial institutions such as banks.

Financing the Government's Short-term Borrowing

The discount market collectively agree to 'cover the tender' – that is, to submit a bid for the entire weekly issue of Treasury bills. This is important since it guarantees that the government's short-term borrowing requirement will always be met. In practice, the discount market is never required to take up the entire weekly issue of Treasury bills because the government will accept higher bids from other individuals and institutions leaving the discount market to take up the residual.

Secondary Market in Short-term Securities

As well as discounting bills of exchange and Treasury bills, the discount houses maintain a secondary market in other short-term securities such as local authority bills and sterling certificates of deposit. This adds to the efficiency with which the financial system functions, since it provides investors with a market for their securities should they wish to dispose of them. Investors are therefore more likely to purchase newly issued securities because the existence of a secondary market makes instant sale possible if this becomes necessary. The absence of such a market implies that investors will be unable to dispose of any securities held and must therefore await maturity before they can redeem their investments for cash.

Provision of Liquid Assets to the Banking Sector

The discount houses accept loans from banks at *call and short notice*. Such funds earn interest for the banks but are highly liquid. In particular, money at call must be repaid within a few hours. The discount houses are therefore clearly useful to the banking sector since they provide an income on surplus funds which the banks might otherwise be unable to lend because of their need to maintain adequate levels of liquidity to meet demands from their depositors.

However, in providing a home for short-term funds, the discount houses also function as a buffer between the Bank of England and the rest of the banking sector. Flows of funds between the government and the bank can fluctuate quite widely on a day-to-day basis, for example as a result of unusually large tax payments. In such cases, a bank which is left short of funds will call in its loans to the discount market and the discount market will in turn seek loans from other banks. If the discount market is unable to obtain replacement funds it will be forced to borrow from the Bank of England in its role as lender of last resort.

Implementation of Monetary Policy

The discount market provides the channel through which the Bank of England implements its monetary policy. In particular, as we shall see in Chapter 25, when the discount houses are forced to borrow from the Bank of England they do not know in advance the terms on which the Bank will make assistance available to the market. By varying the terms on which it gives assistance to the market the Bank of England is able to influence the level of interest rates in the economy generally (see pp. 229–30).

The Retail Banks

The retail banks in the UK are the London, Scottish and Northern Ireland clearing banks and the Girobank. The Banking Department of the Bank of England is also included, but since this is purely for statistical purposes we ignore the Bank of England in this section. The retail banks are so called because they have a large branch network and offer retail services to their customers. Table 24.1 gives some idea of the importance of the different activities in which they are involved.

Let us look at those items in the balance sheet with we are not familiar, beginning with the liabilities side.

Notes outstanding refer to sterling banknotes issued by the Scottish and Northern Ireland clearing banks. Most are backed pound for pound by Bank of England notes.

Sterling deposits consist of either sight deposits or time deposits. The former can be withdrawn on demand whereas notice of withdrawal (7 days, 30 days, etc.) is required before the latter can be withdrawn.

We now turn to the asset side of the balance sheet

Balances with the Bank of England consist of cash ratio deposits and operational deposits. The former are of no economic significance; they are payments banks, along with many other financial insititutions, are forced to make to the Bank of England to provide the Bank with operating income. The latter are used for settlement of inter-bank indebtedness after the clearing of cheques has taken place.

Advances are the most profitable, but least liquid, of a bank's assets. In the main they are loans to customers such as overdrafts and once granted the bank cannot request repayment until the full term of the loan has expired.

Investments primarily consist of holdings of government and government guaranteed securities.

Table 24.1 *Banks in the UK: combined balance sheet of monthly reporting institutions[1] as at 31 December 1990*

LIABILITIES (£m)		*ASSETS (£m)*	
Sterling liabilities		**Sterling assets**	
Notes Outstanding	1678	Notes and Coin	3956
Deposits, of which:		Balances with the Bank of England, of which:	
Slight deposits	169211	Cash ratio deposits	1690
Time Deposits	306653	Operational deposits	3
Certificates of deposit[2]	53296	Special deposits	–
Other sterling liabilities	74272		
		Market Loans	
Other currency liabilities		LDMA, of which:	
		Secured	10466
Deposits, of which:		Unsecured	260
Sight and time deposits	126449	Other UK bank	91066
Certificates of deposit[2]	709973	UK bank CD's	20271
		Building society CD's and time deposits	3337
Other foreign currency liabilities	25106	UK local authorities	625
		Overseas	28706
		Bills, of which:	
		Treasury bills	3242
		Eligible bills	36
		Eligible bank bills	10588
		Other bills	574
		Advances	375999
		Investments	26272
		Other sterling assets	32770
		Other currency assets	
		Advances	152569
		Market loans	445526
		Bills	5642
		Investments	46771
		Other foreign currency assets	5129
Total liabilities	11266331	Total assets	11266331

[1] Generally those with total balance sheet of £100m or more, or eligible liabilities of £10m or more, other than members of the LDMA

[2] and other short-term paper (short-term securities) issued.

Source: *Bank of England Quarterly Bulletin*, February 1991

They are more liquid than advances because they can be sold on the capital market.

Liquidity and Profitability

Banks have obligations to their shareholders and must therefore consider the profitability of their activities. However, they also have obligations to their customers, and in particular must ensure they are **able to meet demands for cash**. The problem is that the most liquid assets they hold are their least profitable assets and their most profitable assets are their least liquid. Until recent years, the emphasis of banking behaviour was firmly on asset management. In other words, they attempted to manage their assets in such a way as to ensure an adequate level of liquidity and the achievement of their profitability targets. However, the introduction of certificates of deposit has enabled banks to shift the emphasis of their activities. They are now more concerned to expand their liabilities so as to increase their profits and to ensure they have sufficient assets to meet liquidity considerations by issuing certificates of deposit.

Accepting Houses

These institutions are sometimes referred to as merchant banks because all the seventeen accepting houses currently operating in the UK are merchant banks. However, merchant banks perform a variety of functions such as underwriting an issue of shares, providing advice on mergers, financing overseas transactions and so on, but only their acceptance business has implications for the money market. Acceptance business simply means that for a fee they will *underwrite* a bill of exchange – that is, guarantee payment on the bill in the event of default by the drawee. This has important implications because once a bill is accepted it becomes a 'first class bill' and it will then be possible to have the it discounted at one of the money market institutions. We may note that although acceptance business is a highly specialised activity, retail banks and other financial institutions will also carry out a certain amount of acceptance business.

The Parallel Money Markets

The *parallel*, or *secondary money markets* are so called to distinguish them from the discount market which is a *primary market*. An important difference between the primary market and the parallel markets is that loans to the latter are *unsecured*: they have no lender of last resort facility and lenders rely on the good name of the institution to which they lend funds as their guarantee that these funds are indeed secure. It is worth noting that although we identify several parallel money markets, in reality the distinction between these markets is blurred because the same institutions participate in many of the different markets and therefore funds flow freely between markets which might otherwise appear quite separate.

The Sterling Inter-bank Market

This is undoubtedly the largest of all the sterling parallel money markets. Almost all financial institutions in the UK participate in some way in the inter-bank market. It is the market in which financial institutions **borrow and lend to each other**. The transactions between participants in the market involve sums of a minimum of £500,000 and in the main are for several millions of pounds. Transactions of £20m are not uncommon in this market. Funds can be borrowed overnight or for periods of up to five years. However, most funds are borrowed for three months or less and a significant amount is borrowed overnight to enable banks and other financial institutions to balance their books at the end of each working day.

It is worth noting that interest rates charged in the inter-bank market are particularly significant and are thought to provide a good indication of the marginal cost of funds to the banking sector. The key rate is the London inter-bank offered rate (LIBOR) which adjusts swiftly to short-term changes in supply and demand conditions and is therefore an indicator of future trends in short-term interest rates in general.

Sterling Certificates of Deposit Market

This market was launched in 1968 and it was originally envisaged that the main participants would be non-bank institutions and individuals. However, as it has evolved, banks and other financial institutions have become active participants in the sterling certificates of deposit market. In this sense, the market consists of both a primary and a secondary element. The banks issue certificates of deposit to investors through the market but existing certificates are also traded between individuals and institutions through the market. The value of transactions has grown from about £1,000m in 1970 to in excess of £300,000m in 1990.

The market is important because it enables banks and building societies to raise *wholesale deposits* (deposits in excess of £1/4m) at fixed rates of interest and for fixed terms, thus reducing the degree of uncertainty over their future interest rate commitment. In addition, by offering a higher rate of interest on their certificates of deposit, banks and building societies can be certain of attracting any additional deposits they require to facilitate liability management.

The Finance House Market

This market specialises in raising wholesale deposits by UK finance houses, from the banking sector and from the wholesale banks in particular. However, funds are also provided in this market by insurance companies, pension funds and non-financial companies. The finance houses usually require fixed term deposits which are used to facilitate purchases on behalf of individuals and organisations who then repay the finance house in instalments.

The Local Authority Market

This is the oldest of all the parallel money markets and dates from 1955. Some negotiable local authority bonds nearing maturity are traded on this market, but of much more significance are local authority bills which are usually issued with an original maturity of three months or six months. Local authority bills are usually issued by tender and have been popular with the discount houses when Treasury bills have been in short supply. In many ways they are regarded as very similar to Treasury bills, and in particular their liquidity has also made them popular with banks.

The Euro-currency Market

The Euro-currency market is simply a market in currencies held outside their country of origin. For example, if a UK exporter accepts payment in dollars for his (her) output and deposits these dollars in a London bank for future use a Euro-dollar deposit will be created. Originally the Euro-currency market was a market in dollars, but it is now a market in many different currencies. It has grown spectacularly since its beginnings some thirty years ago and currently has assets in excess of $4000bn!

Banks which participate in this foreign currency market accept deposits from individuals and firms but are interested only in large or *wholesale* deposits which means upwards of about $100,000. However, they also issue Euro-currency bonds in order to attract deposits which they can on-lend to borrowers. The magnitude of deposits increased dramatically with the rise in the price of oil in 1973–74 and a large part of the increasing OPEC surpluses were deposited in the Euro-currency market. A large part of these surpluses were lent to the developing countries and culminated in the 'debt crisis' of the 1980s.

However, this is not the issue we wish to explore at this stage. Instead we want to focus on the implications for domestic monetary control of a vast and growing Euro-currency market. The Euro-currency market may present difficulties to the authorities at a time when the Bank of England is attempting to restrict the growth of bank lending. For example, if organisations can obtain funds for overseas investment purposes in the Euro-currency market this may well release other funds for use in the domestic economy. Of course, as we shall see on pp. 229–30, the Bank of England, by raising its own rate of interest, can raise all other rates of interest in the domestic economy including Euro-currency rates, and can therefore cut down the demand for funds. However, as we shall see in Chapter 33, an increase in the rate of interest will attract more funds from abroad and can put upward pressure on the exchange rate. Such pressure might well be at odds with government policy, especially since sterling has joined the ERM (see p. 329).

The relationship between the various institutions in the money market is illustrated in Figure 24.3 on p. 224.

Figure 24.3 *The financial system*

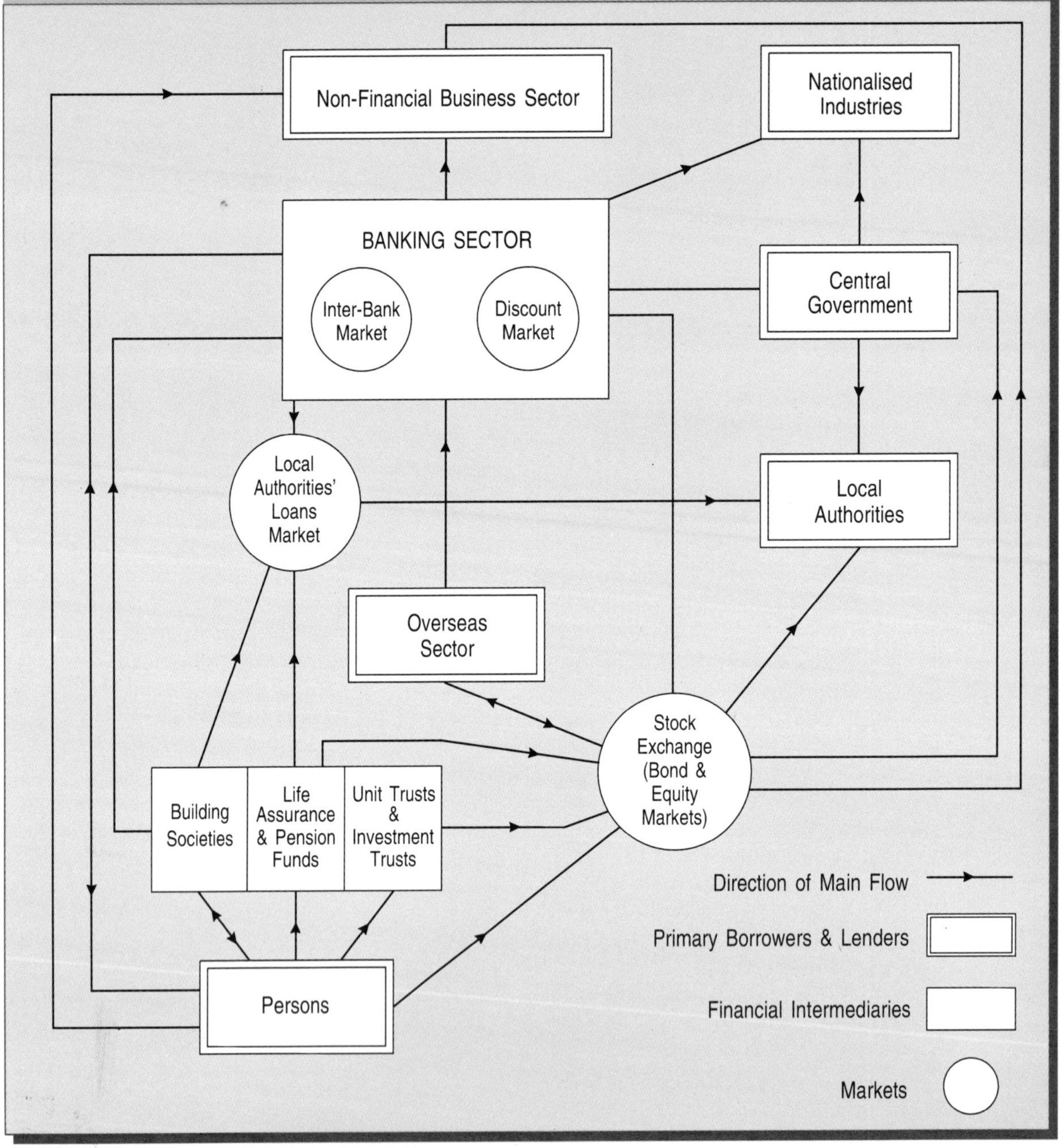

REVIEW QUESTIONS

1 What do the discount houses discount?

2 What do the accepting houses accept?

3 What is the inter-bank market, and why is it important?

4 Does the existence of a Euro-currency market make monetary control more difficult in the UK?

5 What is the purpose of the 'lender of last resort' facility?

6 Why is there a conflict between liquidity and profitability for the retail banks?

CHAPTER 25

MONETARY CONTROL

CONNECTIONS

In Chapter 25 we focus on the techniques of monetary control used by the authorities in the conduct of monetary policy. The reasons for exercising monetary control are discussed in Chapter 28. In discussing monetary control we shall frequently refer to many of the monetary institutions discussed in Chapter 24. We shall also refer to the exchange rate, which is discussed in Chapter 33 and the ERM which is discussed in Chapter 34. We shall also refer to the banking sector in the money supply process as discussed in Chapter 23.

Key Concepts

Broad money
Fiscal policy
High-powered money
LIBOR
Monetary base
Narrow money
Open market operations
Special deposits

Defining the Money Supply

Monetary policy is concerned with the **supply of money in the economy** and the **costs of borrowing it**. As we shall see in Chapter 27, there is a relationship between the rate of money growth – that is, the rate at which the money supply grows – and the rate of inflation. The broad aim of monetary policy is to control the growth of the money supply so as to avoid an excessive rate of inflation. But what exactly do we mean by *the money supply*?

In Chapter 23 we argued that *money is as money does*. This is a very important functional definition of money, but if the authorities aim to control the growth of the money supply it is clear that they must first define which variables it is they are going to control. The problem is therefore to define the range of assets which performs the functions of money. Unfortunately this is easier said than done because some assets perform some, but not all, of the functions of money. The problem is made even more difficult because different assets perform different functions of money.

There is no doubt that notes and coin count as money. They are sometimes referred to as *outside* or *fiat* money to indicate that they are created by the State and are distinct from *inside* or *scriptural* money which are assets to one economic agent but are the liabilities of a bank or other financial intermediary. But which type of deposits function as money? Clearly *sight deposits* are regarded as money because they are acceptable as a means of payment (see p. 208) – that is, they are a *medium of exchange*. However, *time deposits* are subject to *notice of withdrawal* and are not therefore acceptable as a medium of exchange. On the other hand, these deposits, because they earn higher rates of interest than sight deposits, are regarded more as a *store of value* and therefore perform another important function of money. They are sometimes referred to as *quasi-money* and although they are not a medium of exchange, they can quickly be converted into such a medium.

Despite its simplicity, this classification of deposits as either sight deposits or time deposits may be too crude for practical purposes. In particular, it leaves unanswered the question of whether we should include sterling deposits of overseas residents and foreign currency deposits. In fact, we shall see in Chapter 27 that a change in money growth, because of its effect on expenditure, can have an effect on the **rate of inflation**. This is the primary reason why governments monitor and control money growth. But changes in sterling deposits of overseas residents may not have the same effect on expenditure in the domestic economy, and therefore on domestic inflation, as changes in deposits of domestic residents. Similarly foreign currency deposits can usually be spent only in the domestic economy if they are converted into domestic currency. Of course, it could be argued that in the UK foreign currency deposits are convertible without restriction into sterling and so the growth of foreign currency deposits may have an effect on spending in the domestic economy. However, there are charges made on currency conversion and so here again changes in foreign currency deposits may not affect expenditure in the domestic economy *to the same extent* as changes in sterling deposits.

A further problem is that there is a whole range of 'near money' assets which, although they do not function as a medium of exchange, can readily be converted into such a medium. We have seen in Chapter 24 that different securities are traded in organised markets and can therefore easily be converted into the means of payment. However, here again it is not clear what effect the sale of securities will have on the money supply. For example, if one private individual sells a security to a broker and the broker sells the security to another private individual, there will simply be a change in the ownership of bank deposits: effectively one individual will transfer a bank deposit to another individual in payment for the security. There will therefore be no change in the total volume of bank deposits and no change in the money supply. However, the same is not true if a private individual sells the security to a bank. Here, as we have seen on p. 210, payment will be made by the bank *creating a deposit* on itself. In this case, the sale of the security will lead to an increase in the money supply.

Because of the problems in identifying those assets which perform the functions of money, the authorities have different measures of the money supply. These are discussed below, but economists often classify the different money aggregates, as these measures of the money supply are known, as *narrow money* and *broad money*. Narrow definitions of the money supply include those assets which function mainly as a medium of exchange and therefore provide information on changes in immediate spending potential in the economy. Broad money, on the other hand, includes those assets which function more as a store of value and so the broad money aggregates provide information on the overall growth of liquidity in the economy.

Figure 25.1 shows the monetary aggregates currently monitored in the UK and the relationship between them.

The Background to Monetary Policy

We noted earlier that monetary policy has two strands: control of **money growth** and **interest rate** control. But how do the authorities exercise control over these targets of monetary policy? In fact this is a very complicated area, and it is not at all clear how much precision the authorities can exercise over either money growth or the rate of interest. Nevertheless, the authorities do have a profound influence on both of these, and to understand why we need to consider the current institutional mechanisms and techniques of the Bank of England's operations in the money markets.

High-powered Money

We have seen in Chapter 23 that the growth of bank lending is to some extent dependent on the commercial banks obtaining an adequate supply of reserve assets. In fact, the reserve assets of the banking sector consist of notes and coin held by the banks plus their operational deposits at the Bank of England which can be converted into cash on demand. These assets are sometimes collectively referred to as *high-powered money* or the *monetary base* of the banking system. Since cash in circulation is a small proportion of the total money supply, no attempt is made to restrict this and the Bank of England simply responds passively to changes in the public's demand for cash. In other words, the supply of cash is **demand determined** and is never restricted for purposes of monetary control. Operational deposits therefore perform a pivotal role in the implementation of monetary policy.

Open Market Operations

This is the term used to describe the Bank's activities in the money markets, and these activities have a crucial impact on other institutions in the monetary sector such as the commercial banks. To see why, let

Figure 25.1 *Relationships between the monetary aggregates and their components*

Notes and coin in circulation with M4 private sector

plus M4 private sector non-interest-bearing sterling sight bank deposits

plus M4 private sector interest-bearing sterling sight deposits

plus M4 private sector sterling time bank deposits (including sterling certificates of deposit)

plus M4 private sector holdings of building society shares and deposits and sterling certificates of deposit

equals **M4**

plus Holdings by the M4 private sector of money-market instruments, etc. (banks bills, Treasury bills, local authority deposits), certificates of tax deposit and national savings instruments (excludes certificates, SAYE and other long-term deposits)

equals **M5**

Notes and coin in circulation outside the Bank of England

plus Bankers' operational balances with the Bank of England

equals **M0**(1)

plus M4 private sector interest-bearing retail sterling bank deposits with banks and building societies

equals **M2**

plus M4 private sector foreign currency bank and building society deposits

equals **M4c**

(1) M0 is calculated on a weekly averaged basis. All other aggregates are calculated at end-months.

us consider what happens if the Bank makes an open market purchase of securities such as Treasury bills. The Bank does not purchase securities itself but instructs its broker, one of the discount houses, (currently Seccombe, Marshall and Campion plc) to act on its behalf. When securities are purchased, they will be returned to the Bank of England where they will be retired and their sellers will receive cheques drawn against the Bank of England. They will pay these into their accounts at the commercial banks and the commercial banks will present them to the Bank of England for payment. Payment will be made by transferring deposits from the government's account at the Bank of England into the operational deposits of the commercial banks. The opposite happens when an open market sale of securities is made. In this case, cheques are drawn against deposits held by the commercial banks and payment is made to the Bank of England by a reduction in the operational deposits of the commercial banks.

Clearly the Bank's operations in the open market have implications for the supply of base money to the commercial banks through its effect on their operational deposits. However, the Bank makes no attempt in its open market operations to control the supply of base money in order to influence the money supply. It is sometimes erroneously claimed that open market sales of securities, by reducing the operational deposits of the commercial banks, cause a reduction in their lending. In fact, as we saw on p. 226, the commercial banks are not required to maintain any minimum ratio between operational deposits and eligible liabilities. Instead, as we shall see below, open market operations are used to influence **interest rates**.

Bank of England Forecasts of the Daily Position in the Money Market

Although the clearing banks are not required to maintain operational deposits at any minimum level, each individual bank is required to inform the Bank of England of the target level of operational deposits it is aiming at each day. The clearing banks always aim to keep these at a minimum level, because no interest is received on them. If operational deposits rise above a clearing bank's target level, it will immediately seek to switch the excess into income earning assets such as Treasury bills; and if they fall below the target level action, such as the sale of Treasury bills, will be taken to replenish them.

Each working day at 9.45am, the Bank of England announces its estimate of the expected cash position of the banking system. This estimate is derived from two sources. As banker to the government, the Bank is able to prepare an estimate of flows between itself and the private sector – for example, because of tax receipts and government disbursements, the day's take up of Treasury bills (tendered for the previous week), maturities of Treasury bills and so on. The Bank also receives information from the clearing banks about the target level of operational deposits they are aiming at for that particular day. All of this information is used to produce the Bank's estimate of the day's expected cash position in the money market. If necessary, perhaps because of unexpectedly large tax receipts, the Bank will issue a further estimate of the expected cash position in the money market at noon.

Shortages and Surpluses of Funds

In general, as we shall see below, the Bank, through its open market operations, will operate so as to leave the market short of funds. To relieve the shortage the Bank will normally invite the discount houses to offer eligible bills for outright purchase by the Bank. This is the route through which the Bank normally acts as *lender of last resort*, but how does this relieve a shortage of funds? After all, it is the clearing banks who are short of funds. In fact, since all banks must balance their books at the end of the day's trading, an individual bank which is short of funds will bid for deposits in the inter-bank market. However, when one bank borrows in the inter-bank market another bank lends in the inter-bank market. These inter-bank transactions cannot therefore relieve an *aggregate shortage* of funds. In other words, when the market is short of funds further action will be required, and this implies that banks will call in their loans from the discount market and/or sell securities to the discount market.

Conventionally banks withdraw funds from the discount houses before noon though they might offer surplus funds to the discount houses up to the close of business in the afternoon. Because of this the banks often withdraw funds in excess of their estimated needs from the houses in the morning as precautionary balances, and re-lend the excess in the afternoon. The Bank therefore acts only to relieve a shortage in the morning and at noon it will inform the discount houses, through its broker, that it is prepared to consider purchases of eligible bills. The discount houses are given a second opportunity to transact in bills at 2pm when, if the Bank's morning estimate of the likely shortage or surplus of funds in the market for that day has been significantly altered, it will publish a revised estimate. If the discount market requires further assistance later in the day it can borrow directly from the Bank by pledging bills as security for such loans.

If there is a surplus of funds in the market the Bank acts, as indicated above, in the afternoon to absorb it. To do this, the Bank will issue Treasury bills of one or specified maturities and it will invite offers from the discount houses and the clearing banks. The clearing banks are included in this offer otherwise they would be at a disadvantage in relation to the discount market when placing surplus funds. Since the sale of such Treasury bills is for same day settlement, the Bank can always use this technique to create a shortage of funds and therefore compel the discount market to borrow.

The Bank's Procedure for Dealing in Bills

When the Bank transacts business with the discount market it deals only in eligible bills at the short end of the market – that is, short-term eligible bills. The Bank has specified four maturity bands in which it is prepared to deal:

Band 1, 1 – 14 days to maturity
Band 2, 15 – 33 days to maturity
Band 3, 34 – 63 days to maturity
Band 4, 64 – 91 days to maturity

The Bank restricts its dealing to the short end of the market (indeed the Bank frequently deals only in Bands 1 and 2), reflecting its intention of influencing short-term rates of interest. The procedure is for the Bank to invite the discount houses to offer bills for sale at prices of their own choosing (we shall see on p. 239 that there is an inverse relationship between the price of bills and the rate of interest). If the interest rate implied in these offers is acceptable to the Bank it will purchase bills, otherwise the discount houses must revise their offers to the Bank.

Techniques of Monetary Policy

Having outlined the institutional mechanisms and the procedures through which the Bank conducts its operations in the money markets, we turn our attention to the techniques of monetary policy.

Short-term Interest Rates

Normally the Bank maintains short-term interest rates within an undisclosed band. However, the rate of interest it sets is known because of the prices at which it buys eligible bills. In its dealings with the money market, the general aim of the Bank is to smooth the effect of changes in the flow of funds between itself and the clearing banks so as to avoid erratic changes in short-term rates of interest. However, the current focus of monetary policy is short-term interest rates and therefore the authorities sometimes act so as to engineer a change in short-

Box 25.1 How does the Bank's operations at the short end of the market affect mortgage rates?

When the Bank of England acts in the money market it does so at the short end of the market. When it acts to raise short-term rates of interest this increases the attractiveness of short-term assets. As funds are competed away from long-term investments this puts upward pressure on long-term rates. Similarly a decrease in short-term rates will put downward pressure on long-term rates.

This process is referred to as *arbitrage*, and it provides a powerful reason why the Bank, by its operations at the short end of the market, might influence mortgage rates. However, the effect might not always be strong because the impact of changes in short-term rates becomes weaker the longer the time perspective considered. Slight changes in the Bank's Band 1 dealing rate, though they will undoubtedly influence other short-term rates, are unlikely to affect the mortgage rate. Even when the Bank makes a significant cut of perhaps ½ per cent in its Band 1 dealing rate we find that although short-term rates adjust immediately, mortgage rates often change only after a time lag such as a month or even longer in some cases.

term rates. To ensure that the Bank has maximum influence over short-term rates of interest it normally conducts its daily activities in the bill market so as to leave the market short of funds. It can then relieve this shortage on terms of its own choosing.

Ordinarily this will mean that the Bank accepts offers of eligible bills from the discount houses at prices which leave short-term rates of interest unchanged. However, if the Bank wishes to see a change in short-term interest rates it will reject the offers and, since the market is short of funds, the discount houses will be compelled to re-submit offers which imply a change in interest rates to the level consistent with government policy.

It is important to note that although the Bank confines itself to dealing in bands of shorter-term maturities, any change in its dealing rates will affect interest rates across a wide spectrum. When the Bank raises its dealing rates in the bill market, interest rates in general will rise and when the Bank reduces its dealing rates in the bill market, interest rates in general will fall. For example, if the Bank charges a higher rate of interest to the discount market they will raise their own dealing rates with the rest of the banking sector. Additionally, since the banks' base rates are set $^1/_8$ per cent above the Bank of England's Band 1 dealing rate, it follows that as the Bank raises its Band 1 dealing rate, base rates *automatically* follow suit. Furthermore since *all* interest rates administered by the banks are linked to their base rates, all interest rates will move in the direction of the Bank of England's Band 1 dealing rate. Box 25.1 gives some further information on why interest rates tend to move together.

While the Bank's main technique for changing interest rates is to change the rate at which it deals

Box 25.2 Who sets interest rates?

At times it is alleged that the Bank *determines* rates of interest while at other times it is alleged that the market determines interest rates. So where does the truth lie? Who sets interest rates?

At the most basic level, the answer is of course the Bank of England. By convention commercial banks' base rates are maintained at $^1/_8$ per cent above the Bank of England's Band 1 dealing rate. A direct link therefore exists and a rise in the Bank's Band 1 dealing rate will lead to a rise in banks' base rates and therefore to a rise in all other rates of interest. Evidence of the Bank's influence in the market is well documented. For example, in May 1990 the markets held a strong view that sterling was about to join the ERM and on 17 May three-month and twelve-month sterling LIBOR,[1] which had been well above 15 per cent at the beginning of the month, threatened to fall below 15 per cent. However, the Bank took a different view and 'signalled' to the market that a reduction in interest rates would be resisted. The 'signal' was a £250m loan to the discount market at a rate of 15 per cent, rather than purchases of bills at $14^3/_4$ per cent and $14^7/_8$ per cent which were the rates at which assistance had been given earlier in the day. On May 23rd figures for the current account deficit in April were published. The deficit of £1.8bn was worse than expected and in consequence downward pressure on interest rates abated.

Clearly the Bank can exert a powerful influence on interest rates but the Governor of the Bank of England has said: 'There is a popular perception that the monetary authorities dictate the general level of interest rates, and it is of course true that we are able to exert a very considerable influence on it. But the extent of our influence should not be exaggerated. The financial markets are themselves an immensely powerful influence which we can never afford to ignore. At times, if market sentiment is uncertain and if the authorities are relatively confident in their view of the appropriate policy stance, the Bank's lead may be readily followed. But at other times, if we sought to impose a level of rates against strong market opposition, we are liable to be forced to change our stance'.

In fact, as we shall see on p. 245, there are many factors which influence interest rates and if pressure in the market is strong enough the Bank will be forced to bow to this pressure. Clearly the Bank can influence interest rates, but it cannot swim against the tide indefinitely.

[1] LIBOR is the London Inter-Bank Offer Rate. It is an important short-term rate of interest and adjusts quickly to changes in supply and demand conditions in the money markets. It therefore accurately reflects the general level of short-term interest rates. Since it is the rate at which banks lend to each other in the inter-bank market, it reflects the marginal cost of funds to the banks.

with the discount market it does, on occasion, take more direct action to signal its intention. If the Bank wishes to provide a strong signal to the market that it wishes to see a change in short-term interest rates it usually announces on the day of the change that it will not be transacting in bills on that day, but that the discount market can borrow at 2.30pm at a stated rate of interest. Thereafter the Bank will buy bills from the discount houses at the new dealing rate until there is a further change in interest rates.

Special Deposits

Under the current arrangements, monetary sector institutions with eligible liabilities of £10m or more may be obliged to place *special deposits* with the Bank. These deposits earn interest at a rate roughly equivalent to the Treasury bill rate, but are effectively *frozen* at the Bank and cannot be used by the banks for lending purposes. They are therefore a highly effective means of **reducing the liquidity of the monetary sector**. Despite this, no call has been made for special deposits since 1979. A major reason for this is that they apply only to certain institutions (those with eligible liabilities of £10m or more) and therefore tend to encourage the growth of less efficient institutions which are outside the scope of current banking regulations. Nevertheless, this mechanism is still in place and the authorities can, if they wish, issue a call for special deposits.

Fiscal Policy

'Fiscal policy' refers to government expenditure and taxation. However, fiscal policy also has important implications for monetary policy. In particular, when its expenditure exceeds its revenue, the government has a **budget deficit**. This will be financed by borrowing and, as we shall see on p. 328, if this is done through issuing Treasury bills which are bought by the banking sector, there will be an increase in the money supply. When the government has a **budget surplus** (revenue exceeds expenditure) there will be a reduction in the money supply unless the authorities use the surplus to retire debt (that is, buy debt) from the non-bank, non-building society private sector.

As well as its effects on the money supply, fiscal policy may also influence rates of interest. Thus, when the government has a budget deficit, it will issue securities to meet its borrowing requirement. If all other things remain equal – and in particular if there is no reduction in the demand for funds from the private sector – this implies an increase in competition for funds in the money market. This increase in demand for funds will, if all other things remain equal, drive up interest rates. The opposite will happen if the government has a budget surplus. Clearly monetary policy is not independent of fiscal policy.

REVIEW QUESTIONS

1 What is meant by the term 'arbitrage' and why is it important in explaining why the Bank's influence on interest rates is so pervasive?

2 What is meant by the term 'high-powered money'?

3 How will an open market purchase of securities by the government affect the supply of high-powered money?

4 If the government operated a system of monetary base control, that is, if it controlled the supply of high-powered money, how would this affect interest rates?

5 Why does the Bank of England act to influence short-term rather than long-term interest rates?

6 Why do sales of gilts to the non-bank private sector reduce money growth, whereas sales of gilts to the banking sector increase money growth?

7 In what ways are fiscal policy and monetary policy related?

CHAPTER 26

INTEREST RATES

CONNECTIONS

The **rate of interest** is an extremely important concept and is related to a great deal of microeconomic and macroeconomic analysis. We have seen in earlier chapters that it is related to changes in investment and the level of national income. It is also an important part of the government's **monetary policy** and has a powerful impact on a country's **foreign exchange rate**.

Key Concepts

Investment demand for money
Liquidity preference
Loanable funds
Nominal rate of interest
Precautionary demand for money
Real rate of interest
Term structure of interest rates
Time preference
Transactions demand for money
Treasury bill

What is the 'Rate of Interest'?

'Interest' is usually thought of as the amount that must be paid to borrow funds or the amount that is earned if funds are lent. The *rate* of interest expresses this amount as an *annual percentage* of the sum borrowed or lent. For example, if a firm borrows £10,000 for 12 months, and after this time repays a total of £11,000 £1,000 is interest, and the rate of interest is:

$$\frac{£1,000}{£10,000} \times 100 = 10\%$$

Economic commentary in the media frequently refers to changes in the rate of interest as though there was only **one rate of interest**. Our definition above also refers to 'the' rate of interest. In fact, a glance in any high street bank will show that there are **many rates of interest**. An important question to ask is therefore what economists mean by 'the' rate of interest.

Interest rates are related in such a way that if one interest rate is rising, in general all interest rates will be rising and if one interest rate is falling, in general all interest rates will be falling. Because interest rates *in general* move in concert, economists focus on a single rate, such as the Treasury bill rate or the three-month inter-bank rate, to represent the *trend* in interest rates. In other words, whether interest rates *in general* are rising or whether *in general* they are falling is shown by the behaviour of the representative rate. It is this trend movement in all interest rates, illustrated by the behaviour of the representative rate, that economists are referring to when they speak of 'the' rate of interest.

We now know what the rate of interest is, but we do not know what **determines it**. In fact, there is no single theory which explains how the rate of interest is determined in all circumstances. Instead, different theories highlight the importance of different factors that influence the rate of interest. Later we focus on two theories of interest rate determination: the *loanable funds theory* and the *liquidity preference* theory, but first we explain why there are so many rates of interest.

Why are There so Many Rates of Interest?

Different rates of interest arise because of differences in the nature of borrowing and lending. Some of the more important factors causing differences in interest rates are:

Degree of risk: The credit-worthiness of the borrower, and therefore the risk of default, is an important factor influencing this. The greater the degree of risk, the higher the rate of interest banks will charge to compensate for accepting the higher risk.

Duration of loan: If there is no expectation of a reduction in interest rates, the length of time funds are lent will have an important influence on the rate of interest. After all, the longer the period money is lent, the longer the lender forgoes current consumption.

Marketability of the asset: In the financial world it is often the case that when money is lent, securities are exchanged for funds. These securities can be sold in secondary markets. However, some assets are more marketable than others and in general such assets will pay a lower rate of interest than more marketable assets.

Absolute size of the transaction: Financial intermediaries may be prepared to offer a higher rate of interest for relatively large wholesale deposits. This reflects lower unit costs of administration: in other words, the average cost of administering a deposit falls as the size of the deposit increases, and this may encourage institutions to offer higher rates of interest on larger deposits.

The Loanable Funds Theory

This is one of the earliest theories of interest rate determination and is associated with the classical school of economics. It focuses attention on the importance of the demand for funds from those who wish to borrow and the supply of funds from those who wish to lend, in determining the rate of interest.

Demand for Loanable Funds

In the loanable funds theory it is argued that the demand for funds is **inversely related to changes in the rate of interest**. In other words, a *rise* in the rate of interest causes a *reduction* in the demand for funds; and a *reduction* in the rate of interest causes an *increase* in the demand for funds.

At the time the classical theory was developed this was justified because it was assumed that the demand for loanable funds came from the desire of firms for capital investment. After all, there was little government intervention in the economy and no provision for the purchase of consumer durables on credit. It was argued that firms would demand funds for capital investment if it was profitable for them to do so. Since interest is a cost of production it follows that changes in the rate of interest will change the profitability, or expected return, of investment. Specifically, as the rate of interest falls the cheaper it is to borrow funds and therefore, if all other things remain equal, the more profitable it is to invest. The demand curve for loanable funds is therefore the normal shape, showing that the quantity of loanable funds *increases* as the rate of interest *falls*.

Supply of Loanable Funds

The supply of loanable funds is determined by the **level of savings**. In other words, as the rate of interest rises the supply of loanable funds increases, and vice versa. The classical economists argued that this was because individuals had a *time preference* for **current consumption**. This simply means that current consumption is preferable to the *same level* of consumption at some stage in the future. In order to persuade individuals to overcome their time preference for current consumption, and therefore to save, it was necessary to offer a reward in the form of interest for saving. The higher the rate of interest, the greater the future level of consumption made possible by abstaining from current consumption. Because of this it was argued that as the rate of interest rises the more individuals will be persuaded to save. The supply curve for loanable funds is therefore the normal shape, showing that as the rate of interest *increases*, there will be an *increase* in the quantity of loanable funds supplied.

The Determination of the Rate of Interest

The rate of interest is established at that level which equates the **demand for loanable funds with the supply of loanable funds**. In Figure 26.1, demand for loanable funds is shown by *D* and the supply of loanable funds is shown by *S*. The equilibrium rate

Figure 26.1 *Supply and demand for loanable funds*

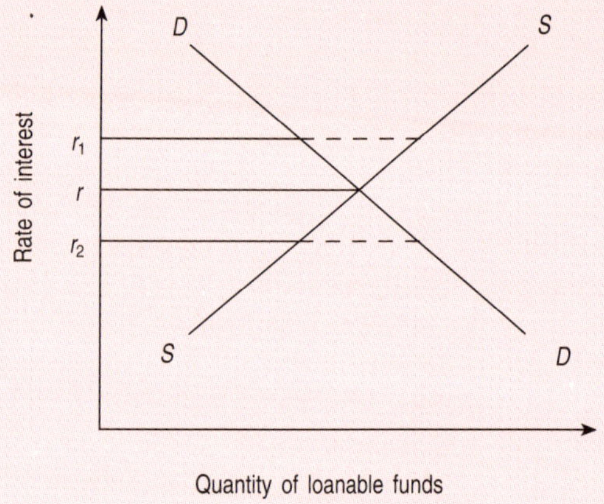

of interest is r since this is the rate at which the demand for loanable funds equals the supply of loanable funds.

Given the supply and demand conditions S and D no other rate of interest is sustainable. For example, at a rate of interest r_1, supply of loanable funds exceeds demand and therefore the rate of interest will fall. At a rate of interest r_2 the opposite happens: demand for loanable funds exceeds supply and the rate of interest rises.

Changes in the Rate of Interest

Once the equilibrium rate of interest is established, there will be no tendency for it to change unless there is a change in at least one of the factors determining demand for loanable funds or supply of loanable funds. Remember that D and S are drawn on the assumption that all factors which affect demand for loanable funds or supply of loanable funds, *except* the rate of interest, do not change. When there is a change in one of these other factors this will cause a *shift in the position* of the supply curve or the demand curve. We saw in Chapter 3 that an increase in demand or an increase in supply occurs when there is an outward movement of the **whole demand curve** or the **whole supply curve**. This means that at any given rate of interest a greater amount of loanable funds is now supplied or demanded than previously. A reduction in demand or supply implies the opposite. In this case, there is an inward movement of the whole supply or demand curve, and therefore fewer loanable funds are now supplied or demanded at any given rate of interest than previously.

Figure 26.2(a) shows the effect on the rate of interest of a change in the demand for loanable funds, and figure 26.2(b) shows the effect of a change in the supply of loanable funds.

Figure 26.2 (a) *The effect of a change in the demand for loanable funds on the rate of interest*

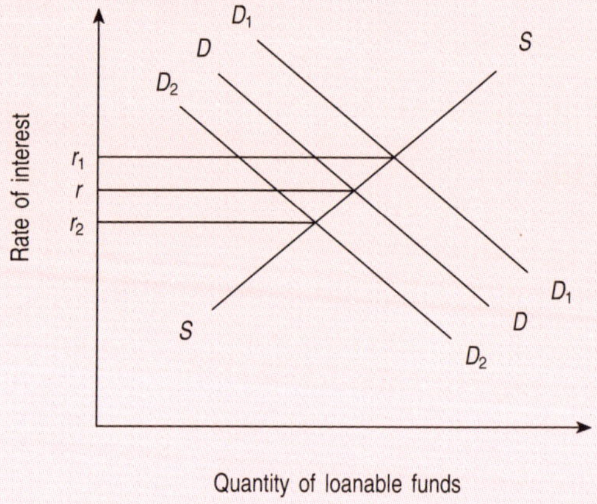

Figure 26.2 (b) *The effect of a change in the supply of loanable funds on the rate of interest*

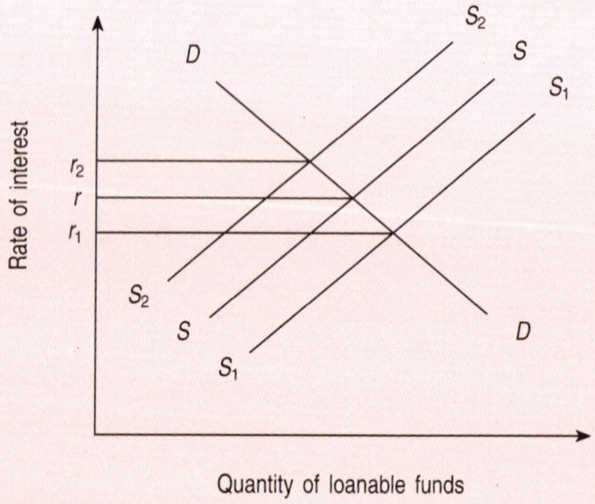

In figure 26.2(a) supply of loanable funds and demand for loanable funds are initially in equilibrium at r. Now if there is an increase in demand for loanable funds this will shift the whole demand curve upwards from D to D_1, and a new equilibrium rate of interest will be established at r_1. A reduction in the demand for loanable funds has exactly the opposite effect. The whole demand curve shifts downwards from D to D_2, and in this case a new equilibrium rate of interest is established at r_2.

Figure 26.2(b) shows the effect of a change in the supply of loanable funds. Supply and demand are again initially in equilibrium at r. An increase in the supply of loanable funds implies a downward shift in the whole supply curve from S to S_1, and a new equilibrium rate of interest will be established at r_1. A reduction in supply shifts the whole supply curve upwards, leading to a new equilibrium at r_2.

Changes in Demand for Loanable Funds

In our discussion of the loanable funds theory we have argued that the demand for loanable funds is derived from the demand of firms for funds with which to finance capital investment. Since firms carry out investment if they expect to make a profit, it follows that anything which changes the expected profitability of capital investment will change the **demand for loanable funds**.

Clearly an important factor is the cost of additional capital which, as we have seen, is partly determined by the rate of interest. However, if all other things including the rate of interest are constant, there are two broad factors which determine the expected profitability of additional investment: the productivity of capital, and the price at which the final output produced from additional capital is sold. In other words, if a firm is considering the purchase of an additional machine it will consider how much extra output the machine will produce, and the price at which this output can be sold. It is these which together determine the additional revenue the firm receives from investing in capital equipment and which can be compared with the cost of purchasing additional capital.

If there is a change in the expected revenue from investing in capital there will be a change in the demand for loanable funds. For example, if technological advances increase the productivity of capital this means that more output will now be produced from a given input of capital. If the price at which this output is unchanged this will increase the expected profitability of investment. Because of this there will be an increase in the demand for loanable funds at any given rate of interest – that is, the demand for loanable funds curve will shift outwards. In terms of Figure 26.2(a), the demand curve will shift from D to D_1, and, all other things remain equal, the rate of interest will rise from r to r_1.

Similarly, if there is a rise in the price of the product which capital is used to produce, and all other things remain equal, there will be an increase in the expected profitability of additional investment, and therefore an increase in the demand for loanable funds. Conversely, a fall in the price of the product which capital is used to produce will lead to a reduction in the expected profitability of additional investment if all other things remain equal. In this case, there will be a reduction in the demand for loanable funds. In terms of Figure 26.2(a), the demand curve will shift inwards from D to D_2 and if all other things remain equal, there will be a rise in the rate of interest from r to r_2.

Changes in Supply of Loanable Funds

It was argued that the supply of loanable funds was provided by household savings. An increase in the rate of interest provided the incentive to increase savings by offering a higher reward for abstaining from current consumption. As the rate of interest increased, the supply of loanable funds increased. However, this relationship is based on the assumption that all other things remain equal. In particular, if the attitude towards saving changes there will be a change in the amount of funds saved at all rates of interest and this will be shown by a shift in the whole of the supply of loanable funds curve. For example, if saving becomes more popular then at any given rate of interest a greater amount of money will be saved than previously. In terms of Figure 26.2(b) the supply of loanable funds curve will shift outwards to S_1 and, if all other things remain equal, there will be a reduction in the rate of interest from r to r_1. The opposite occurs if it becomes less desirable to save. Here the supply of loanable funds curve shifts inwards to S_2 and, if all other things remain equal, there will be an increase in the rate of interest from r to r_2.

A Modern Approach to Loanable Funds Theory

Demand for Loanable Funds

In the classical version of the loanable funds theory outlined above, the demand for loanable funds was derived entirely from the **demand of firms for investment funds**. In practice, funds are demanded for many other purposes. We have seen in Chapter 20 that the economy can be divided into different sectors: the personal sector, the government sector, and so on. We have also seen that over any given period each of these sectors receives income and uses this to finance expenditures. When any sector spends more than it currently receives it is in deficit and must borrow to finance that part of its expenditures not covered by current receipts. For example, when central government expenditure exceeds receipts from taxation and so on (that is, the government has a budget deficit), it borrows to finance this deficit. The same is true for an individual household or firm with a deficit. Those individual units within each sector which have a deficit give rise to a demand for funds with which to finance that deficit.

The inclusion of more than one sector contributing to the demand for loanable funds does not change the basic relationship between the demand for funds and the rate of interest. Admittedly it is unlikely that demand of the public sector for funds will be influenced by changes in the rate of interest. In particular we shall see later that whether the central government has a budget deficit is determined by wider macroeconomic considerations such as the impact of the budget on the level of aggregate demand or its effect on the money supply. These considerations are not influenced by changes in the rate of interest and such changes therefore have little bearing on the demand for funds by the public sector.

However, the same is not true of firms or households. For reasons outlined earlier the demand for investment funds will fall as the rate of interest rises, and vice versa. Similarly, many consumer durables are purchased on credit and therefore by raising the cost of purchasing consumer durables, an increase in the rate of interest might be expected to cut demand for funds by the personal sector. However, the relationship is not clear cut and the demand for consumer durables may be relatively inelastic with respect to changes in the rate of interest. Nevertheless, changes in the rate of interest can sometimes exert a powerful impact on the demand for housing by the personal sector. As the rate of interest rises, the demand for housing falls and therefore the demand for mortgage finance fails. This reasoning allows us to argue that the demand for loanable funds will be inversely related to the rate of interest and therefore the demand for loanable funds curve will be the normal shape.

Supply of Loanable Funds

In the classical version of the loanable funds theory, the supply of loanable funds comes from the households who are persuaded to save more as the rate of interest rises because of the promise of a higher level of consumption in the future. This seems very plausible, but in practice there is no firm evidence that an increase in the rate of interest leads to a significant increase in household saving. Indeed a great deal of saving by the personal sector is on a *contractual* basis, such as premiums on insurance policies and contributions to pension funds. Such contractual saving is unlikely to be affected by changes in the rate of interest.

Nevertheless it is still possible to argue that the supply of loanable funds responds positively to changes in the rate of interest. The main reason for this is that as the rate of interest rises it becomes more profitable for the commercial banks to create deposits. They will therefore be prepared to increase their advances to customers, and this will give the normal shaped supply curve for loanable funds. Additionally, as we shall see on p. 314, as the rate of interest in one country rises, that country attracts funds from abroad. These international flows of funds are very responsive to changes in the rate of interest and the higher the rate of interest rises in one country the greater the quantity of funds that country will attract.

Liquidity Preference Theory

The liquidity preference theory was developed by Keynes, who argued that the rate of interest was not determined by the supply and demand for loanable funds, but by the demand for money to hold and the total money stock – that is, the existing money supply. Keynes identified three motives for holding money or three reasons why individuals and organisations demand money: a *transactions demand*, a *precautionary demand* and a *speculative demand*. Let us analyse each in turn.

The Transactions Demand for Money

Everyone needs to hold some money in order to carry out routine transactions such as paying for bus fares or lunch, purchasing groceries, paying electricity bills and so on. Similarly firms hold transactions balances to meet routine payments such as wages, payment for raw materials and power, and so on.

The transactions demand for money arises because payments and receipts are not perfectly synchronised. If all purchases were made at the same instant income was received, there would be no transactions demand for money. Instead purchases are made in between receipts of income and therefore money balances are held or demanded to meet these anticipated transactions. Let us look at the determinants of the demand for transactions balances.

The Level of Income

One of the main determinants of the demand for transactions balances is the level of income. For most individuals and organisations, and certainly for the community as a whole, as income rises expenditure increases. If we assume that the total nominal value of all transactions in an economy is always four times greater than nominal GNP and that all other things remain equal, the transactions demand for cash will always be a quarter of GNP. As nominal GNP rises, the transactions demand for cash will rise proportionately as shown in Figure 26.3.

Figure 26.3 *The transaction demand for cash and the level of income*

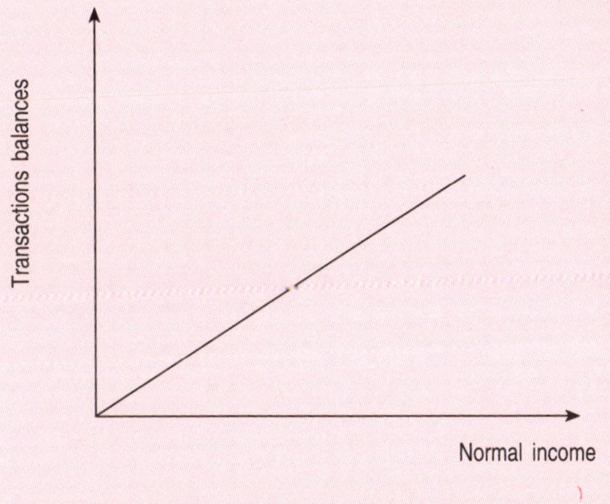

In fact, all other things do not remain constant and it is changes in these other factors that affect transactions demand for money and which explain why, far from rising proportionately, transactions demand for money has fallen over the years. Two of these 'other factors' which exert a powerful influence on the transactions demand for money are the frequency with which income is received, and the frequency with which it is spent.

The frequency with which income is received

Suppose an individual receives £140 per week and spends this at the rate of £20 per day. In this case the average weekly holding of money, or the average weekly demand for transactions balances, would be £70 and the annual level of expenditure would be: £140 × 52 = £7280.

Now if the same individual were to be paid on a four-weekly cycle, income received would be £560 every four weeks. Again if expenditure were spread evenly throughout the four week period at the rate of £20 per day, the average holding of money would increase to £280, but the total level of spending would be unchanged at £7280! In other words there has been no change in this individual's total expenditure, but the average transactions demand for money has increased from £70 to £280 – an increase of 300 per cent! Figure 26.4 illustrates the effect of a change in the frequency of income receipts on the individual's average transactions demand for money.

What is true for the individual in this case is also true for the community as a whole. Changing the frequency with which income is received will change the demand for transactions balances, even if there is no change in the level of income.

The frequency with which expenditures are made

Rather than spending income evenly over any given period such as the four-weekly cycle discussed above, assume our individual spends her entire income in the first half of the month at the rate of £40 per day. Here the average holding of money in the first half of the month is £280, and zero in the remainder, making an average transactions demand for money of £70. This compares with an average transactions demand for money of £280 when expenditures are spread evenly throughout the four week cycle.

Precautionary Demand for Money

The demand for precautionary balances broadly represents money that is held as a precaution against some unforeseen event such as an unanticipated reduction in prices. If we hold only the amount of money which we *anticipate* spending it will be impossible to take advantage of such price reduc-

Figure 26.4 *The effect of a change in the frequency of income receipts on an individual's average transactions demand for money*

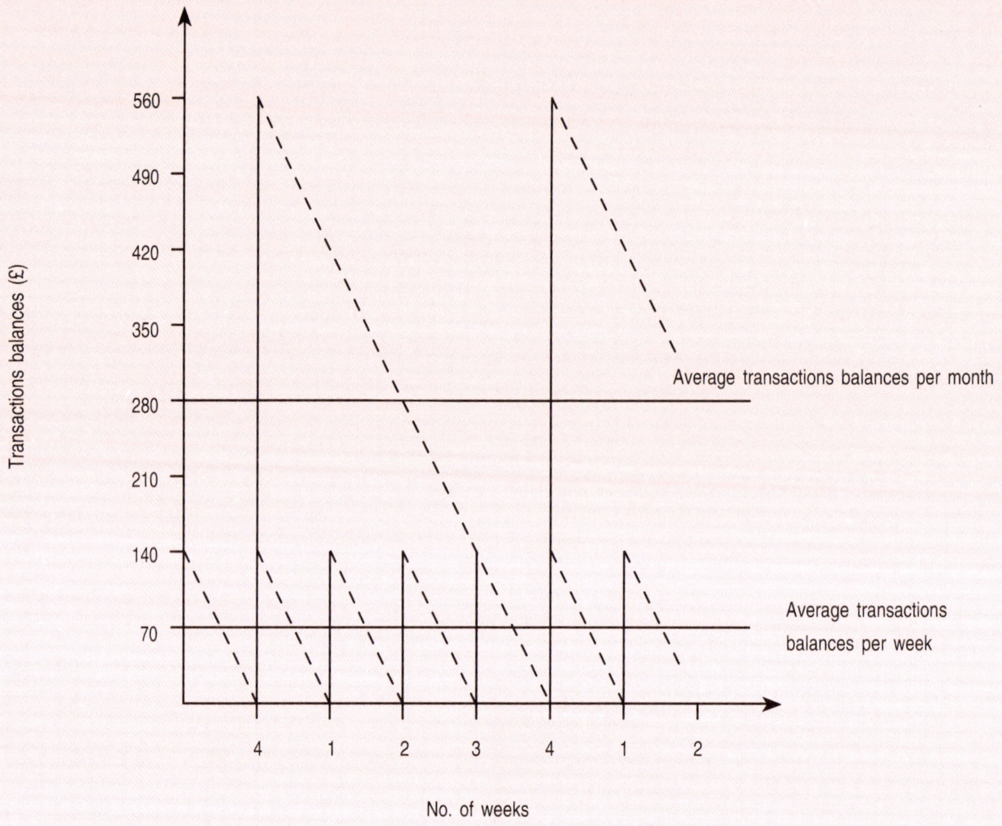

tions. However, precautionary balances are also held as a cushion against an unanticipated interruption in receiving receipts. Firms, in particular, are not always certain when they will receive payment for sales of goods. Late receipt of payments might well create cash flow problems for firms and make it difficult for them to make purchases. To minimise such problems firms and individuals hold precautionary balances.

Again, a major determinant of precautionary balances is likely to be the level of income. For example, an individual with an annual income of £30,000 is likely to hold larger precautionary balances than an individual with an annual income of £5000. However, another factor of considerable importance in modern economies is the availability of overdraft facilities. Firms and individuals probably hold smaller precautionary balances than otherwise because if some unanticipated event requires money which is not held, it can be borrowed from one of the monetary institutions such as a bank.

Speculative Demand for Money

The third motive Keynes identified for holding money was the speculative motive. Basically Keynes considered only two forms of holding wealth: money and bonds. The problem is to decide when money will be preferred to bonds, and vice versa.

The crux of the matter is that, in nominal terms, the value of money is **fixed**. A £1 coin has the same face value tomorrow that it has today. However, the value or price of a bond varies, sometimes rising, sometimes falling. Money is a better store of value if bond prices are expected to fall since bond holders will make a capital loss in these circumstances. Money will therefore be preferred to bonds if bond prices are expected to fall. On the other hand, if bond prices are expected to rise, holders of bonds will make a capital gain, and in these circumstances bonds will be preferred to money.

This is very important because bond prices and interest rates move in opposite directions. A rise in the rate of interest implies a fall in bond prices, and vice versa. This is most easily illustrated if we consider a bond such as a consul (that is, an undated security issued by the UK government which carries an annual return fixed as a percentage of the face value of the consul). Let us say the rate of return is 5 per cent and the nominal price of the consul is £100 This means that for each £100 consul held an investor receives £5 per year. To obtain the market, or current, rate of interest this £5 must be expressed as a percentage of the current market price of the bond.

1 If the bond has a current market price of £80, the current rate of interest is:

$$\frac{£5 \times 100}{£80} = 6.25\%$$

As the price of the bond falls from £100 to £80, the rate of interest rises from 5 per cent to 6.25 per cent.

2 If the bond has a current market price of £125 the current rate of interest is:

$$\frac{£5 \times 100}{£125} = 4\%$$

As the price of the bond rises from £100 to £125 the rate of interest falls from 5 per cent to 4 per cent.

Now at any moment in time each individual investor is assumed to have his own idea about what he considers to be the normal rate of interest in present circumstances. Different investors will have different ideas about what constitutes the normal rate of interest, but each individual investor will be clear in his own mind about his own view. When interest rates are below an investor's view of the normal rate his expectation will be that the *next change* in interest rates will be upwards. Because of the inverse relationship between security prices and the rate of interest, an investor who expected interest rates to rise would also expect bond prices to fall. In these circumstances the investor would prefer money to bonds because holding bonds would involve him in a capital loss. The opposite is true when the rate of interest is above the investor's perception of the normal rate. Here the next expected change in the rate of interest would be downwards, and this implies an expected rise in bond prices. In this case bonds would be preferred to money because when the rate of interest falls bond prices rise and holders of bonds therefore make a capital gain.

Although each individual investor will be convinced in his own mind about the next expected change in the rate of interest, not all investors will necessarily have the same opinion. However, the more the rate of interest continues to move in one direction, the more investors' expectations will converge. Thus the higher the rate of interest moves, the more investors will come to believe that the next change in the rate of interest will be downwards. Since this implies an upward movement in bond prices as the rate of interest rises bonds will increasingly be preferred to money. The opposite is also true. The lower the rate of interest falls, the more investors will come to expect the next change in the rate of interest to be upwards. This implies a fall in bond prices and in these circumstances investors will increasingly prefer money to bonds thus avoiding a capital loss. Figure 26.5 illustrates the speculative, or asset, demand for money.

Figure 26.5 shows that as the rate of interest falls, the quantity of money held as an asset increases. In fact Figure 26.5 implies that there is some rate of interest that is so low the asset demand for money is infinite. This is because the rate of interest is so low that everyone expects the next change in interest rates to be upwards – that is, the next change in bond prices to be downwards. In these circumstances no one will be prepared to hold bonds and therefore the asset demand for money will be infinite.

The Liquidity Preference Curve

The total demand for money, or liquidity preference, curve is given by the sum of the transactions

Figure 26.5 *Speculative or asset demand for money*

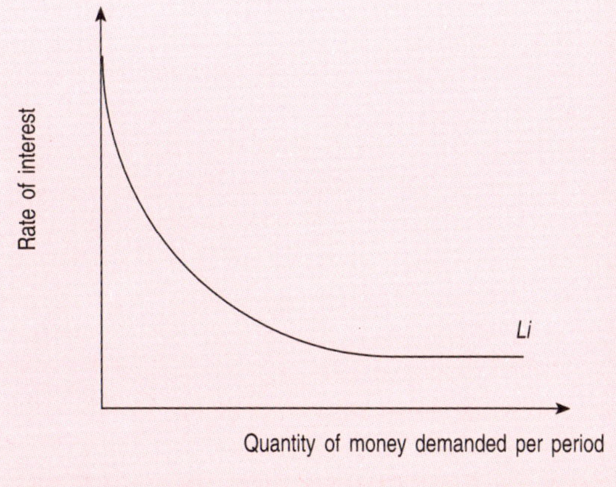

demand, precautionary demand and asset demand for money. Because transactions balances and precautionary balances are held with the intention of being used as and when necessary, they are sometimes grouped together, or aggregated, for analytical purposes and referred to as the demand for *active balances*.

Traditionally it was assumed that the demand for transactions balances and the demand for precautionary balances were not significantly influenced by changes in the rate of interest. In other words, demand for these balances was assumed to be interest rate inelastic. In practice, this may be something of an oversimplification. A rise in the rate of interest increases the opportunity cost of holding money balances which in the main earn no interest. This may encourage some wealthier individuals and larger firms in particular to delay certain transactions and to economise on their holdings of active balances. Nevertheless, there is a limit on the extent to which economies can be made and the assumption of an interest inelastic demand for active balances is not seen as a major criticism of the liquidity preference theory. Figure 26.6(a) shows demand for active balances (L_a).

The asset demand for money, on the other hand, as we have seen is highly responsive to changes in the rate of interest. After all, each time the rate of interest changes investors will assess the new rate against their view of the normal rate they would expect to exist at that point in time. If the existing rate is above their view of what is normal they will prefer to hold less money and more bonds. If the rate is below their view of the normal rate, they will increase their holdings of money and hold fewer bonds. Because money is held as an asset, rather than with the intention of spending it on goods and services, the asset demand for money is sometimes referred to as the demand for *idle balances*. Figure 26.6(b) shows the asset demand for money (L_i). Combining the demand for active balances and the demand for idle balances gives the overall demand for money in the liquidity preference theory. This is shown in Figure 26.6(c) (L_p).

Determination of the Rate of Interest

In the liquidity preference theory it is assumed that the supply of money is fixed by the monetary authorities on a day-to-day basis and in the short run is not responsive to changes in the rate of interest. It is therefore assumed to be interest rate inelastic.

In Figure 26.7 the demand for money is shown by L_p and the money supply is initially represented by *SM*. In this situation the equilibrium rate of interest is *r*. If the rate of interest is below *r*, the demand of money exceeds thesupply of money. In order to increase their holdings of money to the required level, individuals and organisations will sell bonds. This will drive bond prices down and will therefore force the rate of interest up. The opposite occurs if the rate of interest is above *r*.

The authorities cannot exercise day-to-day control over the demand for money. They must therefore choose to control *either* the rate of interest *or* the supply of money, they cannot do both. If the

Figure 26.6 *Overall demand for money in the liquidity preference theory*

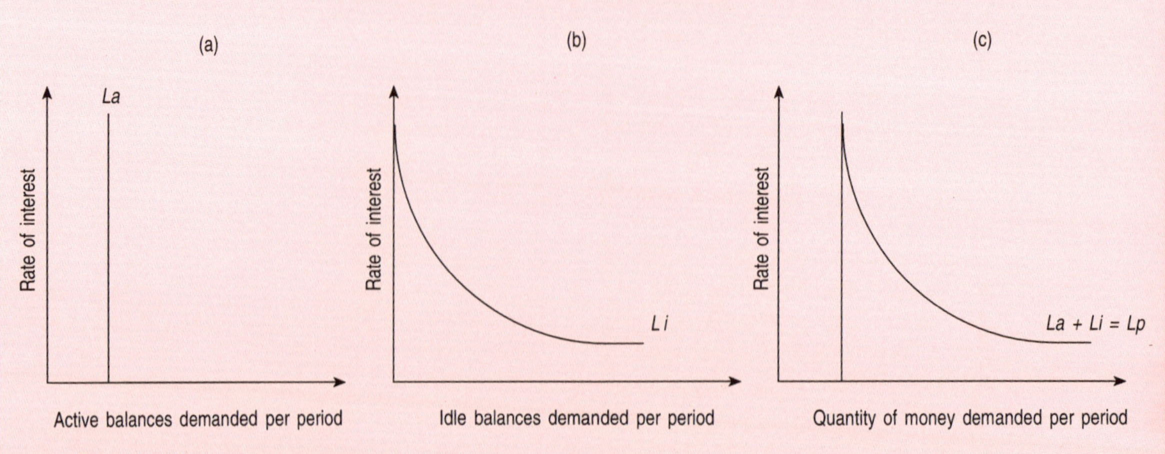

Figure 26.7 *The equilibrium rate of interest*

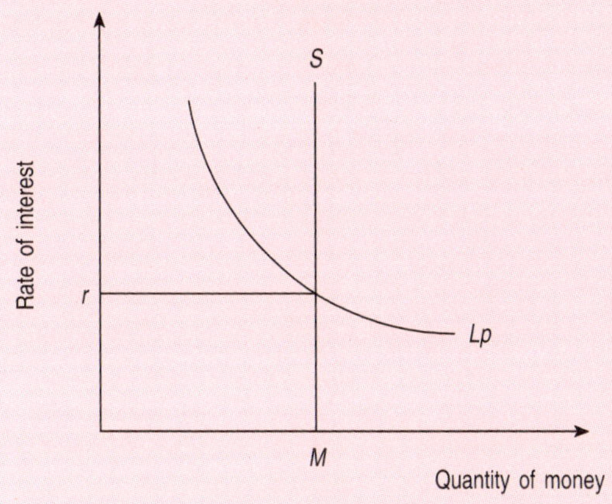

authorities choose to control the rate of interest they must fix the money supply at whatever level brings supply and demand for money into equilibrium at the chosen rate of interest. On the other hand, if they fix the money supply, they must accept whatever rate of interest brings supply and demand for money into equilibrium. Let us look at the effect of changes in the money supply on the rate of interest.

Changes in the Supply of Money

Referring to Figure 26.8 we can see that with demand for money given by L_p and the supply of money given by *SM*, the rate of interest will be r. If the authorities now increase the money supply to *SM*, supply of money will exceed demand for money at the existing rate of interest r. Individuals and organisations will be holding larger money balances than they require. The excess money balances will be used to purchase bonds. The increased demand for bonds will drive up bond prices and will therefore force down the rate of interest. This process will continue until the rate of interest falls to r, when supply and demand for money will again be in equilibrium.

Figure 26.8 *Supply and demand for money in equilibrium*

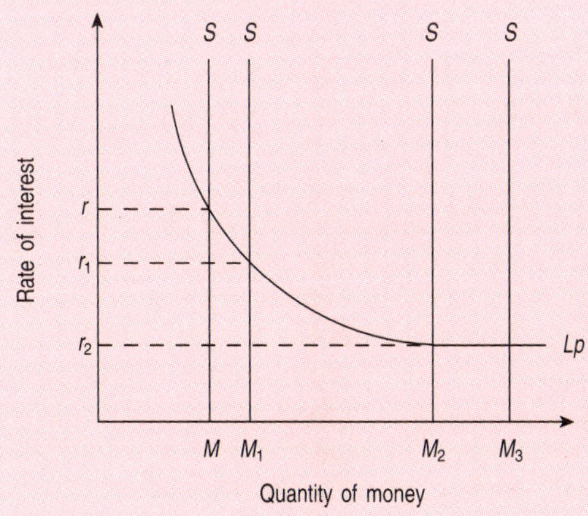

Remember from our earlier discussion of the determination of income on p. 193 that changes in the rate of interest lead to changes in investment, and through this to changes in income. To Keynesians this is the channel through which changes in the money supply bring about changes in other economic variables such as national income. However, what if the money supply is initially at SM_2 and the authorities bring about an increase to SM_3. Here there is no change in the rate of interest which stays constant at r_2. In other words, the entire increase in the money supply is willingly absorbed into idle balances. At r_2 everyone expects the next change in bond prices to be downwards and therefore no-one is prepared to buy bonds. This is the so-called *liquidity trap* and it implies that when the rate of interest is so low that no-one expects it to fall any further, monetary policy is powerless to bring about any change in economic variables because changes in the money supply have no effect on changes in the rate of interest.*

Changes in the Demand for Money

Just as changes in the supply of money can cause changes in the rate of interest, so changes in the demand for money can cause changes on the rate of interest. Figure 26.9 shows the effect of changes in the demand for money on the position of the liquidity preference curve.

The demand for money is initially shown by L_p. An increase in the demand for money is shown by a shift in the demand for money curve from L_p to L_{p1}, and a reduction in the demand for money is shown by a shift from Lp to L_{p2}. Notice that even when the demand for money increases or decreases, the curves converge at some low rate of interest. This simply implies that even though the demand has changed investors still believe that there is some rate of interest that is so low everyone believes that the

*Despite its appealing logic care must be taken when considering the liquidity trap. In reality, there is no firm evidence that a liquidity trap has ever existed!

Figure 26.9 *The effect of changes in the demand for money on the position of the liquidity preference curve*

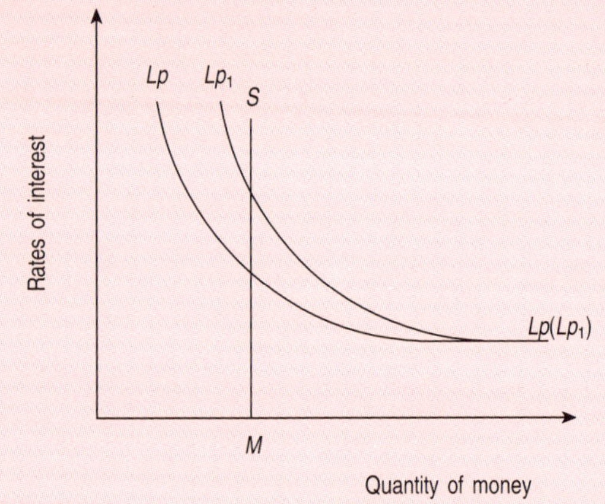

next change in interest rate will be upwards, and therefore holding money is preferable to holding bonds.

There are several factors that may cause a change in the demand for money. We have already seen on pp. 237–8 that changes in income, the frequency with which income is received or spent as well as changes in technology can cause an increase or decrease in the transactions demand for money. If all other things remain equal, an increase in the demand for transactions balances will shift the liquidity preference curve from L_p to L_{p1} and a reduction in the demand for transactions balances will shift it from L_{p1} to Lp. Equally it is possible that there might be a change in the asset demand for money.

Figure 26.10 *The effect of an increase in the demand for money is offset by an accommodating increase in the supply of money*

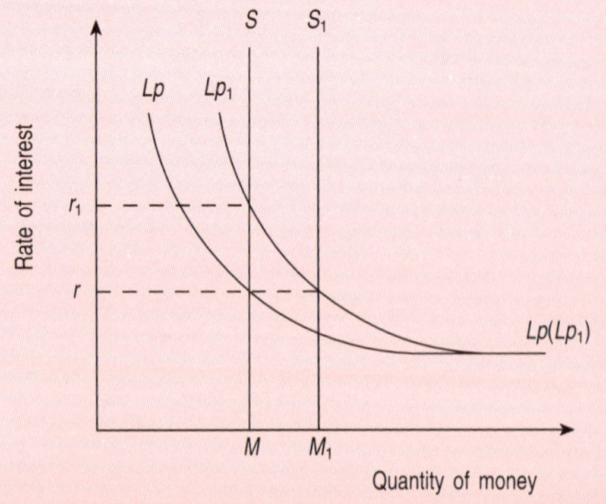

Remember that the asset demand for money depends on the expectations of future changes in the rate of interest of all individual investors. Anything which causes a change in expectations of investors will shift the liquidity preference curve. One factor of importance here is announcements by the government about the future conduct of economic policy. For example, if the government announced that their main economic objective is to cut the rate of inflation this may encourage the belief that interest rates will rise in the future. At any given rate of interest more people will now expect a rise in the rate of interest than previously, and therefore the liquidity preference curve will shift outwards such as when the demand for money curve shifts from L_p to L_{p1} in Figure 26.9.

Stabilising Interest Rates

If all other things remain equal a change in the demand for money will cause a change in the rate of interest. For example, Figure 26.10 shows that if the demand for money changes from Lp to L_{p1} then, if the supply of money is fixed as SM, the rate of interest will rise from r to r_1.

If the authorities wish to stabilise the rate of interest, then each time the demand for money changes they must adjust the supply of money to accommodate the change in demand. In terms of Figure 26.10, if demand for money and supply of money are initially represented by Lp and SM respectively and the authorities wish to stabilise the rate of interest at r, when demand for money increases to L_{p1} the authorities must increase the supply of money to SM_1, thus accommodating the increase in demand for money and avoiding a rise in the rate of interest.

The Term Structure of Interest Rates

We saw on p. 233 that one of the factors which accounts for differences in interest rates is the length of time a security has to run before it matures. The relationship *existing on a particular day* between length of time to maturity and the rate of interest paid on the *same type of securities* is referred to as the *term structure of interest rates*. Although the concept of the term structure of interest rates is widely applied, it is strictly relevant only to fixed interest, fixed term securities such as government gilt edged stock. A typical term structure might appear as:

Years to maturity	1	2	3	4	5	6	7	8
Interest rate (%)	9.6	9.9	10.15	10.30	10.4	10.45	10.45	10.45

When illustrated diagrammatically the term structure of interest rates is referred to as the *yield curve*. Strictly, the yield on a security is not the same as the rate of interest paid on it. However, since both the rate of interest and the yield on a security follow the same basic pattern with respect to time, for simplicity they are often regarded as being synonymous. A typical yield curve is illustrated in Figure 26.11.

Figure 26.11 *A normal yield curve*

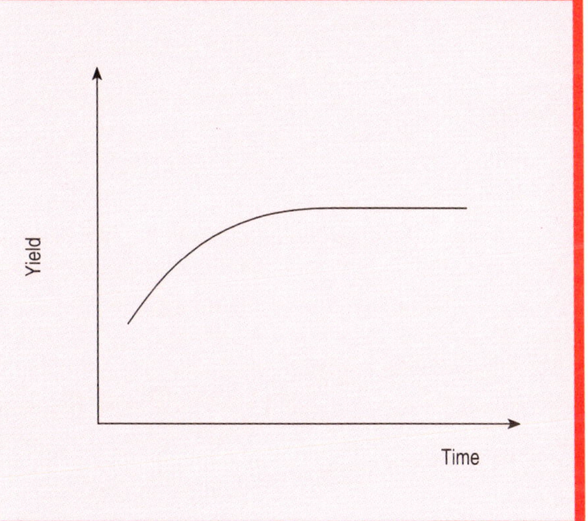

The yield curve illustrated in Figure 26.11 is referred to as a *normal* yield curve and slopes upwards from left to right. The *normal yield curve* indicates that if all other things are equal this is the relationship we would expect to find. In general, the longer the length of time to maturity, the higher the yield that is required to compensate for loss of liquidity. Notwithstanding this, we find that initially the yield rises markedly as length of time to maturity increases, but with each successive increase in length of time to maturity there is a smaller and smaller increase in yield until, beyond a certain number of years to maturity, time has no influence on yield. In other words, beyond a certain number of years to maturity, the yield curve becomes horizontal with respect to time.

Figure 26.12 *The effect on the yield curve of an expected fall in interest rates*

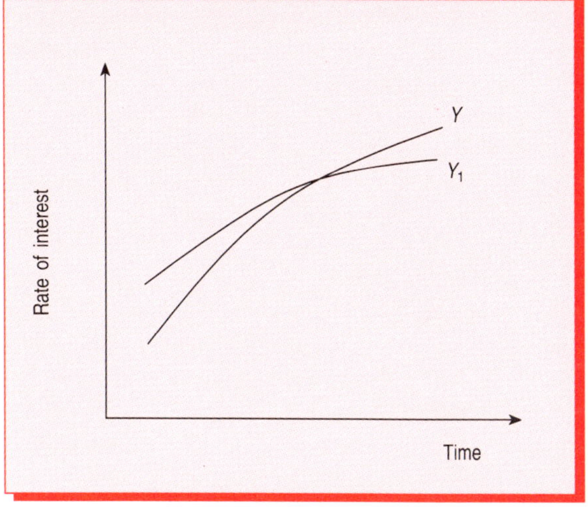

In practice, as Figure 26.12 shows, yield curves do not always conform to the 'normal' shape illustrated in Figure 26.11.

There is no inconsistency between Figure 26.11 and Figure 26.12. Figure 26.11 is drawn on the assumptions that all other factors that affect yields are constant. In the real world, these other factors are not constant. Because of this the precise shape of the yield curve at any particular point in time will depend on several factors. One factor of considerable importance is expectations about future changes in the rate of interest. The importance of changes in expectations on the shape of the yield curve are analysed in the following section.

Expectations and the Yield Curve

If, at a particular moment in time, no-one expects any changes in the rate of interest, we may observe a normal yield curve such as that illustrated in Figure 26.11. Now if expectations change so that there is a widely held belief that interest rates are about to fall, two opposing forces will change the shape of the yield curve.

- Since interest rates are expected to fall, if investors lend long term they will be holding securities with a relatively high yield if their expectation proves correct. Investors will therefore increase the quantity of funds they are prepared to lend long term and will reduce the quantity of funds they are prepared to lend short term.

- For borrowers, the situation is different. If funds are borrowed long term, borrowers are locked into, or borrow at, what will be a relatively high rate after interest rates rise. They will therefore have an incentive to borrow short term until after interest rates have fallen. Borrows will therefore reduce their demand for long term funds and increase their demand for short term funds.

The combined effect of these two forces implies that there will be an increase in the supply of short-term funds and a reduction in demand for such funds. Rates at the short end of the market will therefore fall. At the long end of the market the opposite occurs. There is a reduction in supply of funds and an increase in demand. The effect is to drive down short-term rates and to drive up longer-term rates. In other words, an expected increase in interest rates makes the new yield curve steeper than the 'normal' yield curve. Figure 26.12 illustrates the effect of an expected increase in interest rates on the yield curve. Y is the normal yield curve and Y_1 illustrates the effect of a widely held belief that interest rates are about to rise.

The process works in reverse when there is a widely held belief that interest rates are about to fall. Here, investors will be more interested in lending long term. To do so will lock in a higher rate of interest than will be available after interest rates fall. The supply of long-term funds will therefore increase while the supply of short-term funds will tend to fall. Borrowers, on the other hand, will be more interested in borrowing short term. This will enable them to take advantage of the expected fall in interest rates. If they borrow long term they will be committed to higher interest payments than will be available after interest rates fall. Because of this, demand for funds will increase at the short end of the market and demand will fall at the long end. The combined effect will be to drive interest rates up at the short end of the market and down at the long end. In terms of Figure 26.12, if Y_1 now represents the normal yield curve, Y will represent the yield curve after the change in expectations of a fall in interest rates.

The Nominal Rate of Interest and the Real Rate of Interest

This chapter has mainly been concerned with the *nominal* rate of interest – that is, the money value of interest expressed as a percentage of the amount lent or borrowed. However, because the value of money changes over time economists are often more interested in the *real* rate of interest. This is simply the nominal rate adjusted to take account of inflation, and it is sometimes expressed as:

$$r = i - \mathrm{p}$$

where r is the real rate of interest, i is the nominal rate of interest and p is the rate of inflation. For example, if for one year the nominal rate of interest was 8 per cent and the rate of inflation was 5 per cent, then the real rate of interest was 3 per cent. In other words, if a sum of money had been lent at a nominal rate of 8 per cent, it would buy 3 per cent more goods and services when it was repaid twelve months later.

Box 26.1 Forecasting changes in interest rates

Commercial banks, building societies and large corporations devote considerable resources to forecasting movements in interest rates. They have an incentive to do this. If they can correctly forecast future interest rates they can increase profits by altering their borrowing and lending arrangements in *anticipation* of future rates.

To forecast interest rate movements organisations use mathematical and econometric techniques. However, some simple rules of thumb can help anyone to make a well-informed guess about the future course of interest rates in the UK.

A major factor explaining movements in UK interest rates is the behaviour of sterling against the Deutschemark on the foreign exchange market. If sterling is expected to depreciate against the Deutschemark then UK interest rates will be expected to rise. The reason for this is explained on p. 314 but the main point to note here is that to forecast future changes in interest rates we need to know what causes sterling to depreciate against the Deutschemark. In fact, a major factor here is **relative inflation rates**. If the UK rate of inflation persistently exceeds the German rate of inflation a depreciation of sterling becomes increasingly likely (see pp. 313–14). Another factor is the rate of interest in Germany. If all other things remain equal, an increase in German rates will cause a depreciation of sterling against the Deutschemark (see p. 314). We might also note that if sterling is actually depreciating against the Deutschemark, a cut in interest rates is extremely unlikely.

As well as the international dimension there are domestic factors to consider. If the UK rate of inflation is expected to rise this is likely to increase pressure on interest rates to preserve the real rate, as discussed on p. 244. Again, this begs the question of what causes an increase in the expected rate of inflation. The best long run guide to this is the **rate of growth of the money supply**. If this is rising at a faster rate, inflation will be expected to rise. However, other factors can sometimes give a clue to the likely future course of inflation. In particular, if wage settlements exceed the existing rate of inflation by more than the growth of productivity (about 2–2½ per cent in the UK) this will create the expectation of an increase in the rate of inflation.

These rules of thumb can now be summarised:

(i) If sterling is weak against other ERM currencies, and particularly the Deutschemark, an increase in UK interest rates is a possibility.
(ii) If the rate of inflation exceeds that of the UK's major trading partners, pressure on UK interest rates will be increasing.
(iii) If interest rates in Germany are rising, an increase in UK interest rates is more likely.
(iv) If the rate of inflation in the UK rises, UK interest rates are likely to rise.
(v) If the UK government tightens its monetary policy so as to restrict money growth, this is likely to cause an increase in UK interest rates.

These rules of thumb do not enable us to make precise predictions over the timing or extent of interest movements, but they do give an indication of the likely future trend.

REVIEW QUESTIONS

1 In what circumstances might a rise in the rate of interest persuade an individual to cut down on the amount of money saved per period of time?

2 From your own holdings of cash on a particular day, can you identify the proportion held for precautionary purposes?

3 Taking a bond with no fixed redemption date paying interest at the rate of 5 per cent pa and a nominal price of £100:

(a) What is the current rate of interest if the bond has a current market value of £110?
(b) What would be your answer if the current market price of the bond was £90?
(c) What would be the market price of the bond if the current market rate of interest is 5 per cent?

4 Can (i) the real rate of interest, (ii) the nominal rate of interest, ever be negative? Explain.

5 What does it mean to say the demand for money is interest inelastic?

6 If the community as a whole is holding less money than it desires at the current rate of interest, why will this lead to an increase in the rate of interest?

7 'UK money rates ease as inflation fears weaken.'

Money market rates were around $^1/_8$ to $^3/_{15}$ points lower in late trade as inflation fears faded slightly following today's lower than expected UK Retail Price Index.

A 0.4 per cent rise in the RPI for March giving an annual rate of 7.9 per cent was slightly below market expectations and compared with 7.8 per cent in February. The number eased fears of any immediate rise in base rates, dealers said, 'The market heaved a sigh of relief after today's figures', one money broker said, 'Everybody is certainly more optimistic and upward pressure on rates appears to be off at the moment.'

(a) What is meant by the phrase 'Money market rates were around $^1/_8$ to $^3/_{15}$ points lower'?
(b) Why are 'market expectations' important in the determination of nominal interest rates?
(c) Use your knowledge of the Loanable Funds Theory to explain why a rise in RPI below market expectations would cause a change in the demand for, and supply of, loanable funds which would cause a reduction in the rate of interest.
(d) Does the influence of changes in the RPI on nominal interest rates imply that the Government is unable to control the rate of interest?

CHAPTER 27

MEASURING CHANGES IN THE VALUE OF MONEY

CONNECTIONS

Changes in the value of money are caused by inflation and the main measure of the rate of inflation in the UK is changes in the Index of Retail Prices (RPI). However, changes in the rate of inflation have implications for the level of unemployment, for the balance of payments and for the distribution of income.

Key Concepts

Inflation
Price relative
Retail price index
Tax and price index
The price level
Weighting

Price Relatives

The basic principles involved in measuring changes in retail prices are straightforward. For example, if we consider a single good, good *A*, whose price increases from £5.00 in 1991 to £5.50 in 1992 we can easily measure the percentage change in the price of this good as:

$$\frac{\text{Price in 1992} - \text{Price in 1991}}{\text{Price in 1991}} \times 100$$

$$= \frac{£0.5}{£5.00} \times 100 = 10 \text{ per cent}$$

We can say that the price of good *A* was 10 per cent higher in 1992 than in 1991. Alternatively we could carry out the following calculation:

$$\frac{\text{Price in 1992}}{\text{Price in 1991}} \times 100 = 110$$

The second calculation uses an *index* to measure the price change between 1991 and 1992. This calculation tells us that if the price of good *A* is 100 in 1991, its price rises to 110 in 1992. The numbers 100 and 110 are *index numbers*, and they are used to measure **percentage changes in price from one period to another**.

A comparison when only one set of prices is involved, as in the calculation above, is referred to as a *price relative*. When analysing changes in the price of a single good or when making comparisons between changes in the price of one good and changes in the price of another good over time, price relatives are obviously important. However, economists are often interested in the behaviour of the *general level of prices*, because this provides us with an indication of how the *cost of living* has changed between two periods.

Index Numbers

We have seen above that price relatives can be calculated using index numbers. The same technique can be applied to a range of goods and services to calculate changes in their average price. To do this we must select a *base year* – that is, the year against which we are going to compare price changes. In the base year the prices of all goods we monitor are assigned the value of 100 and price changes in subsequent years are expressed as a **ratio of the base price** – that is, 100.

But which prices shall we monitor? After all, in an economy like the UK there are millions of prices quoted and it would be impossible to monitor them all. In fact, economists consider only the price changes of a representative *basket* of goods and services. Thus when compiling the RPI we monitor the prices of those goods and services which the average family purchases. For simplicity, let us consider only four goods *A*, *B*, *C* and *D* with base year prices of £2, £5, £1, and £3 respectively. Assume that the following year these prices change to £2.5, £6, £0.8 and £6 respectively. These price changes can be used to compute a simple index of prices. Let us refer to the base year as year 1 and the following year as year 2.

Table 27.1 *Index of prices*

	Year 1		Year 2	
Good	Price (£)	Index No.	Price (£)	Index No.
A	2.00	100	2.50	125
B	5.00	100	6.00	120
C	1.00	100	0.80	80
D	3.00	100	6.00	200
		400		525

Average price in year 1 = 400/4 = 100
Average price in year 2 = 525/4 = 131.25

In Table 27.1 the prices of all goods in the base year are expressed as 100. The price changes which take place between year 1 and year 2 are expressed as a ratio of 100. For example, the price of good *A* rises from £2 in year 1 to 2.5 in year 2, and this is reflected in the value of its index number which rises from 100 to 125. If we sum the value of all index numbers and divide by the total number of goods in the basket, we can compute the **arithmetic average price** of the basket of goods. Since the index of prices rises from 100 in year 1 to 131.25 in year 2, we can say that prices were on average 31.25 per cent higher in year 2 than in year 1.

A Weighted Price Index

The simple index of prices illustrated in Table 27.1 might be misleading because the amount of money spent on each good might be different. This is important because total expenditure on a good is an indication of its importance. For example, if good *A* represents a good which is purchased weekly, while good *D* is only purchased annually, the change in the price of good *A* is far more significant than the change in the price of good *D*, despite the fact that the percentage change in the price of good *D* is greater than the percentage change in the price of good *A*!

The relative importance of each item in the index can be allowed for if we allocate each good a *weight* derived from **total spending on each good in the base year**. For example, let us suppose that in the base year, 10 per cent of total expenditure was on good *A*, 30 per cent was on good *B*, 40 per cent was on good *C* and 20 per cent was on good *D*. We can use this information to compute an index of prices which is more representative of the effect of the price changes that have taken place. Table 27.2 illustrates how this can be done.

In this case, we assign each good in the basket an index number as previously, but now this index number is multiplied by the appropriate weight to obtain the weighted index number. We sum the value of these weighted index numbers and then divide by the sum of the weights to obtain our weighted price index. Again in the base year the value of the price index is 100. However, in year 2 we find that the value of the index has increased to 145, indicating that on average the same basket of goods costs the consumer 45 per cent more in year 2 than in year 1.

General Problems with Index Numbers

In compiling an index of prices there are several problems that may reduce the reliability of the index.

The Problem of Weights

We have seen above the impact of using weights to construct an index. However, calculating reliable weights poses a major problem. Different families do not all buy **the same goods and services**, nor do they buy them in the same **proportions**. A family with teenage children will buy different goods and services from a family with younger children. Different sized families will have different expenditure patterns, and so will families with widely differing incomes. For example, changes in the

Table 27.2 *Weighted index of prices*

Good	Year 1 Price (£)	Year 1 Index	Year 1 Weight	Year 1 Weighted index	Year 2 Price (£)	Year 2 Index	Year 2 Weight	Year 2 Weighted index
A	2.00	100	1	100	3.00	150	1	300
B	1.00	100	3	300	2.00	200	3	600
C	2.00	100	4	400	1.50	75	4	300
D	4.00	100	2	200	4.50	125	2	250
				1000				1450

Index of prices in year 1 = 1000/10 = 100
Index of prices in year 2 = 1450/10 = 145

price of food will be less significant to a relatively wealthy family because they will spend a smaller proportion of their income on food than a less wealthy family. This is illustrated in the Engel Curve discussed on pp. 57–8 and there is ample evidence to support its validity.

Which Goods and Services to Include

A representative price index should include those goods and services which are consumed by the groups whose expenditures are monitored. However, there are problems here because some people will not necessarily consume **all the goods and services monitored**. For example, changes in the price of cigarettes may be important to a heavy smoker but they will have no relevance to a non-smoker. To include changes in the price of cigarettes therefore reduces the reliability of the index for non-smokers.

There is another problem because the range of goods and services which become available will **change over time**. Many people now own portable computers, video cameras and whole range of goods not readily available even a few years ago. On the other hand, less red meat and fewer fresh vegetables are now consumed than previously. An index of prices will become less reliable over time unless it is continually revised to take account of changes in the goods and services consumed.

Another problem is that major price changes can often cause changes in the **pattern of consumption**. For example, an increase in mortgage repayments caused by an increase in interest rates may well reduce expenditure on a range of goods and services. The same will happen if the economy moves into recession. These changes in patterns of consumption will reduce the reliability of an index since it will be difficult to take account of them. Once the weights are set it is difficult to change them each time the pattern of consumption changes.

Which Prices to Consider

A further problem when computing an index of prices is to consider those changes in price which consumers **actually pay**. Most goods and services can be purchased from a variety of outlets and prices do not always change in these outlets simultaneously or even by equivalent amounts. There may also be problems in the longer term because of changes in the shopping habits of the population. For example, there is a growing tendency for families to purchase their weekly groceries at large supermarkets and to purchase fewer items from independent retail outlets such as the corner shop. For an index of prices to be reliable, data on prices must be gathered from retail outlets which reflect the changing shopping habits of consumers.

Changes in the Quality of Goods

An index which simply monitors price changes will ignore the effect of changes in the quality of the different goods which consumers buy. Often price changes are accompanied by the introduction of changes in style or design so that a new product is superior to the one it replaces. If you have ever watched a television programme on a black and white television set you will understand that changes in quality can be quite significant. Many other consumer durables, such as washing machines and cars incorporate improvements over time and price changes often reflect the improved quality. It is misleading to monitor price changes without allowing for **quality changes**.

The Retail Prices Index

The principles explained on pp. 247–9 are used to calculate the Retail Prices Index which is published monthly by the Department of Employment and is the main measure of how the average household has been affected by changes in the prices of different goods and services in the UK. It includes 600 separate items and approximately 130,000 price quotations are collected in 180 towns and cities throughout the UK. The weights in the RPI are calculated from the spending patterns of 7000 households representing the different income groups, though pensioners and households on the top 4 per cent of incomes are excluded.

Table 27.3 *Weights assigned to items in the RPI*

Item	Weight (1987)
Food	168
Catering	50
Alcoholic drink	78
Tobacco	36
Housing	160
Fuel and light	55
Household goods	74
Household services	41
Clothing and footwear	72
Personal goods and services	37
Motoring expenditure	132
Fares and other travel costs	23
Leisure goods	50
Leisure services	29
All items	1000

Source: *Employment Gazette*, August 1987

Table 27.3 shows the weights assigned to the different items currently included in the RPI. The total basket of goods in the RPI is divided into 14

Box 27.1 Housing Costs and the RPI

The whole basis for including housing costs in the RPI can be questioned. Owner-occupation is a form of investment. Indeed for many households it is their most important investment. It is argued that investment in property should be excluded from the RPI, just as other forms of investment such as purchases of shares in private sector companies are excluded. Investment has little to do with consumer price movements, which is what the RPI mainly seeks to monitor.

Moreover the way housing is included in the RPI is a contentious issue. A significant element of housing costs are mortgage interest payments which measure the costs of housing for owner-occupiers. However, this makes the RPI quite volatile because mortgage interest payments are sensitive to movements in interest rates generally. In fact, if the government raises interest rates as part of an anti-inflationary policy, the initial effect will be to increase the rate of inflation as measured by the RPI. This is precisely what happened during 1990 when interest rates were consistently increased to damp down consumer demand.

There are other problems with including mortgage repayments in the RPI. If borrowers switch from consumer loans, which are not included in the RPI, and use mortgage finance which is included in the RPI for purchases of consumer durables, total interest payments will fall because mortgage finance is usually cheaper than other finance and interest payments attract tax relief. However, the RPI would increase even without any change in interest rates. This is what happened in the late 1980s. Another problem is that a cut in income tax rates, because it reduces tax relief on mortgage finance, raises the RPI. For example, if gross interest repayment on a mortgage is £600 per month and income tax is reduced from a basic rate of 30 per cent to 25 per cent, net interest payments would increase from £420 per month to £450 per month.

broad groups and the combined weight of these product groups is 1000. Food is given the highest weighting of 168 (that is, 16.8 per cent of the total), reflecting the importance of expenditure on food to the average household.

Given the problems involved in assessing the reliability of an index, an important question to ask is how reliable the RPI is in measuring the effect of changes in prices for the average family?

The Problem of Weights

The weights in the RPI are revised at the beginning of every year from data gathered by the *Family Expenditure Survey* over the previous year to June. For some items such as consumer durables where expenditure can fluctuate widely from year to year, expenditure is averaged over a three-year period. Because of this, it might be argued that the revised weights are out of date at the time they are used in the RPI. Strictly therefore the RPI does not measure changes in prices as they affect *this year's basket of goods* but as they affect *some previous year's basket.* Nevertheless, this is not seen as a major problem because expenditure patterns do not usually alter radically from year to year although if they do, perhaps because relatively high interest rates or recession cause consumers to make changes, this will obviously reduce the reliability of the RPI.

A more serious problem is that the weights might not accurately reflect the experiences of the different income groups in society. We have already noted some of the problems. Families differ in terms of composition and changes in the price of food affects those at the lower end of the income scale more than those at the top end. There is a general consensus that the RPI more accurately reflects the impact of price changes on wealthier groups in society than poorer groups because the former spend more and therefore contribute more to the weighting pattern. This reduces the reliability of the RPI since it clearly does not reflect the impact of price changes on the average family.

Which Goods and Services to Include

The items whose prices are used in the compilation of the RPI are carefully specified in terms of size, style, material composition and so on, or by reference to a a manufacturer's brand and model. In either case, the item chosen is usually one that sells well in the particular retail outlet where prices are recorded. For example, a particular fridge might be thought to provide a better price indicator in Manchester and another in London. In this way, local variations in tastes are allowed for.

Which Prices to Consider

Careful attention is also given to the regions and retail outlets selected for gathering data on prices charged for the different items in the index. Localities are chosen so as to provide a balanced sample of the country as a whole. Similarly retail outlets are chosen so as to reflect the different shopping habits of the population. In other words, data on prices is gathered from supermarkets and small independent retailers. In amalgamating information on the different prices quoted for a particular article to form a price index, the aim is to ensure that the importance of each region and each type of retail outlet reflects its share of total expenditure on the item in question.

Changes in the Quality of Goods

If meaningful comparisons of the RPI are to be made from one year to the next it is important that price quotations should be obtained for the same article. However, we have already noted that quality changes take place over time. To minimise the problem, obsolete goods are dropped from the index in January of each year and replaced by newer, more sophisticated models. The RPI Advisory Committee considers that this will in the main avoid problems caused by quality changes. However, this may not be strictly correct. We have already noted that price changes, whether they are due to quality changes or some other factor, may induce a change in consumption patterns. If this is the case, it again implies that the weights used for computing the index will be inaccurate.

Uses of the RPI

Despite its limitations, the RPI provides the most accurate estimate of how changes in the prices of goods and services affect the population in general. As we shall see in Chapter 28, changes in the RPI are the main measure of the rate of inflation in the UK and, along with information of changes in earnings, the RPI can be used to estimate changes in real income. Changes in the RPI are also used as a basis

Box 27.2 RPI Principles and concepts

Any price index is essentially defined by the answers to three questions:

- **What** does it cover?
- **Who** does it apply to?
- **How** is it calculated?

The principles and concepts underlying the RPI, laid down by successive Advisory Committees, can be summarised under these headings as follows:

What does the RPI cover?
The RPI basket includes practically all the goods and services on which people spend their money, arranged in the following groups: food; alcoholic drink; tobacco; housing; fuel and light; household goods; household services; clothing and footwear; personal goods and services: motoring expenditure: fares and other travel costs: leisure goods: and leisure services. Some expenditure is outside the scope of the index, namely:

- savings, including pension contributions and the capital element of mortgage repayments;
- income tax and payments for services which are non-measurable or highly variable, such as gifts and expenditure on betting.

Taxes on expenditure, for example VAT and excise duties, are included as they are part of the price paid for goods and services affected.

The order in which items are placed in the basket does not affect its total cost. Thus, while the coverage of the index affects its reliability, the structure is incidental and can be adjusted to meet the needs of users.

Who does the RPI apply to?
The RPI reflects the average impact of prices on the great majority of households in the United Kingdom, including practically all wage earners and most salary earners. The index basket is, therefore, determined by the expenditure patterns of a very broad range of households, but two types of household are excluded on the grounds that their spending differs greatly from that of the great majority. These two groups are:

- pensioner households mainly dependent on state benefits
- the 4 per cent of households with the highest incomes

How is the RPI Calculated?
The RPI basket is updated at the beginning of every year to keep abreast of changes in the pattern of household spending, and then fixed for the duration of that year, its cost in January being compared with its cost in each subsequent month up to the following January. A continuous series is produced by linking the latest year's price changes with those for earlier years, the result being called a 'chain' index. The chain is taken back to an arbitrary reference point known as the reference date, at which the value of the index is set at 100. The choice of reference date has no numerical significance: translating from one date to another involves only a simple scaling operation which has no effect on the measurement of price change between any pair of months.

The total cost of the basket is found by collecting the prices charged for a representative selection of items in a representative selection of shops throughout the country. Each selection is designed to ensure that the recorded price movements, taken together, give a good estimate of the change in prices for the whole of the expenditure category in question.

To ensure that the price index is not affected by changes in the amount or quality of goods and services bought the items selected for pricing are specified in detail.

Source: 'A short guide to the retail prices index', *Department of Employment Gazette* (August 1987)

for calculating the required increase in certain payments, such as supplementary benefit, which are *index-linked*.

In addition, many public sector pay increases (such as that for the fire services) as well as tax-free allowances are linked to movements in the RPI. Because of this it has been suggested that a 1 percentage point error in calculating the RPI might add as much as £500m to public sector expenditure in 1987 prices. Similarly, changes in the RPI are an important factor in private sector wage negotiations and any overestimate of inflation might encourage pay demands which might add significantly to the rate of inflation as measured by changes in the RPI.

We shall see in Chapter 28 that inflation can have many undesirable consequences and all governments attach great significance to the control of inflation. Here again the most important statistic is the RPI, and changes in the RPI can be sufficient to trigger a change in policy from the government. In other words, the conduct of economic policy is sometimes crucially influenced by changes in the RPI.

The Tax and Price Index

The RPI measures how households are affected by changes in retail prices; but what people can buy out of their earnings depends on the deductions from their pay for income tax, as well as the prices they pay when spending their take home pay. The *Tax and Price Index* (TPI) shows how the **purchasing power of income is affected by changes in direct taxes**, including national insurance contributions, as well as changes in retail prices.

Changes in prices as measured by changes in the RPI have a weight of about 75 per cent in the TPI. Changes in direct taxes (including national insurance contributions) therefore have a weight of 25 per cent in the TPI. Like the RPI, the TPI is a composite index covering a range of households in different tax positions. Information from the different income groups is aggregated with the intention that the TPI should reflect what is happening on average to the vast majority of households.

To see how the TPI is calculated suppose that between year 1 and year 2 the RPI increased from 100 to 110 whereas an index of direct taxes fell from 100 to 96 because of tax changes announced in the Budget. Whereas the RPI increases by 10 per cent, the TPI increases by only 6.5 per cent, that is:

$$0.75(110) + 0.25(96) = 106.5$$

The TPI is clearly a superior measure of changes in the purchasing power of take home pay, but it has never been as widely used as the RPI. There are many reasons for this. As indicated earlier, the RPI serves many purposes for which the TPI would be unsuitable. In addition, the TPI applies only to tax payers. Many households pay little or no direct tax and so are largely unaffected by tax changes. They are nevertheless affected by changes in the prices of the goods and services which they buy!

REVIEW QUESTIONS

1 Why does a rise in the price level imply a fall in the value of money?

2 How accurately does the RPI measure the change in your own income?

3 What do the weights in the RPI reflect?

Question 4 is based on Table 27.4.

4 (a) Calculate a weighted index of prices for years 1 and 2.

(b) What is the percentage change in the weighted index over the period?

(c) What is the change in the value of money over the period?

Table 27.4 *Changes in prices and the value of money*

	Year 1			Year 2		
Good	Price (£)	Index	Weight	Price (£)	Index	Weight
A	2.00	100	4	2.50	125	4
B	5.00	100	2	6.00	120	2
C	1.00	100	1	0.80	80	1
D	3.00	100	3	6.00	200	3

CHAPTER 28

INFLATION

CONNECTIONS

In Chapter 28 we analyse the **causes** and **consequences** of inflation. We shall be referring to many of the concepts discused in Chapter 27 including the *rate of inflation* and the *retail price index*. We shall also be using the aggregate demand and aggregate supply framework developed in Chapter 22, as well as the concept of the natural rate of unemployment which was also discussed in Chapter 22.

Key Concepts

Cost push inflation
Demand pull inflation
Hyperinflation
Phillips Curve
Quantity theory of money
Velocity of circulation

Inflation is defined as a *continuous rise in the general level of prices*. However, inflation is sometimes defined as a *continuous fall in the value of money*. In fact, both definitions are different ways of saying the same thing. If the average price of goods and services doubles, a given amount of money will only buy half as much: in other words, the value of money has fallen by 50 per cent.

Before we turn our attention to the causes of inflation, it is useful to remember that there are different degrees of inflation. Although the UK has experienced inflation in excess of 20 per cent per annum, it is usually suggested that the degree of inflation the UK experiences, along with most other developed countries, is *creeping* inflation. But what does this mean? In fact, there is no unambiguous definition of creeping inflation – it simply means that inflation, though it causes problems, does not undermine the stability of the economy.

Box 28.1 Inflation and the purchasing power of money

Inflation is usually defined as a **sustained increase in the price level** or a **sustained fall in the value of money**. In fact, these definitions of inflation have exactly the same meaning and are opposite sides of the same coin. For example, if the RPI rises from 180 in year 1 to 240 in year 2, then the rate of inflation between these periods is:

$$\frac{\text{RPI in Yr 2} - \text{RPI in Yr 1}}{\text{RPI in Yr 1}} = \frac{240-180}{180} = 33.3\%$$

Alternatively, we can calculate the change in the **purchasing power of money** that has occurred over the same period. For convenience, let us consider the change in the purchasing power of 100p between year 1 and year 2. This equals

$$\frac{100\text{p} \times \text{RPI in Yr 1}}{\text{RPI in Yr 2}} = \frac{100\text{p} \times 180}{240} = 75\text{p}$$

In other words, when the rate of inflation is 33.3 per cent, the value of money falls by 25 per cent. This is exactly what we would expect because if the value of money falls by 25 per cent, we will require 33.3 per cent more to buy the same amount of goods and services.

Box 28.2 Hyperinflation in the Weimar Republic and Hungary

Hyperinflation occurs when the value of money falls so rapidly that it ceases to perform its functions effectively. It is impossible to put a precise figure on what rate of inflation constitutes hyperinflation. To some extent it depends on **recent experiences of inflation**. For example, if a country has a rate of inflation of 2 per cent per annum in one period and this rises to 6 per cent per annum in the next period, there is an increase in the *rate of inflation* of 200 per cent. Such a rapid increase in the rate of inflation would undoubtedly cause problems but few economists would consider a rate of inflation of 6 per cent to be hyperinflation.

On the other hand there have been cases when the rate of inflation has been so excessive that it has seriously reduced the ability of money to carry out its functions. The most often quoted example of hyperinflation is that which occurred in the Weimar Republic during the 1920s. Some detail on just how severe this inflation was is given in Table 28.1, while Table 28.2 details the changes in the rate of inflation which occurred in Hungary in the 1940s.

Table 28.1 *Inflation in the Weimar Republic 1913–23*

	Wholesale price index
Jan 1913	1
Jan 1920	12.6
Jan 1921	14.4
Jan 1922	36.7
July 1922	101.0
Jan 1923	2785.0
July 1923	74787.0
Aug 1923	944041.0
Sept 1923	23949000.0
Oct 1923	7095800000.0
Nov 1923	750000000000.0

When inflation reaches these degrees economic collapse is certain to follow unless the rate of inflation can quickly be reduced. In Germany during the worst excesses of the hyperinflation workers began to receive their wages several times daily and even then had to run to the retail outlets to spend them before their wages lost their purchasing power. It was said that the cost of lunch could rise 25 per cent while it was being eaten! In these circumstances it is hardly surprising that money ultimately became unacceptable in payment for goods and services and **barter** developed. This is an inefficient way of doing business but it indicates the difficulty faced by producers. Many were forced to close because after selling their products, input prices rose so quickly they were unable purchase additional inputs.

Table 28.2 *Inflation in Hungary: cost of living index (without rent) 1938–46*

		% increase at an annual rate[1]
Mid-1938 = 100		
Mid-1939	100	–
Mid-1941	139	18
Mid-1943	217	25
15 July 1945	9200	527
31 August	17300	15000
30 September	38900	1700000
31 October	250300	5.0×10^{11}
30 November	1545700	3.1×10^{11}
31 December	3778000	4.5×10^{6}
31 January 1946	7089000	1.9×10^{5}
28 February	45845300	5.4×10^{11}
31 March	205060000	6.4×10^{9}
30 April	3575600000	7.9×10^{16}
31 May	1076400000000	5.5×10^{31}
30 June	470300000000000	4.8×10^{33}
31 July	12572000000000000000	1.3×10^{55}

1. Monthly rate of increase compounded at an annual rate

Source: *National Westminster Bank Review* (August 1975)

However, some countries have experienced rates of inflation which are so high that economic stability is undermined. Economists refer to inflation of this degree as *hyperinflation*. The most well-documented case of hyperinflation is that which occurred in the Wiemar Republic of Germany in the 1920s. However, it is not the most serious hyperinflation that has ever occurred. This was experienced by Hungary between 1946–7 (see Box 28.2).

The Quantity Theory of Money

The quantity theory of money is one of the oldest theories in economics. Its basic prediction is that there is a **stable and proportional relationship** between **changes in the money supply** and the **price level**.

The quantity theory of money is based on the *equation of exchange*. One version of the equation of exchange is expressed in the following way:

$$MV_t \equiv PT$$

where: M = the money supply
V_t = the transactions velocity of money
P = the average price of each transaction, and
T = the total number of transactions made.

The transactions velocity of money requires some explanation. It is simply the average number of times the money supply is used to make a transaction. It is an important variable because it is possible for a given money stock to finance a total value of transactions many times greater than the value of the money stock itself. For example, if I spend £5 on an article, the seller receives £5 which he or she can then spend on another article, and so on. In other words, the same £5 finances more than one transaction.

However, there is another version of the equation of exchange which is expressed in the following way:

$$MV_y \equiv PY$$

where: M = the money supply
V_y = the income velocity of money – that is, the average number of times the money supply is used to purchase final output
P = the average price of each unit of final output, and
Y = real income – that is, the total volume of final output produced.

This version of the equation of exchange is referred to as the *income version* as opposed to the *transactions version* explained earlier. The distinction is important because total transactions includes all intermediate transactions *and* all final transactions. Strictly, it would also include the value of all second-hand transactions. The income version of the equation of exchange is therefore more useful to economists since it avoids the problems of double counting (see pp. 157–8) which would occur if we included all transactions, as well as the problem of including transactions in goods produced in previous periods, which would occur if we included transactions in second-hand goods.

Whichever version of the equation of exchange we consider, as it stands it is simply a *truism* or an identity – something which is true by definition. For example, look closely at the income version of the equation of exchange. MV_y is simply total expenditure on final output in the economy over a given period of time. If the money supply is £5000m and, on average, each unit of currency is used four times in the purchase of final output, total expenditure on final output in this economy is £20,000m. PY, on the other hand is the value of final output produced in the economy, (that is, nominal GNP, see p. 159). By definition, this must equal the value of total expenditure on final output. To say that $MV_y \equiv PY$ simply tells us that total expenditure is equal to total receipts.

However, it is alleged that V_y is not related to changes in the money supply and varies only slowly over time. For simplicity, it is therefore sometimes treated as a constant. In addition, those economists who accept the predictions of the quantity theory of money, usually referred to as *monetarists*, argue that in the long run real income does not vary with changes in the money supply. They argue that there is a *natural rate of output* and, that this is determined by such factors as the capital stock, technological progress, size of the labour force and the skills it possesses, mobility of labour and so on. Again these factors are likely to change only slowly over time, and for simplicity the natural rate of output is usually assumed to be constant in the long run.

The implication is that in the long run the price level varies directly with changes in the money supply and the quantity theory of money asserts that *causation* is one way: from money to prices. The prediction of the quantity theory is therefore that an increase in the money supply will, in the long run, lead to a *proportional* increase in the price level. In other words, if the money supply rises by 10 per cent the price level will rise by 10 per cent. Furthermore quantity theorists, or monetarists, argue that an increase in the money supply is the *only* cause of an increase in the price level. These two ideas are often summarised in a single sentence: an increase in the money supply is both a necessary and a sufficient condition for an increase in the price level.

The route through which an increase in the money supply leads to an increase in the price level is referred to as the *transmission mechanism*. The quantity theorists argue that an increase in the money supply will lead to an increase in demand for most goods and services. After all, if the money supply increases, some economic agents must receive the increased money supply and it is reasonable to assume that, in consequence, their spending will increase. However, as we have seen on pp. 198–9, while there may be some increase in the output of goods and services in the short run, in the long run the economy will return to the natural rate and output will revert to its original level. Since V_y is assumed to be constant, an increase in the money supply must therefore lead to an increase in the price level or the equation of exchange will be violated. Since the equation of exchange is an identity, that is, it holds at all times and in all circumstances – such a violation is impossible.

In more technical terms, it is argued that an increase in the money supply will create an imbalance between the supply of money and the demand for money at the existing level of nominal income. This implies that economic agents will be holding more money than they require at the existing level of nominal income. They will therefore spend these excess money balances. In the long run, since no increase in output above the natural rate is possible, increased spending on goods and services will drive up the price level. As the price level rises, demand for money will increase because a higher level of money balances will be required to finance any *given level* of transactions. Equilibrium will be restored when prices have increased to the level required to bring demand for money into line with supply of money. In other words, prices go on rising until the increased supply of money is willingly held.

The Keynesian View of Inflation

Traditionally, the Keynesian view of inflation has identified two broad types of inflation: *demand pull inflation* and *cost push inflation*. However, before we consider these it is important to note that the Keynesians do not dispute the validity of the identity $MV_Y = PY$. Indeed, Keynes and his colleagues at Cambridge made great use of this identity in their work, though they usually presented it in the form $M = kPY$, where k is the inverse of V_Y (that is, $k = 1/V_Y$). However, the Keynesian view is that this identity does not imply causation. They reject the notion that V_Y is stable and that the economy tends to some natural rate of unemployment. In other words, they argue that changes in PY are possible independently of changes in M. This is reflected in the Keynesian analysis of the causes of inflation.

Demand Pull Inflation

Demand pull inflation occurs when aggregate demand is *persistently* rising so that aggregate demand exceeds aggregate supply at the existing price level. In these circumstances it is inevitable that the price level will be *persistently* bid upwards. For this reason, the process of demand pull inflation has been likened to the behaviour of the price level at an auction. Typically the auctioneer sets a relatively low starting price and expects that demand will initially exceed supply for whatever is on sale. This excess demand bids up the price until only one buyer remains. We can illustrate the process of demand pull inflation for the economy as a whole using the aggregate demand and aggregate supply framework developed in Chapter 22.

Remember, that, a Keynesian view of the economy is that at very low levels of output an increase in aggregate demand will lead to an increase in output with the price level unchanged. However, as the economy approaches full employment further increases in demand will lead to upward pressure on prices, although output will still increase. But at full employment there is no longer any scope for an increase in output and at this point any further increase in aggregate demand simply leads to higher price.

In Figure 28.1, AD is the initial aggregate demand curve and AS is the aggregate supply curve. The economy is initially in equilibrium with the price level at P and output is below the full employment level at Y. If aggregate demand now rises to AD_1, the price level will rise to P_1 and, because not all resources were fully employed, output will increase to Y_F, the full employment level. At this point, any further increases in aggregate demand will simply result in rising prices. According to this view of inflation, a *persistent* rise in aggregate demand will generate a *persistent* rise in the price level once the full employment level of output is reached.

Figure 28.1 *The effect of an increase in aggregate demand on the price level*

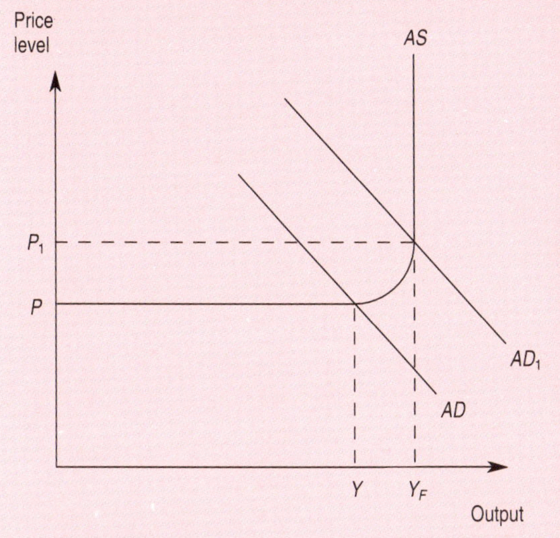

In Chapter 20 aggregate demand was defined in the following way:

$$AD = C + I + G + (X-M)$$

Because of this, many possible sources of an increase in aggregate demand have been identified. For example, a cut in the rate of personal income tax, by increasing disposable income, might lead to a rise in consumption expenditures. A reduction in the rate of interest might be expected to encourage an increase in investment as well as increased consumption spending on consumer durables. The government might increase its own expenditure or bring about a reduction in the exchange rate so as to raise X and reduce M. However, while any of these might cause a one-off change in demand and prices, none of them would cause a *persistent* rise in demand and hence a *persistent* rise in the price level. Nevertheless an increase in any one of them might initiate a rise in prices which, as we shall see on pp. 260–1, might be the proximate cause of inflation.

It should be noted that this view of inflation is not necessarily at odds with the quantity theory of money. If we define full employment as the natural rate of unemployment and argue that the only cause of a rise in demand is an increase in the money supply, the demand pull hypothesis is exactly the same as the quantity theory hypothesis. However, in reality the Keynesians argue that aggregate demand can rise for several reasons, an increase in the money supply being only one possible reason. In other words the Keynesians argue that if there is no change in the money supply, an increase in aggregate demand is still possible if there is an increase in V_Y.

Cost Push Inflation

Cost push inflation occurs when the source of upward pressure on prices is rising costs. Because labour costs account for about 70 per cent of total costs in the UK (see Table 18.1, p. 160) attention has inevitably focused on wage increases as a source of inflation. Indeed the term *wage push inflation* has been coined specifically to refer to periods of inflation when the ultimate cause is thought to be wage increases in excess of productivity increases.

Another reason why the role of wage increases in the inflationary process has been emphasised is because of the nature of the wage bargaining process in the UK. The bargaining period stretches for several months, and it is sometimes argued that there is a tendency for each set of wage negotiations to build on the wage increases already achieved by those workers who have reached agreement earlier in the bargaining year. This behaviour is sometimes referred to as *leapfrogging* and, if it occurs, it would certainly be a source of persistent upward pressure on prices.

However, a word of caution is necessary here. No-one seriously argues that it is possible for workers to negotiate wage increases in excess of productivity increases independently of the state of the economy. Instead, it is usually argued that the ability of workers to obtain wage increases is greater the closer the economy is to full employment and the more likely are skill shortages.

Additionally, wage increases above productivity increases are not the only source of cost increases. For a country like the UK which imports most of its raw materials, a fall in the external value of sterling on the foreign exchanges will have an immediate effect on the price of raw material imports. It is also possible that employers, by increasing their profit margins, may be the source of upward pressure on costs which drives up final prices. Again we can illustrate the effect of rising costs on the price level in terms of the Keynesian aggregate demand and aggregate supply framework.

In Figure 28.2 AD is the aggregate demand curve and AS is the aggregate supply curve. The economy is initially in equilibrium with the price level at P and output at Y_F. If there is now an exogenous increase in costs of production (that is, an increase in costs at all levels of output), the aggregate supply curve will shift

Figure 28.2 *The effect of an increase in costs on the price level*

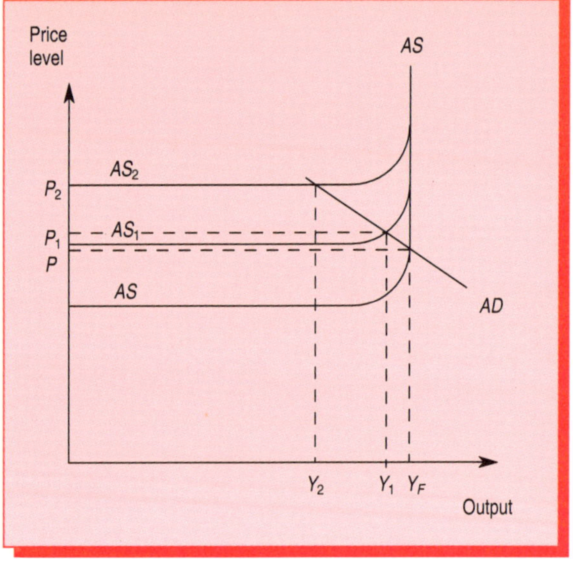

Figure 28.3 *The inflationary spiral*

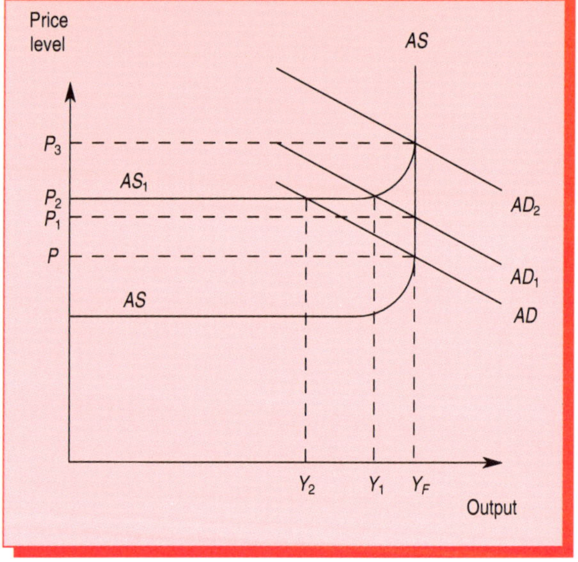

upwards to AS_1 giving a higher equilibrium price of P_1 and lower equilibrium level of income Y_1. If there is a further exogenous increase in costs of production, aggregate supply now shifts to AS_2, and equilibrium is restored when the price level has risen to P_2 with a further reduction in output to Y_2. It is clear that a *persistent* rise in costs of production will generate a *persistent* rise in the price level.

The Inflationary Spiral

In our discussion above of the Keynesian view, we identified two distinct causes of inflation: excess demand at the ruling price level and rising costs of production. In practice, it may not always easy to identify the primary cause of inflation. To see why, let us refer to Figure 28.3.

In Figure 28.3 AD is the initial aggregate demand curve and AS is the initial aggregate supply curve. The economy is initially in equilibrium with the price level at P and output at the full employment level Y_F. If there is an increase in aggregate demand, the economy will initially move to a new equilibrium with the price level at P_1 and output remaining at the full employment level, Y_F. However, the higher price level will result in workers demanding wage increases which, when paid, will raise costs of production and shift the aggregate supply curve upwards to AS_1. This gives a further upward impetus to prices and causes a reduction in output which falls to Y_1. But this is not the final equilibrium position of the economy because the higher wages will be spent and will generate a further increase in aggregate demand which shifts to AD_2. This results in a higher price level P_2 and output returns to the full employment rate Y_F, and so on.

The process described above was *initiated* by an increase in aggregate demand. However, it could equally easily have been initiated by an increase in costs of production. For example, if we refer to Figure 28.3 and again begin with aggregate demand and aggregate supply given by AD and AS respectively, we can see that the economy is initially in equilibrium with the price level at P and output at the full employment level Y_F. Now if there is an exogenous increase in costs caused by an increase in wages, this will shift the aggregate supply curve to AS_1 and the economy will be in equilibrium with a higher price level P_2 and a lower output level Y_2. However, as these higher wages are spent, aggregate demand will shift to AD_2 which will restore full employment, but will result in a further increase in the price level to P_3, and so on.

This is the so-called *inflationary spiral* or *wage–price spiral*. It describes inflation as an interlocking process of cost increases and demand increases. Because of this, it has been argued that once inflation is under way, it is not always easy to identify the underlying cause as either excess demand at the ruling price level or exogenous increases in costs. Furthermore we know from pp. 257–8 that monetarists reject the notion that increases in costs can push up the price level unless there is an increase in the money supply. Box 28.3 provides some explanation of the monetarist rejection of rising costs as a source of inflation.

The Phillips Curve

In 1958, the economist A.W. Phillips published a research paper entitled: *The Relation Between Unemployment and the Rate of Change of Money Wages in the United Kingdom 1861–1957.* This research paper profoundly influenced economic thinking and the formation of economic policy. The main conclusion of this paper was that a *stable* relationship existed between the level of unemployment and the rate of wage change. Other research in this area quickly followed and seemed to confirm Phillips's original findings. Furthermore an equally stable relationship was found to have existed for many years between the rate of change of prices (that is, the rate of inflation) and the level of unemployment. It is this latter relationship which is usually generalised in the Phillips Curve which is illustrated in Figure 28.4

The Phillips curve shows that as the **level of unemployment falls**, the **rate of inflation rises**. Since the basic relationship had been stable for almost a century, it was assumed that it would continue to be stable and therefore the Phillips Curve was interpreted as offering policy makers a menu for policy choice. They could choose lower unemployment if they were prepared to accept higher inflation, or lower inflation if they were prepared to accept higher unemployment. In fact, if the Phillips Curve really was stable, governments could *trade off* one against the other to obtain what they considered to be

Box 28.3 The cost push illusion

If cost push inflation is really a myth, why do consumers hear businessmen rationalise their price increases with: 'I have to raise my price because my costs have risen'. Are businessmen simply trying to pass the buck? No, most businessmen (especially those operating relatively small businesses) believe that higher costs of production are the motivation for raising prices. They seldom identify the real cause – **increased aggregate demand resulting from increased money growth**. The translation of increased aggregate demand into higher prices is frequently concealed in the market place by the existence of inventories. As a result a 'cost-push illusion' is created.

No merchant sells his product at a constant rate; sales in some periods are larger than normal, while sales in other time periods are smaller. In order to hedge against running out of their product during periods of larger than normal sales, merchants typically hold inventories (or buffer stocks). If aggregate demand increases, merchants cannot immediately distinguish this phenomenon from a period in which sales are temporarily above normal: that is, they do not realise immediately that they could raise their price and still make the normal amount of sales. Consequently they will not raise their price immediately, but instead, will draw down their inventories held for an occasion such as this. If these higher than normal sales persist, merchants will increase their purchase rate from suppliers in order to maintain their inventories at the desired level. The firms that supply these merchants thus will experience higher than normal rates of sales, and their inventories will be depleted more rapidly than desired, motivating them to increase the rates at which they purchase from their suppliers.

This process continues filtering down the network of markets until it finally reaches the market of raw materials (the primary inputs used to produce this commodity). In the raw materials markets, the amount available is insufficient to meet the increased amount demanded at the *old* price. Since aggregate demand has increased (not just the demand of one or a few manufacturers), all manufacturers want additional raw materials. As a result, all offer higher prices to suppliers until the price of raw materials is bid up enough to clear the market. Because the higher price of raw materials increases their cost of production, manufacturers will charge wholesalers a higher price for their product, citing increased raw material costs as the reason. Wholesalers will say that the increased manufacturers' price makes it necessary to charge retailers a higher price. And finally, the retailer (merchant), being completely truthful, will tell the consumer that he must charge a higher price because his costs have risen.

Extract from Dallas Batten, 'Inflation: The Cost Push Myth', *Federal Reserve Bank of St Louis Review* (June–July 1981)

Figure 28.4 *The Phillips Curve*

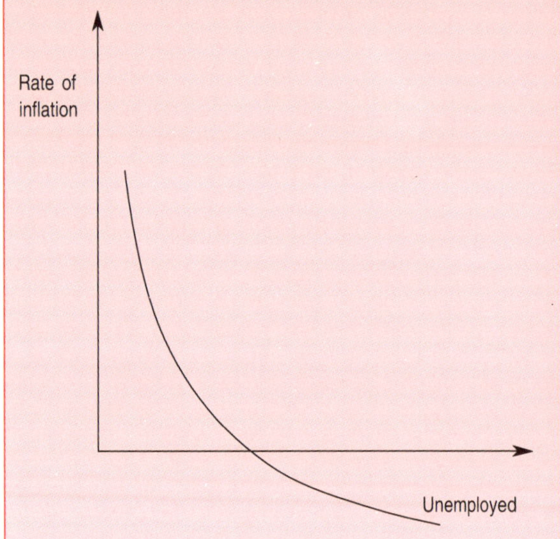

Figure 28.5 *Employment and the real wage*

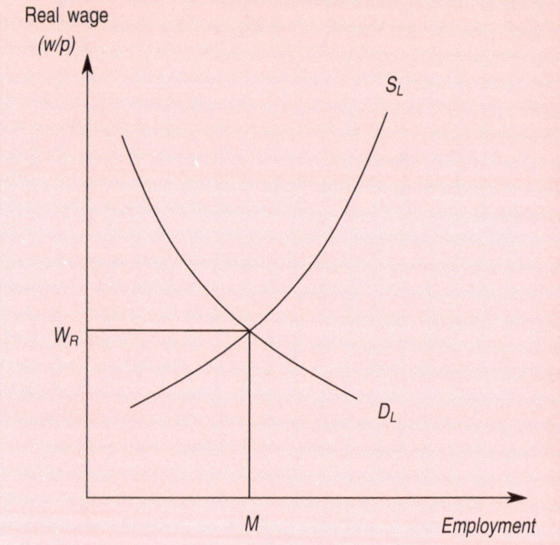

the most desirable position on the curve. In other words, by accepting more of one variable they could have less of the other, and so, by varying the level of aggregate demand, the authorities could achieve what they considered to be the *optimum combination of inflation and unemployment* from the range of alternatives implied in the Phillips Curve.

The Behaviour of Inflation and Unemployment

In his 1968 Presidential Address to the American Economics Association, Friedman (see p. 263) argued that the original relationship implied in the Phillips curve arose because of the confusion which existed between *money wages* and *real wages*. He argued that in wage bargaining employers and employees are not so much concerned with nominal, or money, wages, as with real wages. It is the real wage that determines the purchasing power of money wages and therefore it is the real wage that influences the willingness of workers to supply labour and the willingness of employers to demand labour. To understand the implications of this let us consider

In Figure 28.5 S_L shows the supply of labour with respect to the *real wage*. The supply of labour varies directly with the real wage showing that as the real wage rises, more workers are willing to offer themselves for employment. We would expect this relationship because a higher real wage implies that a given amount of labour time now exchanges for, or buys, a greater volume of goods and services. As the real wage rises, more workers will therefore be attracted into the labour market because the higher real wage obtained from accepting employment enables them to buy more output than previously.

The demand for labour with respect to the real wage is given by D_L in Figure 28.5. The demand for labour varies inversely with the real wage showing that as the real wage falls the demand for labour increases. Again we would expect this relationship because as the real wage rises, the real return to employers, that is real profits, falls. As the real wage rises therefore, firms will demand fewer workers.

The labour market in Figure 28.5 is in equilibrium when the real wage is W_R and M workers are employed. Since the labour market is in equilibrium when M workers are employed, unemployment must be at the natural rate. However, the significant point to note is that the labour market is in equilibrium at a particular *real* wage (W_R), not a particular nominal wage. Furthermore, this real wage will be constant at W_R as long as wages and prices are rising (or falling) at the same rate. This implies that unemployment can be at the natural rate irrespective of the rate of inflation.

The Expectations-augmented Phillips Curve

This line of reasoning led Friedman to formulate his expectations-augmented Phillips Curve. Basically

Figure 28.6 *Short run Phillips Curves and the expectations augmented or long run Phillips Curve*

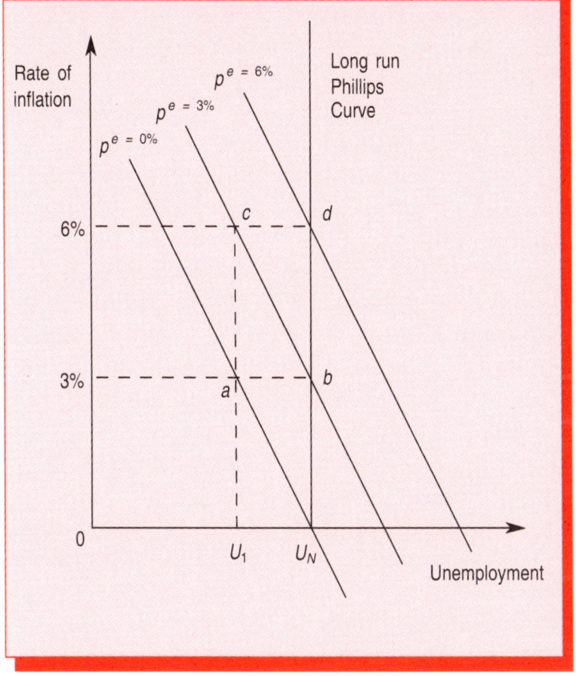

Figure 28.7 *Inflation and unemployment, in the UK, 1976–90*

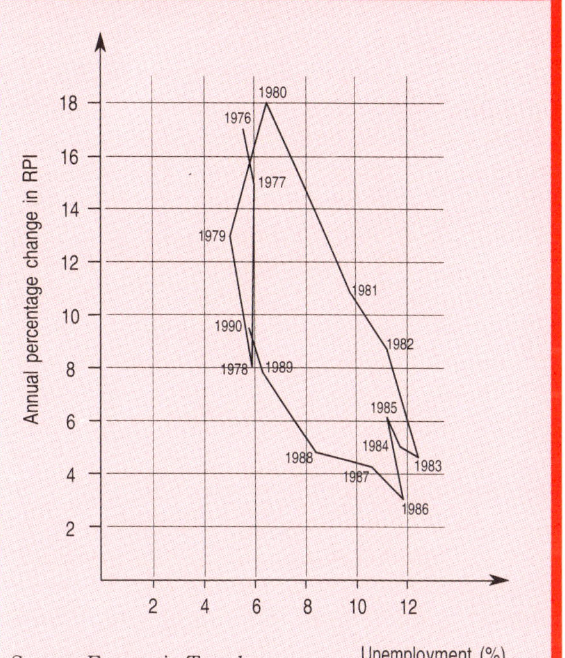

Source: *Economic Trends*

Friedman argued that for each *expected* rate of inflation, there is a unique *short run Phillips Curve*. To understand the importance of this let us consider Figure 28.6 which shows the natural rate of unemployment, U_N, and three short run Phillips Curves. (We shall see below why they are called 'short run Phillips Curves'.) The Phillips Curve $P^{e=0\%}$ is the appropriate curve if the *expected rate of inflation* is zero. Similarly $P^{e=3\%}$ and $P^{e=6\%}$ are the appropriate Phillips Curves if the expected rate of inflation is 3 per cent and 6 per cent respectively.

There is no doubt that Phillips identified a relationship between inflation and unemployment that had been stable over the period he surveyed. However, when the authorities based policy on the Phillips curve they were increasingly less successful in achieving the inflation–unemployment combination they had selected from the range of choices offered by the Phillips Curve. Specifically, it became apparent towards the end of the 1960s that higher rates of inflation were associated with higher rates of unemployment than would have been expected if the relationship identified by Phillips had been stable over time. Figure 28.7 shows the course of inflation and unemployment in the UK between 1976 and 1990.

Figure 28.7 shows that there was no stable relationship between unemployment and inflation in the UK for the period illustrated. The instability of the Phillips Curve after its existence was discovered is in marked contrast to its apparent stability before discovery. At the time, considerable attention focused on the reasons for the apparent breakdown of the Phillips Curve. There is now a consensus that *expectations* played an important role in explaining the existence of the Phillips Curve, and its apparent disappearance. The importance of expectations is considered in the following section.

Real Wages and the Labour Market

Let us assume that unemployment is initially at the natural rate and that the actual rate of inflation is zero. Let us further assume that the economy has not experienced any inflation for some considerable period of time and that no inflation is expected in the future. If for some reason the government now decides that it wishes to reduce unemployment below the natural rate U_N, to U_1 for example. To achieve this it expands the money supply by 3 per cent. What will the effect of this be?

The immediate effect of an increase in the money supply will be an increase in demand for goods and services and firms will experience destocking – that is, their stocks of output will fall to meet the increase in demand. Inevitably the increased demand for goods and services will bid up their prices and since there is no change in wage rates *real profits* will rise. Faced with rising demand and rising real profits, firms will wish to increase output and will hire more workers. To hire more workers firms will be willing to offer higher wages, though such increases in wages will be less than the increase in prices so as to preserve higher real profits. Because the expected rate of inflation is zero, workers will *perceive* these increases in the *nominal wage* as an increase in the *real wage*. In other words, workers suffer from *money illusion*, and therefore interpret a rise in money wages as a rise in real wages because they are unaware of the extent to which prices are rising. Because workers incorrectly interpret the increase in nominal wages as an increase in real wages, they are willing to accept offers of employment and the economy moves up the short run Phillips Curve $P^{e=0}$ to point a. The authorities have therefore achieved their aim of reducing unemployment to U_1.

However, this is not a stable equilibrium position because wage contracts were negotiated when the *expected rate of inflation* was zero, but the *actual rate of inflation* turned out to be 3 per cent. When wage contracts are renegotiated individuals will realise that their expectations of inflation were incorrect and will negotiate wage rises to compensate for the higher rate of inflation. However, once nominal wages increase by 3 per cent, the real profits of employers and the real wage of employees are exactly the same as before the government increased the money supply. The incentive for firms to expand output and employ additional workers therefore disappears and they will cut back on output and the numbers they employ. Similarly, those workers who accepted employment in the mistaken belief that they were being offered a higher real wage will withdraw from the labour market once they realise that there has been no change in the real wage.

However, although the economy moves up the short run Phillips Curve $P^{e=0}$, it does not move back down this curve. Remember the money supply has increased by 3 per cent and the quantity theory of money predicts that this will result in a 3 per cent increase in the price level. Reducing output and the numbers employed does not change this and therefore the actual rate of inflation and expected rate of inflation remain at 3 per cent. The new equilibrium is therefore at point b in Figure 28.6

If nothing else changes, inflation will remain stable at 3 per cent and unemployment will remain at the natural rate. However, if the authorities again try to reduce unemployment to U_1 by increasing the money supply by a further 3 percentage points, the process will be repeated. Employers will experience destocking and rising prices. As real profits rise they will expand output and attract more workers by offering higher nominal wages. Workers will again fail to perceive the rise in prices and will mistakenly believe they are being offered higher real wages. The economy will initially move to point c on the Phillips Curve $P^{e=3\%}$ and subsequently to point d when unemployment will have returned to the natural rate, but the actual and expected rates of inflation are now 6 per cent.

It seems clear that any attempt by the authorities to reduce unemployment below the natural rate by increasing the money supply will simply result in an increase in the rate of inflation in the long run, with no effect on unemployment. In other words, in its original form, the Phillips Curve is a short run phenomenon. The ability of the authorities to reduce unemployment along a short run Phillips Curve depends entirely on their ability to bring about a discrepancy between the actual rate of inflation and the expected rate of inflation. Any given increase in the money supply will achieve this only in the short run and therefore the long run Phillips Curve is vertical at the natural rate of unemployment. The implication is that the authorities must accept ever higher rates of inflation if they attempt to reduce unemployment below the natural rate by increasing the money supply. For this reason the above analysis is sometimes referred to as the *accelerationist hypothesis*.

Figure 28.8 *A short run Phillips Curve for the UK, 1986–90*

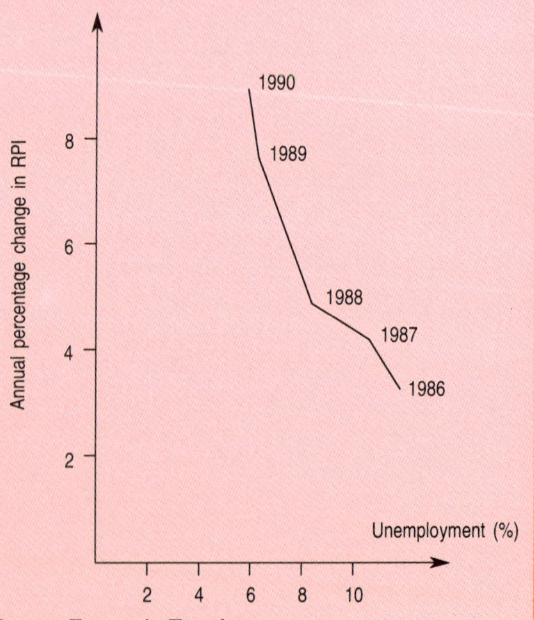

Source: Economic Trends

Milton Friedman (1912–)

Friedman was born in New York, the son of immigrant garment workers. He was an undergraduate at Rutgers University, New Jersey, where he learned the importance of empirical work, and particularly statistical techniques, in testing the validity of economic theories. From Rutgers he went to the University of Chicago where he was awarded an MA and then to Colombia where he gained his Phd in 1946. He then returned to the University of Chicago to take up a teaching appointment and was appointed professor in 1948. He retired from Chicago on reaching 65 but still carries on with his scholarly work at the University of Stanford's Hoover Institution.

Friedman is a brilliantly original thinker and is provocative in his views. He has challenged many of the established beliefs and the originality of his contribution was recognised in 1976 when he was awarded the Nobel prize in economics.

The underlying theme of Friedman's work is that the economy functions most efficiently when it is free of unnecessary government involvement. He views the free operation of markets as the source of economic prosperity and objects to government involvement because he feels that, however well-intentioned such involvement might be, its effect is usually the opposite of the intended effect. For example, he has argued that minimum wages, designed to avoid economic hardship, actually cause unemployment and therefore increase economic hardship for those who become unemployed.

Despite this, Friedman is best known as one of the founders of *monetarism*. The term refers to those economists who believe, among other things, that changes in the rate of inflation can only be caused by changes in the money supply. Friedman apparently dislikes this term and prefers to be called a *quantity theorist* since monetarists base their thinking on the quantity theory of money (see pp. 255–7).

Friedman has been a prolific writer. His best-selling book, *Free to Choose*, written with his wife Rose, is a strong defence of the market economy. However, his most influential book is his *Monetary History of the United States* written with Anna Swartz, in which he argued that the 'Great Depression' of the 1920s and 1930s, far from indicating a problem with free market economies, was, in fact, caused by mismanagement of the monetary system!

Is There an Exploitable Short Run Trade-off?

Despite the implications of the natural rate hypothesis, governments may still be tempted to exploit a short run trade-off between inflation and unemployment. The temptation to exploit this trade-off increases the longer the period that represents the short run. So how long is the short run? Figure 28.8 shows the relationship between inflation and unemployment in the UK between 1986 and 1990.

Even if we accept the accelerationist hypothesis, it is clear that an exploitable short run relationship might last for several years. However, a short run relationship of this duration cannot always be relied upon. Instead it seems reasonable to assume that economic agents will adjust their expectations of inflation more rapidly if they have recently experienced rapid inflation. At relatively low rates of inflation, expectations of future inflation may not adjust so rapidly and therefore we are more likely to find an exploitable short run trade-off. However, we must remember that exploiting any short run relationship will simply lead to higher inflation in the long run.

The Consequences of Inflation

To some extent the consequences of inflation depend on whether it is *anticipated* or *unanticipated*. The distinction is important because if inflation is unanticipated, the actual rate of inflation will differ from the expected rate of inflation. We consider the case of anticipated inflation in Chapter 29. Here we concentrate on the consequences of unanticipated inflation.

Inflation and the Allocation of Resources

The effect of inflation on the allocation of resources has undoubtedly been a major reason why governments have given more emphasis to reducing the rate of inflation in recent years. One way in which inflation adversely affects the allocation of resources is because it causes confusion between *absolute* price changes and *relative* price changes. If demand for a particular product rises, this will cause that product's price to rise and encourage firms to increase output. Rising prices are therefore a signal that society desires more of a particular product and to facilitate this, resources are competed away from alternatives for which society does not have such a strong preference.

When there is no inflation it is easy for the price mechanism to discharge its role of communicating information about society's preferences to producers. However, if *all* prices in the economy are rising, producers will be unable to distinguish between a rise in price caused by an increase in **demand for their good** (a **relative** price rise) and a rise in price as a **result of inflation** (an **absolute** rise in price). They will therefore make the 'wrong' decisions and some firms will increase output in the mistaken belief that society desires more of their product. In consequence, more resources will be attracted into the production of these goods than society really desires. In other words, inflation will cause **inefficiency in the allocation of resources.**

Another way in which inflation will adversely affect the allocation of resources is that it will encourage the growth of instruments and markets whose only function is to protect traders and investors against the effects of inflation. In recent years we have seen the growth of markets such as those in *swaps* and *futures* as a result of a generally higher and more variable rate of inflation. These instruments and markets represent a waste of resources because they would be largely unnecessary if inflation did not exist. This waste of resources might be quite considerable since these markets create jobs for many thousands of people, require the latest computer technology and so on.

Similarly it is likely that inflation, especially if it is at a variable rate, will encourage a diversion of resources into assets which provide a *hedge* against inflation. For many people property provides the most obvious hedge against inflation and this partly explains the attractiveness of home-ownership. The problem is that if savings are diverted into the property sector, less funds will be available for investment in the business sector. Investment in property may well benefit those individuals who own property, but it does not benefit the economy as a whole since it represents investment in non-productive assets. It is sometimes argued that greater investment in the business sector would lead to increased economic growth and an improvement in the standard of living. If inflation leads to resources being diverted into non-productive assets this may adversely affect future living standards.

Inflation and the Balance of Payments

If the UK has a higher rate of inflation than that of its trading competitors, this will make UK exports less competitive on world markets and imports more competitive in the home market. The result will almost certainly be a reduction in demand for UK exports and an increase in demand for imports. This will imply a deteriorating balance of payments position. In fact the effect of inflation on export earnings and import expenditure is a serious problem for those countries with relatively high rates of inflation.

Inflation and Investment

We have seen on p. 235 that the nominal rate of interest is crucially influenced by the rate of inflation. Countries with relatively high rates of inflation also tend to have relatively high rates of interest. Higher rates of interest will raise the cost of borrowing and in response firms may cut back on their investment spending. It is also likely that consumers will postpone purchases of consumer durables and, along with the effects on exports and imports discussed above, this will further discourage investment. Additionally a higher rate of inflation may also be a more variable rate of inflation and, if true, this will most probably discourage investment because it increases uncertainty, for example about the price output will sell for in the future.

Inflation and Employment

On p. 261 we argued that if there is a natural rate of unemployment, the actual level of unemployment will be unaffected in the long run by changes in the rate of inflation. Nevertheless, this view is not accepted by all economists and it is sometimes suggested that inflation may adversely affect the level of unemployment. One way in which this might happen, as argued above, is that if inflation in the UK were greater than the rate of inflation experienced by our main trading competitors, this would make UK exports uncompetitive abroad and imports more competitive in the home market.

Exports would therefore fall and imports would increase as UK consumers turned to cheaper foreign substitutes. The effect would be a fall in domestic output and employment which would be exacerbated because of the effect of this on investment. It would also be exacerbated because of the effect on consumption through the multiplier effect discussed on p. 187. Furthermore, if rising inflation lead to upward pressure on interest rates and a reduction in investment, as discussed above, employment would again be adversely affected. It would also be adversely affected if inflation resulted in a reduction in expenditure on consumer durables because of higher interest rates.

Inflation and the Redistribution of Income

An often quoted effect of inflation is the arbitrary redistribution of income it imposes on society. One way in which this occurs is when borrowers and lenders have entered into fixed contracts. If one individual borrows funds from another individual at a fixed nominal rate of interest, inflation will cause a *redistribution of real income* from the lender in favour of the borrower. This occurs because at the time funds are lent, the lender forgoes a certain amount of current consumption. When inflation occurs and the loan is repaid, the same sum of money will buy less than at the time the loan was made. If the real rate of interest is negative – that is, if the nominal rate of interest is less than the rate of inflation – the borrower will gain at the expense of the lender.

There are other ways in which inflation will redistribute income. For example, some groups receive incomes which are fixed in nominal terms. Some people, such as debenture stock holders in joint stock companies, receive interest income at a constant nominal rate. Others receive occupational pension schemes which have no built-in cost of living provision. For both of these groups inflation will cause a reduction in real income. On the other hand, some groups may be better able to protect themselves against the effects of inflation. For example, those workers who belong to powerful trade unions will be better able to protect their real income from inflation than workers in weaker unions. Similarly those workers paid on commission may be better able to protect their real income than those paid incomes negotiated annually.

Box 28.4 Progressive taxes, inflation and real personal disposable income

When taxes are levied at progressive rates, inflation can cause a reduction in real disposable income. To see how this might happen let us assume that all income earners have a tax free allowance of £4,000. Let us further assume that the first £20,000 of income is subject to income tax at a rate of 25 per cent and that thereafter tax is levied at a rate of 40 per cent. Let us consider an individual with a gross earned income of £30,000. For this individual taxable income is £30,000 – £4,000 = £26,000 and £30,000 and tax liability is (£20,000 × 0.25) + (£6,000 × 0.40) = £7,400. Disposable income is therefore £22,600.

Now if inflation occurs at the rate of 10 per cent and wages also rise by 10 per cent, then gross income will rise to £33,000 and, with unchanged tax rates and tax free allowances, disposable income will rise to £24,400. This implies an increase in disposable income of almost 8 per cent; but prices have risen by 10 per cent. In other words real personal disposable income has fallen!

To avoid this effect tax free allowances are usually increased annually in the government's budget. However, the government is under no obligation to increase tax free allowances and does not always increase them by the amount necessary to preserve the **purchasing power of real personal disposable income**. When this happens the tax system and inflation combine to reduce real personal disposable income and it has sometimes been suggested that as real personal disposable income falls, workers are encouraged to demand higher wage awards. However, the effect of this is counter-productive since it puts further upward pressure on prices and, through the tax system, results in a greater *proportion* of gross income being paid in taxation. The result is a further reduction in real personal disposable income which may encourage a further round of pay demands.

Inflation and Tax Revenue

During periods of inflation, tax revenues received by the government tend to increase even if the government does not change the *rates of taxation*. This is referred to as *fiscal drag*. One reason why tax revenues increase is that inflation implies rising prices and this will be reflected in higher receipts of VAT which is levied at a *constant rate* of 17.5 per cent in the UK. When prices rise, the amount of VAT paid on each unit sold increases. As long as price increases are not more than offset by falling sales, VAT receipts will increase.

However, it is the effect of inflation on the receipts of income tax that attracts most attention. As incomes rise, individuals are forced into higher tax brackets so that *net income* does not rise in line with *gross income*. This, added to the effect of rising prices, may mean that the effect of inflation and a progressive tax system is to reduce real personal disposable income (see Box 28.4).

REVIEW QUESTIONS

1 If prices rise by 10 per cent, by how much does the value of money fall?

2 How does inflation affect the efficiency with which money fulfils its functions?

3 Are the problems of inflation greater if the rate of inflation is variable?

4 What is the prediction made by the quantity theory of money?

5 Why is it often difficult to distinguish between cost push and demand pull inflation?

6 What is meant by the term 'money illusion'?

7 Why is the existence of money illusion important to the derivation of the short run Phillips Curve?

8 What is 'natural' about the natural rate of unemployment?

9 Does the existence of a natural rate of unemployment imply that the government is powerless to influence the level of unemployment?

CHAPTER 29

RATIONAL EXPECTATIONS IN ECONOMICS

CONNECTIONS

In Chapter 29 we build on our knowledge of the long run Phillips Curve and the natural rate hypothesis outlined in Chapter 28 to analyse the effect of economic policy on macroeconomic variables such as the level of output and inflation. We shall also draw on our knowledge of the quantity theory of money as explained in Chapter 28 and we make use of the aggregate demand and aggregate supply framework developed in Chapter 22. We will also refer to liquidity preference theory discussed in Chapter 28.

Key Concepts

Adaptive expectations
Monetary policy
Policy ineffectiveness
The labour market
The goods market
The rate of interest

The Importance of Expectations

The role of expectations is important in analysing economic events and forecasting the probable outcome of different courses of action. Frequently the success or failure of any course of action depends on **how economic agents react** to that course of action. For example, if interest rates are expected to rise in the future, this will influence the *present behaviour* of investors and borrowers. It is likely that their actions will be different to the actions they would take if they expected interest rates to remain unchanged or to fall. It is therefore important to know how economic agents form their expectations because it will then be possible to forecast more accurately the future outcome of a particular course of action. In discussions about how expectations are formed, attention has primarily focused on the effect of policy by the authorities on output, employment and inflation.

Adaptive Expectations

'Adaptive expectations' are expectations which are formed on the basis of **past behaviour**. For example, adaptive expectations implies that economic agents will form their expectations of the future rate of inflation on the basis of the rate of inflation experienced in the past, especially the recent past. If inflation in the recent past has been relatively high, then if expectations are formed in an adaptive manner, economic agents will expect it to be relatively high in the present period.

We have already used the notion of adaptive expectations in explaining the nature of the long run Phillips Curve. Remember that in terms of our analysis on pp. 260–1 it was assumed that economic agents form their expectation of the price level on the basis of their experience of the price level in the previous period. Thus we argued that when the government increased the money supply by 3 per cent, this led to an eventual increase in the rate of inflation from zero to 3 per cent. It also led to a change in the *expected rate of inflation* from zero to 3 per cent! In other words, expectations of inflation *adapted* to the higher rate of inflation that economic agents experienced.

If expectations are formed in this way, then by varying policy from one period to the next the monetary authorities can create a divergence between the *expected* and the *actual* rate of inflation. This will make it possible for the authorities to influence output and employment in the short run as explained on pp. 260–1.

Rational Expectations

Rational expectations is a branch of the *new classical macroeconomics* and provides a different approach to the formation of expectations which has enormously influenced the way economists think about their subject. This branch of economic thinking developed during the 1970s and 1980s and although not all economists accept the most extreme predictions of new classical theory, there is no doubting its effect on macroeconomic thinking. It has contributed particularly to our understanding of the way financial markets such as the foreign exchange market operate, to the way the labour market operates, and to the effect of government policy on output, employment and inflation. So what exactly is meant by the term *rational expectations*?

At the simplest level, expectations are said to be 'rational' when they are formed by using all relevant information to improve predictive accuracy. It is difficult to refute this basic proposition because the alternative is that economic agents ignore relevant information when forming their expectations. However, despite its simplicity this statement has profound implications for economic analysis; but before we go on to consider these it is useful to consider the rational expectations hypothesis in a little more detail.

It is important to be clear at the outset that we are *not* saying that rational expectations always turn out to be correct. Indeed, no matter how rationally expectations are formed, random events will ensure that predictions are at least periodically incorrect. What we are saying is that rational expectations represent the *most probable outcome* of an event that can be forecast from all of the information that is currently available. This is an important point, because it implies that once expectations have been formed they are subject to **continuous revision** to take account of any **new information that becomes available**. In other words, rational expectations are continually updated as new information becomes available.

Proponents of rational expectations argue that, in forming their expectations, economic agents use all relevant information and build up a model to forecast the outcome of events such as changes in the money supply. If the relevant model fails correctly to predict the outcome of such events, rational expectations tells us it will be rejected and replaced by another model, or amended to take account of new information with the aim of improving the predictive accuracy of the model. Forming expectations in this way has two very important implications:

- Economic agents will not make **systematic errors** in forming their expectations. In other words, they will not *repeatedly* omit a relevant variable or repeatedly fail accurately to estimate its effect.
- In the long term economic agents will arrive at the model which **correctly predicts the future outcome of a particular economic event**. Remember that this does not mean that all errors are eliminated. It simply means that the source of error is reduced to random events rather than using an inaccurate model. In other words, any discrepancy between the forecast outcome of an event and the actual outcome are due to random events which, by their very nature, could not have been forecast.

These deceptively simple conclusions have profound implications for the conduct of macroeconomic policy as we shall see in the following sections.

Rational Expectations and Policy Ineffectiveness

We have seen on pp. 260–1, that an unanticipated increase in the money supply causes an unanticipated increase in aggregate demand and through this, an unanticipated rise in the price level. In consequence profits rise and this encourages producers to expand their output. Such an outcome will always result from an *unanticipated* increase in the money supply. However, the rational expectations hypothesis predicts that it will not always be easy for governments to achieve an increase in the money supply which is unanticipated. The corollary of this is that it will not always be easy for governments to influence the level of output and employment by changes in the money supply.

To see why this is so let us take as our basic proposition that the model which most accurately predicts the effect of a change in the money supply on the price level is the *quantity theory of money*. This view is accepted by proponents of the rational expectations hypothesis as well as monetarists. Because the quantity theory of money provides the best available forecast of the effect of a change in the money supply on the price level, rational expectations theorists argue it is the model that will be used by *all* economic agents in forming their expectations. For simplicity we stick with the conventional assumptions adopted on p. 257, that the income velocity of circulation (V_y) is constant and that the natural rate of real income (Y_n) is the long run equilibrium rate of income. We begin with an analysis of the labour market and subsequently we consider the goods market.

The Labour Market

We begin with a labour market which is initially in long run equilibrium so that unemployment in Figure 29.1 is initially at the natural rate U_n and the actual rate of inflation coincides with the expected rate of inflation. For simplicity let us assume this is initially equal to zero. $P^{e=0}$ shows the relevant short run Phillips Curves and P_L shows the long run Phillips Curve.

Now suppose the government increases the money supply in an attempt to reduce the level of unemployment below the natural rate. Because the expected rate of inflation is zero, such an increase in the money supply is unanticipated and government

Figure 29.1 *The effect of an unanticipated increase in the money supply of* x *per cent*

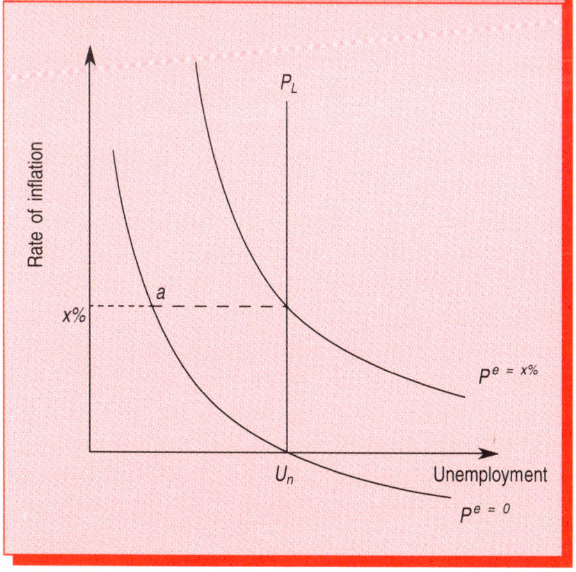

policy will therefore initially be successful. The economy will move up the short run Phillips Curve $P^{e=0}$ to point a, and unemployment will fall below the natural rate. However, as we have seen on p. 261, in the long run unemployment will return to the natural rate and the government will not have achieved a permanent reduction in the level of unemployment. The only long run effect of the increase in the money supply will be an increase in the price level.

But what if the government repeatedly uses this technique – that is, each time unemployment returns to the natural rate, the money supply is increased so as to reduce unemployment? If expectations are formed rationally, those involved in fixing wages and prices, because they form their expectations on the basis of the quantity theory of money, will know that an increase in the money supply has no long run effect on real economic activity and simply leads to higher prices.

To understand the significance of this, assume that the government declares its intention of cutting unemployment and announces an increase in the money supply of x per cent to achieve this. The change in the money supply is now *anticipated* by economic agents. In these circumstances, an increase in the money supply will have no effect on output or employment either in the short or the long run. Firms will simply raise prices proportionately with the anticipated increase in the money supply. Employees will also anticipate the increase in the price level following an increase in the money supply and will demand a proportionate increase in wages. Since all economic agents are assumed to have access to the same information about the behaviour of the money supply and are assumed to use the same model, the quantity theory of money, they will all expect the same increase in the price level.

The implication is that the increase in the money supply leaves real profits and real wages unchanged and therefore has no effect on output and employment. Remember that it is only *unanticipated changes* in the money supply, because of their effect on actual inflation and expected inflation, that have an effect on output and employment. When there is no divergence between actual inflation and expected inflation there is no incentive for firms to expand output and demand more labour. Neither is there any incentive for additional workers to enter the labour market. Output and employment are therefore unchanged despite the increase in the money supply. The result of a perfectly anticipated increase in the money supply of, say, x per cent, is illustrated in terms of Figure 29.2.

Figure 29.2 *The effect of a perfectly anticipated increase in the money supply of* x *per cent on the level of unemployment*

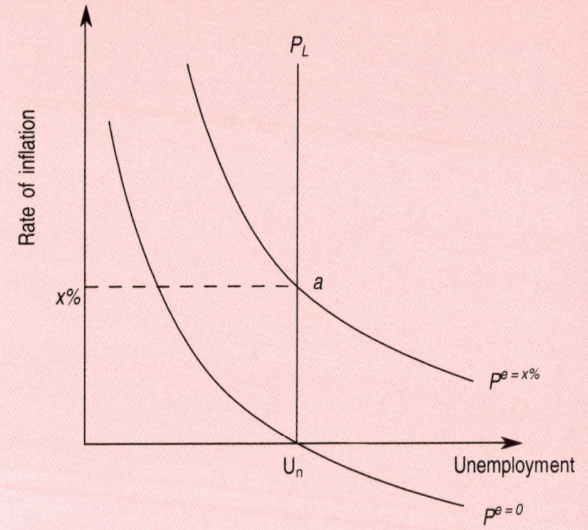

A perfectly anticipated increase in the money supply results in an immediate increase in the rate of inflation of *x* per cent and no change in the level of unemployment

Figure 29.3 *The effect of a perfectly anticipated increase in the money supply on the price level*

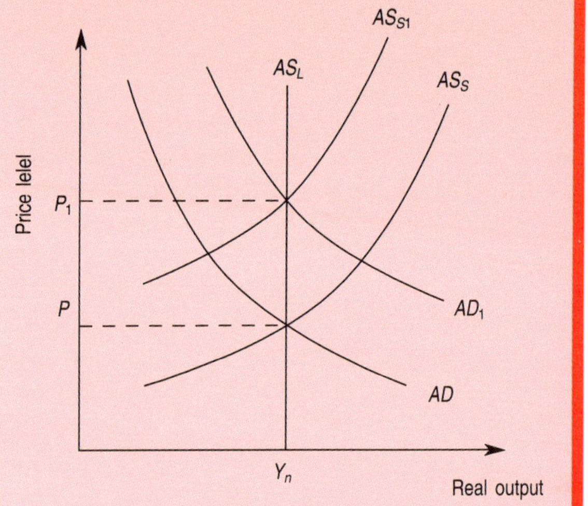

A perfectly anticipated increase in the money supply this results in an immediate increase in the price level but has no effect on real output

Assume that unemployment is initially at the natural rate and that the actual rate of inflation and expected rate of inflation are zero. Now assume that expectations change and economic agents correctly anticipate an increase in the money supply of x per cent as a result of a government announcement to this effect. The effect of an announcement that the money supply will grow by x per cent will create the expectation of an x per cent increase in the price level. The change in expectations will cause all contracts to be renegotiated and instead of the increase in the money supply causing a movement up a short run Phillips Curve, the economy moves immediately to its new long run equilibrium at point *a* on the long run Phillips Curve. According to the rational expectations hypothesis, any anticipated change in the money supply will simply result in a movement up or down the long run Phillips Curve.

It is easy to see the importance of understanding how expectations are formed. If monetary policy is anticipated, it will be ineffective in influencing anything except the price level, even in the short run. This is the famous *policy ineffectiveness* conclusion of the rational expectations hypothesis.

The Goods Market

We can illustrate the same effect using aggregate supply and aggregate demand curves, as in Figure 29.3.

Aggregate demand is initially given by *AD* and aggregate supply is initially given by *AS*. The expected rate of inflation and the actual rate of inflation are equal and the economy is initially in equilibrium with output at Y_n and the price level at *P*. Now if the government announces a target increase in the money supply of x per cent, economic agents will expect the price level to rise by x per cent, partly because the increased money supply implies an increase in aggregate demand. (Aggregate demand shifts from *AD* to AD_1 in Figure 29.3.) Factor prices will also rise, for example, as employees demand higher wages, and this will shift the aggregate supply curve to AS_1. Here again, because the increase in the money supply was perfectly anticipated there was no effect on output or employment. The economy moves from its original long run equilibrium position to its new long run equilibrium position with the price level now at P_1. Here again, announced policy changes are ineffective in influencing anything except the price level.

It is important to note that in Figure 29.3 there is no change in real output, even in the short run, when there is an announcement on target rates of growth for the money supply. This is essentially the same result as indicated in Figure 29.2. Since there is no change in the level of output, there will be no change in the level of employment. When real income is at the natural rate, unemployment must also be at the natural rate. An increase in output above the natural

Box 29.1 The behaviour of the money supply and the rate of interest

The liquidity preference theory outlined on pp. 236–42 implies that an increase in the money supply leads to a reduction in the rate of interest. However, for most of the 1980s the UK experienced relatively high interest rates accompanied by a relatively large rate of growth of the money supply, as shown in Figure 29.4.

Figure 29.4 *Interest rates and growth of the money supply, UK, 1980–9*

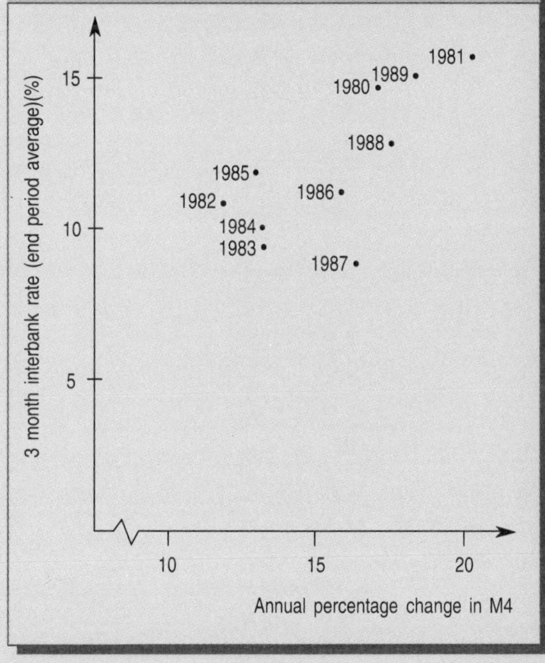

It can be seen that far from reducing interest rates for the period shown, an increase in money growth is more usually associated with higher interest rates. This is difficult to reconcile with the liquidity preference theory, and can more readily be explained in terms of rational expectations.

To see why, let us assume that the actual rate of inflation and the expected rate of inflation are initially zero. In these circumstances if the government increases the money supply it will cause interest rates to fall as the liquidity preference theory predicts. However, the fall in the rate of interest will cause an increase in investment leading to a rise in the level of income and an increase in the demand for money. If there is no further change in the supply of money, the increased demand for money will pull up interest rates. In addition, as income returns to the natural rate, the increase in the money supply will simply be reflected in an increase in the price level.

We have seen on p. 244 that in the long run, the nominal rate of interest is given by the equation $i = r + p$, where i is the nominal rate of interest, r is the real rate of interest and p is the rate of inflation. It is usually agreed that the real rate of interest (r) changes only slowly over time and therefore this equation is the mathematical model which explains the behaviour of interest rates outlined in the previous paragraph. It implies that changes in the **money supply** lead to changes in the **nominal rate of interest**. Now if the government systematically increases the money supply in an attempt to reduce interest rates, economic agents will form rational expectations by substituting π, the expected rate of inflation, for p, the actual rate of inflation.

We know that economic agents will wish to forecast the behaviour of interest rates, because by so doing they can earn a profit if their forecasts are accurate. They can do this because they can borrow funds at a lower rate than they would expect to pay in the future. Indeed the financial institutions such as the commercial banks employ economists and statisticians partly to provide forecasts of interest rates! Accepting the quantity theory of money as the best long run predictor of the price level gives us a relationship between m, the money supply, and p, the price level. When there is an increase in the growth of the money supply, rational economic agents will immediately expect an increase in the price level and therefore an increase in the nominal rate of interest.

In fact, we are not claiming that economic agents adjust their plans instantaneously to new information on the behaviour of the money supply. However, we do feel that such information takes only a little time to affect behaviour because of its impact on expectations and this could account for the behaviour of the money supply and interest rates in the UK during the 1980s.

rate implies a reduction in unemployment below the natural rate, and vice versa.

The Policy Implications of Rational Expectations

We have seen that the main result of the rational expectations doctrine is that announced policy changes have no effect on output or employment. However, care must be taken here. We are not saying that monetary policy cannot influence output and employment. We are simply saying that monetary policy has an effect on output and employment only if it is *unanticipated*. The effect of any anticipated change in monetary policy will be discounted before it has even occurred. However, even unanticipated changes in the money supply have only a short run effect on output and employment. In the long run the effect is entirely on the price level.

What does this imply about the role of monetary policy? Clearly if the government is prepared to vary monetary policy in a random (and therefore unpredictable) way, monetary policy may perform a short term role. However, it is unlikely that governments will wish to vary the money supply in a random way. In the long run this will simply create inefficiency in the allocation of resources (see pp. 263–4).

The new classical school argue that monetary (and fiscal) policies should be targeted to achieve stable rates of inflation. More specifically, governments should aim at a desired rate of inflation rather than a desired rate of unemployment because in the long run monetary policy has no effect on output or employment. Attempts to influence output and employment by varying monetary policy simply lead to higher prices. So what kind of policies should be implemented to achieve price stability?

Many new classical economists argue in favour of the *monetary rule* recommended by Friedman and other monetarists. The central bank would simply announce in advance a target rate of growth for the money supply and would ensure that this target was met. Because the change in the money supply would be anticipated it would not affect output or employment. But if a relatively low target were chosen it would immediately achieve a lower rate of inflation.

Similarly, many economists of the new classical school favour a set rule for *fiscal policy*. Many have argued that on average the budget should be balanced so that on average tax revenue received by the government equals expenditure by the government: in other words, budget deficits in one year should be offset by surpluses in other years. Despite this, all new classical economists argue against large swings in the state of the budget so that relatively large deficits and relatively large surpluses are avoided. A balanced budget is favoured primarily because budget deficits and surpluses bring about changes in the money supply (see p. 238). A balanced budget is therefore seen as a necessary ingredient of any policy to achieve a target rate of growth for the money supply.

Criticisms of the Rational Expectations Hypothesis

A major criticism of the new classical school is that the policy ineffectiveness conclusion explained earlier in this chapter has not yet been proven. This does not necessarily imply that policy will not become ineffective in the future. Remember that rational expectations are formed in such a way that they are subject to continuous revision as new information becomes available. Though policy has not yet proved to be ineffective, it may do so in the future. However, a different view is that policy has not yet proved to be ineffective because the basic assumptions of the new classical school are unsound. So what are these assumptions and why may they be unsound?

Costs of Gathering and Processing Information

The rational expectations hypothesis has been criticised because it assumes that all economic agents have access to the same information. This may not always be the case. There are costs involved in gathering and processing information and therefore not all economic agents can be relied upon to formulate the same prediction. In addition, it has been argued that the authorities will posses more and better information than other economic agents. This will enable the authorities to predict and respond to events which are unanticipated by the public. Since these events are unanticipated by the public, the response of the authorities will also be unanticipated. This will enable the authorities *systematically* to vary unemployment and output above or below the natural rate. This is completely at odds with the predictions of the rational expectations hypothesis.

Wage and Price Inflexibility

Even if economic agents do possess the same information as the monetary authorities, there is some doubt that they will respond in the way predicted by the rational expectations hypothesis. In particular, employees are constrained in their demands for higher wages by existing contracts which can be renegotiated only when the contracts expire. It seems reasonable to assume that the monetary authorities can vary the money supply in response to new information more quickly than contracts can be renegotiated. They can therefore create a discrepancy between the actual rate of inflation, and the rate of inflation that was expected at the time the contracts were originally negotiated. Again this is completely at odds with the new classical school since it implies that monetary policy can be varied to influence output.

Assessment of Rational Expectations

The criticisms of the rational expectations hypothesis discussed above cast doubt on the accuracy of the policy ineffectiveness conclusion. On the other hand, the new classical economists argue that if the authorities have access to more complete information than other economic agents, rather than using this to manipulate output and employment in the short run they should make this information public. In particular, they argue that to do so improves the allocation of resources since it avoids the waste associated with unanticipated inflation. In other words, if the authorities use their informational advantage to reduce unemployment below the natural rate, they will generate higher inflation in the long run and a diversion of resources into instruments and markets designed to avoid the risks of unanticipated price changes (see p. 267).

There is no doubt that the policy ineffectiveness conclusion remains controversial. However, the new classical school cannot be dismissed and the notion of rational expectations plays an important part in macroeconomic thinking. Indeed, in some markets there is convincing evidence that economic agents do form their expectations by considering all relevant information and respond accordingly (see p. 273). Much more work needs to be done on the way expectations are formed and their effect on the macroeconomy, but one thing is certain: rational expectations has fundamentally changed the way economists think about their subject and things will never be the same again!

Box 29.2 The Keynesian, monetarist and new classical approaches compared

We have identified three ways of approaching the determination of national income in this book: the Keynesian approach, the monetarist approach and the new classical approach. There are fundamental differences in each approach although the new classical approach more closely resembles the monetarist approach than the Keynesian approach. To see why, let us compare all three approaches.

The **new classical macroeconomics** provides a way of analysing the effect of government policy on the real economy – that is, the effect of policy on the level of output and employment. The main conclusion of the new classical approach is that when the government systematically uses the same policy actions it has no effect on any macro variables except the price level, even in the short run. Economists who belong to this school advocate that governments abandon any attempt to stabilise the economy by variations in monetary and fiscal policy.

The approach of the new classical school is in marked contrast to the **Keynesian approach**, which advocates a high degree of intervention for stabilisation purposes. The Keynesian view is that governments should increase their own spending and/or reduce taxation to offset a reduction in private sector spending, thus averting the onset of recession. In times of rising private sector spending, the opposite would occur to prevent the economy from 'overheating' and causing an increase in the rate of inflation. The new classical school do not accept that systematic intervention by the authorities achieves anything except a higher rate of inflation in the long run.

The new classical school is clearly closer to the monetarist school than the Keynesian school but even here there are differences. In particular many **monetarists**, including Milton Friedman, argue that expectations are unlikely to be formed in a forward looking way as new classical economists assume. They argue that expectations are more likely to be formed in an adaptive, or backward looking way. If this is correct it is possible for the government systematically to achieve a change in output and employment in the short run by applying broadly the same economic strategies period after period.

It is important to be clear that while monetarists accept the *possibility* of this, it is not something which they advocate. Like new classical economists, they favour a balanced budget along with stable and predictable rates of money growth which are announced in advance. Both the new classical school and the monetarist school are against manipulating monetary and fiscal policies so as to stabilise the economy, and both agree that the long run effect of this is simply a higher rate of inflation.

Does the evidence support the views of any of these schools of thought? In 1980 the government of the UK announced its intention to set declining target rates of growth for the money supply for several years ahead. The aim was to cut inflation from an annual rate approaching 20 per cent to single figures. This was the central theme of the 'Medium Term Financial Strategy' (MTFS). The data in Table 29.1 shows the behaviour of the money supply, the rate of inflation, the level of unemployment and an index of real GDP between 1980 and 1985.

Table 29.1 *Changes in GDP, inflation, unemployment and money growth 1980–5*

	Index of GDP	% change in RPI	Unemployment (%)	Money growth (%)[1]
1980	100.0	17.9	6.0	20.0
1981	98.5	11.9	9.3	14.5
1982	100.3	8.6	10.9	10.0
1983	103.5	4.6	11.9	9.8
1984	106.4	4.0	12.4	9.5
1985	109.9	6.1	12.9	14.8

[1] The figures are for fiscal years. Note that £M3 was a measure of broad money which the government attempted to control as part of the *Medium Term Financial Strategy*. This measure of the money supply is no longer published but included most of the components of M4

Sources: *Economic Trends; Financial Statistics*

For the period shown, the money supply fell and there was indeed a reduction in the rate of inflation. Throughout the period there was a marked rise in the level of unemployment. The behaviour of the price level and the level of unemployment are consistent with a Keynesian and a monetarist interpretation. A fall in the rate of money growth caused a fall in aggregate demand and, through this, a rise in the level of unemployment and a fall in the rate of inflation. Of course, a monetarist interpretation would claim that the rise in unemployment was only temporary and would be reversed to some extent as the economy reverted to the natural rate.

This need not concern us here since we cannot accurately measure the natural rate of unemployment. What is important is that an announced target rate of growth for the money supply did not *immediately* lead to a reduction in the rate of inflation while having relatively little effect on output and employment as the new classical economists might expect. Indeed, between 1980 and 1981 real GDP fell by about 1.5 per cent! This seems to discredit the new classical school. However, we cannot dismiss these views quite so easily.

Remember that the announcement of monetary targets was a departure from existing policy. It was not the systematic application of a given policy. It is therefore possible that economic agents failed to forecast accurately the outcome of policy and that it affected output and employment and for this very reason took longer to affect the price level!

So which interpretation do we accept? The simple answer is that at present we cannot reject any of them on the basis of the evidence. Here again, we are reminded that economics is a young science and that much more work remains to be done!

REVIEW QUESTIONS

1 What is 'rational' about rational expectations?

2 What are 'adaptive expectations'? Are they ever rational?

3 Why might the labour market not adjust instantaneously to new information?

4 If the authorities bring about a random change in the money supply this will have a short run effect on output and employment, but if they vary the money supply systematically it will have no effect on output and employment. Why is this?

5 Are forecasts based on rational expectations always correct?

6 Why might the theory of rational expectations be more relevant in explaining the behaviour of financial markets than the effect of monetary policy on the level of output and employment?

CHAPTER 30

INTERNATIONAL TRADE

CONNECTIONS

In Chapter 30 we will be studying the reasons why countries **specialise and trade with one another**. An important concept in explaining international trade is opportunity cost. We will also refer to the concepts of specialisation, factor returns and mobility.

Key Concepts

Absolute advantage
Comparative advantage
Opportunity cost ratio
Terms of trade
Trading possibility curve

We are all aware that international trade takes place. In Britain we buy French wine; in France people buy British pullovers. However, not everyone is so aware of the effect international trade has on a nation's economy and the welfare of its inhabitants. In fact, for most countries the growth of international trade has been a major factor in the growth of living standards, especially since the Second World War.

Although all countries can benefit from international trade, such trade is more important to some countries than others. In particular, large economies often have a wider range of economic resources which makes it possible for them to satisfy the various demands for output without the need for foreign trade. For example, in the USA imports are about 10 per cent of GNP compared with about 30 per cent for the UK, and over 60 per cent for Belgium. In some cases a country's exports consist largely of a single product – oil from Bahrain and fish products from Iceland, for example. Table 30.1 gives some idea of the size of trade flows.

Table 30.1 *World exports, 1981–9*

	World	Industrial countries
1981	1855.0	1218.5
1982	1716.5	1155.5
1983	1666.7	1139.4
1984	1767.6	1214.2
1985	1807.8	1272.4
1986	1990.4	1485.6
1987	2342.9	1735.1
1988	2686.2	1987.7
1989	2891.7	2127.3

Source: GATT

Theories of International Trade

There are several reasons why countries trade, but the most important is undoubtedly that it allows countries to *specialise* in the production of those goods and services where they are relatively efficient compared with other countries. Because countries specialise where they have greatest relative efficiency, trade can be mutually beneficial. Let us examine the circumstances when this can happen.

The Principle of Absolute Advantage

A country is said to have an *absolute advantage* in the production of a good when it can produce more of that good with a *given amount of resources* than another country. To illustrate this let us make the following simplifying assumptions:

- All firms experience constant returns to scale as output changes.
- There is perfect factor mobility within a country – that is, resources are able to move freely from the production of one good to the production of another.
- There are no costs such as transport costs involved in trading between countries.
- Conditions of perfect competition exist in product and factor markets.
- There are no barriers to trade such as tariffs or quotas (see p. 290).

For simplicity, let us suppose there are only two countries, the UK and Portugal, each possessing resources which can be used to produce two goods, wheat or cars. Assume that the UK can produce 10 tonnes of wheat or 5 cars with x units of resources, and that Portugal can produce 20 tonnes of wheat or 4 cars with the same resources. These production possibilities are set out in Table 30.2

Table 30.2 *Production possibilities for wheat and cars, UK and Portugal*

	Tonnes of wheat that can be produced using x resources	No. of cars that can be produced using x resources
UK	10	5
Portugal	20	4

In the UK, according to the figures in Table 30.2, the production of 1 car has an opportunity cost of 2 tonnes of wheat, while in Portugal the opportunity cost of a car is 5 tonnes of wheat. This implies that the UK has an *absolute advantage* in the production of cars because, with a *given amount of resources* it can produce a greater volume of cars than Portugal. Conversely, Portugal is said to have an *absolute advantage* in the production of wheat because, with a *given amount of resources* it can produce a greater volume of wheat than the UK. In terms of opportunity cost, cars are relatively cheap in the UK and relatively expensive in Portugal, while wheat is relatively expensive in the UK and relatively cheap in Portugal.

In these circumstances, it is possible for both countries to gain from specialisation and trade. To see why this is so, let us look at the effect of specialisation on the total amount produced by the UK and Portugal. For simplicity we assume that each country has a total of $20x$ and initially devotes *half of its resources* ($10x$) to the production of wheat and half to the production of cars. In this case, the two countries' outputs would be

Table 30.3 *Units of output produced without specialisation, UK and Portugal*

	Wheat	Cars
UK	100	50
Portugal	200	40
Total	300	90

Now if each country devotes *all its resources* ($20x$) to the production of the good in which it has an absolute advantage, cars in the UK and wheat in Portugal, how much output is produced? In this case, the two countries' outputs would be as shown in Table 30.4.

Table 30.4 *Units of output produced after specialisation, UK and Portugal*

	Wheat	Cars
UK	0	100
Portugal	400	0
Total	400	100

We can see that when each country specialises in the production of that good in which it has an absolute advantage, the result is a **demonstrable gain in the combined output of both goods**.

The Gains from Trade

The principle of absolute advantage demonstrates that when two countries specialise, their combined output will be increased. However, it does not follow that both countries will *necessarily* gain from trade. Whether this happens depends on the *terms of trade* – that is, the rate at which goods exchange against each other. For specialisation and trade to be mutually beneficial, the terms of trade must lie somewhere *between* the domestic opportunity cost ratios of both countries.

Let us examine this proposition in the context of our example. We saw that in the UK the domestic opportunity cost ratio was 1 car:2 tonnes of wheat, while in Portugal the domestic opportunity cost ratio was 1 car:5 tonnes of wheat. Assume the terms of trade ratio is, say, 1 car:3 tonnes of wheat. This tells us that for each car the UK exports to Portugal, it receives 3 tonnes of wheat in exchange. This compares with only 2 tonnes of wheat for each car given up when wheat is produced domestically. Clearly, when the terms of trade are 1 car:3 tonnes of wheat, the UK can benefit from specialisation and trade. But what about Portugal? In fact, the same reasoning tells us that Portugal also gains. When cars are produced domestically, each car costs 5 tonnes of wheat compared with only 3 tonnes of wheat when cars are purchased from the UK. Portugal therefore also gains from specialisation and trade.

If the terms of trade lie outside of the limits set by the domestic opportunity cost ratios, only one country can gain from specialisation and trade. For example, if the terms of trade are 1 car:6 tonnes of wheat, the UK will gain from trade, but it will be cheaper for Portugal to produce its own cars. The opposite will be true if the terms of trade are, say, 1 car:1 tonne of wheat.

We can illustrate the potential gains from trade diagrammatically in terms of Figure 30.1, which shows a production possibility curve (solid line) for the UK, based on the assumption that the UK has $20x$ resources and experiences constant returns throughout. The gradient of the production possibility curve measures the UK's domestic opportunity cost ratio which is 1 car:2 tonnes of wheat. Figure 30.1 also shows the *trading possibility curve* (dotted line) for the UK, which shows the maximum levels of consumption of cars and wheat attainable after trade, given that 1 car exchanges for 3 tonnes of wheat.

To see the benefits of trade, assume the UK wishes to consume 50 cars. In the absence of trade, the maximum output of wheat that could be produced from its remaining resources would be 100 tonnes. This combination of cars and wheat is shown by point *X* in Figure 30.1. However, if the UK specialises fully in car production (where it has an absolute advantage) and obtains wheat from Portugal in exchange for cars at a rate of exchange of 1 car:3 tonnes of wheat, it can obtain 150 tonnes of wheat in exchange for 50 cars, thus leaving 50 cars for its own consumption. This combination of cars and wheat is shown by point *Y* in Figure 30.1. This point is unobtainable in the absence of trade. By comparing points *X* and *Y* you will be able to confirm that trade has made it possible for the UK to consume an extra 50 tonnes of wheat without any reduction in the amount of cars consumed. More generally, the trading possibility curve shows that more wheat is available for *any given quantity of cars* given up than is available when wheat is produced domestically.

Figure 30.1 *A production possibility curve and a trading possibility curve*

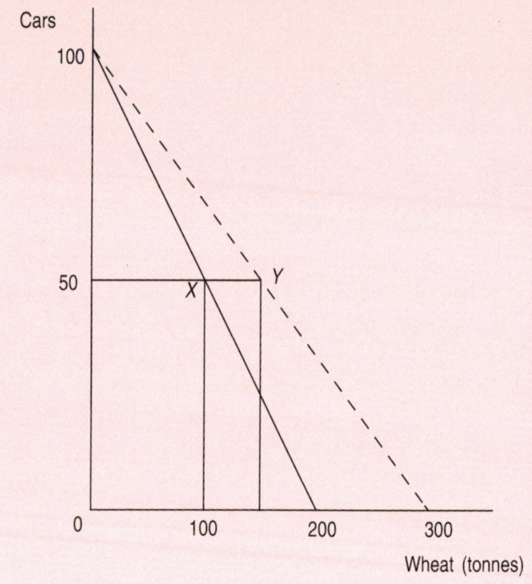

The Principle of Comparative Advantage

In the example on p. 279, where the UK was absolutely more efficient at producing cars and Portugal was absolutely more efficient at producing wheat, specialisation led to an increase in the combined output of both countries compared with self-sufficiency. However, even if one country, say the UK, was more efficient at producing both goods,

Box 30.1

There is ample evidence to support the importance of absolute advantage as an explanation of why international trade might take place. In the mid-nineteenth century, the USA was a leading producer of wooden ships, reflecting an absolute advantage in terms of high productivity of labour and an ample wood supply. The UK on the other hand, was a leading producer of metal ships, reflecting its superiority in the engineering trades. The USA therefore specialised in production and export of wooden, ships while the UK specialised in metal ships. At the present time Indonesia has an absolute advantage in the production of many spices which are exported on a world scale. Table 30.5 provides some interesting detail on the importance of absolute advantage.

Table 30.5 *Specialisation by absolute advantage*

Country	Major primary	% share of visible exports, 1982–4
Brazil	Coffee, soy beans, iron ore	28
Indonesia	Petroleum	62
Mexico	Petroleum	58
Nigeria	Petroleum	96
Pakistan	Rice, cotton	21
Libya	Petroleum	99
Saudi Arabia	Petroleum	100
Venezuela	Petroleum	92
Bolivia	Tin, gas, silver, zinc	91
Chile	Copper	46
Colombia	Coffee	51
Egypt	Petroleum, cotton	79
Ethiopia	Coffee, hides	72
Ghana	Cocoa	46
Guatemala	Coffee, cotton, sugar, bananas	49
Ivory Coast	Coffee, cocoa, wood	53
Jamaica	Alumina, bauxite, sugar	72
Kenya	Coffee, tea, petroleum	67
Malaysia	Rubber, wood, petroleum, palm oil, tin	62
Peru	Copper, petroleum, fish meal, silver, zinc, lead	65
Philippines	Sugar, coconut, copper, wood	30
Sri Lanka	Tea, rubber, coconut	50
Tanzania	Coffee, cotton, sisal	52
Thailand	Rice, rubber, corn, tapioca, sugar	44
Zambia	Copper	89

Source: Nancy Wall, *The World Economy* Economic Briefs (Collins Educational, 1989) p. 10

specialisation could still be advantageous provided that each country could exploit a *comparative advantage* in the production of one of the goods. We can analyse this proposition in terms of a simple model based on the same assumptions as our model of absolute advantage (see Table 30.6).

Table 30.6 shows that the UK has an absolute advantage in the production of both cars and wheat. However, the domestic opportunity cost of producing cars in terms of wheat differs between the UK and Portugal. In the UK, the opportunity cost ratio is 1 car:4 tonnes of wheat whereas in Portugal the domestic opportunity cost ratio is 1 car:5 tonnes of wheat. The UK is therefore *relatively more efficient* at producing cars since it has to give up only 4 tonnes of wheat to produce 1 car, whereas Portugal has to give up 5 tonnes of wheat to produce 1 car. However,

Table 30.6 *Comparative advantage*

	Tonnes of wheat that can be produced using x resources	No. of cars that can be produced using x resources
UK	20	5
Portugal	10	2

David Ricardo (1772–1823)

David Ricardo is widely regarded as the greatest of the classical economists. He was born in Amsterdam, the son of a Jewish broker, but moved to London when he was thirteen. It seems that his formal education ended in Amsterdam and he entered his father's broking business at fourteen. In 1793 he married a Quaker and by Jewish custom his father broke with him, though the two seem to have remained friendly. As a result of the split, Ricardo set up his own brokerage business and was tremendously successful. He retired from business at forty and bought Gatcomb Park, now the home of the Princess Royal.

Ricardo was friendly with James Mill, father of John Stuart Mill, who persuaded him to enter Parliament which he did in 1819. As was customary before the Reform Act of 1832, he did this by purchasing a piece of land which entitled its owner to a seat in Parliament. In Parliament he proved to be a brilliant debater and championed many causes that were against his own personal interest.

Ricardo's interest in economics was aroused after reading *The Wealth of Nations* and though he disagreed with parts of it, it strongly influenced his thinking. His own major work is his *Principles of Political Economy and Taxation* which was published in 1817 and again it was Mill who persuaded him to write it. This was a wide-ranging book on economic theory and in it Ricardo unveiled the *Law of Comparative Advantage* – a concept which survives today (see below). He also outlined what has come to be called the Ricardian theory of rent despite the fact that Ricardo did not discover the analysis and explicitly denied having done so. He did nevertheless considerably develop the analysis and considerably extended its application.

Ricardo's book was tremendously influential and for more than half a century thereafter other economics books written in England were either an elaboration or a commentary on his basic ideas.

Portugal is *relatively more efficient* at producing wheat since it can produce 5 tonnes of wheat for each car given up, whereas the UK can produce only 4 tonnes of wheat for each car given up. In other words, the UK has a *comparative advantage* in the production of cars and Portugal has a *comparative advantage* in the production of wheat – despite having an absolute disadvantage in the production of these goods!

Specialisation and Comparative Advantage

To see how both countries can benefit from specialisation and trade let us again assume that the UK and Portugal each have $20x$ units of resources and specialise completely by committing their $20x$ resources to the production of the good in which each has a comparative advantage (cars for the UK and wheat for Portugal). You might suppose that, compared with self-sufficiency and each country devoting half of its resources to the production of both goods, the outcome would be a demonstrable improvement in the *total output* of both goods. This turns out not to be the case as shown in Table 30.7.

Table 30.7 shows that with complete specialisation the two countries produce in total more cars but *less* wheat than when there is self-sufficiency. This is because the UK has an absolute advantage in the production of both goods, including cars, in which it now specialises. However, an improvement in the total combined output can be demonstrated unam-

Table 30.7 *Self-sufficiency and complete specialisation, UK and Portugal*

(a) Self-sufficiency: units of output produced

	Wheat	Cars
UK	200	50
Portugal	100	20
Total	300	70

(b) Complete specialisation: units of output produced

	Wheat	Cars
UK		100
Portugal	200	
Total	200	100

Table 30.8 *Partial specialisation: units of output produced*

	Wheat	Cars
UK	120	70
Portugal	200	
Total	320	70

biguously if we assume that the absolutely more efficient country, the UK, *partially* specialises in the production of the good in which it has a comparative advantage (cars), while the less efficient country, Portugal, specialises *fully* in the good in which it has a comparative advantage (wheat). If Portugal now devotes 20*x* resources to wheat production, while the UK devotes, say, 14*x* units of resources to car production and 6*x* to wheat production, the outcome is a demonstrable improvement in the combined output of both goods compared with the self-sufficiency case, as shown in Table 30.8.

Because specialisation leads to an improvement in the two countries' total output, it is possible for trade between them to be mutually beneficial even though one country has an absolute advantage in the production of both goods. However, as in the absolute advantage model we studied on p. 279, trade will be mutually beneficial only if the terms of trade lie somewhere between the domestic opportunity cost ratios of both countries. In this case, these are 1 car:4 tonnes of wheat in the UK, and 1 car:5 tonnes of wheat in Portugal. (You can check this by re-reading the analysis on p. 280; and then applying a terms of trade ratio of, say, 1 car:4.5 tonnes of wheat to our current example. You should then compare this with the outcome when the terms of trade lie outside the limits set by respective domestic opportunity cost ratios.)

Criticisms of the Principles of Absolute and Comparative Advantage

The principles of absolute and comparative advantage are models which, we have seen, demonstrate the gains from specialisation and trade. However, remember from p. 279 that these models are based on several *assumptions*. We now examine these to see how realistic they are in the real world.

Constant Costs

Constant costs implies that firms experience constant returns to scale as output expands or contracts. (This assumption was reflected in the use of a straight-line domestic production possibility schedule in Figure 30.1, p. 280.) In the real world, constant costs are unlikely to be experienced and firms are more likely to experience either *decreasing returns to scale* (in which case unit costs will rise as output expands), or *increasing returns to scale*, (in which case unit costs will fall as output expands). In both cases, the domestic opportunity cost ratios will change as output changes, and this will affect the gains from trade.

For example, in terms of our models if Portugal experienced decreasing returns to scale as it produced more wheat, domestically produced cars would become cheaper in terms of wheat. The attractiveness of imported UK cars would therefore diminish and the incentive to specialise fully would disappear. On the other hand, if increasing returns to scale are experienced then, because of falling unit costs as output expands, the gains from specialisation and trade would be greater than those predicted from the constant cost model. There is a tendency for this to happen in manufacturing industry.

Perfect Factor Mobility

The changed output patterns which might be required by specialisation will be possible only if a country's resources are highly mobile. In the short run this is not a very realistic assumption and full specialisation may not be possible. However, in the longer term factor mobility, and hence the scope for international specialisation and trade, will end to increase.

The required movement of factors of production in response to trade opportunities will impose *adjustment costs* on the community. If labour, for instance, is relatively immobile, the outcome of a change in the pattern of production may be a lengthy period of *structural unemployment* for affected workers. The concentrated incidence of such costs, especially when industries are localised, will be in contrast to the widespread benefits of trade in the form of cheaper imports for consumers.

Full Employment of Resources

If a country has unemployed resources it will be operating inside its production possibility curve. The

Box 30.2

There is ample evidence to support the principle of comparative costs as an explanation of international trade and specialisation. Consider Figure 30.2, which gives data on the total labour input required in the production of various goods for the Republic of Korea and the United States.

For the goods listed, the data shows that the United States has an absolute advantage – that is, it requires less labour than the Republic of Korea to produce the same output in every industrial sector illustrated. Even in cotton textiles, where the Republic of Korea is supposed to have a comparative advantage, the United States required fewer man-years to produce $lm worth of output than the Republic of Korea. In the United States in 1980 it took 64 man-years to produce £1m worth of textiles whereas the Republic of Korea required 245 man-years to produce the same amount of textiles – that is, nearly four times as many man years as the United States!

Despite this, in 1980 the Republic of Korea was the second largest developing country exporter of textiles to the United States. Its exports totalled $418.7m, or 16.5 per cent of total United States' imports of textiles from developing countries. To explain this we have to look at the comparative wage rates in the two countries.

In 1980, the average annual wage for the industrial worker in the United States was $16,406, while it was only $2,890 in the Republic of Korea. United States workers therefore earned nearly six times as much as workers in the Republic of Korea. In textiles, a relatively low wage sector in both countries, the wages were

Figure 30.2 *Units of labour required per $m of output: intercountry comparison, man-years, 1980*

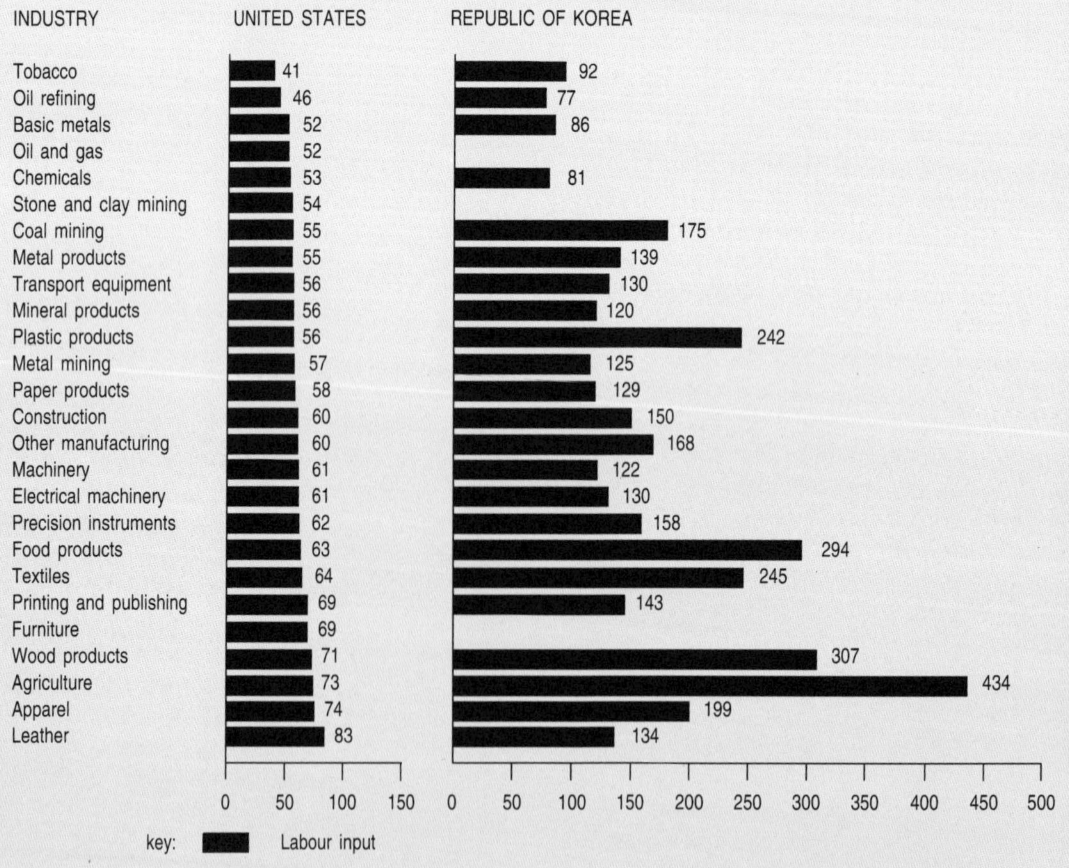

Source: UNIDO input-output data bank

$11,268 and $2430 respectively, a five-fold difference. It is partly the existence of this differential which allows trade to be mutually beneficial.

Further evidence of comparative advantage is given in Table 30.9 which shows the growth of exports for developed and developing countries (see p. 373) between 1983 and 1989. The dominance of the developed countries in manufacturing and the developing countries in primary production is clear.

Table 30.9 *Growth of exports*

	Developed countries		Developing countries	
Annual volume-growth of exports, 1983–9 (%)	6.5		6.5	
Exports by sector, 1987 (%)				
Consumer goods	11		10	
Textiles and clothing	5		10	
Machinery and equipment	45		28	
Semi-manufactures	12		6	
Iron, steel and chemicals	15		6	
Total manufactures		78		60
Raw materials	11		25	
Foodstuffs	11		15	
Total primary products		22		40
Total		100		100

Source: UNIDO

domestic opportunity cost of increasing the output of a given goods will therefore be zero and hence less than the cost of importing the good in question. In these circumstances, it will be more efficient to expand domestic production than to import the good.

Zero Trading Costs

In our model it was assumed that goods could be traded between countries at zero cost. Clearly this is a simplifying assumption and in practice firms which trade internationally do incur trading costs. For example, there are costs involved in foreign currency transactions, insurance cover and so on. However, the main trading cost is usually the cost of transporting goods from one country to another. An important factor here is the *weight: value ratio* of the good being moved. A good with an extremely low weight: value ratio (for example, cut diamonds) will have a trading cost per unit which is not far from the zero-cost assumption in our model. On the other hand, if the weight: value ratio is relatively high (as it is, for example, in the case of gravel), the trading cost per unit may be appreciable. Thus although gravel may be cheaper to produce in England than in Denmark the final cost of English gravel on arrival in Denmark may, due to high transport costs, approach or exceed that of locally produced gravel. The scope for Anglo–Danish trade and specialisation in gravel will therefore be correspondingly reduced. Transport costs also depend on the distance over which a good is traded. Nevertheless, you may be surprised to learn that the current (1991) cost of sending shirt cargo by air from Hong Kong to the UK is as little as 70p per shirt! While costs of trade are never zero, they are not always as high as we might think!

No Trade Restrictions

Our models of trade assume that countries are able to trade freely with one another. In the real world, this is not always so. Countries sometimes protect home industries with import restrictions such as tariffs, quotas, and so on; these hinder or prevent trade and so reduce the potential gains of international specialisation. In this context tariff reductions, achieved especially through GATT (see p. 297) have been one factor behind the growth of world trade which we drew attention to at the start of this chapter.

Intra-industry Specialisation

The notions of absolute and comparative advantage are important in explaining much of the trade which takes place between developed and less developed

Box 30.3 International trade and regional blocs

The 1980s saw an increasing convergence of countries into membership of three large 'regional blocs':

The **European Community (EC)**
North America comprising the USA, Canada and, by 1991, Mexico
East Asia, comprising Japan, Korea, Taiwan, Hong Kong, Indonesia and others

A regional bloc is essentially an area of 'economic integration' with increasing economic links between its member countries. Of the three blocs, the EC and North America have achieved significant economic integration, whereas East Asia remains in the early stages of integration. Has there been a tendency for international trade to become concentrated within regional blocs, at the expense perhaps of trade between countries in different blocs? Let us refer to Table 30.10, which summarises the 1980s pattern of trade within each of the blocs ('intra-bloc trade').

We can see that intra-bloc trade, measured as a proportion of a bloc's total trade, increased significantly in the EC, rose somewhat in North America but did not change significantly in East Asia. Overall, then, the evidence suggests that economic blocs do tend to 'concentrate' international trade.

Remember, though, world trade grew substantially in the 1980s (Table 30.1, p. 278). Thus although the proportion of trade in blocs grew, the *amount* of trade between blocs also expanded. Much of the growth in trade was between the world's industrial countries, so that intra-bloc trade as a proportion of trade between these did not in fact increase. This suggests that regional economic integration may be part of a broader process of integration amongst industrial countries generally.

Table 30.10 *Intra-bloc trade as a percentage of total trade*

	1982	1985	1988
European Community			
Exports	53.9	54.4	59.5
Imports	50.1	52.7	57.7
North America			
Exports	28.3	38.0	34.6
Imports	27.4	28.0	26.7
East Asia			
Exports	31.1	25.9	26.9
Imports	31.1	32.2	35.7

Source: *Bank of England Quarterly Bulletin*, August 1990

countries. Developed countries tend to have an advantage in producing finished manufactured products, which they export to less developed countries. They import in return those goods in which the less developed countries have an advantage – namely, basic manufactures and primary products (see Table 30.9 on p. 285). However, most of the world's trade is between the developed countries themselves, much of it consisting of manufactures, and it is not always easy to explain the pattern of trade that exists in terms of absolute and comparative advantage.

Consider trade in high performance cars, for example. The UK exports Jaguars but simultaneously imports BMWs from Germany. Italy exports Alfa Romeos yet also imports Lotus cars from the UK. We call this *intra-industry specialisation*. Clearly these three countries cannot all have an absolute or comparative advantage in the production of high performance cars. We therefore need a different explanation of trade.

Features of Intra-industry Specialisation

Intra-industry specialisation has three important features.

- It is often based on a **choice of brands** for a given good, whether it is cars or types of beer.
- There are usually substantial **economies of scale** in the production of each brand. Take the case of beer. The UK makes Worthington, Denmark makes Carlsberg and Holland makes Heineken. Yet low cost production is possible for all three brands, since each can be exported on a large scale.
- Intra-industry specialisation is often associated with **innovation in products and processes**.

A Theory of Intra-industry Specialisation

It is clear that such features of intra-industry specialisation as economies of scale and innovation cannot easily be accounted for in terms of absolute or comparative advantage, since both of these models assume *given* conditions of production. What is required is a *dynamic* theory to take account of changing conditions. Recent work in this area[1] stresses that the growth of intra-industry specialisation depends on the presence of four conditions

- advanced and specialised factors of production
- sophisticated and demanding home customers
- efficient suppliers and related industries
- a domestic market consisting of fiercely competing firms who pressure each other in terms of efficiency and product development.

Porter places great stress on the last factor, pointing to many instances where it has supported successful specialisation such as Japanese cars, Swiss pharmaceuticals, Italian ceramic tiles and British motor racing cars.

In Porter's view[1] then, while traditional economic theory may explain Italy's potential as a specialist tile producer, its actual development can best be explained through dynamic factors relating to innovation.

Table 30.11 *Instances of successful international specialisation*

Denmark	pharmaceuticals, specialty electronics, tele-communications equipment
Germany	eyeglass frames, optical instruments, X-ray apparatus
Italy	factory automation equipment
Japan	fax machines, optical instruments, robotics
Switzerland	hearing aids, pharmaceuticals
UK	auctioneering, pharmaceuticals, electrical generation equipment
US	advertising, computer software, accountancy

Source: Porter, *The Competitive Advantage of Nations*, p. 26.

Porter's approach has been used to explain other instances of successful specialisation such as those indicated in Table 30.11.

[1] This section draws heavily on Michael E. Porter, *The Competitive Advantage of Nations* (Macmillan, 1990).

Box 30.4 Specialisation in ceramic tiles

Ceramic tiles are a sophisticated product which is fired and glazed with complex equipment in temperatures up to 1000° Celsius. If you have any in your kitchen there is a fair chance they were made in Italy which produces about one-third of the world's output. Most of Italy's production comes from the town of Sassuola. Italian ceramic tiles are clearly an example of regional specialisation. How can we explain it?

- *Advanced and specialised factors of production*: The Sassuola area is rich in clays which over centuries have been used by skilled craftsmen in the production of earthenware goods. Ceramic tile businesses have been able to exploit this tradition.
- *Sophisticated and demanding home customers*: There has long been a high level of demand for quality tiles by very sophisticated Italian customers, whose needs anticipate those of foreign customers.
- *Efficient suppliers and related industries*: Northern Italian engineering firms are versatile and innovative and have been well able to support the growth of a ceramic tile industry as equipment suppliers, design consultants, and so on.
- *A domestic market of fiercely competing firms*: A high level of income in Sassuola has meant the availability of venture capital and the emergence of a multitude of competing local firms. These firms are constantly 'pressurising' one another into improved performance.

The Italian ceramic tile industry has been so successful that it is now the world leader and well ahead of its nearest rivals, Spain and (West) Germany.

International specialisation can take unexpected forms. Many people who watch grand prix motor car racing probably imagine the cars are built in Japan, the USA or Italy. In fact, 75 per cent, including leading grand prix names such as McLaren, Williams and Lotus are built in the Midlands and southern England!

British racing car production might be another example of intra-industry specialisation. There is a 'choice of brands', for although the UK dominates, there are in fact other producers elsewhere making cars and parts which, while satisfying the grand prix specifications, do differ significantly in design and operation. Innovation of product and process is extremely important in the racing car industry, and the UK is relatively well-endowed with skilled labour.

Source: Porter, *The Competitive Advantage of Nations*

REVIEW QUESTIONS

Question 1 is based on the following extract.

Côte d'Ivoire

Major exports: Cocoa-beans and dirivatives 27%, coffee and extracts 17%, wood 9%, petroleum products 8%, cotton 5% (1989)

Agriculture and forestry: Agriculture provided employment for 79% of the labour force and accounted 30% of GDP and three quarters of export revenues in 1983. The country is the world's leading producer of cocoa and the fifth largest producer of coffee. With cocoa and coffee accounting for 27% and 17% of exports respectively, price movements in these commodities have a major impact on the economy. Crops are sold to the Caisse de Stabilisation et de Soutien des Prix des Productions Agricoles (CSSPA), the government marketing agency, at state regulated prices. The subsequent lowering of these in 1989 may have had an adverse long term impact on production.

In an effort to diversify export crops, the production of cotton, which now acounts for only 5% of exports, palm oil, tropical fruits and rubber is being developed. Self sufficiency remains a major objective. The increase in food crops has made it possible to cut some imports, including rice and wheat. The export of wood, which acounts for 9% of exports, is declining as a result of the progressive depletion of forestry reserves.

Source: Barclays Bank

1 Consider the extract above:

(a) Which hypothesis of specialisation can best account for the observed pattern of crop production?

(b) Why do you think the Côte d'Ivoire is seeking to diversify its exports? To what extent is this likely to be compatible with the stated aim of self-sufficiency?

Question 2 is based on Table 30.12.

Table 30.12 *Value added per worker and wage rate, developed and developing countries*

	Value added per worker (1980 dollars)		Average wage rate (1980 dollars)	
	South	North	South	North
Food products	7,546	28,790	2,054	10,268
Beverages	19,831	47,428	4,126	13,100
Tobacco products	9,263	74,987	1,622	14,057
Textiles	4,913	17,334	1,824	8,164
Wearing apparel	5,961	13,722	2,456	6,946
Leather and fur products	6,450	17,161	2,186	7,856
Footwear	6,985	13,558	2,513	6,629
Wood and wood products	5,174	21,422	1,823	10,037
Furniture and fixtures	6,560	19,916	2,161	9,761
Paper and paper products	12,716	34,660	3,494	14,446
Printing and publishing	9,210	31,258	3,334	14,191
Industrial chemicals	20,624	49,968	4,277	16,875
Other chemical products	15,877	48,084	4,076	14,696
Petroleum refineries	86,262	188,437	8,638	19,971
Miscellaneous petroleum and coal products	23,074	50,703	3,464	13,291
Rubber products	9,794	27,029	2,804	12,956
Plastic products	10,456	26,535	2,953	11,711
Pottery, china and earthenware	6,428	19,672	2,292	9,485
Glass and glass products	9,904	26,790	3,220	11,860
Other non-metal mineral products	9,408	29,589	2,752	11,418
Iron and steel	11,544	32,938	3,423	15,244
Non-ferrous metals	17,717	37,308	4,077	15,291
Metal products	9,377	25,561	3,305	12,278
Non-electrical machinery	10,815	29,606	3,820	14,002
Electrical machinery	10,366	28,500	3,251	13,183
Transport equipment	11,948	29,685	4,129	15,286
Professional and scientific equipment	8,968	33,524	3,243	3,852
industries	7,897	23,041	2,407	9,812

Source: UNIDO

The data in Table 30.12 refer to developed countries ('North') and developing countries ('South').

(a) Calculate for each product the ratio of unit labour costs (South divided by North)

(b) On the basis of this calculation select **six** industries in which South countries would be likely to have:
  (i) a comparative advantage;
  (ii) a comparative disadvantage.

(c) Consult available World Bank and United Nations trade data sources to see to what extent actual trade patterns confirm your prediction.

3 In what circumstances will a country have a comparative advantage in producing a particular good despite having an absolute disadvantage in producing that good?

4 Why might nations not wish to specialise even when they have a comparative advantage in the production of some goods compared with other countries?

CHAPTER 31

FREE TRADE AND PROTECTION

CONNECTIONS

In Chapter 31 we examine the types of, reasons for, and consequences of, **restrictions on trade** between different countries. We shall build on Chapter 30 in particular, but it will also be useful if you are familiar with income determination in an open economy which was covered in Chapters 21. We shall also refer to the Common Agricultural Policy of the EC which is discussed in Chapter 34.

Key Concepts

Exchange controls
General Agreement on Tariffs and Trade (GATT)
Infant industry
Quotas
Tariffs
The new protectionism
Voluntary export restraints (VERs)

Types of Restriction on Trade

Tariffs

A tariff is an **indirect tax placed on imports**. It may be *selective* (that is, imposed on a particular product), or *general* (when it is imposed on a range of products). The effect of any tariff is to raise the price consumers pay for imports, usually with the aim of encouraging them to switch to domestically produced substitutes. Sometimes tariffs are *specific* (that is, levied at a fixed rate), but usually they are *ad valorem* (that is, levied as a percentage of the imported price of a good).

Quotas

An import quota is a **physical restriction** on the *value* or the *volume* of imports allowable within a particular period of time such as a year. When a quota is expressed in volume terms there is often a tendency for the value of the restricted good to increase because foreign exporters concentrate on goods with a higher unit value. For example, in the case of car exports the tendency would be to concentrate on exporting luxury saloons rather than family cars. When a quota is placed on the value of an import, the opposite might occur, with foreign exporters concentrating on the lower end of the market.

Exchange Controls

Exchange controls exist when the residents of a country are required by law to **exchange all foreign currency receipts for domestic currency**. This provides a powerful restriction on trade, because importers may be unable to purchase goods from other countries unless they can obtain foreign currency, and this can be only obtained from the authorities.

Subsidies

Subsidies, as we have seen on p. 49 are **payments by governments to producers and sellers**, and their effect is to reduce the price of goods and services which are granted subsidies. Placing subsidies on particular products can therefore encourage consumers to buy domestic output in preference to imports.

Voluntary Export Restraints (VERs)

These are simply agreements between two countries whereby one country **voluntarily agrees to restrict** the volume of a product that is exported to the other country; this is an increasingly common form of protection.

The 1970s and 1980s saw the introduction of new methods of trade restriction. These are potentially serious because they are not overtly protective and so are not easily removed by international agreement. Four examples of the type of restrictions that now operate are given.

Health and safety standards can be used to protect domestic industry against imports. For example, in 1983 the UK attempted to limit the import of French milk, on the grounds that it did not meet British health regulations. However, the French accused the UK of unfairly protecting its milk industry.

Government contracts can be awarded in favour of domestic producers as a means of restricting imports. This practice is common in the case of civil engineering tenders.

Complex and excessive customs formalities can be used to delay the import of goods. For example, Japanese customs procedures are sometimes so complex that foreign exporters have been known to set up local agencies to handle the problems encountered. This clearly adds to the difficult and expense of exporting to Japan.

Import deposit schemes compel importers to place an advance deposit with the authorities before goods can be imported. By reducing the liquidity of importers this acts as a barrier to trade. Such schemes are common in a number of developing countries.

Box 31.1 The spread of non-tariff barriers in the 1980s

In spite of – and sometimes owing to – the strong growth of world trade over the past two years, the multilateral trading system was subject to considerable strain. Various national actions appeared to strengthen the trend towards bilateralism in trade relationships and led to a proliferation of the already numerous quantitative restrictions on trade. International efforts to strengthen the system continued.

Barriers to trade continued to spread. The number of 'voluntary' export restraints and other export restraint measures recorded by the General Agreement on Tariffs and Trade (GATT) shot up from 135 in September 1987 to about 290 in September 1988. These numbers, moreover, exclude export restrictions under the Multifibre Arrangements (MFA). Some of the measures appear minor and in a few cases restraint measures may only have averted a total import ban. Nevertheless, the proliferation of these measures is evidence of a shift towards bilateralism and managed trade. Eighty-seven of these agreements were obtained by the European Economic Community, 62 by the United States, and 47 by other developed market economies and were aimed at restraining exports from both developing and developed countries. The largest proportion of the restraints were accounted for by textiles and clothing, followed by agriculture and steel. Increasing use is also made of countervailing duties and anti-dumping measures. Developing countries continued to use a wide range of non-tariff barriers as well as tariffs that are often very high and are imposed for balance of payments and other reasons, especially raising government revenue.

Non-tariff barriers now affect a larger proportion of world trade than before. The proportion of non-fuel trade subject to various forms of such barriers increased from 19 per cent in 1981 to 23 per cent in 1987.

The proliferation of such measures has been accompanied by new trade frictions, while many old disputes continued. Trade tension between EEC and the United States increased over the Community's ban on hormone-treated beef. The amount of import from the United States that was affected was only $150 million and the restriction was not considered by the Community as a trade measure. But it resulted in United States retaliation under which punitive import duties were imposed on $100 million worth of Community food exports. EEC counter-retaliated by restricting $360 million worth of United States farm exports.

In another trade conflict, the United States claimed that Japan had not sufficiently opened its market to foreign semiconductors. It therefore refused to lift trade restrictions it had earlier imposed on Japanese exports to the United

States. The protection of Japanese agriculture, despite some recent liberalisation also remained a source of friction between Japan and its major trading partners. The United States, seeking voluntary export restraint, has expressed its intention to impose countervailing duties and quotas on imports of beef, veal and mutton from Australia and New Zealand. A number of countries have complained against restriction by the EEC on imports of apples. The threat of anti-dumping measures forced the Republic of Korea temporarily to stop exporting colour televisions and video cassette recorders to EEC and to accept voluntary restraints on knitwear exports to Japan. EEC enforced one of the largest anti-dumping measures ever taken, imposing duties of up to 44 per cent on Japanese exports of dot-matrix computer printers. In May 1989, the United States announced that it would retaliate against Japan for having failed to open its telecommunications market to United States competition.

However, a number of trade liberalisation measures have also been taken. Under the roll-back commitments made at Punta del Este, the European Economic Community became the first trading group to offer to eliminate quantitative restrictions and import quotas on 121 industrial processed goods, excluding Japanese and Eastern European exports. Japan has agreed to take a number of steps to liberalise its imports of beef, citrus and seven categories of processed food. The Republic of Korea has reduced tariffs, eliminated the licensing system for some imports and relaxed foreign exchange regulations. A ban on imports of beef was replaced by quotas. A number of other developing countries, including Brazil, Columbia, India, Mexico and Pakistan, as well as Australia, New Zealand and Poland have unilaterally reduced tariffs on imports.

A major development during the year was the enactment of the United States Omnibus Trade and Competitiveness Act of 1988. The legislation, which sets rules of trade for the largest trading nation, will have a large impact on the trading system. The United States administration and Congress have viewed it as an instrument of liberalisation of trade. Others, however, have seen its emphasis on reciprocity and provisions for retaliation as a threat to the system of international rules.

The United States administration announced, in early May 1989, a list of countries which it considers to have erected unfair barriers against United States exports. Under the provisions of the law, countries were to be selected from the list for United States sanctions if they failed to remove the barrier within a specified period. Prominent on the list were EEC, Brazil, India and Japan. The announcement of the list has given rise to concerns about increased frictions in international trade.

Source: *United Nations World Economic Survey* (1989)

Arguments for Protection

There are a number of arguments for protection, but at the present time many economists do not consider these arguments to be convincing.

To Improve the Balance of Payments

It is suggested that widespread protection can, through its effect on the level of imports, reduce or eliminate a balance of payments deficit. However, protection does not address the main *causes* of balance of payments difficulties, which generally stem from a lack of competitiveness. In fact, one study[1] has raised the possibility that the use of import restrictions could lead to a significant reduction in a country's exports. In the case examined, it turned out that a tariff which raised import prices by 5 per cent was likely to lead to a 4 per cent increase in export prices. The reason was that import restrictions led directly to higher domestic prices, which in turn were likely to be followed by higher wage awards. Firms selling in the domestic economy would be able to pass on the effects of higher wage costs by charging higher prices, but the same was not true for exporting firms selling in foreign markets. Any attempt by the latter to recoup higher costs by raising prices on the domestic market resulted in a substantial loss of sales as consumers turned to competing products.

[1] K. Clements, and L. Sjaastad, *How Protection Taxes Exporters* (Trade Policy Research Centre, 1985)

For Strategic Reasons

Some industries are considered so important strategically that their continued operation is given high priority. Agriculture is a case in point, for it is argued that it would be inadvisable to become over-dependent on foreign food supplies lest these be threatened in times of war or political instability. Where a strategic industry is not competitive it might therefore be protected. However, defining a 'strategic industry' is a difficult task, and one which is ultimately the responsibility of politicians. Since politicians are sometimes lobbied by particular industries their judgement is not always objective. Moreover, once granted protection is difficult to remove if an industry ceases to be considered strategic.

To Support Infant Industries

An 'infant industry' is a newly formed industry in the early stages of development. Protection could shield such an industry from foreign competition and provide time for it to mature, exploit economies of scale and eventually compete without protection. Although this is an appealing argument, there are two fundamental objections to it.

- It is difficult to formulate **precise criteria** to identify industries which, if granted protection, would eventually become internationally competitive. Governments and their advisers who take these decisions may well select industries for protection which ultimately turn out to be unsuccessful. The acid test of success is long run profitability, and identifying profitable opportunities is the function of the capital market. In other words, it is the role of entrepreneurs, as risk takers, to accept short run losses while a business grows into profitability. If this fails to be the case, the policy implication is that capital market reform should be undertaken – not that young industries should be granted protection.
- The reduction in competition resulting from protection might lead to a **decline in the productive efficiency** of domestic producers. The assertion that protection necessarily reduces efficiency is difficult to test. A 1987 World Bank study of 41 developing countries (that is, those in the early stages of economic development) found that those pursuing protection of domestic mar-

Table 31.1 *Annual average growth of per capita real gross national product, 1973–85*

Free trade				Restricted trade			
Strongly		Moderately		Strongly		Moderately	
Singapore	6.5	Malaysia	4.1	Cameroon	5.6	Bangladesh	2.0
Hong Kong	6.3	Thailand	3.8	Indonesia	4.0	India	2.0
South Korea	5.4	Tunisia	2.9	Sri Lanka	3.3	Burundi	1.2
		Brazil	1.5	Pakistan	3.1	Dominican Republic	0.5
		Turkey	1.4	Yugoslavia	2.7	Ethiopia	−0.4
		Israel	0.4	Colombia	1.8	Sudan	−0.4
		Uruguay	0.4	Mexico	1.3	Peru	−1.1
		Chile	0.1	Philippines	1.1	Tanzania	−1.6
				Kenya	0.3	Argentina	−2.0
				Honduras	−0.1	Zambia	−2.3
				Sengal	−0.8	Nigeria	−2.5
				Costa Rica	−1.0	Bolivia	−3.1
				Guatemala	−1.0	Ghana	−3.2
				Ivory Coast	−1.2	Madagascar	−3.4
				El Salvador	−3.5		
				Nicaragua	−3.9		

Source: *Federal Reserve Bank of St Louis Review* (January–February 1988) kets experienced slower economic growth than those which had adopted free trade policies. The study concluded that protection damaged allocative efficiency by preventing resources from flowing to their most productive uses while reductions in domestic competition had an adverse effect on productive efficiency.

Table 31.1 shows that those countries with open economies (such as Singapore and South Korea) have generally made more economic progress than those countries with protected economies (such as Argentina and Ghana).

Despite this, there do seem to be instances where *particular industries* might have benefited from protection. A case in point is provided by the protection in the 1980s of the Japanese computer semiconductor industry to enable it to compete with that of the United States. One study[1] has shown that without protection the Japanese industry would have been unlikely to survive. Yet with the help of heavy subsidies equivalent to a 36 per cent tariff, three Japanese semiconductor firms were able to develop. The Japanese producers, once they had obtained a foothold in world markets, were able to develop their technical knowhow and eventually overtake their American rivals. Whether they could have achieved this without protection seems doubtful. Successful protection, where it occurs, seems to rest on two important conditions:

- Domestic producers see protection as providing an opportunity for **innovation and cost reduction**.
- The number of domestic producers within the industry in question is sufficiently large to generate **intense competition**.

Arguments Against Protection

Protection and Retaliation

A major objection to protection is that it invites retaliation from other countries. The United States, for instance, has trade laws which give its President authority to retaliate against foreign trade practices, particularly dumping, which 'unfairly' discourage US exporters. In 1986 when Portugal and Spain entered the EC they were required under the terms of its common agricultural policy to increase the proportion of grain purchased from other member coun-

[1] R. Baldwin and P. Krugman, quoted in *The Economist*, 22 September 1990

Figure 31.1 *The effect of a tariff on economic welfare*

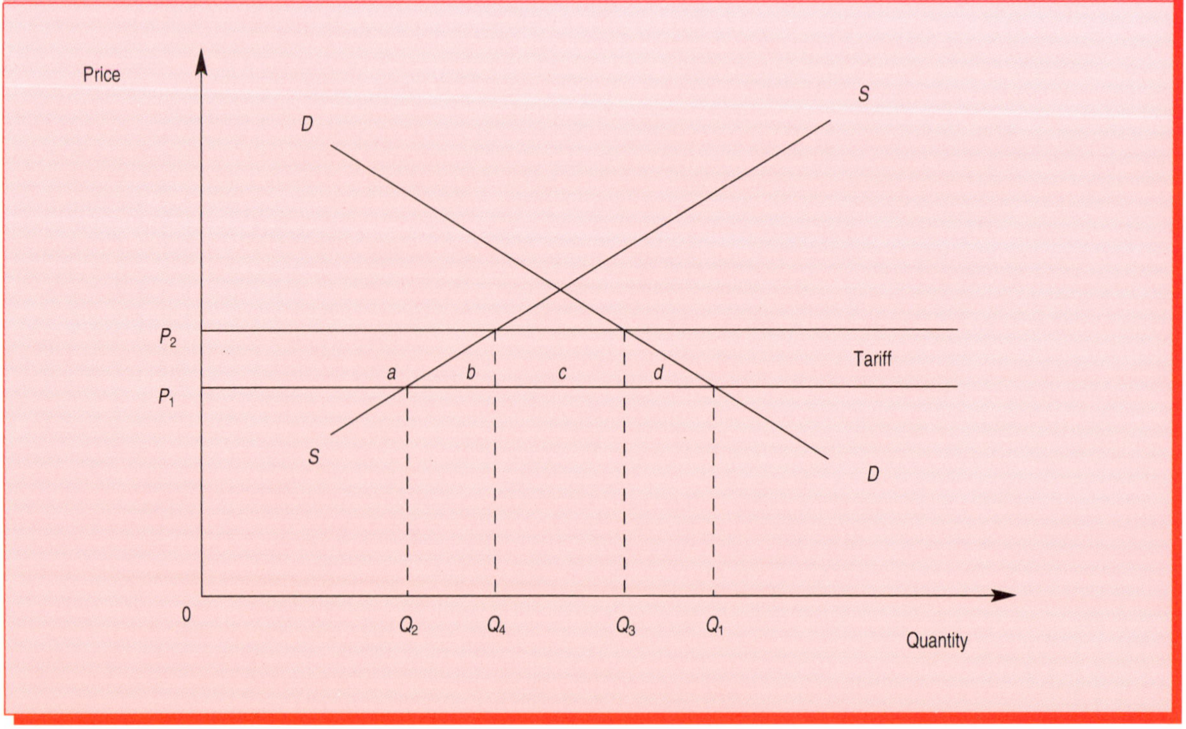

Box 31.2 How the United States retaliated against foreign protection

In 1989 there were new developments in 'managed' trade and bilateralism. The trade policy initiative which attracted attention most was the inclusion of the 'Super' and 'Special' Section 301 provisions in the United States Omnibus Trade and Competitiveness Act of 1988.

The Act enumerates several measures aimed at opening foreign markets to United States exports. Section 301 stems from previous trade legislation which required the enforcement of those United States rights that emanate from trade agreements and specifies the actions to be taken in response to foreign trade practices judged pernicious to United States exports.

Supplemented as of 1989 by 'Super 301', the definition of unfair trade practices has been expanded beyond individual commodities to include general patterns of trading behaviour. The Super 301 provision directs the United States Trade Representative to identify priority practices, which, if eliminated, would significantly increase United States exports, and priority countries, based on the number and pervasiveness of their trade barriers. Once a country has been 'cited', the administration has 12–18 months to negotiate the removal of the barriers. If the talks are unsuccessful, the Government can then levy tariffs of up to 100 per cent on selected imports from the 'offending' country. In 1989, Japan was cited for its refusal to buy United States commercial satellites and super computers and for its barriers to American lumber. India was named for restricting foreign investment and the operation of foreign-based insurance companies, and Brazil for its import-licensing practices. On 30 March 1989, the United States released its inventory of global trade barriers, listing 35 countries and two regional trading blocs which in its view maintained the most important obstacles to American exports. Japan was accused of maintaining the most barriers, followed by the European Community, Canada, the Republic of Korea, India and Brazil. The administration had until the end of April to designate the countries and practices which would be given 'priority' in trade policy in 1990.

The second arm of Section 301 is the 'Special' provision, designed to enhance the Government's ability to negotiate improvements in foreign intellectual property regimes. This statute requires the United States Trade Representative to identify foreign countries denying protection of intellectual property rights and market access to United States firms relying on such protection and to determine which of those are 'priority countries', triggering a six-month investigation. In 1989, significant progress was made in various negotiations and no countries were identified under Special 301. Rather, 25 countries were singled out for special attention, 17 of them being placed on a 'Watch List' and the other 8 on a 'Priority Watch List'.

Activities in which one country unilaterally passes judgement on the trade practices of other countries are not in conformity with the spirit of GATT. Another major example of an attempt to resolve trade problems through bilateral channels is the United States 'Structural Impediments Initiative', which was launched in July 1989 to seek fundamental changes in the workings of the Japanese and United States economies in order to reduce trade barriers. For its part, the United States has verbally agreed to effect concrete economic changes which would meet Japan's demand for a restoration of United States competitiveness, for example by bolstering savings and investment and improving education. The quid pro quo consists of a Japanese pledge to make it easier for foreigners to invest in Japan and to do business there.

Source: *UN World Economic Survey* (1990)

tries. This had the effect of reducing US grain exports by about £1000m per annum. President Reagan retaliated with increased tariffs on EC food exports, such as mineral water and cheeses. In due course, the EC was obliged to modify its protection of agriculture. At about the same time the USA 'named' Brazil and Japan for engaging in unfair trade practices and both these countries bowed to pressure by undertaking a degree of import liberalisation.

The General Case Against Protection

We saw above that the arguments for protection are not in general convincing. However, there is in addition a very important general case against protection. This we shall now examine using Figure 31.1.

In Figure 31.1 the domestic supply and demand curves for a product are *SS* and *DD* respectively. It is assumed that the ruling world price of the product is OP_1, and that in the absence of a tariff, supply on the domestic market will be perfectly elastic at this price. Sales on the domestic market will therefore be OQ_1, of which OQ_2 is supplied by domestic producers, the remainder O_2Q_1 being supplied from imports. Consider now the effect of the imposition of a tariff of P_1P_2 per unit imported. We can see that the price of the good on the domestic market rises to OP_2, total output falls to OQ_3, domestic output extends to OQ_4, and there is a contraction of imports to Q_3Q_4.

The effect of the tariff on the level of economic welfare is three-fold.

- The higher domestic price causes a cut in consumption resulting in a reduction of consumer

Table 31.2 *Relative magnitude of welfare effects, USA*

Case	Consumer losses Totals ($m)	Producer gains Total ($m)	Government gains Tariff revenue ($m)	Overall net loss ($m)
Manufacturing				
Book manufacturing	500	305	0	195
Benezoid Chemicals	2,650	2,250	252	148
Glassware	200	130	54	16
Rubber footwear	230	90	139	1
Ceramic articles	95	25	69	1
Orange juice	525	390	128	7
Canned tuna	91	74	10	7
Speciality steel	520	420	32	68
Non-rubber footwear	700	250	262	188
Colour televisions	420	190	77	153
CB radios	55	14	32	9
Bolts, nuts, large screws	110	60	16	34
Automobiles	5,800	2,600	790	2,410
Motorcycles	104	67	21	16
Agriculture & Fisheries				
Sugar	930	550	5	375
Dairy products	5,500	5,000	5	495
Meat	1,800	1,600	44	156
Fish	560	200	177	183
Mining				
Petroleum	6.900	4,800	70	2,030
Lead & zinc	67	46	11	10

Source: *Federal Reserve Bank of St Louis* (January–February 1988) welfare equal to the area $a + b + c + d$ in Figure 31.1.

- Domestic firms benefit from the higher price and increased sales and experience an increase in producer welfare equal to the area *a*.
- The government benefits from the receipt of tariff revenue equal to area *c*.

There is therefore a net 'deadweight' welfare loss to the economy as a whole equal to areas *b* and *d*. This inevitable loss in welfare constitutes a powerful case against the imposition of tariffs.

Other types of trade restriction have broadly similar welfare effects on domestic consumers and producers. However, unlike tariffs they do not usually generate government revenues, except in so far as higher prices resulting from reduced domestic supply lead to increased indirect tax yields. Table 31.2 shows the relative magnitude of welfare effects for the US economy due to the protection of a number of domestic industries.

We should not be surprised to find that protection reduces a country's level of welfare for, by restricting trade, it inevitably reduces the gains available from international specialisation which we examined in Chapter 30. What is perhaps surprising is the prevalence of protection when, as we have seen, it often operates against the interest of the countries which employ it. One reason for this is that whereas consumer losses resulting from protection are likely to be widespread and therefore individually relatively small, gains to producers are concentrated in scope and very visible. This makes it much easier for producer interests to lobby effectively for protection.

The 'New Protectionism'

The increasing range and use of trade restrictions since the 1970s has sometimes been called the 'new protectionism'. The following reasons have been suggested for its rise:

- As GATT succeeded in reducing the main form of protection, namely tariffs (see p. 290), there was a tendency for its member countries to maintain protection by employing new types of trade restriction, some of which were outside the GATT 'rules'.
- Whereas world economic growth in the 1950s and 1960s was sustained, after this period it was interrupted by a number of periods of recession. Faced with the threat of rising unemployment, many governments sought to promote economic recovery by restricting imports.
- Mature industrial countries were being exposed to rising levels of manufactured exports from Japan and the newly industrialised countries. Consequently import restrictions were deemed necessary to protect domestic industry and employment.
- Some countries (for example the USA) experienced a shift in their comparative advantage in favour of services. However, trade in services has always been subject to many restrictions. Countries exporting services therefore felt less inhibited about restricting manufactured imports.

The main instrument in the new protectionism has been the voluntary export restraint (VER). As we saw on p. 291, a VER is a trade agreement between two countries whereby one 'voluntarily' agrees to restrict to a specific amount the volume of its exports to the other. The increasing use of VERs was connected with a number of practical advantages:

- A VER can be negotiated for a **specific period**.
- A VER is **flexible**, requires no legislation, and can be revised and re-negotiated periodically in the light of changing economic circumstances.
- A VER can be 'targeted' at a **particular exporting country**.
- Responsibility for administering a VER lies with the **exporting countries**.

In the event, the use of VERs has turned out to have unintended consequences. We can examine these in terms of the case study in Box 31.3, which relates to a Japanese restraint on car exports to the USA.

The General Agreement on Tariffs and Trade

We have seen that the arguments for protection are weak and that there is also a strong welfare case against protection. A further drawback of protection is that it might spread indiscriminately between countries on a 'tit-for-tat' basis, leading to a multiple contraction in world income and employment, as in the 'trade wars' of the 1930s. It was for reasons such as these that a very important arrangement known as the General Agreement on Tariffs and Trade (GATT) was set up in 1947 to aim for trade liberalisation. GATT is still in existence, and now has over

Box 31.3 A voluntary export restraint in practice: the US Japanese automobile agreement

One well known example of a voluntary export restraint is the Japanese restraint on automobile exports to the United States. In early 1981, The Japanese imposed restraints to preempt more restrictive measures advocated by many, especially labor groups within the United States. These protectionist pressures increased during the late 1970s and early 1980s as automobile sales by US producers declined and foreign producers captured larger shares of the US market.

With the restraints, the prices paid by U.S. consumers for Japanese automobiles rose. This reduced the competitive pressures on U.S producers and non-Japanese exporters to the United States with the effect of increasing prices for these automobiles, but not as much as the rise in Japanese prices. The higher automobile prices reduced US purchases, but the effects on US and non-Japanese producers were mitigated by the relatively larger rise in the prices of Japanese automobiles and the resulting shift away from Japanese automobiles.

The restraints also induced quality changes as Japanese producers shifted their mix of exports toward larger and more luxurious models that generated more profits per unit. In addition, more 'optional' equipment was installed in each unit. Consequently, the average transaction price of Japanese automobiles increased because of the pure price effect as well as the quality effects associated with the restraints.

In fact, the factors underlying the price change affect the prices of all automobiles sold in the United States and complicate the estimation. For all new cars sold in 1984, Collyns and Dunaway[1] estimated an average increase of $1,649 (17 per cent) which consisted of a pure price effect of $617 per car and a quality effect of $1,032 per car. The higher price led to a reduction in 1984 purchases of approximately 1.5 million.

As suggested above, the export restraints had differential effects. For example, the price increase for domestically produced automobiles of $1,185 (12 per cent) was less than the increase for imports from Japan of $1,700 (22.5 per cent). This relative price change allowed the US producers to increase their market share by 6.7 percentage points, enough to leave domestically produced unit sales unchanged despite a decline of unit sales in the United States. Thus, the US reduction in 1984 purchases of 1.5 million was borne by foreign producers. These production changes were estimated to generate increased US automotive employment in a range from 40,000 to 75,000 jobs.

The higher automobile prices represent one of the losses for consumers. The pure price effect caused US consumers to suffer a loss of consumer surplus of $5.6 billion in 1984. In addition US consumers were worse off to the extent that quotas limited their range of automotive choices. Purchases of increased quality resulting from the quota totaled $10.75 billion in 1984. The welfare loss associated with these quality expenditures was not estimated, but it is clear that this loss is possibly greater than the loss associated with the pure price effect.

The losses of US consumers are primarily transfers from consumers to domestic and foreign producers. Estimates of the benefits for domestic and foreign producers hinge on the assumption about the distribution of the pure price effects. If export restraints led to equivalent pure price effects on domestic and imported cars, then US producers gained $5 billion in 1984 and foreign producers gained $1.5 billion. Of the foreign producers' gain, Japanese producers received $1 billion. On the other hand, if export restraints led to equivalent quality effects, then US producers gained $1.25 billion in 1984 and foreign producers gained $5.5 billion. Of the foreign producers' gain, Japanese producers received $5.25 billion. If accurate, this figure provides an obvious reason why the Japanese government continued the restraints beyond early 1985 when the Reagan administration decided not to request an extension of the agreement.

[1] Collyns and Dunaway, 'The Cost of Trade Restraints: The Case of Japanese Automobile Exports to the United States', *International Monetary Fund Staff Papers* (March 1987)

Source: Cletus C. Coughlin and Geoffrey G. Wood, 'An Introduction to Non-Tariff Barriers to Trade', *Federal Reserve Bank of St Louis Review* (January–February 1989)

100 members who meet at regular intervals to negotiate reductions in trade restrictions.

At the heart of GATT are three important principles:

- *Multilateral bargaining* implies that member *A* agrees to reduce restrictions on imports from *B* provided that *B* simultaneously offers comparable concessions on its imports from *A*.
- *The 'most favoured nation' rule* implies that any reductions in trade restrictions made by *A* and *B* are automatically extended to all other GATT members.
- *Resolution of trade disputes* between member countries should take place by reference to GATT rules.

Other features of GATT include the following:

- *A range of exemptions* which permit the use of trade restrictions to support agriculture and to protect industries experiencing extreme short-term difficulties due to a rapid rise in imports, including cases of 'dumping' of output abroad below its cost of production.
- *Special arrangements* for developing countries, including the use of discriminatory tariffs against developed countries' products, together with preferential export access to their markets.
- *Provisions permitting the formation of trading blocs* (for example, the EC), even though these necessarily involve discriminatory trade arrangements against non-participating countries.

GATT in Operation: the Uruguay Round

GATT trade liberalisation procedures operate through a series of negotiated 'rounds' between member countries. Since the inception of GATT there have been eight such rounds. The first six rounds were mainly concerned with tariff reductions. The seventh, the 'Tokyo Round', was more complex in scope and explored a wider set of issues, including the control and reduction of non-tariff barriers. In terms of tariff reductions the achievements of GATT since 1947 have undoubtedly been impressive. Whereas at the end of the Second World War, average tariff levels in the main industrial countries were as high as 50 per cent, by the completion of the Tokyo Round they had been negotiated to very low levels.

However, this undoubted success in trade liberalisation was subject to three qualifications:

- It applied mainly to **industrial goods** and had little effect on agricultural trade, which has remained outside GATT provisions.
- It took no account of trade in **services**, which is still subject to many restrictions.
- It took no account of the increasing use, particularly in recent decades, of non-tariff restrictions, especially **VERs**.

It was therefore decided that the eighth Uruguay Round of GATT negotiations, which commenced in 1986 and was due to be completed in 1990, would include within its scope trade liberalisation in these three areas.

The Uruguay Round and Agriculture

Many countries, especially industrial countries, strongly protect their agriculture with a combination of tariffs, quotas and subsidies. Such protection not only reduces consumer welfare in these countries, it also seriously disrupts the markets of food exporting countries. In the Uruguay Round GATT members agreed in principle to aim for substantial reductions in agricultural protection. In simple terms, the USA and certain other important agricultural producers wanted an agreement to reduce farm support by at least 75 per cent over ten years. The EC, on the other hand, reluctantly proposed a 30 per cent reduction. Unless agreement was reached there was a danger that negotiations in agricultural trade would break down, thereby threatening other negotiations and undermining the status of GATT itself.

How much would liberalisation of world agricultural trade be worth?

According to an OECD report:

- Protected agriculture is so inefficient in most industrial countries that trade liberalisation would, through its beneficial effects on allocative and productive efficiency, increase real income in these countries by almost 1 per cent, that is £7.2bn.
- The direct cost to these countries of protecting agricultural employment is about £20,000 per job per year.
- Liberalisation of agricultural trade would require less than 1 per cent of the industrial countries' work forces to be displaced.
- Liberalisation of agricultural trade would raise income in many developing countries by enabling them to export up to £30bn more food per year.

The Uruguay Round and the New Protectionism

One of the biggest problems facing GATT has been the proliferation in recent years of bilateral voluntary export regulations, the use of which has seriously undermined the liberal trading regime established under GATT in the postwar years. As we saw on p. 297 one reason for the widespread use of VERs is that they fall outside the terms of reference of GATT. It was proposed in the Uruguay Round that GATT members should agree to phase out VERs and replace them with multilateral import quotas. These would then be progressively reduced and in due course, after perhaps 10 years, abolished. The likelihood of this scheme being adopted will depend on how rapid a rate of import expansion the main developed countries will be prepared to accept.

The Uruguay Round and Trade in Services

Although services such as finance, telecommunications, transport, construction and consultancy now account for one-fifth of world trade, they are not covered by GATT. It is widely accepted that they should be, since protecting suppliers of services is costly in the same way as protecting industry and agriculture. Barriers to trade in services are of two main types. Suppliers of services may be prevented from setting up sales points in countries where they wish to operate. Or they may be prevented from selling them from their home country by restrictions on cross-border sales of services. Proposals considered at GATT included the following:

- Equality of national treatment for foreign and domestic suppliers of services.
- There should be openess or transparency on methods employed by member countries to restrict trade in services.
- No discrimination in trade in services between different GATT members.

Box 31.4 Motives for regional integration

We have seen on p. 297 that GATT experienced difficulty in stemming the rising tide of protectionism in the 1980s. Many countries therefore began to pursue trade liberalisation through the alternative route of regional integration, as the following extract makes clear.

> Recent integration initiatives among industrial countries aim at removing tariff barriers to trade. Gains in efficiency through a reduction in market segmentation caused by a reduction in non-tariff barriers was the major reason for launching the internal market programme in the European Community. The same is true of the United States–Canada Free Trade Agreement which was additionally motivated by Canada's interest to avoid 'administered protection' in its trade with the United States.
>
> Impatience with the slow and cumbersome process of multilateral negotiations has contributed to recent initiatives by industrial countries to liberalise trade on a bilateral basis. It is noteworthy that the bilateral discussions that led to the United States–Canada Free Trade Agreement was initiated following the failure of the 1982 GATT Ministerial Meeting to launch multilateral trade negotiations. The main motivating force behind the trend towards regionalism in the industrial countries thus appears to be the need to reduce non-tariff barriers to trade and to diffuse trade tensions, which is perceived to be easier to achieve on a regional than on a global basis. The expected gains are increased productive efficiency through the achievement of economies of scale, the adoption of cost reducing technologies, and a reduction in market segmentation, which creates monopoly rents and imposes administrative costs.
>
> A different set of reasons seems to underly the trend towards preferential trading among developing countries. Tariffs continue to be more important than non-tariff barriers in these countries. The elimination of tariffs among a group of partner countries is thus viewed as a means of achieving industrialisation through regional import substitution by 'swapping' markets for each other's products.

Regional integration among developing countries has also sometimes aimed at economising on foreign exchange by setting up clearing accounts for intra-area trade. Such internal clearing accounts exist for most regional trading groups among developing countries, including the Latin American Integration Association, the Central American Common Market, and the Caribbean Community. This objective also underlies the recent integration initiatives in Africa. Most recently there has been increased focus on opening markets in a broader way and thus integrating members of preferential trading arrangements into the global trading system.

Source: *United Nations World Economic Survey* (1990)

REVIEW QUESTIONS

1 If trade liberalisation is in a country's own interest, why is protectionism increasing?

2 Some countries impose a 'dubbing tax' on foreign language films. Examine the economic arguments for and against this.

3 When might a country prefer to impose quotas on imports rather than levy a tariff?

4 If the Uruguay Round succeeds, some countries will suffer. Why is this?

5 In what circumstances will the imposition of a quota lead to an increase in import expenditures?

CHAPTER 32

THE BALANCE OF PAYMENTS

CONNECTIONS

The balance of payments is very closely related to movements in the **exchange rate** and, as we shall see in Chapter 33, changes in one of these usually cause a change in the other. There is also an important connection between changes in the balance of payments and changes in the **domestic output of goods and services**. An increase in expenditure on imports and/or a reduction in expenditure on exports will cause a reduction in domestic output and an increase in unemployment. If there is inadequate supply capacity, an increase in demand for exports may lead to domestic inflation. If we accept the natural rate hypothesis these problems will be self-correcting short-term phenomena. If we do not, government policies may be necessary to aid the process of adjustment. There is therefore also an important connection between changes in the balance of payments and the government's **economic policies**.

Changes in the current account (see below) are also connected with changes in the **terms of trade**. If the price of exports rises (falls) relative to the price of imports – that is, the terms of trade move favourably (unfavourably) – this will almost certainly lead to changes in the value of exports and imports of goods and services. The effect of changes in the terms of trade on the current account depends partly on the elasticity of demand for goods and services.

Key Concepts

Accommodating transactions
Autonomous transactions
Balance of trade
Current account
Exports
Imports
Invisible trade
Transactions in assets and liabilities (capital account)
Visible trade

The Balance of Payments

The balance of payments is a statistical presentation of financial transactions between one country and the rest of the world in a given year. Receipts from the rest of the world are referred to as **credits** while payments to the rest of the world are referred to as **debits**. The balance of payments consist of two main sections: the *current account* and the *capital account* (which is also called *transactions in assets and liabilities*). The current account records transactions in goods and services, whereas the capital account mainly records flows of investment funds. However, as we shall see below, the capital account also includes movements in bank deposits used to pay the transactions in the current account.

How Balance of Payments Transactions are Recorded

Balance of payments accounts of the type we are examining are based on the principle of *double-entry bookkeeping* in which each external transaction is entered in the accounts **twice**. For example, if a UK resident imports £10m of cars there is both a debit entry in the balance of payments and a credit entry.

The debit entry on the capital account is payment for the cars while the corresponding credit on the current account is for shipment of the cars. In other words, the current account shows the **original transaction**, the capital account shows how it was **financed**. From an accounting point of view the total of credits must always equal the total of debits and therefore the balance of payments in total must always balance. We can see this in Table 32.1 (p. 304) where debits on the current account total −£14,380m and credits on the capital account total £14,380m. It follows that in an *accounting sense* there is no such thing as a balance of payments 'deficit': it must be the case that a current account deficit will just be offset by an equivalent capital account surplus.

Transactions in the Current Account

The current account records transactions in *visible* and *invisible* trade. Trade in visibles consists of all physical goods traded internationally. The invisible account deals mainly in *services* of various kinds bought from abroad (invisible imports) and sold abroad (invisible exports). Some trade in services, such as the use of British merchant shipping to carry cargo from one country to another, or British insurance firms underwriting risks abroad, are easily identified in the invisible account. However, some items in this account require further explanation.

General government expenditure abroad includes expenditure on such items as defence and the upkeep of embassies.

Interest, profits and dividends consists of payments received on UK investments abroad and paid on foreign investments here.

Transfers are often subdivided into *government transfers* and *private transfers*. Government transfers include foreign aid and annual subscriptions to the institutions of the EC. Private transfers mainly consist of money moved between countries by people living abroad, such as when foreign workers send remittances home.

Table 32.1 (p. 304) shows a summary of the UK balance of payments in 1990. We can see that the *visible balance*, or the *balance of trade*, (−£18,675m) when added to the *invisible balance* (£4295m) gives the *current balance* (−£14,380). For analytical purposes most of the items which make up the current account can be regarded as *autonomous transactions*: they represent transactions undertaken by individuals and organisations for the satisfaction they give.

Transactions in Assets and Liabilities (Capital Transactions)

Transactions in assets and liabilities (the capital account) records transactions in financial assets between one country and the rest of the world. These transactions are often called *capital movements*. *Capital outflows* are given a *negative sign* in the account because they are **debit transactions**. Conversely *capital inflows* as **credit transactions** are given a *positive sign*. Capital movements are undertaken by governments, firms and households and may be long-term or short-term.

It is often convenient to analyse capital transactions in terms of long-term and short-term **capital flows**.

Long-term Capital Flows

Like imports and exports, long-term capital flows are mainly of an *autonomous* nature. We can identify two types of long-term capital flows:

Direct investments are investments in **real assets** such as plant and machinery. The purchase, or construction, by a Japanese firm of a factory in the UK would be an example of an inflow of direct investment into the UK.

Portfolio investments consist of the international sale and purchase of **financial instruments** such as company shares or government bonds.

Short-term capital flows

These consist of lending by, or borrowing from, banks together with private lending and deposits overseas. Short-term capital flows arise mainly because of transactions in the balance of payments current account. This tells us that they are not autonomous but *accommodating* in nature. Suppose, for example, a UK resident imports £5m of Japanese cars and pays for these by depositing funds in a UK branch of the exporter's bank. This transaction will represent an *inflow* of short-term capital for the UK. In the balance of payments accounting terms we would have the following situation:

	£m
Current account: autonomous transaction	−5
Capital account: accommodating transaction	+5

If the exporter subsequently withdraws these funds from his UK bank to pay for purchases made in his own country there will be a capital outflow which will be recorded in 'Transactions of UK

Table 32.1 *UK balance of payments, 1990*

Current Account, £m			
Visible trade			
Exports	102038		
Imports	−120731		
Visible Balance	−18675		
Invisible trade			
Sea transport			
	3847		
	−3591		
Civil aviation		256	
	4358		
	−4674		
		−316	
Travel			
	7784		
	−9916		
		−2132	
Financial and other services			
	15649		
	−5935		
		9714	
General government	432		
Expenditure abroad	−2753		
		−2321	
Interest, profits and dividends			
	81287		
	−77258		
		4029	
Transfers			
	3993		
	−8928		
		−4935	
Invisible balance			4295
Current balance			−14380

Capital Account, £m (transaction in UK assets and liabilities)			
Transactions in assets			
Direct investment overseas	−11702		
Portfolio investment overseas	−12587		
Loans to overseas residents by UK banks	−37246		
Other private lending and deposits overseas	−9462		
Changes in official reserves	−77		
Central government	−1227		
		−72301	
Transactions in liabilities			
Direct investment in UK	18997		
Portfolio investment in UK	5070		
Loans to UK residents from overseas banks	46179		
Other private lending and deposits from overseas	12977		
Other external liabilities of central government	1158		
		84381	
Net transactions			12080
Balancing item			2300
		Total	14380

Source: UK Balance of Payments Pink Book, 1991

banks'. Exactly the opposite happens when UK goods are sold abroad. Sales of UK exports would generate an autonomous inflow on the current account and an accommodating outflow of short-term capital.

Unlike long-term capital, short-term capital transactions are predominantly monetary, and do not correspond to the creation of physical assets. They are therefore potentially highly mobile and can be rapidly moved from one country to another in response to changes in short-term interest rates. For this reason, short-term capital is sometimes referred to as 'hot money'. The unstable nature of hot money can lead to problems when there is a substantial deficit on the current account unmatched by a surplus of long-term autonomous capital (see p. 308).

Capital account transactions can also take the form of changes in the UK's **foreign exchange reserves**. It is this section of the capital account that indicates an overall recorded balance of payments surplus or deficit. When all other flows of funds have been added together a deficit is financed by running down the official reserves of foreign currency and a surplus is added to the reserves of foreign currency.

Table 32.1 (p. 304) shows that in 1990 the official reserves rose by £77m. However, this figure appears as a negative in Table 32.1. Why is this? In fact, it is in keeping with the principle of double entry book-keeping. In adding together all credits and debits any balance of payments surplus will already have been counted once. To show it as an addition to the reserves will therefore be **double counting** – that is, the surplus will be counted twice. In order to ensure the balance of payments sums to zero additions to the reserves are therefore given a negative sign. Exactly the opposite occurs in the case of a deicit. Here changes in the official reserves are given a positive sign.

The Balancing Item

We can see that the UK had a current deficit of £14,380. Hence the inward net value of capital flows must be a surplus of £14,380m. However, after allowing for the change in the foreign exchanges reserves, only £12,080m of net capital inflow is identified as having occurred. Something is wrong: there is a 'missing' £2300m! The reason for this lies in the fact that a balance of payments account is derived from millions of separate transactions, so errors and omissions are inevitable. In 1990 these amounted to the substantial sum of £2300m. This net total of errors and omissions is known as the *balancing item* and is entered into the accounts as shown in Table 32.1. If all the items in the accounts were measured accurately the balancing item would be zero.

One possible explanation for the large balancing item in 1988 is that exports may have been larger than measured in the accounts. It is in fact known that both visible and invisible exports tend to be underrecorded. But it is hard to imagine they would be under-recorded by so much. What is more likely is that in addition a considerable under-recorded **capital inflow**, especially short term, may have taken place in 1988. It is a cause for regret that the balancing item is often so large since this leads to considerable difficulties in interpreting changes in the balance of payments.

The Causes of the UK's Balance of Payments Deficit

Let us look at the data in Figure 32.1 and Table 32.2 below. The overall picture is clear. In the early 1980s the UK had been enjoying a comfortable current account surplus, but by the end of the decade this had deteriorated to a deficit of about £20,000m.

There are many factors which might account for the changes in the UK balance of payments that took place during the 1980s. Here we discuss what are considered to be the most important factors.

Structural Factors

- During the period in question there was a decline in *net oil exports*. These peaked in the mid-1980s but had fallen significantly by 1990. The decline was due to two factors: a reduced volume of oil production as North Sea capacity passed its peak; and a fall in world oil prices.
- There was a decline in *the manufacturing export balance* in the 1980s, due partly to the contraction of the UK manufacturing base. A detailed analysis of *de-industrialisation* would be out of place in this context but one important factor that needs to be stressed is the 'oil-squeeze effect' on manufacturing in the early 1980s. As the UK's expanding oil sector bid for new resources such as capital and labour the market price of these resources tended to rise. As a result, all sectors of the economy, including the manufacturing sector, faced higher input prices, and a corresponding reduction in international competitiveness.

Figure 32.1 *The behaviour of the UK Current Account*

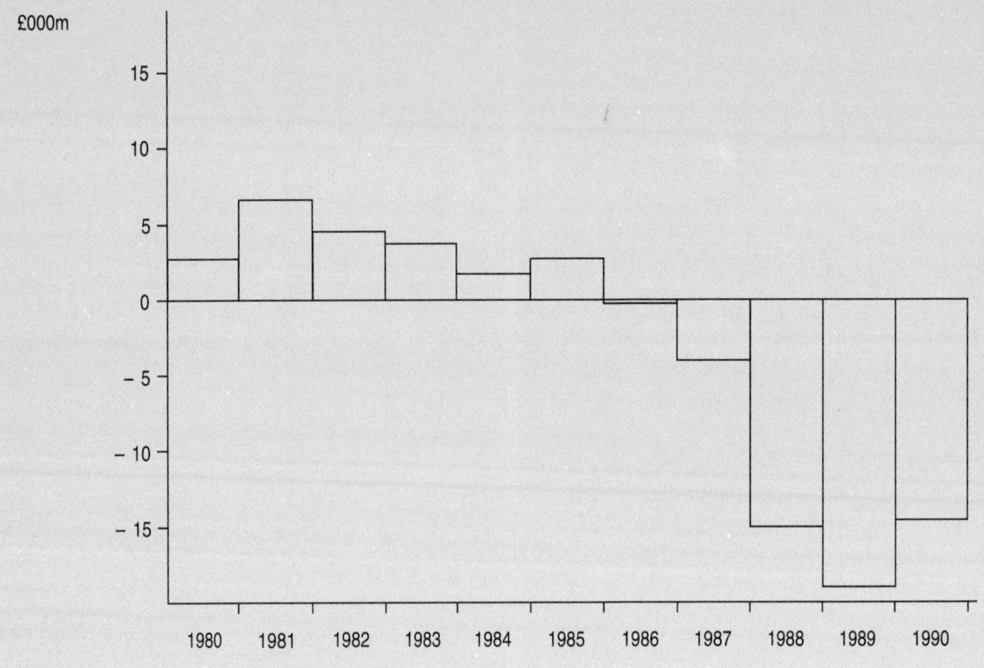

Source: Balance of Payments Pink Book, 1991

In the early 1990s there were indications that *re-industrialisation* might be occurring as the comparative advantage of UK oil production declined and as UK manufacturing became more efficient. This latter development was associated in some instances with inflows of Japanese investment and management, for example in TV production and motor car production, where UK exports began to improve appreciably.

- There was a significant fall in net invisible exports in the late 1980s, as Tables 32.3 and 32.4 show, culminating in a *deficit* in the last quarter of 1989 – the first since Napoleonic times!

Table 32.2 *UK balance of payments deficit, 1986–91*

	1986	1987	1988	1989	Forecasts 1990	1991
Non-oil Trade	−13.4	−15.1	−23.6	−24.4	−19.9	−17.0
Oil Trade	4.1	4.2	2.8	1.4	2.8	3.1
Visible Trade Balance	−9.4	−10.9	−20.8	−23.0	−17.1	−13.9
Services	6.2	5.7	4.2	4.4	5.1	5.7
Interest Profits & Dividends	5.4	4.8	5.5	2.5	2.0	1.8
Transfers	−2.2	−3.4	−3.6	−4.2	−4.3	−4.1
Invisible Trade Balance	9.4	7.1	6.1	2.7	2.8	3.4
Current Account	0.1	−3.8	−14.7	−20.3	−14.3	−10.5

Source: *Barclays Economic Report* (February 1990)

Table 32.3 *Interest, profits and dividends, £m net, 1988Q1–1989Q4*

1988	Q1	1012
	Q2	1485
	Q3	1502
	Q4	1510
1989	Q1	1519
	Q2	366
	Q3	523
	Q4	−750

Source: *Economic Trends*

Table 32.4 *Net invisible exports, 1985–90 (£m)*

	Sea transport	Civil aviation	Travel	Financial	General government	Total
1985	–297	201	571	7510	–1298	6687
1986	–86	–408	–530	9241	–1409	6808
1987	–28	–616	–1020	10029	–1620	6745
1988	–40	–905	–2032	9351	–1800	4574
1989	133	–540	–2412	9753	–2249	4685
1990	256	–316	–2132	9714	–2321	5201

Source: Balance of Payments Pink Book, 1991

One part of the problem was that over the three years 1987–9, the UK current account had been in deficit in total to the tune of about £40,000m. Some of this had been covered by inflows of long-term capital but most had been financed by inflows of short-term capital. By 1989 the rate of interest in the UK had risen to around 15 per cent. Higher interest payments notebly on short term capital therefore increased invisible outflows. However, the invisible balance also suffered from a deterioration in earnings from various services. It is true that under-recording of invisible exports might have been occurring which would make the invisible deficit appear worse than it actually was. Nevertheless the *trend* in the invisible balance during this period was undoubtedly downwards.

Overheating and the UK Balance of Payments

The second main factor leading the UK payments deficit from the late 1980s was *overheating* of the domestic economy. For much of the 1980s demand had grown steadily, though not excessively, in the UK economy. Then around 1987 demand began to rise at a much faster rate. At first output kept pace with rising demand, but in 1988 and 1989 labour shortages and other bottlenecks restricted the growth of output. The outcome was that inflation increased, with exports suffering some loss of competitiveness. More seriously, in order to meet unsatisfied domestic demand, non-oil imports flooded into the UK while non-oil export growth was curtailed. Where did this domestic demand explosion come from? Table 32.5 shows that the increase in demand came mainly from the UK private sector with households and businesses both increasing their expenditure substantially.

Table 32.5 *Increase in domestic demand*

Percentage increase	1982–6 average	1987	1988	1989
Domestic demand	3.3	5.6	7.4	4.1
Consumer expenditure	3.2	6.1	6.5	4.3
Manufacturing investment	4.5	5.1	11.7	9.0
Non-oil gross domestic product	2.6	5.4	5.6	3.6
Non-oil export volume	3.9	5.1	0.9	5.0
Non-oil import volume	7.7	8.2	14.2	9.8
Unemployment (Millions)	2.88	2.82	2.25	1.80
Personal savings ratio (%)	9.9	5.7	4.3	5.2

Source: *Barclays Economic Review* (February 1990)

Why Was the UK Balance of Payments Deficit a Problem?

We saw on p. 303 that in an accounting sense there is no such thing as a balance of payments deficit. It must be the case that a current account deficit will just be offset by an equivalent capital account surplus. However, when economists refer to a 'balance of payments deficit', they have in mind the concept of balance of payments *disequilibrium*. This is connected with *how* a current account deficit might be financed through the capital account. In 1990 the position, if we include the balancing item in capital flows, was:

	£m
Current account balance	–14,380
Net capital inflows	14,380

The key question is this: *what kind* of capital was entering the UK? In fact, during this period there was heavy reliance on short-term capital inflows to accommodate the current account deficit. The problem is that a current account deficit cannot be financed indefinitely by short-term capital inflows since it requires higher and higher domestic interest rates to go on attracting capital inflows. Continually relying on short term capital inflows to finance a current account deficit is therefore a situation of balance of payments *disequilibrium*. Sooner or later it becomes necessary for *balance of payments adjustment* (see p. 316) to take place – that is, for the current account to move out of deficit. Such adjustment would eventually take place through market forces, but the UK authorities have usually taken the view that it is preferable to implement policies designed to achieve adjustment. The types of policy that might be implemented are considered in Chapter 33.

REVIEW QUESTIONS

1 Consider the following data:

	Money values
Visible imports	4000
Balance of trade	200
Invisible imports	3800
Invisible exports	2000
Net long term capital	–2100
Change in foreign exchange reserves	200
Balancing item	nil

(a) On the basis of the data calculate the value of:
  (i) visible exports
  (ii) the invisible balance
  (iii) the current balance
  (iv) net short-term capital

(b) If the country in question has a GNP of 10,000 comment on the significance of its balance of payments situation.

Question 2 is based on the information in Figure 32.2.

How are the types of developments in the motor car industry described above likely to affect the UK's balance of payments in the 1990s:

(a) On the visible account?
(b) On the invisible account?
(c) In transactions in assets and liabilities?

Figure 32.2 *UK motor industry trade deficit cut*

UK motor industry cuts trade deficit

Andrew Cornellus
Business Editor

THE motor industry, which last year accounted for £6 billion of the UK's $20 billion trade deficit, improved its trading performance in the first quarter of this year, but still showed a £1.4 billion deficit in its trade with the rest of the world.

Figures from the Society of Motor Manufactures and Traders published this morning reveal that the industry's first quarter deficit was £151 million down on the first quarter of 1989, making it the second successive quarter when the industry's trading position has improved.

The figures will hearten ministers who have made the issue of improveing the UK's motor industry trading deficit a priority.

This has been done largely by encouraging Japanese manufactures like Nissan, Toyota and Honda to produce cars in Britain for export to the rest of Europe.

According to the SMMT, the improved first quarter trading position was helped by a 9 per cent fall in car imports to the UK, reflecting the overall slowdown in the British car market.

Motor industry exports were also up by 12 per cent at £2.24 billion in the first quarter, helped by stronger sales of car components, heavy trucks and specialist vehicles like tractors and dumper trucks.

The most buoyant markets for the UK exporters were the European Community, particularly France, and on a smaller scale, Japan where the government is slowly relaxing the rules which prevent overseas companies penetrating the Japanese market.

The SMMT says the figures show that Britain's motor industry has continued to play a positive part towards reducing the national trade deficit.

Source: *Guardian* (12 June 1990)

3 Distinguish between the *terms of trade* **and the** *balance of trade*.

4 Why does the balance of payments always balance?

5 Study the following information, which relates to the economies of Italy and Norway, and then answer the questions that follow.

ITALY

'Despite the problems caused by comparatively high inflation . . . Italy has been one of the fastest growing economies in Europe. In 1990 growth is likely to be maintained at around 3%, broadly in line with the European average. Domestic demand growth has slackened . . . Although international competitiveness has deteriorated, Italy should benefit from the trade stimulus of developments in Germany and Eastern Europe.'

A. *Domestic Economy* (% Annual changes)	*Average* 1981–88	1987	1988	1989	*Forecast* 1990
Real GDP	2.2	3.0	3.9	3.0	3.0
Private consumption	2.5	3.9	3.8	3.6	3.3
Public consumption	3.0	3.6	3.0	2.5	2.0
Fixed investment	1.2	6.8	4.9	5.4	5.0
Total domestic demand	2.2	4.6	4.7	3.0	3.4
Consumer prices	10.6	4.7	5.0	6.6	6.0
Money supply	11.2	8.7	8.5	11.0	9.0
Unemployment (%)	10.3	12.0	12.0	12.0	12.0
B. *External*					
Export volume (% change)	3.9	2.0	5.2	9.2	8.0
Import volume (% change)	3.9	9.5	6.9	8.7	8.5
Trade balance (US $bn)	−4.0	−0.1	−0.8	−1.8	−2.7
Current account (US $bn)	−3.0	−1.5	−5.2	−11.0	−13.0

Source: Barclay's Country Report (1990)

NORWAY

'The last three years have seen Norway pass through a difficult period of adjustment following the 1986 oil market collapse (resulting in proportionally the largest current account deficit of any OECD country) ... Weaker domestic demand, assisted by firmer energy prices, has succeeded in returning the current account to surplus. Inflation is also now at, or below, the level of Norway's major competitors.

Prospects for the next few years are favourable, with moderate inflation and a growing current account surplus.'

A. *Domestic Economy* (% Annual changes)	*Average* 1981–88	1987	1988	1989	*Forecast* 1990
Real GDP	2.9	0.9	1.1	2.5	1.5
Private consumption	2.4	−0.8	−2.3	−2.0	1.5
Public consumption	3.4	4.5	0.1	3.0	2.5
Fixed investment	2.9	−0.6	4.0	−3.0	−5.0
Total domestic demand	2.6	−1.0	−0.5	−3.0	0.4
Consumer prices	8.5	8.7	6.7	4.5	4.5
Money supply	12.2	11.2	13.0	6.5	7.0
Unemployment (%)	2.6	2.1	3.2	3.8	4.0
B. *External*					
Export volume (% change)	4.8	8.4	6.5	12.0	6.0
Import volume (% change)	3.7	−2.0	−2.5	−2.5	2.5
Trade balance (US $bn)	1.8	−1.2	−0.7	4.6	5.2
Current account (US $bn)	−0.2	−4.2	−3.7	1.5	2.2

Source: Barclay's Country Report (1989)

(a) For the period 1987 to 1990, compare the balance of payments of the two countries.
(b) What factors might account for their different balance of payments performance?
(c) Determine, and give possible reasons for, Italy's declining invisible balance.
(d) What extra data would you require to determine which country had the sounder overall balance of payments position in the period 1987–90?

CHAPTER 33

EXCHANGE RATE SYSTEMS

CONNECTIONS

In this chapter we analyse the determinants of exchange rates and the implications of exchange rate movements. We shall see that there is an important connection between the exchange rate and the balance of payments. We are also concerned with the implications of exchange rate movements for international trade and protection. We shall see that there is an important connection in the short run between changes in the exchange rate and changes in the rate of interest and in the long run between changes in the rate of inflation in different countries and changes in the exchange rate.

Key Concepts

Appreciation
Depreciation
Devaluation
Effective exchange rate
Fixed exchange rate
Floating exchange rate
Forward rate
International Monetary Fund
J curve
Marshall–Lerner condition
Purchasing power parity
Revaluation
Special Drawing Rights
Spot rate

The Foreign Exchange Market

The foreign exchange market is the intermediary through which **one currency is converted into another** and the *rate* at which currencies can be converted is known as the *rate of exchange*. The rate of exchange is therefore the **price of one currency in terms of another currency**.

Unlike many of the markets in securities or commodities, the foreign exchange market does not have a specific location where all buyers and sellers of foreign currency meet. Indeed, most dealing in foreign exchange is done via the telephone and telex networks although banks and money brokers, who are the main participants in the market, have their own dealing rooms.

There are two markets in foreign exchange: the *spot market* and the *forward market*.

- The **spot market** is the market where deals are struck for *immediate* delivery (usually two working days) of foreign currency. The spot price of foreign currency, or the spot rate, is therefore the price that must be paid to buy currency for *immediate* delivery.
- The **forward** market is the market where currency can be bought or sold *at a rate of exchange agreed today* for delivery at some specified *future date*. Forward rates are quoted continuously for 30-day and 90-day delivery, though forward rates can be agreed for longer periods than this.

The main function of the forward exchange market is to provide traders with the means of eliminating risk due to exchange rate changes. For

Box 33.1 Spot and forward exchange rates

Table 33.1 *Rates of exchange: Pound spot – forward against the pound*

Mar 28	Day's spread	Close	One month	% p.a.	Three months	% p.a.
US	1.7300 – 1.7415	1.7385 – 1.7395	0.91 – 0.89	6.21	2.52–2.49pm	5.76
Canada	2.0050 – 2.0150	2.0105 – 2.0115	0.52 – 0.44cpm	2.86	1.33–1.20pm	2.52
Netherlands	3.3345 – 3.3595	3.3375 – 3.3475	$1 - \frac{7}{8}$cpm	3.37	$2\frac{3}{8}$–$2\frac{1}{4}$pm	2.77
Belgium	60.75 – 61.40	61.15 – 61.25	19 – 16cpm	3.43	46–40pm	2.81
Denmark	11.3125 – 11.4350	11.3950 – 11.4050	$3\frac{1}{2}$–$2\frac{3}{8}$orepm	3.09	$7\frac{7}{8}$–$6\frac{1}{2}$pm	2.52
Ireland	1.1110 – 1.1175	1.1125 – 1.1135	0.24–0.19ppm	2.32	0.54–0.44	1.76
Germany	2.9600 – 2.9625	2.9625 – 2.9675	$\frac{7}{8}$–$\frac{3}{4}$pfpm	3.29	$2\frac{1}{4}$–2pm	2.87
Portugal	259.10 – 261.90	260.90 – 261.90	28–7cpm	0.80	17–65dis	–0.63
Spain	182.80 – 184.75	182.80 – 183.10	2–12cdis	–0.46	18–34dis	–0.57
Italy	2204.05 – 2219.90	2206.75 – 2207.75	4–2lirepm	1.63	7–4pm	1.00
Norway	11.4975 – 11.5945	11.5500 – 11.5600	$2\frac{3}{4}$–$1\frac{5}{8}$gropm	2.27	$6\frac{1}{8}$–$4\frac{3}{4}$pm	1.88
France	10.0345 – 10.1180	10.050 – 10.0600	$2\frac{3}{4}$–$2\frac{5}{8}$cpm	3.21	7–$6\frac{5}{8}$pm	2.71
Sweden	10.6820 – 10.7365	10.7150 – 10.7250	$\frac{3}{4}$–$\frac{1}{2}$orepm	0.70	$\frac{1}{2}$pm–par	0.09
Japan	243.10 – 246.00	245.00 – 246.00	$1\frac{1}{4}$–1ypm	5.50	$2\frac{3}{4}$–$2\frac{1}{2}$pm	4.28
Austria	20.77 – 20.97	20.77 – 20.80	$9\frac{1}{2}$–$8\frac{3}{4}$gropm	5.27	$18\frac{1}{4}$–$16\frac{1}{8}$pm	3.31
Switzerland	2.5250 – 2.5370	2.5250 – 2.5350	$\frac{7}{8}$–$\frac{3}{4}$cpm	3.85	$2\frac{3}{8}$–$2\frac{1}{8}$pm	3.56
Ecu	1.4370 – 1.4490	1.4410 – 1.4420	0.40–0.35cpm	3.12	1.00–0.93pm	2.68

Commercial rates taken towards the end of London trading. Six-month forward dollar 4.35–4.30cpm.
12 Month 6.92–6.82
Source: *Financial Times*

Spot and forward exchange rates at the close of the previous day's trading are quoted in the daily press. In the spot market the rates quoted are for immediate delivery of currency (usually two working days between participants in the foreign exchange markets) and in the forward markets the rates quoted are for delivery of currency in three months or six months. Market makers (that is, those prepared to buy and sell foreign currency) quote two rates: a *bid* rate and an *offer* rate. The bid rate is the rate at which market makers, or dealers, will buy currency and the offer rate is the rate at which they will sell currency. But how are the rates of exchange quoted in the daily press and illustrated in Table 33.1 to be interpreted?

We shall see on pp. 312–13 that in a free market the spot rate is determined by the interacting forces of supply and demand. However, the forward rate is simply the spot rate plus a *premium* or *minus* a *discount*. The forward premium or discount is calculated in the following way:

$$\frac{\text{Spot rate} \times \text{Interest differential} \times \text{No. of days}}{360 \times 100}$$

We can use this general formula to calculate any forward rate of exchange provided we have the appropriate information. For example, to calculate the six-month forward rate for the dollar against the Deutschemark we need the following information:

	Bid	*Offer*
Spot exchange rate (US$ = DM)	1.5050	1.5060
6-month Euro $ interest rate	8.0625%	8.1250%
6-month Euro DM interest rate	8.6875%	8.8125

Premium/discount

$$\text{bid rate} = \frac{1.5050(0.086875 - 0.08125)182}{360} = 0.0043$$

Premium/discount

$$\text{offered rate} = \frac{1.5060(0.088125 - 0.080625)182}{360} = 0.0057$$

In this example, German interest rates are higher than US interest rates implying that forward Deutschemarks are at a discount. This discount is *added* to the spot rates quoted above (and a premium would be *deducted*) because the spot rate is the quantity of Deutschemarks that must be given up to purchase one dollar. Since the Deutschemark is at a discount against the dollar each dollar is worth more Deutschemarks forward than spot. Adding the discounts calculated above gives the dollar/Deutschemark forward. Thus we have:

	Bid	*Offer*
Forward rate US$ + DM	1.5093	1.5117

Source: Bank of England

example, a UK importer of Japanese stereo equipment might agree to make payment of 300m yen on delivery of the stereo equipment in 30 days' time. If the current spot rate is £1 = 300 yen, and the importer does not expect this to change over the next 30 days, the expected purchase price to him of the stereo equipment is £1m. However, if at the time of delivery the spot rate is £1 = 250 yen, then the purchase price to the importer is, in fact, £1.2m. The risk of such a substantial increase in the import price can be averted if the importer agrees to buy yen 30 days' forward at the time he signs the deal to pay for imports in 30 days' time. Typically, forward rates are close to spot rates and we might suppose that at the time the deal is arranged the spot rate is £1 = 300 yen and the 30-day forward rate is £1 = 299.5 yen. If the dealer agrees to buy yen 30 days' forward, then the cost of importing the stereo equipment is fixed at $300/299.5 \times$ £1m = £1,001,670 (approx.). For a relatively small amount the importer has eliminated the risk of higher payments because of exchange rate changes between the time purchase of the goods is agreed, and the time payment has to be made.

However, this leaves unanswered the question of who agrees to supply yen 30 days' forward. One possible source is a Japanese importer of goods from Britain who will require sterling in 30 days' time to honour his import contract. Given the number of transactions involved in international trade, this is not an unrealistic possibility, and banks will therefore quote forward rates in many currencies confident that any agreement to purchase foreign currency forward can be offset by a simultaneous agreement to sell foreign currency forward.

The Determination of Exchange Rates in Free Markets

When there is no intervention in foreign exchange markets, exchange rates are determined by the forces of supply and demand for each currency in the foreign exchange market. Let us consider the determination of the sterling exchange rate against the dollar.

The Demand for Sterling

The demand for sterling on the foreign exchange market is a derived demand: it is derived from the demands of American importers, Americans who wish to invest in UK firms or who wish to hold sterling balances. The demands of all these groups for sterling will give a negatively sloped demand curve showing that at a lower rate of exchange, more sterling will be demanded. The reason for this is that when the rate of exchange is relatively low, British exports are relatively cheap in the USA. For example, if the rate of exchange is £1 = $1, £2m worth of British goods costs an American importer $2m. However, if the rate of exchange is £1 = $2 the *same £2m worth of British goods* now costs the American importer £4m. *As the sterling rate of exchange rises, each unit of sterling costs more dollars.* If we assume the demand for British goods is elastic, as the price in America rises, fewer goods would be demanded and therefore less sterling would be demanded. Similarly, at higher rates of exchange it is more expensive for Americans to invest in real assets in the UK, or to purchase securities, and here again we might expect demand for sterling to vary inversely with the rate of exchange.

The Supply of Sterling

The supply of sterling to the foreign exchange market stems from the demand for dollars by UK residents with which to pay for goods and services imported from the USA, or to invest in the USA, and so on. The supply of sterling is positively sloped, because at relatively low rates of exchange demand for imports will be relatively low. For example, at a rate of exchange of £1 = $1, $4m worth of imports from the USA costs a UK importer £4m. However, at a rate of exchange of £1 = $2, *the same $4m worth of imports* costs a UK importer £2m. *As the sterling rate of exchange rises, each unit of sterling buys more dollars.* If we assume that the demand for imports is elastic, more imports will be demanded as the sterling exchange rate rises and therefore more sterling will be supplied to the foreign exchange market.

Equilibrium in the Foreign Exchange Market

When there is no intervention in foreign exchange markets, exchange rates are freely determined by the forces of supply and demand. In Figure 33.1 the supply of sterling to the foreign exchange market is represented by *SS* and *DD* represents the demand for sterling on the foreign exchange market. Given these schedules it is clear that at any moment in time there

Figure 33.1 *Equilibrium rate of exchange*

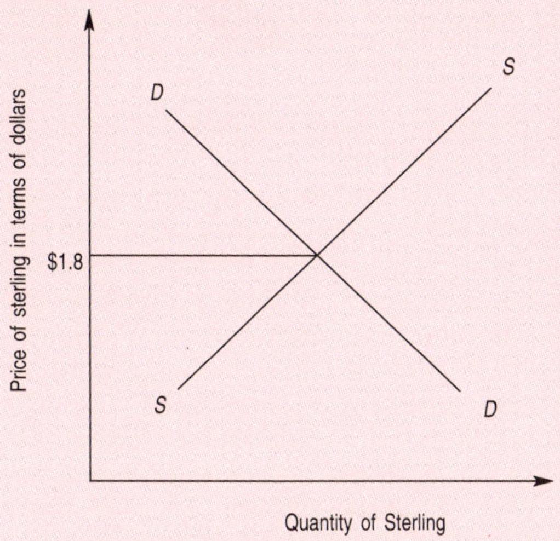

can only be one rate of exchange between sterling and the dollar: that which equates supply of sterling with demand for sterling. This is the equilibrium rate of exchange and in Figure 33.1 this is £1 = $1.8.

At any rate of exchange above £1 = $1.8 there will be a surplus of sterling supplied to the foreign exchange market and this will cause the rate of exchange to fall or *depreciate*. At any rate of exchange below £1 = $1.8 there will be a shortage of sterling on the foreign exchange market and this will cause the exchange rate to rise or *appreciate*. With the supply and demand conditions as given in Figure 33.1, £1 = $1.8 is the only stable exchange rate for sterling.

Factors Causing Movements in Free Market Exchange Rates

In markets where exchange rates float freely equilibrium can be disturbed only if there is a **change in the conditions of demand and/or supply** for a currency on the foreign exchange market – in other words, if there is a shift in the demand and/or supply schedules. So what factors might cause a change a shift in the supply or demand schedules?

Domestic Price Levels and the Exchange Rate

In the long term there is no doubt that changes in domestic price levels exert a major influence on exchange rates and one theory of exchange rates, the *purchasing power parity theory* or the *law of one price*, explains changes in the **external value of a country's currency** purely in relation to changes in the **domestic rate of inflation relative to changes in the foreign rate of inflation**. In terms of the sterling exchange rate, the purchasing power parity theory can be expressed as:

$$\text{Foreign exchange price of £} = \frac{\text{Foreign price level}}{\text{UK price level}}.$$

This is simply a statement to the effect that, in return for a given amount of its own currency, the UK will require enough foreign currency to enable it to buy abroad the same quantity of goods that could be bought internally. The implication is that if the UK price level rises and the foreign price level

Box 33.2 Arbitrage and exchange rates

If on a particular day the exchange rate for sterling against the dollar in London is quoted at £1 = $1.75, then the exchange rate in New York for the dollar against sterling will be quoted at $1 = £0.5714. Any other set of bilateral exchange rates would imply that it was possible for investors to make *riskless* profit simply by changing currency in one financial centre and then converting back to the original currency in another financial centre. For example, if the sterling/dollar rate in London was £1.75 and the dollar/sterling rate in New York was $1 = £0.6, with £1m one could buy dollars in London obtaining $1.75m which could then be sold for sterling in New York to obtain £1.05m. Such opportunities for riskless gain could not exist in reality because as soon as the opportunity arose investors would exploit them. The resultant changes in supply and demand for different currencies would cause changes in bilateral exchange rates so as to eliminate the opportunity for riskless gain.

In fact all foreign currencies are linked together. For example, if we are given the following set of bilateral exchange rates: £1 = $1.75 and £1 = 3DM, then the only possible exchange rate for the dollar and the Deutschemark is $1 = 1.714DM.

remains constant, the external value of sterling will *depreciate*.

We can use our basic supply and demand framework to illustrate the effect of a relatively high rate of inflation in the UK on the sterling/dollar exchange rate. In Figure 33.2 supply and demand for sterling on the foreign exchange market are initially represented by *SS* and *DD* respectively. The equilibrium rate of exchange is therefore initially £1 = $1.80.

If prices in the UK now rise relative to prices in the USA, exports from the UK will become less competitive in the USA and there will therefore be a contraction in demand for UK exports. Because of this there will be a reduction in the amount of sterling demanded *at any given exchange rate* and therefore demand for sterling on the foreign exchange market will shift from *DD* to D_1D_1. However, the higher rate of inflation in the UK also implies that imports from the USA become more competitive in the UK. In consequence UK residents will demand more imports at any *given rate of exchange* and therefore the supply curve for sterling will shift from *SS* to S_1S_1. The combined effect of these changes in demand and supply for sterling is to pull down the sterling exchange rate to a new lower equilibrium of £1 = $1.40 in Figure 33.2.

The effect of different rates of inflation on the exchange rate can be profound, but in reality purchasing power parity between currencies is unlikely to be fully maintained. One reason for this is that many goods and services are purchased domestically, but not traded internationally. They will therefore affect the domestic price level, but will not directly affect the exchange rate.

Figure 33.2 *Inflation and the sterling/dollar exchange rate*

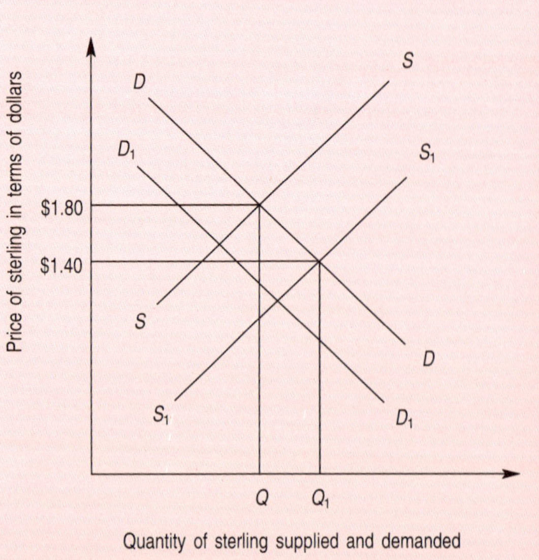

Changes in Real Income

The level of real income is a major determinant of the demand for imports and a rise in real income in one country will lead to a rise in the demand for imports. The extent to which import demand increases depends on the marginal propensity to import, but in a country like the UK, with a relatively high marginal propensity to import, the effect of an increase in real income on import demand will be significant. An increase in demand for imports *at any given rate of exchange* will shift the supply curve for sterling outwards and this implies a depreciation of the exchange rate. Despite this, the relationship between the growth of real income and the exchange rate is unclear and those countries with the fastest rate of growth have the strongest exchange rates.

Changes in Interest Rates

Changes in interest rates exert a powerful short-term influence on exchange rates through their effect on capital flows. For example, if interest rates in the UK rise relative to rates of interest in other countries, the UK will attract capital flows and demand for sterling will increase *at any given rate of exchange*. On the other hand, the higher rate of interest in the UK will encourage domestic residents to invest in the UK rather than abroad. The supply of sterling to the foreign exchange market will therefore fall *at any given rate of exchange*. In a free market the effect of these changes will be to push up the sterling exchange rate. A change in the rate of interest abroad relative to UK rates will have the opposite effect.

Speculation

Speculation on the foreign exchange market is motivated by *expected changes in exchange rates* with speculators hoping to profit by correctly anticipating changes in exchange rates. For example, speculators who consider sterling to be overvalued and who expect an imminent reduction in the foreign exchange price of sterling could make a speculative gain, if their expectations are correct, by selling sterling for dollars, and then converting dollars back

Box 33.3 Covered interest parity

Investments are always covered in the forward markets. Arbitrage operations will ensure this. For example, consider the following quotations taken at the close of business in London on Monday 5 February 1990.

Closing exchange rate	*Spot*	*Forward*
Dollars per pound	1.6885–1.6960	2.72–2.69 (premium)

Interest rate	Eurosterling	Eurodollar
3-month offer rate	$15^1/_{16}$	$8^1/_4$

If all other factors remain unchanged the Eurosterling deposit offers the highest return. However, if the dollar appreciates it might be better to hold dollars. One way to avoid risk is to *hedge investments* in the forward market. Before we see the result of this, two points need clarification:

- In the forward exchange market the dollar is at a premium against sterling. This means that the forward dollar buys more sterling and therefore we have to *subtract* from the spot price to obtain the forward price (Remember that the forward rate shows the number of dollars per pound. In this case, the spread in the forward market would be 1.6613–1.6991.
- The interest rates are annualised so that they do not show what would be earned on a three-month deposit. The three-month equivalents are 3.570% and 2.002% respectively.

Initially the interest rate differential on Eurosterling compared to Eurodollars looks encouraging. If we invest £100 in Eurosterling then in three-months time we have:

$$£100(1.03570) = £103.57$$

Alternatively, if we convert sterling to dollars spot, invest in Eurodollars and repurchase sterling forward in three months 'time', we obtain:

$$100 \times \frac{1.6885(1.02002)}{1.6691} = £103.19$$

Given these quotations it seems possible to make a small profit out of covered investments though, contrary to what might be expected, not from investing in Eurosterling despite the higher interest rate! However, in practice the rates quoted above are not available to the typical investor. They are available only to investors placing sums in excess of £250,000. In addition, once we include transactions costs any possibility of even a small gain disappears. It would be surprising if this relationship did not exist since this would imply that riskless gains could be made!

into sterling after the reduction in the sterling exchange rate.

Fixed Exchange Rates

Exchange rates are fixed when the authorities **fix the amount of foreign currency that can be bought with a given amount of their own currency**. Sometimes fixed exchange rates are known as *pegged* exchange rates because one currency is pegged to another; in such circumstances, it is unusual rigidly to fix exchange rates and small deviations of a specified amount are usually permitted. The way in which these margins of fluctuation operate is discussed in relation to the ERM on pp. 329–30.

In order to maintain a fixed exchange rate, the authorities must intervene in the foreign exchange market to neutralise changes in supply and demand for domestic currency and so avoid movements in the exchange rate. For intervention purposes, the authorities hold *reserves* of foreign currency. and use these to stabilise exchange rates. For example, let us assume that supply and demand for sterling on the foreign exchange market are initially given by *SS* and *DD* respectively in Figure 33.3, and that the authorities have agreed to maintain a fixed exchange rate between sterling and the dollar of £1 = $1.75.

If the UK now experiences a balance of payments deficit, because the demand for imports increases, the supply of sterling to the foreign exchange market will shift from *SS* to S_1S_1. The increased supply of sterling will, in a free market, cause a depreciation of sterling. In order to prevent this the authorities purchase the excess supply of sterling on the foreign exchange market using the official reserves. The effect of this is to shift the demand curve for sterling from *DD* to D_1D_1, thus maintaining the fixed

Figure 33.3 *Maintaining the fixed exchange rate*

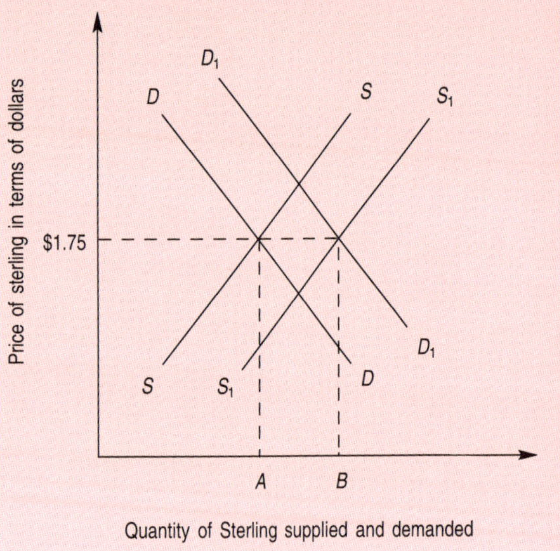

exchange rate of £1 = $1.75. This is the basic process of **exchange rate intervention**. By purchases and sales of sterling, the authorities neutralise any change in the conditions of supply and demand for sterling which would otherwise cause a change in the official exchange rate.

However, intervention of this nature is not a long-term option. After all, the authorities only have a limited amount of reserves. In our example above, to maintain the exchange rate at £1 = $1.75 they purchase an amount of sterling equal to *AB* and this implies a reduction in the official reserves, of $\$1.75 \times AB$. Since the authorities possess limited reserves only a limited amount of intervention is possible to stabilise the exchange rate, and if downward pressure continues the authorities will be forced to take further action. There are several alternatives the authorities might consider.

Increasing the Rate of Interest

One option available to the authorities is to raise the domestic rate of interest. This will stem the outflow of currency but, more importantly, will attract an inflow of foreign currency. However, there are domestic considerations which limit the use of interest rates for intervention purposes in the long term. The higher rate of interest will be unpopular, for example with home-owners, and will depress domestic demand for consumer durables and investment goods and will therefore raise unemployment.

Official Borrowing Abroad

Sometimes the authorities borrow from abroad. The foreign currency obtained by borrowing can be used to supplement the reserves. Again, however, this is not an option that can be pursued indefinitely. Foreign countries will be unwilling to go on lending without limit, especially in the aftermath of the debt crisis (see p. 379).

Deflation of Domestic Demand

Both policies discussed above are essentially short-term policies. If deficits in the balance of payments continue, it will be necessary to pursue a longer-term strategy. The most obvious strategy is to deflate aggregate demand (see pp. 355–6) and so, by reducing the level of national income, reduce the consumption of imports. The level to which import consumption falls depends on the magnitude of the marginal propensity to import. The greater the marginal propensity to import, the greater the reduction in imports following a reduction in national income. However, in the longer term deflation, because of its effect on domestic inflation may encourage exports which will become more competitive abroad, and discourage imports which will become less competitive in the domestic economy.

Devaluation

If other measures fail to remove a balance of payments deficit the authorities will be forced to devalue their currency. This is an **administered reduction in the exchange rate** from one fixed parity to a lower fixed parity. Devaluation raises the price of imports in the domestic economy and lowers the price of exports in the world economy. The aim is to encourage sales of exports and to discourage purchases of imports. The effects of currency changes are considered on pp. 319–21.

Advantages of Floating Exchange Rates

Floating exchange rates are sometimes considered to have several advantages and disadvantages compared with fixed exchange rates. Let us briefly look at these.

Automatic Balance of Payments Adjustment

The principal advantage of free floating exchange rates is that they provide an **automatic mechanism for ensuring balance of payments equilibrium**. If, at the existing rate of exchange, a country's balance of payments moves into deficit, then the quantity of that country's currency supplied to the foreign exchange market will exceed demand for it. The currency will therefore depreciate against other currencies and, in consequence, demand for exports will increase (because they have become cheaper abroad) while demand for imports will fall (because they have become more expensive in the domestic economy). For a country whose balance of payments moves into surplus the mechanism works in reverse. The exchange rate *appreciates*, export sales will decline and import consumption will increase until balance of payments equilibrium is restored. The effectiveness of this mechanism depends on certain assumptions, which are discussed on pp. 319–21.

Freedom in the Choice of Domestic Policies

Because balance of payments adjustment is automatic, the authorities are free to pursue policies in the domestic economy independently of balance of payments considerations. Remember, under fixed exchange rates a country's domestic policies are dictated by the need to achieve equilibrium in the balance of payments. In particular, this may mean pursuing deflationary policies which adversely affect output and employment in the domestic economy when balance of payments deficits are experienced.

Disadvantages of Floating Exchange Rates

Despite these advantages, most of the world's exchange rates are fixed in some way. To see why, let us consider the disadvantages of floating exchange rates

Reduced International Trade

It is sometimes alleged that freely floating exchange rates reduce the volume of international trade because of uncertainty over what exchange rate will exist in the future when contracts fall due for settlement. In other words, since traders cannot know what exchange rates will prevail in the future, they cannot know what actual level of expenditure will be incurred (or what level of revenue will be earned) when contracts are settled. There is probably some truth in this argument but it is easy to exaggerate its importance. After all, we have seen on p. 311 that rates of exchange can be agreed in the forward market, thus eliminating exchange rate risk. Nevertheless, the cost of forward cover may discourage smaller companies from using this option, and the risk of exchange rate movements may therefore discourage such firms from trading internationally.

Exchange Rate Instability

A related issue is that it is sometimes alleged that free floating exchange rates are inherently unstable, and that this instability is due to speculative pressure. It will certainly make it difficult for firms to plan future output and investment levels. The argument is therefore about whether speculation actually destabilises foreign exchange rates. If it does, any resultant overvaluation of a currency will penalise industries in the traded goods sector – that is, exports of goods and domestically produced goods which compete with imports. Consequently, some industries which might otherwise have been viable may be forced permanently to contract and some may even be forced to close.

However, the effect of speculation is by no means certain. Indeed, it has been argued that speculation actually stabilises exchange rates. Speculators act *in anticipation* of exchange rate movements. Therefore if there is a widely held view that a currency is about to appreciate, speculators will buy that currency *before* appreciation and will therefore increase their demand for that currency. If their expectation is correct, when the currency actually appreciates they will sell their holdings of that currency and, by swelling market supply, they will mitigate the extent of any appreciation. The opposite occurs in the case of an expected depreciation.

Increased Inflationary Pressure

Another argument against free floating exchange rates is that since equilibrium in the balance of payments is automatic, the element of discipline on nations to avoid inflationary pressure is reduced. Furthermore, countries whose currencies depreciate will experience rising import prices and, where raw materials or semi-finished products are imported, this implies rising final prices. This is a cost push explanation of inflation and such an approach would not be accepted by monetarists or newclassical economists.

Advantages of Fixed Exchange Rates

The arguments for fixed exchange rates constitute the case against floating rates. The main advantages of maintaining a regime of fixed exchange rates are summarised below.

Reduced Risk

By maintaining a fixed rate of exchange, international buyers and sellers of goods can agree a price and not be subjected to the risk of later changes in exchange rates before contracts are settled. It is argued that those involved in international trade are risk averse and that the existence of exchange rate risk when exchange rates are floating discourages them from exporting or importing.

Discipline in Economic Management

It is argued that under a fixed exchange rate regime, because the burden of adjustment to long-term disequilibrium in the balance of payments is thrown onto the domestic economy, governments have an incentive to avoid a rate of inflation that is out of line with that of their major competitors. This is one of the main reasons for Britain's entry into the ERM (see p. 331).

Elimination of Destabilising Speculation

Because exchange rates are fixed it is sometimes suggested that there is no possibility of speculation causing an overvaluation or an undervaluation of the exchange rate. This is important because any overvaluation or undervaluation of a currency in relation to its underlying equilibrium will affect the allocation of resources. In particular, overvaluation will result in some potentially profitable organisations being forced to close, while undervaluation will enable inefficient organisations to go on trading.

Disadvantages of Fixed Rates

These are important advantages, and the fact that most nations have adopted fixed exchange rates indicates a strong preference for this approach. However, there are disadvantages with fixed exchange rates and these are summarised below.

Balance of Payments Adjustment

A major problem with fixed exchange rates is that they do not provide an automatic mechanism to restore balance of payments equilibrium. The burden of adjustment to a balance of payments surplus or deficit is therefore thrown on to the domestic economy.

Exchange Rate Instability

It is alleged that fixed exchange rates are inherently unstable in the long run because different countries pursue policies which are mutually inconsistent under a system of fixed exchange rates. For example, if one country attaches greater significance to the control of inflation than its trading partners, it is likely to experience a continuing balance of payments surplus. If this surplus persists, it will require persistent adjustment of exchange rates. The problem is that when fixed exchange rates are adjusted, there is an immediate and significant change in costs and prices which may adversely affect economies. Under floating exchange rates the exchange rate gradually moves from one equilibrium to another and there is no immediate and significant change in costs and prices. Rather, there is a series of minor changes allowing a more gradual adjustment in the economy.

International Transmission of Inflation

It is sometimes suggested that fixed exchange rates lead to the transmission of inflation from one country to that of its trading partners. This may happen when inflation in one country leads to an increase in the price of imports in other countries because price differences are not offset by changes in the exchange rate (see p. 27).

The Effective Exchange Rate

When all exchange rates are fixed a devaluation of, say, 10 per cent in the external value of a country's currency implies a devaluation of 10 per cent against all other currencies. For example, with respect to other currencies in the ERM there is no problem with understanding the implications of a change in any of the intra-ERM currencies. However, when exchange rates float, as with sterling against the dollar and the yen, it is possible for the external value of one currency to fall against some currencies but simultaneously to rise against others. In these circumstances, it is misleading to refer to a currency depreciation.

The *effective exchange rate* seeks to answer the question: 'Given all the changes in individual rates of exchange that have taken place, what uniform and unilateral change in the exchange rate of sterling against all other currencies would have had exactly the same overall effect on the UK trade balance?' In simple terms, this implies that if the effective exchange rate for sterling is initially indexed at 100 per cent and subsequently falls to 95, the actual changes in exchange rates that have caused the depreciation will, in time, have the same effect on the visible balance of the UK as a 5 per cent depreciation in sterling against all other currencies, but with all other exchange rates remaining constant.

Depreciation and the Current Balance

Depreciation (or appreciation) of the exchange rate changes the *foreign price of exports* and the *domestic price of imports*. For example, if the exchange rate depreciates from £1 = $2 to £1 = $1.80, a car manufactured in the UK which costs £12,000 in the domestic market will cost $24,000 in the USA before depreciation, and $21,600 after depreciation. A car imported from the USA, on the other hand, costing $26,000 in the USA costs £13,000 in the UK before depreciation, and £14,444 after depreciation. Appreciation will have the opposite effect but whether these price changes succeed in removing a deficit or surplus on the current balance depends on certain conditions. Let us examine these conditions, and for simplicity we consider the case of a current account deficit.

The Elasticity of Demand for Exports and Imports

Elasticity of demand for exports and imports is important because, as we have seen on p. 27, elasticity of demand determines the effect on total earnings of a price change. If demand for exports is elastic, then after depreciation total earnings of foreign currency from export sales will rise because there will be a more than proportionate increase in the volume of goods and services sold. The more elastic the demand, the greater the effect of a given depreciation on export earnings.

On the other hand, since depreciation does not affect the *foreign price* of imports, any reduction in consumption as a result of depreciation will reduce foreign currency expenditure on imports! Of course, the greater the elasticity of demand for imports, the greater the proportional reduction in imports consumed after depreciation, and hence the greater the reduction in foreign currency expenditure.

The critical elasticity condition for depreciation to improve the current balance, the so called Marshall–Lerner condition, is that the **sum of the elasticities of demand for exports and imports should be greater than 1**. In these circumstances, it could be argued that the combined change in export earnings and import expenditure will be such as to improve the current balance. However, other considerations are also important.

Supply of Exports

Even when elasticity of demand conditions are favourable it does not necessarily follow that depreciation will improve the current balance. It is also important to consider the *elasticity of supply* of exports. When there is full employment in the economy, elasticity of supply will be relatively low and it will not be possible to meet an increase aggregate demand with an increase in aggregate supply. If there is full employment in the economy it is sometimes argued that depreciation should be accompanied by deflation of domestic demand, so that resources can be released from the production of non-tradeable goods and services to the production of tradeables – that is, exports and import competing industries.

Time Lags

In the real world the favourable effects of depreciation will take some time to become fully apparent. In the short run, demand elasticities following depreciation may be relatively low: existing contracts must still be honoured and it will take time for producers to increase the supply of import substitutes because of factor immobility and the need to increase capacity. Because of this, it is likely that depreciation will initially have little effect on the quantities of exports and imports bought and sold. This implies that the current balance will initially deteriorate following depreciation because the foreign price of exports will fall whereas the foreign price of imports will be unchanged. The current balance will improve over time only as consumers and producers respond to the changed prices. This is often referred to as the 'J Curve effect', and it is illustrated in Figure 33.4.

Figure 33.4 *The J curve effect*

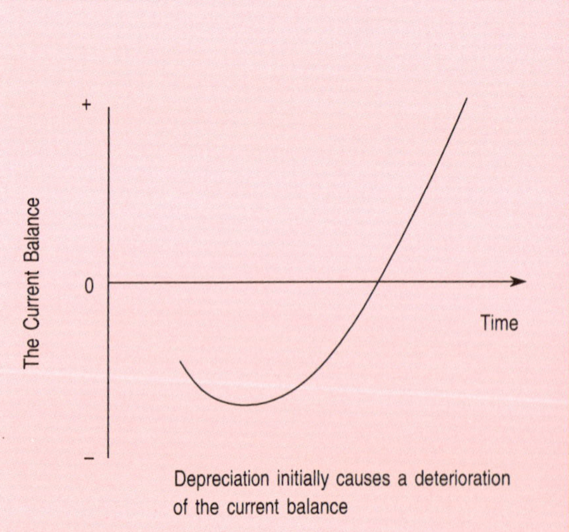

Income Effects

To the extent that depreciation increases exports and reduces imports for the country whose currency depreciates, it will raise incomes in the domestic economy (as injections increase and leakages fall) but will reduce incomes abroad (as injections fall and leakages increase). Whether depreciation is successful in the long term depends on the income elasticity of demand for imports at home and abroad. If demand for imports is relatively income elastic in the domestic economy, as income rises following depreciation there will be a proportionately larger increase in the consumption of imports. On the other hand, if demand for imports abroad is also income elastic, then as incomes fall abroad there will be a proportionately larger reduction in import consumption – that is, exports from the domestic economy will fall. The long run effects of depreciation may not therefore be favourable, depending on the respective income elasticities of demand.

Administered Price Changes

It is possible that exporters and suppliers of imports may administer price changes so as to preserve predepreciation price levels. In particular, multinational companies may do this so as to avoid competition among their own products. However, other firms may adjust prices so as to avoid any retaliatory action by foreign producers. Because of this, following depreciation a company may simply raise the price of its exports *in domestic currency* so as to leave the *foreign currency price* unchanged. If this occurs it will certainly reduce the effect of depreciation on the current account.

Domestic Inflation

One problem following depreciation that is particularly relevant for the UK is that the cost of raw materials increases, and this in turn will raise final prices. This is a potentially serious problem, and inflation in the domestic economy can quickly wipe out the gains from depreciation; in these circumstances any improvement in the terms of trade will be only temporary and deficits will soon reappear.[1]

Attributes of an Effective Monetary System

The main function of an international monetary system is to **promote efficiency in the utilisation of resources**. To do this, the monetary system should provide confidence and encourage countries to specialise. However, it must also provide either a mechanism for dealing with imbalances in the

[1] This argument would not be accepted by either monetarist or new classical economists.

balance of payments or else, in the case of fixed exchange rates, ensure an adequate growth of liquidity to finance emerging balance of payments deficits. This is particularly important because as the value of international trade flows increases, the size of deficits and surpluses will increase. A shortage of liquidity will mean that deficits cannot be financed and therefore the growth of international trade will be restricted.

The International Monetary Fund

The International Monetary Fund (IMF) was established in 1946 as the central institution in the international monetary arrangements agreed at Bretton Woods in 1944. It is simply an organisation of countries which seeks to achieve certain aims, including the following:

- To promote **international monetary co-operation**
- To facilitate the **expansion and balanced growth of world trade**
- To promote **exchange stability** and maintain orderly exchange arrangements among members
- To assist in the establishment of a **multilateral system of payment** and the **elimination of foreign exchange restrictions**
- To provide **temporary international liquidity** to countries with balance of payments deficits.

The last aim, that of providing temporary assistance to countries with balance of payments deficits, has developed into the Fund's major objective. The Fund has available different types of assistance depending on the nature of a country's problem, but most assistance is conditional (that is, given only when countries agree to implement economic policies approved by the Fund which are designed to eliminate the cause of their balance of payments problem).

The Fund obtains the bulk of its finance through a system of **quotas** paid by each of its 150 members. Each country's quota is based on the size of its GDP and its share of world trade, and is paid in the member country's currency. This gives the Fund foreign currency to lend to countries with balance of payments difficulties. However, quotas also serve another purpose: they are used to determine the extent of members' borrowing rights on the Fund and their share of any allocation of SDRs (see p. 322).

The Fund has a basic facility under which credit is available in four 'slices' or tranches, each equivalent to 25 per cent of quota. Effectively, countries 'purchase' foreign currency or SDRs by supplying amounts of their own currency, and receive in exchange foreign currency with which to settle their balance of payments deficit. The first credit tranche is available unconditionally, but access to the subsequent three tranches (the upper tranches) is usually granted only when increasingly stringent conditions, set by the IMF and aimed at removing the cause of the deficit, are met. These conditions usually involve some commitment to **control money growth**. Technically a member's borrowing rights at the Fund are exhausted when the Fund is holding an amount of its currency equal to 200 per cent of its quota, though in practice the Fund has sometimes granted credit in excess of this.

Resources are normally made available under a line of credit known as a *stand-by arrangement*, which specifies the amount and period over which a member can make drawings. This type of assistance is therefore similar to overdraft facilities at a commercial bank. The aim is to reduce unnecessary borrowing and thus economise on the use of Fund resources. Drawings normally take place over a period of one year, but can be made over a period of up to three years. Repayments must begin three years after a drawing is made and must be completed within five years after any drawings are made.

Components of International Liquidity

International liquidity refers to those assets which countries use to settle their international obligations to one another. Such assets are often referred to as *reserve assets*, and for most of the world, excluding those countries which belong to the CMEA,[1] there are four main types of reserve asset: gold, convertible national currencies, reserve positions in the IMF and SDRs. Each of these is discussed in turn and their relative importance is shown in Table 33.2.

---

[1] The Council for Mutual Economic Assistance, also known as COMECON and consisting largely of the USSR and the East European Economies.

Table 33.2 *International reserves*

	SDR (millions)
SDR's	26757
Gold	26875
Reserve positions in the IMF	25004
International currencies	595332
Total	674168

The composition of international reserves as at 31st March 1991

Note: The value of the SDR is caluculated as a weighted average of the international value of the currency of five countries – the USA, UK, Germany, Japan and France

Source: IFS

Gold

This has the longest history of all reserve assets and it is almost universally acceptable in exchange for a country's currency. Despite this, countries prefer to settle their obligations to each other in other assets so that although gold is a reserve asset it is rarely used as a means of settling international obligations.

Convertible National Currencies

When one currency is convertible into others it will automatically become a reserve asset. In world markets the American dollar is the most important reserve asset but other currencies such as the Deutschemark and the yen are widely used.

Reserve Positions in the IMF

As we have seen, countries which are members of the IMF can borrow foreign currency from that organisation. When a country's currency is used by other members of the IMF, the Fund's holdings of that country's currency may fall below the level established in its quota. This results in that country having a reserve position in the Fund which is termed the 'reserve tranche'. The amount in the reserve tranche can be drawn upon conditionally and these drawings need not be repurchased. A country with a reserve position in the IMF therefore has *unconditional* access to additional foreign currency equivalent to the foreign currency value of its reserve tranche which can be used to finance a balance of payments deficit.

Special Drawing Rights (SDRs)

These are reserve assets created by the IMF which can be used by members in their international dealings with one another and in their dealings with various supra-national organisations such as the IBRD or World Bank. SDRs were introduced in 1970 as a supplement to existing reserve assets in response to an anticipated shortage of world liquidity caused by the increasing volume and value of world trade. However, the threatened shortage of world liquidity did not materialise and SDRs are of limited importance as an international asset. It should be noted that SDRs, like the ECU, are a basket currency and are not money in the full sense of the term but are book entries (see pp. 380–3).

REVIEW QUESTIONS

1 Assume the following exchange rates are quoted on a particular day: £1 = 3DM, £1 = $1.8 and $1 = 4DM. How can an investor with £1m make a riskless gain by buying and selling currency on the foreign exchanges?

2 If the forward rate of exchange is at a discount, what does this tell you about the expected future spot rate?

3 Why does a country require reserves of foreign currency when exchange rates are fixed but not when they are floating?

4 When exchange rates are fixed, is the purchasing power parity theory irrelevant?

5 Distinguish between *depreciation* **and** *devaluation***.**

6 Does speculation stabilise or destabilise exchange rates?

Figure 33.5 shows supply and demand for sterling. *SS* and *DD* represent the original supply and demand conditions. In Questions 7–11 begin with the original equilibrium point *E* and identify the new equilibrium point in each case. Assume that all other things remain equal

7 The rate of interest in the UK rises.

Figure 33.5 *Supply and demand for sterling*

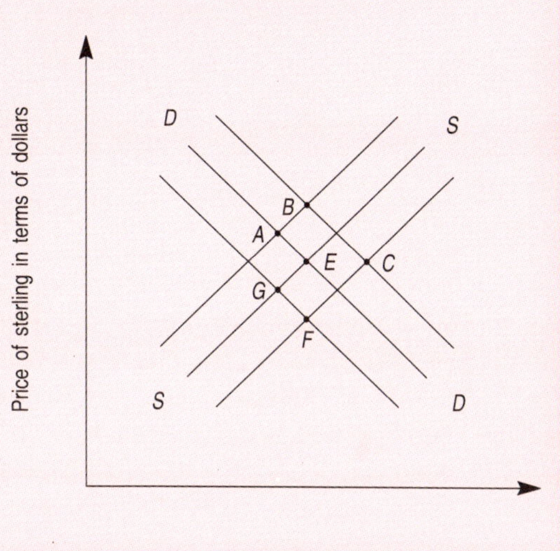

8 The UK restricts the import of cars.

9 Inflation in the UK falls.

10 Inflation abroad rises.

11 There is a sharp increase in the price of oil on world markets.

12 To what extent can the SDR be regarded as money?

CHAPTER 34

EUROPE'S ECONOMIC COMMUNITY

CONNECTIONS

Europe's **Economic Community** is an important, wide-ranging and complex mechanism. We will be making use of a great deal of material covered in other chapters and in particular we shall refer to economies of scale (Chapter 7), international trade and protection (Chapters 30 and 31), the balance of payments and exchange rates (Chapters 32 and 33).

Key Concepts

Common Agricultural Policy CAP)
Customs union
European Monetary System (EMS)
Exchange Rate Mechanism (ERM)
Free trade area

Types of Economic Integration

There are several types of economic integration and we begin our discussion of the EC by considering the different forms integration might take.

- *A free trade area*

In this arrangement the members eliminate tariff barriers among themselves but remain free to set individual tariffs against non-member countries. The European Free Trade Association (EFTA) which consists of Sweden, Norway, Iceland, Finland, Austria and Switzerland, is an example. However, the EC is more than just a free trade area.

- *A customs union*

This is 'tighter' than a free trade area. Not only are tariff barriers eliminated among members, a *common external tariff* is applied against non-members. The EC *is* a customs union.

- *A common market*

This is a customs union plus an important 'extra' – completely free movement of factors of production (labour and capital) between member countries. The EC will become a common market in 1992.

- *Economic union*

This consists of a common market plus *harmonisation* of national economic policies, for example in agriculture, taxation and transport. The EC has already achieved some degree of economic union and in 1992 is set to make further progress.

- *Full economic integration*

This involves economic union plus completely unified monetary, fiscal and social policies, together with the setting up of a supra-national authority whose decisions are binding on member states. There is an influential view, particularly on the Continent, that the EC should move towards full economic integration. Others have argued passionately for the maintenance of a looser EC of independent economic states.

Institutions of the EC

The EC has four main institutions. These are mainly based in Brussels and Luxembourg and are staffed in varying proportions from member countries.

The Council of Ministers

This is the EC's 'cabinet' and its role is to decide EC policies. The Council's ministers are appointed from member states.

The European Commission

This consists of 17 permanent members who represent the Community. The Commission is responsible for initiating policies for consideration by the Council of Ministers. It also administers and implements existing policies.

The European Parliament

In practice, this has little power. It monitors the activities of the Council and the Commission and shares in the making of the Community budget.

The European Court of Justice

This consists of 13 independent judges and rules on cases of EC law including disputes between member countries and the Commission. Incidentally, it is not the same as the European Court of Human Rights.

EC revenues are spent on EC policies, which we discuss in detail on p. 327. For the present, we identity three important areas of policy/expenditure:

The Common Agricultural Policy (CAP), which absorbs over a half of the EC funds.

Regional Policy, which provides financial assistance for EC regions with significant economic problems.

Social Policy, which is mainly concerned with improving living, work and employment conditions.

Financing the EC

The EC has a substantial budget. Its revenues come mainly from four sources:

- A proportion of member countries' value added tax revenues, about 1 per cent, must be put into the EC budget.
- Agricultural imports into the EC pay a protective duty which goes into the EC budget.
- Manufactures imported into the EC are subject to a common external tariff; about a third of this revenue goes into the budget.
- In 1988 it was decided to introduce a new revenue resource in the form of a *uniform rate national contribution* based on member countries' respective GNPs.

Table 34.1 *EC revenue and expenditure, 1988*

EC revenue	(1988) million ecu	%
VAT resource	23,367	54.6
Agricultural & sugar levies	2,782	6.5
Customs duties	8,388	19.6
GNP based resource	6,933	16.2
Other	1,327	3.1
Total	42,797	100.0
EC Expenditure	**million ecu**	**%**
Agricultural support	29,058	65.1
Regional and transport	4,023	9.0
Social fund	3,109	7.0
Energy, technology	1,309	2.9
Repayments and aid to member states	3,730	8.4
Cooperation with developing countries	1,095	2.5
Other	2,324	5.2
Total	44,648	100.0

Source: EC

Why is There an EC?

An important motive for setting up the EC was *political* rather than economic. The aim was to encourage cooperation between member countries and to reduce the likelihood of future European wars. The EC was also designed to secure important economic benefits. Let us begin by examining the customs union aspect of the EC. The effects of a customs union can be divided into two types.

Static Effects

Static effects relate to increased specialisation which becomes possible in a bigger tariff-free market. Each member country will be more able to specialise in goods where it has a comparative advantage and which it can produce more efficiently (see p. 280). A production shift of this kind from a high cost to a low cost source is known as *trade creation.*

In terms of the EC, member countries with relatively large agricultural sectors (France, for instance) might be expected to specialise more in producing foodstuffs while countries like Germany and the UK would concentrate more on manufacturing. Some specialisation along these lines has taken place, and is likely to be reinforced by the accession of more recent members with large agricultural sectors whose economies tend to be 'complementary' to those of earlier EC members. The development of this type of comparative cost specialisation has however been distorted by the operation of the EC's agricultural policy (the CAP, see p. 327). However, most EC members have large manufacturing sectors (including France) which would tend to make broadly similar products. The creation of a large customs union market like the EC increases the scope for the reorganisation of production into more specialised patterns *within industries*: for example, jewellery from Italy, TVs from Holland, wine glasses from France, and so on.

Customs unions can also have *harmful* static effects. These take place when the enlargement of the market shifts some production from low cost to high cost sources.

Suppose the price of a bicycle saddle in the UK, France and Japan respectively is £25, £20 and £16. Suppose there is no customs union and the UK has a £7 tariff on both French and Japanese products. The Japanese saddle will then be cheapest with a UK price of £23. A UK bicycle manufacturer will therefore use the Japanese product. Now suppose the UK and France join in a customs union. The French saddle now enters the UK market tariff free and is priced at £20. But the Japanese saddle continues to pay the tariff and costs £23. The result is that a UK manufacturer will now purchase the French saddle. Production has now switched from the cheapest source, Japan, to a more expensive source, France. *Trade diversion* has taken place and at a world level specialisation has been impaired.

In the case of manufacturing, the EC customs union has probably caused relatively little trade diversion: the external tariff of the EC is low by world standards, tariff-free import arrangements exist with many non-EC countries in the Mediterranean, Caribbean and Africa and there is a tariff-free arrangement with EFTA. In the case of agriculture, though, the CAP undoubtedly generates trade diversion on a massive scale (see p. 327).

Dynamic Effects

The other main effect of a customs union is that it is likely to give rise to *dynamic effects* which develop cumulatively, sometimes over long periods of time. One of these is the development and expansion of existing successful firms via new and increased economies of scale. In smaller national markets firms might be unable to operate at their optimum size. In the case of Italy, for example, exports of design based products and services to other EC members have flourished since the 1970s. Famous names include Ferrari, Lamborghini and Maserate (sports cars), and Armani, Valentino, Verrace and Bellini (fashion design). It is also likely that the creation of a customs union will lead to increased competition which will put firms under pressure to achieve greater efficiency and lower costs. Another factor is that a customs union is likely to attract foreign investment from outside the customs union. Foreign firms who, due to the common external tariff, face restricted export entry to the customs union are likely to set up production units *within* it. This partly explains why, in recent years, the UK has attracted considerable American and Japanese investment, in the car industry for example.

The EC and Factor Mobility

In the sections above we have been looking at the effects of the EC as a customs union. We now need to examine the remainder of the 'Common Market' element: the provision for *free movement of factors of production* between member countries. The gains which arise from factor mobility can be related to the concept of marginal productivity. Suppose the marginal product of an unskilled worker is £5000 in Sicily and £16,000 in Munich. Then the movement of one (employed) worker from Sicily to Munich will increase net EC output by £11,000. In the current 12 member EC, not to mention likely future accessions from Eastern Europe, labour productivity varies greatly so that potential output gains from labour movements are considerable.

There are also potential gains from capital mobility within the EC, with capital being able to move to those sectors where it has the highest productivity. The provision for factor mobility is a central feature of the EC and is due to become fully effective in 1992.

EC Policies

The Common Agriculture Policy (CAP)

We have examined two important aspects of the EC, its customs union arrangement and the provision for factor mobility. We now look at a third aspect – that is, common economic *policies*. The most important of these is in agriculture.

In any advanced economy there is a tendency for farm incomes to be unstable and also to lag behind those in manufacturing and services. This is due to special characteristics of farming: the demand for its products is often price and income inelastic; long run supplies tend to increase substantially due to technical innovations; a multitude of small production units leads to fierce competition between producing units; and resources are relatively immobile – that is, capital and labour tend to 'stick' in farming.

To achieve price and income stability, the EC adopted a policy of price support in agriculture known as the *Common Agricultural Policy* (CAP). This now covers virtually all agricultural production in the EC, although the degree of support is generally higher for 'northern products' (such as cereals). The CAP has the following aims:

- To increase agricultural production
- To ensure a fair standard of living for the agricultural community
- To stabilise agricultural markets
- To ensure supplies to consumers at reasonable prices
- To allow regional specialisation within agriculture in the EC
- To eliminate market distortions.

These aims are to be achieved through the following mechanisms:

- A **guaranteed minimum support price** is set annually for domestic (EC) producers of a given farm product.
- **Variable import duties** (levies) are imposed on agricultural products entering the EC. These are designed to prevent imports from selling below the CAP support price.
- If the level of support results in an **excess supply** of the product in the EC in relation to total demand, then the CAP 'intervention agencies' buy up the excess in order to prevent the EC price falling below the support level.
- Surpluses thus acquired can be **stored and sold** in times of shortage, destroyed, converted into by-products or sold abroad at subsidised prices.

The CAP arrangements can be illustrated in terms of conventional supply and demand analysis. In Figure 34.1 *DD* and *SS* are the domestic (Community) demand and supply curves for a given agricultural product. *SW* indicates the world supply of the product which is assumed to be infinitely elastic at the price OP_W. Without any support intervention the EC would consume OQ_1 units; of this OQ_2 would be produced within the EC and the remainder, Q_2Q_1, imported. Assume the EC now sets a support price of OP_1. The market price now increases to OP_1, leading to three effects. First consumption contracts to OQ_3. Second, domestic supply extends to OQ_4. Third, imports, which are subject to an appropriate variable import levy, contract to Q_3Q_4.

However, suppose the support price is OP_2. At this level EC output is greater than consumer demand – that is, there is an excess supply of the product. As we saw on p. 49 surplus stocks of the product would develop as the intervention agencies bought up supplies to prevent the market price falling below the support price. Alternatively if we assume that all excess supplies are exported directly by EC farmers, an export subsidy will be required equal to the area *abcd*. In practice, the CAP has led to overproduction of many agricultural products resulting in large

Figure 34.1 *Supply and demand analysis of the CAP arrangements*

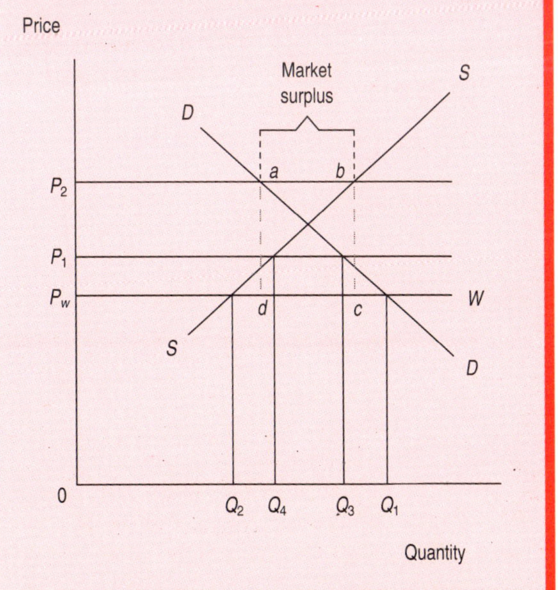

stocks of unsold agricultural output that are manifested in butter 'mountains', wine 'lakes', and so on. In order to correct this it would be necessary to reduce support prices in order to discourage farm production and encourage consumption. Unfortunately political pressures have made this difficult to achieve. One example of this is the events leading to the 1990 Anglo–French 'lamb war'. Moreover, to the extent that CAP support leads to high and stable farm prices it provides an incentive to *invest in an expansion of production*. This in turn tends to depress market prices and bring about the need for even greater CAP support and intervention.

The Cost of the CAP

The CAP has undoubtedly produced some benefits for EC farmers but, as we have just indicated, it has also created problems. Moreover in financial terms the costs of implementing the CAP have been very considerable, particularly for the UK. This is because the UK pays much more into the CAP scheme than its relatively small farming sector receives back in support. In 1990 the net financial transfer for the UK on this account was running at a debit of about £2000m. Some idea of the financial costs of the CAP is given in Table 34.2.

Table 34.2 *CAP financial support, 1988*

	million ecu
Cereals	3,313
Oils, fats	5,318
Milk, cheese	5,434
Red meat	3,284
Disposal of stocks	1,714
MCAs	494
Other	9,501
Total	29,058

Source: EC

The CAP has also been costly from a *welfare* point of view. Figure 34.1 on p. 327 reminds us that the effect of the CAP is essentially to force EC consumers to buy *high cost* European food compared with *cheap imports* which would otherwise be available. In other words, the CAP tends to cause *trade diversion*. You can study further the welfare losses from tariffs and other forms of protection on p. 296.

'Green Exchange Rates' and MCAs

An important feature of the CAP is the requirement for common agricultural prices throughout the community. These prices are expressed in the EC's unit of account, the ecu (see p. 329) and then converted through exchange rates into each member's national currency. Suppose that the current CAP price of butter is 1 ecu per kilo and that the exchange rate of the French franc is 1 ecu equals 10 French francs. The price of butter in France will therefore be 10 Francs per kilo. Now if the French franc is devalued by 10 per cent against the ecu, the price of butter in francs will increase to 11 francs. On the one hand this would be to the detriment of French consumers. On the other it would constitute an 'unfair' increase in revenue for French farmers compared to other farmers in the EC.

To prevent this effect it was agreed that agricultural prices would be maintained at pre-devaluation levels. In our example, the price of French butter would be maintained at 10 Fr per kilo. However, a French farmer would still be able to *export* butter to other EC countries at a price of 1 ecu, that is, 11 francs. A French consumer meanwhile would prefer French butter at 10 francs, rather than imported butter which would now cost 11 francs (1 ecu). The effect would be to encourage French exports of butter and to discourage French imports of butter. In order to prevent such distortions in agricultural trade, a system of variable border taxes and subsidies known as *monetary compensation amounts* (MCAs) was introduced to equalise the prices of exports, imports and domestically produced food. In our example a border tax to raise price by 1 franc per kilo would be placed on French butter exports and a subsidy to reduce price by 1 franc per kilo would be placed on French butter. Exactly the opposite would happen if a member's exchange rate was revalued.

The use of MCAs means that agricultural trade within the EC is based on exchange rates which are *fixed* against the ecu and are known as *green rates*. However, since exchange rates within the EC are not rigidly fixed, changes in members' exchange rates against the ecu will lead to changes in agricultural prices. The effect of the MCA arrangements is to break up the EC agricultural market into separate national markets which, on the basis of frontier taxes and subsidies, are enabled to operate at different price levels. Clearly this outcome is at variance with the whole concept of a customs union in agricultural products.

Reforming the CAP

The basic problem of the CAP is that it results in agricultural surpluses which requires an increasing level of subsidy. The main thrust for reform must therefore come from reduced support. Not surprisingly it has proved difficult to persuade the agricultural lobby that this is the case. However, there is now mounting international pressure for reform – for example, from the USA through GATT (p. 299). In the face of this, reform is inevitable. It is the *extent* of such reform that is in doubt. Some progress has been made in this direction.

EC Regional Policy

A number of EC areas suffer from low economic activity and high unemployment. In some areas this is due to the decline of traditional industries – for instance, steel in the North of England and the German Ruhr. In other areas it reflects a general underdevelopment, as in Southern Italy. EC regional policy began in 1975 with the setting up of the European Regional Development Fund, which is supported from the EC budget. By the mid-1980s the Fund was spending about £1000m annually. Assistance is mainly for specific projects or in industry or for infra-structure improvements. The UK has been a major recipient of EC regional aid.

EC Social Policy

EC social policy has developed because of the problems caused by changes in the allocation of resources from increased specialisation and labour movement within the EC. 'Social policy' is defined in a rather narrow sense to cover mainly employment and working conditions involving three main areas:

- The 1983 Social Fund finances **industrial training**, especially for women, migrant workers, the disabled and the young.
- Special policies aim to improve **working rights and conditions**, for example those relating to working women and accident prevention.
- Policy to encourage **industrial democracy** through increased worker participation, disclosure of business accounts, and so on.

In the context of the reforms of 1992, the proposed Delors Social Charter represents a major and controversial development in social policy.

The European Monetary System (EMS)

Two essential conditions for the maintenance of a common market are that member countries maintain **exchange rates** which are **fixed against each other** and that member countries have **similar rates of inflation**. To facilitate this the European Monetary System (EMS) was established in 1979 to create a 'zone of monetary stability'. This simply means stable prices and exchange rates among member countries. Participation in the EMS therefore requires a *collective approach* towards achieving lower, and common, rates of domestic inflation and stability of exchange rates.

How the EMS Works

The principal feature of the EMS is its Exchange Rate Mechanism (ERM). The ERM is an arrangement to maintain stability of exchange rates between member currencies in the EMS. The ERM consists of two systems which operate side by side. First, each member currency has a 'central exchange rate' in terms of the *European Currency Unit* (ecu) which is the unit of account of the EMS. The ecu is composed of a 'basket of member countries' currencies, weighted according to their trading importance within the EC. In 1990 the value of an ecu was approximately 70 pence (see Table 34.3). Each member currency is allowed to fluctuate only within a margin of plus or minus 2¼ per cent of its central ecu rate.

Secondly, the system of ecu central rates generates a 'grid' of bilateral exchange rate 'parities' between member currencies. Each member is obliged to maintain its exchange rates against each of the other ERM currencies within a permitted margin of fluctuation of 2¼ per cent either side of the parities in the grid. (In the case of Spain and the UK this margin is currently 6 per cent.) At the time of writing, for instance, the pound sterling must be kept within a range of 2.83–3.13 German Marks to the pound. Not all EC members participate fully in the EMS; in particular, the currencies of Greece and Portugal do not at present participate in the ERM,

Table 34.3 *Value of an ecu, 1990*

	Units of national currency in ecu basket	£ central parity in other currencies	Units of £ in ecu basket	National currency weights in ecu (%)
Belgium/Luxembourg franc	3.431	60.85	0.056389	8.1
Danish crown	0.1976	11.25	0.017560	2.5
French franc	1.332	9.89	0.134629	19.3
German mark	0.6242	2.95	0.211594	30.4
Irish pound	0.008552	1.10	0.007766	1.1
Italian lira	151.8	2207.25	0.068773	9.9
Dutch guilder	0.2198	3.32	0.066127	9.5
Spanish pesata	6.885	191.75	0.035906	5.2
Pound sterling	0.08784	1.00	0.087840	12.6
Greek drachma	1.44	294.60	0.004888	0.7
Portuguese escudo	1.393	256.47	0.005431	0.8
£/ECU central rate			0.696904	100.0

Note: Column 1 is fixed, but columns 2, 3 and 4 can change as currencies depart from their central parities

Source: *Lloyds Bank Economic Bulletin*, No. 143, November 1990

though it is anticipated they will do so at some future stage.

The ecu rate and the parity rate are clearly very similar but there is an important operational difference. The main role of the ecu rate is to provide an early warning *divergence indicator* that a member country's exchange rate threatens to 'break out' of the permitted margin against other currencies in the grid. This indicator is triggered when the value of a currency moves away from the ecu rate by more than three-quarters of its permitted 2¼ per cent margin. If this happens the presumption is that the member concerned will take action, initially by buying or selling its currency, to prevent it currency moving further out of line and eventually outside its parity grid margins. In the longer term the divergence indicator serves to identify member countries who may be pursuing policies which are unduly expansionary or contractionary in relation to those of other members. In these circumstances, the offending member is expected to adjust its economic policies so as to make them more compatible with those of other ERM members and thus remove pressure on its exchange rate.

Let us look at the operation of the ERM in a little more detail. Suppose the ecu divergence 'trigger' indicates an unacceptable fall in a member currency's exchange rate. The possible responses of the country in question can be examined in sequence:

1. It must take immediate action to **stabilise** its exchange rate by using its official reserves in the way explained on p. 315 It might also bolster this by changes in its rate of interest, which provide a very effective short run mechanism for manipulating exchange rates (see p. 316).
2. In the case of downward pressure on a country's currency which is likely to last for some time the country's central bank may obtain **extra reserves** from an EMS 'kitty' of foreign exchange, known as the European Cooperation Fund, which consists of currencies contributed by member countries. These reserves can be used by the country in question to support its currency on the foreign exchange market.
3. A persistent weakness of the currency is likely to lead to that country's authorities using **deflationary** policies to bring domestic costs and prices more into line with those of other member countries.
4. If none of the measures described so far are successful in keeping the currency in line with its ecu rate, it will be necessary for EMS members to agree to a **downward realignment**

(devaluation) of its exchange rate against the ecu, and hence against the other member currencies. (In the case of too 'strong' a currency an upward realignment may be necessary.) Since 1979, when the EMS was set up there have been twelve currency realignments.

Has the EMS Been a Success?

The EMS was designed to achieve a zone of monetary stability – that is, stable exchange rates and convergence of domestic prices. Has it succeeded? The difficulty is to know how the economies of the member countries would have developed if they had not been in the EMS. As far as exchange rate stability is concerned, intra-EMS exchange rates did in fact fluctuate less after the EMS was set up in 1979. The evidence also suggests that exchange rate realignments, when they have been necessary, seem to have worked smoothly. Except for one, they were carried out without any currency crisis and were mainly accompanied by 'economic convergence'; by this we mean that the effect of realignment was to help bring into line levels of economic activity among member countries. 'Full' EMS currencies have also tended to fluctuate less against major non-EC currencies like the dollar and the Japanese yen than have non-EMS currencies

With respect to price stability the EMS again seems to have successful record. Table 34.4 shows not only that, unlike the UK, the leading member countries' inflation rates declined in the 1980s, they also tended to converge. It is significant also that the cost of reducing inflation, *in terms of higher unemployment*, was lower among full EMS members than it was, for example, in the case of the UK. This is an indication that member countries were pursuing domestic policies which were mutually consistent and that economic convergence was taking place.

Despite this, we must not forget that European economic convergence has been taking place outside the EMS as well. First, there has been growing interdependence between the EC and other European economies. Second, many European countries, after the 1970s inflation problem, came to a shared view of anti-inflationary policy and accordingly adopted similar economic policies. Third, there has been a growing dominance of the (West) German economy which has tended to 'set the going rate' in terms of price stability. Given the influence of the German Mark and West German economy generally, it could perhaps be argued that the EMS has really been a 'German Mark system'. On balance, therefore, the evidence on convergence is inconclusive.

Table 34.4 *Inflation rates before and after EMS (%)*

	1973–9	1980–7	1988	1989	1990
Britain	16.6	6.1	4.9	7.8	10.0
West Germany	4.8	2.8	1.2	2.8	3.3
France	10.7	7.1	2.7	3.5	3.5
Italy	17.6	11.0	5.0	6.6	5.8

Source: Nigel M. Healey, The great EMS debate 1990 vintage, *BIS Financial Review*, May 1990

The UK and the ERM

The UK became a full member of the EMS when it joined the exchange rate mechanism in October 1990. Prior to becoming a full member the UK had not participated in the ERM. A major factor in the decision to join the ERM was the relatively high rate of inflation in the UK compared to other European nations. At the time of entry, it was argued that under the ERM a government cannot, except as a last resort, accommodate inflation with a currency devaluation, as happens when exchange rates float. Therefore businesses and worker groups are under much greater pressure to resist high wage settlements and any other factors which, by leading to higher costs and prices, could reduce the competitiveness of products, and thus threaten reductions in sales, profits and employment. It was further argued that lower levels of inflation would remove downward pressure on sterling against other EC currencies and the dollar, thus removing the need for destabilising increases in the rate of interest to avoid depreciation of sterling.

1992: The Removal of Barriers to Trade

The EC was designed as a common market – that is, a customs union plus a provision for free factor mobility. In 1986 the Single European Act proposed the abolition by 1992 of all barriers to the movement of goods and services and of labour and capital – that is, the creation of a common market by the end of 1992.

The 1986 Act identified three types of barriers to trade.

Box 34.1 The EMS and economic policy

Concerning the EMS, an important question to ask is that if, under the full EMS scheme, national interest rates are related to exchange rates, what policy instrument is available to a national government for regulating internal domestic demand? The answer has to be changes in government spending and taxation – that is, *fiscal policy*. UK experience in this respect is instructive. In 1987 and 1988 the UK Chancellor of the Exchequer pursued an 'informal' ERM policy with sterling, by 'shadowing' the main EMS currency, the German Mark. At one stage much higher oil prices, by implying increased import payments and a deteriorating trade balance, led to a significant fall in the exchange rate of currencies of high oil importing countries such as Italy. The pound sterling on the other hand for a time strengthened, on account of the UK's position as a net oil exporter. However, about this time the UK economy was beginning to 'overheat' through excessive growth of domestic demand (p. 307). Unfortunately, the Chancellor was unable to use disinflationary fiscal policy in the shape of higher taxation, since this would have interfered with his supply side policies (p. 363). He was therefore obliged to use the interest rate instrument *both* to stabilise the pound against the Mark *and* to control domestic demand. Since the pound was 'strong' against the other EMS currencies at this time the Chancellor had to aim for a sharp fall in UK interest rates. This led to an increased inflationary expansion of domestic demand which contributed to later UK balance of payments difficulties (p. 307). These problems also caused political difficulties for the Chancellor because they increased tension with the Prime Minister, Mrs Thatcher. Eventually the Chancellor felt forced to resign.

Excessive customs formalities and administrative procedures: The Act proposed standardisation of documentation and the removal of all frontier formalities within the EC, including passport and customs checks. The aim of this reform would be to speed up business procedures and reduce costs.

Technical barriers: One example of these is differing health and safety standards for goods and services between different members. Another is 'closed procurement' when government contracts are confined to domestic suppliers, in breach of the EC directive that such tenders should be open to firms in all member countries. A third technical barrier is the variety of procedures between member countries in the provision of financial services like banking, insurance and accounting. All such barriers lead to a fragmentation of markets. The Act proposed harmonisation in all respects, including procurement policy. The aim is to achieve increased competition and lower costs.

Differing rates of indirect taxes between member countries: Differing rates of indirect taxation can have a profound effect on trade flows and it is anticipated that harmonisation of indirect taxes would lead to greater competition and lower costs. However, such harmonisation is proving difficult since member countries have a wide variety of VAT practices and excise duty rates. In practice, member countries are likely to be allowed to delay harmonisation of indirect taxes.

The total gain from all three types of reform described above has been estimated at about 6 per cent of member countries' GNP.

1992 will also introduce measures aimed at freeing the EC market in labour and capital. Professional qualifications gained in one member country will thus have to be recognised in all member countries. This means, for example, that a British osteopath or Dutch accountant will legally be able to practise anywhere in the EC. With regard to capital movements there are provisions for full financial integration in terms of: abolition of all exchange controls inside the EC; free trade in financial services like banking, insurance and accountancy; and standardisation of banking practices across the EC, to include harmonisation with those in Japan and in the USA.

1992 and European Monetary Union

Will the EC be a genuinely unified market after 1992? One view is that the 1992 reforms will make full sense only in the context of European monetary union (EMU). Several forms of EMU have been proposed. The most radical is the *Delors Central Bank proposal*, which would have three elements.

- The development of the ecu which is at present mainly an EC unit of account, into an **operational working currency unit** which would eventually replace existing national currencies.

An Economic Commission survey in 1989 found that 90 per cent of industrialists questioned would favour the creation of a single European currency to facilitate their business operations.

- The setting up of an **independent European central bank** to regulate interest rates and monetary policy in the EMS as a whole. The bank would also have the role of lender of last resort for the European banking system and would therefore need the power to produce and supply ecus on the required scale.
- EMU would probably require **binding procedures** to prevent member countries running fiscal deficits which would undermine EMU monetary policies. If a country refused to implement appropriate fiscal policy the EC might apply **sanctions** like withholding EC regional funds.

It has been estimated that for the Community as a whole, the savings in foreign exchange transactions from the creation of EMU would be in the region of $18bn. This represents a considerable opportunity cost to EC countries because these resources have alternative uses. More specifically, for the UK it is clear that remaining outside EMU would involve considerable disadvantages. It has been suggested that the UK would lose influence in European monetary policy and that the proposed European central bank might be set up in Frankfurt rather than London. It is also likely that the City of London would lose some business to other EC financial centres and that foreign capital might be less likely to enter the UK as a base for EC operations.

This represents a powerful case for UK membership of EMU. However, a major disadvantage of EMU is the implied loss of *policy sovereignty*. In

Box 34.2 1992 and your next car

The 1992 single market provisions are intended to make businesses more efficient. Will this mean, for example, cheaper cars in Britain? The EC thinks so. A report in 1988 pointed to the many barriers which keep what could be the world's biggest car market so fragmented:

- Very different levels of VAT, plus in some countries special taxes on new cars
- Widely differing equipment standards (exhausts, dip switches, and so on)
- National government subsidies for Fiat, Renault, the former British Leyland and others
- Various import restrictions on Japanese cars.

The report concluded that following the beneficial effects of removing these barriers after 1992 a new car could be 5 per cent cheaper. But this may not be so:

- The EC is pushing for **design harmonisation** in tyres, windscreens and towing weights, but there are still disagreements in other areas, for example exhaust emissions.
- There is **overcapacity** in Europe's car market and a probability that open competition would drive out at least one major high cost manufacturer, leaving the survivors to compete and benefit from economies of scale. However, this might not happen. The EC is preparing local investment aid schemes aimed at curbing job losses which may have the effect of propping up high-cost car firms.
- There is considerable **fragmentation of consumer taste** within Europe. Many French and Italian motorists for example like 'nippy' medium-sized cars; Danes and Germans, on the other hand, often prefer heavy safe models, often estates. At present there does not seem much potential demand for a 'Eurocar'.
- Will the UK, Italy, France, Spain and Portugal continue to impose **'voluntary' export quotas** on direct imports of low cost cars from Japan? EC discussions for the removal of these are making only slow progress.
- Will Japanese cars produced in the UK be allowed **free market access** to other countries in the EC? (Nissan, Toyota and Honda intend by 1995 to export to Europe one-half of the 500,000 cars they will be making annually in the UK.) The answer could be 'no', because there is continuing strong opposition from France, Italy and other countries.
- There is no agreement in sight for **complete harmonisation of VAT and other taxes** on the sale of cars.

In the event, then, 1992 is probably going to introduce some extra competition and efficiency in the European car markets including the UK. But the car you buy and the price you pay may not after all be very different.

other words, if there is a single European currency then no country which participated in the scheme could pursue an independent monetary policy because it would have no control over the money supply or the rate of interest. Given that changes in monetary policy have considerable influence on the economy, it is no surprise that some people are strongly opposed to EMU.

Opponents of full EMU have suggested a more gradual monetary evolution in the EC. This has been the line taken by the UK government. As an alternative to EMU they have proposed the continuation of national currencies, the evolution of the EMS into a system of more rigidly fixed exchange rates and the development of increased cooperation between central banks on EMS, especially the development of a *hard ecu*.

The UK 'Hard Ecu' Proposal

Although by the early 1990s there was a strong momentum for European monetary union the UK government remained cautious on the issue, being prepared to concede only that if future governments desired it, monetary union might eventually come about. The UK government was also concerned about the route by which possible monetary union might be achieved. Under the Delors plan which we examined above, all the national currencies would at an agreed date be replaced by a single European currency, the ecu. The UK government, however, favoured a more gradual 'evolutionary' route towards monetary union, based on the creation of a 'hard ecu' which would be convertible at a guaranteed exchange rate into the various national currencies. The hard ecu would be issued by a European Monetary Fund in exchange for deposits of national currency. During a transition period towards possible monetary union each EC country would have two legally acceptable currencies, a common hard ecu and its own currency.

If economic agents chose to use the hard ecu on a sufficient scale it would evolve as a viable common currency in its own right alongside the national currencies. This would amount to a market vote of confidence in the hard ecu and the stage would be set for monetary union and the replacement of national currencies by the ecu. If, on the other hand, the hard ecu were to fail to gain market acceptance, the goal of European monetary union would be seen to be unrealistic and could be rejected. The merit of the hard ecu plan would thus be that it would 'test' the feasibility of monetary union. If successful both the hard ecu plan and the Delors plan would culminate in the same outcome, namely a single European currency, only the route would be different.

However, most EC countries continued to favour the Delors plan and tended to view the hard ecu plan as a UK tactic to obstruct and delay monetary union. In 1991 hopes rose on the prospects for eventual monetary union, following a proposal at the EC Commission by Delors for a special treaty clause which would permit the EC to proceed towards union while at the same time allowing the UK to defer a final decision on participation. This would give time for UK opinion on monetary union to evolve and for the British government to reconsider its attitude.

1992 and EC Competition Policy

When a single market develops on a European scale, economies of scale are likely to lead to a reduced number of firms and increased market concentration. It will therefore no longer be appropriate for member countries to pursue individual monopoly and mergers policies. It is proposed that the EC Competition Directorate should become responsible for a unified EC policy on competition, monopolies and mergers (see UK Monopoly Policy, p. 99).

REVIEW QUESTIONS

1 What is 'common' in a common market?

2 Why is free competition in transport important in stabilising a single market?

3 Why will the development of the single market by 1992 lead to an increase in cross border mergers?

4 Is full economic union in Europe possible without monetary union?

5 Since their respective inceptions, EFTA has contracted and lost membership while the EC has expanded and gained membership. What political and economic reasons can you think of to account for this?

6 If you were a Japanese business manager how would you view the likely development of the EC in the 1990s? How would you be likely to respond?

7 Which UK industries do you consider most likely to benefit from the 1992 changes, and which could be adversely affected? Explain your answers.

8 Prepare a case for the siting of a future European Central Bank in London rather than Frankfurt, Paris or some other continental financial centre.

9 What do we mean by the terms 'trade creation' and 'trade diversion'? Examine these concepts in the context of the EC.

10 Why was the UK slow to become a full member of the EMS, and why has it been resisting the idea of European monetary union?

11 What UK professions are likely to experience increased opportunities on the Continent as a result of the 1992 measures aimed at 'freeing' the labour market? How might your likely chosen profession be affected?

CHAPTER 35

PUBLIC FINANCE AND TAXATION

CONNECTIONS

There are important links between topics covered in Chapter 35 and concepts from several branches of economics, including: the price mechanism (Chapter 4); income distribution (Chapter 17); and stabilisation policy (Chapter 36).

Key Concepts

- *Ad valorem* tax
- Budget
- Capital gains tax
- Capital transfer tax
- Direct tax
- Income tax
- Indirect tax
- National Debt
- Progressive tax
- Tax incidence
- Value added tax (VAT)

Public Finance is the branch of Economics concerned with the **revenue, expenditure and debt operations of governments**, and the impact that these measures have on the economy. Let us begin by examining the reasons for government expenditure.

Why do Governments Spend?

Pareto Optimality

We have seen in Chapter 4 that markets can fail to allocate resources optimally. With respect to government spending it is particularly important to note that the free operation of market forces will lead to underprovision of public goods and merit goods. Governments spend to ensure the provision of these, and by doing so it is argued that they will improve the allocation of resources.

Redistribution of Income

Government expenditure is often aimed at creating a more equal distribution of income. Again, the free operation of market forces will encourage inequality in the distribution of income and wealth and by providing pensions to retired persons or by subsidising the consumption of certain goods the government aims to redistribute income.

Stabilisation

Since 1945 government's have actively persued certain economic aims (see p. 353). To achieve these aims, they have sometimes increased their own spending on goods and services with a view to increasing the level of aggregate demand in the economy.

Balanced distribution of industry

As part of their regional policy governments offer grants aimed at encouraging firms to move to certain parts of the country in preference to others. As an incentive governments offer grants to firms which locate in certain assisted areas.

Public Corporations

Some public corporations such as the BBC receive government funding as a matter of course, but those set up to administer the nationalised industries also qualify for government funding when they run at a loss. In the 1970s losses associated with the nationalised industries ran into hundreds of millions of pounds and although losses are certainly lower in the 1990s they have still occurred. When a nationalised industry runs at a loss, consumers of its product effectively receive a subsidy from the Exchequer.

Why do Governments Levy Taxes?

The most obvious answer to this question is 'to provide revenue for the government'. However, economists are also interested in the deeper question of *why* governments require revenue. There are *three* main reasons for taxation.

Allocation

Historically, this is the oldest reason for taxation. If, in ancient Egypt, a Pharaoh wished to build a pyramid, then he would levy a tax and *allocate* the sums raised towards pyramid building. Today, revenue is raised for spending on all sorts of things: education, defence, health, social services, and many others. The government also uses the tax system to modify the operation of the market. In particular, demerit goods can be taxed to correct market failure. This aspect of taxation is therefore concerned with allocation.

Distribution

The distribution of income and wealth depends on a number of factors, some of which were discussed in Chapter 17. The tax system can be used by a government to make adjustments in order to correct to some extent what might be seen as deficiencies in the distribution of income and wealth. Ever since the time of Adam Smith, over two centuries ago, people have been discussing ways of making the tax system more equitable. However, it was only around 1900 that governments began seriously to consider using public finance to help redistribute incomes.

Stabilisation

This is the most recent purpose of taxation. Many economists believe that taxes can be used as a tool, or instrument, of economic policy, and this is due largely to the work of Keynes in the 1930s. Macroeconomic objectives, as we shall see in Chapter 36, include stable prices, full employment, steady growth and equilibrium in the balance of payments and exchange rates. There is, at present, some debate between Keynesians and monetarists over whether the tax system can, or should be, used to control the economy by influencing aggregate demand.

These three purposes of taxation are interlinked. Any tax will have effects on allocation, distribution and stabilisation, and some taxes are more efficient than others at achieving any one of these three aims. It could be argued, for example, that if it is believed that inflation is caused by excess demand, then an increase in income tax would be more efficient than an increase in VAT. This is because income tax affects disposable income and therefore has a clear effect on aggregate demand, whereas VAT has the immediate effect of increasing retail prices, which increases the cost of living and may help cause a wage–price spiral, thus exacerbating the problem of inflation.

The Budget

The Budget is the annual occasion when the Chancellor of the Exchequer presents his plans for raising revenue for the year ahead to Parliament. The Budget proposals are given legal force in the Finance Act. The Budget is *balanced* when revenue is expected just to cover expenditure. A *Budget surplus* implies that revenue exceeds expenditure and a *Budget deficit* implies that expenditure exceeds revenue. Although there have been two occasions in recent years (1988–99 and 1989–90) when a Budget surplus has been achieved, in general there is a Budget deficit. The tax revenues raised in 1990–91 are shown in Table 35.1

The way in which this is financed has attracted attention in recent years. Clearly if the government

Table 35.1 *Tax revenues raised, 1990–1*

	Government Revenue (£m) 1990–91 forecast	
Inland Revenue		
Income tax	55.0	
Corporation tax	20.7	
Petroleum tax	1.1	
Capital Gains tax	2.1	
Inheritance tax	1.2	
Stamp duty	1.9	
Total Inland Revenue		81.9
Customs and Excise		
VAT	32.1	
Petrol etc	9.7	
Tabacco	5.4	
Alcohol	4.9	
Betting	1.0	
Car Tax	1.5	
Customs duties	1.9	
Agriculture	0.1	
Total Customs		56.7
Vehicle duties	3.0	
Oil royalties	0.7	
Rates	12.2	
Others	4.4	
Total taxes		159
National Insurance	35.9	
Community charge	11.2	
Interest	6.4	
Trading Surplus	3.0	
other receipts	3.1	
Total receipts		218.6

Source: Treasury 1990

spends more than it takes in revenue the difference must be made good by borrowing. Borrowing to finance a Budget deficit is the main component of the *Public Sector Borrowing Requirement* (PSBR) and, as we have seen in Chapter 24, government borrowing involves the issue of securities. If the government issues Treasury bills and these are bought by the monetary sector, this may have a serious impact on the growth of the money supply because there will be an increase in the liquidity of the financial intermediaries buying Treasury bills, and this will create the potential for them to expand their lending.

The National Debt

The *National Debt* is the **total amount of outstanding government debt**. In 1990 National Debt stood at £200,000m. At present there seems little chance that this debt will ever be repaid and there is sometimes some discussion of the possible *burden* this imposes on the community. It is sometimes alleged that there is a burden imposed on the present generation who pay taxes to finance interest payments to holders of the debt by the previous generation, who benefited from government spending which was financed by borrowing. In other words, it is sometimes argued that one generation passes on the burden of meeting repayments on a debt, which the previous generation incurred, to a future generation.

In fact, a moment's reflection will show that this argument is unsound. The generation who pay taxes to meet interest payments on the debt is the *same generation* which receives those interest payments. Rather than a burden being imposed on the community there is simply a redistribution of income *within* the community. In this sense, no burden is imposed on one generation by a previous one.

However, what if the holders of the National Debt are not residents of the UK? Overseas residents, as well as domestic resident, hold government debt. In this case, there is something of a burden imposed on the present generation by a previous one. When the debt was incurred, the UK was able to finance a balance of payments deficit by borrowing abroad. The generation which borrowed abroad was therefore able to consume more than it produced, the difference consisting of the excess of imports over exports. However, the present generation is taxed to meet repayments on the debt, but receives no interest because this is paid overseas. In this sense, the National Debt does represent a burden. Nevertheless only about 10 per cent of the National Debt is held abroad and therefore, in the main, tax payments and interest receipts from debt holdings are simply a redistribution of income.

Classification of Taxes

In the main, economists distinguish between *direct taxes* and *indirect taxes*. We consider each in turn.

Direct Taxes

These are taxes on **income**. The principal examples are *Personal Income Tax* (a tax on the income of individuals, which in the UK is collected by HM Board of Inland Revenue); *National Insurance Contributions* (which are used to pay for the NHS, state pensions, and other welfare benefits, and are in effect an additional tax on personal incomes); and *Corporation Tax* (a tax on the income, or profits, of companies).

Indirect Taxes

Indirect taxes are taxes on **expenditure**. In the UK they are collected by HM Customs and Excise. The principal examples are Value Added Tax (VAT) and excise duties, such as those levied on alcohol, tobacco and petrol. Indirect taxes are taxes can be *general* or *specific*. VAT is described as a *general* tax as it is levied on a wide range of goods and services (although there are important exceptions, such as books, children's clothing and fresh food which at present are *zero-rated*). A *specific* (or selective) tax is levied on certain commodities only – for instance, the duty on petrol. Note that usually the selective tax is *additional* to the general tax, so that people buying petrol pay both VAT and Petrol Duty.

Indirect taxes can also be *flat-rate* or *ad valorem* (percentage of value). A flat-rate tax is imposed as an absolute sum of each unit sold; an example would occur if a tax of 50p were imposed on a bottle of wine, whatever the price of the bottle. If, however, a tax of 15 per cent on the price of the bottle were imposed, then this would be described as an *ad valorem* tax, and the amount of tax paid would increase as price increases. VAT is an important example of an *ad valorem* tax.

Since indirect taxes will affect the retail price of the commodities on which they are imposed, they can have a strong effect on the allocation of resources by affecting the pattern of consumer demand.

The distinction between *direct* and *indirect* taxes is not always clear-cut, and can lead to some disagreement among economists; however, there is one important respect in which they differ: the *incidence* of indirect taxes can be transferred, while the *impact* of direct taxes cannot be separated from their incidence. We explain fully what this means on p. 344.

The Principles of Taxation

During the introduction of the Poll Tax there was much debate about the advantages and disadvantages of such a tax. Adam Smith's *canons of taxation* were first written down over two centuries ago, but they are still used today to provide criteria against which taxes can be judged, although it is necessary to supplement the canons to take account of changes in society and the role of the government in the modern economy.

Few economists would disagree with the proposition that a tax should be: *convenient, certain, cost-effective, equitable and supportive of government policy*. The first four of these correspond closely to Adam Smith's canons, and the fifth is a post-Keynesian addition. Let us look at each of these five criteria in turn.

Convenience

The business of paying taxes should be as painless and trouble-free as possible, from the point of view of the taxpayer. Britain's Pay As You Earn system certainly meets this requirement. Income Tax is deducted by the employer so that the employee receives income *net of tax* – that is, after tax has been deducted. Before the introduction of PAYE, people received a bill for tax and sent a payment to the tax collector every six months. This was obviously less convenient that PAYE, and had the added disadvantage that some people found it difficult to resist the temptation to spend the money that they should have been putting aside to meet this liability.

VAT, like other indirect taxes, is another convenient tax, from the point of view of the member of the public as a *taxpayer*. However, retailers and other business people who have to keep detailed VAT accounts might have a different point of view.

Certainty

The taxpayer should have some knowledge, in advance, of his or her liability for tax. It follows that the tax regulations should be as straightforward and easily understood as possible. On the whole, most people find the income tax system fairly easy to understand, provided that there is nothing too unusual about their personal circumstances. People who wish to claim special tax allowances, or who are self-employed, often find it economic to employ an accountant to guide them through the tax laws.

Corporation Tax has a certain amount of uncertainty, mainly because profits by their very nature are unpredictable, and there is not much that anyone can do to alter this fact of life.

Cost-effectiveness

A tax should produce revenue efficiently, without too much of the proceeds being swallowed up by the administrative costs of collection. Personal Income Tax and VAT appear to meet this requirement: it has been estimated that their collection costs amount to somewhere in the region of 1p in the pound, with income taxes slightly more expensive to collect than VAT. These taxes are therefore quite cost-effective.

Equity

'Equity' is concerned with the *fairness* of the tax system. Unfortunately, it is not always easy to define 'fair', but many people would agree that equity implies that taxpayers should make similar sacrifices. In order to try to ensure that people make similar sacrifices, two situations can be identified: *horizontal equity* and *vertical equity*.

Horizontal Equity

This is to do with the treatment of people in similar financial positions. The principle is that people in similar circumstances who have similar finances should pay similar amounts of tax. In order to achieve horizontal equity it is necessary to decide on two things: first, *what* is to be taxed and secondly, *who* is to be taxed? In other words, to achieve horizontal equity it is necessary to group activities together to decide on a *tax base* and individuals together to form a *tax-paying unit*.

The tax base is the activity which is to be taxed. Earning is a taxable activity (for income tax), and so is spending (for VAT). Owning a car is an activity which exposes the motorist to an array of taxes, and in some countries wealth is taxed.

The tax-paying unit refers to the person or other legal entity liable for tax. The government might tax individuals, married couples, families, households, companies, or other institutions. Income tax has traditionally been assessed on couples, but changes in income tax law and the introduction of the Council Tax suggest that the trend today is towards individual taxation.

Figure 35.1 *Vertical equity*

	TAX PAID BY A PERSON EARNING: (per time period)					
	£100		£1000		£10,000	
	Amount (£)	(%)	Amount (£)	(%)	Amount (£)	(%)
Regressive Tax (e.g., poll tax of £10)	10	10	10	1.0	10	0.1
Proportional Tax (e.g., a contribution of 10% of income)	10	10	100	10	1000	10
Progressive Tax (e.g., an Income Tax with average rates of 10, 20 and 50%)	10	10	200	20	5000	50

Vertical Equity

Vertical equity is to do with the treatment of people in different financial circumstances. Figure 35.1 shows some of the alternative ways of attempting to achieved vertical equity in the taxation of personal incomes.

There is general agreement among economists that taxes should be based on the *ability to pay*. They reach this conclusion by reference to the *law of diminishing marginal utility* (see p. 51). Incomes give us the power to purchase goods and services, and as we increase our consumption total utility rises, but marginal utility falls. The marginal utility of a pound's worth of spending power sacrificed by a high income earner is therefore less than the marginal utility lost by a low income earner when a pound is taken away in tax. This implies that for the similarity of sacrifice which was mentioned earlier to be achieved, taxes should be *progressive* (they should take an increasing proportion of income as income rises). However, there is considerable debate about the *degree* of progression that is desirable. We consider some of these arguments later in this chapter.

Support of Government Policy

As discussed on p. 353, government policy has a range of microeconomic and macroeconomic aims. As far as possible, taxes should support these aims. If, for example, the government wishes to encourage saving, then it might be argued that income tax should be reduced (to increase disposable income) and VAT should be increased (to reduce the fraction of that disposable income which is spent, and therefore increase saving). Obviously, there is plenty of scope for disagreement among economists over whether particular courses of action will have the predicted effect, but one of the *aims* of a tax should be to support the government's economic policy.

Income Tax in the UK

The Rate of Tax

In the UK, the amount of tax paid on a given level of income depends on two factors: *tax allowances* and *tax rates*. An allowance is a sum of money which a person is allowed to earn free of tax; the tax rate is the percentage of taxable income which is deducted by the government.

Every year, usually in March, the Chancellor of the Exchequer makes his annual *Budget Statement*. The Chancellor usually announces any new tax laws or amendments to existing legislation on this occasion, and also announces tax allowances and tax rates for the following year. Figure 35.2 shows the tax allowances and tax rates announced in the 1989 Budget.

In addition to the personal allowances shown, a person might receive additional allowances for such things as essential clothing or equipment required for work.

There is an important difference between the marginal rate of tax and the average rate of tax. The marginal rate of tax increases in steps which are known as tax bands or brackets, for example, in 1989/90, the single person's tax allowance was £2785 and up to this point income is taxed at a marginal rate of 0 per cent. If he or she earns £5001 he or she moves into the 25 per cent tax band. This does *not* mean that the *whole* of the £5001 is taxed at the higher rate, only the *marginal* (extra) pound. Similarly, when he or she earns £25,701 or more he or she pays tax at a marginal rate of 40 per cent, but only on each extra pound earned. It follows from this that the average rate of tax rises much more smoothly, not in steps, and is *always* lower than the marginal rate.

Although the UK system of income tax is a progressive system, the degree of progression has been reduced in recent years. In 1979 the highest marginal rate was 83 per cent, currently it is only 40 per cent.

The Effects of Income Tax

Redistribution effect: An important consequence of having a progressive income tax is that it *redistributes* incomes from the better off to the less well off members of society. This effect is obvious if, on the one hand, the rich pay more tax while the poor receive transfer payments (welfare benefits transferred by the government from the taxpayer to the recipient). However, it is important to realise that it is not necessary for a cash payment to the poor to be paid in order for a redistribution of income to take place. This is because all of us, rich or poor, receive benefits in *kind* from the government: we can all benefit from public and merit goods such as the NHS and public education. It is possible to put a monetary value on these benefits in kind (economists sometimes refer to this as the *social wage*). If high income earners benefit from the social wage to the same extent as low income earners, and at the same time contribute a higher proportion of their earnings to the Exchequer, then in effect there has been a redistribution of incomes even though no cash has necessarily been transferred from one group to another. If, of course, we superimpose a system of cash benefits on top of the progressive tax system, then we increase the redistributive effects.

Disincentive effect: It is argued that high marginal rates of income tax, by taking a larger proportion of any additional income received, can cause a *disincentive effect* in various ways. They may discourage people who are on social security from seeking work, or those in work from working longer hours, or seeking promotion to more responsible positions. Young people may be discouraged from studying to achieve higher qualifications, and those with qualifications may be encouraged to join the 'brain drain', taking their talents out this country to places where tax rates are lower.

Tax avoidance effect. Another symptom of the disincentive effect is possibly the grow of *tax avoidance* (which should be distinguished from tax evasion, which is illegal). Tax avoidance involves the use of lawyers and accountants to find loopholes in the tax laws to reduce tax burdens, and it would clearly be an unhealthy state of affairs for a tax system to encourage this to become a growth industry.

The Poverty Trap Effect

There is perhaps more general agreement among economists about the possibility that the tax and benefit system can produce a disincentive effect in the form of a *poverty trap*. It is argued that people who are unemployed or are employed on a low incomes face, in effect, abnormally high marginal rates of tax. This is because when an unemployed worker starts earning, or when a low paid worker obtains a job with a slightly higher wage rate, these people rapidly lose welfare benefits, such as cash

Figure 35.2 *Personal allowances and income tax rates, UK, 1989–90*

Personal allowances 1989/90

		£
Married man		4,375
Single person		2,785
Wife's earned income relief		2,785
Additional personal allowance		1,590
Age allowance		
– single or widowed person	(age 65–74)	3,400
– married couple	(age 65–74)	5,385
– single or widowed person	(age 75 and over)	3,540
– married couple	(age 75 and over)	5,565
– income limit for age allowance		11,400
Widow's bereavement allowance		1,590
Relief for blind person (each)		540

Income Tax rates 1989/90
Rates of tax applying to all income:

Band of taxable income £	Rate of tax %	Tax on band £	Cumulative tax £
0–20,700	25	5,175	5,174
over 20,700	40		

The PAYE tables will give effect to these changes on the first pay date after 17 May 1989.

Source: HM Treasury

Figure 35.3 *Tax/benefit changes and the poverty and unemployment traps (married man with job and two children)*

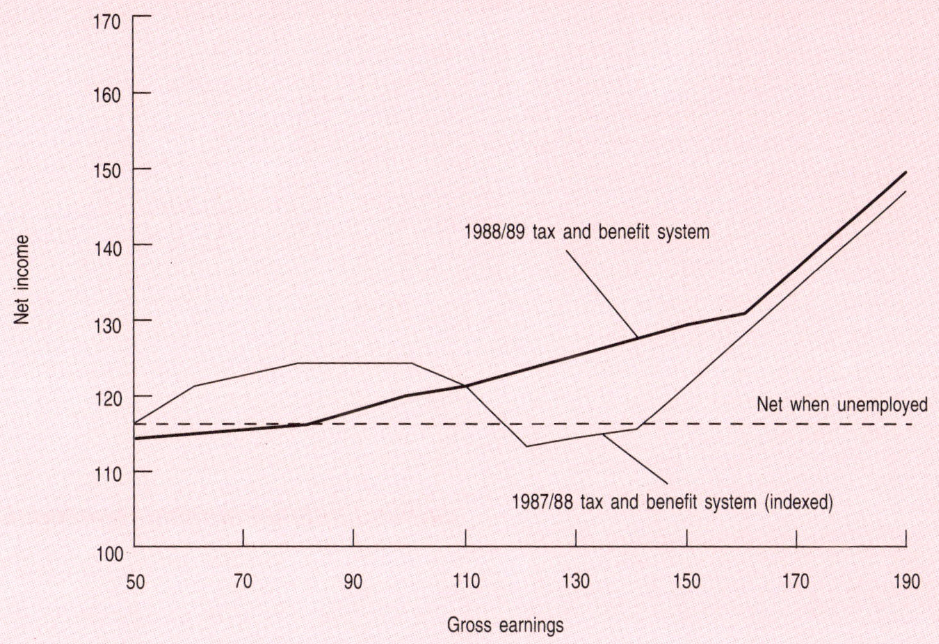

Source: Fiscal Studies

support, assistance with housing costs, or benefits in kind such as help with children's clothing or free school meals. Thus, a pound earned in extra gross income can be worth much less than a pound in its net effect: in certain circumstances families have been known to be *worse off* with a breadwinner in work than out of work, and people obtaining jobs with a higher gross pay have found themselves suffering a fall in disposable income. Figure 35.3 shows how at some salary levels an increase in gross income can lead to a fall in net income, when state benefits are lost.

A poverty trap means that instead of acting as a platform upon which the less well off can build, the tax and benefit system presents a ceiling above which they cannot rise. Some economists and politicians have a simple solution: reduce state benefits.

The graph in Figure 35.3 suggests that the poverty trap in Britain was reduced to some extent by the Social Security Review of 1988, but it can be argued that this was achieved by lowering the real value of assistance to the very poor, rather than by assisting all the lower paid to improve their earning positions.

Some Less Well-known Taxes

Whereas most people come into contact with Income Tax and VAT, there are some taxes which affect a relatively small percentage of the population.

Capital Gains Tax (CGT)

This is a tax on the difference between the price at which certain assets are bought and the price at which they are sold. These assets include such things as stocks and shares, but exclude such things as a family house. There is an exemption limit (which with effect from 6 April 1989 was £6000). This means that gains arising from the selling of an asset will not be taxed unless the gain exceeds £6000. The tax is progressive, with two bands, at 25 per cent and 40 per cent. The justification for having such a tax is that a capital gain increases the *spending power* of an individual in much the same way as an increase in income, and therefore, in order to achieve horizontal equity, it should be taxed.

Inheritance Tax

This is a tax levied on the value of the estate of a deceased person. The threshold below which no tax was payable following the 1989 Budget stood at £118,000. The rate of tax is currently 40 per cent. Before 1986 this tax was known as Capital Transfer Tax, which was really a more accurate description, since it is also levied on lifetime gifts (although at a lower rate of 20 per cent).

Although it was earlier suggested that most people will go through their lives unaffected by Capital Gains Tax and Inheritance Tax it is worth bearing in mind that this assertion may well be proved false by social and economic trends, such as the encouragement of wider share ownership, and the effect on the value of legacies of rising house prices.

The Impact and Incidence of Indirect Taxes

The *impact* of a tax is on the person legally responsible for paying money over to the tax collecting authority. The *incidence* of a tax is on the person who suffers a loss in real income as a result of the tax. (Some economists prefer to use the terms *formal incidence and effective incidence*, but the basis of the distinction is the same.) With direct taxes, such as income tax, it is clear that the impact and incidence are upon the same person: generally, there is (unfortunately) no known method of transferring the burden of our income tax onto some other person. The possibility cannot be entirely ruled out, but it would not be regarded as normal. However, with direct taxes, it is not just possible but probable that at least part of the burden will be transferred. If, for example, the government imposes an indirect tax on *producers*, they can attempt to transfer the incidence of the tax to *consumers*, by raising price. Consumers, on the other hand, can attempt to force producers to accept a lower revenue than desired by preventing them from passing on the full incidence of the tax to consumers.

Figure 35.4 shows how supply and demand theory can be applied in order to illustrate this.

The starting position is shown by the intersection of the supply curve S and the demand curve D at point E, with a starting price of P_E and a quantity demand and supplied of Q_E.

The government imposes a flat-rate tax of t pence per unit on the production of the commodity, thus putting the *impact* on producers. From the producer's

Figure 35.4 *Impact and incidence of taxation*

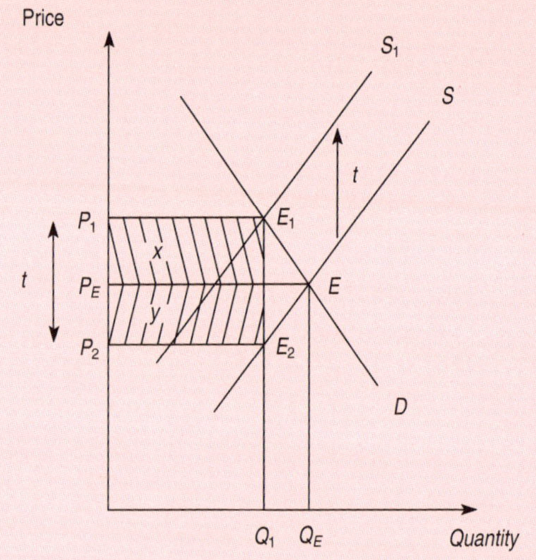

point of view this is equivalent to an increase in costs; the supply curve therefore shifts to the left, indicating that at each and every price the suppliers are less willing to supply than before the tax. The vertical distance between the two supply curves S and S_1 is t; the new equilibrium point is E_1, and the new market price is P_1, with a quantity demanded and supplied of Q_1. However, the revenue received by producers for each good sold, has fallen to P_2.

In Figure 35.4 the hatched area x represents the consumers' share of the tax, and the hatched area y represents the producers' share, with $x + y$ being the total tax revenue to the government.

It is important to note that the way in which the incidence of a tax is distributed between producers and consumers depends, at least in part, on the price elasticities of demand and supply for the product. If the consumers have a low elasticity of demand, then they are likely to be in a weak position *vis à vis* the producers. A low elasticity of demand is likely to mean that consumers regard this good as having few substitutes, and makes them more likely to carry on consuming after substantial price increases – this enables producers to pass on the incidence of tax in the form of higher shop prices. A low elasticity of supply, on the other hand, puts producers in a weak position compared with consumers, because it means that producers have little control over their output: whatever the change in market price they have to produce more or less the same quantity as before, at least in the short run. This means that if consumers resist an attempted price increase, the producers may well be forced to bring prices down again, accepting a lower revenue per good rather than be left with unsold goods.

By careful inspection of Figure 35.4 it can be seen that the relative sizes of areas x and y depend upon the gradients of the demand curve D and supply curve S. If, for example, we were to reduce the gradient of D, making it less elastic at each price, then area x (the consumers' share of tax) would increase. If the demand curve were vertical (perfectly inelastic), then consumers would pay all of the tax.

We can state mathematically that the consumers' share of the tax, Tcs, is inversely proportional to the elasticity of demand Ed, or

$$Tcs = k/Ed \text{ (where } k \text{ is constant), and therefore}$$
$$k = Ed.\ Tcs \qquad (1)$$

Similarly, the producers' share of the tax, Tps, is inversely proportional to the elasticity of supply, Es, or

$$Tps = k/Es, \text{ and therefore}$$
$$k = Es.Tps \qquad (2)$$

Combining equations (1) and (2) we have

$$Ed.\ Tcs = Es.Tps$$

or

$$Tcs/Tps = Es/Ed$$

Thus it is the ratio of elasticity of supply to elasticity of demand which is important in determining incidence, the group with the lower elasticity paying the greater share of the tax (the word 'lower' here ignores the fact that elasticities of demand are strictly speaking negative: we are treating all elasticities as being positive numbers).

When following the news after Budget Day, it is often possible to see this process happening in practice. The Chancellor may, for instance, increase the tax on petrol; suppliers will attempt to pass on all or most of the tax by increasing prices at the pump. In the short run, the petroleum industry is likely to have a low elasticity of supply; it is difficult to switch oil wells and petrol refineries on and off at will. If consumers can resist this price increase by refusing to buy (if they have a fairly high elasticity of demand), then after a while prices will fall, but probably not to their original level. The incidence is therefore shared by producers and consumers, the final share out depending on the *ratio* between the elasticities of demand and supply (at least in *part*, remembering that in the real world there may be other influences on price, besides simple supply and demand relationships, such as the interaction between members of an oligopolistic market).

Direct Taxes Versus Indirect Taxes

During the first few years of the Thatcher government, the beginning of a year-by-year attempt to reduce direct taxation was accompanied by a large increase in VAT to a single rate of 15 per cent. There has therefore been a shift in emphasis away from direct taxes in favour of indirect taxes. What are the consequences of this shift? What we are actually asking here, in effect, is whether or not we wish to accept the consequences of making the tax system *less progressive*.

Arguments in Favour of Indirect Taxes

Compared with direct taxes, indirect taxes leave the taxpayer with **more of his or her income intact**, and give the taxpayer more choice in spending this disposable income. The taxpayer is not taxed until he or she decides to spend. This arguably encourages saving.

There are fewer of the **disincentive effects** which are discussed and in Box 35.2 on p. 351.

There is a **reduced need for tax allowances**, which have been criticised for being arbitrary and distorting market forces. It could be argued, for example, that the income tax concessions given in the UK to house-buyers have caused resources which might have been devoted to manufacturing or exporting to be diverted towards house-building. It is also often said that direct taxes are more likely than indirect taxes to be discriminatory. The UK tax system, for instance, has been accused of discriminating in favour of married men and against other groups.

On the other hand, some indirect taxes can also be seen to be arbitrary. Some EC countries, for example, impose VAT on food, whereas Britain does not.

Arguments in Favour of Direct Taxes

These are related to the ability to pay, whereas indirect taxes tend to be **regressive**. Most economists would probably regard this argument as overwhelming, and are unlikely to be persuaded that it is outweighed by any number of disadvantages. There is room for debate about the *degree* of progressiveness, but not on the *principle* of progression. Economic theory tells us that economic rent can be taxed without any disincentive effect on the supply of labour, but the difficulty, of course, is in identifying economic rent and applying tax at a suitable rate (see p. 151).

There is an **automatic redistribution of income** from the better off to the less well off (and as we have seen, there is no need for any cash transfer in order to achieve this).

Direct taxes are an efficient method of **stabilising** the economy, as they have a clear effect on people's disposable income. While it is possible that the rates of indirect taxes can be varied more rapidly than those of direct taxes, there might be circumstances, as discussed on p. 341, where the use of indirect taxes to stabilise the economy would be inappropriate. While monetarists tend to reject the idea of using taxes of any description for stabilisation purposes, critics of the economic policies of the Conservative government in the late 1980s and early 1990s might argue that many problems arose from its refusal to use income tax increases to control aggregate demand, preferring to rely on high interest rates instead. Thus the CBI, for example, stated that it would have preferred lower interest rates to encourage investment by firms, accompanied by higher personal taxes to discourage consumer demand, especially for imported goods.

Box 35.1 Public spending in the UK

Public spending is a sizeable portion of the British economy: total public spending amounts to about 40 per cent of national income. It covers expenditure on social security benefits, on the National Health Service, on defence, on education, on law and order, on the environment, and on a range of other programmes.

The Government's objective for total public spending is that it should, over time, take a declining share of national income, thus allowing scope for reducing the burden of taxation. The Government is continually looking for improvements in value for money in public spending, so that the quality of public services can be improved while the total cost is reduced.

General government expenditure 1990–91†	£billion
Public expenditure planning total	**180½**
Local authorities self-financed expenditure	14½
Central government debt interest	17½
Other adjustments	3½
General government expenditure	**216**
Privatisation proceeds	−5½
General government expenditure excluding privatisation proceeds	**221½**

†General government expenditure and the planning total are both measured net of certain receipts. Most receipts, eg. taxes, are treated as revenue but certain fees and charges are treated as negative public expenditure

Source: *Financial Statement and Budget Report 1991–92*, March 1991

Measures of public spending

There are several ways of measuring public spending. A broad measure is *general government expenditure (GGE)*. This covers spending by both central and local government, but excludes transfers between them, such as central government grants to local authorities. It includes money the government makes available to nationalised industries and other public corporations, and the interest the government pays on its own outstanding debt. It also includes the proceeds of privatising public concerns.

This is the measure used in the Government's Medium Term Financial Strategy (MTFS) published each year with the Budget. The MTFS sets the Government's public spending plans in the context of the economy as a whole and the revenues available to finance them. For some purposes, including setting the Government's objective of reducing the share of public spending as a proportion of national income, it is preferable to focus on *GGE excluding privatisation proceeds*. The latest estimate of this total in the financial year which has just ended (from 1 April 1990 to 31 March 1991) is £221½ billion. this was just over 40 per cent of the UK's gross domestic product (GDP) – the total value of all the goods and services produced in a year by the nation as a whole. This ratio fell by 7 percentage points between 1982–83 and 1990–91. It is projected to rise a little in 1991–92, but a downward trend is expected to resume the following year.

Not all public spending is susceptible to direct control by the Government, for instance that part of local authorities' spending which they finance from their own income, or debt interest. The Government therefore also defines a narrower measure known as the *planning total* which excludes such items. This is the aggregate on which the Government focuses in setting its future spending plans. In 1990–91 it is £180½ billion.

The table on page 346 shows the size of all these totals in 1990–91.

There are various ways of looking at public spending. It is interesting to look at who plans it, who spends it, what it is spent on and what impact it has. The chart on the following page shows public spending broken down in these four different ways.

Who plans it – spending by government department

By far the biggest programme is that of the Department of Social Security, with a quarter of the total in 1990–91. This is mostly spending on pensions and other social security benefits. Three other large programmes each account for around 10 per cent of the total. These are spending by the Department of Health, mainly on the National Health Service in England; by the Ministry of Defence, including the armed forces; and by the Department of the Environment, including grants to local authorities in England.

Who spends it – spending by sector

As the second column in chart 1 on the following page shows, over 70 per cent of GGE is spent by *central government* itself; that is, by government departments like the Department of Social Security, and by public bodies such as regional health authorities, and the armed forces.

Local authorities accounted for just over a quarter of general government expenditure in 1990–91. Around 40 per cent of their day-to-day spending is on education. But significant amounts are also spent on housing, personal social services (eg. meals on wheels), law and order and protective services, environmental services (eg. refuse collection) and transport.

The public sector also covers public corporations, including nationalised industries, but their expenditure doesn't come within the definition of GGE. Public corporations generate most of their income from trading activities, but may also receive support from central government. Only government grants and loans to public corporations count towards GGE. (The planning total also includes their borrowing from the private sector, and hence all their finance from outside business.) Nationalised industries are subject to annual reviews, both of the programmes of investment they undertake and of their financing in general.

What it is spent on – expenditure by function

This analysis draws together all public spending in a particular field, such as health or education, irrespective of the body actually spending the money. Health spending, for instance, is undertaken not only by the Department of Health in England, but also by the Scottish, Welsh, and Northern Ireland Offices. And local authorities, as well as the Department of Education and Science and other departments, spend money on education. The third column of chart 1 shows that social security spending accounted for rather over a quarter of GGE excluding privatisation proceeds in 1990–91, education and health about 12½ per cent and defence about 10 per cent.

What impact it has – spending by economic category

The economic impact of public spending varies according to its economic category. About 30 per cent of GGE takes the form of *current grants to persons*. These are mainly transfers to individuals, such as pensions, social security benefits and student grants, amounting to about £68 billion in 1990–91. Nearly half, about £104 billion, is made up of *public sector pay* and *other current spending*, Of this, just under two thirds is taken up by the pay of some 5 million people employed by central government and local authorities. *Net capital spending* on purchases of assets, goods and services, buying ambulances and equipment for the police, investment in hospitals and roads and so on – takes up about 5 per cent of GGE, or £12 billion. This figure is net of the proceeds of sales

CHART 1: THE PLANNING TOTAL AND GENERAL GOVERNMENT EXPENDITURE: HOW IT IS PLANNED AND SPENT, 1990–91

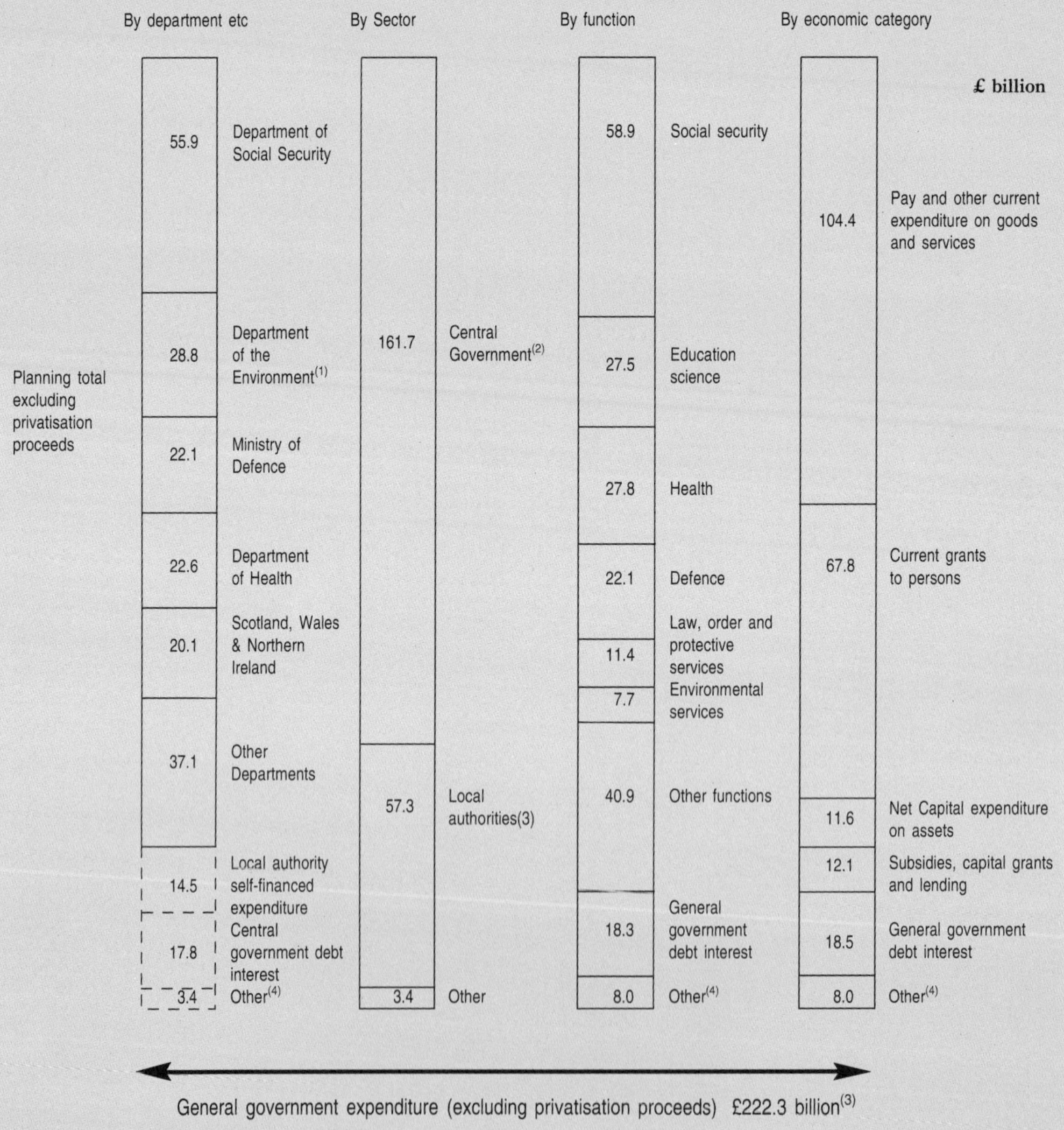

(1) Includes revenue support grant and non-domestic rate payments and certain transitional grants to local authorities in England. Comparable items are included in the figures for Scotland and Wales

(2) Includes grants, subsidies and net lending to public corporations, including nationalised industries, of £3.7 billion. It also includes central government debt interest (£17.8 billion)

(3) The total is made up of £42.7 billion financed by support from central government and £14.5 billion financed from local authorities' own resources. It includes local authority debt interest (£5.2 billion)

(4) Includes the national accounts adjustments. The differences in these figures reflect the different treatment of local authority debt interest and market and overseas borrowing of public corporations in the analyses of GGE by function and economic category

(5) The figures in this table are based on detailed estimates of spending in 1990–91 published in February this year. They differ slightly from the latter estimates quoted in table 1

Source: *Statistical Supplement to the Autumn Statement*, February 1991 by central government and local authorities of capital assets, such as land or buildings: so the total gross contribution of the public sector to increasing the nation's stock of physical assets is much greater – it was about £30 billion in 1990–91. The rest of GGE comprises transfers to the corporate sector, such as grants to private sector companies and nationalised industries; and debt interest payments.

The public expenditure survey

Public spending is planned through an annual review known as the "public expenditure survey". In the survey the government reviews its existing plans for the two coming years, and draws up new plans for the following year. In the 1991 survey, which has just started, last year's plans for 1992–93 and 1993–94 will be reviewed and a plan for 1994–95 will be formulated for the first time.

The Minister in charge of public spending is the Chief Secretary to the Treasury. Like the Chancellor he is a member of the Cabinet.

The starting point for the annual survey is the set of cash plans agreed the previous year. In the spring and summer Ministers of spending departments review their programmes and consider whether they wish to make changes in priorities. they also need to consider whether the cost of existing policies will have changed – for example, if forecasts of inflation or unemployment have changed, this will affect spending on social security payments. The Treasury, meanwhile, will also consider whether it has any changes to propose to departments, and will discuss these with the departments concerned.

In early summer, Ministers write to the Chief Secretary setting out their proposals for changes from previous plans. The Treasury scrutinises these proposals and holds detailed discussions with departments. In particular it looks at the reliability of departments' costings, what it is proposed that any extra money should achieve in terms of increased or better quality output, and whether there are more cost-effective ways of meeting departments' objectives.

In July, the Chief Secretary presents to the Cabinet an overall assessment of the outlook for public spending, taking account of proposals made by departments and of the latest assessment of economic prospects. The total of departments' bids often exceeds the government's assessment of the appropriate level for total public spending. The Cabinet then agrees broad objectives for the survey, and accordingly instructs the Chief Secretary to discuss with individual Ministers how to bring the new plans into line with these objectives.

To help local authorities plan their budgets for the coming financial year, the Secretaries of State for the Environment, Scotland, and Wales make statements in July or August on the amount of grant the government intends to make available to them, and on the government's assessment of what each authority needs to spend to achieve an adequate level of current services, known as total standard spending.

Detailed discussions begin in September between the Chief Secretary and spending Ministers. In these negotiations – the "bilaterals" – the Chief Secretary aims to settle levels of spending on individual programmes which are compatible with the Cabinet's objectives for total public spending.

The bilaterals usually run through September and early October. If spending Ministers and the Chief Secretary cannot reach agreement on a particular issue, it may be referred to the "Star Chamber", a small group of Ministers, chaired by a senior Cabinet Minister, for resolution.

The new plans are then put before Cabinet, which is the final arbiter for any unresolved issues. if they are approved, the way is then clear for the Chancellor to present the results in his Autumn Statement to Parliament, usually in November.

The Autumn Statement sets out the government's new spending plans for the three survey years, together with the latest information on public spending in the current financial year. It also gives the Treasury's latest forecast for the UK economy.

In the past this was followed by a public expenditure White Paper in January, in which the Treasury set out each department's plans in detail. From 1991, however, this has been replaced by a series of detailed reports by individual departments on their spending plans. At the same time, the Treasury publishes a supplement to the Autumn Statement which includes further detailed statistical analyses of the public spending plans.

Controlling public spending

Once the spending plans for the coming year have been agreed, a system of control is necessary to ensure that they are met and that the agreed total is not exceeded. To this end the planning total contains an unallocated *reserve* (£3½ billion for the current financial year, 1991–92, or about 1.7 per cent of the planning total). This allows for unforeseen contingencies to be financed without breaking the agreed planning total. Any increases in programmes have to be met from the reserve, and they have to be agreed by the Chief Secretary.

The primary instrument of control of individual spending programmes during the year is the setting of *cash limits*. A limit is set on the amount of cash that can be spent on a particular programme, regardless of unexpected fluctuations in costs. Cash limits are normally aligned with the annual Supply Estimates, by which Parliament grants authority to the Government to spend money. Of course spending on certain programmes, such as social security, is determined by demand, eg. the number of people claiming benefits; it would not be practicable to try to apply cash limits to these programmes.

Cash limits are intended to encourage efficient management and cost control. Once set the limits are changed only in exceptional circumstances. These is usually some underspending on cash limits – perhaps because departments treat them as ceilings on spending rather than targets. For capital expenditure, where the timing of spending can be difficult to manage precisely, departments are able to carry forward some underspending into the following year.

There are also separate controls on each department's spending on Civil Service *running costs*. Running costs limits fall within departmental cash limits. The main element of running costs is the pay bill but accommodation, personnel overheads and office service costs are also included. The method of control is similar to that provided by cash limits, and departments may, under certain conditions, carry forward into the following year underspending of up to 0.5 per cent of the running costs limit.

Source: *Economic Briefing* (May 1991)

Box 35.2

A method which economists use to consider the problem of the disincentive effect of taxes involves the concept of *demand for leisure*. This enables us to apply ideas with which we are familiar from demand theory (see p. 52). Figure 35.5 shows a framework which can be used to analyse an individuals choice between work and leisure. We assume a wage rate of £5 an hour and that initially no income tax is paid.

The budget line *MN* shows the different combinations of income and leisure which this person can choose; his or her tastes and preferences for leisure or income can be illustrated by indifference curves. Given his or her preferences he or she occupies the equilibrium position *E*, working a 10-hour day (having 14 hours leisure) and taking home £50.

Suppose the government now introduces an income tax of 20 per cent, so that the after-tax wage is now £4 per hour. The number of hours offered for work depends on the relative strength of the income effect compared with the substitution effect (which, in turn, depends on the extent to which the individual is willing to sacrifice leisure for income). These tastes and preferences affect the shape and position of the indifference curves on the indifference map. In our example, the individual has an incentive effect, and chooses to work for more hours; but it would be a simple matter to redraw the indifference map to demonstrate an *disincentive* effect, with the higher tax encouraging the individual to work shorter hours. This underlines the fact that economic theory is generally inconclusive with regard to the existence of the so-called disincentive effect.

Figure 35.5 *Choices between income and leisure*

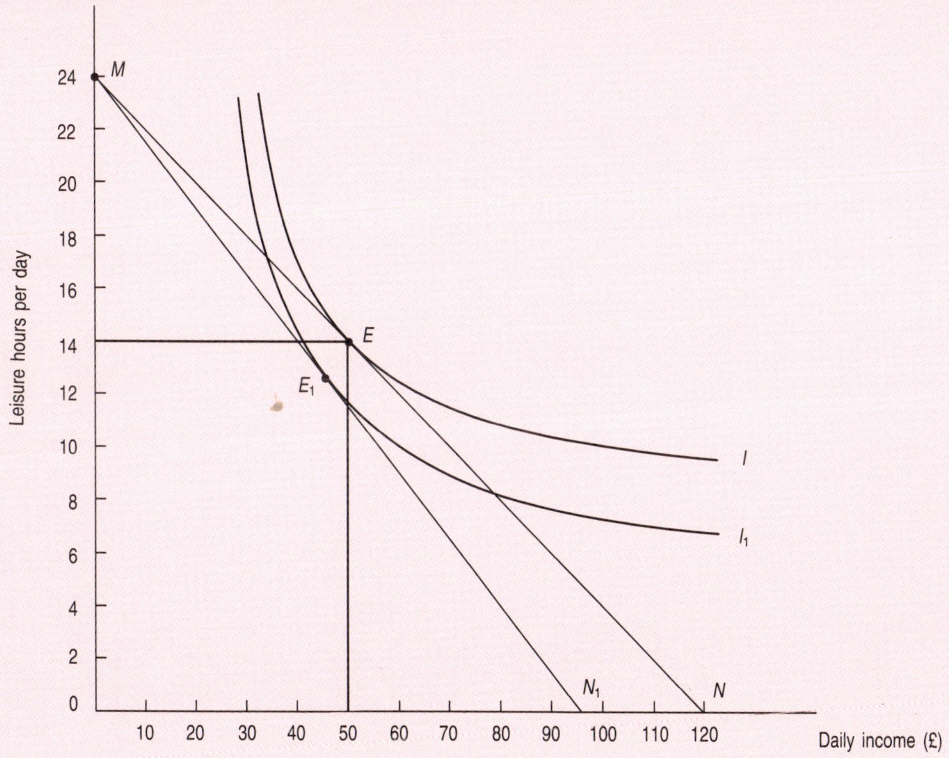

Following the tax the budget line changes from *MN* (point *N* at £120) to MN_1 (point N_1 at £96). The new equilibrium point E_1 shows a reduction in leisure hours.

REVIEW QUESTIONS

1 Summarise the arguments for and against the proposition that progressive taxes have disincentive effects.

2 What is the 'poverty trap'?

3 Using supply and demand curves, show how the incidence of an indirect tax is shared between producers and consumers when the *impact* **is initially on** *consumers*.

4 The UK tax system discriminates heavily against earned income, but leaves wealth relatively untouched. Why is this?

5 Is the National Debt a debt the nation owes itself?

6 How is the PSBR related to the Budget deficit?

CHAPTER 36

STABILISATION POLICY

CONNECTIONS

In Chapter 36 we examine the aims and methods of **Keynesian demand management techniques**. We shall refer to many of the concepts discussed in Chapters 18–22 which deal with the measurement and determination of income. We shall also be concerned with the rate of inflation, the level of unemployment and the state of the balance of payments.

Key Concepts

Aggregate demand management
Economic growth
Deflationary gap
Fiscal policy
Full employment
Incomes policy
Inflationary gap
Monetary policy

The Objectives of Stabilisation Policy

Stabilisation policy implies **stabilising the level of aggregate demand** to achieve certain macroeconomic objectives. These are usually classified as:

- a high and stable level of **employment**
- price **stability**
- equilibrium in the **balance of payments** with a stable **exchange rate**
- steady **economic growth** with improving **living standards.**

Some people would add a fifth objective: that of redistributing income and wealth to create **greater equality**. However, questions about the desirability of greater equality are more relevant to politicians than economists and we do not discuss this issue here. Let us briefly consider each of the policy objectives listed above in turn.

Employment

What constitutes a 'high and stable level of employment' is, of course, a matter of opinion. Nevertheless governments are concerned to ensure that a level of employment which is acceptable to the electorate is achieved. There are social reasons for this, but unemployment also represents an economic waste since unemployed workers could add to the amount of output available for consumption. In addition, we have seen in Chapter 28 that there is a short run trade off between inflation and unemployment and therefore to some extent any employment target is influenced by what constitutes an acceptable rate of inflation.

Price Stability

Similar problems exist in trying to define 'stable prices'. Does 'stable' mean an unchanging price level or does it mean the achievement of some average change in the price level achieved over some period of time? Again we know from Chapter 28 that there are wastes associated with inflation and therefore governments aim at an acceptable rate of inflation

Box 36.1 Recession deepens in the UK

In the United Kingdom, the recession deepened in the fourth quarter of 1990 with continuing falls in retail sales and manufacturing production. Unemployment rose by an average of nearly 60,000 in the three months to December, comparable with the average monthly rise during the recession of 1980/81. The weakness in demand has also been evident in the trade figures, reducing the monthly visible deficit from £1.8bn to less than £1bn in the fourth quarter.

The falling trend in retail sales has reflected a rise in the personal savings ratio – 8.8% in the third quarter, double the figure of two years earlier. A sustained shift to higher rates of saving and investment would be welcome, but the present rise probably reflects consumers' reaction to the surge in inflation and to reduced transactions in the housing market. In the meantime, weak consumer demand is contributing to recession. And with company finances under pressure, the consensus of recent forecasts is that the recessionary conditions which emerged last year are likely to persist into 1991.

Comparisons are inevitably drawn with the situation in the early 1980s. Although there are similarities, the major factors contributing to recession then are not present in the same degree now. That recession was associated with a loss of labour cost competitiveness of around 50% over 1978–1981; static world demand following the second oil shock; and a violent swing in the stock cycle, in part due to changes in the tax treatment of stock holding. Non-oil output fell by around 2% in each of two successive years. In 1991, the outlook is for a recession that is both shorter and less severe. Sterling's real appreciation against all currencies – and particularly the DM – has been much less than in the early 1980s; the world economy seems unlikely to slow as much as in the early 1980s; and the stock cycle should be a less significant factor. Nevertheless, either the situation in the Gulf or the pressures on the company sector, could prompt a sharper cutback than forecasts currently suggest.

Source: *Bank Briefing* (February 1991)

given that changes in the rate of inflation have implications for the level of employment. During the 1980s it was frequently alleged that the UK government's aim was a rate of inflation of zero per cent. However, governments are seldom so forthright in specifying a target rate of inflation.

Balance of Payments

We have already discussed the notion of balance of payments equilibrium in Chapter 32. 'Equilibrium' only can exist if autonomous credits equal autonomous debits. The problem is identifying the *time period* within which autonomous credits must equal autonomous debits.

Economic Growth

Economic growth occurs when a country increases its productive capacity and its national income. The *rate of increase* of the national income of a country provides a measure of how the standard of living of its people is changing although, as we argued in Chapter 18, there are a number of limitations on the usefulness of national income statistics in reflecting living standard: if Country *A* has twice the national income of Country *B*, this does not necessarily mean that the average citizen of *A* has twice the standard living of a counterpart living in *B*. Similarly, economic growth rates do not *necessarily* indicate improvements in living standards. Economists increasingly stress the *costs* associated with growth (pollution, social stress, and so on) that can outweigh the benefits. Indeed, the costs of economic growth are coming under increasing scrutiny and there is growing public concern over the environment and the depletion of natural resources. Nevertheless, governments recognise that if a high and stable level of employment is to be achieved, if an adequate supply of goods and services is to be produced, and if demands for the provision of public services is to be met, then this can be achieved only through economic growth.

The rate of economic growth is determined by the quantity and quality of a country's *factors of production*: whether its land is fertile, or its climate conducive to production: whether its labour force is well skilled; whether its capital equipment is efficient, and so on. It also depends on the availability of natural resources, the state of technical knowledge,

Figure 36.1 *The deflationary and inflationary gaps*

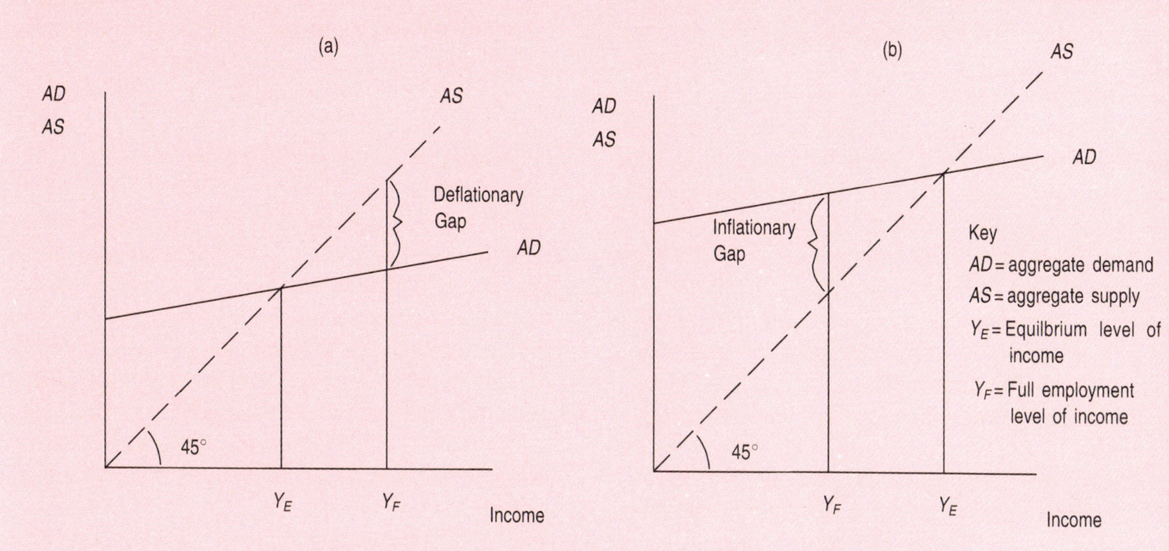

and such matters as the country's political stability, and the attitude of the public to such influences as investment and entrepreneurship. The UK has persistently had growth rates significantly lower than those of its western European neighbours. Periodic balance of payments crises and spurts of inflation have led to the application deflationary policies which may have discouraged investment and hence reduced the growth rate.

However, in making international comparisons it is necessary to examine national income levels as well as *rates of growth*. The fact that developing countries like Korea can achieve far higher rates of growth than the UK is significant for the countries concerned, because it implies that on the whole their citizens can hope to achieve higher living standards. On the other hand, a relatively small percentage growth in the UK represents a far higher *absolute* increase in national income compared with most developing countries, which are starting from a much lower base.

Demand Management Techniques

The objectives of government policy have changed, and there have been considerable changes in the *priority* given to the different objectives, as well as to the means of achieving them. Neo-Keyneisans tend to believe that the government's first priority should be to tackle unemployment, whereas monetarists, for example, regard inflation as an overriding concern from which all other economic evils, such as unemployment, eventually flow. Whether one objective should have priority over any other is a matter that is properly decided through the ballot box. We are concerned with the policies governments use to achieve their objectives, and in this chapter we focus on *demand management techniques*, which is the approach used in the UK until the end of the 1970s. In Chapter 37 we focus on *supply-side techniques*.

Demand management techniques are essentially short run techniques – that is, they take the supply-side conditions of the economy, such as its productive capacity and the full-employment level of income, as given. If the equilibrium level of income is estimated to be below the full employment level of income, then there is a *deflationary gap* which can be closed by increasing injections and/or reducing leakages to raise the equilibrium level of income. This is illustrated in Figure 36.1(a). If, on the other hand, planned levels of expenditure are such that the equilibrium level of income exceeds the full employment level of income there is an *inflationary gap* which can be eliminated by increasing leakages and/or reducing injections, thus reducing the equilibrium level of income as illustrated in Figure 36.1.

The main techniques of demand management can be classified as being techniques of *monetary policy* or *budgetary policy* (or *fiscal policy*). In practice, the distinction between monetary policy and fiscal policy is not always clear cut.

Monetary policy involves the use of techniques which affect the growth rate of the money supply and the rate of interest. Since a large proportion of the money supply is in effect created by the banking sector (see Chapter 25), monetary policy includes various methods which are available for controlling bank credit, not all of which are necessarily used simultaneously. As a technique for bringing about short run changes in aggregate demand, it was previously thought that changes in the availability or price of credit would have an impact. As we have seen on p. 225, attention now focuses on the long run effects of changes in money growth, and many economists now argue against the use of monetary policy to bring about short run changes in aggregate demand..

Budgetary policy involves varying government expenditure and taxation with the intention of changing aggregate demand to the desired level. Budgetary policy can either be *reflationary*, with reduced taxes and increased government spending (and the likelihood of a budget deficit); or it can be *deflationary*, with increased taxes and reduced government spending (bringing with it the possibility of a budget surplus). Of course, any attempt by the authorities to achieve a desired level of aggregate demand implies an ability accurately to assess and forecast the **actual level of aggregate demand**. However, in recent years, doubts have been expressed about the precision of economic forecasts, and even with sophisticated statistical techniques, including computer models of the economy, recent Chancellors of the Exchequer have expressed reservations about the reliability of economic models.

Incomes Policies

An *incomes policy* is a policy for restraining incomes with the aim of reducing the rate of inflation. By restricting the growth of incomes demand and costs are simultaneously restrained. During the 1960s and 1970s, successive UK governments pursued policies of this type, and in order to make them more acceptable to the workforce they were sometimes accompanied by some form of price restraint. In such cases, they were known as *prices and incomes policies*.

In the 1980s and 1990s these policies have fallen into disfavour, and there has been no formal incomes policy since 1979. Typically policies used in the UK have involved a *wage freeze*, or the establishment of a maximum allowable pay rise. They were usually introduced in response to a perceived crisis: a dramatic increase in the rate of inflation or a large balance of payments deficit.

The main problem with any attempt to establish an arbitrary limit on pay increases is that it eliminates the scope for collective bargaining. By freezing the existing pattern of wage differentials the labour

Figure 36.2 *The Neo-Keynesian 'box'*

Problem area (1)	Monetary policy (2)	Budgetary policy (3)	Other options (4)
Inflation	Restrictive	Deflationary	Prices and incomes policy
BOP deficit (falling £)	Restrictive	Deflationary	Prices and incomes policy, import controls, Devaluation
BOP surplus (rising £)	Expansive	Reflationary	Revaluation
Unemployment	Expansive	Reflationary	Incomes policy (no price control)
Low Growth	Expansive	Reflationary	Remove controls

market is unable to respond to structural changes caused by the decline of some industries and the expansion of others. Expanding industries are unable to offer higher wages in order to attract the additional workers they require while workers have no incentive to leave declining industries. The implication is that economic growth will be adversely affected.

Governments have sometimes attempted to alleviate this problem by introducing concessions for so called *special cases*. The problem, of course, is how to define criteria against which a 'special case' can be judged. If one group of workers are awarded a pay rise that breaches the maximum allowable increase because they are adjudged to represent a special case, other workers will almost certainly resent this unless they also are judged to be a special case. If all groups are awarded special case status, incomes policy cannot succeed in restricting the growth of incomes. On the other hand it is difficult to see how incomes policy can succeed in the long run without public support. If there is resentment, once the policy is removed there will tend to be a wage scramble when those who were not awarded special status will no doubt attempt to restore the traditional pattern of wage differentials.

Incomes policies may also be resented for other reasons. Policies that focus mainly on wage restraint are usually viewed with suspicion by the labour force since other factor rewards, in particular profits, are not always similarly restricted. In addition, some individuals are better able than others to protect themselves against income restraint. An increase in perks such as a staff discount or increasing the amount of overtime offered to workers are ways of avoiding restraint. Another way is to upgrade jobs so that workers receive a pay rise because of promotion.

Demand management policies are summarised in Figure 36.2.

Column (1) shows five different problem areas. The inclusion of a balance of payments surplus as a 'problem' may cause some surprise. It is more obvious that a balance of payments deficit is a problem, when a country's exports fail to pay for its imports. However, it should be noted that if one country or group of countries is persistently in surplus, then this must logically mean that other countries or groups of countries are persistently in deficit. For example, in the early 1970s the huge surpluses of the oil exporting countries was matched by huge deficits in the oil importing countries. Modern thinking therefore tends to regard equilibrium in the balance of payments as a desirable objective, so that modest surpluses and deficits tend to cancel each other out over a period of years.

Figure 36.3 *The effect of demand management on the balance of payments*

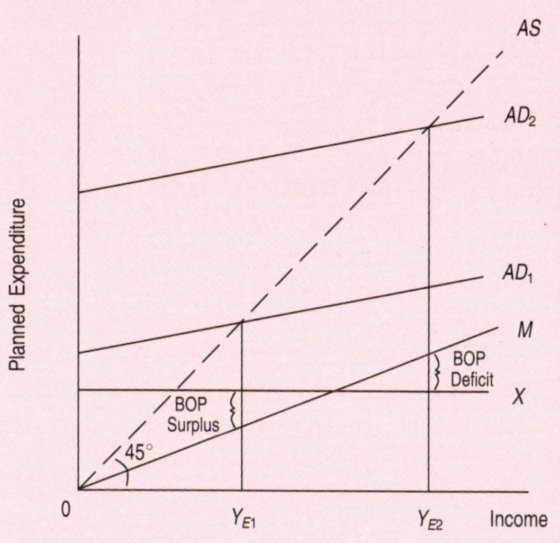

Columns (2) and (3) show how monetary and budgetary policies can be used to tackle the different problem areas, either by increasing or reducing the level of aggregate demand. Column (4) shows some further options (sometimes known as *direct policies*), which can sometimes be used as an alternative to monetary and budgetary policies.

Conflict between Policies

In Figure 36.3 national income is initially in equilibrium where aggregate demand, AD_1, equals aggregate supply at YE_1. We assume here that exports are exogenously determined – that is, they do not depend on the national income of the country in question; rather they are determined by incomes in **other countries**. It is reasonable to suppose that imports are endogenously determined – that is, they vary directly with national income since higher incomes will enable economic agents to purchase increased quantities of goods and services from abroad, and vice versa. For the sake of simplicity, we assume that the imports graph is a straight line rising from the origin. At YE_1 there is a balance of payments surplus, because exports are greater than imports at this level of income.

Suppose aggregate demand now increases, perhaps through an increase in government spending or investment which directly increases injections. The line AD_1 shifts to AD_2. However, some of the increased demand will be reflected in higher spending on imports. As shown in Figure 36.3, at the new equilibrium level of income YE_2 there is a balance of payments deficit. This move from surplus into deficit will be more pronounced if the country has a high marginal propensity to import and the gradient of the *M* function is therefore greater. This helps to explain the tendency of the British economy to experience *stop-go* cycles. During the *go* phase of the cycle, demand is expanded and output increases. However, increasing incomes leads to an increase in imports and a balance of payments deficit. In order to deal with this the stop phase of the cycle is implemented, and the government of the day introduces measures to reduce the level of aggregate demand. As output falls unemployment rises. Eventually governments attempt to cut unemployment and the cycle enters the *go* phase again.

Why do Policies Conflict?

It is sometimes alleged that there is a conflict between the different policy objectives we have outlined. Why is this? Why cannot all macroeconomic aims be achieved by a single all-embracing policy? It is because measures to achieve one objective often prevent the achievement of another objective, at least in the short run. As indicated in Figure 36.2 on p. 356, for instance, tax reductions aimed at increasing employment through higher aggregate demand may have the effect of increasing expenditure on imports, and thus causing balance of payments problems; increased interest rates aimed at reducing aggregate demand and discouraging imports may have the effect of increasing the exchange rate and thus making it more difficult to sell exports, and so on.

Neo-Keynesian analysis stresses the idea of *trade-offs*. Keynes himself realised that running a budget deficit in order to reduce unemployment could be inflationary, but he regarded a mild rate of inflation as an acceptable price to pay for achieving full employment. We have already examined this trade-off in Chapter 28 using the Phillips Curve. Figure 36.3 shows the trade-off between full employment and equilibrium in the balance of payments, which has been another significant part of the economic history of the UK.

REVIEW QUESTIONS

1 Are high interest rates an effective anti-inflationary policy, or do they cause inflation?

2 If a government wishes to increase taxes to reduce inflation, which would be the more effective: income tax or Value Added Tax? Justify your answer.

3 Is it realistic to expect governments to achieve the aims of macroeconomic policy? Discuss the proposition that governments should neither be praised for all successes, nor blamed for all failures.

4 Do demand management policies ignore the supply side of the economy?

CHAPTER 37

SUPPLY-SIDE POLICIES IN THE UK

CONNECTIONS

In Chapter 37 we shall be studying a number of 'supply-side' policies. We shall draw on material already covered in earlier chapters in the book, and in particular it would be useful for you to have a clear understanding of labour markets and collective bargaining (Chapter 14), the theory of taxation (Chapter 35), enterprise (Chapter 15), monopoly, oligopoly and 'contestable markets' (Chapters 11 and 13) and aggregate supply (Chapter 22).

Key Concepts

Deregulation
Incentives
Minimum wages
Privatisation
Tax distortion
Training
Unemployment trap

The Advent of 'Supply-side' Economics

In Chapter 36 we saw how demand management can be used to regulate the level of economic activity. However, by the 1970s a number of economists were beginning to have doubts about the effectiveness of demand management policies. The view, examined on p. 260, that any attempt to reduce unemployment below the natural rate by expanding aggregate demand ultimately would lead only to an increase in the rate of inflation gained more widespread acceptance . Economists therefore turned their attention towards *improvements in aggregate supply* as a vehicle for better macro-economic performance. The policies which evolved have been referred to as *supply-side policies*. In essence, these aim to establish a framework of conditions which, by improving the workings of markets and increasing competition and incentives, lead to **greater economic efficiency**. In other words, the aim of supply-side policies is to make markets operate more efficiently and thus increase the economy's **aggregate supply potential**.

In 1979 a Conservative government was elected and began to implement supply-side policies. We shall be examining these under four main headings: labour market reform, tax reform, deregulation and privatisation. However, it is important to stress that adopting supply-side policies is not something peculiar to the UK economy. From the late 1970s onwards governments the world over increasingly adopted supply-side policies.

Reforming the Labour Market

There are a number of 'barriers to employment' which can make labour markets inflexible and prevent them from responding fully to changing economic conditions. These barriers are:

- Excessive pay levels
- The unemployment trap
- Poor industrial relations
- Inadequate labour skills
- Inappropriate attitudes to employment

Let us now examine each of these barriers in turn, and see how government policies were created to deal with them.

Barriers to Employment: Excessive Pay Levels

One possible barrier to employment is the existence of wage levels which are excessive in terms of labour supply and demand. We saw in Chapter 14 that collective bargaining by trade unions might lead to workers being priced out of jobs. In effect the labour market then becomes separated into two groups: *insiders* who are employed, and *outsiders* who are willing to accept work but who are currently unemployed. Wage bargaining is undertaken by insiders, who generally act in their own interest, without considering that of outsiders. When, as in the UK recession of the early 1990s, an economic shock leads to an increasing number of workers becoming unemployed, that is, outsiders, they remain unemployed because insiders will not accept wage cuts to increase employment. Supply-siders argue that the outcome of this wage inflexibility is a higher natural rate of unemployment and a reduction in the economy's potential aggregate supply. There is a school of thought, associated particularly with the Austrian economist Hayek, which advocates the progressive abolition of trade unions. There are two main objections to this approach. First, some labour markets are dominated by powerful employers. In the absence of a trade union the wage-setting process could then easily result in a monopolistic wage 'mark-down'. Secondly, trade unions perform important social and industrial functions outside of collective bargaining.

In the 1980s successive UK governments undertook the following measures to improve wage flexibility.

Trade Union Reform

Trade union reform was aimed at reducing the collective bargaining strength of trade unions and making them more responsive to the wishes of their members.

- The 1980 and 1982 *Employment Acts* outlawed secondary strikes and secondary picketing, and limited primary picketing to six workers. These Acts also introduced secret ballots and made 'closed shops' more difficult to enforce.
- The 1984 *Trade Union Act* extended the use of compulsory secret ballots before industrial action and for election of officers. The provision of secret ballots before industrial action was soon put to the test. Ballots of car workers and rail drivers had the effect of preventing strikes which had been proposed by union leaders. On the other hand, where strike action was undertaken, it could become more effective when supported by the authority of a secret ballot.
- The 1988 *Employment Act* ended legal protection for 'closed shops' and further tightened the provisions for secret balloting in the case of proposed strikes and union elections.

Minimum Wage Regulations

The government took the view that *minimum wages*, set by government wage councils, might restrict employment by pricing workers out of jobs. Accordingly legislation was enacted in 1986 which had the effect of removing workers under the age of 21 from Wage Council protection and reducing the scope for enforcement of minimum wages.

Barriers to Employment: the Unemployment Trap

The operation of the tax and benefit system may have contributed to labour market inflexibility. The existence of 'out of work' benefits in effect constitutes a minimum wage which may deter unemployed workers from seeking employment. If an unemployed person takes on a job he (she) and his (her) family will face both higher taxes and a reduction or withdrawal of benefits. This can produce *effective marginal rates of tax* which are relatively high, and in excess of 100 per cent in some cases. The result is that some workers are financially better off if they are unemployed than if they obtain employment. This effect is referred to as the *unemployment trap*. To weaken this trap, the government introduced the following measures

- **Taxation of unemployment benefits**, so as to reduce the loss of benefit for low wage workers entering employment.
- **Withdrawal of benefits** for unemployed persons who fail to take up training placements.
- **Selective 'targeting' of benefits** at those in genuine need, with the aim of reducing the

incidence of the unemployment trap on other unemployed groups.

The proposition that a relatively high level of out of work benefits *actually* deters a significant number of people from taking up employment is hard to prove. Anecdotal evidence from job centres certainly indicates the existence of job applicants who in fact prefer to remain unemployed on benefit rather than take up employment. On the other hand, adverts for low-pay jobs frequently elicit large numbers of applications from the unemployed, which reminds us that many people prefer even a low pay job to the alternative of being unemployed.

Barriers to Employment: Poor Industrial Relations

It has been alleged that one of the main barriers to employment in the 1970s was poor industrial relations. Frequent strikes and widespread restrictive practices led to situations in which management time and energy, which should have been devoted to production and marketing, was dissipated in solving labour disputes. It was further alleged that the UK's poor reputation damaged export prospects and deterred foreign investment in the UK. The implication is that poor industrial relations resulted in lost employment opportunities. In the 1980s the number of days lost through strikes fell significantly while widespread gains in productivity attest to the decline in restrictive practices. The sources of this improvement in industrial relations are complex but it is claimed that the government's trade union reforms helped lead to a major change in attitudes such that trade unions increasingly recognised that their members' interests are not served by conflict and that effective working practices are the best guarantee of jobs.

Barriers to Employment: Inadequate Labour Skills

Although unemployment in 1988 in the UK was around 2m, there were some 700,000 unfilled vacancies in the economy, and widespread reports of employers being unable to find the workers they needed to expand their businesses and take advantage of new markets. One factor behind this 'mismatch' of labour supply and demand was the existence of inappropriate attitudes among employers and employees: we examine this point below. Another factor, which we now examine, was the absence among many unemployed people of up to date skills which employers required. Training and retraining were therefore increasingly regarded as important in raising productivity and reducing unemployment.

In the 1980s government measures aimed at improving the UK labour force's skills were introduced. A *Youth Training Scheme* was introduced to provide training placements for school and college leavers. On completion of this scheme, 60 per cent of trainees found employment or went into further education. Policies were also introduced to shape the school education curriculum into a form more suited to the needs of industry, for example the *Technical and Vocational Educational Initiative* (TVEI) was designed to provide more computer based and industry related courses.

One of the problems with training in the UK is that those best qualified to undertake it – namely businesses themselves – have often been reluctant to do so, partly for fear that expensively trained employees might leave and take their skills elsewhere, possibly to rival firms. In Germany, by contrast, businesses seem to be much more willing to undertake and finance training on an ambitious scale, particularly in the shape of post-school apprenticeships (two-thirds of German workers have a training qualification, compared with one-third of UK workers).

In 1988 the UK government set out a radical new framework for industrial training with the aim of facilitating access to training throughout the working life for every member of the workforce. In broad outline, the new training initiative involves the setting up of a National Training Agency to develop new training schemes and to promote greater investment by employers in the skills of the workforce. As far as possible these arrangement were to be locally based and involved acceptance of increased responsibility by employers for undertaking and financing training.

Barriers to Employment: Inappropriate Attitudes to Employment

A 1988 White Paper examined employment barriers which could result from unsuitable attitudes. It was found that employers were often reluctant to recruit people who had been out of work for more than a few months, whatever their qualifications and previous

Box 37.1 Where training has pride of place

A measure of the extraordinary success of vocational training in Germany is that businessmen and chambers of commerce alike regard it as normal.

The German system, rooted in company culture, is based more on tradition than regulation. Moreover, come rain or shine, the number of firms involved in vocational training and the amount of money spent on it, continues to rise.

'Every German firm of repute regards it as its duty to take on apprentices and offer vocational training', says Rolf Raddatz, head of apprenticeship training at the German Chamber of Commerce in Bonn. 'There is no obligation, just a commitment. It is a crucial part of a firm's corporate image.'

Western German strength in training has long been cited as one of the key reasons for the economy's strength. Geerd Woortmann, head of vocational training at the Chamber of Commerce, explains why. 'If you are in a country with high costs you know that you stand little chance on price competition. Your best option, therefore, is quality, but you only maintain that with quality labour. Then price becomes a secondary factor. This is an argument that never fails to convince firms.'

This quality has to be maintained all the way down the production line. Mr Woortmann stresses the need for 'fitness in the firm', something largely achieved by constantly keeping the workforce moving ahead with training.

The most recent survey by the chambers of commerce showed that in 1989 West German private industry spent some DM55bn on vocational training (DM28bn on apprenticeships and DM27bn on further training); and that four-fifths of firms felt that in the future they would be doing much more. Only 8 per cent of German firms did not have their own vocational training facilities.

Moreover, it proved that small firms spent relatively more on further training that did big ones. The sums spent on such training by firms in Germany, where there is no obligation to do so – on average DM1,800 per worker in 1987 – were far higher than comparable budgets in France, where there are obligatory contributions, says Mr Woortmann.

'You cannot order vocational training so that workers go to classes just to fulfil a plan', he says. 'It must come from perceived needs and have a purpose in the firm. Only that way does it forge relationships in a company.'

Germany's vocational training rests broadly on two systems: the so-called 'dual system' of apprenticeship, whereby school leavers are trained for two to three years in basic skills, mainly on the job in a firm, but with weekly theoretical classes run by outside institutions such as a chamber of commerce; and the *weiterbildung* (further qualification) which can be done at any stage later on, at a firm's or an employee's initiative.

No firm is obliged to take on apprentices, and after the training period is up there is no obligation to keep any of them on. Many firms, especially small ones, continually train a few apprentices that they will not need. 'The system is therefore highly flexible. The main thing is that youngsters get properly qualified.'

How deeply rooted the system is in industry can be gauged by the fact that even in the late Seventies, when the German economy was in trouble, firms kept taking apprentices.

Crucial to the success of this system is its emphasis on 'learning by doing' in the firm, rather than on a school-based training. 'Firms are less keen to take on people trained in special schools outside, for they have then to be re-adapted to real work conditions', says Mr Raddatz. 'Firms are continually investing in new plant, so apprentices train on the most modern machinery. Outside schools are often way behind.

Apprentices spend most of their time in the firm, and only about 10 hours a week on an external course. Even for the later 'further training', most firms, even small ones, try to offer as much of their own training as possible. 'You cannot forge a company culture in a classroom', says Mr Woortmann.

The challenge for the future is transplanting this tradition into the east, where 'company culture' as the west knows it has been totally erased.

Source: John Eisenhammer, *The Independent* (7 May 1991)

Training in the clothing industry: How does Britain compare with Germany?

Even before the (1990) recession there was considerable evidence to suggest that Britain has a training crisis.

A study that appeared in the National Institute Economic Review in May 1989 showed a remarkable skills gap between clothing manufacturers in Britain and West Germany. The details bear repetition. While the industries are of comparable size:

- Ten times more German workers achieve qualifications to basic City and Guilds standards; 3.5 times as many reach higher levels.
- In the past eight years the number reaching City and Guilds craft standard in the British clothing sector has fallen from 900 to 400.
- The standards to be reached by the end of the second year of the British Youth Training course are below those reached by German trainees in the first six months of the two or three year course.

The researchers, Hilary Steedman and Karen Wagner, argued that our performance in the clothing industry was probably typical of British companies facing stiff foreign competition. They found that while German wages in the industry were between 50 and a 100 per cent higher in Germany than in Britain, German companies had faced up to competitors by concentrating on high quality goods, produced in small batches at high prices. The implication was that because of low skill levels, British companies were forced to compete with those in the Third World producing large quantities cheaply.

Source: *The Independent* (2 October 1991)

experience. Among the unemployed there was evidence that a significant number of benefit claimants were not actively looking for work and some were claiming fraudulently while working at least part time in the *black economy* (see p. 162). The government set in hand two measures to improve employment opportunities for the unemployed

- All new claimants for benefit would be **interviewed** by employment service staff to advise on jobs and to monitor availability for work.
- Claimants would be required to undergo **regular checks on their availability** for work.

Barriers to employment make labour markets inflexible and reduce the supply-side potential of the economy. The main strands of the UK labour market reform may be summarised as follows.

Barrier to employment	*Labour market policy*
Excessive pay levels	Trade union reform
'Unemployment trap'	Reshaping of out of work benefits
Poor industrial relations	Trade union reform
Poor labour skills	Reform of training and education, including setting up of National Training Agency
Inappropriate employment attitudes	More stringent conditions for out of work benefits

Tax Reform

Tax Reform in the 1980s: Reducing the 'Tax Wedge'

Supply-side policies aim to encourage economic efficiency by establishing conditions which improve markets and which increase competition and incentives. One factor which may affect incentives is the level of direct taxation, which tends to act as a 'wedge' between economic agents' *earned income* and their net of tax *disposable income*. In particular, high marginal income tax rates may create a significant disincentive on additional effort. The implication is that a lower level of tax would create an incentive for increased effort. It is also claimed that a smaller tax wedge reduces the unemployment trap, thus giving unemployed workers greater incentive to accept employment. There may be several other favourable effects of a lower tax wedge. It is claimed that it may encourage saving (by increasing disposable income) and investment (by increasing the after-tax return to investors). It is also claimed that a lower tax wedge might encourage pay demands, since any *given* wage award will result in a larger increase in disposable income, and discourage tax evasion and the operation of the black economy.

Reducing the size of the direct tax wedge was a central element in UK supply-side policies. By 1988 basic and top rates of income tax had been reduced

Box 37.2 At last, the labour market is working

Something has happened in the British labour market: it is starting to respond in a flexible way, as it has to if the current downward movement of interest rates and inflation is to be sustained.

That interest rates, which were cut yesterday by ½ per cent to 12½ per cent, are set to fall further is hardly in dispute. Inflation, too, will decline very rapidly through this year, though yesterday's small decline of the retail price index to 8.9 per cent was disappointing. But these reductions can be sustained only if wage increases decline too. In the past few weeks there is evidence that this is happening.

Throughout the 1980s one of the puzzling, worrying features of the way we organise our industrial affairs was the extent to which wage settlements refused to follow inflation downwards. During the early 1980s recession many workers continued to obtain quite large increases in nominal pay, while their colleagues lost their jobs. Then, as the recovery got under way, firms were happy to pay their workers – and indeed their directors – well above the rate of inflation. Successive government ministers fretted about this phenomenon, did their best to hold down public sector pay and criticised the private sector. But most commercial companies were generating enough growth in profits not to have to worry.

Even last year, when the boom was clearly over, pay settlements continued to rise fast. Just why that should have happened was not at all clear. The trade unions – which might reasonably have shouldered much of the blame for the excessive wage settlements in the early 1980s – had been subdued. Pay was still rising fast in areas such as the City where the unions never had much hold. Perhaps companies felt that they could escape the full effect of such settlements by putting up their prices in the home market, and by a devaluation of sterling in their export markets.

Then quite suddenly at the end of last year, something seemed to change. As 1991 has progressed, there has been an inexorable downward shift in pay settlements. The CBI's log shows them declining from 9 per cent in the fourth quarter of last year to 8.3 per cent in the first quarter of this, but that understates the shift, for the most recent settlements have been lower still.

Indeed the really novel feature of this wage round is the way in which more and more companies have deferred wage rounds altogether. In some cases this is simply a question of delaying a pay increase for a couple of months. But commercial giants such as IBM, Philips and, just this week, Trusthouse Forte, have formally frozen pay for up to six months. The Guardian newspaper has sought to freeze pay for a year.

More remarkable still is the experience at Thomas Cook. In January it gave average increases in pay of 11.5 per cent. This month it brought in pay cuts of up to 10 per cent with directors taking the largest bite. Suddenly we seem to be winning the prize that eluded this country through the whole of the 1980s: establishing a wage bargaining system that ensures companies adjust pay to what they can afford, instead of following some national 'going rate'.

If this is right, then it quite transforms the economic prospects for this country through the rest of this century. The aim of ERM membership is to provide a discipline which will shift Britain from being a relatively high inflation, high interest rate economy, with all the inefficiencies and injustices that entails. That discipline carries inevitable costs. But those costs can be much reduced if the country can improve its pay bargaining system.

The Government has recently been pondering what it should do to assist this process: should it, for example, engineer some form of annual national wage round? But the evidence of recent weeks points in exactly the opposite direction. A combination of recession at home and the discipline of ERM membership is imposing just the sort of flexibility that an efficient market economy needs.

Largest hotel chain freezes staff's pay

Trusthouse Forte, Britain's largest hotel chain, has become the latest company to freeze the pay of its staff.

THF, which dos not recognise unions in hotels, has told its 25,000 employees that wage rises will be postponed from April until October; some workers have also been put on short time working. The situation will be reviewed monthly, THF said.

Room occupancy has been hit by the recession and even more severely by a sharp decline in visitors because of the Gulf War and the perceived risk of terrorism. Management grades, whose pay is usually reviewed in November, will probably have to wait until the beginning of next year for a rise.

All main board members, include Rocco Forte, chief executive, whose salary in the latest set of accounts amounted to £211,622 have forgone increases due last month. Other companies introducing pay pauses include IBM, Michelin, Philips and some regions in the road haulage companies industry.

Source: Hamish McRae, *The Independent* (23 March 1991)

to 25 per cent and 40 per cent respectively compared with 33 per cent and 83 per cent in 1979. However, whether this will reduce any disincentive effect is debatable. For example, a 1980 survey by the Institute for Fiscal Studies found that most male employees on average incomes would be unlikely to work more following a cut in income tax. However, married women and high income earners probably would work more.

Tax reductions, in conjunction with reform of social security benefits, have also been undertaken to reduce the unemployment trap. Under 1987 tax and benefit arrangements, a typical jobless person accepting employment would gain little extra net income up to a gross earnings level of £140. In 1988 a combination of reduced income tax and reform of social benefits led to a significant reduction in the unemployment trap (see Figure 37.1).

Supply-side economists also claim that direct tax cuts can increase the incentive to save and invest. In the case of savings a reduction in the tax wedge not only increases households' disposable income, out of which savings are drawn, it also improves the net of tax interest rate earned by savings; both effects tend to encourage saving. In the case of investment a reduction in corporation tax could encourage investment by increasing the level of business funds available for investment and by raising the value of net of tax funds flow from any given investment project (see p. 190).

Clearly a lower level of direct taxes could have beneficial effects on the incentives to work, save and invest. However, they might also have undesirable side effects. In particular, tax reductions lead to lower tax revenues in the short run, higher budget deficits and hence increased government borrowing. One likely outcome of this is higher interest rates, which could have an adverse effect on investment. In addition, by increasing disposable income lower taxes encourage an immediate expansion of consumption and aggregate demand, whereas the supply-side benefits of tax reductions usually take much longer to develop. The resulting tendency for aggregate demand to outstrip aggregate supply at the existing price level is likely to create the very inflationary pressures that supply-side policies are designed to avoid! Opponents of supply-side economics point to rising interest rates and inflation in the UK following the tax cuts of 1987 and 1988 as evidence of such harmful side effects.

Tax Reform: Reducing the Tax Distortion

A second element in UK 1980s tax policy was reform aimed at reducing *tax distortion*. This occurs when a tax has unintended and undesirable effects. To give one example, in the UK in 1979 rates of tax on investment income were considerably higher than

Figure 37.1 *The unemployment trap*

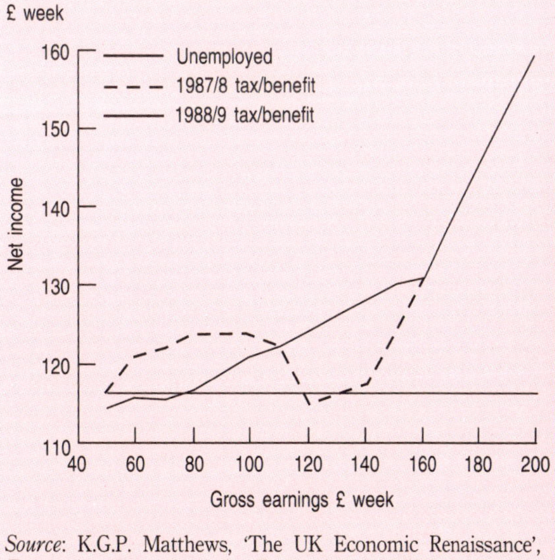

Source: K.G.P. Matthews, 'The UK Economic Renaissance', *Economics (Journal of the Economics Association)* Autumn 1989, p. 106 (adapted)

those on income tax, which had the effect of arbitrarily reducing people's willingness to undertake financial investment in businesses. Secondly, preferential tax relief on premiums paid for life assurance and pension contributions discouraged people from putting their savings into investment which, in the absence of such tax distortions, would sometimes have provided better rates of return.

Measures undertaken in the 1980s to reduce tax distortion included

- Reduction of tax rates on investment income
- Reduction of capital gains tax to the level of basic income tax
- Abolition of tax relief on life assurance

One notable source of tax distortion, however, remained in place: tax relief for home owners on interest paid on mortgages and other forms of home loan. The effect of this was to attract funds to property construction and development, at the expense of other investment areas.

Deregulation

'Deregulation' is the term used to describe the removal of government regulations on the activities of the business sector. Government regulations are usually introduced to protect the safety of consumers and workers. However, in practice they often result in arrangements between producers to restrict competition in the industry. In the 1980s UK governments embarked on a policy of removing regulations. Two examples of this are the ending of legal monopolies for solicitors in the conveyancing of house property and for qualified opticians in the sale of spectacles. A third is the deregulation of the London Stock Exchange which took place with the much publicised 'Big Bang' of October 1986 and which provided opportunities for London to compete more effectively with other exchanges.

Let us examine deregulation of bus services in the UK. Regulation here had been based on a system of 'closed licensing' which limited the number of operators in a given area of service. Closed licensing was intended to prevent wasteful duplication of services and to help in the enforcement of safety regulations. However, it also had the effect of restricting competition, since new businesses wishing to enter the market often found it difficult to obtain licences. To protect bus passengers against possible exploitation, the government had introduced a system of controlled fares. However, these were often set at levels which eroded operators' profits. This contributed to a decline in the number of services, despite a rising level of government subsidies for operators.

Deregulation took the form of introducing open licensing, allowing operators to set up new services, including the long distance market, which up to that point had been a monopoly of the state owned National Bus Company. Increased competition between operators quickly led to improved efficiency and a growth in passenger traffic. However, while fares on long distance services fell appreciably, those for local services showed little change. Some commentators believed that deregulated competition might, through the effect of insolvencies and mergers, eventually lead back to monopolistic market structures. Advocates of deregulation disputed this, arguing that it would be prevented by the *potential* entry of new competitors now made possible by open licensing (see *contestable markets*, p. 98).

Deregulation of UK bus services took place in 1980 and 1986. The main points can be summarised as follows:

- 'Open licenses' were introduced allowing **new operators** to set up services.
- **Controlled fares** were **abolished**.
- Government subsidies for **socially necessary services** continued, but general network subsidies were abolished.
- The National Bus Company, a state owned enterprise which dominated long distance services, was transferred to private ownership and broken down into **independent competing subsidiaries**.

Privatisation

The fourth strand of supply-side policy which we shall examine is *privatisation*. There are many definitions of privatisation but here we mean the transfer of ownership of a business from the public (state) sector to the private. This is done through the formation of a **public limited company** and the sale of its shares to private investors.

Privatisation in the UK took place in two main stages. In the first, from 1979 to the autumn of 1984, most of the businesses privatised (for example, British Petroleum, British Aerospace, Jaguar and Sealink) were engaged in 'workable competition' with private sector rivals. The second stage of privatisation, from the autumn of 1984 onwards,

Box 37.3 Deregulated bus services in two Indian cities

Comparing the performance of public bus companies in two Indian cities illustrates how prudent management, financial independence, and competition can combine to produce efficient and commercially viable public systems.

The Calcutta State Transport Corporation (CTSC) has a fleet of some 1,100 buses, of which usually less than 700 are in operation, mainly for want of repair and maintenance and sometimes because of lack of drivers. It has a high staffing ratio of 20.7 per operational bus. The CSTC has also been plagued by fare evasion estimated at more than 15 per cent of revenue. The resulting combination of low productivity with fare inadequacies and evasion necessitates a subsidy of about $1 million a month. By contrast, the city's 2,200 private buses – operated mainly by small companies or individual owners grouped into several route associations – have been able to survive financially without subsidy and to maintain low staffing ratios and high fleet availability. The drivers and conductors of private buses receive a percentage of revenue, which gives them a strong incentive to combat fare evasion. As a result the fare losses of private bus operations are extremely low, and their operating costs are about half those of the CSTC and are more than covered by revenues.

The Cheran Transit Corporation (CTC) in Coimbatore, a city of about 1m inhabitants, is one of fourteen publicly owned bus corporations in the state of Tamil Nadu – all of which are financially viable and efficient. The CTC does not have an exclusive franchise but operates in direct competition with private buses. The corporation operates with a very high level of efficiency: more than 95 per cent of the fleet is regularly in service, and the staffing ratio of 7.3 per operating bus is comparatively low for public bus corporations. Despite very low fares ($0.04 for a five-kilometre trip), the CTC is able to make a profit ($750,000 in fiscal 1984–85), which enables it to expand its fleet in line with demand. Much of the success of the CTC must be attributed to its dynamic and accountable management and to relatively consistent state government support for adequate and timely fare revisions. Also the CTC pursues prudent commercial policies, comprehensively monitors and costs its services, and has incorporated staff incentives that are common among its private competitors, including bonuses based on revenue gains and savings that result from a higher rate of bus use and better fare collection as well as an annual bonus for accident-free driving.

Source: World Bank

was dominated by the sale of *public monopolies* such as British Telecom, British Gas and the British Airports Authority. Most of these businesses were transferred intact into the private sector – that is, there was no attempt to break them up into competing units. The transfer to private ownership was therefore sometimes accompanied by new government regulations designed to protect consumers against possible monopoly exploitation (see p. 391).

The aims of privatisation can be summarised as follows:

- *To raise finance for the government*: In the case of the UK the scale of privatisation revenues has been substantial, totalling over £36bn by 1991. These receipts helped make possible a reduction in the public sector borrowing requirement, which was a major part of the government's macroeconomic strategy for most of the 1980s.
- *To increase the extent of share ownership*: Shares in newly privatised companies were offered at a discount to increase their attractiveness to potential investors. However, although share ownership certainly widened following privatisation, there is little evidence that it deepened, and most shareholders have ownership in only a single company.
- *To increase allocative and productive efficiency*: As part of their anti-inflationary policy successive UK governments often prevented state controlled industries from raising their prices fully in line with costs. However, as we have seen on p. 91, when prices are prevented from increasing, too much of these particular goods is consumed in relation to the optimum. As privatised businesses these enterprises would charge free market prices which it is argued would lead to improved allocative efficiency. Governments also

Box 37.4 Privatisation – who benefits?

Financial institutions benefit. Privatisation involves the formation of a public company and the issue of its shares to investors by financial institutions such as issuing houses and underwriters. Table 37.1 gives for four major privatisations a breakdown of issuing institutions' income. As we can see the costs of privatisation can be substantial.

Table 37.1 *The costs of four UK privatisations*

	British Telecom (£m)	British Gas (£m)	British Airways (£m)	Rolls Royce (£m)
Underwriting/placing commissions	74	60	8	13
Selling commissions	13	9	3	4
Clearing bank costs	20	45	8	11
Marketing (includes advertising	14	40	6	4
Advisor's fees	6	5	4	2
Overseas offer	30	23	5	–
Total	157	182	34	34

Source: Institute of Economic Affairs

The government benefits. Privatisation has generated substantial amounts of finance for UK governments. Table 37.2 gives a summary of privatisation receipts up to 1991.

Do consumers benefit? There is much less certainty about the extent to which consumers have benefited from privatisation. We have seen that a central aim of privatisation is to improve efficiency and to make the benefits available to consumers in the form of lower prices and better standards of service. But has this occurred on a scale sufficient to justify the cost of privatisation? Let us take the case of BT as an example.

Privatising BT cost £157m, which was equivalent to 2.3 per cent of its annual sales at that time. This suggests that, say, five years of improved efficiency resulting in one-half a percentage point reduction in charges would provide sufficient consumer benefit to justify the initial cost of privatisation. Did BT achieve this? We see below that, following privatisation, BT was required by OFTEL to keep price increases to 3 per cent (later 4½ per cent) below the rate of inflation. The fact that BT was able to achieve this cut in real prices suggests worthwhile benefits to consumers from BT's privatisation. Confirmation of BT's efficiency improvement is provided by a 1988 London Business School survey, which showed that BT's rate of productivity growth increased from 2.0 to 2.5 per cent annually in the mid-1980s. It seems clear that in the case of BT privatisation did improve productive efficiency and offer worthwhile benefits to consumers.

Table 37.2 *UK privatisations*

Business	Date	£m
British Aerospace	1981/2, 1984/5	389
Cable and Wireless	1981/2, 1984/5	1020
Britoil	1982/3, 1983/4, 1985/6	1053
Enterprise Oil	1984/5	382
British Telecom	1984/5, 1985/6, 1986/7	3682
British Gas	1986/7	5600
British Petroleum	1979/80,1981/2, 1983/4, 1987/8	10054
British Airports Authority	1987/8	1275
Rolls Royce Aero Engines	1987/8	1080
British Steel	1988/9, 1989/90	2400
Water	1989/90, 1990/1	2200
Electricity	1990/1, 1991/2	4000
Other		3556
Total		36691

Source: HMSO

However, the issue is not as easily solved as that for while it is true that efficiency improved dramatically at BT and most other privatised businesses, the same is also true for most of those businesses which remained in state-ownership, notably British Steel whose productivity increased by an impressive 12.4 per cent annually. The LBS survey concluded that deregulation and competition had led to efficiency gains in privatised and non-privatised organisations. The extent to which the consumer benefited from privatisation rather than deregulation is therefore an unanswered question.

varied investment in public sector organisations as a means of adjusting aggregate demand to the desired level. Here again, since investment decisions were not entirely related to the demands of consumers, allocative efficiency was impaired. There is also no doubt that such political interference made long-term planning in these organisations very difficult, and contributed to their relatively poor performance.

As well as improving allocative efficiency it was felt that privatisation would improve productive efficiency. It was argued that lack of competition in many public sector markets and the availability of state subsidies to fund losses encouraged inefficiency in public sector organisations. It was felt that opening such markets up to competition and compelling organisations to obtain finance from the capital market would result in greater productive efficiency. Failure to keep costs and prices down would result in declining sales and therefore lost jobs, including managerial positions. The latter would be further at risk because organisations which are managed incompetently are prime targets for a takeover by other organisations. The arguments are very plausible, but whether privatisation actually results in improved productive efficiency is difficult to test though in many cases productivity has increased considerably after privatisation compared with levels achieved before privatisation.

The Privatisation of British Telecom

As an example we now consider the privatisation in 1985 of the first of the big public monopolies – British Telecom (BT).

Telecommunications refers to the telephone system and data communications which now include 'faxing'. In 1979 all such services were provided by the General Post Office (GPO) a state-owned business with a legal monopoly. However, in the early 1980s the government decided to transfer the provision of telecommunications to a newly created state-owned enterprise, British Telecom (BT). It also *deregulated* the market and allowed new businesses to apply for telecommunication licences with the aim of improving efficiency through increased competition. As a result a new telecommunications business, Mercury Communications, was set up. In 1985 the government went further and privatised BT with the aim of further improving efficiency.

One result of competition between BT and Mercury was increased innovation in the form of a rapid expansion of new products such as car telephones and more sophisticated receivers. However, increased competition did not lead to any significant reduction in consumer charges. In fact, there was a danger that the two businesses might collude to exploit their market duopoly so as to raise customer charges. To prevent this the government set up a regulating agency, the Office of Telecommunications (OFTEL) to oversee BT's and Mercury's pricing practices. OFTEL introduced a system of regulation limiting phone charge increases in any given year to 3 per cent *below* the going rate of inflation. (In 1988, this was changed to 4½ per cent.) In 1990 the government announced new plans aimed at further increasing competition in the UK telecommunications market.

Before we move on to a consideration of the effect of supply-side policies it is important to stress that *deregulation* and *privatisation* are not the same thing. Deregulation simply implies that markets are opened up to competition, while privatisation involves a change in the ownership of assets. The problem is that privatisation and deregulation sometimes occur simultaneously. For example, the deregulation of bus services also involved the privatisation of the state-owned National Bus Company and the privatisation of British Telecom was associated with measures aimed at deregulating the telecommunications market. Privatisation and deregulation are therefore both intended to promote competition and both tend to reduce the level of state influence on the economy.

Supply-side Policies : Have They Worked?

The central aim of supply-side policies is to establish conditions which make markets more efficient and thus increase the economy's aggregate supply poten-

Table 37.3 *Growth of labour productivity*

	Output per head		
	1960–70	1970–80	1980–90
	(Average annual % changes)		
Whole economy	2.4	1.3	2.5
Manufacturing industry	3.0	1.6	5.2

Source: A. Maynard, 'Britain's Economic Recovery', *Economics*, (*Journal of the Economics Association*), Autumn 1989, p. 98

Table 37.4 *International comparison of output per head*

Whole economy	1960–70	1970–80	1980–90
	(Average annual % changes)		
UK	2.4	1.3	2.5
USA	2.0	0.4	1.2
Japan	8.9	3.8	2.9
Germany	4.4	2.8	1.8
France	4.6	2.8	2.0
Italy	6.3	2.6	2.0
Canada	2.4	1.5	1.4
G7 average	3.5	1.7	1.8

UK data from CSO. Other countries' data from OECD except 1988 which are calculated from national GNP or GDP figures and OECD employment estimates

Manufacturing industry	1960–70	1970–80	1980–90
	(Average annual % changes)		
UK	3.0	1.6	5.2
USA	3.5	3.0	4.0
Japan	8.8	5.3	3.1
Germany	4.1	2.9	2.2
France	5.4	3.2	3.1
Italy	5.4	3.0	3.5
Canada	3.4	3.0	3.6
G7 average	4.5	3.3	3.6

UK data from CSO. Other countries' data from OECD except France and Italy which use IMF employment data. 1988 data for France and Italy cover first three quarters only.

Source: A. Maynard, 'Britain's Economic Recovery', *Economics*, (*Journal of the Economics Association*), Autumn 1989, p. 98

tial. One way we can see if this has occurred is in terms of *productivity* – that is, the efficiency with which an economy uses inputs to produce output. In particular, we focus on labour productivity, which is defined as the **average output produced by each employed person in the economy**. This can be calculated by dividing the total (real) output of the economy by the numbers employed. It has been claimed that the supply-side policies of the 1980s were so successful as to have resulted in a UK 'productivity miracle'. Has there then been one? The growth of labour productivity in the manufacturing sector and for the economy as a whole is set out in Table 37.3

We can see that the evidence is inconclusive. On the one hand it is clear that *manufacturing productivity* growth in the 1980s was appreciably greater than in the 1960s and 1970s. This is important because an economy like the UK's is unlikely to achieve strong total growth without a corresponding improvement in the manufacturing sector. Moreover, changes in manufacturing productivity are an important element in determining the international competitiveness of our products, a point we return to on p. 371. However, Table 37.3 also shows that

Figure 37.2 *Indicators of competitiveness, UK, 1970s and 1980s*

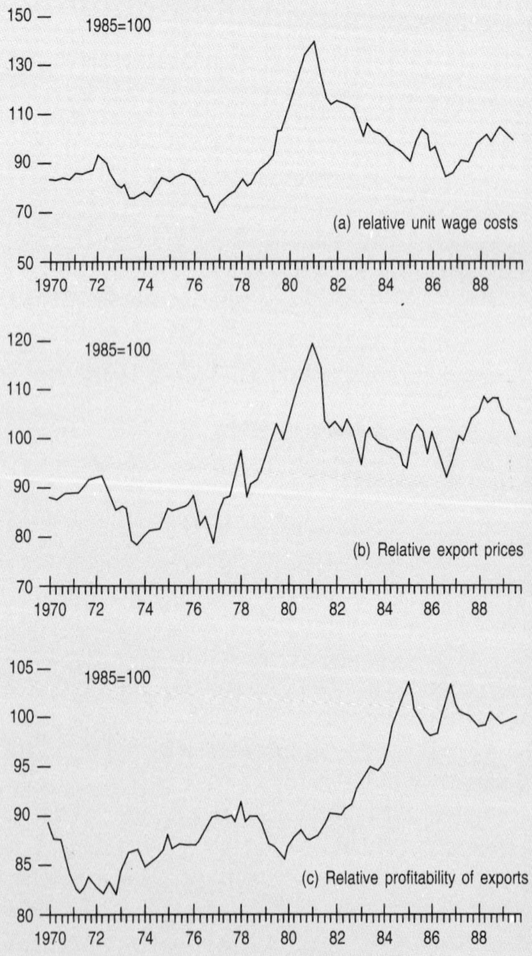

Source: *Barclays Bank Review*, based on CSO and Barclays estimates

productivity growth for the *whole economy* in the 1980s, while much superior to that observed in the 1970s, was little better than the rate achieved in the 1960s: hardly an indication of a productivity miracle!

What is perhaps more significant is the UK's performance in *relation to its major international competitors*. Table 37.4 shows that UK productivity growth was relatively poor compared with other major countries in the 1960s and 1970s. However, in the 1980s UK manufacturing productivity growth out performed that of all others while growth for the economy as a whole was second only to that of Japan! On this basis therefore there was, if not a miracle, at least a significant improvement in the UK supply-side performance.

The supply-side policies which we have been examining in this chapter are likely to remain in place for many years to come, and the real test of supply-side success will be whether the UK's improved productivity growth can be sustained in the long term. By the start of the 1990s, it was becoming evident that continuing supply-side gains and low inflation would prove difficult to maintain. There are several reasons for this. For example, we noted on p. 361 that one of the chief supply-side weaknesses of the UK is the shortage of labour skills, and this remains a serious cause for concern.

UK Competitiveness in the 1980s

In general, unless it is unduly affected by changes in money wage costs and exchange rates, a country's international competitiveness will tend to improve when its productivity increases faster than that of its competitors. Figure 37.2 presents some indicators of UK competitiveness in the 1970s and 1980s.

These indicators are not entirely consistent. However, the general impression is one of declining UK competitiveness in the late 1970s, followed by an improving trend from about 1981 when, we can assume, the government's early supply-side policies were beginning to 'bite'. However, at the end of the decade, there was evidence of a decline in competitiveness. In particular UK productivity growth was slowing down inflationary pressures were increasing. Clearly it is difficult to prove the success or otherwise of supply-side policies, but many commentators believe that they did contribute to the favourable rate of economic growth experienced by the UK in the 1980s. Whether they can have a similar effect in the 1990s remains to be seen.

Box 37.5 Was there an economic miracle in the 1980s?

In the political run up to the 1992 General Election the Government continued to claim that an economic miracle had occurred in the 1980s but, as the following extract shows, the Labour opposition maintained that the miracle was bogus and that the sacrifices of supply-side economic policies had been in vain.

Economic Miracle 'Bogus'

The Labour Party last night seized on a formal Treasury admission that 12½ years of Conservative rule have produced an average annual economic growth rate of only 1.75 per cent, bolstering the Opposition's claims that the Tory economic miracle is 'totally bogus' – and exposed by renewed recession.

As unemployment rose by a spectacular 100,000, to 2,092,700, and Neil Kinnock dubbed John Major 'the Prime Minister of Unemployment' the shadow chancellor, John Smith, highlighted the Treasury's figures given in Commons exchanges by the Economic Secretary, John Maples.

In separate developments on the economic front, Labour last night promised no early income tax cuts but no tax rises for most people either, and hammered home its election theme that the 1980–82 recession was not 'a once and for all sacrifice' as people had been told. This time Mr Kinnock said in Scotland, it was not confined to northern smokestack industries.

On a familiar Commons battleground, Mr Maples earlier produced the lowest average growth figure yet – 1.75 per cent for 1979–91 – because Labour's Stan Orme had asked to include 1991s projected growth figure of minus 2 per cent. The outcome contrasted with an average 2.09 per cent figure for 1979–90 produced – in an answer to the former chancellor Nigel Lawson – only last week.

'Growth at under 2 per cent is a very poor result of 12 years of Conservative economic management. This is significantly below the growth trend of the British economy in the 1960s and 1970s,' said Mr Smith, claiming it showed how far Britain had slipped towards 'the bottom of the European economic league'.

Labour's irritation stems from Mr Lawson's hyperbolic mid-80s talk about Britain's economic miracle outstripping West Germany's – attributing the recession of 1980–82 to the failings of the last Labour Government, which fell in May 1979 after a decade in which UK growth averaged 2.4 per cent, lower than booming competitors in an oil-disrupted period.

Growth in 1979 of 2.8 per cent came at the peak of an economic cycle and some economists would argue that a fairer measure is from trough to trough, in this case 1981–91, which produces a 2.1 per cent average. The Tory defence rests on a better relative performance by Britain in the Eighties, though it was bolstered by North Sea oil.

Either way it throws some cold water on flashier claims made for Thatcherism. And in a speech in Dundee last night, Mr Kinnock derided what he called the 'cosmetic change to the new Toryism – a hole 12 years long and millions of lost jobs, thousands of closed companies, billions of wasted assets wide.'

He complained that the Government's record alternated 'between clobbering demand and production with high interest rates and then letting credit and consumption rip', and rubbed the point home by recalling that in 1987, when the last election was held, inflation and growth were both around 4 per cent, compared with 8.2 per cent inflation and 2 per cent growth now.

In Labour's party political broadcast last night, John Smith said: 'I don't think for a period of years we can afford to cut personal taxation' and that money available from economic growth should go on education and training. He said that tax increases would only affect the better off.

- Recent GNP growth figures are 1979 (2.8 per cent); 1980 (– 2); 1981 (– 1.2); 1982 (1.7); 1983 (3.8); 1984 (1.8); 1985 (3.8); 1986 (3.6); 1987 (4.4); 1988 (4.2); 1989 (1.7); 1990 (0.5) and 1991 (projected at – 2).

Source: Michael White, *Guardian*, 18 April 1991

REVIEW QUESTIONS

1 Distinguish between demand-side and supply-side policies.

2 How might supply-side policies affect (i) economic growth, (ii) the balance of payments?

3 Has deregulation increased the number of 'contestable markets' in the UK?

4 'Since privatisation simply transfers monopolies from the public sector to the private sector it has no effect on efficiency'. Do you agree with this statement?

CHAPTER 38

DEVELOPMENT AND THE PROBLEMS OF THE LESS DEVELOPED COUNTRIES

CONNECTIONS

In Chapter 38 we shall be examining the **economics of developing countries**. We shall be making use of many concepts discussed earlier in the book including population (Chapter 14), enterprise (Chapter 15), free trade and protection (Chapter 31) and supply-side policies (Chapter 37).

Key Concepts

Developed country
Developing country (formerly called a less-developed country)
Economic aid
Economic development
Newly industrialised country (NIC)

What is a Developing Country?

About one-fifth of the world's population lives in *developed industrial economies* with relatively high levels of real income per head. The remainder of the world's population lives in *low to middle income economies* which are classified as *developing countries*. These comprise most of Africa, Asia and Latin America, much of the Middle East, and parts of southern and eastern Europe. Table 38.1 (on p. 375) gives some examples of countries at different stages of economic development, based on the criterion of GDP (income) per head.

Despite this classification, income data could be considered an unrealistic yardstick of development, because it fails to take account of other factors which affect the quality of life (see p. 164). To this end, the United Nations introduced in 1990 a measure known as the *Human Development Index* (HDI). This consists of a weighted combination of three indicators: the purchasing power of real income; life expectancy; and levels of literacy. Table 38.1 shows that on the basis of human development the 'gap' between rich and poor countries looks somewhat narrower, though a significant gap still exists.

The Sources of Economic Development

We define 'economic development' as sustained growth in income per head over a considerable period of time. This is usually associated with profound **structural changes** in an economy. We find that growth is associated with conditions which favour improvements in the quantity and quality of factors of production and the efficiency with which they are combined. The main sources of such improvements are summarised below.

- *Physical investment*: The process of net investment (that is, additions to the nation's stock of physical capital) may take place in two ways. One is *capital widening*, where extra capital is applied to an increased amount of labour, but the amount of capital per worker remains broadly unchanged. This does not necessarily lead to any

Box 38.1 The rising tide of world poverty

Poverty in the developing countries is on the rise. Between 1970 and 1980 the number of people with inadequate diets in developing countries (excluding China) increased from 650 million to 730 million. Since 1980 matters have turned from bad to worse: economic growth rates have slowed, real wages have dropped, and growth in employment has faltered in most developing countries. Precipitous declines in commodity prices have cut rural incomes, and governments have reduced their real spending on social services.

Comprehensive data on poverty are lacking, especially for the most recent years, but scattered information from individual countries confirms the general impression of deteriorating social conditions in many developing countries. A recent study found that the number of people below the poverty line increased at least up to 1983–84 in Brazil, Chile, Ghana, Jamaica, Peru, and the Philippines. It also found that there has been a sharp and widespread reversal in the trend toward improved standards of child health, nutrition, and education. Other sources show that in twenty-one out of thirty-five low-income developing countries, the daily calorie supply per capita was lower in 1985 than in 1965. Between 1979 and 1983 life expectancy declined in nine Sub-Saharan African countries. In Zambia deaths from malnutrition among infants and children doubled during 1980–84, and in Sri Lanka, the calorie consumption of the poorest tenth of the population fell 9 per cent between 1979 and 1982. In Costa Rica falling real wages during 1979–82 increased the incidence of poverty by more than two-thirds. Real per capita public spending on health and education in low-income developing countries stagnated between 1975 and 1984. For six low-income countries the number of physicians per capita decreased between 1965 and 1981, and enrolment ratios for primary education declined in twelve low-income Sub-Saharan African countries.

Source: World Bank

increase in output per worker. The other way is *capital deepening*, where investment leads to an increase in the amount of capital per worker: This is often associated with innovation which, if successful, leads to considerable increases in labour productivity. Contrary to popular belief, investment levels in developing countries are sometimes relatively high and may compare well with those in mature industrial countries. Unfortunately the rapid population growth which is a characteristic of most developing countries means that investment in these countries often leads to capital widening rather than capital deepening. Moreover, the efficiency of investment is often comparatively low in developing countries.

- *Human investment*: Education, health and training are often described as human investment because they play an important part in raising the productivity of labour. Unfortunately low levels of human capital are a feature of many developing countries.
- *Innovation*: There is little doubt that this is an important factor in economic development. It may take a number of forms, including improved organisation and management, better communications, and so on. However, the most important aspect of innovation is probably the application to different uses of existing technology. In the case of computer technology, for instance, three important applications in the UK have been: stock control in large supermarket chains, information processing in the City, and robotics in motor car manufacturing.
- *Reallocation of resources*: Economic development is very much associated with changes in the distribution of a country's labour force. As development takes place there is a tendency for labour to shift from low productivity uses in primary production, including agriculture, to high productivity uses in manufacturing and service industries. Where manufacturing and service opportunities are lacking, however, movements of labour often simply lead to increasing urban poverty.

In general, the more productive and mobile resources are, the more economic development will be encouraged. Unfortunately governments in a number of developing countries have adopted policies which, while intended to foster economic development, have had the opposite effect, primarily because of the way in which they have **distorted**

Table 38.1 *Economic development*

	Population 1986 (m)	GNP *per capita* (1986) ($)	Annual growth of GDP: (%) (1980–6)	Life expectancy (years) (1987)	Adult literacy rate (%) (1985)	HDI index
Low income Economies						
Niger	6.6	260	– 2.6	45	14	0.10
India	781.4	290	4.9	59	43	0.40
China	1054.0	300	10.5	70	69	0.71
Lower middle income economies						
Bolivia	6.6	600	– 3.0	54	75	0.52
Nigeria	103.0	640	– 3.2	51	43	0.32
Turkey	51.6	1110	4.9	65	74	0.75
Upper middle income economies						
Argentine	31.0	2350	– 0.8	71	96	0.91
South Korea	41.5	2370	8.2	70	95	6.90
Hong Kong	5.4	6910	6.0	76	88	0.93
High income oil exporters						
Saudia Arabia	12.0	6950	– 3.4	64	55	0.70
Kuwait	1.8	13890	– 0.9	73	70	0.83
Industrial market economies						
United Kingdom	56.7	8870	2.3	76	99	0.972
West Germany	60.9	12080	1.5	75	99	0.972
United States	241.6	17480	3.1	76	96	0.961

Source: World Bank, UN

the operation of markets and **restricted the mobility of resources**.

Characteristics of Developing Countries

It would be wrong to assume that the world's developing countries are uniform in their characteristics. Each is different and has its own peculiar difficulties. Nevertheless, they often have a number of characteristics in common. These can be summarised as follows.

- Low **productivity in agriculture**.
- Low **levels of human capital** in terms of health, education and training, resulting from a poor social infrastructure.
- Low **domestic savings**.
- High **capital–output ratios**.
- General **unemployment**, particularly in rural areas where the marginal product of labour in agriculture is very low and probably zero in some cases.
- Rapid **population expansion**.
- Poor **infrastructure**, in terms of road, rail and telephone networks, an inefficient banking sector, and so on. A poor communications network

Box 38.2 The problem of underdevelopment

In the 1980s many developing countries experienced economic difficulties which resulted in a decrease in per capita income. The situation was particularly serious in Africa, as the following extract shows:

> In many countries rigid economic and social structures inhibited rapid adaptation to the changed environment of the late 1970s and early 1980s. In a large number of countries, the magnitude of the shocks – escalation of interest rates and a major drop in the prices of commodity exports – overwhelmed adjustment programmes. In others, the difficulties stemmed mostly from the inability to expand agricultural – in particular food – production. Finally, in several countries, prolonged armed conflicts adversely affected economic activities and diverted a considerable amount of resources from development.
>
> In developing countries with rigid economic structures and no mechanisms to buffer large segments of the population from an abrupt worsening of the economic situation, the impact of an adverse shock to the economy can be very painful. In the 1980s natural disasters such as droughts and floods further strained the capacity of several economies.
>
> About two-thirds of the developing countries experienced a decrease in their per capita income in the period 1980–1989. In more than half of these countries, the decline was more than 10 per cent and in two out of the five it exceeded 20 per cent. The magnitude of the decline and the number of countries affected by it are without precedent in the post-war period. The consequences of falling incomes have often been devastating: standards of living have deteriorated; nutritional conditions have worsened; revenues from excise taxes and direct taxes have been negatively affected, limiting the scope of Governments for compensatory measures; and investments have fallen, thus reducing the potential for growth in the medium to long term.
>
> The growth of output in Africa during 1989 is estimated at 2.8 per cent (see Table 38.2) which, for the third consecutive time, was a slight improvement over the previous year's performance. Despite the improvement, the increase in output fell just short of population growth, adding another year to a decade of economic decline.
>
> The collapse of cocoa and coffee prices was a severe blow to the export earnings of producers such as Burundi, the Central African Republic, Cote d'Ivoire, the Gambia, Ghana, Rwanda and Uganda. As part of their structural adjustment programmes, several of these countries had raised the domestic producer prices of these commodities in an effort to increase production and hence exports. However, such moves were frustrated by developments in the international market: in some countries, such as Cameroon and Cote d'Ivoire, producer prices had to be reduced by as much as 50 per cent in 1989. Ghana lost $200 million as a result of the drop in cocoa prices, while the loss experienced by 25 countries belonging to the Inter-African Coffee

implies that it is difficult and expensive to transport raw materials and finished products, while an inefficient banking sector can leave industry short of funds with which to finance production.

It is frequently suggested that a further characteristic of developing countries is that they tend to be lacking in **natural resources**. In fact, while this is true of some developing countries (Bangladesh, for instance), it is not true of many other poor countries (Ghana for instance). Moreover, some of the most successful developing countries, the newly industrialised countries (NICs), are largely lacking in natural resources – Singapore and Hong Kong for instance.

Choice of Development Strategy

Development Through Primary Production

The African countries are typical of many developing countries in employing a high proportion of resources in primary production. This suggests that following the principles of absolute and comparative advantage, the natural development route for these countries might be to specialise in the production and export of primary products – such as, in the case of Ghana, cocoa and minerals. This was in fact the

Organisation was around $250 million in 1989 (over $100 million by Uganda alone) and might reach $1.5 billion in 1990.

The World Bank report identified three major reasons for the crisis in sub-Saharan Africa: low levels of investment, low rates of return (in part a consequence of inadequate past investment in, and maintenance of, infrastructure and services) and rapid population growth. Capital formation in sub-Saharan Africa fell from over 20 per cent of GDP at the beginning of the 1980s to 15 per cent in 1989; this is insufficient to maintain existing capital, as evidenced by the decaying public buildings, deteriorating transport system and collapsing social services throughout the continent. In order to restore growth, strategies have to focus on reviving investment and making it efficient.

The vastness and diversity of the African continent defies any attempt to apply a standard formula for policy measures designed to achieve agricultural transformation. Measures which might prove effective in addressing certain issues in some countries can prove futile, and even have perverse effects, in others. To avoid such pitfalls, reform programmes have to be internally generated and command widespread support.

Source: UN, *World Economic Survey*

Table 38.2 *Economic indicators in two groups of developing countries*

	1961–73	1973–80	1980–89
Investment as a percentage of GDP			
Sub-Saharan Africa	16	21	16
South Asia	18	21	24
Return on investment (%)			
Sub-Saharan Africa	31	14	3
South Asia	23	23	24
Population growth (%)			
Sub-Saharan Africa	2.6	2.8	3.1
South Asia	2.4	2.4	2.3
GDP growth per person (%)			
Sub-Saharan Africa	2.1	− 0.1	− 2.7
South Asia	1.3	2.1	3.0

Source: *The Economist* (9 December 1989) (adapted)

route followed by a number of 'yesterday's' developing countries before they developed into mature industrial economies: the United States, Canada and Australia for example. However, there are problems with this route.

- *Adverse trends in primary product prices*: The trend in the relative price of non-oil primary products has been downwards in recent decades. The reasons for this are partly the development of substitutes, partly the low income elasticity of demand by users and partly an expansion in the supply of many primary products, particularly due to technical advances in production. The net effect has therefore been a decline in market price, compared with manufactured products, and this trend is likely to continue in the future.
- *Fluctuating primary product prices*: A second disadvantage of a concentration on primary products is that although the trend in prices is downwards, prices tend to fluctuate widely because supply and demand tend to be relatively price inelastic. A relatively small change in either demand or supply can therefore cause quite substantial changes in price. As Box 38.2 shows, the effect of this on earnings can be very serious for developing countries, which often have a heavy export concentration in a few primary products. In Zambia, for example, where 80 per cent of export earnings are from copper, a 50 per cent reduction in world copper prices can have a devastating effect on domestic income, employment and the balance of payments.

Development Through Industrialisation

Economic development through industrialisation can take two broad forms.

- *Import substitution*: This is a strategy of using tariffs and other forms of trade restriction to replace imports with **domestic production**. Import substitution is pursued because developing countries wish to reduce their dependence on primary production. However, this approach has not always been successful in encouraging development. One reason is that the countries concerned find themselves specialising in industries where, as explained earlier, they are likely to

Table 38.3 *The 'Asian Dragons'*

	South Korea	Taiwan	Singapore	Hong Kong
GNP *per capita* (US$) 1987	2690	–	7940	8070
Growth of GNP *per capita* (% pa)				
1965–87	6.4	–	7.2	6.2
Growth of manufacturing value added				
1964–73	21.0	18.2	17.8	12.1
1973–83	11.7	8.3	5.4	10.1
Manufacturing value added as a % of GDP				
1964	9.8	21.2	17.1	24.4
1983	33.2	41.9	21.3	33.6
Inflation 1980–87 (% pa)	5.0	–	1.3	6.7
Savings as a % of GDP 1987	38	–	40	31
Growth of manufacturing output (% pa)				
1965–73	49.8	44.7	23.1	20.5
19773–85	21.4	18.3	18.2	13.0

Source: *Economic Review*, Data Supplement (1990)

have a comparative disadvantage. Another reason is that their domestic industries, being sheltered from foreign competition, fail to develop efficiently (see p. 293). The outcome for many, notably in sub-Saharan Africa, has been an undue reliance on growth via expansion of

Figure 38.1 *Investment as a percentage of GDP*

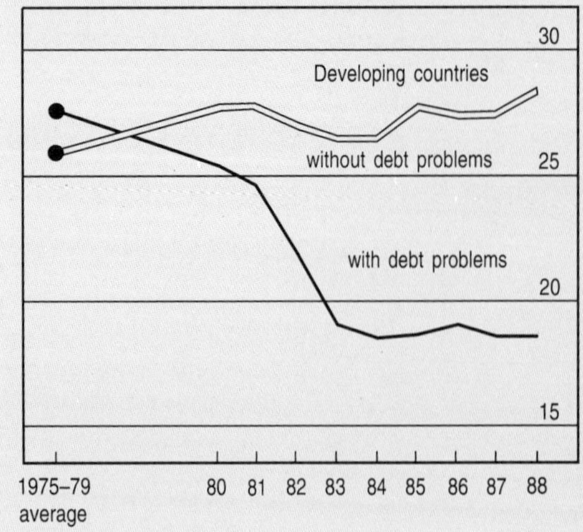

Source: *The Economist* (20 May 1989)

domestic demand. This has often led to inflation rather than economic growth.

- *Manufacturing export growth*: While import substitution involves insulation from the world economy, the strategy of growth through manufacturing exports implies exposure to foreign competition. In the early stages of this strategy exports tend to consist of labour-intensive low quality manufactures such as textiles. Later, as the country in question achieves increasing industrial maturity, the range of successful exports is likely to widen and include capital goods and high quality consumer goods. This has proved to be the case in newly-industrialised countries such as Mexico, Brazil and the 'Asian Dragons' (South Korea, Taiwan, Hong Kong and Singapore). The main threat to this strategy has been the rise of the 'new protectionism' (see p. 297).

The Asian Dragons have attracted much attention, and their success in comparison with other developing countries may be due to several factors including:

- A high level of **human capital**, particularly in terms of educational attainment, making for adaptable and efficient management and labour.

- A high level of **domestic saving and investment**.
- A readiness on the part of entrepreneurs to undertake **innovation** and **accept change**.
- Macroeconomic policies which have held **inflation at relatively low levels by world standards.**
- **Outward looking development strategies**: in South Korea and Taiwan, protection of domestic industry has been falling steadily while in the case of Hong Kong and Singapore it is virtually non-existent.
- The existence of **relatively free domestic markets** with a **low degree of government intervention**. (South Korea is the exception here. Its government has been highly interventionist, controlling domestic industry through financial regulation and vast holding companies.).

Development Through Foreign Borrowing

Borrowing from abroad might be a sound strategy if the funds obtained are employed productively, so that extra output and exports are eventually generated to service and pay off foreign debt. In practice, this has not always been the case. In the 1980s many developing countries found themselves with a severe foreign debt problem, due to three main factors:

- **Increasing balance of payments deficits** resulting from higher oil prices and lower primary product prices.
- High **world interest rates**.
- A **poor rate of return on investments** financed by foreign borrowing.

A number of such countries, notably Brazil, Argentina and Mexico, were lent new funds by creditor countries or were allowed to 'reschedule' their debts – that is, pay back the original loan over an extended period. In this way, cases of debt default (failure to repay debt) were largely avoided. However, as a result, **debt interest charges** have increased substantially.

Increasing interest charges are a problem because they can cause *debt overhang*. This occurs when a country is unable to service its foreign debts in full, and the amount it can afford to pay depends on its economic performance. If its exports increase, much of the benefit goes to creditors abroad. The effect is to depress the return on domestic investment and weaken the incentive to invest. Falling investment in turn retards economic development and export potential. Some evidence of this is given in Figure 38.1, which shows that the rate of investment among developing countries with debt problems did indeed fall significantly in the 1980s.

Table 38.4 *Aid to developing countries*

	£bn at 1985 prices		
	1980	1985	1986
Bilateral aid	27.7	28.6	28.0
Multilateral aid	7.3	8.5	7.7
Total	35.0	37.1	35.7

Source: UN

In 1989 an important initiative, known as the *Brady Plan*, was launched to deal with the problem of developing countries' debt. The main proposals of the Plan can be summarised:

- *Reduced debt servicing*: Foreign creditors (who include banks, governments and international financial institutions) will agree to consider on a case-by-case basis **reductions in interest charges** on foreign debts.
- *Buyback*: Debtor countries will be allowed to **buy back foreign debt** at a discount for cash. Much of this debt is now of little value, trading on secondary security markets (see p. 86) at discounts of up to 70 per cent.
- *International funding*: The World Bank and the IMF, together with the government of Japan, will provide funds of $30bn to $35bn to support debt rescheduling and debt service reductions.

In 1990 Mexico, Uruguay, The Philippines and other countries negotiated deals under the Brady Plan. However, the position over the foreign debt of Argentina and Brazil was more equivocal. Both of these countries had been paying only a part of the debt servicing falling due, and had incurred interest arrears of around $8bn each. Foreign creditors were insisting that some of these arrears should be paid ahead of any Brady-type deal.

Development Through Foreign Aid

Economic aid can be divided into two categories: *bilateral aid* and *multilateral aid* (see Table 38.4). Bilateral aid is arranged between two countries: *donor* and *recipient*. Such aid is often 'tied' in the sense that it can be spent only on specific products supplied by the donor country. This is a considerable disadvantage for the recipient if these products are more expensive than alternatives. *Multilateral aid*, on the other hand, mainly comes from international agencies such as the IBRD, the International Monetary Fund and the European Community. Since aid from these agencies is not tied to a specific donor country it allows recipients more freedom to choose where they place their orders.

Economic aid may contribute to economic development in three ways:

- It can provide resources to **raise the level of investment** undertaken in the market sector.
- It can provide resources to **enlarge and improve social and industrial infrastructure**.
- It can be tied to **economic reform** in recipient countries.

Economic aid can have a profound effect on recipient countries, and there have been many instances where aid has encouraged development. For example, in the late 1960s a bilateral aid arrangement was made between the UK and Kenya for the purpose of building and improving small roads in the tea-growing areas of central Kenya. Better transport made it possible for farmers to move fresh tea to the processing factories, thus increasing their earnings and making possible new investments in tea-growing and other commercial crops. These roads also made it possible for children to attend local town schools. In addition, by taxing tea processing, the Kenyan government was able to generate revenues which could be used to promote other areas of economic development.

Despite this, there is concern among economists at the failure of aid in many cases to yield lasting economic development. It has even been suggested that aid can reduce the recipient country's prospects for development. The main criticisms of the use of foreign aid for development are:

- The provision of free or cheap resources reduces the incentive for recipient countries to use them **effectively**. For example, aid has sometimes been used on prestige projects, such as unnecessary and unprofitable airlines, which do little to improve living standards.
- Economic aid is not always **necessary** for development. Some developing countries, notably the Asian Dragons, have achieved rapid development with little or no aid.
- Economic aid is sometimes used to support policies which **hinder** economic development – for example, state regulation of markets and collectivisation of agriculture.
- Resources provided through aid may be dissipated through **theft** and **corruption**.

These weighty criticisms imply that it might be preferable for developing countries to rely more upon private capital flows where there is a greater incentive to ensure that the resources used earn an adequate return. However, aid might still be preferable to private capital for several reasons:

- Foreign private capital is not necessarily used **more effectively** by developing countries than aid would be. The 1980s international debt crisis exposed many badly-conceived and executed private capital projects.
- Unlike private investment funds, economic aid can be directed to take favourable account of **divergences between private and external benefits**. For example, improving the infrastructure might assist economic development yet involve financial loss.
- While it is admitted that in the past aid was sometimes associated with inappropriate policies in recipient countries, increasingly **aid is now being tied to economic reform**, resulting in improved economic performance.

The IBRD and Development Aid

The International Bank for Reconstruction and Development (IBRD) (or World Bank, as it is commonly known) was established to provide long-term assistance to countries undergoing economic reconstruction and development. IBRD member countries are required to subscribe capital to the IBRD on the basis of a *quota* which is related to the member's national income and position in world trade. However, members are required to pay only a small proportion of their subscribed capital. The remainder constitutes a *guarantee fund* which provides the IBRD with security, enabling it to raise substantial additional funds on the world's capital markets. The IBRD normally charges interest at near-commercial

Box 38.3 Policy reform in Sub-Saharan Africa

In contrast to other developing regions, Sub-Saharan Africa has shown consistently weak economic performance over an entire generation. To make matters worse, during the 1980s per capita income has fallen to about three-quarters of the level reached by the end of the 1970s. Rapid population growth and external shocks have contributed to this, but weak economic performance has now begun to erode the region's productive base and human resources. By the mid-1980s gross investment levels in many countries were too low to maintain the capital stock, and health care and education are now deteriorating.

However, many African governments have started to improve past policies. Their reform efforts can best be described as a slow process of important policy change that is gaining momentum. Changes cover a broad range of policies in many countries. Although reform was initially prompted by the austerity of the early 1980s, many African leaders now recognise that further reforms are essential for improved economic performance. At the UN Special Session on Africa in 1986, African governments submitted a Program of Action for African Economic Recovery and Development. That program recognises the failures of past policies and stresses the need for sustained reform.

Commitment and action vary among countries. On balance, however, about half of the countries in Sub-Saharan Africa are already committed to serious reform. In some areas, especially where institutional and managerial changes are involved, progress is difficult to quantify. In other areas, such as fiscal and monetary policies and price incentives – where better data are available – the signs of progress are clear. A number of countries have made positive adjustments. These include lowering real exchange rates, reducing fiscal deficits, and raising export crop prices. Policy reform has been greatest in countries whose adjustment programs have been sufficiently strong and sustained to be supported by World Bank program lending. Other countries have sometimes allowed policies to worsen.

Most adjusting countries have also taken steps to restructure public employment, rationalise and improve management in public enterprises; lift price and trade controls, both domestically and externally; and strengthen government economic management – especially in public investment programming.

The severity of Africa's structural economic imbalances and the vulnerability of African economies to the external environment often obscure the impact of reform efforts on economic performance. Moreover, it takes considerable time to increase growth, and progress is often spread unevenly across countries and sectors. Although comparisons between countries with and without strong reform programs can be made difficult by the uneven effects of exogenous factors such as export prices and weather, evidence shows that adjustment is generally conducive to growth. For example, excluding countries recently affected by strong external shocks (both positive and negative), growth in reforming countries accelerated from an average of 1 per cent during 1980–85 to nearly 4 per cent during 1986–87. By contrast, growth in non-reforming countries, also 1 per cent in the earlier period, barely increased during 1986–87. In most cases reform has helped to alleviate poverty by raising agricultural incomes and improving the efficiency of public spending on infrastructure and key social services.

Reform efforts in Africa are impressive. But given the uncertain global prospects and severe constraints such as high population growth, countries with adjustment programs must deepen existing reforms. Others still need to adopt and implement adjustment programs. Industrial countries and multilateral financial institutions, in turn, must persevere in their support of African adjustment through increased aid and debt relief.

Source: World Bank

rates on its loans, but it does enable developing countries to acquire funds which might not otherwise be available to them.

In addition, the IBRD has created the International Development Association (IDA) to provide loans at concessionary rates of interest in certain circumstances to countries that might find it impossible to pay the rates normally charged by the IBRD. The IDA's funds are normally directed at government projects, or private sector ventures supported by governments, in the very poorest developing countries where income per head is less than about $500 per year (see Table 38.5). In 1987 the IDA lent £14bn for 127 such projects. IDA loans are very flexible and

Box 38.4 How do Nigerian manufacturers cope with inadequate infrastructure services?

Nigerian manufacturers face frequent interruptions of publicly provided services such as water, electricity, telecommunications, transport, and waste disposal. When available, the services are often of poor quality. This is a waste of public funds that also adds significantly to the cost of manufacturing.

Nigerian manufacturers therefore make capital investments in services such as electricity and water for themselves. According to the Nigerian Industrial Development Bank (NIDB), frequent power outages and fluctuations in voltage affect almost every industrial enterprise in the country. To avoid production losses as well as damage to machinery and equipment, firms invest in generators. A milk processing firm, for example, needed its own generators because voltage surges or gaps in supply could threaten vital equipment. One large textile manufacturing enterprise estimates the depreciated capital value of its electricity supply investment as $400 per worker. If extrapolated to all 6,000 Nigerian manufacturing firms, such an amount (at current prices) could pay for capital equipment to improve transmission and distribution for the entire country, including the residential sector. Similarly companies invest in boreholes and water treatment plants. Typically as much as 20 per cent of the initial capital investment for new plants financed by the NIDB is spent on electric generators and boreholes.

The cost of poor telecommunications is reflected in numerous small expenditures, such as motorcycles for couriers and radio systems, and in time wasted, as managers and sales people travel to deliver messages or hold conversations that would take moments over a working phone line. In Lagos long commuting times caused by inefficient bus services have led firms and workers to rely on private transport as much as possible.

Although necessary, many of these self-provided infrastructure investments are inefficient, because they are too small. Since possibilities for input substitution are limited, firms that make capital expenditures to provide their own services have higher production costs. Better public provision of infrastructure would reduce the losses; policy options are already being studied and developed.

Source: World Bank.

Box 38.5 Entrepreneurial talent in Bangladesh

It is sometimes suggested that a major problem for many developing countries is the lack of entrepreneurial talent. In some cases this is no doubt correct particularly in socialist economies where the state has directed production and the independent entrepreneur has virtually ceased to exist. However, it is by no means always true.

In 1979 Mr Quader, a Bangladeshi entrepreneur started a collaboration with a South Korean sewing machine manufacturer to produce and market its products in Bangladesh. As part of the agreement Quader's workers were sent to South Korea for training by the parent organisation. The Bangladeshi factory was so successful that it was able to cancel its Korean tie-up and 'go independent'. By 1987 Quader's business was producing 2.3m shirts with a value of $5.3m. There was only one problem for Quader. He kept losing his Korean-trained employees who were going off to start their own businesses! In 1985 Bangladesh had 700 clothes-exporting factories and clothing had now become the country's leading export.

Based on an article in *The Economist* (23 September 1989)

can be used for both industrial and infrastructure projects. The former are required to yield a satisfactory financial rate of return, while for the latter a satisfactory economic or social rate of return is all that is required.

Recent years have seen two new developments in IBRD policy towards developing countries:

- The provision of **Structural Adjustment Loans** for developing countries experiencing chronic balance of payments and debt problems.
- A requirement that the granting of loans is conditional on recipient countries adopting **programmes of economic reform to support improved economic performance.**

The increasing emphasis on reform reflects the growing importance of supply-side (see p. 359) considerations in encouraging efficiency in the allocation of resources. By contrast, earlier IBRD aid programmes were often associated with grandiose and ultimately unsuccessful schemes of state planning. One of the most notorious of these was the 'African socialism' policy adopted in Tanzania, which by directing independent peasant farmers into inefficient collective farms, seriously damaged agriculture and converted Tanzania from a food exporter into a food importer.

Population Expansion in the Developing Countries

In the twentieth century there has been a dramatic expansion in world population. Much of this has occurred in the developing countries and has been due to two broad factors:

- A continuing high level of 'demographic fertility' – that is, **a large number of children per family**.
- **A much reduced level of mortality**, because of advances in medical care. Some developing countries are currently experiencing annual population expansion rates of up to 4 per cent. If this continued, a country's population would increase 55 times in 100 years! Fortunately there are indications that population expansion in the developing countries may be slowing down, and we examine this below.

Figure 38.2 gives some idea of the actual and projected growth of world population into the next century.

Population Expansion is a Development Problem

There are a number of ways in which rapid population expansion may impair economic development:

- A reduced level of resources per head makes the choice more difficult between satisfying **present consumption** and undertaking investment which is necessary to assist **future economic development**.
- In economies which are highly dependent on agriculture, population expansion may slow the transfer of labour **out of low productivity agriculture into manufacturing and service industries**. (For example, the rural labour force in Kenya is expected to double in the next 30 years.)
- Population expansion is an important factor encouraging **urban growth**, for although the

Table 38.5 *IDA aid commitments by region*

	1981–84		1985–87		1988	
	Amount ($m)	Commitments	Amount ($m)	Commitments	Amount ($m)	Commitments
Africa	935	33	1329	42	1728	51
Asia	1811	63	1751	55	1551	46
IBRD/IDA countries	1269	44	1232	39	1138	34
IDA only	543	19	519	16	412	12
Other	131	5	122	4	108	3
Total	2878	100	3201	100	3387	100

Source: Jeffrey A. Katz, *Finance and Development* (June 1989) absolute number of people remaining in rural areas is likely to rise, the *proportion* of population living in towns also increases. Rapid urban growth, however, poses severe economic and social challenges in terms of infrastructure requirements. Failure to meet these, particularly if it is coupled with a lack of manufacturing opportunities, often leads to widespread urban poverty.

- A country with high fertility and low mortality will have a large proportion of **young people** in its population. For example, the average age in Egypt is currently less than 20. This implies a high dependency ratio, with resources being used to care for children rather than being directly available for economic development.

Figure 38.3 shows two population pyramids: one for the UK, a typical developed country, and one for India, a typical developing country.

Figure 38.2 *Past and projected world population*

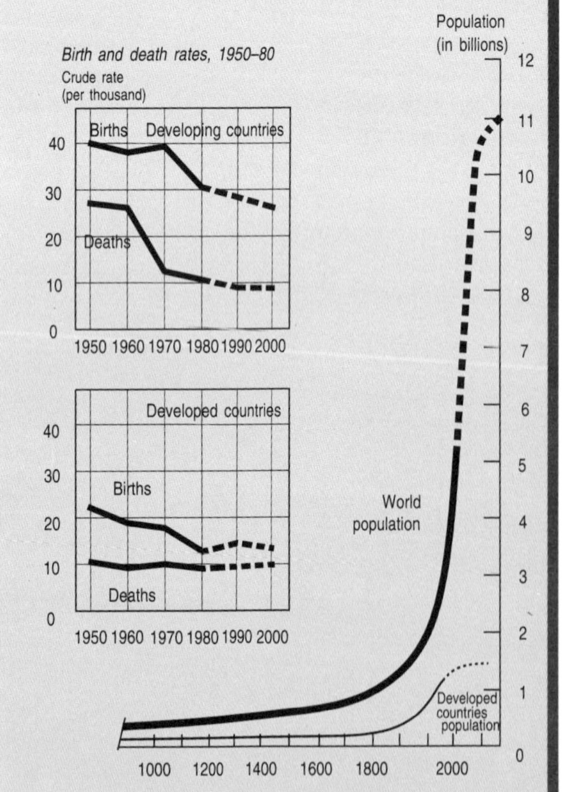

Source: *Finance and Development* (September 1989)

Figure 38.3 *Age structure*

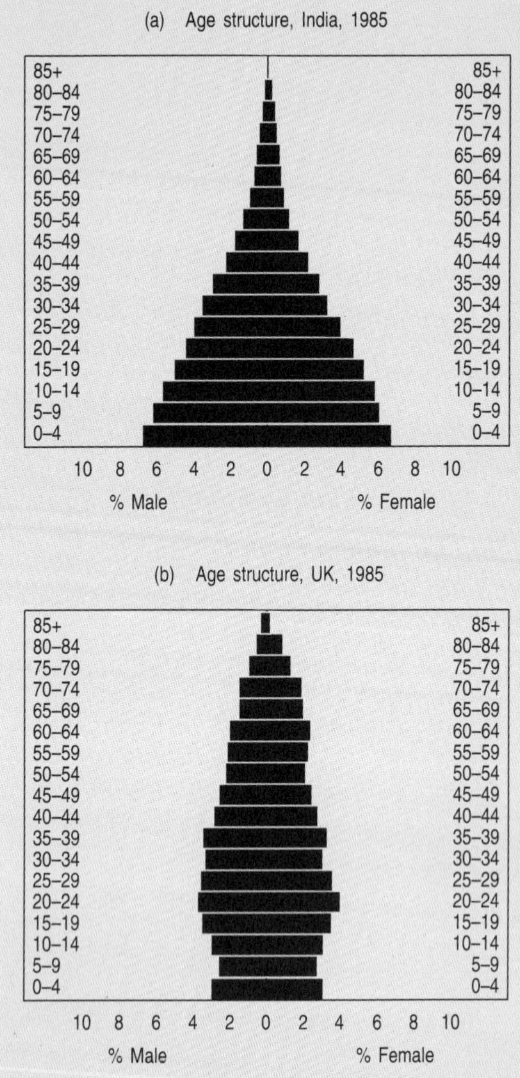

Source: *Philips Certificate Atlas* (1987)

Population Policy in Developing Countries

We have seen that population expansion constitutes a major problem for today's developing countries. How then can such expansion be reduced? Given the low and falling level of mortality there, the key to slower population expansion in developing countries must lie with lower fertility – that is, smaller family size. This may take place in two ways. First, the experience of countries like South Korea, Singapore and Hong Kong in the 1960s strongly suggests that a natural reduction in family size tends to take place when, with economic development, improvements occur in income, literacy and social conditions. Secondly, *population policy* has had some success in reducing fertility. In developing countries it is often the very poorest people, with particularly low income, education and social status, who have the largest families. Population policy seeks to address this problem by providing:

- Better **education and employment opportunities**, especially for women.
- Better information about methods of **family planning**.
- Improved access to **family planning facilities**, since many modern methods of contraception are effective only in conjunction with medical support schemes.

Recent experience suggests that countries pursuing active population policies (for example, India, China and Egypt) are more likely to experience a reduction in both fertility and population expansion than others at a similar stage of economic development, but without population policies (for example, Pakistan, Zambia and Brazil).

Unfortunately, even if, as now seems likely, fertility does continue to fall in a number of developing countries (with the notable exception of sub-Saharan Africa), rapid population expansion will not quickly come to an end. This is because the large numbers of young people now entering child-bearing age will constitute a 'base' for large absolute increases in population well into the next century – a process known as *population momentum*.

REVIEW QUESTIONS

1 Why is an efficient banking sector important for developing countries?

2 Why is unemployment 'disguised' when a worker's marginal product is zero?

3 Who is responsible for the international debt crisis, and what should be done about it?

4 'Successful aid depends upon liberal trade'. Do you agree with this statement?.

5 With reference to a particular country, examine the economic and social effects of underdevelopment.

6 Could emigration help solve the problem of economic underdevelopment?

7 Examine the role of Third World pressure groups such as 'UNCTAD'.

8 What criteria and data would you use to decide if:
(a) Hong Kong (b) Russia, were developed or developing countries?

9 Is there a 'Third World'?

10 Why might it be in the interest of creditor countries to reduce the debt burden of developing countries?

11 Do all developing countries face similar problems in seeking to achieve economic development?

12 Both Mexico and United States have a high level of foreign debt: why is this more of a problem for the former than for the latter?

13 'With every mouth God sends a pair of hands'. How relevant is this comment to the economic effects of population expansion in developing countries?.

GLOSSARY

Absolute advantage: A situation in which one nation can produce a given output at a lower resource cost than its trading competitors

Accelerator theory of investment: A theory which relates changes in the level of investment to changes in the national income

Accommodating capital movements: Those transactions in the balance of payments that are necessary to finance the difference between revenue from the sale of exports and expenditure from the purchase of imports

Accounting profit: The difference between expenses of a firm and the revenue it raises from the sale of output; no allowance is made in accounting profit for the opportunity cost of the resources used in production

Activist strategy: The view that deliberate changes in monetary and/or fiscal policy can be used to stimulate aggregate demand during a recession and restrain aggregate demand during a boom so as to minimise economic instability

Adaptive expectations hypothesis: The view that economic agents base their future expectations on the basis of their experiences, particularly their recent experiences

Aggregate demand: The total value of all planned expenditures on the output of a particular economy over a given time period

Aggregate demand schedule (curve): A curve indicating an inverse relationship between the price level and the total volume of goods and services demanded in an economy

Aggregate supply: The total value of all goods and services produced in an economy over a given time period

Aggregate supply schedule (curve): A curve indicating a positive relationship between the output of an economy and the price level

Allocative efficiency: When the price of the last unit produced is exactly equal to its opportunity cost of production

Anticipated inflation: An increase in the general level of prices that is widely expected by economic agents

Appreciation: An increase in the value of the domestic currency against other currencies on the foreign exchange market which is caused by a change in market forces

Arbitrage: Any activity whereby profit is earned simply by buying a commodity at one price and re-selling it at another

Automatic stabilisers: Changes in taxes and transfer payments that occur automatically as nominal GNP rises or falls

Autonomous variables: Those variables which do not vary directly with the level of income.

Average cost: Total cost divided by total output

Average product: Total product (output) divided by number of variable inputs (usually workers)

Balance of payments: A record of earnings from abroad from the sale of goods and services as well as capital inflows and expenditures on goods and services bought from abroad and capital outflows

Balanced budget: A situation where government expenditure is exactly equal to government revenue

Base year: A year chosen for purposes of comparison on which index numbers are based

Black economy – *see* Underground economy

Black market: Goods sold at prices that contravene legally established minimum prices

Bond: A security given in recognition of a debt on which interest is paid and which will be redeemed at some future date

Break-even point: The level of output at which a firm's revenue is exactly equal to its expenditure

Budget deficit: A situation where government expenditure exceeds government revenue

Budget line: A line showing the different combinations of goods and services that can be purchased at given prices with a given income

Budget surplus: A situation where government revenue exceeds government expenditure

Capital: Any man-made aid to production

Capitalism: An economic system based on the private ownership of productive resources in which goods and services are allocated through the operation of free markets

Cartel: An agreement among sellers of a product to coordinate their levels of production in such a way as to increase the profits of members; effectively a cartel will aim to create a monopoly in the market

Central bank: The bank whose major responsibilities are control of the money supply and supervision of the banking system.

Collective bargaining: The process whereby trade unions negotiate collectively the wages and conditions of their members, rather than allow one person to negotiate individually with the employer

Collusion: Agreements among firms to avoid competitive price changes; the most rigid form of collusion is a cartel

Commercial bank: A privately owned institution which accepts deposits and makes loans with the aim of making profits from its activities

Complements: Goods which are jointly consumed such as cereal and milk

Concentration ratio: The total sales of a small group of firms; the most commonly used ratios in the UK are the three-firm and five-firm concentration ratios

Conglomerate merger: the combining of firms which operate in different markets under single ownership

Constant returns to scale: When a change in the input of all factors of production leads to an equiproportionate change in output

Consumer equilibrium: When a consumer cannot increase total utility by changing the range of goods and services currently consumed

Consumer surplus: The difference between the maximum amount a consumer would be willing to pay and the amount that is actually paid for a good or service

Contestable market: A market in which the costs of entry and exit are low so that there is little risk to firms which enter the market

Cost-benefit analysis: A technique of investment appraisal in the public sector which evaluates the full social costs and social benefits of a project

Cost push inflation: A rise in the general level of prices caused by a rise in costs

Counter-cyclical policy: A policy aimed at moving the economy in the opposite direction of the business cycle; aggregate demand is stimulated during the downturn of the cycle and contracted during the upturn

Cross elasticity of demand: The ratio of the change in the price of one good to the change in demand for another good

Crowding-out effect: The reduction in private investment caused by an increase in public sector investment

Crude birth rate: The number of live births per year per thousand of population

Crude death rate: The number of deaths per year per thousand of population

Current account: A record of all transactions which involve the purchase or sale of goods and services abroad as well as international transfer payments

Cyclical unemployment: The portion of unemployment that is attributable to a decline in a country's total production; cyclical unemployment rises during a recession and falls during a boom

Demand deposits: Those deposits which can be withdrawn from a bank on demand; they are often referred to as *sight* deposits

Demand pull inflation: A rise in the general level of prices caused by a rise in demand at the existing price level

Depreciation: A decrease in the value of the domestic currency against other currencies on the foreign exchange market which is caused by a change in free market forces

Depression: An extended period of heavy unemployment during which the level of output is well below potential

Derived demand: Demand for one item which derives from the demand for another item; the demand for any factor input is a derived demand

Devaluation: A movement of the domestic currency against foreign currencies from one fixed parity to a lower fixed parity; such a movement is the result of an official act of policy rather than the result of free market forces

Dividend: That part of a company's profits distributed to its shareholders

Discounting: Calculating the present value of a future payment or return by using a rate of interest

Diseconomies of scale: When a change in all factor inputs leads to a less than proportional change in output

Disposable income: Personal income less personal taxes

Dissaving: Consumption which is financed by drawing on past savings; in effect, it is the difference between income and consumption when consumption exceeds income

Division of labour: The breaking up of a productive process into different tasks, each done by a different worker

Dumping: The sale of a good by a foreign supplier in one country at a price below the price at which the supplier sells it in the home market

Econometrics: The application of statistical methods to economic problems

Economic good: Any good that is produced from scarce resources; only economic goods have an opportunity cost

Economies of scale: When a change in all factor inputs leads to a more than proportional change in output

Entrepreneur: A profit-seeking, decision-taking bearer of risks; it is the entrepreneur who decides how resources are to be combined into output

Equilibrium: A state of balance that is self-perpetuating in the absence of a disturbance

Euro-currencies: Currencies deposited with a European bank outside their country of origin

Exchange rate: The rate at which domestic currency can be exchanged for foreign currency

Expansionary fiscal policy: An increase in government expenditure and/or a reduction in taxation aimed at increasing the level of aggregate demand

Externalities: The spillover effects of consumption and production which affect non-consumers and/or non-producers. Externalities might be beneficial or detrimental to the well-being of those on whom they are imposed

Factor markets: The markets in which the factors of production – land, labour and capital – are bought and sold.

Factors of production: The inputs of natural resources, labour, capital and entrepreneurship used in producing goods and services

Fiat money: Money which is not backed by some commodity such as gold which has some intrinsic value

Financial intermediary: A financial institution which accepts funds from savers and makes loans to borrowers

Fiscal policy: The use of government spending and taxation policies for the achievement of macroeconomic goals

Fixed cost: Cost that does not vary with output

Fixed exchange rates: A system of exchange rates where currencies have a fixed value against other currencies

Floating exchange rates: A system of exchange rates where the value of a currency against any other currency changes in response to changes in free market forces

Foreign exchange market: Those institutions which buy and sell foreign currency including commercial banks and foreign exchange dealers.

Fractional banking: A banking system in which banks maintain a minimum ratio between certain assets and their total liabilities

Free goods: Those goods such as fresh air which do not embody scarce resources

Frictional unemployment: Unemployment due to a mismatch between qualified workers seeking employment and obtaining a suitable position

General Agreement on Tariffs and Trade (GATT): An organisation consisting of most non-'communist' countries which aims to reduce barriers to trade

Gross National Product (GNP): The total annual value of output produced by a nation's resources

High-powered money: That component of the money stock that is directly under the control of the central bank. In the UK it consists of cash in circulation with the public and operational deposits at the Bank of England

Homogeneous: Alike in all respects

Horizontal integration: The combining under a single ownership of firms at the same stage of producing the same good

Hyperinflation: Very rapid and sustained inflation

Import quota: A restriction on the volume of a particular good that can be imported within a particular period of time

Income effect: That part of an increase in the amount consumed of a good whose price has fallen that is attributable to the increase in real income that results from the fall in price

Income elasticity of demand: The ratio of the percentage change in demand for a good to the percentage change in income

Income multiplier: The ratio of the change in the equilibrium level of income to the change in injections

Incomes policy: A policy that limits the increase in wages in an attempt to limit the rate of inflation

Indifference curve: A curve that shows different combinations of goods which give the consumer equal satisfaction

Inferior goods: Goods for which the income elasticity of demand is negative

Inflation: A continuous rise in the price level

Injection: Spending in the economy other than consumption spending

Innovation: The introduction of new products and processes; it often stems from the application of inventions

Intermediate good: A good that is not sold to the ultimate user and which is used as an input in the production of final goods and services

International Monetary Fund (IMF): An organisation set up to make loans to countries with a balance of payments deficit which they are unable to finance themselves; most loans are conditional on recipients adopting a particular set of economic policies

Inventories: Stocks of unsold goods and raw materials

Investment: The flow of resources into the production of new capital

Invisible: The export or import of a service such as tourism, transport or banking

J curve effect: The tendency for a depreciation of a country's currency against other currencies initially to worsen the trade deficit before an improvement is discernible

Kinked demand curve: A demand curve that is relatively elastic for a price rise and relatively inelastic for a price reduction

Labour force: The portion of the population that is aged between the minimum school-leaving age and the age of retirement; for definitions of the labour force it is immaterial whether members of this group are employed or unemployed

Law of comparative advantage: A principle which states that individuals, regions and nations can gain by specialising in the production of those goods where they have a lower opportunity cost than other individuals, regions and nations.

Law of demand: A principle which states that there is an inverse relationship between the price of a product and the quantity consumers will demand

Law of diminishing marginal utility: A principle which states that as consumption of a good or service increases each successive unit consumed will give less satisfaction than the preceding unit

Law of diminishing returns: A principle which states that as more units of a variable factor are used with a fixed amount of another factor a point will be reached when output rises at a slower rate: that is, marginal product will decline

Law of supply: A principle which states that there is a direct relationship between the price of a good and the amount that will be offered for sale

Leakage: That part of national income not devoted to consumption of domestic output

Less developed country: Low income countries characterised by rapid population growth and extreme poverty for the majority of the population; there is usually a large agricultural sector, a high degree of inequality, illiteracy and poor medical provision

Liquid asset: An asset which is easily and quickly converted into the means of payment without the risk of loss

Long run: A time period during which it is possible to vary the input of all factors of production; in the long run, there are no fixed factors

Macroeconomics: The branch of economics that deals with overall aggregates in the economy such as output, inflation and employment

Marginal cost: The change in total cost when one more unit is produced

Marginal physical product: The change in total output when one more variable factor (usually labour) is employed

Marginal propensity to consume: The proportion of each increase in income that is spent on additional consumption

Marginal propensity to save: The proportion of each increase in income that is saved

Marginal rate of substitution: The rate at which one good or service can be substituted for another good or service without loss of satisfaction

Marginal revenue: The change in total revenue that results from the sale of an additional unit of output

Marginal revenue product: The change in total revenue that results from the employment of an additional variable factor (usually labour)

Marginal tax rate: The amount of additional earnings that must be paid in tax

Marginal utility: The change in total utility that is received when consumption increases by a single unit

Market: Any arrangement which brings buyers and sellers into contact.

Market failure: The failure of the market system to allocate resources in an optimum way; this implies that there are unreaped gains to society

Market mechanism: A method of allocating resources which allows consumers freely to express their preferences for output by what they purchase; individuals are free to own private property and can undertake production in their quest for profit

Market structure: The characteristic features of markets such as the number of suppliers, the ease of entry and exit and the extent of product differentiation

Microeconomics: That branch of economics which deals with individual units such as the individual consumer, the individual market and the individual firm

Minimum efficient scale: The smallest level of output at which average cost is at a minimum

Monetarists: Those economists who believe that changes in the money supply cause changes in nominal GNP which, in the long run, is reflected in a higher rate of inflation

Monetary base – *see* High-powered money

Money supply: Those assets which function particularly as a means of payment and unit of account; in the UK money supply consists mainly of cash and bank deposits

Money supply multiplier: The ratio of bank deposits to reserves held by the banking sector

Monopolistic competition: A market in which there are large numbers of sellers each selling a product which is slightly differentiated from that of rival suppliers

Monopoly: The sole supplier of a good or service; this might be a single firm or a small group of firms who coordinate their activities so as to function as the sole supplier of a good or service

Monopsony: A market in which there is only one buyer

Multinational: A firm which invests in more than one country and produces and markets its products in different countries

Multiplier – *see* Income multiplier *and* Money supply multiplier

National income: The total of all incomes received by the factors of production during a year; it is therefore the value of all output produced during the same period

Natural monopoly: A market situation in which average cost falls over large ranges of output so that the market is most efficiently served by a single supplier

Natural rate of output: The long run equilibrium level of output in an economy

Natural rate of unemployment: The long run equilibrium level of unemployment; it is also the only level of unemployment that is consistent with a non-accelerating rate of inflation

Nominal values: Measurements of economic values in market prices

Normal good: A good which consumers demand more of when they experience an increase in income; this implies that an increase in income causes a rightward shift of the demand curve

Normal profit: The opportunity cost of the entrepreneur. It is the minimum reward the entrepreneur will accept to remain in a particular industry

Normative statements: Statements which are matters of opinion which cannot be proved or disproved by reference to the facts

Oligopoly: A market structure when there are a small number of producers such that the actions of one firm have implications for other firms in the industry; the market is therefore characterised by interdependence between firms

Open economy: An economy which engages in international trade

Open market operations: The purchase or sale of securities by the central bank

Opportunity cost: The cost of doing one thing measured in terms of the alternative forgone; in particular, resources have alternative uses and if they are used to produce one thing the opportunity cost is the alternative they might otherwise have produced

Patent: The exclusive right to produce a particular good or use a particular process

Perfect competition: A market structure in which there are many buyers and many sellers of a homogeneous product; there are no barriers to entry or exit from the market and no individual buyer or seller has, by his actions, any influence on price

Permanent income hypothesis: The hypothesis that consumption depends on some estimate of expected long run income rather than current income

Personal disposable income: The income that is available to individuals after payment of taxes

Phillips Curve: A curve showing an inverse relationship between the rate of inflation and the level of unemployment

Policy-ineffectiveness proposition: The view that systematic or predictable changes in government policy will have no effect on macroeconomic variables

Positive statements: Statements which can be proved or disproved by reference to the facts

Price ceiling: A legal maximum price that can be charged for a particular product

Price discrimination: The practice of charging different prices for the same product

Price elasticity of demand: The ratio of the percentage change in demand for a good to the percentage change in its price

Price elasticity of supply: The ratio of the percentage change in supply for a good to the percentage change in its price

Price leadership: A situation in oligopolistic markets where one firm sets the price for a particular product and other firms simply follow suit

Production possibility curve: A curve showing the maximum output that an economy can produce given its existing resources and a given level of technology

Productivity: The average output per worker
Profit – *see* Accounting profit
Progressive tax: A tax where the marginal rate exceeds the average rate
Protectionism: Policies aimed at protecting domestic industry from foreign competition
Public goods: Goods and services which cannot be supplied to one person but not to others and which once they are provided have zero marginal cost
Purchasing power parity theory: A theory which implies that a country's nominal exchange rate is determined by its rate of inflation relative to the rate of inflation abroad
Quantity theory of money: A theory which implies that changes in the money supply cause proportional changes in the price level
Rational expectations: Expectations which are formed by considering all relevant information rather than just past experiences
Real values: The measurement of a variable after it has been adjusted to take account of price movements
Recession: A reduction in real GNP for two successive quarters; it is characterised by falling output and rising unemployment
Reflation: An expansion of aggregate demand during a recession
Regressive tax: A tax which takes a larger percentage of income from the less well-off members of society
Resources: Factors of production
Saving: Disposable income that is not spent on consumption
Scarcity: A situation in which society desires more output than is currently available
Short run: A period of time when there is at least one fixed factor of production
Social cost: The private cost of production plus the value of any externalities
Special Drawing Rights (SDRs): Assets created by the IMF which give holders unconditional drawing rights
Stagflation: Rising inflation occurring simultaneously with falling output
Strike: A withdrawal of labour which is authorised by a trade union
Structural unemployment: That portion of unemployment caused by a reduction in demand for a particular product
Substitutes: Goods that are related in such a way that a rise in the price of one good causes an increase in demand for the other
Substitution effect: That part of an increase in the quantity of a good demanded whose price has fallen which is attributed to consumers substituting cheaper goods for relatively more expensive goods
Sunk cost – *see* Fixed cost
Supply curve: A curve showing a positive relationship between price and the quantity supplied
Tariff: A tax levied on imports of goods
Tax incidence: The way in which the burden of a tax is shared between different parties
Terms of trade: The ratio of export prices to import prices
Time deposits: Deposits which are subject to notice of withdrawal before they can be withdrawn
Transfer payments: Payments made by the state which are not in return for some productive activity or the result of purchases of goods or services
Underground economy: Economic activity which is concealed from the authorities with the aim of avoiding tax liability
Unemployment: Those who register as available for employment
Unit elasticity of demand: When the percentage change in price of a good is exactly equal to the percentage change in the quantity of that good demanded
Utility: The economist's term for satisfaction derived from consumption
Variable cost: Those costs which vary directly with output
Vertical integration: A merger between firms at different stages of the same productive process; vertical integration may be backwards towards the raw material suppliers or forwards towards the retail outlets
Vicious circle of poverty: A feature of low income countries, 'low income' implies low ability to save, which implies low investment, which implies low income growth, which implies low ability to save, and so on.
Visibles: Exports or imports of goods
Withdrawals – *see* Leakages
Working population: The total of the employed, the self-employed and the unemployed seeking work

INDEX

N

O

P

U

V

W

X

Y